Love the Great Outdoors?

Life Insurance
Company

MAKE LIFE A PRIORITY

PUT A PLAN IN PLACE FOR THE FUTURE WITH LIFE INSURANCE

You insure your automobile, your home, and your most valuable possessions.

But have you taken the steps to help protect your most precious asset:
Your life and the lives of those most important to you?

AAA Life Insurance Company offers you additional peace of mind.

▼ **Term Life**   ▼ **Permanent Life**   ▼ **Annuities**

Get a FREE Quote Today! Visit AAALife.com

Washington

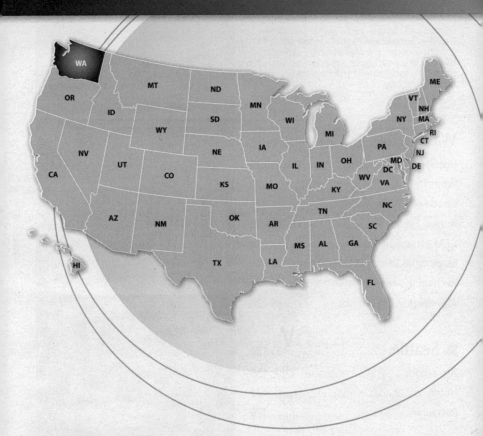

Published by AAA Publishing
1000 AAA Drive, Heathrow, FL 32746-5063
Copyright AAA 2019, All rights reserved

Advertising Rate and Circulation Information: (407) 444-8280

Printed in the USA by Quad/Graphics

This book is printed on paper certified by third-party standards for sustainably managed forestry and production.

Printed on recyclable paper.
Please recycle whenever possible.

Stock #4661

CONTENTS

Get more travel information
at AAA.com/travelguides
and AAA.com/traveltips

Attractions, hotels, restaurants and other travel experience information are all grouped under the alphabetical listing of the city in which those experiences are physically located—or the nearest recognized city.

Washington

Featured Information

free to
rock the boat

TripAssist travel insurance allows you to go with the flow. It can free you up to make the most of your vacation. Nothing will hold you back knowing that you and your travel plans are safe.

Talk to your AAA Travel Agent today for more information.

Global Assistance
Allianz (Ⅲ)

relax

Get the credit card with
unlimited rewards.

The card that gets you there™

With a AAA Member Rewards Visa® credit card you can earn **3x points** on eligible travel and AAA purchases, **2x points** on gas, grocery store and drugstore purchases, and **1 point** per **$1** on all other purchases.*

There are no spending tiers, no rotating categories, no limit to the points you can earn—and you don't have to enroll. Just make purchases, earn rewards and relax.

Visit any participating AAA branch or AAA.com/creditcard.

AAA Member Rewards

4000 1234 5678 9123

4000

VALID THRU 00/00

CHRIS L MARTIN

VISA Signature

Using Your Guide

AAA TourBook guides are packed with travel insights, maps and listings of places to stay, play, eat and save. For more listings, more details and online booking, visit **AAA.com/travelguides**.

Helping You Make the Connection

Look for this symbol 🔗 throughout the guides for direct links to related content.

A to Z City Listings

Cities and places are listed alphabetically within each state or province. Attractions, hotels and restaurants are listed once — under the city in which they are physically located.

Cities that are considered part of a larger destination city or area have an expanded city header. The header identifies the larger region and cross-references pages that contain shared trip planning resources:

- Destination map – outline map of the cities that comprise a destination city or area
- Attraction spotting map – regional street map marked with attraction locations
- Hotel/restaurant spotting map and index – regional street map numbered with hotel and restaurant locations identified in an accompanying index

Cities that are not considered part of a larger destination city or area but have a significant number of listings may have these resources within the individual city section:

- Attraction spotting map
- Hotel/restaurant spotting map and index

Location Abbreviations

Directions are from the center of town unless otherwise specified, using these highway abbreviations:

Bus. Rte.=business route
CR=county road
FM=farm to market
FR=forest road
Hwy.=Canadian highway
I=interstate highway
LR=legislative route
R.R.=rural route
SR/PR=state or provincial route
US=federal highway

About Listed Establishments

AAA/CAA Inspected & Approved hotels and restaurants are listed on the basis of merit alone after careful evaluation and approval by full-time, professionally trained AAA inspectors. An establishment's decision to advertise in the TourBook guide has no bearing on its evaluation or rating; nor does inclusion of advertising imply AAA endorsement of products and services.

Information in this guide was believed accurate at the time of publication. However, since changes inevitably occur between annual editions, please contact your AAA travel professional, visit **AAA.com/travelguides** or download the free AAA Mobile app to confirm prices and schedules.

Attraction Listing Icons

- SAVE AAA Discounts & Rewards® member discount
- 🔌 Electric vehicle charging station on premises. Domestic station information provided by the U.S. Department of Energy. Canadian station information provided by Plug'n Drive Ontario.
- GT Guided Tours available
- 🏕 Camping facilities
- 🍴 Food on premises
- ⊗ Recreational activities
- 🐾 Pet friendly (Call for restrictions/fees.)
- 🛇 Picnicking allowed

In select cities only:

- 🚇 Mass transit station within 1 mile. Icon is followed by station name and AAA/CAA designated station number within listing.

🔻GEM AAA/CAA travel experts may designate an attraction of exceptional interest and quality as a AAA GEM — a *Great Experience for Members®*. See GEM Attraction Index (listed on CONTENTS page) for a complete list of locations.

Consult the online travel guides at **AAA.com/travelguides** or visit AAA Mobile for additional things to do if you have time.

Hotel Listing Icons

May be preceded by CALL and/or SOME UNITS.

Member Information:

- SAVE Member rates: discounted standard room rate or lowest public rate available at time of booking for dates of stay.

ECO Eco-certified by government or private organization.

⊑ Electric vehicle charging station on premises. Domestic station information provided by the U.S. Department of Energy. Canadian station information provided by Plug'n Drive Ontario.

⊠ Smoke-free premises

In select cities only:

🚇 Mass transit station within 1 mile. Icon is followed by station name and AAA/CAA designated station number within listing.

Services:

✈ Airport transportation

🐾 Pet friendly (Call for restrictions/fees.)

🍴 Restaurant on premises

🍴• Restaurant off premises

🍽 Room service for 2 or more meals

🍸 Full bar

🎠 Child care

BIZ Business center

♿ Accessible features (Call property for available services and amenities.)

Activities:

🎰 Full-service casino

🏊 Pool

💪 Health club or exercise room on premises

In-Room Amenities:

HS High-speed Internet service

$HS High-speed Internet service (Call property for fees.)

📶 Wireless Internet service

$📶 Wireless Internet service (Call property for fees.)

📶 No wireless Internet service

🎬 Pay movies

🔲 Refrigerator

🔲 Microwave

🔲 Coffeemaker

🔲 No air conditioning

🔲 No TV

🔲 No telephones

Restaurant Listing Icons

SAVE AAA Discounts & Rewards® member discount

ECO Eco-certified by government or private organization.

⊑ Electric vehicle charging station on premises. Domestic station information provided by the U.S. Department of Energy. Canadian station information provided by Plug'n Drive Ontario.

🔲 No air conditioning

♿ Accessible features (Call property for available services and amenities.)

🚭 Designated smoking section

B Breakfast

L Lunch

D Dinner

24 Open 24 hours

LATE Open after 11 p.m.

🐾 Pet friendly (Call for restrictions/fees.)

In select cities only:

🚇 Mass transit station within 1 mile. Icon is followed by station name and AAA/CAA designated station number within listing.

Map Legend

For attraction and hotel/restaurant spotting maps, refer to the legend below to identify symbols and color coding.

Roads/Highways

Interchange	
Free	
Toll	
	Controlled access
	Controlled access toll
	Local toll
	Primary
	Secondary
	Local unpaved
	Under construction
	Tunnel
	Pedestrian only
	Auto ferry
	Passenger ferry
	Scenic byway

Areas of Interest

✈ ✈	Incorporated city
	Int'l/Regional airport
	Park
	Recreation sites
	Forest
	Natural lands
	Military
	Historic
	Native American
	Beach
	Marsh

Route Shields

Interstate	95 95 Business	Trans-Canada
Federal	Primary 22 Secondary 22	Provincial Autoroute Primary 22 Secondary 22
State	① ①	Mexico ① ①
County	1 1	Historic 66

Boundaries

International	Time zone
State	Continental Divide

Points of Interest

★ National capital	o	Town
★ State/Prov capital	⚑	Campground
■ AAA/CAA club location	▼	Winery
■ Feature of interest	⊛	Customs station
⚜ GEM attraction	■	Historic
⑫ Hotel listing	△	Mountain peak
③ Restaurant listing	—●— Stations	Rapid transit
🎓 College/University	—●—	Metromover

Understanding the Diamond Ratings

Hotel and restaurant evaluations are unscheduled to ensure our professionally trained inspectors encounter the same experience members do.

- When an establishment is Diamond Rated, it means members can expect a good fit with their needs. The inspector assigns a rating that indicates the type of experience to expect.
- While establishments at high levels must offer increasingly complex personalized services, establishments at every level are subject to the same basic requirements for cleanliness, comfort and hospitality. Learn more at **AAA.com/diamonds**.

Hotels	Restaurants
Budget-oriented, offering basic comfort and hospitality.	Simple, economical food, often quick-serve, in a functional environment.
Affordable, with modestly enhanced facilities, décor and amenities.	Familiar food, often cooked to order, served in casual surroundings.

Distinguished, multifaceted with enhanced physical attributes, amenities and guest comforts.	Trendy cuisine, skillfully prepared and served, with expanded beverage options, in an enhanced setting.

Refined, stylish with upscale physical attributes, extensive amenities and high degree of hospitality, service and attention to detail.	Distinctive fine-dining. Creative preparations, skillfully served, often with wine steward, amid upscale ambience.
Ultimate luxury, sophistication and comfort with extraordinary physical attributes, meticulous personalized service, extensive amenities and impeccable standards of excellence.	Leading-edge cuisine of the finest ingredients, uniquely prepared by an acclaimed chef, served by expert service staff led by maître d' in extraordinary surroundings.

Guest Safety

Inspectors view a sampling of rooms during evaluations and, therefore, AAA/CAA cannot guarantee the presence of working locks and operational fire safety equipment in every guest unit.

Contacting AAA/CAA About the TourBook Guide

Tell us what you think about the content and format of the TourBook guide or about your experience at a listed hotel, restaurant or attraction. If your visit to an attraction, hotel or restaurant listed by AAA/CAA doesn't meet your expectations, please tell us about it **during your visit or within 30 days**. Be sure to save your receipts and other documentation for reference. Or, maybe you'd like to recommend a place you visited and would like AAA inspectors to consider.

Use the easy online form at **AAA.com/MemberFeedback** to send us the details.

Alternatively, you can email your comments to: memberrelations@national.aaa.com or submit them via postal mail to: AAA Member Comments, 1000 AAA Dr., Box 61, Heathrow, FL 32746.

Mount St. Helens

Washington

The only state named for a president, Washington is like a book that spans several genres. You've got history and drama, romance and adventure. It appeals to a broad audience by combining a natural setting forged over millennia with the up-to-the-minute technology of the information age.

The dramatic, snowcapped peaks of the Cascades pierce clouds. At 14,411 feet, Mount Rainier is the loftiest peak in the Cascade Range and Washington's highest point. Simultaneously built up by lava flows and torn down by eruptions in an endless cycle stretching over millions of years, its flanks are sheathed in a mantle of snow and glacial ice. This mighty mountain is the Evergreen State's most prominent landmark.

Subterranean tubes tunnel through massive lava flows at Ape Cave Geologic Site, within Mount St. Helens National Volcanic Monument. At 8,365 feet, Mount St. Helens is a pipsqueak only in comparison. It used to

Pike Place Market, Seattle

be 1,312 feet taller, but the cataclysmic 1980 eruption that literally blew its top off replaced the summit with a horseshoe-shaped crater.

Human history doesn't go back nearly as far; just a mere 12,000 or so years. Many cities share their names with Native American tribes: Chinook, Colville, Nooksack, Okanogan, Puyallup, Quinault, Spokane, Walla Walla and Yakima. Reservations in Marysville, Neah Bay, Taholah and Toppenish preserve and celebrate tribal culture, and petroglyphs near Clarkston, Dallesport, Snoqualmie, Spokane and Yakima depict the state's earliest inhabitants.

Modern history hinges on a single event: the Klondike gold rush of 1897. Washington's role as a gateway to Alaska and the Great White North furthered a peaceful relationship between Canada and the United States. It also introduced legions of fortune seekers to wondrous natural landscapes. Although few hit the proverbial mother lode, many of them found a reason to stay.

And then there's Seattle. Relatively young—it was founded in the early 1850s—the city is surrounded by three lakes, a bay, a sound and scenery that fully justify its reputation as a place blessed with stunning views. Seattle has landmarks like the endearingly kitschy Space Needle, perhaps the best farmers market in the country (that would be Pike Place Market) and is headquarters for corporate giants like Amazon.com and Microsoft. Oh, and everyone runs on caffeine; there's a Starbucks, a Tully's or an independent coffee shop on practically every corner.

Searching for Warm Fuzzies

Wine and roses provide a hint of romance. Located astride the same latitudes as the wine-producing regions of France, Washington has more than 650 wineries, many of them concentrated in the Yakima, Columbia and Walla Walla valleys. The intoxicating summer perfume of roses wafts through the air at the Woodland Park Rose Garden in Seattle and at Manito Park in Spokane.

You may also find that certain *je ne sais quoi* in a variation on the theme: breweries and bulbs. Sample locally brewed beer and ale at brewpubs in Seattle and Woodinville. Displays of daffodils, hyacinths and especially tulips blanket Roozengaarde and the Skagit Valley Bulb Farm's Tulip Town, both in Mount Vernon. April brings gardeners who drool over the extravagant flower displays at the popular Skagit Valley Tulip Festival.

Feel the sand between your toes as you admire the sunset at Ocean Shores. Take a San Juan Islands cruise and catch a glimpse of orca and minke whales, porpoises and harbor seals. Or hike to Marymere Falls in Olympic National Park along a winding trail through a serene old forest of moss-covered trees. They're all guaranteed to put you in a warm, fuzzy mood.

Recreation

There isn't much you *can't* do in a state that sets so much land aside for parks and wilderness areas. Hikers and mountain bikers experience trestles and tunnels while cycling along the 100-mile portion of the Palouse to Cascades State Park Trail that roughly parallels I-90 from Cedar Falls (near North Bend) to the Columbia River (near Vantage), following the roadbed of the Chicago-Milwaukee-St. Paul-Pacific Railroad. Some 38 miles of hiking trails meander through forests, sand dunes and along rocky headlands at Deception Pass State Park, at Puget Sound's northern end.

The rugged terrain of Mount Spokane makes for particularly challenging mountain biking. The Centennial Trail, open to hikers, bikers and inline skaters, follows the Spokane River for 37 miles from Nine Mile Falls, near Spokane, east to the Idaho state line. (You can keep going if you want.) You'll experience beautiful vistas while hiking at Wallace Falls State Park, north of Gold Bar; Larrabee State Park, south of Bellingham on the west side of Chuckanut Mountain; and Lake Chelan State Park, west of Chelan.

The 150-mile Cascadia Marine Trail, extending from Olympia north to Point Roberts, is ideal for an extended canoeing getaway. You'll need to pay a Washington State Parks nightly camping fee to camp at shoreline sites along the route. For more information contact the Washington Water Trails Association; phone (206) 545-9161.

Turn the excitement up a notch and challenge river rapids. Expert rafters and kayakers can put in at the upstream end of the Green River gorge in Kanaskat-Palmer State Park, northeast of Enumclaw. Raging rivers racing through canyons in the Cascades make for exciting white-water rafting. Regional outfitters are based along the Methow, Skykomish and Wenatchee rivers. For a tamer excursion, check out the Elwha River in Olympic National Park.

The back country at Crystal Mountain entices expert skiers with its chutes and steep bowls. Stevens Pass, near Skykomish, beckons snowboarders. Gifford Pinchot, Mount Baker-Snoqualmie, Okanogan and Olympic national forests boast hundreds of miles of trails for cross-country skiing, snowshoeing and snowmobiling. And a lighted tubing hill at Fields Spring State Park, south of Anatone in the state's southeastern corner, is a winter blast.

Walla Walla Valley

Historic Timeline

1792	Capt. George Vancouver, sent to find the Northwest Passage and map the unknown region, arrives at Puget Sound.
1805	The epic westward journey of explorers Meriwether Lewis and William Clark ends at the Pacific Ocean.
1889	Washington enters the Union as the 42nd state.
1897	Seattle booms as it becomes an outfitting point of departure for Klondike gold rush fortune seekers.
1909	Women are granted the vote, more than a decade before many other states follow suit.
1942	Grand Coulee Dam, one of the largest concrete structures in the world, is completed.
1962	Seattle hosts the Century 21 Exposition world's fair.
1971	Ubiquitous coffee retailer Starbucks opens its first store at Seattle's Pike Place Market.
1975	Computer software giant Microsoft is founded by Seattle native Bill Gates.
1980	The eruption of Mount St. Helens devastates the surrounding area.
2007	Pike Place Market celebrates its centennial.

What To Pack

Temperature Averages Maximum/Minimum	JANUARY	FEBRUARY	MARCH	APRIL	MAY	JUNE	JULY	AUGUST	SEPTEMBER	OCTOBER	NOVEMBER	DECEMBER
Ilwaco	49 / 37	51 / 37	53 / 39	55 / 41	59 / 46	62 / 50	65 / 52	66 / 52	66 / 48	60 / 43	52 / 40	48 / 36
Oroville	32 / 21	41 / 26	54 / 31	65 / 37	73 / 44	79 / 50	86 / 54	85 / 54	75 / 46	60 / 36	43 / 30	33 / 24
Seattle	47 / 36	51 / 37	55 / 39	59 / 43	65 / 48	70 / 53	75 / 56	75 / 57	70 / 53	60 / 46	52 / 40	47 / 36
Spokane	34 / 25	40 / 26	49 / 32	57 / 37	67 / 44	74 / 50	83 / 56	83 / 56	73 / 47	58 / 37	42 / 30	32 / 23
Walla Walla	41 / 30	46 / 32	55 / 37	63 / 42	70 / 48	79 / 54	89 / 61	88 / 61	78 / 53	64 / 43	49 / 35	39 / 29
Yakima	39 / 23	47 / 26	56 / 30	64 / 34	72 / 42	80 / 48	88 / 53	87 / 52	78 / 44	64 / 34	48 / 27	36 / 21

From the records of The Weather Channel Interactive, Inc.

Good Facts To Know

ABOUT THE STATE

POPULATION: 6,724,540.

AREA: 71,298 square miles; ranks 18th.

CAPITAL: Olympia.

HIGHEST POINT: 14,411 ft., Mount Rainier.

LOWEST POINT: 5 ft. below sea level, Ebey Island, Snohomish County.

TIME ZONE(S): Pacific. DST.

GAMBLING

MINIMUM AGE FOR GAMBLING: 18.

REGULATIONS

TEEN DRIVING LAWS: No unrelated passengers under age 20 are permitted for the first 6 months; a maximum of three unrelated passengers under age 20 are permitted for the following 6 months. Nighttime restrictions: 1 a.m.-5 a.m. Restrictions may be lifted at age 17. For more information phone (360) 902-3900.

SEAT BELT/CHILD RESTRAINT LAWS: Seat belts are required for the driver and all passengers ages 16 and over. Children ages 8-15 and taller than 4'9" must use a child restraint or seat belt. Child restraints are required for children under age 8 and less than 4'9" tall. Children under age 13 must be in the rear seat if practical. AAA recommends the use of seat belts and appropriate child restraints for the driver and all passengers.

CELLPHONE RESTRICTIONS: All drivers are prohibited from texting or using a hand-held cellphone while driving. Drivers are banned from holding a personal electronic device or using a finger to interact with a device while driving, beyond a one-touch activation of an app or function. Instruction permit and intermediate license holders may not use a wireless communication device while driving.

HELMETS FOR MOTORCYCLISTS: Required for all riders.

RADAR DETECTORS: Permitted. Prohibited for use by commercial vehicles.

MOVE OVER LAW: Drivers are required to vacate the lane nearest police, fire and rescue vehicles stopped on the side of the road and using audible or flashing signals. The law also applies to recovery vehicles, including tow trucks. If unable to vacate the lane, drivers are required to slow down.

FIREARMS LAWS: Vary by state and/or county. Contact Washington State Department of Licensing, Firearms Licensing, P.O. Box 9649, Olympia, WA 98507; phone (360) 664-6616.

HOLIDAYS

HOLIDAYS: Jan. 1 ▪ Martin Luther King Jr. Day, Jan. (3rd Mon.) ▪ Lincoln's Birthday, Feb. 12 ▪ Washington's Birthday/Presidents Day, Feb. (3rd Mon.) ▪ Memorial Day, May (last Mon.) ▪ July 4 ▪ Labor Day, Sept. (1st Mon.) ▪ Election Day, Nov. (1st Tues. following 1st Mon.) ▪ Veterans Day, Nov. 11 ▪ Thanksgiving, Nov. (4th Thurs.) ▪ Christmas, Dec. 25.

MONEY

TAXES: Washington's statewide sales tax is 6.5 percent, with cities and counties each allowed to add increments. Cities and counties may levy lodgings taxes of up to 3 percent except in Seattle, the rest of King County, Pierce County and Wenatchee, where lodgings taxes are higher. The statewide tax on automobile rentals is 5.9 percent, with cities and counties each allowed to add up to 3 percent.

VISITOR INFORMATION

INFORMATION CENTERS: State welcome centers open May through September are at Custer ▪ Oroville ▪ Megler ▪ and Maryhill. The Information center in Vancouver, at the northbound I-5 Gee Creek Rest Area, is open all year.

FURTHER INFORMATION FOR VISITORS:
Scenic Washington State
215 W. Holly St.
Suite H24
Bellingham, WA 98225
(800) 544-1800

NATIONAL FOREST INFORMATION:
Outdoor Recreation Information Center
222 Yale Ave. N.
Seattle, WA 98109
(206) 470-4060
(877) 444-6777 (national forest reservations)

FISHING AND HUNTING REGULATIONS:
Department of Fish and Wildlife
1111 Washington St. S.E.
Olympia, WA 98501
(360) 902-2200
TTY (800) 833-6388

RECREATION INFORMATION:
Washington State Parks and Recreation Commission
1111 Israel Rd. S.W.
Tumwater, WA 98501
(360) 902-8500
(888) 226-7688 for camping reservations

Washington Annual Events

Please call ahead to confirm event details.

Visit **AAA.com/travelguides/events** to find
AAA-listed events for every day of the year

WINTER

Dec.
- Argosy Christmas Ship Festival
  Seattle / 206-623-1445
- Bellevue Magic Season / Bellevue
  425-450-3777
- A Victorian Country Christmas
  Festival / Puyallup /
  253-770-0777

Jan.
- Bavarian Icefest / Leavenworth
  509-548-5807
- Seattle Boat Show / Seattle
  206-634-0911
- Lake Chelan Winterfest / Chelan
  800-424-3526

Feb.
- Northwest Flower & Garden Show
  Seattle / 253-756-2121
- Spokane International Film Festival
  Spokane / 888-411-7743
- Wintergrass Music Festival /
  Bellevue / 253-428-8056

SPRING

Mar.
- Winthrop Balloon Roundup / Winthrop
  509-996-2125
- Penn Cove MusselFest / Coupeville
  360-678-5434
- Irish Festival / Seattle /
  253-237-2811

Apr.
- Daffodil Festival / Tacoma
  253-627-6176
- Dogwood Festival of the Lewis-Clark
  Valley / Clarkston / 208-792-2447
- Skagit Valley Tulip Festival / Mount
  Vernon / 360-428-5959

May
- Washington State Apple Blossom
  Festival / Wenatchee /
  509-662-3616
- Lilac Festival / Spokane
  509-535-4554

SUMMER

June
- Berry Dairy Days Festival /
  Burlington / 360-757-0994
- Fremont Fair / Seattle
  206-694-6706

July
- Bite of Seattle / Seattle
  425-283-5050
- Sequim Lavender Festival / Sequim
  360-681-2035
- Seattle Seafair / Seattle
  206-728-0123

Aug.
- Washington State International
  Kite Festival / Long Beach /
  800-451-2542
- A Taste of Edmonds / Edmonds
  425-670-1496
- Morton Loggers' Jubilee / Morton
  360-496-6362

FALL

Sept.
- Wooden Boat Festival / Port
  Townsend / 360-385-3628
- Washington State Fair / Puyallup
  253-841-5045
- Bumbershoot: Seattle's Music & Arts
  Festival / Seattle / 206-281-8111

Oct.
- Dungeness Crab & Seafood Festival
  Port Angeles / 360-452-6300
- Mahogany and Merlot Vintage Boat
  and Car Show / Chelan
  509-682-8023

Nov.
- Christmas Arts & Crafts Show
  Spokane / 509-924-0588
- Hometown Holidays / Ellensburg
  509-925-2002
- Christkindlmarkt / Leavenworth
  425-445-6183

Pioneer Square Historic District

Seattle Japanese Garden

Deception Pass State Park, Oak Harbor

Seattle skyline

Mount Rainier National Park

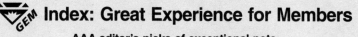

Index: Great Experience for Members

AAA editor's picks of exceptional note

LeMay—America's
Car Museum

Lake Chelan

Washington Park
Arboretum

The Museum of Flight

See Orientation map on p. 26 for corresponding grid coordinates, if applicable.
*Indicates the GEM is temporarily closed.

STAY CONNECTED

TO ALL THE THINGS MEMBERSHIP CAN DO FOR YOU

- member discounts around you
- cheapest gas nearby
- Diamond Rated hotels and restaurants
- travel information and reservations
- roadside assistance

Download today. Connect every day.
AAA.com/mobile | CAA.ca/mobile

Washington
Atlas Section

ROAD Atlas 2019

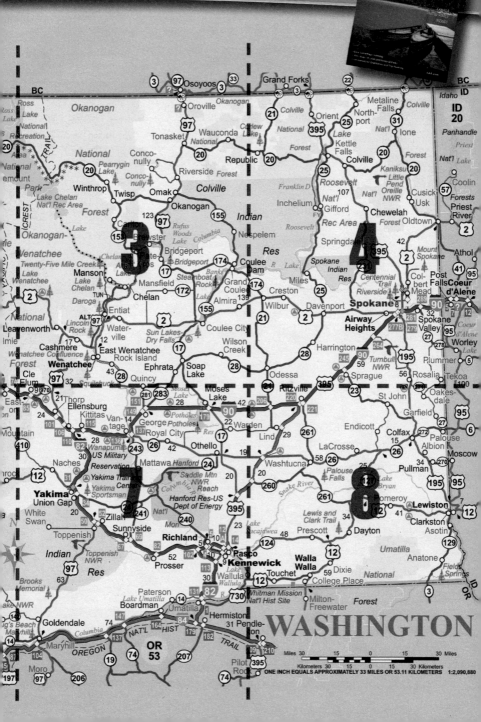

WASHINGTON

Miles 30   15   0   15   30 Miles
Kilometers 30   15   0   15   30 Kilometers
ONE INCH EQUALS APPROXIMATELY 33 MILES OR 53.11 KILOMETERS   1:2,090,680

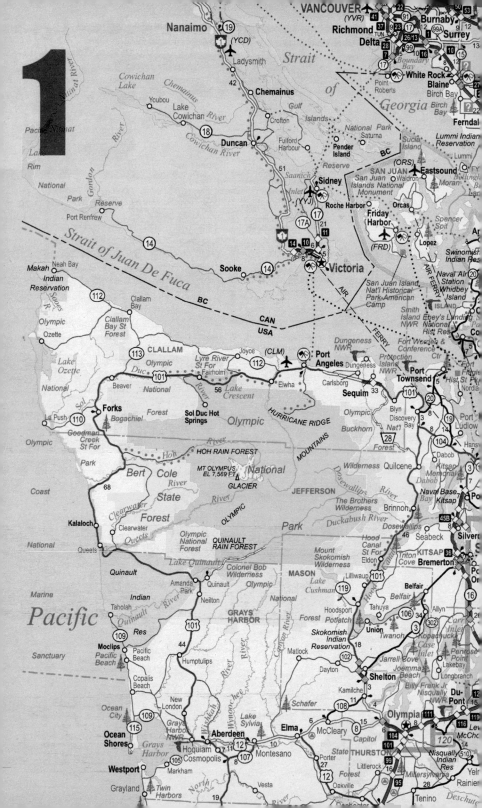

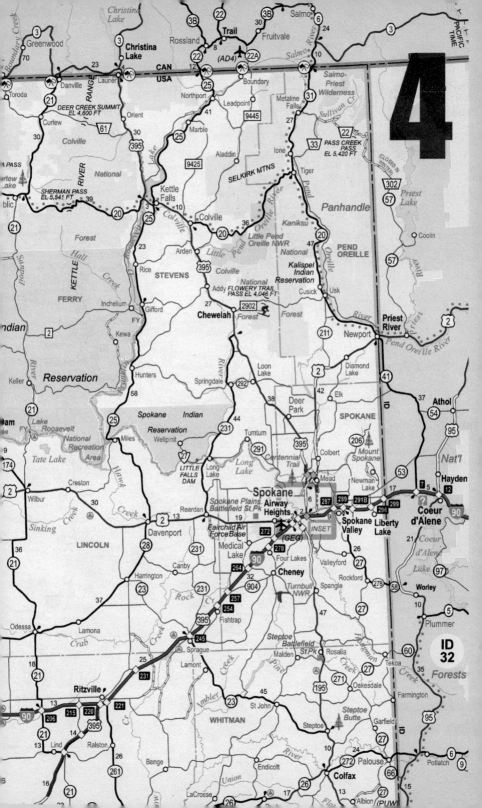

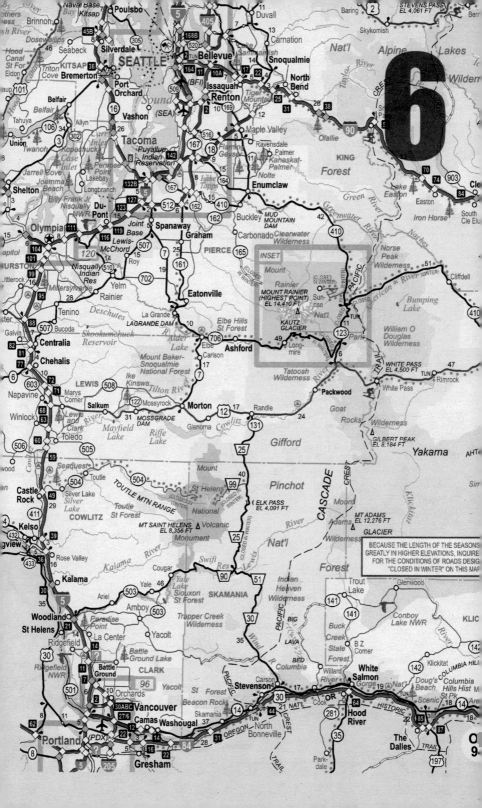

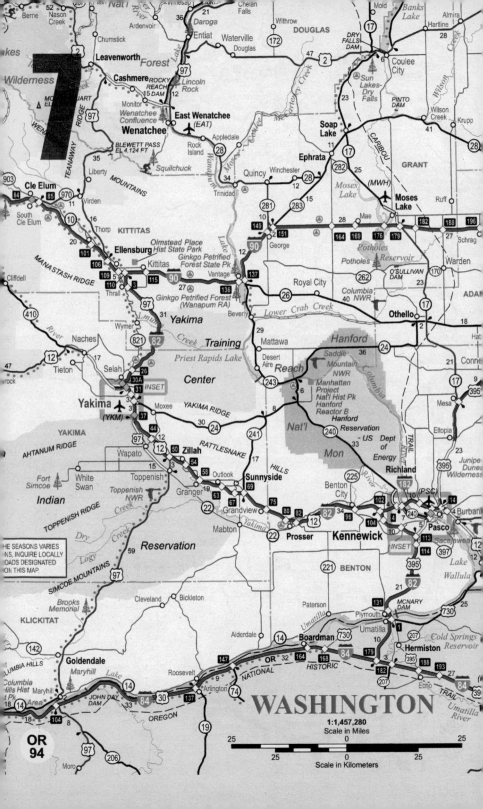

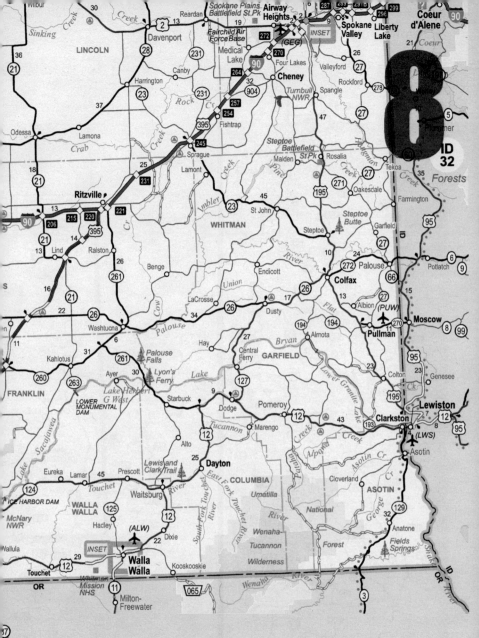

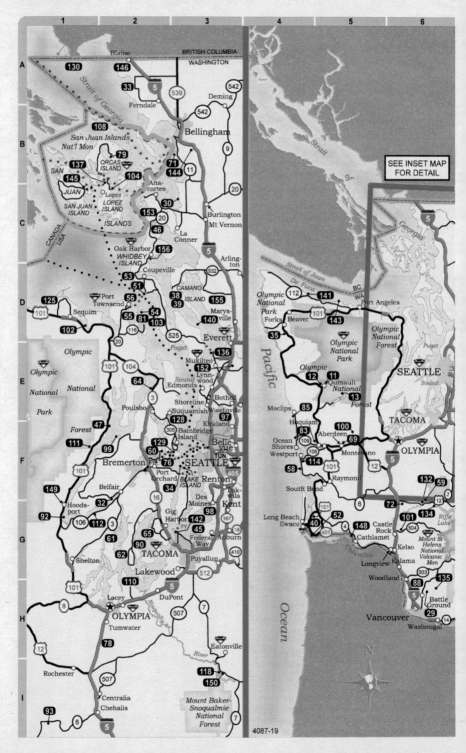

4087-19

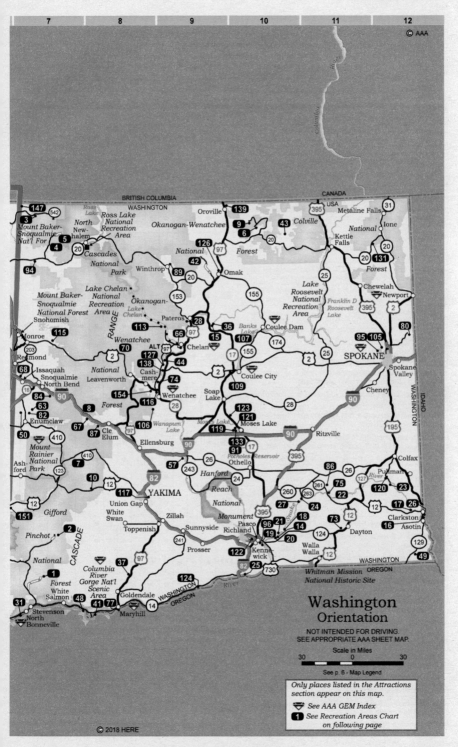

© AAA

BRITISH COLUMBIA
WASHINGTON
CANADA
USA

Oroville

Okanogan-Wenatchee

National   Forest

Colville

Metaline Falls

National

Ione

Kettle
Falls

Chewelah

Newport

Mount Baker-
Snoqualmie
Nat'l For

Ross
Lake

North
New-
halem

Ross Lake
National
Recreation
Area

Cascades
National
Park

Winthrop

Lake Chelan
National
Recreation
Area

Okanogan-
Lake
Chelan

Pateros

Omak

Lake
Roosevelt
National
Recreation
Area

Franklin D
Roosevelt
Lake

Coulee Dam

Forest

SPOKANE

Spokane
Valley

Mount Baker-
Snoqualmie
National Forest

Snohomish

Monroe

Redmond

Issaquah
North Bend

Wenatchee

National

Leavenworth

Cash-
mere

Chelan

Banks
Lake

Coulee City

Cheney

IDAHO
WASHINGTON

Snoqualmie
Forest

Enumclaw

Cle
Elum

Wenatchee

Wanapum
Lake

Soap
Lake

Moses Lake

Ritzville

Colfax

Pullman

Mount
Rainier
National
Park

Ashford

Ellensburg

Potholes
Reservoir

Othello

Hanford

Reach

National

Monument

Dayton

Clarkston
Asotin

YAKIMA

Union Gap
White
Swan

Zillah

Toppenish

Sunnyside

Prosser

Pasco
Richland

Kenne-
wick

Walla
Walla

Whitman Mission
National Historic Site

WASHINGTON
OREGON

Gifford

Pinchot

National

Forest
White
Salmon

Columbia
River
Gorge Nat'l
Scenic
Area

Goldendale

Maryhill

Stevenson
North
Bonneville

CASCADE

RANGE

Columbia

River

Washington
Orientation

NOT INTENDED FOR DRIVING.
SEE APPROPRIATE AAA SHEET MAP.

Scale in Miles
30   0   30

See p. 6 - Map Legend

*Only places listed in the Attractions
section appear on this map.*

See AAA GEM Index

See Recreation Areas Chart
on following page

© 2018 HERE

Recreation Areas Chart

The map location numerals in column 2 show an area's location on the preceding map.

Find thousands of places to camp at AAA.com/campgrounds

	MAP LOCATION	CAMPING	PICNICKING	HIKING TRAILS	BOATING	BOAT RAMP	BOAT RENTAL	FISHING	SWIMMING	PET FRIENDLY	BICYCLE TRAILS	WINTER SPORTS	VISITOR CENTER	LODGE/CABINS	FOOD SERVICE
NATIONAL PARKS (See place listings.)															
Mount Rainier (F-7) 378 square miles. Scenic. Boating (no motors), cross-country skiing, snowshoeing.		•	•	•	•			•		•	•	•	•	•	•
North Cascades (C-7, C-8) 505,000 acres. Bird-watching, canoeing, horseback riding, kayaking, mountain climbing; guided tours.		•		•	•			•					•		
Olympic (E-1) 922,650 acres. Bird-watching, cross-country skiing; interpretive talks.		•	•	•	•	•	•	•	•	•			•	•	•
NATIONAL FORESTS (See place listings.)															
Colville (C-11) 1,100,000 acres. Northeastern Washington. Cross-country skiing, hunting, scuba diving, snowmobiling, tubing; horseback riding trails.		•	•	•	•	•		•	•	•		•			
Gifford Pinchot (G-7) 1,368,300 acres. Southwestern Washington. Cross-country skiing, mountain climbing, snowmobiling, snowshoeing, tubing; horse rental.		•	•	•	•	•		•	•	•	•	•	•	•	•
Goose Lake (G-7) 7 acres 13 mi. w. of Trout Lake via SR 141, FR 24 and FR 60. Bird-watching, boating (no motors).	❶	•	•	•	•			•	•	•					
Takhlakh Lake (G-7) 32 mi. s.e. of Randle via SR 131, FR 23 and FR 2329. Mountain views. Boating (electric motors only).	❷	•	•	•	•			•	•	•					
Mount Baker-Snoqualmie (D-7, I-3) 1,724,229 acres. Northwestern Washington. Cross-country skiing, horseback riding, hunting, mountain biking, sledding, skiing, snowboarding, snowmobiling, water skiing.		•	•	•	•	•		•	•	•	•	•	•	•	•
Douglas Fir Campground (C-7) 2 mi. e. of Glacier on SR 542. Boating (no motors).	❸	•	•	•	•			•		•					
Horseshoe Cove Campground (C-7) 14 mi. n. of Concrete on Baker Lake. Horseback riding, snowshoeing.	❹	•		•	•	•		•	•	•					
Shannon Creek Campground (C-7) 24 mi. n. of Concrete on Baker Lake. Water skiing.	❺	•		•	•	•		•	•	•					
Okanogan-Wenatchee (C-8, D-8) 3,906,000 acres. North-central Washington. Nature trails.		•	•	•	•	•		•	•	•	•	•	•	•	•
Bonaparte Lake (C-10) 16 acres 7 mi. n.w. of Wauconda via SR 20 and CR 4953. Boating (no motors); nature trails.	❻	•	•	•	•			•	•	•					
Bumping Lake (F-7) 19 acres 3 mi. s. of Goose Prairie.	❼	•		•	•	•	•	•	•	•					
Kachess Lake (E-8) 92 acres 15 mi. n. of Easton via I-90 and FR 49. Nature trails.	❽	•		•	•	•		•	•	•					
Lost Lake (C-10) 23 acres 17 mi. n.w. of Wauconda via SR 20, CR 4953, FR 32 and FR 33. Boating (no motors); amphitheater, nature trails.	❾	•	•	•	•			•		•					
Rimrock Lake Area (F-8) at Rimrock off US 12. Water skiing.	❿	•		•	•	•		•	•	•					
Olympic (D-5, E-1) 632,324 acres. Northwestern Washington. Horseback riding, hunting.			•	•	•	•		•	•	•			•	•	•
Falls Creek Campground (E-5) 3 acres 3 mi. e. of US 101 on Quinault Lake. Water skiing; nature trails.	⓫	•	•	•	•			•	•	•					
Willaby Campground (E-4) 7 acres 2 mi. e. of US 101 on Quinault Lake. Nature trail.	⓬	•	•	•	•			•	•	•					
Wynoochee Lake-Coho (E-5) 2,777 acres 1 mi. w. of Montesano on US 12, then 37 mi. n. on FR 22 (Old Wynoochee Valley Rd.).	⓭	•	•	•	•	•		•	•	•					
NATIONAL RECREATION AREAS (See place listings.)															
Lake Chelan (D-8) 62,000 acres. North central Washington. Horse rental, houseboat rental.			•	•	•	•	•	•		•			•	•	•
Lake Roosevelt (D-11) 100,059 acres. Northeastern Washington. Hunting, water skiing; houseboat rental.			•	•	•	•		•	•	•				•	•
Ross Lake (C-8) 118,000 acres. Northwestern Washington.		•	•	•	•	•	•	•	•	•				•	
ARMY CORPS OF ENGINEERS															
Charbonneau Park (G-10) 244 acres 8 mi. e. of Burbank on SR 124, then 2 mi. n. on Sun Harbor Dr. to Charbonneau Rd. Marina	⓮	•	•		•	•		•	•	•					

Recreation Areas Chart

The map location numerals in column 2 show an area's location on the preceding map.

Find thousands of places to camp at AAA.com/campgrounds

	MAP LOCATION	CAMPING	PICNICKING	HIKING TRAILS	BOATING	BOAT RAMP	BOAT RENTAL	FISHING	SWIMMING	PET FRIENDLY	BICYCLE TRAILS	WINTER SPORTS	VISITOR CENTER	LODGE/CABINS	FOOD SERVICE
Chief Joseph Dam (D-9) 864 acres off SR 17 in Bridgeport.	15		•		•	•		•					•		
Chief Looking Glass (G-12) 17 acres in Asotin on SR 129.	16	•	•	•	•			•			•				
Chief Timothy (G-12) 282 acres 8 mi. w. of Clarkston on US 12. Water skiing.	17	•	•	•	•	•		•	•	•			•	•	•
Fishhook (G-11) 46 acres 15 mi. e. of Burbank on SR 124, then 4 mi. n. on Page Rd.	18	•	•		•	•		•	•						
Hood Park (G-10) 99 acres 3 mi. s. of Pasco on US 12/395 at SR 124. Beach, playground.	19	•	•		•	•		•	•	•					
Ice Harbor Lock and Dam (G-10) 524 acres 5 mi. e. of Burbank off SR 124 to 2763 Monument Dr.	20	•	•		•	•		•					•		
Levey Park (G-10) 50 acres 10.5 mi. e. of Pasco on Pasco-Kahlotus Rd., then 1 mi. s. on Levey Rd. Boat moorage.	21	•	•		•	•		•							
Little Goose Lock and Dam (F-11) 16,364 acres 8 mi. n.e. of Starbuck off US 12 on Little Goose Dam Rd.	22		•		•	•		•	•						
Lower Granite Lock and Dam (F-12) 14,863 acres 28 mi. n. of Pomeroy on Almota Ferry Rd.	23		•		•	•		•					•		
Lower Monumental Lock and Dam (G-11) 14,726 acres 7 mi. s. of Kahlotus on Devil's Canyon Rd.	24		•		•	•		•							
McNary Lock and Dam (G-10) 17 acres 1.5 mi. e. of Umatilla, Ore., on US 730, then 1 mi. n. on McNary Dam Rd.	25		•		•	•		•					•		
Swallows Park (G-12) 64 acres 1 mi. s. of Clarkston on SR 129.	26		•		•	•		•	•	•	•				
Windust Park (G-10) 54 acres 10 mi. n.e. of Pasco on Pasco-Kahlotus Rd., then 5 mi. s.e. on Burr Canyon Rd.	27	•	•		•	•		•	•	•					
STATE															
Alta Lake (D-9) 174 acres 2 mi. s.w. of Pateros off SR 164. Golf (18 holes), sailboarding, scuba diving, snowmobiling, water skiing, windsurfing.	28	•	•	•	•	•		•	•	•		•			•
Battle Ground Lake (H-6) 280 acres 3 mi. n.e. of Battle Ground off SR 502. Bird-watching, boating (no motors), scuba diving; dock, equestrian camping and trails.	29	•	•	•	•			•	•	•				•	•
Bay View (C-2) 25 acres 7 mi. w. of Burlington via SR 20. Beach-combing, bird-watching, fishing (saltwater), sailboarding, scuba diving, water skiing.	30	•	•	•		•		•	•	•				•	
Beacon Rock (H-7) 5,100 acres 35 mi. e. of Vancouver via SR 14. Rock climbing, mountain biking.	31	•	•	•	•	•		•		•	•				
Belfair (G-2) 65 acres 3 mi. w. of Belfair at 3151 N.E. SR 30. Bird-watching, clamming, crabbing, fishing (fresh and saltwater), snorkeling, windsurfing.	32	•	•					•	•	•					
Birch Bay (A-2) 194 acres 1 mi. s. of Birch Bay at 5105 Helweg Rd. Bird-watching, clamming, crabbing; amphitheater, interpretive trail.	33	•	•	•				•	•	•	•				
Blake Island Marine (F-2) 475 acres 4 mi. w. of Seattle via boat. Clamming, fishing (saltwater), scuba diving; boat moorage, Native American village.	34	•	•	•				•		•			•	•	•
Bogachiel (D-4) 123 acres 6 mi. s. of Forks at Bogachiel on US 101. Bird-watching.	35	•	•	•				•		•					
Bridgeport (D-9) 748 acres .75 mi. n. of Bridgeport via SR 17. Bird-watching, golf (nine holes), sailboarding, water skiing.	36	•	•	•	•	•		•	•	•					•
Brooks Memorial (G-8) 700 acres 12 mi. n.e. of Goldendale off US 97. Bird-watching, mountain biking; amphitheater.	37	•	•	•				•		•		•			
Cama Beach (D-3) 463 acres 14 mi. s.w. of Stanwood on Camano Island. Historic. Bird-watching, clamming, crabbing, kayaking; guided tours, interpretive programs, museum.	38	•	•	•			•	•	•	•			•	•	•
Camano Island (D-3) 173 acres 14 mi. s.w. of Stanwood on Camano Island. Scenic. Bird-watching, clamming, crabbing, fishing (saltwater), sailboarding, scuba diving, water skiing; amphitheater.	39	•	•	•	•	•		•	•	•					

Recreation Areas Chart

The map location numerals in column 2 show an area's location on the preceding map.

Find thousands of places to camp at AAA.com/campgrounds

	MAP LOCATION	CAMPING	PICNICKING	HIKING TRAILS	BOATING	BOAT RAMP	BOAT RENTAL	FISHING	SWIMMING	PET FRIENDLY	BICYCLE TRAILS	WINTER SPORTS	VISITOR CENTER	LODGE/CABINS	FOOD SERVICE
Cape Disappointment (G-4) 1,882 acres 3 mi. s.w. of Ilwaco via SR 100. Historic. Clamming, crabbing, fishing (fresh and saltwater); dock, Lewis & Clark Interpretive Center, lighthouse.	40	•	•	•	•	•		•	•	•			•	•	•
Columbia Hills (H-8) 3,338 acres 17 mi. e. of White Salmon off SR 14. Bird-watching, rock climbing, windsurfing; amphitheater, Native American petroglyphs.	41	•	•	•	•	•		•	•	•					
Conconully (C-9) 81 acres 18 mi. n.w. of Omak off US 97. Cross-country skiing, dog sledding, mountain biking, snowmobiling, snowshoeing, water skiing; dock.	42	•	•		•	•	•	•	•	•	•	•	•		
Curlew Lake (C-10) 87 acres 10 mi. n.e. of Republic on SR 21. Snowmobiling, water skiing; amphitheater, dock.	43	•	•		•	•	•	•	•	•		•			
Daroga (E-9) 90 acres 6 mi. n. of Orondo. Tennis, water skiing; ballparks.	44	•	•	•	•	•		•	•	•	•				
Dash Point (G-3) 398 acres 5 mi. n.e. of Tacoma on SR 509. Boating (no motors), mountain biking, sailboarding.	45	•	•	•	•			•	•	•	•				
Deception Pass (C-2) 4,134 acres 9 mi. n. of Oak Harbor on Whidbey Island. Clamming, crabbing, scuba diving, white-water kayaking; dock, horseback riding trails.	46	•	•	•	•	•	•	•	•	•	•		•	•	•
Dosewallips (F-1) 1,039 acres at Brinnon off US 101. Clamming, crabbing, fishing (fresh and saltwater), scuba diving.	47	•	•	•				•	•	•					
Doug's Beach (H-7) 400 acres 2 mi. e. of Lyle. Bird-watching, kayaking, windsurfing.	48		•					•	•	•					
Fields Spring (G-12) 825 acres 5 mi. s. of Anatone off SR 129. Bird-watching, cross-country skiing, sledding, snowmobiling, snowshoeing; amphitheater, sports fields.	49	•	•	•						•	•	•	•		
Flaming Geyser (F-7) 480 acres 1.75 mi. s. of Black Diamond on SR 169, then 2.75 mi. w. on S.E. Green Valley Rd. Bird-watching, kayaking (white-water), volleyball; horseback riding trail, interpretive trail, playground.	50		•	•	•			•	•	•					
Fort Casey Historical (D-2) 998 acres 3 mi. s. of Coupeville off SR 20. Fishing (saltwater), scuba diving.	51	•	•	•	•	•		•		•			•		
Fort Columbia Historical (G-5) 593 acres 1 mi. s. of Chinook on US 101. Historic.	52		•	•						•			•	•	
Fort Ebey (D-2) 649 acres 3 mi. w. of Coupeville off SR 20. Historic. Beachcombing, bird-watching, mountain biking, paragliding, scuba diving.	53	•	•	•				•		•	•		•		
Fort Flagler Historical (D-2) 783 acres 11 mi. n.e. of Port Hadlock on Marrowstone Island. Historic. Clamming, crabbing, scuba diving; museum.	54	•	•	•	•	•		•	•	•	•		•	•	•
Fort Townsend Historical (D-2) 414 acres 3 mi. s. of Port Townsend off SR 20. Historic. Crabbing, fishing (saltwater), scuba diving.	55	•	•	•	•			•	•	•					
Fort Worden (D-2) 434 acres 1 mi. n. of Port Townsend via Cherry St. Historic. Scuba diving.	56	•	•	•	•	•		•	•	•	•		•	•	•
Ginkgo Petrified Forest (Wanapum Recreation Area) (F-9) 7,470 acres 3 mi. s. of Vantage on the Columbia River. Bird-watching, water skiing; concerts (seasonal), museum.	57	•	•	•	•	•		•	•	•			•		
Grayland Beach (F-4) 412 acres on SR 105 in Grayland. Beachcombing, clamming, crabbing, fishing (saltwater).	58	•	•	•				•	•	•				•	
Ike Kinswa (F-6) 421 acres 5 mi. n.w. of Mossyrock via US 12. Mountain biking, windsurfing, water skiing; dock.	59	•	•	•	•	•		•	•	•				•	•
Illahee (F-2) 75 acres 3 mi. n.e. of Bremerton on SR 306. Beachcombing, clamming, crabbing, fishing (saltwater), scuba diving, water skiing; boat moorage, dock.	60	•	•	•	•	•		•	•	•					
Jarrell Cove (G-2) 67 acres 15 mi. n.e. of Shelton off SR 3 on Hartstene Island. Beachcombing, clamming, crabbing, fishing (saltwater), sailboarding, scuba diving, water skiing, windsurfing; boat moorage, dock.	61	•	•	•	•			•	•	•	•				

Recreation Areas Chart

The map location numerals in column 2 show an area's location on the preceding map.

Find thousands of places to camp at AAA.com/campgrounds

	MAP LOCATION	CAMPING	PICNICKING	HIKING TRAILS	BOATING	BOAT RAMP	BOAT RENTAL	FISHING	SWIMMING	PET FRIENDLY	BICYCLE TRAILS	WINTER SPORTS	VISITOR CENTER	LODGE/CABINS	FOOD SERVICE
Joemma Beach (G-2) 106 acres 4 mi. s.w. of Lakebay on Case Inlet. Beachcombing, crabbing, fishing (saltwater), scuba diving, water skiing.	62	•	•	•	•	•		•		•					
Kanaskat-Palmer (E-7) 320 acres 11 mi. n.e. of Enumclaw. Bird-watching, white-water kayaking and rafting.	63	•	•	•				•	•	•	•				
Kitsap Memorial (E-2) 58 acres 6 mi. n. of Poulsbo off SR 3. Beachcombing, clamming, crabbing, fishing (saltwater), scuba diving.	64	•	•	•				•	•	•				•	
Kopachuck (G-2) 109 acres 7 mi. w. of Gig Harbor via Rosedale St. and Kopachuck Rd. Beachcombing, clamming, crabbing, fishing (saltwater), scuba diving, water skiing.	65		•	•	•			•	•	•					
Lake Chelan (D-9) 127 acres 9 mi. w. of Chelan off US 97 Alt. Scuba diving, water skiing.	66	•	•		•	•		•	•	•			•		
Lake Easton (F-7) 516 acres at Easton off I-90. Boating (no motors), cross-country skiing, dog sledding, mountain biking, snowmobiling; dock.	67	•	•	•	•	•		•	•	•	•	•			
Lake Sammamish (E-7) 510 acres 2 mi. n.w. of Issaquah via I-90. Bird-watching; sports fields.	68		•	•	•	•	•	•	•	•					•
Lake Sylvia (F-5) 252 acres 1 mi. n. of Montesano off US 12. Bird-watching, boating (no motors), mountain biking; fishing pier.	69	•	•	•	•			•	•	•					
Lake Wenatchee (E-8) 489 acres 22 mi. n. of Leavenworth off SR 207. Beachcombing, cross-country and downhill skiing, horseback riding (guided), mountain and ice climbing, snowmobiling, water skiing, white-water kayaking; dock.	70	•	•	•	•	•	•	•	•	•	•	•			
Larrabee (B-3) 2,683 acres 6 mi. s. of Bellingham on SR 11. Clamming, crabbing, fishing (fresh and saltwater); amphitheater.	71	•	•	•	•	•		•		•	•				
Lewis and Clark (G-6) 616 acres 12 mi. s.e. of Chehalis off I-5 exit 68. Horseback riding trails, interpretive trail.	72	•	•	•				•		•					
Lewis and Clark Trail (G-11) 37 acres 4 mi. w. of Dayton on US 12. Historic. Bird-watching, cross-country skiing, snowshoeing; sports fields.	73	•	•	•				•	•	•		•	•		
Lincoln Rock (E-9) 86 acres 6 mi. n.e. of Wenatchee via US 2. Cross-country skiing, water skiing; boat moorage, dock.	74	•	•	•	•	•		•	•	•	•			•	
Lyons Ferry (F-11) 168 acres 20 mi. s.e. of Washtucna off SR 261 at 620 Marmes Rd. Bird-watching, water skiing; interpretive displays.	75		•	•	•	•	•	•	•						
Manchester (F-2) 111 acres 6 mi. n.e. of Port Orchard via Beach Dr. Fishing (saltwater), mountain biking, scuba diving.	76	•	•	•				•		•	•	•			
Maryhill (H-8) 81 acres 12 mi. s. of Goldendale on US 97. Beachcombing, sailboarding, water skiing, windsurfing; dock.	77	•	•	•	•	•		•	•	•					
Millersylvania (H-2) 842 acres 10 mi. s. of Olympia off I-5 exit 95. Bird-watching, mountain biking; dock.	78	•	•	•	•			•	•	•				•	•
Moran (B-2) 5,252 acres on Orcas Island, reached by ferry from Anacortes. Bird-watching, boating (no motors), mountain biking; horse trails.	79	•	•	•	•			•	•	•				•	•
Mount Spokane (D-12) 13,919 acres 30 mi. n.e. of Spokane via US 2 and SR 206. Cross-country and downhill skiing, mountain biking, snowmobiling, snowshoeing; fire lookout, horseback riding trails.	80	•	•	•						•	•	•			•
Mystery Bay (D-2) 10 acres 1 mi. n. of Nordland off SR 116. Beachcombing, bird-watching, clamming, crabbing, scuba diving; boat moorage.	81		•		•	•		•		•					
Nolte (E-7) 111 acres 6 mi. n.e. of Enumclaw off SR 169. Bird-watching, boating (no motors).	82		•	•				•	•	•					
Ocean City (F-4) 170 acres at the n. edge of Ocean Shores off SR 115. Interpretive center. Beachcombing, bird-watching, clamming, scuba diving; marina.	83	•	•					•	•	•			•		
Olallie (E-7) 2,336 acres 6 mi. e. of North Bend via I-90. Bird-watching, mountain biking, rock climbing; waterfalls.	84		•	•				•		•	•				

Recreation Areas Chart

The map location numerals in column 2 show an
area's location on the preceding map.

**Find thousands of places to camp
at AAA.com/campgrounds**

	MAP LOCATION	CAMPING	PICNICKING	HIKING TRAILS	BOATING	BOAT RAMP	BOAT RENTAL	FISHING	SWIMMING	PET FRIENDLY	BICYCLE TRAILS	WINTER SPORTS	VISITOR CENTER	LODGE/CABINS	FOOD SERVICE
Pacific Beach (E-4) 10 acres in Pacific Beach. Beachcombing, clamming, fishing (saltwater), kayaking, surfing.	85	•	•	•				•	•	•					
Palouse Falls (F-11) 105 acres 17 mi. s.e. of Washtucna off SR 261. Bird-watching.	86	•	•	•						•					
Palouse to Cascades (F-8) 4,956 acres at the corner of 6th St. and Milwaukee Ave. in South Cle Elum. Bird-watching, cross-country skiing, horseback riding, rock climbing; interpretive center.	87	•	•	•				•		•	•	•			
Paradise Point (H-6) 88 acres 19 mi. n. of Vancouver off I-5 exit 16. Amphitheater.	88	•	•	•	•			•	•	•					
Pearrygin Lake (D-9) 1,185 acres 5 mi. n.e. of Winthrop off SR 20. Bird-watching, cross-country skiing, fat-tire snow bicycling, snowmobiling, snowshoeing, water skiing; dock.	89	•	•	•	•	•	•	•	•	•				•	•
Penrose Point (G-2) 165 acres 1 mi. e. of Lakebay off SR 302. Beachcombing, bird-watching, clamming, crabbing, fishing (saltwater), mountain biking, scuba diving, water skiing; boat moorage, dock.	90	•	•	•	•			•	•	•	•				
Potholes (F-10) 775 acres 10 mi. s.e. of Moses Lake on SR 17, then 14 mi. w. on SR 262. Bird-watching, water skiing, white-water kayaking; dock.	91	•	•	•	•	•	•	•	•	•					
Potlatch (G-1) 125 acres n. of Shelton off US 101. Beachcombing, clamming, crabbing, fishing (saltwater), sailboarding, scuba diving, water skiing; boat moorage.	92	•	•	•	•			•		•					
Rainbow Falls (I-1) 139 acres 18 mi. w. of Chehalis on SR 6. Bird-watching, horseback riding.	93	•	•	•				•	•	•	•				
Rasar (D-7) 169 acres 19 mi. e. of Burlington on SR 20. Bird-watching; amphitheater.	94	•	•	•				•	•	•					
Riverside (D-11) 12,000 acres 6 mi. n.w. of Spokane off SR 291. Historic. Scenic. Bird-watching, cross-country skiing, kayaking, rock climbing, snowmobiling, snowshoeing, water skiing, wildlife viewing; dock, horse trails, off-road vehicle area, petroglyphs.	95	•	•	•	•	•	•	•	•	•	•	•			
Sacajawea (G-10) 284 acres 3 mi. s.e. of Pasco off US 12. Historic. Water skiing; dock; interpretive center.	96		•	•	•	•		•	•	•			•		•
St. Edward (E-3) 316 acres 2 mi. s. of Kenmore on Juanita Dr. N.E. Historic. Bird-watching, horseback riding, mountain biking, water skiing; playground.	97		•	•				•		•	•				
Saltwater (G-3) 137 acres 2 mi. s. of downtown Des Moines off Marine View Dr. Beachcombing, camping (seasonal), clamming, fishing (saltwater), scuba diving, volleyball, windsurfing; artificial reef, playground.	98	•	•	•				•		•	•				•
Scenic Beach (F-2) 88 acres 12 mi. n.w. of Bremerton at Seabeck. Beachcombing, bird-watching, fishing (saltwater), sailboarding, scuba diving, water skiing.	99	•	•		•			•	•	•					
Schafer (F-5) 119 acres 8 mi. n. of Satsop on the Satsop River. Bird-watching, rafting.	100	•	•	•				•	•	•					
Seaquest (G-6) 475 acres 5 mi. e. of Castle Rock off I-5 exit 49. Bird-watching; amphitheater, lodging (yurts), museum.	101	•	•	•						•			•	•	
Sequim Bay (D-1) 92 acres 7 mi. s.e. of Sequim off US 101. Beachcombing, bird-watching, clamming, crabbing, scuba diving; boat moorage.	102	•	•	•	•	•		•	•	•					
South Whidbey (D-2) 347 acres 10 mi. s. of Coupeville on Whidbey Island. Beachcombing, bird-watching, clamming, crabbing, fishing (saltwater), scuba diving.	103	•	•	•				•		•					
Spencer Spit (B-2) 200 acres on the e. side of Lopez Island. Beachcombing, clamming, crabbing, fishing (saltwater); scuba diving, bike rental, guided kayak tours.	104	•	•	•	•	•	•	•		•					
Spokane River Centennial Trail (D-12) 40 mi. along the Spokane River between Nine Mile Falls and the Idaho state line. Bird-watching, cross-country skiing, mountain biking, snowshoeing, white-water kayaking.	105		•					•	•	•	•	•	•		

Recreation Areas Chart

The map location numerals in column 2 show an area's location on the preceding map.

Find thousands of places to camp at AAA.com/campgrounds

	MAP LOCATION	CAMPING	PICNICKING	HIKING TRAILS	BOATING	BOAT RAMP	BOAT RENTAL	FISHING	SWIMMING	PET FRIENDLY	BICYCLE TRAILS	WINTER SPORTS	VISITOR CENTER	LODGE/CABINS	FOOD SERVICE
Squilchuck (F-8) 249 acres 7 mi. s. of Wenatchee on Squilchuck Canyon Rd. Cross-country skiing, mountain biking, sledding, snowshoeing, tubing.	106	•	•							•	•	•			
Steamboat Rock (D-10) 5,043 acres 11 mi. s. of Grand Coulee on SR 155. Bird-watching, fishing (ice), ice climbing, mountain biking, rock climbing, scuba diving, snowshoeing, water skiing; dock, fishing pier, horseback riding trails.	107	•	•	•	•	•		•	•	•	•	•			•
Sucia Island Marine (B-2) 564 acres 2.5 mi. n. of Orcas Island. Accessible only by boat. Fishing (saltwater), scuba diving; dock.	108	•	•	•	•	•		•		•					
Sun Lakes-Dry Falls (E-10) 4,027 acres 4 mi. s.w. of Coulee City off SR 17. Bird-watching, golf (nine holes), water skiing; amphitheater, dock.	109	•	•	•	•	•	•	•	•	•					•
Tolmie (H-2) 105 acres 8 mi. n.e. of Olympia off I-5 exit 111. Beachcombing, bird-watching, clamming, crabbing, fishing (saltwater), scuba diving; underwater park.	110		•	•	•			•	•	•					
Triton Cove (F-1) 29 acres 5 mi. n. of Eldon on US 101 on Hood Canal. Bird-watching, crabbing, fishing (saltwater), scuba diving; dock.	111	•			•	•		•	•	•					
Twanoh (G-1) 182 acres 5 mi. e. of Union on SR 106. Beachcombing, clamming, crabbing, fishing (saltwater), tennis, water skiing; beach, boat moorage, dock.	112	•	•	•	•	•		•	•	•					•
Twenty-Five Mile Creek (D-8) 235 acres 25 mi. w. of Chelan on 25 Mile Creek Rd. Bird-watching, mountain biking, scuba diving, water skiing; marina.	113	•	•	•	•	•		•	•	•					•
Twin Harbors (F-4) 172 acres 3 mi. s. of Westport on SR 105. Beachcombing, clamming, fishing (saltwater), scuba diving.	114	•	•	•				•		•					
Wallace Falls (D-7) 4,735 acres 2 mi. n.e. of Gold Bar off US 2. Mountain biking, rock climbing, snowshoeing, white-water kayaking.	115	•	•	•	•			•	•	•	•	•	•	•	
Wenatchee Confluence (E-8) 197 acres 3 mi. n. of Wenatchee. Fishing (seasonal), tennis, water skiing, windsurfing; ballparks; beach, interpretive trail, sports courts.	116	•	•	•	•	•		•	•	•	•				
Yakima Sportsman (F-8) 266 acres 1 mi. e. of Yakima off I-82 exit 34. Bird-watching, horseback riding.	117	•	•	•				•	•	•					
OTHER															
Alder Lake (I-3) 385 acres 5.5 mi. s.w. of Elbe off SR 7 on Pleasant Valley Rd. Boat moorage.	118	•	•		•	•		•	•						
Blue Heron Park (F-9) 78 acres 3.5 mi. s.w. of Moses Lake at 111 Westshore Dr. Disc golf (nine holes); barbecue grills, playground.	119		•		•	•		•	•						
Boyer Park (F-12) 140 acres 23 mi. w. of Pullman via SR 194. Hunting; beach, food (seasonal).	120	•	•											•	•
Cascade Park (E-10) 30 acres 3 mi. n.w. of Moses Lake at 2001 W. Valley Rd. Water skiing; boat moorage, playground.	121	•	•		•	•		•	•						
Columbia Park (G-10) 400 acres in Kennewick at 5111 Columbia Park Tr. Archery, disc golf, golf (18 holes); tennis; ballpark, interpretive trail, memorials, playground (aquatic), ropes course, train ride, skate park.	122	•	•	•	•	•		•	•	•	•				
Connelly Park (E-10) 5 mi. n. of Moses Lake, w. of SR 17 on McConihe Rd. Playground.	123		•					•	•						
Crow Butte (G-9) 275 acres 13 mi. w. of Paterson on SR 14. Water skiing, windsurfing.	124	•	•		•	•		•	•						
Dungeness Landing County Park (D-1) 6 acres (and 13 acres of tideland) 5 mi. w. of Sequim on US 101, then 4 mi. n. on Kitchen Rd. Bird-watching; horseback riding trails.	125	•	•	•	•	•			•						
Eastside Park (C-9) 77 acres .25 mi. w. of Main St. on Omak Ave. in Omak. Swimming (pool); carousel, garden, skate park, sports courts, swimming pool.	126	•	•					•	•					•	
Entiat City Park (E-8) 40 acres just off US 97A at 2461 Lakeshore Dr. in Entiat. Open mid-May to early Sept. Playground.	127	•	•		•	•		•	•	•					

Recreation Areas Chart

The map location numerals in column 2 show an area's location on the preceding map.

Find thousands of places to camp at AAA.com/campgrounds

	MAP LOCATION	CAMPING	PICNICKING	HIKING TRAILS	BOATING	BOAT RAMP	BOAT RENTAL	FISHING	SWIMMING	PET FRIENDLY	BICYCLE TRAILS	WINTER SPORTS	VISITOR CENTER	LODGE/CABINS	FOOD SERVICE
Fay Bainbridge Park (E-3) 17 acres 6 mi. n. of Bainbridge Island at 15446 Sunrise Dr. Scenic. Clamming, crabbing, scuba diving; beach, boat moorage.	128	•	•		•	•		•		•					
Fort Ward Park (F-2) 137 acres 4 mi. s.w. of Bainbridge Island at 2241 Pleasant Beach Dr. Historic. Beachcombing, bird-watching, crabbing, fishing (saltwater), sailboarding, scuba diving, water skiing.	129		•	•		•		•		•	•				
Lighthouse Marine Park (A-1) 21 acres on s.w. corner of Point Roberts at 811 Marine Dr. Clamming, whale watching; beach, boardwalk, observation tower.	130	•	•		•	•		•							
Little Pend Oreille NWR (C-12) 41,568 acres 25 mi. e. of Colville via SR 20. Bird-watching, cross-country skiing, horseback riding, hunting, snowshoeing.	131	•	•	•				•	•			•	•		
Mayfield Lake County Park (F-6) 51 acres 3 mi. w. of Mossyrock on US 12. Volleyball; beach, horseshoe pits, playground.	132	•	•	•	•	•		•	•						•
Montlake Park (F-10) 10 acres at Beaumont and Linden aves. in Moses Lake. Water skiing; boat moorage.	133		•	•	•	•		•	•				•		
Mossyrock Park (G-6) 272 acres 3 mi. e. of Mossyrock via Aljune and Swofford rds. Fish cleaning station, food (seasonal), horseshoe pits.	134	•	•	•	•	•		•	•						•
Moulton Falls Regional Park (G-6) 387 acres 3 mi. s. of Yacolt on CR 16. Historic. Swimming (river); waterfalls.	135		•	•											
Mukilteo Lighthouse Park (E-3) 18 acres at 609 Front St. in Mukilteo. Scuba diving; fire pits, lighthouse.	136		•		•	•		•		•					
Odlin County Park (B-1) 80 acres on n. side of Lopez Island. Bird-watching, clamming; beach, boat moorage.	137	•	•		•	•		•							
Orondo River Park (E-8) 5 acres 3 mi. n. of Orondo at 21553 SR 97. Water skiing; boat moorage.	138	•	•		•	•			•	•					
Osoyoos Lake Veteran's Memorial Park (C-10) 47 acres 1 mi. n. of Oroville on US 97. Bird-watching, ice-skating, water skiing; beach, fish cleaning station, horseshoe pits.	139	•	•		•	•		•	•						•
Phil Simon Memorial Park (D-3) In Langley on Whidbey Island off Wharf St. Dock, marina.	140		•		•	•		•							
Pillar Point County Park (D-5) 4 acres 35 mi. w. of Port Angeles off SR 112. Beachcombing, bird-watching, clamming.	141	•	•		•	•		•							
Point Defiance Park (G-3) 702 acres in Tacoma off Pearl St. Scuba diving, tennis; beach, fishing pier, gardens.	142		•	•	•	•	•	•	•	•	•				•
Salt Creek County Park (D-5) 196 acres 15 mi. w. of Port Angeles off SR 112. Historic. Bird-watching, kayaking, scuba diving, surfing; beach, horseshoe pits, sports courts.	143	•	•	•				•		•					
Samish Park (B-3) 26 acres 10 mi. s. of Bellingham off I-5 exit 246 on North Lake Samish Dr. Canoeing; fishing dock.	144		•	•	•		•	•	•						
San Juan County Park (B-1) 12 acres on w. side of San Juan Island. Scuba diving, whale-watching (seasonal); beach (gravel).	145	•	•	•	•	•				•	•	•			
Semiahmoo County Park (A-2) 300 acres at the entrance to Semiahmoo Spit on the w. side of Drayton Harbor in Blaine. Beachcombing, bird-watching, clamming, sailing, water skiing; museum.	146		•		•			•	•				•	•	
Silver Lake Park (C-7) 411 acres 4 mi. n. of Maple Falls off SR 542 at 9006 Silver Lake Rd. Horse rental, playground.	147	•	•	•	•	•	•	•	•			•	•	•	
Skamokawa Vista Park (G-5) 75 acres .5 mi. w. of Skamokawa on SR 4. Beachcombing; baseball, basketball, horseshoe pit, tennis.	148	•	•		•	•		•							•
Skokomish Park At Lake Cushman (F-1) 603 acres 7 mi. n.w. of Hoodsport via SR 119. Scuba diving, water skiing.	149	•	•	•	•	•		•	•						
Sunny Beach Point (I-3) 9 acres on Alder Lake off SR 7. Open mid-May to mid-Sept. (water levels permitting). Water skiing.	150		•		•			•	•						
Taidnapam Park (G-7) 5 mi. e. of Morton on US 12, s. on Kosmos Rd., then 4 mi. e. on Champion Haul Rd. Boat ramp (seasonal), playground.	151	•	•		•	•		•	•	•					

Recreation Areas Chart

The map location numerals in column 2 show an area's location on the preceding map.

 Find thousands of places to camp at AAA.com/campgrounds

	MAP LOCATION	CAMPING	PICNICKING	HIKING TRAILS	BOATING	BOAT RAMP	BOAT RENTAL	FISHING	SWIMMING	PET FRIENDLY	BICYCLE TRAILS	WINTER SPORTS	VISITOR CENTER	LODGE/CABINS	FOOD SERVICE
Thornton A. Sullivan Park (E-3) 35 acres 5 mi. s. of Everett on 112th St., S.E. Disc golf (nine holes), ping-pong; beach, nature trails, playground.	152	•	•					•	•	•					
Washington Park (C-2) 220 acres 4 mi. w. of Anacortes on Sunset Ave. Scenic drive. Beach.	153	•	•	•	•	•		•	•						
Wenatchee River County Park (E-8) 10 acres 10 mi. n.w. of Wenatchee on US 2/97. Open Apr.-Oct. Ping-pong, white-water rafting; ballparks, playground.	154	•	•		•	•			•			•			
Wenberg County Park (D-3) 45 acres 4 mi. n. of Marysville via I-5, then 8 mi. w. off SR 531. Water skiing; beach, playground.	155	•	•		•	•		•	•		•				•
Windjammer (City Beach) Park (C-2) 28 acres .25 mi. e. of SR 20 in Oak Harbor on Whidbey Island. Swimming (lagoon); dock, playgrounds, sports courts, windmill.	156	•	•			•		•	•						

Make the Connction

AAA guidebooks are just the beginning. Open the door to a whole lot more on **AAA.com**. Get extra travel insight, more information and online booking.

 Find this symbol for places to look, book and save on AAA.com.

ABERDEEN (F-5) pop. 16,896, elev. 10'

Named for the Scottish city, Aberdeen wraps around the head of expansive Grays Harbor at the mouths of the Chehalis and Wishkah rivers. The settlement grew up around a sawmill established in 1884. By 1910 dozens of lumber and shingle mills lined the harbor and the population rose to 17,000.

Aberdeen is the home port for two tall sailing ships. The *Lady Washington*, built in the city in the late 1880s, is a full-scale replica of the late 18th-century merchant brig that was the first American-flagged vessel to round Cape Horn; in 2007 it was named the Official Ship of the State of Washington. A companion vessel, the *Hawaiian Chieftain*, was built in Lahaina, Hawaii in 1988. Tours and local sailing excursions are offered when the ships are in port; for more information phone (360) 532-8611 or (800) 200-5239.

Handsome Victorian and Craftsman-style homes grace Aberdeen's hillside residential district north of downtown. Sam Benn Park, E. 9th and N. I streets, offers tennis courts, disc golf, a playground, a rose garden and a network of pathways through landscaped rolling hills; phone (360) 537-3230.

Greater Grays Harbor, Inc.: 506 Duffy St., Aberdeen, WA 98520. **Phone:** (360) 532-1924 or (800) 321-1924.

A HARBOR VIEW BED & BREAKFAST   (360)533-7996

♥♥♥♥ Historic Bed & Breakfast. **Address:** 111 W 11th St 98520

BEST WESTERN PLUS ABERDEEN   (360)537-7460

♥♥♥
Hotel
$139-$249

AAA Benefit: Members save up to 15% and earn bonus points!

Address: 701 E Heron St 98520 **Location:** Waterfront. Just e on US 12, cross street to Kansas St; downtown. **Facility:** 87 units, some efficiencies. 3 stories, interior corridors. **Terms:** cancellation fee imposed. **Pool:** heated indoor. **Activities:** hot tub, exercise room. **Guest Services:** coin laundry.

WHERE TO EAT

BREAKWATER SEAFOOD & CHOWDER HOUSE
                    360/532-5693

♥ Seafood. Quick Serve. **Address:** 306 S F St 98520

🔗 For more details, rates and reservations: AAA.com/travelguides/hotels

AIRWAY HEIGHTS pop. 6,114, elev. 2,398'

• Hotels & Restaurants map & index p. 187

DAYS INN & SUITES SPOKANE AIRPORT
                    (509)244-0222

♥♥ ♥♥
Hotel
$78-$200

Address: 1215 S Garfield Rd 99001 **Location:** I-90/US 2 exit 277 to US 2, 4 mi w. **Facility:** 61 units. 2 stories (no elevator), interior corridors. **Parking:** winter plug-ins. **Activities:** exercise room. **Guest Services:** coin laundry, area transportation. **Featured Amenity:** full hot breakfast.

NORTHERN QUEST RESORT & CASINO
                    (509)481-6000   39

♦♦♦ ♦♦♦
Hotel
$179-$369

Address: 100 N Hayford Rd 99001 **Location:** I-90 exit 277B (US 2), 4.3 mi w toward Fairchild Air Force Base/Davenport/Spokane International Airport, then 1 mi n. **Facility:** With an on-site casino, sports lounge, cigar bar and spa, guests will find more entertainment options than they could imagine—even outdoor concerts. Enjoy rooms with four-jet showers and great views. 250 units. 10 stories, interior corridors. **Terms:** check-in 4 pm, 3 day cancellation notice-fee imposed. **Amenities:** video games, safes. **Dining:** 6 restaurants, also, Masselow's Steakhouse, see separate listing, entertainment. **Pool:** heated indoor. **Activities:** sauna, hot tub, exercise room, spa. **Guest Services:** valet laundry, area transportation.

WHERE TO EAT

MASSELOW'S STEAKHOUSE   509/242-7000   46

♥♥♥ ♥♥♥
Pacific Northwest
Fine Dining
$23-$53

AAA Inspector Notes: With a modern tribute to the Kalispel Indian tribe showing through in the décor, the restaurant's menu also resonates a tribute with regional offerings such as elk, bison, beef, pork, chicken and seafood. Be sure to try the seasonal dessert. **Features:** full bar. **Reservations:** suggested. **Address:** 100 N Hayford Rd 99001 **Location:** I-90 exit 277B (US 2), 4.3 mi w toward Fairchild Air Force Base/Davenport/Spokane International Airport, then 1 mi n; in Northern Quest Resort & Casino. **Parking:** on-site and valet.

Prime grade steaks and award winning wine list.

ANACORTES (C-2) pop. 15,778, elev. 75'

Anacortes occupies the northern end of hilly Fidalgo Island, which is linked by bridges to Whidbey Island to the south and the mainland to the east. Settled in the 1860s, the town was first called Ship Harbor, but in 1876 town promoter Amos Bowman had it changed to a Spanish-sounding version of "Anna Curtis," his wife's maiden name.

From the 1,270-foot summit of Mount Erie, 5 miles south via Heart Lake and Mt. Erie roads, view-sextend to the Cascades, Olympics and San Juan Islands. Campbell Lake, at the base of the mountain, is unusual; not only is it on an island, but it has an island inside of it as well. Washington Park *(see Recreation Areas Chart)*, 4 miles west on wooded Fidalgo Head, offers beaches and hiking trails; phone (360) 293-1927.

Anacortes Community Forest Lands occupy 2,800 acres of the island's interior. Fifty miles of multi-use trails wind through woods, passing meadows, wetlands and lakes. A trailhead kiosk with a trail map is located on A Avenue south of 37th Street. For more information phone the Anacortes Parks Department at (360) 293-1918.

Washington State Ferries, 2100 Ferry Terminal Rd., offers daily car ferry service to the San Juan Islands and Sidney, British Columbia. Reservations for vehicles on the Anacortes-to-Sidney ferry are highly recommended. May through September parking is $10 per day, $20 for 2 days, $25 for 3 days and $40 for 7 days; parking fees are half off the rest of the year. For ferry information phone (206) 464-6400, or (888) 808-7977 in Wash.

Skagit County maintains a toll car ferry service from the foot of I Avenue to Guemes Island. The fare is $10-$12 for a car and driver; $4 for single passenger. Phone (360) 293-6356.

Anacortes Chamber of Commerce: 819 Commercial Ave., Suite F, Anacortes, WA 98221. **Phone:** (360) 293-7911.

DECEPTION PASS TOURS is at 5596 SR 20, 2 mi. n. of Deception Pass Bridge. The bridge, which connects Whidbey and Fidalgo islands, is one of the Pacific Northwest's scenic wonders. Completed in 1935, it spans the narrow passage through which Joseph Whidbey, master of the HMS *Discovery* and Capt. George Vancouver's chief navigator, sailed in the spring of 1792, proving that it was not a small bay but rather a deep and turbulent channel (hence the name) connecting the Strait of Juan de Fuca with the Saratoga Passage.

One-hour tours aboard the jet-driven catamaran *Island Whaler* travel through Deception Pass to Canoe Pass and Rosario Strait—known for its large porpoise population—before heading into Bowman Bay. Tour guides relate the history of the bridge and the Puget Sound islands and provide information about the region's wildlife, which includes bald eagles, seals and the giant Pacific octopus. This is a fun way to get an up-close look at an impressive engineering feat and feast your eyes on some gorgeous water views. Whale-watching tours also are available in the spring and summer.

Hours: Cruises depart daily on the hour 11-6, July 1-Oct. 1; Thurs.-Mon. on the hour 11-6, Apr.-June. Whale-watching tours depart Sat. at 10 a.m. **Cost:** $39.95; $34.95 (ages 3-12 and 62+). Whale-watching tours $89; $79 (ages 0-12 and 65+).

Tickets can be purchased at the office or at the booth in the parking lot at the south end of Deception Pass Bridge, where passengers receive boarding passes and directions to the dock; arrive 15 minutes prior to departure time. **Phone:** (360) 679-7222 or (888) 909-8687. [GT]

MYSTIC SEA CHARTERS departs from the Cap Sante Marina, Dock A (710 Seafarers Way). Scenic excursions aboard the 100-foot *Mystic Sea*, a passenger vessel with a heated, enclosed aft deck, cruise the waters of the San Juan Islands. Whale-watching trips for orca, humpback and minke whales are offered seasonally.

Time: Allow 6 hours, 30 minutes minimum. **Hours:** Trips depart daily at 10:45, mid-May to early Oct.; passengers must arrive by 10. **Cost:** Fare $105; $95 (ages 65+); $85 (military with ID); $69 (ages 3-17 and students with ID); $49 (ages 3-17); $29 (ages 0-2). A fuel surcharge may apply. Reservations are required. **Phone:** (360) 588-8000 or (800) 308-9387. [T]

ANACO BAY INN	360/299-3320

♥♥ Extended Stay Hotel. **Address:** 916 33rd St 98221

MAJESTIC INN & SPA	(360)299-1400

♥♥♥ Hotel. **Address:** 419 Commercial Ave 98221

MARINA INN   (360)293-1100

♥♥ 💎
Hotel
$74-$169

Address: 3300 Commercial Ave 98221 **Location:** Just s of downtown. Located in a commercial area. **Facility:** 52 units. 2 stories (no elevator), interior corridors. **Terms:** 3 day cancellation notice. **Activities:** limited exercise equipment. **Guest Services:** coin laundry. **Featured Amenity:** continental breakfast.

[SAVE] [BIZ] 🛜 ✕ 🛎 🖥 💻

SWINOMISH CASINO & LODGE	360/588-3600

♥♥♥ Hotel. **Address:** 12885 Casino Dr 98221

WHERE TO EAT

ADRIFT RESTAURANT	360/588-0653

♥♥ American. Casual Dining. **Address:** 510 Commercial Ave 98221

ANTHONY'S AT CAP SANTE MARINA	360/588-0333

♥♥♥ Seafood. Casual Dining. **Address:** 1207 Q Ave 98221

CALICO CUPBOARD CAFE & BAKERY	360/293-7315

♥♥ American. Casual Dining. **Address:** 901 Commercial Ave 98221

FRIDA'S GOURMET MEXICAN CUISINE	360/299-2120

♥♥ Mexican. Casual Dining. **Address:** 416 1/2 Commercial Ave 98221

ROCKFISH GRILL/ANACORTES BREWING	360/588-1720

♥♥ American. Casual Dining. **Address:** 320 Commercial Ave 98221

THAI SEASON RESTAURANT	360/293-4004

♥♥ Thai. Casual Dining. **Address:** 710 Commercial Ave 98221

ARLINGTON (D-3) pop. 17,926, elev. 120'
• Part of Seattle area — see map p. 124

Located just below the confluence of the north and south forks of the Stillaguamish River, Arlington dates from the early 1860s, when settlers farmed the rich soils of the river valley. This former lumbering center once ranked among the nation's top producers of shingles. The Stillaguamish Valley Pioneer Museum, 20722 67th Ave. N.E., has exhibits about local history as well as a huge collection of old photographs; phone (360) 435-7289.

Arlington-Smokey Point Chamber of Commerce: 104 N. Olympic Ave., Arlington, WA 98223. **Phone:** (360) 659-5453.

BEST WESTERN PLUS ARLINGTON/MARYSVILLE
(360)363-4321

♥♥♥ 🔷🔷
Hotel
$129-$209

Best Western PLUS. **AAA Benefit:** Members save up to 15% and earn bonus points!

Address: 3721 172nd St NE 98223 **Location:** I-5 exit 206, 0.4 mi e. **Facility:** 100 units, some efficiencies. 4 stories, interior corridors. **Terms:** check-in 4 pm, cancellation fee imposed, resort fee. **Pool:** heated indoor. **Activities:** hot tub, exercise room. **Guest Services:** valet and coin laundry. **Featured Amenity: full hot breakfast.**

SAVE 🛎↑ CALL 🛗 ☕ 💪 BIZ
📶 ⊠ 🚭 🖨 💻 / SOME UNITS 🐾

WYNDHAM GARDEN HOTEL   (360)657-0500
♥♥♥ Hotel. **Address:** 16710 Smokey Point Blvd 98223

ASHFORD (F-7) pop. 217, elev. 1,770'

Located just outside the Nisqually entrance to Mount Rainier National Park, Ashford was settled in the 1880s. Initially a sawmill settlement, it became the main gateway to the park when the Tacoma Eastern Railway reached town in 1904. In the early days most park visitors came by rail; passenger train service continued until 1926, the same year the road leading to the park was paved. Cozy bed-and-breakfast properties are popular with national park visitors. The Ex-Nihilo: Recycled Spirits of Iron Sculpture Park is 3 miles west at 22410 SR 706.

Mt. Rainier Visitor Association: 30027 E. SR 706, P.O. Box 214, Ashford, WA 98304. **Phone:** (360) 569-0910 or (877) 617-9951.

ALEXANDER'S LODGE   360/569-2300
♥♥ Historic Country Inn. **Address:** 37515 SR 706 E 98304

ASOTIN (G-12) pop. 1,251, elev. 760'

Originally named Has-Hu-Tin (a Native American word meaning "eel"), Asotin was renamed by an act of the state legislature in 1886. The town is at the southern end of the Clearwater and Snake River National Recreation Trail, a 19-mile paved route that follows the river shoreline north through the Clarkston-Lewiston area. Chief Looking Glass Park (see Recreation Areas Chart), 305 1st St., features the 1899 Full Gospel Church with an original white oak pump organ. The Snake River Road continues south 21 miles to the mouth of the Grande Ronde River, at the northern entrance to Hells Canyon.

AUBURN (G-3) pop. 70,180, elev. 79'
• Hotels & Restaurants map & index p. 201
• Part of Seattle area — see map p. 124

Originally named Slaughter after Lt. William A. Slaughter, who was killed in a Native American skirmish, the town of Auburn acquired its present name in 1893, a salute to the same-named town in New York. In 1912 the Northern Pacific Railroad made Auburn its western freight terminus, prompting many large locomotive shops to open. Major employers today include Boeing and the federal government's General Services Administration.

Emerald Downs, half a mile east of SR 167 on 15th St. N.W. to 2300 Emerald Downs Dr., offers Thoroughbred racing mid-April to late September; free stable tours are given Saturday mornings by appointment. Phone (253) 288-7000 for racetrack information, or (253) 288-7711 for tours.

Note: Policies concerning admittance of children to pari-mutuel betting facilities vary. Phone for information.

Auburn Area Chamber of Commerce: 25 2nd St. N.W., Auburn, WA 98001. **Phone:** (253) 833-0700.

Shopping: Outlet Collection Seattle, junction SRs 18 and 167, offers more than 100 outlet stores, including Ann Taylor, Burlington Coat Factory, Marshalls, Nordstrom Rack and Old Navy.

FLAMING GEYSER STATE PARK is 2 mi. e. on SR 18, .5 mi. e. on S.E. Auburn-Black Diamond Rd., then 8 mi. e. on S.E. Green Valley Rd. to 23700 S.E. Flaming Geyser Rd. The 480-acre park is named for an old coal test hole that has an 8-inch methane flame. The Steelhead Trout Imprinting Project holds young fish in a series of ponds to instill the habit of homing. A playground is on the grounds. See Recreation Areas Chart. **Hours:** Daily 8-dusk. **Cost:** Park admission $10 (per private vehicle); Discover Pass, valid for 1 year, $30 (per private vehicle). **Phone:** (253) 735-8839. 🐾 🍴

SOOS CREEK BOTANICAL GARDEN AND HERITAGE CENTER is 4 mi. n.e. on SR 18 to the S.E. 304th St. exit, w. .5 mi. on S.E. 304th St., then n. on 132nd Ave. S.E. to the entrance at 29308 132nd Ave. S.E. Located on the site of a 160-acre homestead settled in 1890, this garden's themed areas include the Rain Garden, Heritage Flowers, Cedar Grove and the Vegetable Demonstration Garden. Birds twitter in the Louie/Christensen Aviary. The Soos Creek Heritage Center has historical photographs, maps and antiques that document farm life on the Soos Creek Plateau dating back to 1890.

(See map & index p. 201.)

Time: Allow 1 hour, 30 minutes minimum. **Hours:** Wed.-Sat. 10-3, mid-Mar. to mid-Nov. **Cost:** $5. **Phone:** (253) 639-0949.

BEST WESTERN PLUS MOUNTAIN VIEW AUBURN INN
(253)887-7600 **36**

Hotel
$99-$309

Best Western PLUS. **AAA Benefit:** Members save up to 15% and earn bonus points!

Address: 401 8th St SW 98001 **Location:** SR 18 exit C St, just s, then just w. Auburn, 46. **Facility:** 124 units. 4 stories, interior corridors. **Terms:** cancellation fee imposed. **Pool:** heated indoor. **Activities:** hot tub, exercise room. **Guest Services:** valet and coin laundry, area transportation. **Featured Amenity:** full hot breakfast.

SAVE · 🍴 · 🛜 · 🛁 · BIZ · HS · 🛜
✕ · 🛗 · 📷 · 🖥 · /SOME UNITS · 🐾 · 🚐

COMFORT INN-AUBURN (253)333-8888 **35**
Hotel. **Address:** 1 16th St NE 98002

LA QUINTA INN & SUITES AUBURN (253)804-9999 **37**
Hotel. **Address:** 225 6th St SE 98002

WHERE TO EAT

SUN BREAK CAFE 253/939-5225 **27**
American. Casual Dining. **Address:** 22 A St SW 98001

BAINBRIDGE ISLAND (F-3) pop. 23,025, elev. 89'
• Hotels & Restaurants map & index p. 170
• Part of Seattle area — see map p. 124

The Bainbridge Island community of Winslow traces its beginnings to the late 19th century, when it was a shipbuilding center for schooners. Eagle Harbor still hums with the activities of the Washington State Ferries maintenance yard; daily ferries connect the island to nearby Seattle.

The Walkabout, a mile-long foot path, parallels the Winslow waterfront. A footbridge leads to Eagle Harbor Waterfront Park and a fishing pier. Six miles north at 15446 Sunrise Dr. is Fay Bainbridge Park (see Recreation Areas Chart), a well-known Puget Sound recreation area. Despite—or because of—its hilly terrain and scenic vistas, the island is a popular spot for bicycling.

Bainbridge Island Chamber of Commerce: 395 Winslow Way E., Bainbridge Island, WA 98110. **Phone:** (206) 842-3700.

Shopping: Downtown Winslow, Winslow Way and Madison Avenue, offers a variety of shops, galleries and eateries.

BAINBRIDGE ISLAND MUSEUM OF ART is a quarter mile n. of the ferry terminal at 550 Winslow Way E. Six galleries on two floors present 12 to 16 changing exhibits a year, including displays from the permanent collection. The focus is on works by artists from the Puget Sound region. **Time:** Allow 30 minutes minimum. **Hours:** Daily 10-6. Closed Thanksgiving and Christmas. **Cost:** Free. **Phone:** (206) 842-4451. 🍴

BLOEDEL RESERVE is 6.5 mi. n.w. of the ferry dock on SR 305, then .4 mi. n. on Agatewood Rd. N.E., then .6 mi. e. to 7571 N.E. Dolphin Dr. This 150-acre former private estate was once owned by Angela Collins, widow of John Collins, Seattle's sixth mayor. Prentice and Virginia Bloedel purchased it, lived in the house for 32 years and then bequeathed everything to the public so that visitors could come and enjoy nature's beauty in a relaxed, tranquil setting.

Guests are greeted at the gatehouse and provided with a map that serves as a guide to the 2-mile tour of the grounds, encompassing meadows, ponds, protected woodlands, various moss and Japanese gardens and a bird marshland. The gardens are all meticulously landscaped and benefit from Puget Sound's mild, moist climate. The estate home, built in the style of a French country house, functions as a visitor center and has displays relating to the history of the reserve.

Trails wind through a dense forest of Douglas fir, western red cedar, western hemlock and moss-encrusted maples. Be sure and stroll through the Glen, which is ablaze in late spring and early summer with blooming rhododendrons. Perennials, bulbs, wildflowers and more than 15,000 cyclamen plants—one of the largest plantings in the world—add their own beauty, making this one of the most enchanting spots in the entire reserve.

Picnicking and pets are prohibited. **Time:** Allow 1 hour, 30 minutes minimum. **Hours:** Tues.-Sun. 10-4 (also Thurs.-Sun. 4-6, Memorial Day-Labor Day). Closed Jan. 1, Thanksgiving and Christmas. **Cost:** $17; $12 (ages 65+ and military with ID); $10 (ages 13-18 and students with ID); $6 (ages 5-12). **Phone:** (206) 842-7631.

THE MARSHALL SUITES (206)855-9666 **14**
Hotel. **Address:** 350 NE High School Rd 98110

WHERE TO EAT

DOC'S MARINA GRILL 206/842-8339 **12**
American. Casual Dining. **Address:** 403 Madison Ave S 98110

HITCHCOCK 206/201-3789 **10**
Pacific Northwest. Casual Dining. **Address:** 133 Winslow Way E 98110

THE STREAMLINER DINER 206/842-8595 **11**
American. Casual Dining. **Address:** 397 Winslow Way E 98110

BATTLE GROUND (H-6) pop. 17,571, elev. 290'
• Hotels p. 40 • Restaurants p. 40

Battle Ground's name refers to an incident that occurred in 1855, when a group of Native Americans being detained at Fort Vancouver staged an escape. In the ensuing skirmish their chief was killed, and a band of volunteer soldiers permitted the escapees to give him the dignity of a traditional burial. The volunteers were subsequently hounded by other soldiers stationed at the fort for not waging battle against the fugitives. Although there never was a "battle ground," the name was adopted when the town was established in 1902.

Three miles northeast of Battle Ground off SR 502 is Battle Ground Lake State Park (see Recreation Areas Chart). The site is believed to be a caldera formed by the collapse of a volcanic cone.

Battle Ground Chamber of Commerce: 1710 W. Main St., Suite 113, Battle Ground, WA 98604. **Phone:** (360) 687-1510.

BEST WESTERN PLUS BATTLE GROUND INN & SUITES   (360)687-8881

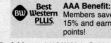

Hotel
$92-$175

Best Western PLUS. AAA Benefit: Members save up to 15% and earn bonus points!

Address: 1419 W Main St 98604 **Location:** At SW 15th Ave; downtown. **Facility:** 46 units. 3 stories, interior corridors. **Terms:** cancellation fee imposed. **Pool:** heated indoor. **Activities:** hot tub, exercise room. **Guest Services:** coin laundry.

WHERE TO EAT

BURGERVILLE   360/687-7308
American. Quick Serve. **Address:** 217 W Main St 98604

MILL CREEK PUB   360/723-5223
American. Casual Dining. **Address:** 1710 SW 9th Ave, Suite 101 98604

BEAVER (D-4) elev. 390'

Beaver was settled in 1891 in a location at the southern end of Lake Pleasant, in the Sol Duc Valley. After rail lines were built into the woods, the town became a booming logging camp.

SOL DUC HATCHERY INTERPRETIVE CENTER is 4 mi. w. on US 101, then 1 mi. s.w. on Mary Clark and Pavel rds. to 1423 Pavel Rd. Juvenile salmon can be observed. **Time:** Allow 30 minutes minimum. **Hours:** Daily 8-4:30. **Cost:** Free. **Phone:** (360) 327-3246.

BELFAIR (F-2) pop. 3,931, elev. 46'
• Part of Olympic National Park area — see map p. 100

Located at the head of Hood Canal's southern hook, Belfair sprang up in the 1880s as a supply center for area logging operations. Belfair State Park (see Recreation Areas Chart), 3 miles west at 3151 N.E. SR 300, has beach access along Hood Canal and interpretive displays about shellfish,

water quality and the life cycle of salmon. You can see spawning salmon in Big Mission and Little Mission creeks during the fall; phone (360) 275-0668.

Tahuya State Forest, west of Belfair off SR 300, is a 23,100-acre "working forest." Dozens of miles of multi-use trails and forest roads provide recreation opportunities for hikers, mountain bikers, horseback riders, motorcyclists, and ATV and four-wheel-drive vehicles. For information phone the Department of Natural Resources at (360) 825-1631 or (360) 801-5097.

North Mason Chamber of Commerce: 30 N.E. Romance Hill Rd., Suite 103, P.O. Box 416, Belfair, WA 98528. **Phone:** (360) 275-4267 or (360) 275-0600.

SELAH INN   360/275-0916
Bed & Breakfast. **Address:** 130 NE Dulalip Landing 98528

BELLEVUE (F-3) pop. 122,363, elev. 100'
• Hotels p. 42 • Restaurants p. 44
• Hotels & Restaurants map & index p. 160
• Part of Seattle area — see map p. 124

The traditional role of this Eastside (i.e., east of Lake Washington) community, scenically wedged between Lake Washington and Lake Sammamish, has been that of Seattle's younger, unassuming sibling. Less than 30 years ago Bellevue was a suburban town, a bedroom community for Seattleites who wanted a little peace and quiet. No more—now there are not one but two impressive downtown skylines within spitting distance of Puget Sound.

Bellevue's first high-rise rose in 1983. More went up in the 1990s. Today a small (at least by Seattle standards) but growing forest of skyscrapers defines the city's profile. Take a walk around downtown Bellevue and you'll see steel-and-glass behemoths like the twin 42-story luxury condominium development Bellevue Towers and Avalon Meydenbauer, an upscale high-rise apartment complex, rising like vertical mushrooms from a particularly fertile forest floor.

Bellevue Downtown Park, just west of Bellevue Way N.E. between N.E. 4th and N.E. 8th streets, is an expansive 21-acre greensward in the heart of downtown. A half-mile path encircles grass lawns, and a stepped canal of flowing waters ends in a 240-foot-wide waterfall that spills into a reflecting pool. The big, open lawn is great for kite flying and a nice spot for a picnic. The park is lovely in April when flowering trees are in bloom.

There also are tucked-away little nooks where you can enjoy the Northwest's robust natural beauty. A prime example is little Meydenbauer Beach Park, perched on the shore of Meydenbauer Bay at 419 98th Ave. N.E. It's just a couple of blocks west of Bellevue Downtown Park; take 98th Avenue N.E. off Lake Washington Boulevard N.E. (Don't let the green directional signs leading away from Lake Washington Boulevard and the bay fool you; just follow them and you'll get to the parking lot.) From

(See map & index p. 160.)

there it's a short jaunt down to the waterfront via a paved walkway that passes beneath tall trees.

A little slip of a beach looks out over Meydenbauer Bay, an indentation along the Lake Washington shoreline. A whaling company was based here until the 1940s; it's been supplanted by the expensive craft moored at the adjacent Meydenbauer Bay Yacht Club. Tony homes climb the wooded hillsides above the bay. This pretty, well-kept park has a fishing dock, a picnic area and restrooms.

Two cool public art installations are at the Bellevue Transit Center, downtown at 10850 N.E. 6th St. "High Road" comprises three spherical shapes that appear to be walking on stilts; "Windswept" is an illuminated-from-within aluminum sculpture mounted atop an elevated platform that also serves as a bench. Bellevue's public transportation nerve center is a convenient base from which you can board Sound Transit express buses for travel throughout the Seattle-Tacoma-Everett-Bellevue metro area. Sound Transit's 550 Express makes the run to downtown Seattle in 30 minutes. For schedule and fare information phone (206) 398-5000 or (888) 889-6368.

Visit Bellevue Washington: 11100 N.E. 6th St., Third Floor, Bellevue, WA 98004. **Phone:** (425) 450-3777.

Shopping: The "Bellevue Collection," which consists of three separate complexes, anchors downtown shopping. Lincoln Square, on Bellevue Way N.E. between N.E. 6th and N.E. 8th streets, has specialty retailers and stores selling upscale home furnishings and accessories. Everything about this complex is sleek, from the post-modern interior design (lots of gleaming stainless steel) to the water that glides in shimmering sheets down a 65-foot vertical glass shaft to a pool bristling with sinuous emerald-green glass tubes ("Lincoln Square Fiori," the work of Dale Chihuly). Another Chihuly piece, the spectacular, three-tiered "End of the Day Chandelier," hangs above the Lincoln Way entrance and is strikingly illuminated at night.

A similar lineup of shops is at the adjacent Bellevue Place, inside the Hyatt Regency Bellevue at 900 Bellevue Way N.E. An elevated pedestrian walkway connects Lincoln Square to Bellevue Square across the street. In addition to anchor stores Macy's and Nordstrom, this destination mall has some 200 shops and restaurants. The Gunnar Nordstrom Gallery, 800 Bellevue Way N.E., is an intimate space that displays contemporary fine art. Regional artist Bill Braun's works are huge favorites here. His *trompe l'oeil* paintings are incredibly realistic: simply rendered montages of flowers, houses and butterflies that look just like a child's construction paper art project. You won't believe your eyes.

The Bellevue Farmers Market sets up Thursdays 3-7 in the First Presbyterian Church parking lot at 1717 Bellevue Way N.E., mid-May to mid-Oct. Local farmers offer organic fruits and veggies, hazelnuts,

honey, fresh seafood and homemade baked goods. Regularly scheduled events include chef demos, hands-on activities for kids and fiddle and banjo hoedowns.

The Shops at the Bravern fills an angled space between N.E. 8th Street and 110th Avenue N.E. Neiman Marcus, Hermès, Gucci, Salvatore Ferragamo, Tory Burch and other upscale stores are in a landscaped setting reminiscent of a European village.

Just south of the Bellevue Collection is Old Bellevue, a stretch of Main Street where shopping is a stroll-along-the-sidewalk-and-browse affair. The mix of shops and boutiques runs the gamut from quaint to trendy. Stop at Belle Pastry, known for oh-so-fresh-baked baguettes, brioches and croissants.

MarketPlace @ Factoria, just southeast of the I-90/I-405 junction, has the usual lineup of outlet mall stores, from T.J. Maxx and DSW Shoe Warehouse to Nordstrom Rack and Old Navy. Crossroads Bellevue, 15600 N.E. 8th St., is another popular shopping destination, with Barnes & Noble, Old Navy and a farmers market held on Tuesdays, June through September.

BELLEVUE BOTANICAL GARDEN is at 12001 Main St. in Wilburton Hill Park. A half-mile nature trail traverses this 53-acre tract of rolling hills, native woodlands, meadows and bogs. Another trail, the Ravine Experience, winds for three-tenths of a mile through second-growth forest and crosses a 150-foot long suspension bridge. Gardens illustrate the use of ground covers, alpine plants, perennials, drought tolerant plants, ferns and Northwest native plants. A Japanese-influenced garden honors Yao, Bellevue's sister city in Japan.

Time: Allow 1 hour, 30 minutes minimum. **Hours:** Garden open daily dawn-dusk. Visitor center daily 9-4. Guided 90-minute tours depart Sat.-Sun. at 2, Apr.-Oct. **Cost:** Free. **Phone:** (425) 452-2750. GT

KIDSQUEST CHILDREN'S MUSEUM is at 1116 108th Ave. N.E. Exhibits engage children up to age 10 with such interactive galleries as On the Go, which has a kid-friendly, full-scale Peterbilt semi-truck cab, the Treehouse and the Bellevue Mercantile. The Water Gallery explores both fun and practical uses of H2O, while the Tot Orchard keeps toddlers entertained. There also is a 2.5-story Atrium Climber. **Time:** Allow 1 hour minimum. **Hours:** Tues.-Thurs. and Sat. 9-5, Fri. 9-8, Sun. noon-5. Closed Jan. 1, Easter, July 4, Thanksgiving and Christmas. **Cost:** $12; $11 (ages 60+ and military with ID); free (ages 0-1). **Phone:** (425) 637-8100.

LAKE HILLS GREENBELT, 15416 S.E. 16th St., is a 150-acre wildlife corridor and park featuring two lakes, 3 miles of hiking trails, agricultural areas and demonstration gardens. The ranger station has displays of native animals and plants; it also showcases sustainable building products. The Urban Demonstration Garden hosts master gardener workshops. **Hours:** Grounds open daily dawn-dusk. Ranger station open Tues.-Sat. noon-4. Guided

(See map & index p. 160.)

tours depart Sat. at 2. Master gardener workshops offered Wed. and Sat. at various times; phone ahead to confirm schedule. Closed major holidays. **Cost:** Free. **Phone:** (425) 452-7225 or (425) 452-6885. GT 𝒜

AC HOTEL BY MARRIOTT SEATTLE BELLEVUE/ DOWNTOWN   (425)625-2450 65

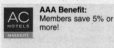

Contemporary Hotel
$72-$453

AC HOTELS MARRIOTT

AAA Benefit: Members save 5% or more!

Address: 208 106th Pl NE 98004 **Location:** I-405 exit 13 (NE 4th St), 0.4 mi w, then just s. **Facility:** 234 units. 7 stories, interior corridors. **Terms:** check-in 4 pm, cancellation fee imposed. **Amenities:** safes. **Activities:** exercise room. **Guest Services:** valet laundry.

SAVE ▼ CALL 🦽 👪 BIZ 🛜 ✕ 📶 💻

BELLEVUE CLUB HOTEL   425/454-4424 72

Boutique Hotel
Rates not provided

Address: 11200 SE 6th St 98004 **Location:** I-405 exit 12, 0.4 mi nw. **Facility:** The first thing you'll notice is the meticulous landscaping around this elegant hotel. Artwork by international and local artists is proudly displayed in the public spaces. 66 units. 4 stories, interior corridors. **Parking:** on-site (fee) and valet. **Amenities:** safes. **Dining:** 3 restaurants. **Pool:** heated outdoor, heated indoor. **Activities:** sauna, hot tub, steamroom, tennis, game room, health club, spa. **Guest Services:** valet laundry, area transportation. **Featured Amenity: continental breakfast.**

SAVE 🍴 🏋 ▼ 🛗 CALL 🦽 👪 BIZ HS 🛜 ✕ 📶 /SOME UNITS 🐾 🍽 💻

COURTYARD BY MARRIOTT-BELLEVUE DOWNTOWN   (425)454-5888 62

Hotel
$84-$483

COURTYARD

AAA Benefit: Members save 5% or more!

Address: 11010 NE 8th St 98004 **Location:** I-405 exit 13B, just w. **Facility:** 253 units. 5 stories, interior corridors. **Parking:** on-site (fee). **Terms:** cancellation fee imposed. **Amenities:** safes. **Pool:** heated indoor. **Activities:** exercise room. **Guest Services:** valet and coin laundry.

SAVE ECO 📶 🍴 ▼ CALL 🦽 🛜 👪 BIZ HS 🛜 ✕ 📶 💻 /SOME UNITS 🍽

COURTYARD BY MARRIOTT BELLEVUE/REDMOND   (425)869-5300 55

 Hotel. **Address:** 14615 NE 29th Pl 98007

AAA Benefit: Members save 5% or more!

EMBASSY SUITES BY HILTON SEATTLE - BELLEVUE   (425)644-2500 76

Hotel
$129-$400

EMBASSY SUITES by HILTON

AAA Benefit: Members save 5% or more!

Address: 3225 158th Ave SE 98008 **Location:** I-90 exit 11 westbound; exit 11A (SE Eastgate Way/156th Ave SE) eastbound, just ne. **Facility:** 240 units. 5 stories, interior corridors. **Terms:** check-in 4 pm, 1-7 night minimum stay, 3 day cancellation notice-fee imposed. **Amenities:** safes. **Pool:** heated indoor. **Activities:** hot tub, exercise room. **Guest Services:** valet and coin laundry, area transportation. **Featured Amenity: full hot breakfast.**

SAVE 🍴 🏋 ▼ CALL 🦽 🛜 👪 BIZ 🛜 ✕ 📶 📶 💻 /SOME UNITS 🐾

EXTENDED STAY AMERICA-SEATTLE-BELLEVUE-DOWNTOWN   425/453-8186 70

🅥🅥 Extended Stay Hotel. **Address:** 11400 Main St 98004

FAIRFIELD INN & SUITES BY MARRIOTT SEATTLE BELLEVUE/REDMOND   (425)869-6548 56

Hotel
$69-$344

Fairfield

AAA Benefit: Members save 5% or more!

Address: 14595 NE 29th Pl 98007 **Location:** I-405 exit 14 (SR 520), 2.3 mi e to 148th Ave NE (north exit), then just nw. **Facility:** 144 units. 3 stories, interior corridors. **Terms:** cancellation fee imposed. **Pool:** heated indoor. **Activities:** exercise room. **Guest Services:** valet and coin laundry. **Featured Amenity: breakfast buffet.**

SAVE 🍴 CALL 🦽 🛜 👪 BIZ 🛜 ✕ 📶 📶 💻 /SOME UNITS 🐾 HS

HAMPTON INN & SUITES BY HILTON BELLEVUE DOWNTOWN-SEATTLE   425/453-4100 67

🅥🅥🅥 Hotel. **Address:** 11405 NE 2nd Pl 98004

AAA Benefit: Members save 5% or more!

HILTON BELLEVUE   (425)455-1300 71

Hotel
$109-$459

Hilton HOTELS & RESORTS

AAA Benefit: Members save 5% or more!

Address: 300 112th Ave SE 98004 **Location:** I-405 exit 12, just nw. **Facility:** 353 units. 10 stories, interior corridors. **Parking:** on-site (fee). **Terms:** check-in 4 pm, 1-7 night minimum stay, 3 day cancellation notice-fee imposed. **Amenities:** safes. **Pool:** heated outdoor. **Activities:** hot tub, exercise room. **Guest Services:** valet and coin laundry, rental car service, area transportation.

SAVE 📶 🍴 🏋 ▼ CALL 🦽 🛜 👪 BIZ HS 🛜 ✕ 📶 💻 /SOME UNITS 🐾

HILTON GARDEN INN SEATTLE/BELLEVUE DOWNTOWN   425/454-0070 59

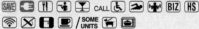 Hotel. **Address:** 10777 NE 10th St 98004

AAA Benefit: Members save 5% or more!

(See map & index p. 160.)

HYATT HOUSE SEATTLE/BELLEVUE

(425)747-2705 **74**

▼▼▼ **Extended Stay Contemporary Hotel**
$109-$609

HYATT house™

AAA Benefit: Members save 5% or more!

Address: 3244 139th Ave SE 98005 **Location:** I-90 exit 11 westbound, 0.9 mi w, just n; exit 10B eastbound, just n, 0.7 mi e, then just n. **Facility:** 160 units, some efficiencies. 5 stories, interior corridors. **Pool:** heated indoor. **Activities:** hot tub, exercise room. **Guest Services:** valet and coin laundry, area transportation. **Featured Amenity:** breakfast buffet.

SAVE ◻ ◻ CALL ◻ ◻ ◻ BIZ HS ◻ ◻
◻ ◻ ◻ / SOME UNITS ◻

HYATT REGENCY BELLEVUE

(425)462-1234 **60**

▼▼▼▼ **Contemporary Hotel**
$159-$429

HYATT REGENCY™

AAA Benefit: Members save 5% or more!

Address: 900 Bellevue Way NE 98004 **Location:** I-405 exit 13 (NE 8th St), 0.6 mi w. **Facility:** Centrally located, this urban oasis serves as an anchor of The Bellevue Collection—a Pacific Northwest premier shopping, dining and entertainment destination, all connected by skybridges. 732 units. 20-24 stories, interior corridors. **Parking:** on-site (fee) and valet. **Terms:** check-in 4 pm. **Amenities:** safes. **Dining:** 2 restaurants, also, 13 Coins Restaurant, see separate listing. **Pool:** heated indoor. **Activities:** exercise room. **Guest Services:** valet laundry, boarding pass kiosk.

SAVE ECO ◻ ◻ ◻ CALL ◻ ◻ ◻ BIZ HS
◻ ◻ ◻ ◻ ◻ / SOME UNITS ◻

LA RESIDENCE SUITE HOTEL

(425)455-1475 **61**

▼▼▼ **Extended Stay Hotel**
$139-$229

Address: 475 100th Ave NE 98004 **Location:** I-405 exit 13B, 0.9 mi w on NE 8th St, then just s. **Facility:** 19 kitchen units, some two bedrooms. 4 stories, interior corridors. **Terms:** cancellation fee imposed. **Activities:** bicycles, exercise room. **Guest Services:** coin laundry. **Featured Amenity:** continental breakfast.

SAVE ◻ BIZ HS ◻ ◻ ◻
◻ ◻ / SOME UNITS ◻

RED LION HOTEL BELLEVUE

(425)455-5240 **69**

▼▼ **Hotel**
$88-$298

Address: 11211 Main St 98004 **Location:** I-405 exit 12, 0.4 mi n on 114th St. **Facility:** 181 units. 2 stories (no elevator), interior corridors. **Parking:** on-site (fee). **Terms:** check-in 4 pm, cancellation fee imposed, resort fee. **Pool:** heated outdoor. **Activities:** exercise room. **Guest Services:** valet laundry, rental car service, area transportation.

SAVE ◻ ◻ ◻ ◻ BIZ ◻
◻ ◻ ◻ ◻ / SOME UNITS ◻

RESIDENCE INN BY MARRIOTT SEATTLE BELLEVUE

(425)882-1222 **57**

▼▼▼ Extended Stay Hotel. **Address:** 14455 NE 29th Pl 98007

AAA Benefit: Members save 5% or more!

RESIDENCE INN BY MARRIOTT SEATTLE BELLEVUE/DOWNTOWN

(425)637-8500 **73**

▼▼▼ Extended Stay Hotel. **Address:** 605 114th Ave SE 98004

AAA Benefit: Members save 5% or more!

SEATTLE MARRIOTT BELLEVUE

(425)214-7600 **66**

▼▼▼ Contemporary Hotel. **Address:** 200 110th Ave NE 98004

AAA Benefit: Members save 5% or more!

SHERATON BELLEVUE HOTEL

(425)455-3330 **68**

▼▼▼ **Hotel**
$215-$472

Ⓢ **Sheraton**

AAA Benefit: Members save 5% or more!

Address: 100 112th Ave NE 98004 **Location:** I-405 exit 12 northbound; exit 13 southbound, just s. **Facility:** 178 units. 7 stories, interior corridors. **Terms:** cancellation fee imposed. **Amenities:** safes. **Activities:** exercise room. **Guest Services:** valet laundry, area transportation.

SAVE ◻ ◻ ◻ CALL ◻ ◻
BIZ ◻ ◻ ◻ ◻ ◻
/ SOME UNITS ◻ ◻

SILVER CLOUD HOTEL-BELLEVUE EASTGATE

(425)957-9100 **75**

▼▼▼ Hotel. **Address:** 14632 SE Eastgate Way 98007

SILVER CLOUD INN-BELLEVUE DOWNTOWN

(425)637-7000 **58**

▼▼▼ Hotel. **Address:** 10621 NE 12th St 98004

W BELLEVUE

(425)709-9000 **64**

▼▼▼▼ Contemporary Hotel. **Address:** 10455 NE 5th Pl 98004

AAA Benefit: Members save 5% or more!

THE WESTIN BELLEVUE

(425)638-1000 **63**

▼▼▼▼ **Contemporary Hotel**
$175-$435

WESTIN HOTELS & RESORTS

AAA Benefit: Members save 5% or more!

Address: 600 Bellevue Way NE 98004 **Location:** I-405 exit 13 (NE 4th St), 0.6 mi w, just n on Bellevue Way NE, then just e. **Facility:** Located in Lincoln Square—a shopping, entertainment and business hub—this hotel occupies floors two through 19 of a 42-story tower. The linens are luxurious and the service pampering. 337 units. 42 stories, interior corridors. **Parking:** on-site (fee) and valet. **Terms:** cancellation fee imposed. **Amenities:** safes. **Dining:** 3 restaurants. **Pool:** heated indoor. **Activities:** hot tub, exercise room, spa. **Guest Services:** valet laundry, boarding pass kiosk.

SAVE ◻ ◻ ◻ CALL ◻ ◻ ◻ BIZ $HS ◻
◻ ◻ ◻ / SOME UNITS ◻ ◻ ◻

(See map & index p. 160.)

WHERE TO EAT

13 COINS RESTAURANT   425/455-1313
American. Casual Dining. **Address:** 900 Bellevue Way NE 98004

ANDIAMO RISTORANTE ITALIANO   425/452-9602 (81)
Italian. Casual Dining. **Address:** 938 110th Ave NE, Suite 1 98004

BIS ON MAIN   425/455-2033 (96)
International. Fine Dining. **Address:** 10213 Main St 98004

BURGERMASTER   425/827-9566
Burgers. Quick Serve. **Address:** 10606 NE Northup Way 98004

CACTUS BELLEVUE SQUARE   425/455-4321 (89)
Tex-Mex. Casual Dining. **Address:** 535 Bellevue Square 98004

CARMINE'S-BELLEVUE   425/786-0160 (94)
Italian. Fine Dining. **Address:** 88 102nd Ave NE 98004

CHACE'S-PANCAKE CORRAL   425/454-8888 (97)
American. Casual Dining. **Address:** 1606 Bellevue Way SE 98004

THE CHEESECAKE FACTORY   425/450-6000 (86)
International. Casual Dining. **Address:** 401 Bellevue Square 98004

DANIEL'S BROILER, BELLEVUE PLACE   425/462-4662 (79)
Steak. Fine Dining. **Address:** 10500 NE 8th St, Suite 2100 98004

EARLS KITCHEN + BAR   425/452-3275
American. Casual Dining. **Address:** 700 Bellevue Way NE 98004

EL GAUCHO   425/455-2715 (92)
Steak. Fine Dining. **Address:** 450 108th Ave NE 98004

FOGO DE CHAO   425/450-4004 (91)
Brazilian Steak. Casual Dining. **Address:** 440 Bellevue Way NE 98004

GOLDBERG'S FAMOUS DELICATESSEN   425/641-6622 (98)
American. Casual Dining. **Address:** 3924 Factoria Blvd SE 98006

HENRY'S TAVERN BELLEVUE   425/697-9800 (88)
American. Casual Dining. **Address:** 500 Bellevue Way NE, Suite 310 98004

JOHN HOWIE STEAK   425/440-0880 (87)
Steak. Fine Dining. **Address:** 11111 NE 8th Ave 98004

MAGGIANO'S LITTLE ITALY   425/519-6476 (80)
Italian. Casual Dining. **Address:** 10455 NE 8th St 98004

MCCORMICK & SCHMICK'S   425/454-2606 (82)
Seafood. Fine Dining. **Address:** 700 Bellevue Way NE, Suite115 98004

NINE O BAR & GRILL   425/214-9000 (99)
American. Casual Dining. **Address:** 14632 SE Eastgate Way 98007

PALOMINO RESTAURANT   425/455-7600 (85)
Mediterranean. Fine Dining. **Address:** 610 Bellevue Way NE 98004

PEARL SEAFOOD & OYSTER BAR   425/455-0181 (84)
American. Casual Dining. **Address:** 700 Bellevue Way NE 98004

P.F. CHANG'S CHINA BISTRO   425/637-3582 (83)
Chinese. Fine Dining. **Address:** 525 Bellevue Square 98004

PURPLE CAFE AND WINE BAR   425/502-6292 (93)
American. Casual Dining. **Address:** 430 106th Ave NE 98004

RUTH'S CHRIS STEAK HOUSE   425/451-1550 (78)
Steak. Fine Dining. **Address:** 565 Bellevue Square 98004

SEASTAR RESTAURANT & RAW BAR   425/456-0010 (95)
Seafood. Fine Dining. **Address:** 205 108th Ave NE, Suite 100 98004

TAJ PALACE OF INDIA   425/643-4200 (77)
Indian. Casual Dining. **Address:** 2331 140th Ave NE 98005

WILD GINGER ASIAN RESTAURANT & SATAY BAR   425/495-8889 (90)
Asian. Casual Dining. **Address:** 508 Bellevue Way NE 98004

BELLINGHAM (B-3) pop. 80,885, elev. 60'
• Restaurants p. 47

Bellingham was named for the bay it overlooks, a body of water in turn named by Capt. George Vancouver's 1792 expedition in honor of Sir William Bellingham, a controller in the British Navy who had personally checked Vancouver's supplies prior to the explorer's departure from England. The city's business district rises behind the docks at the head of the bay.

The Bellingham Cruise Terminal, at the foot of Harris Avenue, is the southern terminus of the Alaska Marine Highway's weekly ferry service to Ketchikan, Juneau and other ports in the Alaska panhandle; for information phone (360) 676-2500 or (800) 642-0066.

The Mount Baker Theatre, 104 N. Commercial St., opened as a movie palace in 1927. The Art Deco-Moorish interior and original pipe organ that once provided accompaniment to silent film showings are still a part of the building; phone (360) 734-6080 for ticket information. The wooded campus of Western Washington University, established in 1893, crowns the heights just south of downtown. Brochures detailing a self-guiding campus tour are available at the visitor center.

Bellingham has an impressive collection of Victorian and craftsman-style homes, particularly in the residential neighborhoods north and south of the downtown area. The Eldridge historic district on the near north side of town is noted for its stately mansions.

Bellingham/Whatcom County Tourism: 904 Potter St., Bellingham, WA 98229. **Phone:** (360) 671-3990 or (800) 487-2032.

Shopping: Fairhaven, the restored business district centered on 12th Street and Harris Avenue, features a variety of specialty shops, boutiques, galleries and restaurants. The Bellingham Farmers Market sets up at the Village Green noon to 5 on Wednesdays, June through August, and at East Chestnut Street and Railroad Avenue 10 to 3 on Saturdays, April through mid-December. A cluster of antique and second-hand stores is on Holly Street between Commercial Street and Central Avenue.

Bellis Fair, at I-5 exit 256, has more than 75 stores, including anchors JCPenney, Kohl's and Macy's.

CHUCKANUT DRIVE is 3 mi. s. on I-5 to exit 250, then 1 mi. w. on SR 11. This scenic highway is 21 miles long and winds for 8 miles along the rocky shore of Samish Bay at the cliffside of 1,900-foot Chuckanut Mountain. Originally a dirt logging road that opened in 1896, it became the original route of the Pacific Highway, the primary north-south highway in western Washington. Magnificent views extend out across the bay to the San Juan Islands. In places a dense forest canopy arches over the roadway; maples and alders blaze with color in the fall. 🍴

SPARK MUSEUM OF ELECTRICAL INVENTION is at 1312 Bay St. The museum's collection covers human achievements dating as far back as 1580. Among the many notable inventors saluted are Thomas Edison, Benjamin Franklin and Guglielmo Marconi. The focal point is a 10-foot Tesla coil—for the uninitiated, a type of circuit transformer used to produce electricity—that is said to be the largest example of the device west of Chicago.

Visitors can experience the power of lightning during the 40-minute MegaZapper Electrical Show; not recommended for ages 0-4. Also on display is a full-scale replica of the *Titanic's* radio room. A library features schematics, rare books and magazines from radio's Golden Age.

Time: Allow 1 hour minimum. **Hours:** Wed.-Sun. 11-5 or by appointment. MegaZapper Electrical Show Sat.-Sun. at 2:30. Closed Jan. 1, Thanksgiving and Christmas. **Cost:** $8; $5 (ages 0-11). Galleries and MegaZapper Electrical Show $12; $9 (ages 5-11). **Phone:** (360) 738-3886. GT

SQUALICUM HARBOR is 1 mi. n.w. on Roeder Ave. to 722 Coho Way. One of the largest marinas on Puget Sound, Squalicum Harbor features promenades, a 2,500-gallon marine life tank and a variety of restaurants. A boat launch and visitor moorage are available for a fee. **Hours:** Daily dawn-dusk. **Cost:** Free. **Phone:** (360) 676-2542. 🍴

Marine Life Center is in Squalicum Harbor at 1801 Roeder Ave. The center is an open-air, covered exhibit featuring marine animals from the waters of Northern Washington. The touch pool allows visitors to touch live specimens of sea stars, hermit crabs, anemones and sea cucumbers. The main observation pool holds 1,500 gallons of sea water; among the marine creatures on display are rockfish, perch, sea stars and a spiny-headed fish called a sculpin.

One aquarium is home to a giant Pacific octopus. **Hours:** Daily 10-6, June-Aug.; 11-5, rest of year. **Cost:** Donations. **Phone:** (360) 671-2431.

WESTERN GALLERY AND OUTDOOR SCULPTURE COLLECTION is on the Western Washington University campus, 1 mi. w. via I-5 exit 252, then s.w. on Bill McDonald Pkwy. to the visitor information center in the Campus Services building. Visitors will find 29 works by national and international artists focusing on various themes. The mostly contemporary sculptures are displayed throughout the campus. A self-guiding tour brochure is available from the visitor center. The Western Gallery, in the Fine Arts Complex, features changing contemporary art exhibitions.

Time: Allow 1 hour minimum. **Hours:** Gallery open Mon.-Fri. 10-4 (also Wed. 4-8), Sat. noon-4, early Oct.-late May. Gallery closed between school sessions. Visitor information center open Mon.-Fri. 7:15 a.m.-8 p.m., mid-Sept. to mid-June; 7:15-5, rest of year. Outdoor sculpture collection accessible daily during daylight hours. **Cost:** Free. **Parking:** $2 (per hour); $10 (all day). **Phone:** (360) 650-3900.

WHATCOM MUSEUM is at 250 Flora St. (at Grand Ave.). This complex on the north side of downtown preserves the region's artistic and cultural legacy. The Lightcatcher Building has a two-story, curved translucent wall framing a courtyard. Rotating exhibits focus on nature, Northwest history and local artists. Displays at the all-ages Family Interactive Gallery demonstrate how people connect with art, nature and the environment. A block away at 121 Prospect St. is Old City Hall. An 1892 red-brick Victorian structure topped by a clock tower, it has a distinctive four-cornered cupola.

Time: Allow 1 hour minimum. **Hours:** Lightcatcher Building open Wed.-Sun. noon-5. Family Interactive Gallery open Wed.-Sat. 10-5, Sun. noon-5. Old City Hall open Wed.-Sun. noon-5. Closed Jan. 1, Thanksgiving, Christmas Eve and Christmas. **Cost:** $10; $8 (ages 6-17, ages 62+, and military and college students with ID); $5 (ages 2-5). **Phone:** (360) 778-8930. 🍴

BAYMONT INN & SUITES BY WYNDHAM   (360)671-6200

◈◈◈
Hotel
$79-$124

Address: 125 E Kellogg Rd 98226 **Location:** I-5 exit 256A, 1 mi ne via Meridian St. **Facility:** 70 units, some efficiencies. 3 stories, interior corridors. **Pool:** heated outdoor. **Activities:** limited exercise equipment. **Guest Services:** valet and coin laundry.

SAVE CALL 🚫 🏊 BIZ 📶 ✕
🛏 📷 💻 / SOME UNITS 🐾

BEST WESTERN HERITAGE INN   (360)647-1912

Hotel
$109-$169

AAA Benefit: Members save up to 15% and earn bonus points!

Address: 151 E McLeod Rd 98226 **Location:** I-5 exit 256A, just se. **Facility:** 90 units, some kitchens. 3-4 stories (no elevator), interior corridors. **Terms:** cancellation fee imposed. **Pool:** heated outdoor. **Activities:** hot tub, exercise room. **Guest Services:** valet and coin laundry, area transportation. **Featured Amenity: full hot breakfast.**

THE CHRYSALIS INN & SPA   (360)756-1005

Boutique Hotel
$179-$359

Address: 804 10th St 98225 **Location:** Waterfront. I-5 exit 250, 1.3 mi nw on Old Fairhaven Pkwy, 0.6 mi n via 12th and 11th sts, just w on Taylor Ave, then just n. Close to railway tracks. **Facility:** A respite for the body, mind and soul, this hotel overlooks Bellingham Bay. All rooms have water views in addition to a gas fireplace. Sometimes trains lumber by on the nearby tracks. 43 units. 3 stories, interior corridors. **Terms:** check-in 4 pm, cancellation fee imposed. **Dining:** Keenan's at the Pier, see separate listing. **Activities:** steamroom, spa. **Guest Services:** valet laundry.

COMFORT INN BELLINGHAM   (360)738-1100

Hotel. **Address:** 4282 Meridian St 98226

ECONO LODGE INN & SUITES   (360)671-4600

Hotel. **Address:** 3750 Meridian St 98225

FOUR POINTS BY SHERATON BELLINGHAM HOTEL & CONFERENCE CENTER   (360)671-1011

Hotel
$65-$186

FOUR POINTS BY SHERATON
AAA Benefit: Members save 5% or more!

Address: 714 Lakeway Dr 98229 **Location:** I-5 exit 253 (Lakeway Dr), just se. **Facility:** 132 units. 4 stories, interior corridors. **Terms:** cancellation fee imposed. **Amenities:** safes. **Dining:** 2 restaurants. **Pool:** heated indoor. **Activities:** hot tub, exercise room. **Guest Services:** valet and coin laundry, area transportation.

HOLIDAY INN EXPRESS-BELLINGHAM   (360)671-4800

Hotel
$99-$219

Address: 4160 Meridian St 98226 **Location:** I-5 exit 256A, 0.7 mi e. **Facility:** 101 units. 3 stories, interior corridors. **Terms:** cancellation fee imposed. **Pool:** heated indoor. **Activities:** hot tub. **Guest Services:** valet laundry, area transportation. **Featured Amenity: full hot breakfast.**

HOLIDAY INN HOTEL & SUITES-BELLINGHAM   360/746-6844

Hotel. **Address:** 4260 Mitchell Way 98226

HOME2 SUITES BY HILTON, BELLINGHAM AIRPORT   (360)734-3111

Extended Stay Hotel
$119-$299

HOME2 SUITES BY HILTON
AAA Benefit: Members save 5% or more!

Address: 805 Home Ln 98226 **Location:** I-5 exit 257, just n. **Facility:** 105 efficiencies. 4 stories, interior corridors. **Terms:** 1-7 night minimum stay, 3 day cancellation notice-fee imposed. **Pool:** indoor. **Activities:** hot tub, game room, exercise room. **Guest Services:** valet and coin laundry, area transportation. **Featured Amenity: continental breakfast.**

HOTEL BELLINGHAM AIRPORT   (360)676-7700

Hotel
$109-$249

Address: 3985 Bennett Dr 98225 **Location:** I-5 exit 258, just nw. **Facility:** 132 units. 4 stories, interior corridors. **Pool:** heated outdoor. **Activities:** limited exercise equipment. **Guest Services:** valet and coin laundry, area transportation.

HOTEL BELLWETHER   (360)392-3100

Hotel. **Address:** One Bellwether Way 98225

LA QUINTA INN & SUITES BELLINGHAM   (360)738-7088

Hotel. **Address:** 1063 W Bakerview Rd 98226

OXFORD SUITES BELLINGHAM   (360)676-1400

Hotel
$95-$700

Address: 4051 Meridian St 98226 **Location:** I-5 exit 256A, just n. **Facility:** 99 units, some kitchens. 6 stories, interior corridors. **Terms:** check-in 4 pm, 2-14 night minimum stay - seasonal and/or weekends, 30 day cancellation notice-fee imposed. **Amenities:** Some: safes. **Pool:** heated indoor. **Activities:** sauna, hot tub, steamroom, exercise room. **Guest Services:** valet and coin laundry, area transportation. **Featured Amenity: breakfast buffet.**

SPRINGHILL SUITES BY MARRIOTT BELLINGHAM   (360)714-9600

Hotel
$85-$262

SPRINGHILL SUITES MARRIOTT
AAA Benefit: Members save 5% or more!

Address: 4040 Northwest Ave 98226 **Location:** I-5 exit 257, just n. **Facility:** 122 units. 5 stories, interior corridors. **Terms:** cancellation fee imposed. **Pool:** heated indoor. **Activities:** hot tub, exercise room. **Guest Services:** complimentary and valet laundry, area transportation. **Featured Amenity: full hot breakfast.**

TOWNEPLACE SUITES BY MARRIOTT BELLINGHAM
(360)714-9700

Extended Stay Hotel
$74-$286

TOWNEPLACE SUITES MARRIOTT **AAA Benefit:** Members save 5% or more!

Address: 4050 Northwest Ave 98226 **Location:** I-5 exit 257, just n. **Facility:** 83 units, some two bedrooms, efficiencies and kitchens. 5 stories, interior corridors. **Terms:** cancellation fee imposed. **Amenities:** safes. **Pool:** heated indoor. **Activities:** hot tub, exercise room. **Guest Services:** complimentary and valet laundry, area transportation. **Featured Amenity: full hot breakfast.**

[SAVE] [icons] CALL [icons] [BIZ] [HS] [icon]
[icons] / SOME UNITS [icon]

WHERE TO EAT

ANTHONY'S AT SQUALICUM HARBOR 360/647-5588
Seafood. Casual Dining. **Address:** 25 Bellwether Way 98225

ANTHONY'S HEARTHFIRE GRILL SQUALICUM HARBOR
360/527-3473
American. Casual Dining. **Address:** 7 Bellwether Way 98225

ASLAN BREWING CO. 360/778-2088
American. Brewpub. **Address:** 1330 N Forest St 98225

BOUNDARY BAY BREWERY & BISTRO 360/647-5593
American. Brewpub. **Address:** 1107 Railroad Ave 98225

CHUCKANUT BREWERY & KITCHEN 360/752-3377
American. Brewpub. **Address:** 601 W Holly St 98225

COLOPHON CAFE 360/647-0092
American. Casual Dining. **Address:** 1208 11th St 98225

D'ANNA'S CAFE ITALIANO 360/714-0188
Italian. Casual Dining. **Address:** 1317 N State St 98225

DIRTY DAN HARRIS STEAKHOUSE 360/676-1011
Steak. Casual Dining. **Address:** 1211 11th St 98225

HUNDRED NORTH 360/594-6000
American. Casual Dining. **Address:** 100 N Commercial St 98225

KEENAN'S AT THE PIER 360/392-5510
Pacific Northwest. Casual Dining. **Address:** 804 10th St 98225

THAI HOUSE RESTAURANT 360/734-5111
Thai. Casual Dining. **Address:** 187 Telegraph Rd 98226

BLAINE (A-2) pop. 4,684, elev. 77'

Blaine is a port of entry on Drayton Harbor just south of the British Columbia border. First settled in 1856, it enjoyed a fleeting boom during the Fraser River gold rush. After the Homestead Act began attracting farmers to the area, Blaine became a dairy supply center and fishing port.

Peace Arch Historical State and Provincial Park, on I-5 at the international border, commemorates more than 100 years of harmony between the United States and Canada. The inscriptions on the arch, erected in 1921, read "Children of a Common Mother" and "Brethren Dwelling Together in Unity;" phone (360) 332-8221.

Occupying a former 19th-century fishing fleet bunkhouse at 9261 Semiahmoo Pkwy., the Alaska Packers Association Cannery and Fishing Museum houses an exhibit describing the Alaska Packers Semiahmoo Cannery, which operated for more than a century before closing in 1985. The museum also features a scale model fish trap, a restored Bristol Bay fishing boat, and photos and paintings that document local history; phone (360) 371-3558. The museum is in Semiahmoo County Park, where the tidal flats offer beachcombing and bird-watching opportunities *(see Recreation Areas Chart)*.

The 1946 passenger ferry *MV Plover*, which once carried cannery workers across Drayton Harbor between Blaine and Semiahmoo Spit, now transports tourists and residents along the same route. The 11-minute westbound trip from Blaine departs from the Visitor's Dock at Blaine Marina, across the street from Blaine Marine Park. Scenic sights include Semiahoo Bay, British Columbia's Coast Mountains, basking harbor seals, eagles and various shorebirds. The return trip takes 23 minutes.

The ferry operates Friday through Sunday (also July x), Memorial Day weekend to Labor Day. Departure times are on the hour from the Visitor's Dock and on the half-hour from the wharf at Semiahmoo Resort. The ride is free, but donations are accepted. For additional information phone the visitor information center.

Blaine Visitor Information Center: 728 Peace Portal Dr., Blaine, WA 98230. **Phone:** (360) 332-4544 or (800) 624-3555.

SEMIAHMOO RESORT, GOLF AND SPA 360/318-2000
Resort Hotel. **Address:** 9565 Semiahmoo Pkwy 98230

BLAKE ISLAND (F-3)
• Part of Seattle area — see map p. 124

BLAKE ISLAND MARINE STATE PARK is 8 mi. from Seattle's downtown waterfront; tour boats depart from Pier 55 in Seattle. The 475-acre park offers 8 miles of hiking trails, beach access and panoramic views of the Seattle skyline and surrounding mountains *(see Recreation Areas Chart)*. Deer and bald eagles are among the wildlife found in the park, which is also the location of Tillicum Village.

The park is accessible only by private boat or tour boat. **Hours:** Daily 8-dusk. **Cost:** Free. Private boat moorage $5 per foot or a minimum of $70; buoys $15 a night. **Phone:** (360) 731-8330 for park information, or (206) 623-1445 for tour boat reservations.
[GT] [icons]

BOTHELL (E-3) pop. 33,505, elev. 72'
• Hotels p. 48 • Restaurants p. 48
• Hotels & Restaurants map & index p. 160
• Part of Seattle area — see map p. 124

Named for pioneer David Bothell, this greater Seattle suburb began its existence as a settlement on

(See map & index p. 160.)

the banks of the Sammamish River in the early 1870s, initially prospering as a lumbering and agricultural center. Bothell's Canyon Park district, along I-405 north of the city, is a center for high-tech businesses.

The Bothell campus of the University of Washington/Cascadia Community College at 17819 113th Ave. N.E., dates from 1889 and encompasses a wetlands area crisscrossed with several miles of paved trails. Visitors can walk along an elevated section of boardwalk where native species have been planted; signs and photographs describe the restoration process. The Town-Gown Loop, a 2.7-mile trail featuring 20 interpretive plaques, links the campus with downtown Bothell.

Greater Bothell Chamber of Commerce: 23716 8th Ave. S.E., Suite I-1, Bothell, WA 98021. **Phone:** (425) 485-4353.

Shopping: Country Village, 1.5 miles north via SR 527, has 45 specialty shops and galleries in an outdoor setting of landscaped gardens, ponds and shady pathways where you can feed wandering chickens; phone (425) 483-2250. A farmers market sets up Fridays from noon to 6, June through September.

Downtown Bothell's Main Street earns the adjective "quaint," with a plentiful selection of small shops and restaurants along a two-block stretch spruced up with pretty landscaping and colorful banners. On a scale of one to 10, the browsing potential ranks high at Bothell Jewelers & Collectibles, 10130 Main St. This establishment has everything from rhinestone brooches and vintage belt buckles to Hummel and Goebel collector plates, antique leather postcards and Beatles memorabilia; phone (425) 487-2900.

COMFORT INN & SUITES   (425)402-0900   **28**
🌢🌢 Hotel. **Address:** 1414 228th St SE 98021

COUNTRY INN & SUITES BY RADISSON   425/485-5557   **31**
🌢🌢 Hotel. **Address:** 19333 N Creek Pkwy 98011

EXTENDED STAY AMERICA-SEATTLE-BOTHELL-WEST
                               425/402-4252   **27**
🌢🌢 Extended Stay Hotel. **Address:** 923 228th St SE 98021

HILTON GARDEN INN SEATTLE/BOTHELL
                               425/486-0400   **26**
🌢🌢🌢 Hotel. **Address:** 22600 | **AAA Benefit:**
Bothell Everett Hwy 98021 | Members save 5% or more!

HOLIDAY INN EXPRESS BOTHELL-CANYON PARK
                               425/483-8100   **29**
🌢🌢🌢 Hotel. **Address:** 22922 15th Ave SE 98021

RESIDENCE INN BY MARRIOTT SEATTLE NE
                               (425)485-3030   **30**
🌢🌢🌢 Extended Stay Hotel. **Address:** 11920 NE 195th St 98011 | **AAA Benefit:** Members save 5% or more!

WHERE TO EAT

BEARDSLEE PUBLIC HOUSE   425/286-1001   **53**
🌢🌢 American. Gastropub. **Address:** 19116 Beardslee Blvd, Suite 201 98011

BONEFISH GRILL   425/485-0305   **52**
🌢🌢🌢 Seafood. Fine Dining. **Address:** 22616 Bothell Everett Hwy 98021

BURGERMASTER   425/486-8980
🌢 Burgers. Quick Serve. **Address:** 18626 Bothell Everett Hwy 98012

LOMBARDI'S   425/892-2931   **51**
🌢🌢 Italian. Casual Dining. **Address:** 19409 Bothell Everett Hwy 98012

BREMERTON (F-2) pop. 37,729, elev. 10'
• Hotels & Restaurants map & index p. 170
• Part of Seattle area — see map p. 124

Named for Seattle real estate entrepreneur William Bremer, Bremerton is home to Naval Base Kitsap - Bremerton, the northern outpost of the Pacific Fleet. The base also is responsible for the city's largest industry, the Puget Sound Naval Shipyard.

Harborside Fountain Park, just south of the ferry terminal on First Street, overlooks the waterfront. It features five copper-plated fountains shaped like submarine sails. North of the ferry terminal, Bremerton Boardwalk offers a promenade along the shoreline, which is indented with bays and inlets.

The highlight of the 🌢 Armed Forces Festival, held in mid-May, is a parade through downtown Bremerton that salutes past and present veterans. Other events include the Pepsi Armed Forces Festival Golf Tournament, a military culinary arts competition and a pancake breakfast.

Washington State Ferries connects Bremerton with Seattle; phone (206) 464-6400, or (888) 808-7977 in Wash. The Kitsap Transit passenger toll ferry links Bremerton with Annapolis and Port Orchard; phone (360) 373-2877 or (800) 501-7433.

Bremerton Chamber of Commerce: 286 Fourth St., Bremerton, WA 98337. **Phone:** (360) 479-3579.

Shopping: Kitsap Mall, 9 miles north in Silverdale, has 120 stores, including JCPenney, Kohl's, Macy's and Sears.

USS *TURNER JOY* (DD-951) NAVAL MEMORIAL MUSEUM SHIP is n. of the ferry terminal on the Bremerton Waterfront at 300 Washington Beach Ave. The ship serves as an educational facility and as an exhibit honoring the US. Navy. The *Turner Joy,* a Forrest Sherman Class destroyer commissioned in 1959, saw action in the Gulf of Tonkin incident of 1964, earning nine battle stars. Decommissioned in November 1982, the ship remains close to its original configuration. A self-guiding tour provides access to most of the ship and involves climbing steep stairways; comfortable walking shoes are recommended.

(See map & index p. 170.)

Time: Allow 1 hour minimum. **Hours:** Daily 10-5, Mar.-Oct.; Wed.-Sun. 10-4, rest of year (weather permitting). Last admission 30 minutes before closing. Closed Jan. 1, Easter, Thanksgiving and Christmas. **Cost:** $15; $13 (ages 62+ and retired military with ID); $11 (ages 13-17); $7.50 (active military and dependents with ID); $6 (ages 5-12); free (active military in uniform with ID). **Phone:** (360) 792-2457. GT

FAIRFIELD INN & SUITES BY MARRIOTT SEATTLE
BREMERTON   (360)377-2111   **2**
▼▼▼ Hotel. **Address:** 239 4th St
98337   AAA Benefit:
                                   Members save 5%
                                   or more!

HAMPTON INN & SUITES BY HILTON BREMERTON
                          360/405-0200   **3**
▼▼▼ Hotel. **Address:** 150 Washington Ave 98337   AAA Benefit:
                                   Members save 5%
                                   or more!

SUPER 8-BREMERTON   (360)377-8881   **1**

▼▼
Hotel
$70-$80

Address: 5068 Kitsap Way 98312 **Location:** SR 3 exit Kitsap Way, just ne; 4.2 mi w of ferry terminal. **Facility:** 75 units. 3 stories (no elevator), interior corridors. **Amenities:** *Some:* safes. **Guest Services:** coin laundry. **Featured Amenity:** continental breakfast.

⟨SAVE⟩ 🛎 CALL ♿ 📶 ✕ 🖂
🛄 🖥 /SOME UNITS 🐾

WHERE TO EAT

ANTHONY'S AT SINCLAIR INLET   360/377-5004   **3**
▼▼▼ Seafood. Casual Dining. **Address:** 20 Washington Ave
98337

BOAT SHED   360/377-2600   **1**
▼▼ American. Casual Dining. **Address:** 101 Shore Dr 98310

BREMERTON BAR & GRILL   360/627-8081   **2**
▼▼ American. Casual Dining. **Address:** 190 Pacific Ave
98337

BURLINGTON (C-3) pop. 8,388, elev. 36'

Founded as a logging camp in the 1880s, Burlington became an important rail junction served by both the Great Northern and Northern Pacific lines. Named for the city in Vermont, the town serves as a commercial center for the surrounding farms that produce peas, cauliflower, seed crops and flower bulbs.

Burlington Chamber of Commerce: 520 E. Fairhaven Ave., Burlington, WA 98233. **Phone:** (360) 757-0994.

Shopping: Cascade Mall, off I-5 exit 229, offers more than 40 stores including Macy's. Next to the mall, The Outlet Shoppes at Burlington has more than 30 stores.

CANDLEWOOD SUITES-BURLINGTON   360/755-3300
▼▼▼ Extended Stay Hotel. **Address:** 1866 S Burlington Blvd
98233

FAIRFIELD INN & SUITES BY MARRIOTT BURLINGTON
                          (360)757-2717
▼▼▼ Hotel. **Address:** 9384 Old
Hwy 99 N 98233   AAA Benefit:
                                   Members save 5%
                                   or more!

HAMPTON INN & SUITES BY HILTON BURLINGTON
                          360/757-7100
▼▼▼ Hotel. **Address:** 1860 S Burlington Blvd 98233   AAA Benefit:
                                   Members save 5%
                                   or more!

HOLIDAY INN EXPRESS HOTEL & SUITES   360/755-7338
▼▼▼ Hotel. **Address:** 900 Andis Rd 98233

WHERE TO EAT

BOB'S BURGERS & BREW   360/757-9097
▼▼ American. Casual Dining. **Address:** 9394 Old Hwy 99
North Rd 98233

SAKURA JAPANESE STEAKHOUSE & SUSHI BAR
                          360/588-4281
▼▼ Japanese. Casual Dining. **Address:** 1830 S Burlington
Blvd 98233

CAMANO ISLAND (C-2) elev. 361'

Wooded Camano Island, named for late 18th-century Spanish explorer Jacinto Camaño, is just 17 miles long and tapers from a width of about 7 miles at the north end to a mile-wide southern point. SR 532 bridges the narrow saltwater channel west of Stanwood that separates the island from the mainland. A network of paved roads crisscrosses the island, providing access to Cama Beach Historical State Park, Camano Island State Park *(see Recreation Areas Chart)* and half a dozen county parks.

Utsalady, 1 mile off SR 532 on the island's north shore, is its most historic community. The first European settlers arrived here in 1853, and by the 1870s the town was a busy log exporting and shipbuilding center and the prime port for nearby mainland settlements. Dotted with summer cabins and second homes, Camano today is largely residential and remains decidedly—and delightfully—rural.

Camano Island's tranquility has long attracted artists, including many who have taken up permanent residence. Among the members of the Camano Island Arts Association is Dale Chihuly's famous Pilchuk Glass School. The Camano Island Studio Tour, which takes place Mother's Day weekend and the weekend following, allows visitors to experience the area's scenic beauty while visiting artist studios and attending a juried art show; phone (425) 263-2813.

Camano Island Chamber of Commerce: 848 N. Sunrise Blvd., Camano Island, WA 98282. **Phone:** (360) 629-7136.

CAMAS pop. 19,355

CAMAS HOTEL
360/834-5722

Historic Boutique Hotel
Rates not provided

Address: 405 NE 4th Ave 98607 **Location:** Jct NE Cedar St; downtown. **Facility:** This intimate, European-style hotel has cozy rooms and sparkling white bathrooms. Located in the heart of the city, it offers convenient access to window shopping and a variety of restaurants. 24 units. 3 stories (no elevator), interior corridors. *Bath:* some shared. **Parking:** street only. **Guest Services:** coin laundry. **Featured Amenity:** continental breakfast.

SAVE 🍴 📶 ✕ 🛄 💻 / SOME UNITS 🐾 ☎

WHERE TO EAT

BURGERVILLE
360/834-3289
American. Quick Serve. **Address:** 518 NE 3rd Ave 98607

ROOTS RESTAURANT & BAR
360/260-3001
Pacific Northwest. Casual Dining. **Address:** 19215 SE 34th St 98607

CASHMERE (E-8) pop. 3,063, elev. 795'

Named for south Asia's fabled Vale of Kashmir, Cashmere, in the heart of Wenatchee Valley, is surrounded by fruit orchards. The town's roots can be traced back to a Roman Catholic mission established in 1863. With its lampposts and covered sidewalks, the downtown business district has a bit of a pioneer look. The sandstone towers of Peshastin Pinnacles State Park, 2 miles northwest on US 2/97 at 7201 N. Dryden Rd., are a popular rock climbing area; phone (509) 884-8702.

Cashmere Chamber of Commerce: 103 Cottage Ave., P.O. Box 834, Cashmere, WA 98815. **Phone:** (509) 782-7404.

Shopping: Browse for antiques at two large malls: Antique Mall at Cashmere, 603 Cotlets Way near the Cashmere Museum & Pioneer Village; and Apple Annie Antique Gallery, 100 Apple Annie Ave.

CASHMERE MUSEUM & PIONEER VILLAGE is just off US 2 at 600 Cotlets Way. This museum recreates the history of the Columbia River Indians before the arrival of white settlers; its collection of artifacts is considered among the best in the Northwest.

The village comprises 20 authentic pioneer structures, including a smithy, assay office, school, hotel, general store, saddle shop, doctor and dentist office, saloon, jail and post office. Also on display is a Great Northern Railway caboose, ticket office and section house. A working water wheel is on the bank of the Wenatchee River. **Time:** Allow 1 hour minimum. **Hours:** Mon.-Sat. 10-4, Sun. noon-4, Apr.-Oct. **Cost:** $7; $6 (ages 62+); $4.50 (ages 6-17); free (ages 0-5 and active military with ID). **Phone:** (509) 782-3230.

VILLAGE INN MOTEL
509/782-3522
Motel. **Address:** 229 Cottage Ave 98815

CASTLE ROCK (G-6) pop. 1,982, elev. 59'

The town's namesake, a 150-foot-high rock, was a landmark for Cowlitz Indians and Hudson's Bay Co. traders as early as 1832. Castle Rock prospered as a Cowlitz River steamboat port and trading center for valley farms. A local sawmill was the first to produce cedar shingles from the western red cedar that grows in abundance in the region.

Castle Rock marks the beginning of the Spirit Lake Memorial Highway (SR 504), a scenic route that leads past the areas affected by the eruption of Mount St. Helens in 1980. The Mount St. Helens Visitor Center at Silver Lake *(see attraction listing p. 90)* is 5 miles east of I-5 exit 49.

Castle Rock Chamber of Commerce Visitor Center: 147 Front Ave. N.W., Castle Rock, WA 98611. **Phone:** (360) 274-6603.

TIMBERLAND INN & SUITES
360/274-6002

Motel
Rates not provided

Address: 1271 Mount St. Helens Way 98611 **Location:** I-5 exit 49, just ne. **Facility:** 40 units. 2 stories (no elevator), exterior corridors. **Guest Services:** coin laundry.

SAVE HS 📶 ✕ 🛄 💻

CATHLAMET (G-5) pop. 532, elev. 53'

Cathlamet is a picturesque riverside settlement linked with rural Puget Island and known as Little Norway for its largely Scandinavian population. Of interest is the 1895 Pioneer Church, built into a rock outcropping that overlooks the village. The last remaining ferry service on the lower Columbia River operates between Puget Island—accessible by bridge from town—and Westport, Ore. Phone (360) 795-3301 for ferry information.

Displays at the Wahkiakum County Historical Museum, 65 River St., include Northwest Indian artifacts, farm implements, guns and logging equipment. The museum is open weekends May through October; phone (360) 849-4353.

A once endangered population of white-tailed deer, thought to be extinct in the 1930s, lives within Julia Butler Hansen Refuge for the Columbian White-tailed Deer. The refuge covers 4,757 acres on the mainland and several islands in the Columbia River below Cathlamet. Wildlife often can be seen from Steamboat Slough and Brooks Slough roads, especially in the morning and evening when the deer feed in the pastures. Motorists should watch for animals in or near roadways. Phone (360) 795-3915 for information.

CENTRALIA (I-2) pop. 16,336, elev. 188'

Along with neighboring Chehalis, Centralia forms the commercial center of the rich Chehalis Valley farmland and nearby timberlands. More than a dozen outdoor murals depicting 19th-century Centralia grace downtown buildings.

Aside from offering a wide range of recreational activities, walking trails and playing fields, Fort Borst Park includes several historical sites. Located at the confluence of the Skookumchuck and Chehalis rivers, the 101-acre park occupies land homesteaded by Joseph Borst; the Borsts were among the first pioneer families to settle this area in the 1850s.

Shopping: The Centralia Outlets, on both sides of I-5 exit 82, has more than 25 stores. Antique stores are along Tower Avenue, downtown between Locust and Maple streets. Dealers sell their wares at the Centralia Square Antique Mall, 201 S. Pearl St.; phone (360) 736-6406.

GREAT WOLF LODGE	360-273-7718
❤❤❤ Resort Hotel. **Address:** 20500 Old Hwy 99 SW 98531	
MOTEL 6-#394	(360)330-2057
❤ Motel. **Address:** 1310 Belmont Ave 98531	
PEPPERMILL EMPRESS INN	360/330-9441
❤❤ Hotel. **Address:** 1233 Alder St 98531	

WHERE TO EAT

BERRY FIELDS CAFE 360/736-1183

❤❤❤

American Casual Dining $5-$15

AAA Inspector Notes: Adjoining an antiques mall, the restaurant enables guests to rest their feet after a morning of browsing selections of Depression glass. Portions of fresh food are on the generous side; a salad is a meal, and sandwiches can easily serve two or work as leftovers. A slice of freshly made pie provides a sweet finish. **Address:** 201 S Pearl St 98531 **Location:** At Pearl and Locust sts; downtown. [B] [L]

BURGERVILLE 360/736-5212
❤ American. Quick Serve. **Address:** 818 Harrison Ave 98531

COUNTRY COUSIN 360/736-2200
❤❤ American. Casual Dining. **Address:** 1054 Harrison Ave 98531

MCMENAMINS OLYMPIC CLUB HOTEL & THEATER 360/736-5164
❤❤ American. Casual Dining. **Address:** 112 N Tower Ave 98531

CHEHALIS (I-1) pop. 7,259, elev. 196'

Chehalis was established in 1873 when the Lewis County seat was moved from Claquato. First named Saundersville, the town's name was changed in 1879. The historic neighborhood along Pennsylvania Avenue features a variety of architectural styles. Claquato Church, on Stern Road, is one of the oldest churches in the state. The 1858 structure functioned for a time as Claquato Academy; the bronze bell in the belfry was cast in Boston in 1857 and shipped around Cape Horn.

Centralia-Chehalis Chamber of Commerce: 500 N.W. Chamber of Commerce Way, Chehalis, WA 98532. **Phone:** (360) 748-8885 or (800) 525-3323.

CHEHALIS-CENTRALIA RAILROAD & MUSEUM is w. of I-5 exit 77 on SR 6, then s. on Riverside Dr. to 1101 S.W. Sylvenus St. The railroad offers steam train excursions through the Chehalis Valley to Millburn and Ruth. Brunch and dinner trains and special seasonal trips also are available; phone for details.

Time: Allow 2 hours minimum. **Hours:** Trips to Millburn depart Sat.-Sun. at 1 and 3, late May-late Sept. Trips to Ruth depart Sat. at 5, late May-late Sept. **Cost:** Ruth round-trip fare $17; $16 (ages 62+); $14 (ages 4-15). Millburn round-trip fare $14; $13 (ages 62+); $11 (ages 4-15). Dinner train $50. **Phone:** (360) 748-9593. [GT]

VETERANS MEMORIAL MUSEUM is at 100 S.W. Veterans Way. Dedicated to America's veterans, the museum houses displays of military memorabilia from wars as early as the American Revolution. Small arms, a variety of uniforms, cavalry-era saddles and even a 1942 Stuart tank are exhibited. Visitors can watch videos of veterans recounting their experiences. A 30-foot by 60-foot American flag covering one wall was donated by the crew of the USS *Abraham Lincoln*.

Time: Allow 1 hour minimum. **Hours:** Tues.-Sat. 10-5 (also Sun. 1-5, June 1-Labor Day weekend). Closed major holidays. **Cost:** $6; $5 (ages 65+ and military veterans with ID); $4 (ages 6-18 and students with ID); free (ages 0-5 and active military with ID). **Phone:** (360) 740-8875. [GT]

BEST WESTERN PLUS PARK PLACE INN & SUITES (360)748-4040

❤❤❤
Hotel
$129-$169

Best Western PLUS **AAA Benefit:** Members save up to 15% and earn bonus points!

Address: 201 SW Interstate Ave 98532 **Location:** I-5 exit 76, just se. **Facility:** 60 units. 3 stories, interior corridors. **Terms:** cancellation fee imposed. **Pool:** heated indoor. **Activities:** hot tub, bicycles, exercise room. **Guest Services:** coin laundry.

HOLIDAY INN EXPRESS & SUITES CHEHALIS 360/740-1800
❤❤❤ Hotel. **Address:** 730 NW Liberty Pl 98532

WHERE TO EAT

SPIFFY'S RESTAURANT & BAKERY 360/262-3561
❤❤ American. Casual Dining. **Address:** 110 US 12 98532

CHELAN (E-9) pop. 3,890, elev. 1,238'
• Hotels p. 52 • Restaurants p. 52

Chelan, set amid orchards and vineyards at the southern end of its 55-mile-long namesake lake, has been a resort since the beginning of the 20th century. Dry, warm summers draw crowds to its three public beaches. Recreational activities include swimming, boating, water skiing and parasailing. Hang gliding and paragliding are popular at Chelan Sky Park, south of town via Chelan Butte Rd.

More than a dozen colorful murals decorate the exteriors of many downtown buildings. The 12-acre Chelan Riverwalk Park offers a paved 1-mile loop along the Chelan River. Area scenic drives include SR 150 northwest to Manson, and the road along the lake's south shore to Twenty-five Mile Creek State Park *(see Recreation Areas Chart)*. The sunny hillsides flanking the lake have become an emerging grape growing region, and wine touring is increasingly popular.

Lake Chelan Chamber of Commerce: 216 E. Woodin Ave., P.O. Box 216, Chelan, WA 98816. **Phone:** (509) 682-3503 or (800) 424-3526.

LAKE CHELAN fills a glacier-carved trough on the eastern flank of the Cascade Range. One of the most scenic spots in the Pacific Northwest, the 55-mile-long lake extends from the semi-arid benchlands near the Columbia River northwestward into the alpine heart of the North Cascades. At nearly 1,500 feet deep, the lake is one of the continent's deepest, while the surface is some 1,100 feet above sea level, while portions of the bottom lie 400 feet below sea level.

Snowcapped peaks, some towering more than 8,000 feet, flank the upper reaches. Roads follow both banks of the lower reaches. This clear blue lake is fed by a number of streams, some fed by glaciers clinging to the mountains.

Two state parks are on the south shore. Lake Chelan State Park *(see Recreation Areas Chart)* is 9 miles west off US 97 Alt. and SR 971. Nine miles farther up S. Lakeshore Drive is Twenty-five Mile Creek State Park *(see Recreation Areas Chart)*. **Phone:** (509) 687-3710 for Lake Chelan State Park, or (509) 687-3610 for Twenty-five Mile Creek State Park.

Lake Chelan Boat Co. departs from the dock at 1418 W. Woodin Ave. The company has been carrying passengers on the lake since the 1890s. Service is offered on the *Lady of the Lake II* and the *Lady Express* year-round between Chelan and Stehekin, in Lake Chelan National Recreation Area *(see place listing p. 77)*. Excursions are offered on both vessels mid-June to mid-September and on a rotational basis the rest of the year. Stops, which vary depending on the trip, are made at Fields Point Landing, Prince Creek, Lucerne and Moore Point.

Pets must be transported in approved kennels, which can be rented at the dock. **Hours:** Round-trips depart daily at 8:30, May 1-Oct. 15; Wed. and Fri.-Mon. at 10, in Apr. and Oct. 16-Oct. 31; Mon., Wed. and Fri. (and Sun., Nov.-Dec.) at 10, rest of year. Additional sailings are offered seasonally; phone for details. Closed Christmas. **Cost:** Round-trip fare $40.50-$61; $20.25-$30.50 (ages 2-11). A fuel surcharge may apply. Reservations are recommended. **Phone:** (509) 682-4584, (509) 682-2224 for a recorded schedule, or (888) 682-4584 for reservations. GT

CAMPBELL'S RESORT ON LAKE CHELAN   509/682-2561
Resort Hotel. **Address:** 104 W Woodin Ave 98816

LAKESIDE LODGE & SUITES   509/682-4396

Hotel
Rates not provided

Address: 2312 W Woodin Ave 98816 **Location:** Waterfront. West end of town. Adjacent to city park. **Facility:** 93 units, some efficiencies and kitchens. 2-4 stories, exterior corridors. **Parking:** winter plug-ins. **Terms:** check-in 4 pm. **Pool:** heated outdoor, heated indoor. **Activities:** hot tub, beach access, exercise room. **Guest Services:** coin laundry. **Featured Amenity:** breakfast buffet.

WHERE TO EAT

CAMPBELL'S BISTRO & PUB & VERANDA
509/682-4250

American
Casual Dining
$10-$36

AAA Inspector Notes: *Historic.* Located on the shores of Lake Chelan, the upstairs is a casual café and pub while the lower level is a more full-service experience. The veranda is popular during the summer. Come enjoy a dark porter beer and slow-roasted prime rib. For breakfast try the popular eggs Benedict or apple-oat pancakes. **Features:** full bar, patio dining, happy hour. **Address:** 104 W Woodin Ave 98816 **Location:** On Lake Chelan; in Campbell's Resort on Lake Chelan. B L D

LA BRISA   509/682-5633
Mexican. Casual Dining. **Address:** 246 W Manson Hwy 98816

CHENEY (E-12) pop. 10,590, elev. 2,373'

Rolling grasslands dotted with lakes and pine woods surround (CHEE-nee), which sprang up with the arrival of the railroad from Spokane in 1881. First called Willow Springs, then Depot Springs, the town's present name honors the director of the Northern Pacific Railroad. Impressed by this, Benjamin P. Cheney donated $10,000 toward the founding of an academy in 1882; this school became the nucleus of Eastern Washington University.

The architecturally interesting Interurban Railway Depot is at Second Street and College Avenue. A collection of Victorian homes at Third and F streets includes an elaborate Queen Anne-style residence built in 1904.

The Columbia Plateau State Park Trail follows an abandoned rail line through a scenic landscape of pine forest, grasslands and lakes that includes Turnbull National Wildlife Refuge. The northernmost 4 miles of the trail are paved; the remainder of the 23-mile section the runs through Cheney is crushed rock. The north trailhead begins at Fish Lake, 4 miles east on SR 904; phone (509) 646-9218.

West Plains Chamber of Commerce: 510 1st St., Cheney, WA 99004. **Phone:** (509) 747-8480.

HOLIDAY INN EXPRESS HOTEL & SUITES-CHENEY UNIVERSITY AREA   509/235-1100
Hotel. **Address:** 111 Betz Rd 99004

WHERE TO EAT

EL RODEO   509/235-5679
♦♦ Mexican. Casual Dining. **Address:** 505 2nd St 99004

CHEWELAH (D-11) pop. 2,607, elev. 1,671'

Both Protestant and Roman Catholic missionaries traveled this part of the state in the mid-19th century; a plaque at the First Congregational Church, downtown at Park and Webster streets, commemorates the first Protestant sermon given in the Pacific Northwest. An original hand-hewn log cabin standing at 309 Third St. is the site of a Native American agency established in Chewelah in 1873.

Chewelah Chamber of Commerce: 401 S. Park St., Suite E, P.O. Box 94, Chewelah, WA 99109. **Phone:** (509) 935-8595.

NORDLIG MOTEL   509/935-6704
♦
Motel
Rates not provided

Address: 101 W Grant Ave 99109 **Location:** North edge of town on US 395. Across from a city park. **Facility:** 14 units. 2 stories (no elevator), exterior corridors. *Bath:* shower only. **Parking:** winter plug-ins. **Featured Amenity:** continental breakfast.

SAVE ▮▮ CALL 🔊 📶 ✕ ▮
📷 / SOME UNITS 🐾

CLARKSTON (G-12) pop. 7,229, elev. 807'

Clarkston was the final in a series of name changes for this town in Washington's southwestern corner. Residents of neighboring Lewiston, Idaho, named their town for Clark's partner Meriwether Lewis. The noted explorers, assisted by the Nez Perce Indians, spent time at the confluence of the Snake and Clearwater rivers. Petroglyphs dating back some 6,000 years can be seen along Snake River Road, which follows the river south of town; directions are available at the Lewis Clark Valley Chamber of Commerce, 502 Bridge St.; phone (509) 758-7712 or (800) 933-2128.

The presence of the Snake River guarantees a variety of recreational opportunities, including boating, camping, fishing and swimming. Hikers and bikers take advantage of the Clearwater and Snake River National Recreation Trail, a paved stretch that runs along 19 miles of river shoreline in the Clarkston-Lewiston area.

Kiwi Air offers scenic helicopter flights that show off the region's spectacular landscape of valleys, canyons, upland prairies and mountains. Flights depart from the Kiwi Air helipad on Port Drive (at 9th Street). For information and reservations phone (509) 751-9000.

Local tour companies offer 1- and 2-day jet boat excursions and 3- and 5-day river float trips through Hells Canyon. Reservation information is available from the Visit Lewis Clark Valley visitor center.

The ♦ Dogwood Festival of the Lewis-Clark Valley features events throughout the month of April, including an art festival, a dog show, a car show, foot races and a family fun fair; phone (208) 792-2447.

Visit Lewis Clark Valley: 847 Port Way, Clarkston, WA 99403. **Phone:** (509) 758-7489 or (877) 774-7248.

BEAMERS HELLS CANYON TOURS departs from the Beamers Tour Dock behind the Quality Inn at 700 Port Dr. in Clarkston, Wash. This tour company offers jet boat excursions through Hells Canyon—North America's deepest river gorge. The full-day tour provides opportunities to view three mountain ranges, three states and five rivers. Half-day tours and other excursions also are available. **Hours:** Trips offered daily, May-Sept.; Sat.-Sun. only, Mar.-Apr. and in Oct. Departure times vary; phone ahead. **Cost:** Full-day tour $219; $10 (ages 0-8 with paid adult). Half-day trip $139; free (ages 0-8 with paid adult). Reservations are required. **Phone:** (509) 758-4800 or (800) 522-6966. GT ▮▮

BEST WESTERN RIVERTREE INN   (509)758-9551
♦♦♦
Motel
$110-$170

 Best Western.

AAA Benefit: Members save up to 15% and earn bonus points!

Address: 1257 Bridge St 99403 **Location:** 0.9 mi w of Snake River Bridge on US 12. **Facility:** 61 units. 2 stories (no elevator), exterior corridors. **Parking:** winter plug-ins. **Terms:** cancellation fee imposed. **Pool:** heated outdoor. **Activities:** sauna, hot tub, picnic facilities, exercise room. **Guest Services:** coin laundry.

SAVE ▮▮ 🍴 ♿ BIZ HS 📶
✕ ▮ 📷 📺 / SOME UNITS 🐾

QUALITY INN & SUITES CONFERENCE CENTER
                                            (509)758-9500
♦♦ Hotel. **Address:** 700 Port Dr 99403

WHERE TO EAT

HAZEL'S GOOD EATS   509/758-8861
♦♦ Breakfast Sandwiches. Casual Dining. **Address:** 601 Bridge St (US 12) 99403

QUAY RESTAURANT   509/758-9500
♦♦ American. Casual Dining. **Address:** 700 Port Dr 99403

ROOSTER'S WATERFRONT RESTAURANT & BAR
                                            509/751-0155
♦♦ American. Casual Dining. **Address:** 1010 Port Way 99403

STATION 3 FAMILY RESTAURANT & LOUNGE   509/758-3288
♦♦ American. Casual Dining. **Address:** 916 6th St 99403

TOMATO BROTHERS ITALIAN STEAK HOUSE   509/758-7902
♦♦ Italian. Casual Dining. **Address:** 200 Bridge St 99403

CLE ELUM (F-8) pop. 1,872, elev. 1,905'

Cle Elum means "swift water" in the Kittitas Indian language, and that's an apt description of the river of the same name, which flows out of Lake Cle

Elum 8 miles to the northwest. The town originated from a gold claim in 1883; 3 years later coal was discovered and the settlement gained a sawmill, a school and a stop on the Northern Pacific Railroad line. The last coal was mined here in 1963.

This is the gateway to a vast recreation area encompassing the Okanogan-Wenatchee and Mount Baker-Snoqualmie national forests, and as a result nearly every conceivable outdoor recreational activity can be enjoyed. One particularly popular activity is a 3- to 4-hour raft trip down the 16-mile stretch of the Yakima River between Cle Elum and Thorp.

The 4.7-mile Coal Mines Trail follows a former Northern Pacific branch line from Flagpole Park in Cle Elum through Roslyn to the town of Ronald. Interpretive panels along the way describe the region's mining heritage.

Kittitas County Chamber of Commerce—Cle Elum Visitor Information Center: 312 W. 1st St., Cle Elum, WA 98922. **Phone:** (509) 925-2002 or (888) 925-2204.

PALOUSE TO CASCADES STATE PARK TRAIL can be accessed at the corner of 6th St. and Milwaukee Ave. in South Cle Elum. The linear park encompasses 212 miles of the Palouse to Cascades State Park Trail, which follows a historic railway line along the scenic Yakima River and over the Cascades into western Washington. The park includes 110 miles of hiking, biking and horse trails and winds through fir and pine forests, negotiates rolling farmlands and steep canyons, runs atop lofty railroad trestles and even ventures into tunnels along the way. Cross-country skiing is popular in winter; a Sno-Park permit is required November 15 through April 30. *See Recreation Areas Chart.*

The trailhead is part of the South Cle Elum Rail Yard National Historic District. Information panels along the Rail Yard Trail, which loops through the site, describe area history. The former Milwaukee Road Depot now functions as an interpretive center. A waiver form (available at each tunnel entrance) is required to enter the tunnel. **Hours:** Daily 6:30 a.m.-dusk, Memorial Day weekend-Labor Day; 8-dusk, rest of year. **Cost:** Park admission $10 (per private vehicle); Discover Pass, valid for 1 year, $30 (per private vehicle). **Phone:** (509) 656-2230 or (360) 902-8844. 🅰 🆇 🌲

BEST WESTERN SNOWCAP LODGE   (509)674-0200

🔻🔻🔻
Hotel
$119-$150

BW **Best Western.** **AAA Benefit:** Members save up to 15% and earn bonus points!

Address: 809 W Davis St 98922 **Location:** I-90 exit 84 eastbound, just n; exit westbound, 0.6 mi w, then just s. **Facility:** 50 units. 2 stories (no elevator); interior corridors. **Terms:** check-in 4 pm, cancellation fee imposed. **Pool:** heated indoor. **Activities:** hot tub, exercise room. **Guest Services:** complimentary laundry.

SAVE 📶 CALL 🅶 🔜 🛅 BIZ
HS 🛜 ✖ 🅱 🖼 🖵

SUNCADIA RESORT   509/649-6460

🔻🔻🔻
Resort Hotel
Rates not provided

Address: 3600 Suncadia Tr 98922 **Location:** I-90 exit 80, 2 mi n, then 0.3 mi w. **Facility:** This property boasts panoramic views of the Cascade Mountains and is a great place for outdoor enthusiasts. Rooms here are not your typical rentals and come with upscale furnishings and décor. 300 units, some two bedrooms, three bedrooms, efficiencies, kitchens, houses and condominiums. 2-6 stories, interior corridors. **Parking:** on-site and valet, winter plug-ins. **Terms:** check-in 4 pm. **Amenities:** safes. **Dining:** 2 restaurants, also, Portals, see separate listing. **Pool:** heated outdoor, heated indoor. **Ac-**

tivities: sauna, hot tub, steamroom, self-propelled boats, fishing, regulation golf, par 3 golf, tennis, cross country skiing, sledding, ice skating, recreation programs, bicycles, playground, lawn sports, picnic facilities, trails, health club, spa. **Guest Services:** complimentary laundry, area transportation.

SAVE 📶 🔜 🍽 CALL 🅶 🔜 🛅 BIZ HS 🛜
✖ 📷 🖵 /SOME UNITS 🖼 🅱 🖵

TIMBER LODGE INN   (509)674-5966
🔻🔻 Motel. **Address:** 301 W 1st St 98922

WHERE TO EAT

THE COTTAGE CAFE & FIRESIDE LOUNGE
509/674-2922

🔻🔻🔻
American Casual Dining
$4-$19

AAA Inspector Notes: *Classic.* A local favorite since 1935, this unpretentious restaurant specializes in family-style home cooking. It is hard to find a time when the place is not busy. The on-premises bakery churns out temptations such as pies, sweet rolls and other desserts; the cinnamon roll is a must. **Features:** full bar. **Address:** 911 E 1st St 98922 **Location:** I-90 exit 85, 1.1 mi w on SR 903.

B L D LATE CALL 🅶

MA MA VALLONE'S STEAK HOUSE & INN   509/674-5174
🔻🔻 Steak. Casual Dining. **Address:** 302 W 1st St 98922

PORTALS   509/649-6473
🔻🔻🔻 Pacific Northwest. Fine Dining. **Address:** 3600 Suncadia Tr 98922

COLFAX (F-12) pop. 2,805, elev. 1,974'

Settled in 1870, Colfax lies at the heart of The Palouse, a hilly region renowned for its fertile soils. The town is the seat of Whitman County, one of the nation's most productive wheat, barley, dry pea and lentil growing areas. In the late 1890s, Eastern Washington communities sponsored an immigrant bureau in

Chicago, and chartered special trains to carry home-steaders to the area. The handsome, turn-of-the-20th-century brick and stone buildings lining Main Street attest to the prosperity of that period.

The Perkins House, 623 N. Perkins Ave., built in 1884 by town founder James Perkins, features period furnishings and memorabilia. The adjacent log cabin was built in 1870. For information phone Colfax Chamber of Commerce.

Colfax Chamber of Commerce: 623 N. Perkins Ave., P.O. Box 706, Colfax, WA 99111. **Phone:** (509) 553-9729.

BEST WESTERN WHEATLAND INN   (509)397-0397

♦♦♦♦
Hotel
$110-$130

Best Western. **AAA Benefit:** Members save up to 15% and earn bonus points!

Address: 701 N Main St 99111 **Location:** 0.6 mi n of downtown. **Facility:** 50 units, some kitchens. 2 stories (no elevator), interior corridors. **Parking:** winter plug-ins. **Terms:** cancellation fee imposed. **Pool:** heated indoor. **Activities:** hot tub, picnic facilities, exercise room. **Guest Services:** coin laundry. **Featured Amenity:** full hot breakfast.

SAVE 🕪 ➷ 🏃 BIZ HS 📶
✕ 🍴 🖥 🖨 / SOME UNITS 🐾

WHERE TO EAT

PALOUSE HYDE OUT TAVERN   509/397-9561
♦♦ American. Casual Dining. **Address:** 215 N Main St 99111

SOL VALLARTA   509/397-6762
♦♦ Mexican. Casual Dining. **Address:** 205 N Main St 99111

TOP NOTCH CAFE   509/397-4569
♦♦ Breakfast Sandwiches. Casual Dining. **Address:** 210 N Main St 99111

COLUMBIA RIVER GORGE NATIONAL SCENIC AREA (B-7)

Following the Columbia River in both Oregon and Washington, the scenic area consists of 292,500 acres of sheer cliffs, mountainous forestland, hilly deciduous woods and grassy plains. The Oregon section extends from the Sandy River near Troutdale about 80 miles east to the Deschutes River. Rain forests and waterfalls, characteristic of the area's western end, give way east of the mountains to oak woods and grasslands.

Before settlement brought towns and dams, the rapids near The Dalles were impassable, requiring a difficult portage around the river and its enclosing cliffs. By 1913 plans were underway to create a scenic roadway, now the Historic Columbia River Highway *(see attraction listing),* similar to Charlemagne's winding roads through the Rhine Valley.

The Columbia provides a wide travel corridor and recreational playground. Through a collaboration of preservation and developmental interests, many public recreational areas have been set aside for hiking, camping, fishing, rock climbing, wildlife viewing and other activities. Phone (541) 308-1700 for more details, including safety information.

◥ **COLUMBIA GORGE INTERPRETIVE CENTER MUSEUM,** 990 S.W. Rock Creek Dr. in Stevenson, Wash., features displays about the natural and cultural history of the region. Exhibits depict Native American lifestyles, the fur trading era and the harnessing of the gorge's natural resources.

Highlights include a 37-foot-high, full-scale replica of a 19th-century fish wheel, a restored 1893 Corliss steam engine that served as the power source for sawmills, a collection of rosaries said to be the world's largest, a railroad exhibit and a diorama of a Native American dip-net fisher. "Cedar Trees," an outdoor installation, features three 30-foot-high carved sculptures by Native American artist Dudley Carver. "Forged Through Time" is a 15-minute video documenting the Ice Age floods and geological formation of the Columbia River Gorge.

Time: Allow 1 hour minimum. **Hours:** Daily 9-5. Closed Jan. 1, Thanksgiving and Christmas. **Cost:** $10; $8 (ages 60+ and students and military with ID); $6 (ages 6-12); $30 (family, two adults plus two dependent children). **Phone:** (509) 427-8211 or (800) 991-2338.

◥ **HISTORIC COLUMBIA RIVER HIGHWAY** is e. of Portland; for the best views of the gorge, enter the area from the w. at I-84 exit 17. Portions of the scenic highway split and become parallel roads: The upper level, old US 30, is the older, more scenic route; the lower level, I-84, is an interstate highway.

The highway provides panoramic views of the Columbia River Gorge from the Vista House at Crown Point State Scenic Viewpoint *(see attraction listing)* and, near Portland, at Women's Forum State Scenic View. East of the latter park, Larch Mountain Road runs 14 miles to a view at Sherrard Point, where a short trail accesses views of mounts Adams, Hood, Jefferson, Rainier and St. Helens.

The other 22 miles of this scenic road travel through the gorge, with 2,000-foot-tall cliffs, unusual rock formations and 11 waterfalls. **Hours:** Daily 24 hours. Interpretive center daily 9-5. Phone ahead to confirm schedule. **Cost:** Free. **Phone:** (541) 308-1700, or (503) 695-2372 for the Multnomah Falls Lodge Visitor Center. 🍴

HISTORIC COLUMBIA RIVER HIGHWAY STATE TRAIL will stretch 73 mi. from Troutdale to The Dalles when completed. Currently 65 miles of the scenic recreation trail are finished and open to bicyclists. Portions follow the Historic Columbia River Highway and, temporarily, I-84, while other parts are closed entirely to motorized traffic and are open to pedestrians and wheelchair users, including the Bonneville and Twin Tunnels segments.

The Bonneville Segment connects John B. Yeon State Scenic Corridor and Bridge of the Gods in Cascade Locks. At either end of the Twin Tunnels Segment, which is more than 4 miles long, are visitor centers and trailheads, both named for Sen. Mark O. Hatfield. The Mosier Twin Tunnels, for which this section was named, are original highway tunnels constructed in 1921 and restored in 2004. Visitors can see graffiti left behind by drivers stuck in the tunnels during a November 1921 snowstorm and tunnel windows offering views of the gorge below.

Hours: Daily dawn-dusk. Mark O. Hatfield West Visitor Center daily 10-2. **Cost:** Free. Day-use parking $5. **Phone:** (541) 387-4010 or (800) 551-6949.

MULTNOMAH FALLS RECREATION AREA is at 55000 E. Historic Columbia River Hwy. One of Oregon's most recognized scenic landmarks, stunning Multnomah Falls plunges a dramatic 542 feet off a cliff before flowing over a second 69-foot drop. Combined with a less precipitous 9-foot descent between the two, the total height of the falls is 620 feet, making it the highest along the Columbia River Highway. The graceful concrete arch of the Benson Bridge spans the top of the lower falls, completing the iconic image that appears in countless postcards and tourist photos.

Thanks to underground springs, the falls flow year-round although rainfall and melting snow unleashes a deafening torrent in spring. At the base of the falls, Multnomah Falls Historic Lodge, built in 1925, offers a restaurant as well as a visitor center with exhibits and information about the area's trail network.

The paved Multnomah Falls Trail leads a quarter mile to the Benson Bridge and then steeply ascends for another mile to an overlook above the falls. Hikers can complete a loop back to the lodge via the Larch Mountain Trail, which passes other waterfalls, including pretty Wahkeena Falls.

Note: Parking lots for the falls can be accessed from both Historic Columbia River Highway and I-84, but expect large crowds and plenty of competition for spaces in late spring and summer. **Hours:**

Daily 24 hours. Visitor center daily 9-5. **Cost:** Free. **Phone:** (503) 695-2372.

VISTA HOUSE AT CROWN POINT STATE SCENIC VIEWPOINT is about 3 mi. e. of Corbett off I-84 exit 22 at 40700 E. Historic Columbia River Hwy. The view from Crown Point and the Vista House overlook offers a 30-mile panorama of the Columbia River Gorge from 733 feet above sea level. Vista House was built soon after the scenic highway was dedicated in 1916. **Hours:** Park open daily 24 hours. Vista House open daily 9-6, mid-Mar. through Labor Day; daily 10-4, day after Labor Day-late Nov. (weather permitting); Fri.-Sun. (hours vary), rest of year. Phone ahead to confirm schedule. **Cost:** Donations. **Phone:** (503) 695-2240 or (503) 344-1368.

COLVILLE NATIONAL FOREST (C-11)

Elevations in the forest range from 1,289 ft. at the Columbia River Dam to 7,309 ft. at Gypsy Peak. Refer to AAA maps for additional elevation information.

In northeastern Washington, Colville National Forest covers about 1,100,000 acres. In the approximate center of the forest is Roosevelt Lake; Grand Coulee Dam is to the south. The Columbia River courses through this wilderness area. Gardner Cave, in the forest's eastern half, has stalagmite and stalactite formations that can be toured.

In the northeast corner of the forest, east of Metaline Falls, is the 43,000-acre Salmo-Priest Wilderness Area. No motorized vehicles are permitted, but FRs 22, 20 and 270 and Sullivan Creek Road, south of Metaline Falls off SR 31, all lead to trailheads where visitors can continue into the wilderness area on foot. These roads are closed due to weather conditions from mid-November to early or mid-June.

Brochures and maps outlining several of the forest's self-guiding automobile and hiking routes are available at ranger stations in Kettle Falls, Metaline Falls, Newport and Republic. For additional information contact the Forest Supervisor's office, 765 S. Main St., Colville, WA 99114; phone (509) 684-7000. *See Recreation Areas Chart.*

CONCRETE pop. 705, elev. 435'

OVENELL'S HERITAGE INN AND LOG CABINS   360/853-8494
Cabin. **Address:** 46276 Concrete Sauk Valley Rd 98237

COULEE CITY (E-10) pop. 562, elev. 1,584'

Coulee City is the former junction of railroad and stagecoach lines that ran along the Columbia River. According to Guy Waring, a 19th-century pioneer and author, trains and coaches were deliberately scheduled *not* to connect with each other, forcing passengers to spend the night in town. The little town is the only place between Soap Lake and Coulee Dam where east-west travelers can cross the Grand Coulee. Dramatic rock cliffs flank the town north and south of town.

SUN LAKES-DRY FALLS STATE PARK is 3 mi. s.e. off SR 17 at 34875 Park Lake Rd. N.E. Huge floods rushing across eastern Washington during the last ice age carved a network of gashes, the largest of which is Grand Coulee. Dry Falls, Grand Coulee's central feature, was once a 3.5-mile-wide cataract over which water plunged about 400 feet. For those not wishing to attempt the moderately rough road through the park, Dry Falls is visible from both SR 17 and the interpretive center. See Recreation Areas Chart.

Time: Allow 1 hour minimum. **Hours:** Park open daily 6:30 a.m.-dusk, May-Sept.; 8-dusk, rest of year. Interpretive center open daily 9-5, May-Sept.; Fri.-Tues. 9-4, Mar.-Apr. and in Oct. Interpretive center closed major holidays. **Cost:** Park admission $10 (per private vehicle); Discover Pass, valid for 1 year, $30 (per private vehicle). **Phone:** (509) 632-5583 or (509) 632-5214.

COULEE DAM (D-10) pop. 1,098, elev. 1,145'

Coulee Dam, as well as the adjacent communities of Electric City, Elmer City and Grand Coulee, sprang from the desert in 1933 to house laborers building the Grand Coulee Dam. The project, which was completed in 1942, employed more than 8,000 workers. The dam was built on the site of Seaton's Ferry, a remote Columbia River crossing; the ferry operated from 1920 to 1934.

Crown Point, 2 miles west on SR 174, offers a panoramic view of the dam from a vantage point 626 feet above the Columbia. Within Bicentennial Park, adjacent to North Dam Park on SR 155, are the Gehrke Windmills, a collection of more than 50 windmills created from colorfully painted pieces of castaway iron.

GRAND COULEE DAM is off SR 155. The dam harnesses the Columbia River for irrigation, power and flood control. Said to be one of the largest concrete structures in the world, it is 550 feet high, 500 feet wide at its base, 5,223 feet long and contains nearly 12 million cubic yards of concrete. Behind the dam Lake Roosevelt extends 151 miles upstream to the Canadian border. Twelve giant pumps lift water from this reservoir to Banks Lake.

The massive face is illuminated by a 36-minute laser light show presented during the summer. Good viewpoints for watching this spectacle are at the visitor center, at Douglas Park and Crown Point. The Grand Coulee Dam Visitor Center, on SR 155 on the west bank below the dam, has interactive displays. A 45-minute film, Man-made Marvel, details the dam's construction process. Visitors can take a guided 45-minute tour of the pump generating plant.

Purses, backpacks and packages are not permitted on the tour. **Time:** Allow 2 hours minimum. **Hours:** Visitor center open daily 8:30 a.m.-11 p.m., Memorial Day weekend-July 31; 8:30 a.m.-10:30 p.m., in Aug.; 8:30 a.m.-9:30 p.m., in Sept.; 9-5, rest of year. Tours are given on the hour daily 10-5, late May-Aug. 31; at 10, noon, 2 and 4, Apr. 1-late May and Sept.-Oct. Laser light show presented nightly at 10, Memorial Day weekend-July 31; at 9:30, in Aug.; at 8:30, in Sept. Closed Jan. 1, Thanksgiving and Christmas. **Cost:** Free. **Phone:** (509) 633-9265. GT

LAKE ROOSEVELT NATIONAL RECREATION AREA—see place listing p. 77.

COLUMBIA RIVER INN (509)633-2100

Motel $118-$129

Address: 10 Lincoln Ave 99116 **Location:** On SR 155 at visitor center. **Facility:** 35 units, some two bedrooms and kitchens. 2 stories (no elevator), exterior corridors. **Parking:** on-site and street, winter plug-ins. **Terms:** cancellation fee imposed. **Pool:** heated outdoor. **Activities:** sauna, hot tub, exercise room. **Guest Services:** coin laundry.

SAVE / SOME UNITS

COUPEVILLE (D-2) pop. 1,831, elev. 2'

An easy and popular day trip from Seattle, Coupeville is located on Whidbey Island (see place listing p. 216). Established in 1853, it is one of the oldest communities in the state, with several homes that date to the mid-19th century. Three old blockhouses built to defend Puget Sound and settlers' homes from the Coast Salish Indians can be visited. West of town is Madrona Way, a 4-mile scenic route that winds along the shore of Penn Cove. The drive is named for the Pacific madrona, a dark evergreen tree with shaggy, cinnamon-colored bark.

Coupeville Chamber of Commerce: 905 N.W. Alexander St., Coupeville, WA 98239. **Phone:** (360) 678-5434 or (360) 678-5664.

Shopping: Antique shops, art galleries, crafts stores and souvenir shops line Front Street between Alexander and Center streets downtown.

ANCHORAGE INN BED & BREAKFAST (360)678-5581
Bed & Breakfast. **Address:** 807 N Main St 98239

CAPTAIN WHIDBEY INN 360/678-4097
Historic Country Inn. **Address:** 2072 Captain Whidbey Inn Rd 98239

COMPASS ROSE 360/678-5318
Historic Bed & Breakfast. **Address:** 508 S Main St 98239

GARDEN ISLE GUEST COTTAGES & VACATION RENTALS
360/678-5641
Cottage. **Address:** 207 NW Coveland St 98239

WHERE TO EAT

CHRISTOPHER'S ON WHIDBEY 360/678-5480
Pacific Northwest Seafood. Casual Dining. **Address:** 103 NW Coveland St 98239

FRONT STREET GRILL 360/682-2551
Regional American. Casual Dining. **Address:** 20 Front St 98239

KNEAD & FEED 360/678-5431
Deli. Casual Dining. **Address:** 4 Front St NW 98239

DAYTON (G-11) pop. 2,526, elev. 1,606'
• Hotels p. 58 • Restaurants p. 58

Dayton was founded in 1871 along the bank of the Touchet (TOO-she) River. Flour milling was the first industry, and the town prospered as a trading center for surrounding farms, ranches and timberlands. First, Second and Third streets south of Main Street are lined with historic homes built in architectural styles ranging from Gothic, Italianate and Queen Anne to Craftsman.

Dayton Chamber of Commerce: 166 E. Main St., Dayton, WA 99328. **Phone:** (509) 382-4825 or (800) 882-6299.

Self-guiding tours: The depot and chamber of commerce have walking tour maps describing Dayton's historic districts; phone (509) 382-2026 or (509) 382-4825.

BEST WESTERN PLUS DAYTON HOTEL & SUITES
(509)382-4790

Hotel
$110-$190

Best Western PLUS
AAA Benefit: Members save up to 15% and earn bonus points!

Address: 507 E Main St 99328 **Location:** Just e of downtown. **Facility:** 50 units. 3 stories, interior corridors. **Terms:** cancellation fee imposed. **Pool:** heated indoor. **Activities:** hot tub, picnic facilities, exercise room. **Guest Services:** coin laundry. **Featured Amenity:** full hot breakfast.

THE WEINHARD HOTEL   (509)382-4032
Historic Boutique Hotel. **Address:** 235 E Main St 99328

WHERE TO EAT

WEINHARD CAFE & BAKERY   509/382-1681
American. Casual Dining. **Address:** 258 E Main St 99328

DEMING (B-3) pop. 353, elev. 207'

The Salish-speaking Nooksack people have lived in this area for thousands of years. European settlement began in the 1880s, and the town was named for George Deming, owner of the land development company.

Raspberries, strawberries and Christmas trees are local specialties. Deming Homestead Eagle Park, 3 miles east on SR 542, then south to 8160 Truck Rd., is a good vantage point for watching bald eagles feeding on spawned-out salmon from December into February; phone (360) 599-2776.

WINERIES
• **Mount Baker Vineyards and Winery** is on SR 542 at 4298 Mount Baker Hwy. **Hours:** Daily noon-5. Closed Christmas. **Phone:** (360) 592-2300. GT

THE NORTH FORK BREWERY & PIZZERIA   360/599-2337
Pizza. Brewpub. **Address:** 6186 Mt Baker Hwy (SR 542) 98244

DES MOINES (G-3) pop. 29,673, elev. 89'
• Hotels & Restaurants map & index p. 160
• Part of Seattle area — see map p. 124

On the eastern shore of Puget Sound, Des Moines was settled in 1867. The city was named for the Des Moines City Improvement Co. and prospered as a major sawmill center in the late 1800s.

The Des Moines Marina, west of SR 509 at 22307 Dock Ave. S., has a 670-foot public fishing pier. Guest moorage, boat launch facilities and gasoline are available; phone (206) 824-5700. Two miles south of downtown on Marine View Dr. S. is popular Saltwater State Park. Encompassing a 1,400-foot-long beach and a deep, forested ravine, it offers opportunities for bird-watching, camping, picnicking, hiking, windsurfing and scuba diving (see Recreation Areas Chart); phone (253) 661-4956.

DES MOINES BEACH PARK, 4 blks. w. of SR 509 via S. 223rd St. to 22030 Cliff Ave. S., is a 20-acre park that includes the Covenant Beach Historic District with meadows, woodlands, hiking trails, 635 feet of saltwater beach and a salmon-bearing stream that empties into Puget Sound. The district, which operated as a church retreat for more than 50 years, still reflects its Swedish architectural heritage. **Hours:** Daily dawn-dusk. **Cost:** Free. **Phone:** (206) 870-6527.

FOUR POINTS BY SHERATON SEATTLE AIRPORT SOUTH
(253)642-0100 128

Hotel
$95-$307

FOUR POINTS BY SHERATON
AAA Benefit: Members save 5% or more!

Address: 22406 Pacific Hwy S 98198 **Location:** I-5 exit 149, just w on Kent-Des Moines Rd, then just n. Located in a commercial area. **Facility:** 225 units. 7 stories, interior corridors. **Parking:** on-site (fee). **Terms:** cancellation fee imposed. **Amenities:** safes. **Pool:** heated outdoor. **Activities:** exercise room. **Guest Services:** valet and coin laundry.

WHERE TO EAT

ANTHONY'S HOMEPORT DES MOINES   206/824-1947 129
Seafood. Casual Dining. **Address:** 421 S 227th St 98198

SALTY'S AT REDONDO BEACH   253/946-0636 130
Seafood. Casual Dining. **Address:** 28201 Redondo Beach Dr S 98198

DUPONT (H-2) pop. 8,199, elev. 246'
• Part of Seattle area — see map p. 124

Although DuPont is a product of the 20th century, Native Americans resided in this area 5,000 years ago. The first Europeans gazed upon the Puget Sound shoreline in 1792. The Hudson's Bay Company built a storehouse at the mouth of Sequalitchew Creek in 1832, and a year later constructed Fort Nisqually, a trading post that became the nucleus of early European settlement in the region. Puget Sound's first steamship, the side-wheeler S.S. *Beaver,* began serving the fort in 1837. Two years later Americans established the Nisqually Methodist Episcopal Mission, attracting the first U.S. citizens.

In 1906 the E.I. duPont deNemours Co. acquired a tract of land for the manufacture of black powder and high explosives, which led to the creation of a company town. Weyerhauser purchased the site after the dynamite plant closed in 1976 and developed Northwest Landing, a planned community of curving boulevards, parks and Craftsman-style homes that is now a National Historic District.

DuPont City Hall: 1700 Civic Dr., DuPont, WA 98327. **Phone:** (253) 964-8121.

BEST WESTERN LIBERTY INN DUPONT   (253)912-8777

◆◆◆
Hotel
$89-$159

Best Western. **AAA Benefit:** Members save up to 15% and earn bonus points!

Address: 1400 Wilmington Dr 98327 **Location:** I-5 exit 118, just nw on Center Dr, then just ne. **Facility:** 72 units. 3 stories, interior corridors. **Terms:** check-in 4 pm, cancellation fee imposed. **Pool:** heated indoor. **Activities:** hot tub, limited exercise equipment. **Guest Services:** valet and coin laundry.

SAVE CALL ♿ ⛵ BIZ 🛜 ✕ 🖪 📺 🖵

FAIRFIELD INN & SUITES BY MARRIOTT TACOMA DUPONT
(360)334-3314

◆◆◆ Hotel. **Address:** 1515 Wilmington Dr 98327

AAA Benefit: Members save 5% or more!

HAMPTON INN & SUITES BY HILTON, DUPONT 253/912-4444

◆◆◆ Contemporary Hotel. **Address:** 800 Station Dr 98327

AAA Benefit: Members save 5% or more!

HOME2 SUITES BY HILTON, DUPONT   253/912-1000

◆◆◆ Extended Stay Hotel. **Address:** 600 Station Dr 98327

AAA Benefit: Members save 5% or more!

WHERE TO EAT

FARRELLI'S WOOD FIRE PIZZA   253/912-5200

◆◆ Pizza. Casual Dining. **Address:** 1590 Wilmington Dr 98327

EAST WENATCHEE pop. 13,190

CEDARS INN, EAST WENATCHEE   509/886-8000

◆◆
Hotel
Rates not provided

Address: 80 Ninth St NE 98802 **Location:** Just e of SR 28. **Facility:** 94 units. 3 stories, interior corridors. **Terms:** check-in 4 pm. **Pool:** heated indoor. **Activities:** hot tub, bicycles, exercise room. **Guest Services:** coin laundry. **Featured Amenity:** full hot breakfast.

SAVE 🍴 CALL ♿ ⛵ 🐾 BIZ 🛜 ✕ 🖪 📺 🖵 / SOME UNITS 🐾

WHERE TO EAT

MAI LEE THAI   509/884-1412

◆◆ Thai. Casual Dining. **Address:** 595 Grant Rd 98802

EATONVILLE (H-3) pop. 2,758, elev. 810'

Founded in 1889, Eatonville was named for pioneer settler Thomas C. Van Eaton. Large-scale milling began after the railroad arrived in 1904, and the town became an important lumbering center. Pack Forest, 3 miles southwest of town on SR 7, is a 4,300-acre tract used by the University of Washington's College of Forest Resources to discover, teach and demonstrate concepts of sustainable forestry. There are more than a dozen miles of multiuse trails. The 1927 log Gatehouse displays a section of Douglas fir cut in 1933 that measures nearly 10 feet in diameter; phone (253) 692-4160.

NORTHWEST TREK WILDLIFE PARK is 6 mi. n. on SR 161 to 11610 Trek Dr. E. This 725-acre park features animals native to the Pacific Northwest. A naturalist-guided tram tour through this 435-acre free-roaming area allows visitors to see moose, caribou, elk, bison and other animals in their natural habitats. A walk-through area features forest dwellers, grizzly bear and black bear habitat and other large predator exhibits. Kids' Trek features a nature discovery center and nature-themed playground. A picnic pavilion also is available.

The park's Zip Wild Adventure features a variety of challenges, including barreling along ziplines, climbing a 30-foot wall, crawling across a cargo net and negotiating a narrow, zigzagging bridge. Participants tackle one of five courses at their own pace.

Time: Allow 3 hours minimum. **Hours:** Park opens daily at 9:30, mid-Mar. to early Oct.; Fri.-Sun. at 9:30, rest of year. Closing times vary. Zip Wild Adventure daily 10-5, mid-June to early Sept.; Sat.-Sun. 10-4, early May to mid-June and early-late Sept. Closed Thanksgiving, Christmas Eve and Christmas. Phone ahead to confirm schedule. **Cost:** Park admission $23; $21 (ages 65+ and military with ID); $15 (ages 5-12); $11 (ages 3-4). Zip Wild Adventure admission (includes safety equipment and access to a practice course) $21.95-$69.95 per person. Participants must be 5 years of age or older, be at least 38 inches tall and weigh less than 275 pounds; reservations are required. **Phone:** (360) 832-6117, or (360) 832-7163 for Zip Wild Adventure reservations and information. GT 🏕

PIONEER FARM MUSEUM AND OHOP INDIAN VILLAGE is at 7716 Ohop Valley Rd. E. This 1880s farm offers guided tours with such hands-on activities as milking and other household and farm chores similar to those that were routinely undertaken more than 100 years ago. There are pony rides for children as well. Guides conduct 1.5-hour tours and provide narration about pioneer life. Hour-long guided tours of Ohop Indian Village also are offered.

Time: Allow 2 hours minimum. **Hours:** Daily 11-4, Father's Day-Labor Day; Sat.-Sun. 11-4, Mar. 15-day before Father's Day and day after Labor Day-day before Thanksgiving. Ohop Indian Village tours are conducted Fri.-Sun. at 1 and 2:30, Father's Day-Labor Day. **Cost:** Museum $11; $10 (ages 3-18 and 62+). Indian village tour $10.50; $9.50 (ages 3-18 and 62+). Combination pioneer museum/Indian village tour $20.50; $18.50 (ages 3-18 and 62+). **Phone:** (360) 832-6300. GT 🏕

MILL VILLAGE MOTEL (360)832-3200

WV WV
Motel
$130-$160

Address: 210 Center St E 98328 **Location:** Just e of jct SR 161. **Facility:** 32 units. 2 stories (no elevator), exterior corridors. **Featured Amenity:** continental breakfast.

SAVE ᵀᴵ• BIZ 🛜 ✕ 🖥 🖵

🖵 / SOME UNITS 🐾

EDMONDS (E-3) pop. 39,709, elev. 120'

• Hotels & Restaurants map & index p. 160
• Part of Seattle area — see map p. 124

Legend has it that when logger George Brackett petitioned to establish the town of Edmonds in 1890, he added the names of his two oxen to the list to achieve the required number of petitioners. He named the town in honor of Vermont Sen. George Franklin Edmonds, but misspelled the name.

Along the Puget Sound waterfront are beaches, a marina and a public fishing pier. The Olympic Mountains provide a distant backdrop. More than a dozen colorful murals decorate the exterior walls of downtown buildings along Main Street and on cross streets from the waterfront to Fifth Avenue; they depict the city's beautiful natural setting, history and people. The strollable downtown features vintage street lamps, quaint cafes and boutiques.

Just north of the ferry dock is Brackett's Landing Beach, where scuba divers take advantage of Edmonds Underwater Park, a 27-acre underwater dive park. Washington State Ferries provide frequent daily service to Kingston; phone (206) 464-6400, or (888) 808-7977 in Wash.

A Taste of Edmonds, a 3-day festival occurring the second weekend in August, is a great way to celebrate summer in this waterfront city. There are three stages for live entertainment—the Main Stage, the Beer Garden Stage and the Kids Stage—plus art and craft booths, food vendors, beer and wine gardens and kiddie rides. The festivities take place at Civic Playfield, 310 6th Ave. N.

Edmonds Visitors Center : 121 5th Ave. N., P.O. Box 146, Edmonds, WA 98020. **Phone:** (425) 776-6711.

Shopping: Art galleries, antique shops, specialty stores and restaurants cluster along Main Street in downtown Edmonds. A Summer Market is held Saturdays 9-3, late June to early October, at 5th and Main streets.

EDMONDS HISTORICAL MUSEUM, 118 N. 5th Ave., chronicles the settlement and growth of Edmonds and southern Snohomish County. Special

(See map & index p. 160.)

exhibits include a working model of a shingle mill, an original 1922 jail cell and a marine room displaying the city's maritime heritage. The museum occupies the former 1910 Carnegie Library/City Hall and offers changing regional history exhibits. **Time:** Allow 1 hour minimum. **Hours:** Wed.-Sun. 1-4. **Cost:** $5; $2 (ages 65+ and students with ID). **Phone:** (425) 774-0900.

BEST WESTERN PLUS EDMONDS HARBOR INN
(425)771-5021 138

Hotel
$135-$150

Best Western PLUS.

AAA Benefit: Members save up to 15% and earn bonus points!

Address: 130 W Dayton St 98020 **Location:** Just s at Port of Edmonds. Located in Harbor Square Business Park. **Facility:** 91 units. 2-3 stories, interior/exterior corridors. **Terms:** cancellation fee imposed. **Pool:** heated outdoor. **Activities:** hot tub, exercise room, massage. **Guest Services:** valet and coin laundry. *(See ad this page.)*

WHERE TO EAT

ARNIES AT EDMONDS   425/771-5688 139
Seafood Steak. Casual Dining. **Address:** 300 Admiral Way, Suite 211 98020

CHANTERELLE   425/774-0650 137
American. Casual Dining. **Address:** 316 Main St 98020

GIRARDI'S OSTERIA   425/673-5278 140
Italian. Casual Dining. **Address:** 504 5th Ave S 98020

SALT & IRON   425/361-1112 138
American. Casual Dining. **Address:** 321 Main St 98020

SCOTT'S BAR & GRILL   425/775-2561 141
American. Casual Dining. **Address:** 8115 Lake Ballinger Way 98026

ELLENSBURG (F-8) pop. 18,174, elev. 1,577'
• Hotels p. 62 • Restaurants p. 62

Ellensburg, situated in the middle of the Kittitas Valley, is noted for its cattle ranches and farms raising hay, corn and other crops. The valley once was considered a neutral area where the otherwise hostile Wenatchee, Nez Perce and Yakama Nation tribes hunted and fished together in peace.

After the Northern Pacific Railroad built its transcontinental line through the valley in 1886, farming expanded and Ellensburg boomed, becoming so prosperous that in 1889 it was a serious contender for the state capital. On the north side of town, Central Washington University is home to the Donald L. Garrity Japanese Garden. Rockhounds visit in search of elusive blue agates, which are found in this region. From May through September, the Yakima River is a popular rafting stream both above and below Ellensburg.

The Kittitas County Fair/Ellensburg Rodeo, held over Labor Day weekend, features an old-fashioned county fair in addition to a rodeo that has grown from a friendly competition among ranch hands to major league status (more than $400,000 in prize money). Some 20,000 enthusiastic fans from around the state come to watch ropers, wrestlers and Xtreme bull riders show their stuff in various events, making this the state's largest rodeo. Another popular rodeo event is the Western Parade through downtown, described as "one of the horsiest around."

▼ *See AAA listing this page* ▼

The Kittitas County Fair dates back to 1885. The fairgrounds, off 9th Avenue, also are a national historic district. Festivities include mechanical bull riding and a pedal tractor pull for kids, agricultural exhibits, the re-created Frontier Village, live music and a carnival.

The Kittitas County Barn Quilt Trail loops through the valley surrounding Ellensburg, passing colorful quilt blocks on the sides of more than 100 historic and working barns.

Kittitas County Chamber of Commerce: 609 N. Main St., Ellensburg, WA 98926. **Phone:** (509) 925-2002 or (888) 925-2204.

CLYMER MUSEUM & GALLERY is at 416 N. Pearl St. Exhibiting the works of Western artist John Ford Clymer, the collection includes cover illustrations for the *Saturday Evening Post* and oils depicting wildlife and Western themes. The museum also features changing exhibits. **Time:** Allow 30 minutes minimum. **Hours:** Mon.-Fri. 11-5, Sat. 11-3 (also Sat. 3-4, May-Oct.). Closed Jan. 1, Easter, Memorial Day, July 4, Labor Day, Thanksgiving and Christmas. **Cost:** Free. **Phone:** (509) 962-6416.

BEST WESTERN PLUS ELLENSBURG HOTEL
(509)925-4244

Hotel
$94-$300

Best Western PLUS **AAA Benefit:** Members save up to 15% and earn bonus points!

Address: 211 W Umptanum Rd 98926 **Location:** I-90 exit 109, just n on Canyon Rd, then just w. **Facility:** 55 units, some efficiencies. 3 stories, interior corridors. **Terms:** cancellation fee imposed. **Pool:** heated indoor. **Activities:** hot tub, exercise room. **Guest Services:** valet and coin laundry.

SAVE ⏱ CALL 🚭 🛁 ♿ BIZ
HS 🛜 ✖ 🔌 🖥 🖨
/SOME UNITS 🐾

COMFORT INN ELLENSBURG   (509)925-7037
Hotel. **Address:** 1722 S Canyon Rd 98926

ECONO LODGE   509/925-9844
Motel. **Address:** 1390 N Dollarway Rd 98926

HAMPTON INN BY HILTON ELLENSBURG   509/933-1600
Hotel. **Address:** 2705 Triple L Loop 98926   **AAA Benefit:** Members save 5% or more!

HOLIDAY INN EXPRESS   509/962-9400
Hotel. **Address:** 1620 S Canyon Rd 98926

WHERE TO EAT

SUGAR THAI CUISINE   509/933-4224
Thai. Casual Dining. **Address:** 306 N Pine St 98926

YELLOW CHURCH CAFE   509/933-2233
American. Casual Dining. **Address:** 111 S Pearl St 98926

ENUMCLAW (F-7) pop. 10,669, elev. 742'

After encountering a severe thunderstorm in the area, Duwamish Indians referred to a nearby mountain as Enumclaw, or "thundering mountain." The name stuck when the town was established in 1885.

The pastureland surrounding Enumclaw is a noted horse raising area, producing more than 20 breeds, including Thoroughbreds, Morgans, Paso Finos and paints. January through June are the best months to see foals romping in their paddocks.

Enumclaw Area Chamber of Commerce: 1421 Cole St., Enumclaw, WA 98022. **Phone:** (360) 825-7666.

FEDERATION FOREST STATE PARK is 18 mi. e. to 49201 SR 410. The park consists of 619 acres of old growth forest with nature trails and picnic areas. Exhibits at the Catherine Montgomery Interpretive Center illustrate the state's seven contrasting life zones. Gardens outside the center showcase edible and poisonous native plants and flora from six of Washington's nine biosystems. **Hours:** Daily 8 a.m.-dusk, early Apr.-early Oct. Phone for information about guided tours. **Cost:** Park admission $10 (per private vehicle); Discover Pass, valid for 1 year, $30 (per private vehicle). Interpretive center free. **Phone:** (360) 663-2207 or (360) 902-8844. GT 🎏

LEE RESTAURANT & LOUNGE   360/825-3761
American. Casual Dining. **Address:** 1110 Griffin Ave 98022

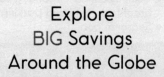

EPHRATA pop. 7,664, elev. 1,277'

BEST WESTERN RAMA INN   (509)754-7111

Hotel
$110-$150

Best Western.

AAA Benefit: Members save up to 15% and earn bonus points!

Address: 1818 Basin St SW 98823 **Location:** On SR 28; west end of town. **Facility:** 70 units, some kitchens. 2 stories, interior corridors. **Pool:** heated indoor. **Activities:** sauna, hot tub. **Guest Services:** coin laundry. *(See ad this page.)*

SAVE ⍰ CALL ⍰ ⍰ HS ⍰ ⍰ ⍰ ⍰ ⍰ /SOME UNITS ⍰

EVERETT (E-3) pop. 103,019, elev. 21'

• Hotels p. 64 • Restaurants p. 65
• Part of Seattle area — see map p. 124

Eastern capitalists selected Everett's deepwater port as the site for a major industrial center in the early 1890s. The Panic of 1893 dashed their dreams, but by 1900 Minnesota timber entrepreneur Frederick Weyerhaeuser had established a sawmill on the fledgling town's waterfront, and within a decade the mill was among the world's largest. Timber was king in early Everett, with over a dozen lumber and shingle mills operating. Labor disputes plagued the city in the early days, however, culminating in the Everett Massacre in 1916, when seven men were shot and an unknown number drowned.

Everett's economy, once dependent on forest products, is today dominated by service industries, aerospace and the military. Boeing selected an abandoned air force base south of the city as the site for its 747 manufacturing plant in the mid-1960s, and the Everett Naval Station was established on the downtown waterfront in the early 1990s.

Many of the city's neighborhoods overlook Port Gardner, the Olympics and the Cascades. Quite a few of the mansions lining Rucker and Grand avenues north of downtown were formerly owned by timber barons. Grand Avenue Park, at 1800 Grand Ave. between 16th and 19th streets, contains a plaque commemorating the 1792 landing of Capt. George Vancouver on the shoreline below.

Jetty Island, off the northern end of the waterfront, is at the channel entrance of the Snohomish River. The man-made island, 2 miles long by 200 yards wide, is home to 45 species of birds as well as a herd of California sea lions from October to June. Accessible by private boat year-round, the island also can be accessed via a free ferry service that operates daily (weather permitting), July 1-Labor Day. Ferries depart from the 10th Street boat launch off W. Marine View Drive; phone (425) 257-8304 or (425) 257-8300.

Shopping: Everett Mall, 5 miles south on S.E. Everett Mall Way, has Burlington and Sears. Everett Marina Village, on the waterfront at the foot of 18th Street, is a renovated portion of the waterfront district that recalls an 1890s village.

FLYING HERITAGE & COMBAT ARMOR MUSEUM is at the s.e. corner of Paine Field. From I-5 southbound take exit 189, go w. on SR 526, s. on Airport Rd., w. on 112th St. S.W., then n. on 30th St. W. to 109th St., following signs; from I-5 northbound take exit 186, go w. on 128th St. S.W. to Airport Rd., w. on 112th St S.W., then n. on 30th St. W. to 3407 109th St., following signs.

▼ See AAA listing this page ▼

The collection includes 19 meticulously restored, rare World War II-era fighter planes from the United States, the United Kingdom, Germany, Japan and the former Soviet Union. Each plane represents a technological advancement in manned flight; many are the last examples of their type known to exist, and most are in flying condition. A highlight is the Messerschmitt 163B Komet, the world's first rocket-powered fighter.

Fly days, scheduled noon to 1 on selected dates from June to early October (weather permitting, phone for details), offer an opportunity to see two of these historic fighter craft take to the sky. Flights can be observed from an observation area adjacent to the runway. Guided tours are available by reservation. **Time:** Allow 1 hour minimum. **Hours:** Tues-Sun. 10-5 (also Mon. 10-5, Memorial Day-Labor Day). Closed Thanksgiving and Christmas. **Cost:** $16; $14 (ages 65+ and veterans and military with ID); $12 (ages 6-17). **Phone:** (877) 342-3404. [GT]

FUTURE OF FLIGHT AVIATION CENTER & BOEING TOUR—see Mukilteo p. 91.

IMAGINE CHILDREN'S MUSEUM is at 1502 Wall St. The museum's three floors of hands-on exhibit areas explore science, literacy, math, history and art. Highlights include Tall Timbers Rooftop Adventure, featuring a rooftop play structure with panoramic views and a dinosaur fossil dig area; AirMazing Laboratory, where kids learn about the effects of air movement; and Wildlife Clinic, an area for kids to play veterinarian.

Time: Allow 1 hour minimum. **Hours:** Tues.-Wed. 9-5, Thurs.-Sat. 10-5, Sun. 11-5. Closed Jan. 1, Easter, Memorial Day, Labor Day, Thanksgiving and Christmas. **Cost:** $10.20; $5.10 (to all Thurs. 3-5); free (ages 0-12 months). **Phone:** (425) 258-1006.

BEST WESTERN CASCADIA INN   (425)258-4141

Hotel
$89-$199

Best Western. **AAA Benefit:** Members save up to 15% and earn bonus points!

Address: 2800 Pacific Ave 98201 **Location:** I-5 exit 193 northbound; exit 194 southbound, just w. **Facility:** 134 units. 3 stories, interior corridors. **Terms:** cancellation fee imposed. **Pool:** heated outdoor. **Activities:** hot tub. **Guest Services:** valet and coin laundry, area transportation.

[SAVE] [icons] CALL [icons]

BEST WESTERN PLUS NAVIGATOR INN & SUITES
(425)347-2555

Hotel
$119-$229

Best Western PLUS. **AAA Benefit:** Members save up to 15% and earn bonus points!

Address: 10210 Evergreen Way 98204 **Location:** I-5 exit 189, 1 mi w on SR 526 to Evergreen Way, then 1.6 mi s. **Facility:** 102 units, some efficiencies and kitchens. 3-4 stories, interior corridors. **Terms:** cancellation fee imposed. **Pool:** heated indoor. **Activities:** hot tub, exercise room. **Guest Services:** complimentary and valet laundry, area transportation.

[SAVE] CALL [icons] / SOME UNITS

COURTYARD BY MARRIOTT SEATTLE NORTH/EVERETT
(425)259-2200

Hotel. **Address:** 3003 Colby Ave 98201

AAA Benefit: Members save 5% or more!

DELTA HOTELS BY MARRIOTT SEATTLE EVERETT
(425)339-2000

Hotel. **Address:** 3105 Pine St 98201

AAA Benefit: Members save 5% or more!

EXTENDED STAY AMERICA-SEATTLE-EVERETT-SILVERLAKE
425/337-1341

Extended Stay Hotel. **Address:** 1431 112th St SE 98208

HAMPTON INN BY HILTON SEATTLE/EVERETT DOWNTOWN
425/349-4466

Hotel. **Address:** 2931 W Marine View Dr 98201

AAA Benefit: Members save 5% or more!

HOLIDAY INN EXPRESS HOTEL & SUITES   425/609-4000

Hotel. **Address:** 131 128th St SW 98204

INN AT PORT GARDNER, AN ASCEND HOTEL COLLECTION MEMBER   (425)252-6779

Boutique Hotel
$119-$189

Address: 1700 W Marine View Dr 98201 **Location:** Waterfront. I-5 exit 193 northbound, 1.2 mi w on Pacific Ave, then 1.2 mi n; exit 194 southbound, 1.2 mi w on Everett Ave, then 1 mi n; in Everett Marina Village. **Facility:** The hotel has comfortable rooms with views of a lovely marina and Puget Sound. A number of restaurants are an easy walk away. 33 units. 3 stories, interior corridors. **Guest Services:** valet laundry. **Featured Amenity:** continental breakfast.

[SAVE] [icons] CALL [icons] / SOME UNITS

LA QUINTA INN EVERETT
(425)347-9099

Hotel
$69-$124

Address: 12619 4th Ave W 98204 **Location:** I-5 exit 186, just nw. **Facility:** 73 units. 3 stories, interior corridors. **Pool:** heated outdoor. **Guest Services:** coin laundry. **Featured Amenity:** continental breakfast.

SAVE ⬆ CALL ♿ 🛏 BIZ 📶
✕ 🗄 🖥 🖨 /SOME UNITS 🐾

WHERE TO EAT

ANTHONY'S HOMEPORT EVERETT   425/252-3333
Seafood. Casual Dining. **Address:** 1726 W Marine View Dr 98201

ANTHONY'S WOODFIRE GRILL   425/258-4000
American. Casual Dining. **Address:** 1722 W Marine View Dr 98201

BURGERMASTER   425/347-5700
Burgers. Quick Serve. **Address:** 7909 Evergreen Way 98203

CAPERS + OLIVES   425/322-5280
Italian. Casual Dining. **Address:** 2933 Colby Ave 98201

EMORY'S ON SILVER LAKE   425/337-7772
American. Casual Dining. **Address:** 11830 19th Ave SE 98208

LOMBARDI'S   425/252-1886
Italian. Casual Dining. **Address:** 1620 W Marine View Dr 98201

SCUTTLEBUTT BREWING CO.   425/257-9316
American. Brewpub. **Address:** 1205 Craftsman Way 98201

EVERSON pop. 2,481

HERB NIEMANN'S STEAK & SCHNITZEL HOUSE
360/966-2855
Steak. Casual Dining. **Address:** 203 W Main St 98247

FEDERAL WAY (G-3) pop. 89,306, elev. 500'

- Restaurants p. 66
- Hotels & Restaurants map & index p. 201
- Part of Seattle area — see map p. 124

Part of the Seattle-Tacoma metropolitan area, Federal Way spreads over a series of wooded ridges above Puget Sound. The name is a reference to federally funded SR 99 (formerly Pacific Highway South), built through the area in 1929.

West Hylebos Wetlands Park, 411 S. 348th St., has a 1-mile nature trail that winds through a forest and a bog. Dash Point State Park, 6 miles west of SR 99 on SR 509, has 11 miles of hiking trails and 3,000 feet of Puget Sound shoreline at the base of a wooded bluff *(see Recreation Areas Chart)*.

Federal Way Chamber of Commerce: 31919 1st Ave. S., Suite 202, Federal Way, WA 98003. **Phone:** (253) 838-2605.

Shopping: Macy's is the anchor store at The Commons at Federal Way, 1 mile west of I-5 exit 143 at the southeast corner of SR 99 and S. 320th Street.

PACIFIC BONSAI MUSEUM is .25 mi. e. of northbound I-5 exit 142A via SR 18 to the Weyerhaeuser Way exit, then .25 mi. n. following signs; from southbound I-5 take exit 143, then e. on S. 320th St. a quarter mi., then s. 1 mi. on Weyerhaeuser Way following signs. This 1-acre facility was established as a symbol of the importance of trading relationships with Pacific Rim countries. The collection includes more than 60 bonsai trees from the United States, Canada, Japan, Korea, China and Taiwan. Several of the trees are more than 500 years old. Bonsai-themed fine art also is on display. **Time:** Allow 30 minutes minimum. **Hours:** Tues.-Sun. 10-4. Closed Jan. 1, Thanksgiving, Christmas Eve and Christmas. **Cost:** Donations. **Phone:** (253) 353-7345.

RHODODENDRON SPECIES BOTANICAL GARDEN is .25 mi. e. of northbound I-5 exit 142A to the Weyerhaeuser Way exit, then .25 mi. n., following signs; from southbound I-5 take exit 143, then .25 mi. e. on S. 320th St., then s. 1 mi. on Weyerhaeuser Way, following signs to 2525 S. 336th St. This 24-acre garden features more than 700 species of rhododendron from around the world. The alpine section displays rhododendrons and other plants adapted to survive the harsh growing conditions of high altitudes. The Rutherford Conservatory houses tropical rhododendron and some of the most rare companion plants. Of special interest is the Rhododendron Big Leaf Forest, Blue Poppy Meadow and Victorian Stumpery.

Time: Allow 1 hour minimum. **Hours:** Tues.-Sun. 10-4. Closed Jan. 1, Thanksgiving, Christmas Eve and Christmas. **Cost:** $8; $5 (ages 65+ and students with ID); free (ages 0-11 and military with ID). **Phone:** (253) 838-4646.

BEST WESTERN PLUS SEATTLE/FEDERAL WAY
(253)529-4000 **17**

Hotel
$129-$189

Best Western PLUS. **AAA Benefit:** Members save up to 15% and earn bonus points!

Address: 32124 25th Ave S 98003 **Location:** I-5 exit 143, just sw. **Facility:** 165 units, some two bedrooms. 8 stories, interior corridors. **Terms:** cancellation fee imposed. **Pool:** heated indoor. **Activities:** hot tub, exercise room. **Guest Services:** valet and coin laundry, area transportation.

SAVE 🍴 🍷 🛏 🖥
BIZ 📶 ✕ 🗄 🖥 🖨
/SOME UNITS 🐾

CLARION HOTEL FEDERAL WAY-SEATTLE
(253)941-6000 **13**
Hotel. **Address:** 31611 Pete von Reichbauer Way S 98003

COMFORT INN FEDERAL WAY-SEATTLE (253)529-0101 **14**
Hotel. **Address:** 31622 Pacific Hwy S 98003

(See map & index p. 201.)

COURTYARD BY MARRIOTT SEATTLE-FEDERAL WAY
(253)529-0200 **16**
♥♥♥ Hotel. **Address:** 31910
Gateway Center Blvd S 98003

AAA Benefit:
Members save 5%
or more!

HAMPTON INN & SUITES BY HILTON FEDERAL WAY
253/946-7000 **15**
♥♥♥ Hotel. **Address:** 31720
Gateway Center Blvd S 98003

AAA Benefit:
Members save 5%
or more!

QUALITY INN & SUITES   (253)835-4141 **18**

♦♦♦
Hotel
$90-$160

Address: 1400 S 348th St 98003 **Location:** I-5 exit 142B, 0.5 mi w. **Facility:** 65 units, some efficiencies. 3 stories, interior corridors. **Pool:** heated indoor. **Activities:** exercise room. **Guest Services:** coin laundry. **Featured Amenity: full hot breakfast.**

SAVE CALL ♿ ⚲ 📶 BIZ HS
📶 ✕ 🅿 📷 💻

WHERE TO EAT

BILLY MCHALE'S   253/839-4200 **20**
♥♥ American. Casual Dining. **Address:** 1320 S 324th St, Suite A10 98003

RAM RESTAURANT & BREWERY   206/878-6694
♥♥ American. Casual Dining. **Address:** 31920 Gateway Center Blvd S 98003

THE ROCK, WOOD FIRED PIZZA & SPIRITS
253/835-7625 **21**
♥♥ Pizza. Casual Dining. **Address:** 34817 Enchanted Pkwy S 98003

VERRAZANOS ITALIAN RESTAURANT   253/946-4122 **19**
♥♥ Italian. Casual Dining. **Address:** 28835 Pacific Hwy S 98003

FERNDALE (A-2) pop. 11,415, elev. 30'

Ferndale, in the northwest corner of the state, was so named in 1872 when the area's first schoolteacher noticed clumps of ferns surrounding the schoolhouse. The town is a trade center for area farms.

Ferndale Visitor Information Center: 2007 Cherry St., P.O. Box 1254, Ferndale, WA 98248. **Phone:** (360) 384-3042.

HOVANDER HOMESTEAD PARK is 1 mi. s. via Hovander Rd. to 5299 Nielsen Ave. This 350-acre park encompasses the 1903 restored Hovander House, an interpretive center, barn, milk house and children's farm zoo. The house is furnished with antiques, and the barn has displays of vintage farming equipment.

The grounds feature a beautiful flower garden, native plant and vegetable gardens, a greenhouse and (for the benefit of gardeners) a weed identification garden, all maintained by the Master Gardeners of WSU. From May through October animals like draft horses, cows, sheep, goats and pigs—many on loan from nearby farms—can be seen, and some can be fed. Ducks, chickens, turkeys, geese, rabbits and peacocks are year-round residents. Stroll the boardwalk on Tennant Lake, hike the park's trails or go canoeing. A variety of gardening workshops are scheduled throughout the year.

Dogs are allowed in on-leash areas of the park. **Time:** Allow 1 hour minimum. **Hours:** Grounds open daily 8 a.m.-dusk. House open Fri.-Sun. 12:30-4:30, Memorial Day-Labor Day. The house is not always open during scheduled times; phone ahead to confirm. The boardwalk may be closed during designated hunting season. **Cost:** House $1; 50c (ages 0-12). **Phone:** (360) 384-3444 or (360) 733-2900.
✕ 🐾 🅰

PIONEER PARK is at 2004 Cherry St. Buildings dating 1870-95 form one of the most notable collections of original pioneer log cabins in the Northwest. Among the dozen structures are a post office, barn, church, granary, schoolhouse, stagecoach inn, veteran's museum, jail and homesteads. Artifacts depict life during the pioneer era, and costumed guides conduct tours. During the Olde Fashioned Christmas celebration the buildings are decorated and horse-drawn carriage rides are offered. **Time:** Allow 1 hour minimum. **Hours:** Park open Mon.-Fri. 9-5, Sat.-Sun. 9-dusk. Guided tours of the historic buildings are available Tues.-Sun. 11:30-4:30, May 15-Sept. 15. **Cost:** Tour $5; $3 (ages 6-12). **Phone:** (360) 384-6461. GT

SILVER REEF HOTEL CASINO SPA   360/383-0777

♦♦♦
Contemporary
Hotel
Rates not provided

Address: 4876 Haxton Way 98248 **Location:** I-5 exit 260, 3.6 mi w on Slater Rd. **Facility:** Guests enjoy modern and very spacious guest rooms with the convenience of being right above a rejuvenating spa. Several restaurants and a full-service casino are on site. 206 units. 6 stories, interior corridors. **Terms:** check-in 4 pm. **Dining:** 4 restaurants, also, The Steak House at Silver Reef, see separate listing. **Pool:** heated indoor. **Activities:** sauna, hot tub, steamroom, trails, exercise room, spa. **Featured Amenity: continental breakfast.**

SAVE 🐾 🍴 🧖 🍸 CALL ♿
⚲ 📶 HS 📶 ✕ 💻
/ SOME
  UNITS 🅿 📷

WHERE TO EAT

THE STEAK HOUSE AT SILVER REEF   360/543-7178
♥♥♥ Steak Seafood. Fine Dining. **Address:** 4876 Haxton Way 98248

FIFE pop. 9,173
- Hotels & Restaurants map & index p. 201
- Part of Seattle area — see map p. 124

EMERALD QUEEN HOTEL & CASINO
(253)922-2000 **21**

Hotel
$121-$259

Address: 5700 Pacific Hwy E 98424 **Location:** I-5 exit 137, just ne. **Facility:** Expect contemporary guest rooms and a full-service slots casino, while a shuttle provides service to a sister casino with table games. Guests must pass through the casino to reach the hotel lobby. 103 units. 4 stories, interior corridors. **Amenities:** safes. **Dining:** 3 restaurants. **Pool:** heated outdoor. **Activities:** hot tub, exercise room. **Guest Services:** valet laundry, area transportation.

FORKS (D-4) pop. 3,532, elev. 375'
- Part of Olympic National Park area — see map p. 100

This important Olympic Peninsula logging community takes its name from the forks of the three nearby rivers: the Bogachiel, Calawah and Sol Duc. Forks began in the late 1870s as an agricultural community; commercial logging followed a decade later. In addition to providing the town's name, area rivers support spectacular runs of steelhead trout during the summer and winter, attracting anglers.

More recently, Forks has gained fame as the primary setting for the phenomenally successful "Twilight" series of novels by Stephenie Meyer. Props, costumes and two motorcycles from the "Twilight" movies are on display at the Rainforest Arts Center, 11 N. Forks Ave. The collection is open Thurs.-Mon. 10-4, Tues.-Wed. by appointment; phone the Forks Chamber of Commerce, (360) 374-2531.

Forks Chamber of Commerce/Visitor Information Center: 1411 S. Forks Ave., P.O. Box 1249, Forks, WA 98331. **Phone:** (360) 374-2531 or (800) 443-6757.

MANITOU LODGE   360/374-6295
Bed & Breakfast. **Address:** 813 Kilmer Rd 98331

MILLER TREE INN BED & BREAKFAST   360/374-6806
Historic Bed & Breakfast. **Address:** 654 E Division St 98331

MISTY VALLEY INN BED AND BREAKFAST   (360)374-9389
Bed & Breakfast. **Address:** 194894 US 101 98331

PACIFIC INN MOTEL   360/374-9400
Motel. **Address:** 352 S Forks Ave 98331

WHERE TO EAT

THE IN PLACE   360/374-4004
American. Casual Dining. **Address:** 320 S Forks Ave 98331

GIFFORD PINCHOT NATIONAL FOREST (G-7)
- Attractions map p. 87

Elevations in the forest range from 200 ft. at Columbia River to 12,276 ft. at Mount Adams. Refer to AAA maps for additional elevation information.

Straddling the Cascade Range from Mount Rainier to the Columbia River Gorge National Scenic Area, Gifford Pinchot National Forest covers 1,312,000 acres of mountains, meadows, caves, canyons and streams. On opposite edges of the forest, restless 8,364-foot Mount St. Helens and glacier-clad, 12,276-foot Mount Adams tower above the lesser peaks; the fields of wild huckleberries scattered through the forest and surrounding Mount Adams lure thousands of pickers in late summer.

Forest roads are usually open from late May through November; however, many are narrow and winding and should be traveled with care. Check current road and weather conditions carefully. For information about Mount St. Helens contact the Forest Supervisor's office at (360) 891-5000 or Mount St. Helens National Volcanic Monument *(see place listing p. 88)* at (360) 449-7800.

Of the forest's seven wilderness areas, Goat Rocks and Mount Adams are the largest. Self-issued permits, available at trailheads and ranger stations, are required to enter the Indian Heaven, Mount Adams, Goat Rocks, Trapper Creek, Tatoosh and Glacier View wilderness areas. The forest is home to many species of animals; common birds are ducks, grouse, ravens and Steller and Canada jays. Salmon and trout inhabit the many streams.

Of particular interest are the Big Lava Beds, 14 miles west of Trout Lake on FR 60. The unusual formations originated from a 500-foot-deep crater in the northern part of the lava bed. Ice Cave, 6 miles southwest of Trout Lake on SR 141, is one of numerous lava tubes in an area known as the Big Trench Cave System. Ice usually remains in the 400-foot cave until late summer.

Another interesting volcanic feature is the Palisades, which is visible from US 12, 2.5 miles east of the SR 123 junction. The Clear Fork of the Cowlitz River has cut a deep gorge into an ancient lava flow, exposing an impressive 486-foot-high cliff of columnar basalt. Trails can be followed on foot or horseback.

Gotchen Creek Cabin, a former ranger station constructed in 1909, is the oldest structure in the forest. The cabin can be viewed Friday through Wednesday from late July to late September. Contact the Mt. Adams Ranger Station in Trout Lake for information; phone (509) 395-3402.

The Pacific Crest National Scenic Trail runs through the forest on its way from Mexico to Canada. Canoes and boats with small motors are permitted on some lakes; watch for speed restrictions. Snowmobiling, snowshoeing and cross-country skiing are popular winter pastimes. Fishing and hunting are permitted in season. Downhill skiing is available late November to early April at White Pass, east of Packwood on US 12.

A Northwest Forest Pass, available at ranger stations, is required for parking at most trailheads in the forest. A day pass costs $5 per vehicle; an annual pass costs $30. Recreation information is available at ranger stations in Amboy, Randle and Trout Lake. Contact the Forest Supervisor's Office, Gifford Pinchot National Forest, 1501 E. Evergreen Blvd., Vancouver, WA 98661; phone (360) 891-5000 or TTY (360) 891-5003. *See Recreation Areas Chart.*

GIG HARBOR (G-2) pop. 7,126, elev. 60'
• Part of Seattle area — see map p. 124

Five miles northwest of Tacoma via the Narrows Bridge, Gig Harbor is a picturesque city with a bayfront that manages to retain the flavor of a small fishing village. Washington's "Maritime City" centers on its namesake body of water, a long, narrow inlet of Puget Sound. Seeking refuge from a storm in 1841, members of the Charles Wilkes expedition discovered the bay by chance and named it for their gig, a type of sailing longboat. After the turn of the 20th century many immigrants from islands off the Croatian coast formed the nucleus of the town's fishing industry.

Boats still fill the harbor and marinas, and docks line the shore. Downtown businesses cluster along the southern half of Harborview Drive, which runs along the west side of the bay for just over a mile. Finholm Marketplace, a second business district at the north end of the bay along N. Harborview Drive, is the site of Gig Harbor's original location.

Net sheds are an architectural legacy of the early days. Sixteen historic net sheds dating from 1910 to the 1950s still stand along the city's west shoreline. Built out of rough, hand-hewn fir, they were used to store fishing nets and gear.

Skansie Brothers Park, 3207 Harborview Dr. at Rosedale Street, includes a fishermen's memorial, the classic 1910 Skansie Netshed, the 1908 Andrew Skansie House and Jerisich Dock, a pedestrian-only pier and public boat moorage. The park is a venue for outdoor summer concerts. The Eddon Boat Building, 3805 Harborview Dr., is where the Thunderbird sailboat was developed. The yard still builds and repairs boats and offers activities relating to Gig Harbor's maritime heritage.

Ferry Landing Park, at the southern end of Harborview Drive, overlooks the narrow harbor entrance. Finholm View Climb, next to Finholm Market at 8826 N. Harborview Dr., rewards exertion with a quintessential view of the bay (plus Mount Rainier as a backdrop). The 1.5-mile Waterfront History Walk, paralleling Harborview and N. Harborview drives, features 48 interpretive markers. A brochure outlining the walk is available at the chamber of commerce and local businesses.

Check around town for skippered charter sailboat outings as well as pleasure, fishing boat, sailboat, sea kayak, paddle boat and jet ski rentals. Destiny

Harbor Tours offers 90-minute and 2-hour sightseeing trips departing from Gig Harbor Rent-a-Boat at 8829 N. Harborview Dr.; phone (253) 225-6306.

Gig Harbor Chamber of Commerce: 3125 Judson St., Gig Harbor, WA 98335. **Phone:** (253) 851-6865.

Shopping: Downtown along the waterfront, Harborview Drive and Finholm Marketplace feature specialty shops and art galleries. There are more shops and galleries in the Kimball Business District, on Kimball Drive just off Pioneer Way. April through September a farmers market is held Thursdays 3-7 in Skansie Brothers Park off Harborview Drive, Saturdays 8:30-2 at 5503 Wollochet Dr. N.W. and Sundays 11-4 at 4701 Point Fosdick Dr. N.W.

HARBOR HISTORY MUSEUM is at the n. end of the downtown waterfront at 4121 Harborview Dr. The main gallery has permanent themed exhibits on local history, south Puget Sound Native Americans, pioneer settlers, water transportation, early industrial development, commercial fishing and bridging the Tacoma Narrows. Video kiosks featuring thousands of historic images and hands-on displays augment the exhibits.

The Maritime Gallery displays the restored 65-foot fishing vessel *Shenandoah* (currently under restoration) and the hull of a Thunderbird, a type of sailboat developed in Gig Harbor in 1958. Outside is the restored Midway Schoolhouse. The one-room school operated from 1893 to 1941; it contains period furnishings, books and charts.

Hours: Tues.-Sat. 10-5, Sun. noon-5. Closed Jan. 1, Easter, July 4, Thanksgiving, Dec. 24-27 and Dec. 31. **Cost:** $7; $6 (ages 65+ and students and active military with ID); $5 (ages 6-17). **Phone:** (253) 858-6722.

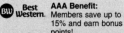

WHERE TO EAT

ANTHONY'S AT GIG HARBOR   253/853-6353
♦♦♦ Seafood. Casual Dining. **Address:** 8827 Harborview Dr N 98332

THE GREEN TURTLE   253/851-3167
♦♦ Pacific Rim. Casual Dining. **Address:** 2905 Harborview Dr 98335

GOLDENDALE (H-8) pop. 3,407, elev. 1,509'

Settled in 1872, Goldendale stands in a broad upland valley commanding panoramas of Cascade volcanoes Mount Hood and Mount Adams. Pioneer ranchers raised sheep and cattle, but after the arrival of the railroad in 1903, wheat farming prevailed. The many Victorian houses surrounding the central business district reflect the town's early prosperity.

Greater Goldendale Area Chamber of Commerce: 903 E. Broadway, Goldendale, WA 98620. **Phone:** (509) 773-3400.

GOLDENDALE OBSERVATORY STATE PARK is 1.5 mi. n. of Main St. at 1602 Observatory Dr. The observatory houses a 24.5-inch reflecting telescope, one of the largest of its kind in the country available for public use. In addition to various telescopes, visitors also have access to a 152mm Lunt H-Alpha Solar telescope for viewing the sun. **Hours:** Thurs.-Sun. 1-11:30, Apr.-Sept.; Fri.-Sun. 1-9, rest of year. Guided tours depart on the hour. Last admission 2 hours before closing. **Cost:** Park admission $10 (per private vehicle); Discover Pass, valid for 1 year, $30 (per private vehicle). **Phone:** (509) 773-3141. GT

THE GLASS ONION   509/773-4928
♦♦♦ American. Casual Dining. **Address:** 604 S Columbus Ave 98620

ST. JOHN'S BAKERY & CAFE   509/773-6650
♦ Greek. Quick Serve. **Address:** 2378 US 97 98620

HANFORD REACH NATIONAL MONUMENT (F-9)

Established by presidential proclamation in June 2000, Hanford Reach National Monument embraces 195,000 acres of federal lands on two sides of the Hanford Reservation in south-central Washington. The monument protects the Hanford Reach, the last free-flowing stretch of the Columbia River in the United States above Bonneville Dam. With summer temperatures routinely reaching 100 degrees Fahrenheit and annual rainfall less than 7 inches, this is the hottest and driest part of the state. The area supports a unique community of plants and animals.

Hanford Reach comprises two separate sections. The 120,000-acre northeast portion preserves the left bank of the Columbia River, including Saddle Mountain National Wildlife Area and the Wahluke Slope and White Bluffs area. The gravel bars along this stretch of river harbor spawning grounds for the largest surviving population of wild salmon in the Columbia basin.

The 60,000-acre Wahluke Unit is open to the public. Visitors can use a boat launch, hike several trails and view the surrounding region from a scenic overlook atop Saddle Mountain; no camping is permitted. The White Bluffs Overlook, 19 miles east of the SR 243 junction on SR 24, then 8.5 miles south via gravel White Bluffs Boat Launch Road, offers a panoramic view encompassing the bluffs, the river and a series of former plutonium production reactors on the Hanford site. The boat launch is open to motorized boats November through June; non-motorized boats year-round.

The other segment of the monument lies southwest of SR 240. It constitutes the Fitzner-Eberhardt Arid Lands Ecology Reserve, Washington's largest remaining shrub-steppe landscape. Due to its environmentally sensitive nature, this section is closed to the public.

Hanford Reach National Monument, open daily dawn-dusk, is administered by the U.S. Fish and Wildlife Service. Information is available from their Burbank office at 64 Maple St., Burbank, WA 99323; phone (509) 546-8300.

HOODSPORT (G-1) pop. 376, elev. 70'
• Part of Olympic National Park area — see map p. 100

First settled in 1880, Hoodsport lies at the base of the Olympic Mountains on the shore of Hood Canal, the westernmost arm of Puget Sound. Clams, oysters and shrimp are harvested from area waters. SR 119 leads west to Lake Cushman, a popular recreation area in the southeast corner of Olympic National Park.

Hood Canal Visitor Information Center: 150 N. Lake Cushman Rd., Hoodsport, WA 98548. **Phone:** (360) 877-2021.

WINERIES
• **Hoodsport Winery** is at N. 23501 US 101. **Hours:** Daily 10-6. Closed Thanksgiving and Christmas. **Phone:** (360) 877-9894 or (800) 580-9894. GT

HOQUIAM (F-5) pop. 8,726, elev. 10'

Forest products have been a staple of Hoquiam's economy since its first sawmill opened in 1882. The city's name derives from the Chehalis Indian word Ho-qui-umpts, meaning "hungry for wood." Grays Harbor is a natural outlet for the area's prime export. The tidal flats lining the harbor west of town shelter migrating shorebirds in spring and fall.

Built in the late 1920s, the 7th Street Theatre, 313 7th St., was the first theater in the state to show talking motion pictures; phone (360) 537-7400.

ILWACO (G-4) pop. 936, elev. 11'

Protected by tall headlands to the west, Ilwaco lies northeast of Cape Disappointment and just inside the mouth of the Columbia River—the location of one of the most treacherous river bars in the world. Over the course of more than 200 years, the hazardous conditions at the Columbia bar and along the nearby coast have claimed hundreds of vessels, earning area waters the nickname "Graveyard of the Pacific."

Cape Disappointment Coast Guard Station and Lighthouse, 3.7 miles southeast off US 101, is the home of one of the largest search and rescue facilities in the state; it also houses the Coast Guard's only heavy-weather Motor Lifeboat School. A local landmark is the Colbert House, built in Chinookville in 1872 and moved by barge to its present-day location at the corner of Spruce and Quaker streets.

Ilwaco is a popular sport fishing port. Charter operators specialize in guided fishing trips for salmon, halibut, tuna, bottom fish and sturgeon; the prime fishing season is May through October. A Washington fishing license, available from charter operators, is required.

CAPE DISAPPOINTMENT STATE PARK is 3 mi. s.w. off US 101. Capt. John Meares named this headland in 1788, which reflected his feelings upon not discovering the fabled Northwest Passage. The park is part of Lewis and Clark National Historical Park, and within its boundaries is Fort Canby; built in 1852, it guarded the entrance to the Columbia River and was Washington's first military installation.

Trails lead through the forest to isolated coves and broad sandy beaches. The park offers a wide range of recreational activities. The Cape Disappointment Lighthouse, commissioned in 1856, is the oldest lighthouse in the state. *See Recreation Areas Chart.*

Hours: Daily 6:30 a.m.-dusk. Lighthouse tour departs daily, May-Sept. **Cost:** Park admission $10 (per private vehicle); Discover Pass, valid for 1 year, $30 (per private vehicle). Lighthouse tour $2.50; free (ages 7-17). Reservations are required for lighthouse tours; children under 7 not permitted on tour. **Phone:** (360) 642-3078, or (360) 642-3029 for lighthouse tour reservations. GT 🅰 🍴 🐾 🏕

Lewis & Clark Interpretive Center, within Cape Disappointment State Park, 3 mi. s.w. off US 101, traces the 8,000-mile trek embarked on and led by Meriwether Lewis and William Clark. Exhibits portray the expedition party's medical treatment, food, entertainment, self-disciplinary measures and the contributions of the Chinook and other tribes toward the trip's success. Sketches by the explorers and artifacts collected on the expedition are displayed; and a multimedia presentation depicts the highlights of the journey. Also of interest are maritime and military exhibits.

Wear comfortable walking shoes; it's a 200-yard uphill trek to the center. **Time:** Allow 1 hour minimum.

Hours: Daily 10-5, Apr.-Oct.; Wed.-Sun. 10-5, rest of year. Closed Jan. 1, Thanksgiving and Christmas. **Cost:** $5; $2.50 (ages 7-17). Park admission $10 (per private vehicle); Discover Pass, valid for 1 year, $30 (per private vehicle). **Phone:** (360) 642-3029.

North Head Lighthouse, within Cape Disappointment State Park, 3 mi. s.w. off US 101, was built in 1897 and crowns its namesake promontory overlooking the Pacific. In 1853 the sailing ship *Vandalia* foundered on the rocks just north of the light on Beards Hollow. Tours of the lighthouse are offered. **CLOSURE INFORMATION:** The lighthouse is undergoing restoration and is scheduled to reopen June 2019. The grounds remain open.

Note: Children under 7 years are not permitted on the lighthouse tour. **Hours:** Daily 10-5:30, May 1-Labor Day; hours vary rest of year. Phone ahead to confirm schedule. **Cost:** Lighthouse $5; $2.50 (ages 7-17). Park admission $10 (per private vehicle); Discover Pass, valid for 1 year, $30 (per private vehicle). **Phone:** (360) 642-3078 or (360) 642-3029. GT

WILLAPA NATIONAL WILDLIFE REFUGE headquarters is 8.5 mi. n. of jct. US 101 and US 101 Alt. at 3888 US 101. The refuge encompasses 14,000 acres of marshland, upland forests, pastures and tidal estuaries. Long Island has a stand of 1,000-year-old red cedars and tidal marshes that support deer, bears, elks, coyotes and beavers. More than 180 species of migratory birds have been sighted among the salt marshes and shifting dunes of Leadbetter Point at the entrance to Willapa Bay. The refuge also includes the adjoining tidal flats at the southern tip of Willapa Bay.

Camping is permitted on the Long Island Unit, but it is accessible by private boat only. **Time:** Allow 4 hours minimum. **Hours:** Daily dawn-dusk. **Cost:** Free. **Parking:** $10 (Leadbetter Unit Parking Area only). **Phone:** (360) 484-3482. 🅰

IONE (C-12) pop. 447, elev. 2,090'

Ione has always been a timber town. Pend Oreille River steamboats linked Washington's northeastern corner with the outside world from the late 1880s until the railroad arrived in 1909. A sawmill built by the Panhandle Lumber Co. opened in this small community in 1901 and by 1909 employed 700 workers; a smaller mill continues to operate on the site. The era of river transportation is fondly recalled during Down River Days the last full weekend in July. The festivities include a parade, a cowboy breakfast and snowmobile races—on the water.

No road can provide comparable vistas, but if you can't take the train ride Box Canyon Viewpoint, 4 miles north of Ione on SR 31, offers a gander at the rugged canyon scenery; it overlooks a narrow, rocky gorge spanned by a railroad bridge.

ISSAQUAH (E-7) pop. 30,434, elev. 98'
- Hotels & Restaurants map & index p. 160
- Part of Seattle area — see map p. 124

The Seattle Pacific and Lakeshore Railroad's extension to nearby Squak Mountain in the late 1800s triggered a major coal mining boom and the settlement of the community of Gilman. The town's name was changed to Issaquah, a Coast Salish Indian word meaning "sound of waterfowl," in 1899.

Greater Issaquah Chamber of Commerce: 155 N.W. Gilman Blvd., Issaquah, WA 98027. **Phone:** (425) 392-7024.

Self-guiding tours: A map outlining a walking tour of historic downtown Issaquah is available at the Gilman Town Hall Museum, the Issaquah Depot Museum and the chamber of commerce.

Shopping: Gilman Village, south of I-90 exit 17 at Gilman Boulevard and Juniper Street, is a complex of restored pioneer houses that contains restaurants and specialty shops. Hand-dipped chocolates are made at Boehm's Chocolate Factory, 255 N.E. Gilman Blvd.

COUGAR MOUNTAIN ZOO is at 19525 S.E. 54th St. on Cougar Mountain. The 12-acre facility focuses on distinctive and endangered species while promoting conservation through education. Daily lectures, animal enrichment activities and demonstrations are offered. **Hours:** Daily 10-4:30, Dec. 1-23; daily 11-3, Dec. 26-30; Wed.-Sun. 9:30-5 (or dusk), rest of year. Closed Jan. 1, Thanksgiving, Christmas Eve, Christmas and Dec. 31. Phone ahead to confirm schedule. **Cost:** $13.50; $12.50 (ages 62+); $9.50 (ages 2-12). **Phone:** (425) 391-5508 or (425) 392-6278.

HILTON GARDEN INN SEATTLE/ISSAQUAH 425/837-3600 **81**
♦♦♦ Hotel. **Address:** 1800 NW Gilman Blvd 98027   **AAA Benefit:** Members save 5% or more!

HOLIDAY INN SEATTLE ISSAQUAH 425/392-6421 **79**
♦♦♦ Hotel. Rates not provided. **Address:** 1801 12th Ave NW 98027 **Location:** I-90 exit 15, 0.3 mi n on 17th Ave NW, then just e. **Facility:** 100 units. 2 stories, interior corridors. **Pool:** heated outdoor. **Activities:** hot tub, exercise room. **Guest Services:** valet and coin laundry, area transportation.

HOMEWOOD SUITES BY HILTON SEATTLE/ISSAQUAH 425/391-4000 **80**
♦♦♦ Extended Stay Hotel. **Address:** 1484 Hyla Ave NW 98027   **AAA Benefit:** Members save 5% or more!

SPRINGHILL SUITES BY MARRIOTT SEATTLE ISSAQUAH (425)427-6000 **82**
♦♦♦ Hotel. **Address:** 1185 NW Maple St 98027   **AAA Benefit:** Members save 5% or more!

WHERE TO EAT

BIG FISH GRILL   425/369-4334 **104**
♦♦ Seafood. Casual Dining. **Address:** 984 NE Park Dr 98029

FINS BISTRO   425/392-0109 **106**
♦♦♦ Seafood. Casual Dining. **Address:** 301 Front St N 98027

FLAT IRON GRILL   425/657-0373 **103**
♦♦ American. Casual Dining. **Address:** 317 NW Gilman Blvd 98027

ISSAQUAH BREWHOUSE   425/557-1911 **107**
♦♦ American. Casual Dining. **Address:** 35 W Sunset Way 98027

JAK'S GRILL   425/837-8834
♦♦ Steak. Casual Dining. **Address:** 14 Front St N 98027

RAM RESTAURANT AND BREWERY   425/313-0415
♦♦ American. Casual Dining. **Address:** 965 NE Park Dr 98029

TRIPLE XXX ROOTBEER DRIVE-IN   425/392-1266 **105**
♦ Burgers. Casual Dining. **Address:** 98 NE Gilman Blvd 98027

WILDFIN AMERICAN GRILL - ISSAQUAH 425/427-0127 **102**
♦♦ American. Casual Dining. **Address:** 835 NW Gilman Blvd 98027

KALAMA (G-6) pop. 2,344, elev. 210'

Founded in the 1840s, Kalama is named for Hawaiian native John Kalama, who settled in the area after marrying the daughter of a Nisqually chief. In addition to being a busy shipping center, Kalama claims two superlatives: a 149-foot single-tree totem pole, in Marine Park, and the first fish hatchery in the state. The latter has been replaced by two newer hatcheries. Nearly 100 antique dealers are in malls and individual shops on N. 1st Street.

The Kalama Transportation Interpretive Center, off I-5 exit 30 at 110 W. Marine Dr., has exhibits and displays detailing Kalama's first inhabitants, the Cowlitz tribe, early settlers and the city's transportation history; phone (360) 673-2325.

KALAMA BURGER BAR   360/673-2091
♦ American. Quick Serve. **Address:** 49 Ivy St 98625

KELSO (G-6) pop. 11,925, elev. 26'
- Hotels p. 72 • Restaurants p. 72

The dramatic and much lauded run of smelt up the Cowlitz River in January and February has earned Kelso the title Smelt Capital of the World. Also plentiful are steelhead trout and sturgeon, making Kelso an important fishing and canning center.

Kelso-Longview Chamber Visitor Center: 105 N. Minor Rd., Kelso, WA 98626. **Phone:** (360) 423-8400.

Shopping: JCPenney serves as the anchor store at Three Rivers Mall, just west of I-5 exit 39 at Allen Street and SR 4.

COWLITZ COUNTY HISTORICAL MUSEUM is at 405 Allen St. The primary exhibit portrays settlement and transportation from before European settlement to the present. Displays include portions of a loggers' bunkhouse, a re-created railroad depot, historical photographs, a reassembled log cabin with period furnishings, a canoe and Cowlitz Indian artifacts.

The museum also maintains a changing historical exhibit on the first floor of the County Administration Building at 207 4th Ave. N. **Time:** Allow 30 minutes minimum. **Hours:** Museum open Tues.-Sat. 10-4. County Administration Building open Mon.-Fri. 8:30-5. **Cost:** Donations. **Phone:** (360) 577-3119 or TTY (800) 833-6384.

BEST WESTERN ALADDIN INN　　　(360)425-9660

♦♦ Hotel
$99-$250

BW Best Western.
AAA Benefit: Members save up to 15% and earn bonus points!

Address: 310 Long Ave 98626 **Location:** I-5 exit 39, 1.1 mi w via Allen and W Main sts, then just n on 5th Ave NW. **Facility:** 77 units, some kitchens. 2 stories (no elevator), interior corridors. **Terms:** cancellation fee imposed. **Pool:** heated indoor. **Activities:** exercise room. **Guest Services:** coin laundry. **Featured Amenity: full hot breakfast.**

SAVE ▯🍴 ☎ 👪 BIZ HS 🛜 ⊠ ▯ 🖥 🖵 / SOME UNITS 🐾 📺

COMFORT INN　　　(360)425-4600

♦♦ Hotel
$91-$149

Address: 440 Three Rivers Dr 98626 **Location:** I-5 exit 39, 0.3 mi w on Allen St, 0.3 mi s. Adjacent to Three Rivers Mall. **Facility:** 57 units. 2 stories (no elevator), interior corridors. **Pool:** heated indoor. **Activities:** hot tub, limited exercise equipment. **Guest Services:** valet laundry. **Featured Amenity: continental breakfast.**

SAVE ▯🍴 ☎ BIZ 🛜 ⊠ ▯ 🖥 🖵

MOTEL 6 KELSO　　　(360)425-3229
♦ Motel. **Address:** 106 Minor Rd 98626

RED LION HOTEL & CONFERENCE CENTER
KELSO/LONGVIEW　　　(360)636-4400
♦♦ Hotel. **Address:** 510 Kelso Dr 98626

SUPER 8 - KELSO　　　(360)423-8880
♦♦ Hotel. **Address:** 250 Kelso Dr 98626

BURGERVILLE　　　360/501-4354
♦ American. Quick Serve. **Address:** 600 W Main St 98626

KENNEWICK (G-10) pop. 73,917, elev. 362'

The region where Kennewick (which means "winter paradise" in the Yakama Nation tongue) now stands was nothing but arid land with a carpet of bunch grass until the late 1800s, when the first of a series of irrigation projects began to convert sagebrush country into farmland. In 1957 the Kennewick Highland irrigation project was completed; it now supplies water to more than 20,000 acres that support crops of alfalfa, corn and beans. Reinforced by the huge hydroelectric dams harnessing the lower bend of the Columbia River, Kennewick's economy also is supported by chemical and agricultural processing.

Kennewick, Pasco and Richland *(see place listings p. 106 and p. 116)* form the urban Tri-Cities area. Despite the desertlike climate (annual rainfall is less than 8 inches), water is a major feature of the landscape. The Columbia—here three-quarters of a mile wide—flows from north to south. Between Kennewick and Richland it receives the Yakima River. And just downstream from Pasco the Snake, mightiest of the tributaries, joins its parent stream.

It's no surprise, then, that Kennewick is the departure point for various scenic and recreational cruises. Columbia Park *(see Recreation Areas Chart)* extends 4.5 miles along the river. There are several access points off SR 240. Facilities include an aquatic playground, playing fields, a miniature railway, a golf course and a fishing pond. Columbia Park's Regional Veterans Memorial features a 40-foot-high granite slab, said to be the tallest free-standing piece of granite in the U.S.

On the grounds of the Southridge Sports and Events Complex, off US 395 at 2901 Southridge Blvd., is a 9/11 Memorial consisting of a piece of steel that fell more than 1,000 feet from the upper levels of one of the World Trade Center towers on September 11, 2001. Nearby is the Gesa Carousel of Dreams, a restored 1910 Charles Carmel carousel with 45 colorful, hand-carved horses. The carousel was originally located in St. Joseph, Mich., and is set in a glass and wooden structure for year-round operation; phone (509) 378-3257.

Visit Tri-Cities: 7130 W. Grandridge Blvd., Suite B, Kennewick, WA 99336. **Phone:** (509) 735-8486 or (800) 254-5824.

Shopping: The major shopping mall in the Tri-Cities area is Kennewick's Columbia Center, 3 miles north of I-82 exit 109 at 1321 N. Columbia Center Blvd.; anchor stores are JCPenney, Macy's and Sears.

BAYMONT INN & SUITES BY WYNDHAM KENNEWICK
509/736-3326

▼▼ Hotel. **Address:** 4220 W 27th Pl 99337

BEST WESTERN PLUS KENNEWICK INN   (509)586-1332

Hotel
$129-$279

AAA Benefit: Members save up to 15% and earn bonus points!

Address: 4001 W 27th Ave 99337 **Location:** I-82 exit 113 (US 395), 0.8 mi n. **Facility:** 88 units, some kitchens. 3 stories, interior corridors. **Parking:** winter plug-ins. **Terms:** cancellation fee imposed. **Pool:** heated indoor. **Activities:** sauna, hot tub, exercise room. **Guest Services:** valet and coin laundry.

[SAVE] [▮↑] CALL [♿] [🏊] [♨] [BIZ] [📶] [✕] [🛗] [🖥] [🖨]

/ SOME UNITS [🐾] [HS]

CLOVER ISLAND INN   509/586-0541

▼▼ Hotel. **Address:** 435 Clover Island Dr 99336

COMFORT INN BY CHOICE HOTELS KENNEWICK
(509)783-8396

▼▼ Hotel. **Address:** 7801 W Quinault Ave 99336

FAIRFIELD INN BY MARRIOTT   (509)783-2164
▼▼ Hotel. **Address:** 7809 W Quinault Ave 99336

AAA Benefit: Members save 5% or more!

HAMPTON INN BY HILTON KENNEWICK AT SOUTHRIDGE
509/820-3023

▼▼ Hotel. **Address:** 3715 Plaza Way 99338

AAA Benefit: Members save 5% or more!

HILTON GARDEN INN KENNEWICK/TRI-CITIES
(509)735-4600

Hotel
$109-$219

🏨 Hilton Garden Inn

AAA Benefit: Members save 5% or more!

Address: 701 N Young St 99336 **Location:** 1 mi s of SR 240, just e. **Facility:** 120 units. 3 stories, interior corridors. **Terms:** 1-7 night minimum stay, 3 day cancellation notice-fee imposed. **Pool:** heated indoor. **Activities:** hot tub, bicycles, exercise room. **Guest Services:** valet and coin laundry. **Featured Amenity:** full hot breakfast.

[SAVE] [➕] [▮↑] [Y] CALL [♿] [🏊]

[♨] [BIZ] [HS] [📶] [✕] [🛗] [🖥] [🖨]

KENNEWICK SUPER 8 BY WYNDHAM   (509)736-6888

Hotel
$65-$100

Address: 626 N Columbia Center Blvd 99336 **Location:** 1.1 mi s of SR 240. **Facility:** 95 units. 3 stories, interior corridors. **Terms:** 3 day cancellation notice. **Pool:** heated indoor. **Activities:** hot tub. **Guest Services:** coin laundry. **Featured Amenity:** continental breakfast.

[SAVE] [▮↑] CALL [♿] [🏊] [BIZ] [📶]

[✕] [🛗] [🖥] [🖨] / SOME UNITS [🐾]

LA QUINTA INN & SUITES KENNEWICK   (509)736-3656
▼▼ Hotel. **Address:** 2600 S Quillan Pl 99338

QUALITY INN BY CHOICE HOTELS   (509)735-6100
▼▼ Hotel. **Address:** 7901 W Quinault Ave 99336

RED LION INN & SUITES KENNEWICK   509/396-9979
▼▼ Hotel. **Address:** 602 N Young St 99336

SPRINGHILL SUITES BY MARRIOTT KENNEWICK/TRI-CITIES
(509)820-3026

Hotel
$89-$227

SPRINGHILL SUITES MARRIOTT

AAA Benefit: Members save 5% or more!

Address: 7048 W Grandridge Blvd 99336 **Location:** SR 240 exit Columbia Center Blvd, 0.8 mi s to W Quinalt Ave, 0.3 mi se, then just e. Connected to Three Rivers Convention Center. **Facility:** 116 units. 5 stories, interior corridors. **Terms:** cancellation fee imposed. **Pool:** heated indoor. **Activities:** hot tub, exercise room. **Guest Services:** valet and coin laundry. **Featured Amenity:** breakfast buffet.

[SAVE] [▮↑] [Y] CALL [♿] [🏊] [➕] [BIZ] [📶] [✕] [🛗]

[🖥] [🖨]

WHERE TO EAT

BANGKOK RESTAURANT   509/735-7631
▼▼ Thai. Casual Dining. **Address:** 8318 W Gage Blvd, Suite A 99336

BELLA ITALIA RISTORANTE   509/783-1701
▼ Italian. Fine Dining. **Address:** 7000 W Okanogan Pl 99336

BETWEEN THE BUNS   509/987-1091
▼ Hot Dogs. Quick Serve. **Address:** 3902 W Clearwater Ave, Suite 120 99336

BOB'S BURGERS & BREW   509/987-1060
▼ American. Casual Dining. **Address:** 3609 Plaza Way 99337

CARMINE'S FAMILY STYLE ITALIAN DINING   509/396-7890
▼▼ Italian. Casual Dining. **Address:** 525 W 1st Ave 99336

CASA MIA ITALIAN RESTAURANT   509/582-0440
▼▼ Italian. Casual Dining. **Address:** 2541 W Kennewick Ave 99337

CEDARS RESTAURANT & LOUNGE   509/582-2143
▼▼ American. Casual Dining. **Address:** 355 Clover Island Dr 99336

CG PUBLIC HOUSE   509/783-0128
▼▼ New American. Casual Dining. **Address:** 9221 W Clearwater Ave #A 99336

FOODIES BRICK & MORTAR   509/591-0424
▼▼ American. Casual Dining. **Address:** 308 W Kennewick Ave 99337

GRAZE KENNEWICK   509/221-1020
▼ Sandwiches. Quick Serve. **Address:** 8530 W Gage Blvd 99336

ICE HARBOR BREWING COMPANY AT THE MARINA
509/586-3181
▼▼ American. Brewpub. **Address:** 350 Clover Island Dr 99336

MASALA NORTH & SOUTH INDIAN CUISINE   509/737-9999
▼▼ Indian. Casual Dining. **Address:** 3321 W Kennewick Ave, Suite 100 99336

THAI ELEPHANT   509/396-9152
▼▼ ▼▼ Thai. Casual Dining. **Address:** 6030 W Clearwater Ave 99336

TWIGS BISTRO & MARTINI BAR   509/735-3411
▼▼▼▼ American. Casual Dining. **Address:** 1321 N Columbia Center Blvd 99336

KENT (G-3) pop. 92,411, elev. 43'
- Hotels & Restaurants map & index p. 160
- Part of Seattle area — see map p. 124

Settled in the 1880s, Kent was first called Titusville in honor of the town's first mayor, James Titus. Hops were the area's major crop, and in 1890 the town was renamed for Kent County, the English hop-growing center. After disease decimated the hop yards in 1895, dairying became the major industry. The opening of a Boeing plant in 1965 turned Kent into a manufacturing center.

Pacific Raceways, 31001 144th Ave. S.E., offers NHRA drag and road racing on a 2.25-mile track; phone (253) 639-5927. The ShoWare Center, 625 W. James St., is the home ice for the Seattle Thunderbirds hockey team; for ticket information phone (253) 239-7825.

Kent Chamber of Commerce: 524 W. Meeker St., Suite 1, Kent, WA 98032. **Phone:** (253) 854-1770.

HYDROPLANE AND RACEBOAT MUSEUM is at 5917 S. 196th St.; take I-5 exit 152 e. via Orillia Rd. and S. 200th St., which curves into S. 196th St. This fascinating collection of artifacts from the sport of powerboat racing includes ten restored, operational hydroplanes dating from the 1940s to the 1980s. Other displays showcase books, trophies and race memorabilia. Visitors also can see the powerboat restoration area and engine room. **Time:** Allow 1 hour minimum. **Hours:** Tues.-Sat. 10-4 (also Tues. and Thurs. 4-8). **Cost:** $10; $5 (ages 6-16 and 60+). Guided tour free. **Phone:** (206) 764-9453. GT

BEST WESTERN PLUS PLAZA BY THE GREEN
                                            (253)854-8767   134

▼▼▼▼
Hotel
$119-$249

Ⓑⓦ **Best Western PLUS** **AAA Benefit:** Members save up to 15% and earn bonus points!

Address: 24415 Russell Rd 98032 **Location:** I-5 exit 149 southbound; exit 149A northbound, 2 mi ne via Kent Des Moines Rd (SR 516) and Meeker St. Adjacent to golf course. **Facility:** 97 units. 2 stories, interior corridors. **Terms:** cancellation fee imposed. **Activities:** bicycles, exercise room. **Guest Services:** valet and coin laundry, area transportation. **Featured Amenity: full hot breakfast.**

 SAVE ⊞ ⫫ ☀ BIZ 🛜 ⊠ 🛢 ▣

COMFORT INN KENT   (253)872-2211   133
▼▼ ▼▼ Hotel. **Address:** 22311 84th Ave S 98032

HAMPTON INN & SUITES BY HILTON SEATTLE/KENT
                                            253/872-8811   132
▼▼▼▼ Hotel. **Address:** 21109 66th Ave S 98032

AAA Benefit: Members save 5% or more!

RED LION INN & SUITES KENT   253/520-6670   135
▼▼ ▼▼ Hotel. **Address:** 25100 74th Ave S 98032

TOWNEPLACE SUITES BY MARRIOTT-SEATTLE SOUTHCENTER   (253)796-6000   131
▼▼▼▼ Extended Stay Hotel. **Address:** 18123 72nd Ave S 98032

AAA Benefit: Members save 5% or more!

WHERE TO EAT

MITZEL'S AMERICAN KITCHEN   253/395-3635   133
▼▼ ▼▼ American. Casual Dining. **Address:** 22330 84th Ave S 98032

RAM RESTAURANT AND BREWERY   253/520-3881
▼▼ ▼▼ American. Casual Dining. **Address:** 512 Ramsay Way 98032

THAI CHILI RESTAURANT   253/850-5887   134
▼▼ ▼▼ Thai. Casual Dining. **Address:** 120 Washington Ave N 98032

KETTLE FALLS (C-11) pop. 1,595, elev. 1,625'

Native Americans once gathered in great numbers to fish for salmon at the Kettle Falls cataract on the Columbia River, now beneath the waters of Lake Roosevelt. In 1825, the Hudson's Bay Company established a gristmill at nearby Myers Falls, making this the first European settlement in Washington east of the Cascades. The town was relocated to its present site in the 1930s as the reservoir formed behind Grand Coulee Dam.

Kettle Falls Visitor Center: 425 W. 3rd St., P.O. Box 119, Kettle Falls, WA 99141. **Phone:** (509) 738-2300.

KIRKLAND (F-3) pop. 48,787, elev. 100'
- Restaurants p. 76
- Hotels & Restaurants map & index p. 160
- Part of Seattle area — see map p. 124

There aren't too many towns that can boast a lovely lakefront setting *and* a downtown that's pedestrian friendly in the best sense of the term. And happily, Kirkland has both. No other place in the greater Seattle area has as many waterfront parks as this city on Lake Washington's northeastern shore. On a clear day you can see downtown Seattle across the lake, with the distant Olympic Mountains beyond.

Visit on a sunny summer day to take full advantage of the parks. Downtown's Marina Park is just a few steps off Lake Street at 25 Lakeshore Plaza Dr. It has a sandy beach and an open-air pavilion as well as a marina, and the lake views are outstanding. Celebrate the opening day of boating season in early May, or catch a music performance in July and August. A short distance north of Marina Park is Waverly Beach Park (take Central Way west to Market Street, turn right, go north a block to Waverly Way, turn left and continue to the end of the street). It has a bigger beach, a designated swimming area enclosed by a U-shaped dock (good for sunbathing on warm days), and a sweeping view of Lake Washington's northern reaches.

(See map & index p. 160.)

Juanita Bay Park (from downtown, take Market Street/98th Avenue north to 2201 Market St.) encompasses 110 acres of wooded wetland, meadow and marsh areas. It's a good spot for bird-watchers to roam around. The diversity of vegetation in this urban wildlife habitat area can be seen from the boardwalk nature trails that wind along the shoreline. South of downtown, Houghton Beach Park, 5811 Lake Washington Blvd. N.E., is ideal for families; there's a shallow swimming area for kids, a playground, picnic tables, beach volleyball and a public dock for fishing.

You can hardly turn around in Kirkland without bumping into a bronze sculpture or two. There's a bevy of them along the waterfront. At the Marina Park dock, "Coming Home" depicts an embracing family; nearby, along Lakeshore Plaza Drive, "Puddle Jumpers" is made up of six hand-holding, leaping kids—including two with feet suspended in mid-air. This one is pure poetry in motion. Three more youngsters play "Leap Frog" at Marsh Park, just off Lake Washington Boulevard N.E.

There are plenty more sculptures on Kirkland's downtown streets. "Cow and Coyote" near the corner of Central Way and Lake Street is just what the name says: a coyote rakishly perched atop the hind end of a seemingly oblivious cow. Take a seat next to "Betty Lou"; she's the nonchalant gal sitting on a bench at the corner of Kirkland Avenue and Main Street.

The Kirkland Wednesday Market sets up from early June through late September at Marina Park. Produce vendors offer a bounty of seasonal, locally grown fruits and veggies—sweet corn, baby lettuces, summer squash, heirloom tomatoes, blackberries, gooseberries, nectarines and more—plus flowers, jam, baked goods and crafts.

The Kirkland Art Walk takes place the second Friday of the month from 5 to 8 p.m., when a handful of downtown galleries spotlight new artists. For more information phone (425) 889-8212. Kirkland Uncorked, held in mid-July, focuses on fine Washington food and wine. This 3-day "festival of style and taste" features a tasting garden that pairs Washington wines with gourmet nibbles. The festivities also include live jazz and light classical performances, luxury boats that can be toured and the CityDog modeling contest for pooches, with proceeds going to a shelter for homeless animals. It all takes place at Marina Park.

You'll be lucky to find on-street parking downtown in summer, but it's free. There are parking lots with both free and metered spaces at Marina Park, on Lake Street S. and on Main Street. You can park free for 4 hours in the municipal parking garage beneath the Kirkland Library (entrances are on 3rd Street and Kirkland Avenue).

Greater Kirkland Chamber of Commerce: 440 Central Way, Kirkland, WA 98033. **Phone:** (425) 822-7066.

Shopping: The Howard/Mandville Gallery, 120 Park Ln., is one of the largest of several downtown art galleries, with paintings, sculpture and prints by regional and nationally known artists. Emerging as well as established contemporary Northwest artists exhibit at the Parklane Gallery, 130 Park Ln.

Interspersed among the galleries are a slew of specialty shops and boutiques. Fashionistas will approve of Hepburn Boutique, 140 Park Ln., and Zarza Style Boutique, 732 Market St. Kirkland Urban, just off Central Way about half a mile west of I-405 exit 18, is a mixed-use development currently under construction with a scheduled opening in early 2019. A multi-screen theater and restaurants will share space with specialty shops.

Nightlife: The Wilde Rover Irish Pub & Restaurant, 111 Central Way, is named after Irish playwright, novelist and poet Oscar Wilde. It offers a full menu of evening entertainment, from live music to a trivia contest on Wednesdays. Hoist a Guinness Stout and offer the traditional Irish drinking toast: "Sláinte!"; pronounce it "slanj" and you'll be in the ballpark. Phone (425) 822-8940.

The Central Club (124 Kirkland Ave.) is a popular gathering spot for everybody from bikers to Microsoft geeks. There's live music here on Wednesday night; phone (425) 827-0808.

KIRKLAND ARTS CENTER is .2 mi. n. at 620 Market St. Housed in the Peter Kirk Building, built in 1892, the center's art gallery displays a variety of works by artists from across the country with a focus on contemporary Northwest art. **Hours:** Tues.-Fri. 11-6, Sat. 11-5. **Cost:** Free. **Phone:** (425) 822-7161.

BAYMONT INN & SUITES BY WYNDHAM

(425)822-2300 **35**

◈◈◈
Hotel
$79-$159

Address: 12223 NE 116th St 98034 **Location:** I-405 exit 20A northbound; exit 20 southbound, just e; in Totem Lake area. **Facility:** 104 units. 3 stories, exterior corridors. **Terms:** check-in 4 pm. **Pool:** heated outdoor. **Activities:** hot tub, exercise room. **Guest Services:** coin laundry. **Featured Amenity:** continental breakfast.

SAVE ｜｜＋ CALL ⚡ 🏊 🐕 BIZ
🛜 ✕ 🛏 🖼 🖵

COMFORT INN-KIRKLAND   (425)814-1792 **34**
◈◈ Hotel. **Address:** 12204 NE 124th St 98034

THE HEATHMAN HOTEL   425/284-5800 **36**
◈◈◈◈ Boutique Hotel. **Address:** 220 Kirkland Ave 98033

LA QUINTA INN & SUITES SEATTLE BELLEVUE/KIRKLAND
(425)828-6585 **38**
◈◈◈ Hotel. **Address:** 10530 NE Northup Way 98033

🔗 **For complete hotel, dining and attraction listings: AAA.com/travelguides**

(See map & index p. 160.)

WOODMARK HOTEL & STILL SPA   (425)822-3700   **37**

Boutique Hotel
$198-$334

Address: 1200 Carillon Point 98033 **Location:** Waterfront. On Lake Washington Blvd, 1 mi n of SR 520. **Facility:** Take in pretty views of Lake Washington from many of this hotel's rooms, which sit on the lake's eastern shore. A couple of shopping and dining choices are just a short stroll from the hotel. 100 units. 4 stories, interior corridors. **Parking:** on-site (fee) and valet. **Terms:** check-in 4 pm, cancellation fee imposed, resort fee. **Amenities:** safes. **Dining:** 3 restaurants. **Activities:** self-propelled boats, bicycles, exercise room, spa. **Guest Services:** valet laundry, area transportation.

SAVE ⊠ ⊠ ⊠ CALL ⊠ ⊠ BIZ HS ⊠ ⊠
⊠ ⊠ ⊠ /SOME UNITS ⊠

WHERE TO EAT

BIG FISH GRILL   425/827-2722   **63**
♥♥ Seafood. Casual Dining. **Address:** 10426 NE Northup Way 98033

CACTUS KIRKLAND   425/893-9799   **59**
♥♥ Tex-Mex. Casual Dining. **Address:** 121 Park Ln 98033

CAFE JUANITA   425/823-1505   **56**
♥♥♥♥ Northern Italian. Fine Dining. **Address:** 9702 NE 120th Pl 98034

CAFE VELOCE   425/814-2972   **57**
♥♥ Italian. Casual Dining. **Address:** 12514 120th Ave NE 98034

HECTOR'S   425/827-4811   **60**
♥♥ American. Casual Dining. **Address:** 112 Lake St S 98033

RISTORANTE PARADISO   425/889-8601   **58**
♥♥♥ Regional Italian. Casual Dining. **Address:** 120 Park Ln 98033

SHAMIANA   425/827-4902   **62**
♥♥ Indian. Casual Dining. **Address:** 10724 NE 68th St 98033

TRELLIS   425/284-5900   **61**
♥♥♥ Pacific Northwest. Fine Dining. **Address:** 220 Kirkland Ave 98033

LACEY   (H-2) pop. 42,393, elev. 185'

Lacey, a suburban community just east of Olympia, was first called Woodland in honor of pioneer Isaac Woods. By the 1890s Lacey boasted a sawmill, resort hotel and the region's major horse racing track. Tudor-style buildings dominate the campus of St. Martins University, founded in 1895 by the Order of St. Benedict. Tolmie State Park *(see Recreation Areas Chart)*, 4.5 miles west of I-5 exit 111, features 1,800 feet of shoreline on Puget Sound, a saltwater marsh and a 2.5-mile nature trail. The near-shore waters are popular with scuba divers.

The Chehalis Western Trail is a recreation trail following the route of a logging railroad that operated from 1926 into the mid-1980s. The paved, 6.5-mile north segment, suitable for horseback riding, connects Martin Way and Lindsley Lane S.E. with Puget Sound at Woodard Bay. Offering walkers, runners, bikers and roller bladers views of Mount Rainier, the 16-mile paved south segment connects 14th Avenue S.E. at Chambers Lake with SR 507, 2

miles west of Rainier, where it connects with the 14.5-mile Yelm-Tenino Trail.

Lacey South Sound Chamber: 8300 Quinault Dr. N.E., Suite A, Lacey, WA 98516. **Phone:** (360) 491-4141.

BEST WESTERN PLUS LACEY INN & SUITES
(360)456-5655

Hotel
$99-$300

BW **Best Western PLUS**   **AAA Benefit:** Members save up to 15% and earn bonus points!

Address: 8326 Quinault Dr NE 98516 **Location:** I-5 exit 111 (Marvin Rd), just ne. **Facility:** 85 units. 4 stories, interior corridors. **Terms:** cancellation fee imposed. **Pool:** heated indoor. **Activities:** hot tub, exercise room. **Guest Services:** valet and coin laundry. **Featured Amenity:** breakfast buffet.

SAVE ⊠ ⊠ ⊠ ⊠ BIZ HS
⊠ ⊠ ⊠ ⊠ ⊠ /SOME UNITS ⊠

CANDLEWOOD SUITES   360/491-1698
♥♥♥ Extended Stay Hotel. **Address:** 4440 3rd Ave SE 98503

COMFORT INN   (360)456-6300
♥♥ Hotel. **Address:** 4700 Park Center Ave NE 98516

HOLIDAY INN EXPRESS HOTEL & SUITES   360/491-7985
♥♥♥ Hotel. **Address:** 4460 3rd Ave SE 98503

WHERE TO EAT

FARRELLI'S PIZZA AND POOL   360/493-2090
♥♥ Pizza. Casual Dining. **Address:** 4870 Yelm Hwy SE 98503

RAM RESTAURANT AND BREWERY   360/923-5900
♥♥ American. Casual Dining. **Address:** 8100 Freedom Ln NE, Suite C 98516

LA CONNER   (C-3) pop. 891, elev. 50'

This picturesque fishing port dates back to the founding of a trading post in 1868. In the late 19th century dikes and drainage works transformed the boggy marshlands of the nearby Skagit Flats into fertile farmland. Hops and oats were early boom crops; today flower bulbs are an important crop. The 1869 Magnus Anderson Cabin, at the corner of 2nd and Commercial streets, is the oldest building in town.

The west side of 1st Street provides views of docks and boats on the Swinomish Channel. The west bank of the channel is part of the Swinomish Indian Reservation, established in 1855. The La Conner Marina, 613 N. 2nd St. at the northern end of town, has nearly 500 open and covered moorage slips for recreational craft; phone (360) 466-3118.

La Conner Chamber of Commerce: 511 Morris St., Suite 3, P.O. Box 1610, La Conner, WA 98257. **Phone:** (360) 466-4778 or (888) 642-9284.

Shopping: There are clothing stores, art galleries and specialty shops on 1st Street between Morris and Douglas streets.

MUSEUM OF NORTHWEST ART is at 121 S. 1st St. Focusing on the visual art of the Pacific Northwest, the museum displays changing exhibits of paintings, glass and sculpture. **Time:** Allow 1 hour minimum. **Hours:** Tues.-Sat. 10-5, Sun.-Mon. noon-5. Closed Thanksgiving and Christmas. **Cost:** Donations. **Phone:** (360) 466-4446.

HOTEL PLANTER	360/466-4710

🔻🔻 Historic Hotel. **Address:** 715 1st St 98257

LA CONNER CHANNEL LODGE	360/466-1500

🔻🔻🔻 Hotel. **Address:** 205 N 1st St 98257

LA CONNER COUNTRY INN	360/466-1500

🔻🔻 Country Inn. **Address:** 107 S 2nd St 98257

THE WILD IRIS INN	360/466-1400

🔻🔻🔻 Bed & Breakfast. **Address:** 121 Maple Ave 98257

WHERE TO EAT

CALICO CUPBOARD CAFE & BAKERY	360/466-4451

🔻🔻 American. Casual Dining. **Address:** 720 S 1st St 98257

FARMHOUSE RESTAURANT	360/466-4411

🔻🔻 American. Casual Dining. **Address:** 13724 La Conner Whitney Rd 98273

LA CONNER BREWING COMPANY	360/466-1415

🔻🔻 American. Brewpub. **Address:** 117 S 1st St 98257

LA CONNER SEAFOOD & PRIME RIB HOUSE	360/466-4014

🔻🔻 Seafood Steak. Casual Dining. **Address:** 614 S 1st St 98257

NELL THORN WATERFRONT BISTRO & BAR
360/466-4261

Continental Casual Dining $10-$38   **AAA Inspector Notes:** This great new waterfront location serves the same, reasonably priced dishes made from top-quality, fresh organic and local ingredients. Everything down to the tartar sauce is made from scratch, in house. Among menu items are preparations of seafood, duck and beef. Each meal starts with crusty organic sourdough bread and should finish with a tempting dessert. Seasonally changing hours are listed on the website. **Features:** full bar, patio dining, happy hour. **Reservations:** suggested. **Address:** 116 S First St 98257 **Location:** Downtown.

Ⓛ Ⓓ

LAKE CHELAN NATIONAL RECREATION AREA (D-8)

Forming the southern tip of the North Cascades National Park Service complex, Lake Chelan National Recreation Area is accessible only by trail, boat or charter float plane from Chelan *(see place listing p. 51)*. The approximately 62,000-acre area is at the northern end of Lake Chelan, one of the deepest lakes in the country and one of Washington's largest inland bodies of fresh water.

Deer, bears and marmots are among the animals that live in the mountains surrounding the Stehekin Valley. The only town within the recreation area is remote Stehekin, whose name means "the way through" in the Chelan Indian tongue.

Park rangers lead naturalist walks and conduct a variety of educational programs. Recreational opportunities range from short day hikes to overnight camping to strenuous mountain climbing; boating and fishing are popular in Lake Chelan and nearby streams.

Several trails traverse the area; most follow the creeks that flow into the Stehekin River. A particularly spectacular site is Rainbow Falls. Raft trips, kayak tours and trail rides are offered by Stehekin Valley Ranch, 3 blocks from Stehekin Landing; phone (509) 682-4677 or (800) 536-0745.

Shuttle bus service operates from Stehekin to various trailheads late May to early October. The Golden West Visitor Center has information about camping permits, trail conditions, transportation and recreation opportunities. The center is open daily 8:30-5, late May-late Sept.; daily 10-2, late Sept. to mid-Oct.; Mon.-Fri. 12:30-2, Sat.-Sun. 10-2, early May-late May. Hours vary rest of year. Phone (360) 854-7365, ext. 14. *See Recreation Areas Chart.*

LAKE ROOSEVELT NATIONAL RECREATION AREA (D-11)

Stretching from the Grand Coulee Dam along Franklin D. Roosevelt Lake toward the Canadian border in northeastern Washington, this area encompasses 100,059 acres. Geologic formations in much of the region are the result of intense volcanic activity followed by cataclysmic ice age floods. Natural vegetation ranges from sage to pine forests. Numerous wildflowers grace the southern lava flows and terraces along the lake. Deer are common; beavers and muskrats frequent the shores.

Franklin D. Roosevelt Lake is a popular recreation area. Activities include boating, swimming, water skiing, camping, fishing and hunting. A state license is required for fishing or hunting; jet skis have been banned from the lake. The park contains 34 developed recreation sites. Houseboat rentals are available at nearby marinas.

Points of interest in the recreation area include St. Paul's Mission at Kettle Falls Historical Center in Kettle Falls and Fort Spokane. For more information contact Lake Roosevelt National Recreation Area, 1008 Crest Dr., Coulee Dam, WA 99116-1259; phone (509) 754-7800 or (509) 754-7893 for the Fort Spokane Visitor Center. *See Recreation Areas Chart.*

FORT SPOKANE is 25 mi. n. of Davenport on SR 25 to 44150 District Office Ln. N. This 19th-century military outpost was built to ensure peaceful relations between Colville and Spokane Indians and white settlers. A visitor center and museum are in the brick guardhouse, one of four remaining outpost buildings. A self-guiding trail follows the old parade grounds. Historical interpretive programs are offered in the summer.

Time: Allow 1 hour, 30 minutes minimum. **Hours:** Grounds open daily dawn-dusk. Museum open daily 9:30-5, Memorial Day weekend-Labor Day; by appointment, May 1-Memorial Day weekend and Labor Day weekend-Sept. 30. Phone ahead to confirm schedule. **Cost:** Free. **Phone:** (509) 754-7893.

LAKEWOOD (G-3) pop. 58,163, elev. 260'
- Hotels & Restaurants map & index p. 201
- Part of Seattle area — see map p. 124

McChord Air Force Base and the U.S. Army's Fort Lewis, two of the country's largest armed forces installations, adjoin this Tacoma suburb on the south. Fort Steilacoom, on Steilacoom Boulevard at the western edge of town, was established in 1849 on land rented from the Hudson's Bay Co. The army vacated the fort in 1868. Two years later an insane asylum, later a state mental hospital, was established in its place. All that remains of the military post are several houses, a cemetery and the parade ground; the site is now a 340-acre recreation area.

Lakewood Area Chamber of Commerce: 6310 Mt. Tacoma Dr. S.W., Suite B, Lakewood, WA 98499. **Phone:** (253) 582-9400.

LAKEWOLD GARDENS is 9 mi. s. on I-5 to exit 124, then 1 mi. w. to 12317 Gravelly Lake Dr. S.W. Garden highlights of this 10-acre former private estate include formal parterres and topiaries, Japanese maples and rhododendrons, a giant Douglas fir that creates its own shade garden, an 18th-century sculptured lion fountain and a medieval Knot Garden with unusual plants. Self-guiding tours are available. The Georgian-style manor also is open to visitors.

Pets are not permitted. **Hours:** Wed.-Sun. 10-4, Apr.-Sept.; hours vary, rest of year. Closed major holidays, Thanksgiving weekend and the last 2 weeks in Dec. Phone ahead to confirm schedule. **Cost:** $9; $7 (ages 62+ and students and military with ID); free (ages 0-12). **Phone:** (253) 584-4106 or (888) 858-4106. 🎫

BEST WESTERN LAKEWOOD   (253)584-2212 ㉔

♦♦♦ Motel $99-$250

BW Best Western. **AAA Benefit:** Members save up to 15% and earn bonus points!

Address: 6125 Motor Ave SW 98499 **Location:** I-5 exit 125, 2 mi nw on Bridgeport Way SW, just left on Gravelly Lake Dr, then first right. **Facility:** 78 units. 2 stories (no elevator), exterior corridors. **Terms:** cancellation fee imposed. **Pool:** heated outdoor. **Guest Services:** coin laundry. **Featured Amenity: continental breakfast.**

SAVE CALL 🛗 ➦ BIZ HS 📶
✉ 🍴 📷 📺

HOLIDAY INN EXPRESS HOTEL & SUITES TACOMA SOUTH-LAKEWOOD   253/582-7000 ㉖
♦♦♦ Hotel. **Address:** 11751 Pacific Hwy SW 98499

🔥 **Dreaming of s'mores and starry nights? AAA.com/campgrounds**

TOWNEPLACE SUITES BY MARRIOTT TACOMA LAKEWOOD
(253)582-1055 ㉕
♦♦♦ Extended Stay Hotel. **Address:** 11725 Pacific Hwy SW 98499

AAA Benefit: Members save 5% or more!

WHERE TO EAT

RAM RESTAURANT AND BREWERY   253/584-3191
♦♦ American. Casual Dining. **Address:** 10019 59th Ave 98499

LEAVENWORTH (E-8) pop. 1,965, elev. 1,164'

Leavenworth is at the base of the Cascade Mountains near the western end of the Wenatchee Valley. Established in 1890, it prospered as a logging and fruit packing center. By the early 1960s community leaders decided to promote Leavenworth as a tourist destination by capitalizing on its scenic setting. Gradually the town was remodeled to look like a Bavarian village, right down to the alpine-inspired architecture and flower-filled window boxes and hanging baskets.

Leavenworth Carriage Company offers horse-drawn carriage and sleigh rides; phone (509) 421-0679. Art displays are featured in Front Street Park on weekends from May to October; phone (509) 548-5809. A bridge in Waterfront Park leads to nature trails on 15-acre Blackbird Island. A mile northwest of Leavenworth, US 2 parallels the Wenatchee River through the scenic Tumwater Canyon, which blazes with color in the fall.

Area recreational opportunities include hiking, fishing, swimming, horseback riding, white-water rafting, snowmobiling and skiing. The Wenatchee River between Leavenworth and Monitor is one of Washington's most popular white-water rafting streams, with relatively calm stretches alternating with class III and IV rapids. The rafting season extends from May through September.

Befitting its stature as a year-round tourist destination is the town's packed events calendar. The most popular event is the Christmas Lighting Festival, held on the three weekends (Friday through Sunday) before Christmas. At 4:30 each Friday afternoon Santa arrives at the gazebo on Front Street and distributes goodies to kids. On Saturday and Sunday the festivities begin with appearances by Father Christmas, Saint Nicholas and Santa Claus, followed by live music and entertainment that continues all afternoon and into the evening. The lighting ceremony begins both days at 4:30, transforming the buildings and trees along Front Street into a twinkling fantasyland of colored lights.

The holidays aren't the only festive time of year, however. MAIFEST in mid-May salutes Leavenworth's Bavarian heritage with traditional costumes, a dance and a parade. Also in mid-May is the Spring Bird Fest, when birders congregate for bird-watching hikes, guided trips and a songbird concert. In mid-June the International Accordion Celebration presents 4 days of varied music, including jazz, ethnic and classical. On weekends in October the quintessential Bavarian celebration Oktoberfest reigns supreme with art displays, music, food and—last but not least—plenty of drink.

Leavenworth Summer Theater offers performances July through August in three venues including the Leavenworth Ski Hill Amphitheater, 10698 Ski Hill Dr.; Hatchery Park Amphitheater, 7875 E. Leavenworth Rd.; and Leavenworth Festhalle Theater, 1001 Front St. Children under 5 are not permitted; phone (509) 548-2000 for schedule and tickets.

Leavenworth Chamber of Commerce: 940 US 2, P.O. Box 327, Leavenworth, WA 98826. **Phone:** (509) 548-5807.

Shopping: Specialty shops line Front Street in downtown Leavenworth.

BAVARIAN LODGE   (509)548-7878

WWWW
Hotel
$142-$201

Address: 810 US Hwy 2 98826 **Location:** Downtown. **Facility:** 90 units. 4 stories, interior corridors. **Parking:** winter plug-ins. **Terms:** 3 day cancellation notice. **Pool:** heated outdoor. **Activities:** hot tub. **Featured Amenity: full hot breakfast.**

DER RITTERHOF MOTOR INN   509/548-5845
WW Motel. **Address:** 190 US Hwy 2 98826

ENZIAN INN   (509)548-5269
WWW Hotel. **Address:** 590 US Hwy 2 98826

FAIRBRIDGE INN & SUITES LEAVENWORTH   509/548-7992
WW Hotel. **Address:** 185 US Hwy 2 98826

HAMPTON INN & SUITES BY HILTON LEAVENWORTH
                                                 509/470-9798
WWW Hotel. **Address:** 301 Ward Strasse 98826

AAA Benefit: Members save 5% or more!

HAUS ROHRBACH PENSION   509/548-7024
WW Bed & Breakfast. **Address:** 12882 Ranger Rd 98826

HOWARD JOHNSON BY WYNDHAM - LEAVENWORTH
                                                 (509)548-4326
WW Hotel. **Address:** 405 US Hwy 2 98826

ICICLE VILLAGE RESORT   (509)548-7000

WWWW
Hotel
$129-$429

Address: 505 W US HWY 2 98826 **Location:** 0.5 mi w. **Facility:** 154 units, some condominiums. 2-3 stories, interior corridors. **Terms:** check-in 4 pm, 7 day cancellation notice-fee imposed. **Dining:** J. J. Hill's Fresh Grill, see separate listing. **Pool:** heated outdoor. **Activities:** hot tub, miniature golf, bicycles, playground, game room, lawn sports, picnic facilities, exercise room, spa. **Guest Services:** coin laundry. **Featured Amenity: full hot breakfast.**

LINDERHOF INN   (509)548-5283
WW Motel. **Address:** 690 US Hwy 2 98826

OBERTAL INN   509/548-5204
WW Motel. **Address:** 922 Commercial St 98826

WHERE TO EAT

THE ALLEY CAFE   509/548-6109
WW Italian. Casual Dining. **Address:** 214 8th St 98826

ANDREAS KELLER RESTAURANT   509/548-6000
WW German. Casual Dining. **Address:** 829 Front St 98826

J. J. HILL'S FRESH GRILL   509/548-8000

WWW
American Casual Dining
$12-$28

AAA Inspector Notes: The dining area features a distinctive railroad theme. The varied menu includes ribs, steak, seafood and some German specialties, which pair with wines from a list that includes several local varieties. **Features:** full bar, patio dining, happy hour. **Reservations:** suggested. **Address:** 505 W US 2 98826 **Location:** 0.5 mi w; in Icicle Village Resort. [D]

KING LUDWIG'S   509/548-6625
WW German. Casual Dining. **Address:** 921 Front St 98826

KRISTALL'S RESTAURANT & LOUNGE   509/548-5267
WW American. Casual Dining. **Address:** 280 US Hwy 2 98826

PAVZ CAFE BISTRO   509/548-2103
WW German. Casual Dining. **Address:** 833 Front St 98826

SANDY'S WAFFLE HAUS   509/548-6779
WW American. Casual Dining. **Address:** 894 US Hwy 2 98826

SOUTH   509/888-4328
WW Latin American. Casual Dining. **Address:** 913 Front St 98826

VISCONTI'S - LEAVENWORTH   509/548-1213
WWW Italian. Casual Dining. **Address:** 636 Front St 98826

LIBERTY LAKE pop. 7,591

BEST WESTERN PLUS LIBERTY LAKE INN
                                                 (509)755-1111

WWW
Hotel
$125-$145

BW Best Western PLUS. **AAA Benefit:** Members save up to 15% and earn bonus points!

Address: 1816 N Pepper Ln 99019 **Location:** I-90 exit 296 (Liberty Lake), just n. **Facility:** 76 units. 4 stories, interior corridors. **Parking:** winter plug-ins. **Terms:** cancellation fee imposed. **Pool:** heated indoor. **Activities:** hot tub, exercise room. **Guest Services:** coin laundry.

QUALITY INN & SUITES BY CHOICE HOTELS   (509)340-3333
WW Hotel. **Address:** 2327 N Madson Rd 99019

WHERE TO EAT

HAY J'S BISTRO   509/926-2310
WWW American. Casual Dining. **Address:** 21706 E Mission Ave 99019

TRUE LEGENDS GRILL   509/892-3077
WW American. Sports Bar. **Address:** 1803 N Harvard Rd 99019

LONG BEACH (G-4) pop. 1,392, elev. 10'

A popular oyster farming and vacation center, Long Beach is at the southern end of Long Beach Peninsula, known for 25 miles of hard sand beach. Area sports include surf fishing, swimming, boating and deep-sea fishing. Among the peninsula's scenic viewpoints are Cape Disappointment and North Head lighthouses *(see Ilwaco p. 69)*, North Jetty and Beard's Hollow. More than 200 ships have wrecked off Cape Disappointment.

The 8.5-mile Lewis & Clark Discovery Trail runs from Long Beach to Ilwaco. The main access point is at the foot of Bolstad Street, off SR 103. The trail includes a 12-foot-wide elevated boardwalk extending along 2,300 feet of beachfront. It has three observation platforms with interpretive displays of natural history, including a restored skeleton of a 38-foot gray whale.

The blue summer sky above Long Beach is filled with multicolored kites of every size and shape during the Washington State International Kite Festival, which takes place the third week in August. Championship kite fliers from around the world come here to demonstrate their skills and compete in competitions, while novices can attend kite-building workshops.

Long Beach Peninsula Visitors Bureau: 3914 Pacific Way (jct. US 101 and SR 103), Seaview, WA 98644. **Phone:** (360) 642-2400 or (800) 451-2542.

WORLD KITE MUSEUM is 3 blks. w. of SR 103 at 303 Sid Snyder Dr. The museum displays hundreds of kites from around the world and throughout history. Exhibits change regularly. **Time:** Allow 30 minutes minimum. **Hours:** Daily 11-5, Apr.-Sept.; Fri.-Tues. 11-5, rest of year. Closed Christmas. **Cost:** $5; $4 (ages 60+); $3 (ages 3-15). **Phone:** (360) 642-4020.

ANCHORAGE COTTAGES   360/642-2351
▼▼ Cottage. **Address:** 2209 Boulevard N 98631

BEST WESTERN LONG BEACH INN   (360)642-8988

▼▼▼▼
Contemporary Hotel
$109-$400

(BW) **Best Western. AAA Benefit:** Members save up to 15% and earn bonus points!

Address: 500 Ocean Beach Blvd 98631 **Location:** On SR 103; downtown. **Facility:** 50 units. 3 stories, interior corridors. **Terms:** check-in 4 pm, cancellation fee imposed. **Activities:** exercise room. **Guest Services:** coin laundry.

SAVE CALL 🛗 🛁 BIZ 🛜 ✕
📶 🍳 🖥 / SOME UNITS 🐾

🔵 **For more details, rates and reservations: AAA.com/travelguides/hotels**

BOARDWALK COTTAGES   360/642-2305
▼▼ Cottage. **Address:** 800 Ocean Beach Blvd S 98631

THE BREAKERS   360/642-4414

▼▼▼
Vacation Rental Condominium
Rates not provided

Address: 210 26th St NW 98631 **Location:** Oceanfront. Just w of SR 103; north end of downtown. **Facility:** All guest rooms offer balconies or patios, and many have views of the ocean. 130 condominiums. 3 stories (no elevator), exterior corridors. **Terms:** check-in 4 pm. **Pool:** heated indoor. **Activities:** hot tub, bicycles, playground. **Guest Services:** coin laundry.

SAVE 🛥 🛜 ✕ 🚲 📶 🖥
🖨 / SOME UNITS 🐾

RODEWAY INN & SUITES   (360)642-3714
▼▼ Motel. **Address:** 115 3rd St SW 98631

WHERE TO EAT

BENSON'S BY THE BEACH   360/642-3300
▼▼ American. Casual Dining. **Address:** 504 Pacific Ave S 98631

CASTAWAYS SEAFOOD GRILLE   360/642-4745
▼▼ American. Casual Dining. **Address:** 208 S Pacific Ave 98631

CHEN'S CHINESE RESTAURANT   360/642-8288
▼▼ Chinese. Casual Dining. **Address:** 400 Pacific Ave 98631

DOOGER'S SEAFOOD & GRILL   360/642-4224
▼▼ Seafood. Casual Dining. **Address:** 900 Pacific Ave S 98631

EL COMPADRE   360/642-8280
▼▼ Mexican. Casual Dining. **Address:** 1900 Pacific Ave N 98631

LONG BEACH THAI CUISINE   360/642-2557
▼▼ Thai. Casual Dining. **Address:** 1003 Pacific Ave N 98631

LOST ROO   360/642-4329
▼▼ American. Casual Dining. **Address:** 1700 Pacific Ave S 98631

LONGVIEW (G-6) pop. 36,648, elev. 13'

Founded in 1923 on the site of an abandoned settlement known as Monticello, Longview was named for timber entrepreneur R.A. Long, who selected the riverside location for a deepwater port and forest products complex. The city, one of the largest planned communities in the country, was designed with a distinctive curving grid of streets interspersed with parks. R.A. Long Park (the Civic Center) is flanked by many of the city's earliest buildings, most built in the Georgian style, including the 1926 library and the 1923 Monticello Hotel.

Across from the hotel, at 18th Avenue and Olympia Way, is a memorial to a group of settlers who met here in 1852 to petition the U.S. Congress to create a territory north of the Columbia River separate from Oregon. Members of the "Monticello Convention" saw their wish granted the following year with the creation of the Washington Territory. Another historic site is south of town at the mouth of the Cowlitz River; Lewis and Clark's Corps of Discovery camped there in 1805.

Just north of R.A. Long Park, spanning Olympia Way at Civic Center, is Nutty Narrows, said to be the world's first bridge for squirrels. A local resident built the bridge in 1963 to provide the critters with safe passage over the busy thoroughfare. Longview has become something of a "squirrel bridge capital." Since 2011 four more bridges have been built, and another is in the works.

LAKE SACAJAWEA PARK is bordered by Ocean Beach Hwy. and 15th Ave. on the n. and s. and Kessler and Nichols blvds. on the e. and w. Designed by landscape architects in the early 1920s, the park reflects the "City Beautiful" movement of the early 20th century. The centerpiece of the park is 52-acre Lake Sacajawea. Grassy lawns dotted with groves of trees and gardens flank its curving shore, which is encircled by 3.5 miles of trails.

More than 100 species of trees from around the world are on the grounds, as are azalea and rhododendron gardens. A wooden bridge leads to a 1-acre island and the Japanese Garden, which features lanterns, gates, stonework and bamboo screens. **Hours:** Daily dawn-dusk. **Cost:** Free. **Phone:** (360) 442-5400. 🅰️

COUNTRY FOLKS DELI   360/425-2837
▼▼ American. Casual Dining. **Address:** 1329 Commerce Ave 98632

LOPEZ ISLAND (C-2)

One of the islands that make up the San Juan Islands, Lopez Island also is one of the least visited. But for those who crave solitude it offers miles of back roads leading through farms and rolling woodlands and a rugged coast marked with steep cliffs and isolated coves. Mackeye Harbor was the site of the town of Richardson, a bustling fishing port at the turn of the 20th century.

The flat and rolling landscape has made the island particularly popular with cyclists. Camping and beach access is available at Odlin County Park *(see Recreation Areas Chart)* and Spencer Spit State Park *(see Recreation Areas Chart)*; Agate Beach County Park also provides beach access at low tide.

THE GALLEY RESTAURANT & LOUNGE   360/468-2713
▼▼ American. Casual Dining. **Address:** 3365 Fisherman Bay Rd 98261

LUMMI ISLAND

THE WILLOWS INN ON LUMMI ISLAND   360/758-2620
▼▼▼▼ Pacific Northwest. Fine Dining. **Address:** 2579 West Shore Dr 98262

LYNNWOOD (E-3) pop. 35,836, elev. 370'
• Restaurants p. 82
• Hotels & Restaurants map & index p. 160
• Part of Seattle area — see map p. 124

The area's tall, virgin timber attracted loggers in the early 1900s. Later the Seattle-Everett interurban trolley line provided a reliable transportation link, and

by 1917 the Puget Mill Co. was marketing 5- and 10-acre plots on their logged lands as far away as Chicago. Part of their marketing effort was the 32-acre Alderwood Manor Demonstration Farm, which provided would-be farmers hands-on experience in rural life; it featured a fish hatchery, gardens and a hotel.

Scriber Lake Park, 5322 198th Street S.W., offers winding paths, native vegetation and an unusual floating walkway. The 13-mile paved Interurban Trail links Lynnwood with Everett.

Snohomish County Tourism Bureau Visitor Center: 19921 Poplar Way, Lynnwood, WA 98036. **Phone:** (425) 776-3977 or (888) 338-0976.

Shopping: Alderwood Mall, 3000 184th St. S.W., has more than 130 stores, including JCPenney, Macy's and Nordstrom.

BEST WESTERN ALDERWOOD   (425)775-7600 **15**

▼▼▼ **Hotel** $99-$199

 Best Western. **AAA Benefit:** Members save up to 15% and earn bonus points!

 Address: 19332 36th Ave W 98036 **Location:** I-5 exit 181B northbound, just w on 196th St SW, then just n; exit 181 (SR 524 W) southbound, just nw. **Facility:** 140 units. 4 stories, interior corridors. **Terms:** check-in 4 pm, cancellation fee imposed. **Pool:** heated outdoor. **Activities:** hot tub, exercise room. **Guest Services:** coin laundry. **Featured Amenity:** full hot breakfast.

SAVE 🛄 🖥️ BIZ 📶 ✕ 🛅 📠 💻 / SOME UNITS HS

COURTYARD BY MARRIOTT SEATTLE NORTH-LYNNWOOD-EVERETT   (425)670-0500 **19**
▼▼▼ Hotel. **Address:** 4220 Alderwood Mall Blvd 98036   **AAA Benefit:** Members save 5% or more!

EMBASSY SUITES BY HILTON HOTEL SEATTLE NORTH/LYNNWOOD   425/775-2500 **20**
▼▼▼ Hotel. **Address:** 20610 44th Ave W 98036   **AAA Benefit:** Members save 5% or more!

HAMPTON INN & SUITES BY HILTON SEATTLE-NORTH/LYNNWOOD   (425)771-1888 **16**

▼▼▼ **Hotel** $139-$308

 Hampton by Hilton **AAA Benefit:** Members save 5% or more!

 Address: 19324 Alderwood Mall Pkwy 98036 **Location:** I-5 exit 181B northbound, 0.6 mi n; exit 181 (SR 524 E) southbound, 0.5 mi e on 196th St SE, then just n. **Facility:** 152 units, some efficiencies. 4 stories, interior corridors. **Terms:** check-in 4 pm, 1-7 night minimum stay, 3 day cancellation notice-fee imposed. **Amenities:** safes. **Pool:** heated indoor. **Activities:** hot tub, exercise room. **Guest Services:** complimentary and valet laundry, area transportation. **Featured Amenity:** full hot breakfast.

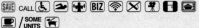 SAVE CALL 🛄 🖥️ 🖥️ BIZ 📶 ✕ 🎾 🛅 📠 💻 / SOME UNITS 🐾

HOLIDAY INN EXPRESS NORTH SEATTLE LYNNWOOD   (425)672-1234 **17**
▼▼▼ Hotel. **Address:** 2515 196th St SW 98036

(See map & index p. 160.)

HOMEWOOD SUITES BY HILTON SEATTLE/LYNNWOOD
425/670-8943 **13**

♥♥♥ Extended Stay Hotel. **Address:** 18123 Alderwood Mall Pkwy 98037

AAA Benefit: Members save 5% or more!

LA QUINTA INN LYNNWOOD   (425)775-7447 **18**

♥♥♥
Hotel
$69-$159

Address: 4300 Alderwood Mall Blvd 98036 **Location:** I-5 exit 181A northbound, just w; exit 181 (SR 524 W) southbound, 0.5 mi w on 196th St SW, just s on 44th Ave SW, then just e. **Facility:** 101 units. 5 stories, interior corridors. **Pool:** heated indoor. **Activities:** hot tub, limited exercise equipment. **Guest Services:** valet and coin laundry. **Featured Amenity: full hot breakfast.**

SAVE ⊇ BIZ 🛜 ✕ 🛏 ▣ / SOME UNITS 🐾

RESIDENCE INN BY MARRIOTT-SEATTLE
NORTH/LYNNWOOD   (425)771-1100 **14**

♥♥♥ Extended Stay Hotel. **Address:** 18200 Alderwood Mall Pkwy 98037

AAA Benefit: Members save 5% or more!

WHERE TO EAT

ANTHONY'S SEAFOOD GRILL ALDERWOOD MALL
425/771-4665 **46**

♥♥ Seafood. Casual Dining. **Address:** 3000 184th St SW, Suite 870 98037

CLAIM JUMPER   425/778-5700

♥♥ American. Casual Dining. **Address:** 18725 33rd Ave W 98037

MOONSHINE BBQ   425/672-9592 **47**

♥♥ Barbecue. Casual Dining. **Address:** 4911 196th St SW 98036

P.F. CHANG'S CHINA BISTRO   425/921-2100 **45**

♥♥♥ Chinese. Fine Dining. **Address:** 3000 184th St, Suite 912 98037

TALAY THAI RESTAURANT   425/670-1340 **48**

♥♥ Thai. Casual Dining. **Address:** 4520 200th St SW, Suite 208A 98036

MARYHILL (H-8) pop. 58, elev. 180'

Maryhill was founded in 1907 by Samuel Hill, who thought the sunny site had the makings of an agricultural utopia. An eccentric lawyer and pacifist Quaker, Hill also was a talented road and monument builder; his works include the Peace Arch Historical State and Provincial Park in Blaine *(see place listing p. 47)* and the Columbia River Scenic Highway on the Oregon side of the Columbia River Gorge.

In 1913 Hill also built the 3.6-mile Maryhill Loops Road, just east of the junction of US 97 and SR 14. The twisting byway was the first in Washington to be paved and is a favorite of pedestrians and bicyclists.

MARYHILL MUSEUM OF ART is 2.7 mi. w. of US 97 at 35 Maryhill Museum Dr. The museum occupies an ornate mansion built by Northwest entrepreneur Samuel Hill. Although dedicated by Queen Marie of Romania in 1926, it did not open until 1940. European and American paintings are complemented by a collection of Auguste Rodin sculptures and watercolors and 18th-century Russian icons.

Other highlights include Hill photographs and memorabilia, Native American basketry and artifacts, the 1945 Théâtre de la Mode French fashion mannequin gallery, international chess sets and personal items donated by Queen Marie, including items by Fabergé. The works displayed in the Special Exhibitions Gallery are changed during the season.

The 5,300-acre grounds include an outdoor sculpture garden and a Lewis & Clark overlook with interpretive panels. **Time:** Allow 1 hour minimum. **Hours:** Daily 10-5, Mar. 15-Nov. 15. **Cost:** Grounds and garden free. Museum $12; $10 (ages 65+); $9 (college students with ID); $5 (ages 7-18); $30 (family, two adults and related children ages 7-18). **Phone:** (509) 773-3733. 🍴 ⊞

STONEHENGE MEMORIAL is 1 mi. e. of jct. US 97 and SR 14, then .7 mi. s. On a cliff overlooking the Columbia River, this concrete reproduction of the famous and mysterious prehistoric monument in Wiltshire, England, was built in 1918 as a memorial to the men of Klickitat County killed in World War I. It was constructed 40 years before the position of Stonehenge was decoded for astronomical measurement and therefore is not exact. Also at the site is the crypt of the monument's builder, Maryhill founder Samuel Hill, and the Klickitat County War Memorial. **Hours:** Daily 7 a.m.-dusk. **Cost:** Free.

MARYSVILLE (D-3) pop. 60,020, elev. 15'
• Part of Seattle area — see map p. 124

In 1877 James P. Comeford built a trading post on Ebey Slough and thus founded the town of Marysville. One of the earliest logging locomotives was built here in 1883. The Tulalip Indian Reservation, established in 1855, is the site of the oldest Roman Catholic mission on Puget Sound.

Greater Marysville-Tulalip Chamber of Commerce: 8825 34th Ave. N.E., Suite C, Marysville, WA 98271. **Phone:** (360) 659-7700.

Shopping: Seattle Premium Outlets, west of I-5 exit 202, features more than 100 stores including Ann Taylor, Banana Republic, Burberry, Gap Factory and Tommy Hilfiger.

HIBULB CULTURAL CENTER AND NATURAL HISTORY PRESERVE is .5 mi. w. of I-5 exit 199, then s. to 6410 23rd Ave. N.E. The center tells the story of the Tulalip Tribes, which include the Snohomish, Snoqualmie and Skykomish peoples as well as other tribes designated by the 1855 Point Elliott Treaty. Canoe Hallway—with floor tiles that recall the Snohomish River, a major means of navigation—contains a priceless collection of tribal artifacts and three rare cedar canoes, and also links the museum galleries.

The main gallery has exhibits spotlighting salmon and the western red cedar, the latter crafted into clothing, houses, baskets and canoes. Other exhibits depict how tribal life changed after the 1855 treaty. Interactive displays and story art panels complement the exhibits.

In the Longhouse visitors can watch a 10-minute video and listen to recorded tribal stories. The 50-acre grounds, a nature preserve, encompass groves of cedar, fir and hemlock trees, estuary wetlands and streams inhabited by salmon.

Time: Allow 1 hour minimum. **Hours:** Tues.-Fri. 10-5 (also first Thurs. of the month 5-8), Sat.-Sun. noon-5. Closed most federal and tribal holidays. **Cost:** $10; $7 (ages 50+); $6 (ages 6-17 and military with ID); free (first Thurs. of the month); $25 (family, two adults and up to four children). **Phone:** (360) 716-2600. GT

HOLIDAY INN EXPRESS HOTEL & SUITES-MARYSVILLE
360/530-1234
▼▼▼ Hotel. **Address:** 8606 36th Ave NE 98270

TULALIP RESORT CASINO   360/716-6000
▼▼▼▼
Contemporary Hotel
Rates not provided
Address: 10200 Quil Ceda Blvd 98271 **Location:** I-5 exit 200, just w, then 0.9 mi n. **Facility:** Native American artwork adorns the elevator landings on each floor as well as inside the large guest rooms. Bathrooms, too, are spacious with a spa like feel and feature body spray-jets in the shower. 370 units. 12 stories, interior corridors. *Bath:* shower only. **Parking:** on-site and valet. **Terms:** check-in 4 pm. **Amenities:** safes. **Dining:** 7 restaurants, entertainment. **Pool:** heated indoor. **Activities:** sauna, hot tub, steamroom, exercise room, spa. **Guest Services:** valet laundry, area transportation.

WHERE TO EAT

RAM RESTAURANT AND BREWERY   360/653-7721
▼▼ American. Casual Dining. **Address:** 10520 Quil Ceda Blvd 98271

METALINE FALLS (C-12) pop. 238, elev. 2,100'

Prospectors who settled on the west bank of the Pend Oreille River founded Metaline Falls in 1909. Several historical buildings here were designed by Spokane architect Kirtland Cutter. Occupying a 1912 school, The Cutter Theatre, 302 Park St., hosts live performances and showcases an art gallery, a mining exhibit and the Rural Schools Museum. Guided tours of the theater are available on weekends in the summer; phone (509) 446-4108.

North of Metaline Falls the Pend Oreille River flows through remote Z Canyon, so named for its zigzag shape. In places the canyon walls are upwards of 400 feet high but only two dozen feet apart. Sullivan Lake recreation area and the Salmo-Priest Wilderness are just east of town.

MOCLIPS (E-4) pop. 207, elev. 43'
• Part of Olympic National Park area — see map p. 100

Moclips is the northernmost of a string of beach towns along the Pacific between Point Grenville and

Ocean Shores. The Northern Pacific Railroad opened its North Beach line in 1905, serving shingle mills and small beach resorts. The queen of these resorts was the 300-room Moclips Beach Hotel, built on pilings at the edge of the sea. Storm waves destroyed the hotel and much of the town in 1911. The shingle mills are long gone, too, but Moclips is still a popular beach getaway.

The beach south of the mouth of the Moclips River was formerly called Moonstone for its once-plentiful agate beds. North of the river the beach curves to the rocky headland of Point Grenville. A Spanish expedition commanded by Bruno Heceta landed here on July 14, 1775, claiming the land in the name of King Carlos III. The Quinault Indian Reservation begins at the northern edge of town. **Note:** Access to beaches within the reservation by non-tribal members is prohibited.

OCEAN CREST RESORT AND RESTAURANT   (360)276-4465
▼▼ Hotel. **Address:** 4651 SR 109 98562

WHERE TO EAT

OCEAN CREST RESORT AND RESTAURANT   360/276-4465
▼▼▼ American. Casual Dining. **Address:** 4651 SR 109 N 98562

MONROE (E-7) pop. 17,304, elev. 72'
• Restaurants p. 84
• Part of Seattle area — see map p. 124

The earliest homesteaders settled the rich river bottomlands along the Snohomish and Skykomish rivers in 1858. Originally called Park Place, the town was renamed for President James Monroe in 1889. It prospered first as a logging center, then later as a farming community. Scenic Stevens Pass Highway (US 2) follows the Skykomish River east into the Cascade Range.

Evergreen Speedway, located at the Evergreen State Fairgrounds a mile west of town on US 2 at 14405 179th Ave. S.E., offers racing and NASCAR-sanctioned events Saturdays from late March to late October; phone (360) 805-6100.

Monroe Chamber of Commerce: 125 S. Lewis St., P.O. Box 69, Monroe, WA 98272. **Phone:** (360) 794-5488.

BEST WESTERN SKY VALLEY INN   (360)794-3111
▼▼▼
Hotel
$109-$240

 Best Western. **AAA Benefit:** Members save up to 15% and earn bonus points!

Address: 19233 SR 2 98272 **Location:** West end of town. Located behind Burger King restaurant. **Facility:** 58 units. 3 stories, interior corridors. **Terms:** cancellation fee imposed. **Pool:** heated outdoor. **Activities:** hot tub. **Guest Services:** coin laundry. **Featured Amenity:** continental breakfast.

EVERGREEN INN & SUITES   (360)863-1900
♦♦ Hotel. **Address:** 19103 SR 2 98272

WHERE TO EAT

ADAM'S NORTHWEST BISTRO & BREWERY   360/794-4056
♦♦♦ American. Gastropub. **Address:** 104 N Lewis St 98272

TUSCANO'S ITALIAN KITCHEN   360/805-5453
♦♦ Italian. Casual Dining. **Address:** 14919 N Kelsey St 98272

MONTESANO (F-5) pop. 3,976, elev. 66'

Founded in the 1850s near the confluence of the Chehalis and Wynoochee rivers, Montesano is a trading center for regional farming and lumber businesses. The Grays Harbor County Courthouse's indoor murals depict area history, including Capt. Robert Gray's discovery of Grays Harbor in 1792. Saturday and Sunday afternoons the Chehalis Valley Historical Museum, 7 blocks west of Main St. at 703 W. Pioneer Ave., documents the role of the area's forest products industry; phone (360) 249-5800.

Montesano is known as the origin of commercial forestry's tree-farm system. Weyerhaeuser established the Clemons Tree Farm in 1941; today the farm sprawls over 200,000 acres. Lake Sylvia State Park *(see Recreation Areas Chart)*, 1 mile north of town off US 12 exit 104, is the site of the county's first sawmill. Along the park's 2-mile Sylvia Creek Forestry Trail, 15 interpretive markers describe how a working forest is managed; phone (360) 249-3621.

MORTON pop. 1,126

SEASONS MOTEL   (360)496-6835

♦♦♦
Motel
$130-$180

Address: 200 Westlake Ave 98356 Location: Jct US 12 and SR 7. **Facility:** 49 units. 2 stories (no elevator), exterior corridors. **Featured Amenity:** continental breakfast.

[SAVE] [↑↑] [BIZ] [≋] [✕] [▯] [▣] [▣] / SOME UNITS [🐾]

MOSES LAKE (F-10) pop. 20,366, elev. 1,060'

Eighteen-mile-long Moses Lake consists of three main arms with 120 miles of shoreline. Recreational activities include fishing, swimming, water skiing and boating. The lake takes its name from Chief Moses, one of the Northwest's most influential Native American tribal leaders; the chief traveled to Washington, D.C., to confer with President Rutherford B. Hayes.

Established along the lake in 1910, the town of Neppel was named for the wife of a Milwaukee-based German language newspaper that promoted the new settlement. When the community incorporated in 1938, the name Moses Lake was adopted. World War II brought an army air force base to the area and an influx of Japanese-American families

forced to relocate inland in 1942. The postwar irrigation works of the Columbia Basin Project began the region's agricultural transformation.

The 13,500-foot runway at the former Larson Air Force Base, established to protect Grand Coulee Dam and the Hanford Atomic Energy Commission site, is one of the nation's longest. Boeing, the U.S. military and several air carriers use the facility for heavy jet testing and training.

Moses Lake Chamber of Commerce: 324 S. Pioneer Way, Moses Lake, WA 98837. **Phone:** (509) 765-7888 or (800) 992-6234.

AMERISTAY INN & SUITES   509/764-7500
♦♦ Hotel. **Address:** 1157 N Stratford Rd 98837

BEST WESTERN PLUS LAKE FRONT HOTEL
                                           (509)765-9211

♦♦♦
Hotel
$139-$169

Best Western PLUS.
AAA Benefit: Members save up to 15% and earn bonus points!

Address: 3000 Marina Dr 98837 **Location:** Waterfront. I-90 exit 176, just nw. **Facility:** 133 units. 2-3 stories (no elevator), interior corridors. **Parking:** winter plug-ins. **Terms:** check-in 4 pm, cancellation fee imposed. **Pool:** heated outdoor. **Activities:** sauna, hot tub, boat dock, fishing, exercise room. **Guest Services:** valet and coin laundry.

[SAVE] [↑↑] [⅄] CALL [🐾] [▣]
[BIZ] [≋] [✕] [▯] [▣] [▣] / SOME UNITS [🐾]

COMFORT SUITES BY CHOICE HOTELS MOSES LAKE
                                           (509)765-3731

♦♦♦
Hotel
$110-$209

Address: 1700 E Kittleson Rd 98837 **Location:** I-90 exit 179, just nw. **Facility:** 60 units, some kitchens. 3 stories, interior corridors. **Parking:** winter plug-ins. **Pool:** heated indoor. **Activities:** hot tub, picnic facilities, exercise room. **Guest Services:** valet and coin laundry. **Featured Amenity:** breakfast buffet.

[SAVE] [↑↑] CALL [🐾] [▣] [↑↑] [BIZ]
[HS] [≋] [✕] [▯] [▣] [▣] / SOME UNITS [🐾]

FAIRFIELD INN & SUITES BY MARRIOTT-MOSES LAKE
                                           (509)765-0500
♦♦♦ Hotel. **Address:** 2380 S Maiers Rd 98837

AAA Benefit: Members save 5% or more!

HOLIDAY INN EXPRESS & SUITES MOSES LAKE
                                           509/766-8000
♦♦♦ Hotel. **Address:** 2300 S Maiers Rd 98837

INN AT MOSES LAKE   509/766-7000
♦♦ Hotel. **Address:** 1741 E Kittleson Rd 98837

RAMADA BY WYNDHAM MOSES LAKE   (509)766-1000
♦♦ Hotel. **Address:** 1745 E Kittleson Rd 98837

WINGATE BY WYNDHAM MOSES LAKE   509/766-2000
♦♦♦ Hotel. **Address:** 1735 E Kittleson Rd 98837

EL RODEO RESTAURANT   509/765-0606
♥♥ Mexican. Casual Dining. **Address:** 1075 W Broadway Ave 98837

MICHAEL'S ON THE LAKE   509/765-1611
♥♥ Steak Seafood. Casual Dining. **Address:** 910 W Broadway 98837

PHO SAIGON   509/765-1233
♥♥ Vietnamese. Casual Dining. **Address:** 115 W 3rd Ave 98837

PORTERHOUSE STEAKHOUSE   509/766-0308
♥♥ Steak. Casual Dining. **Address:** 217 N Elder St 98837

THAI CUISINE   509/766-1489
♥ Thai. Casual Dining. **Address:** 601 S Pioneer Way, Suite H 98837

MOUNT BAKER-SNOQUALMIE NATIONAL FOREST (D-7, I-3)
• Attractions map p. 87

Elevations in the forest range from 280 ft. along the Skykomish River east of Gold Bar to 10,778 ft. at the summit of Mount Baker. Refer to AAA maps for additional elevation information.

Mount Baker-Snoqualmie National Forest covers the western slopes of the Cascades from the Canadian border to the northern boundary of Mount Rainier National Park, its 1,724,229 acres encompassing some of the state's most rugged wilderness. Mount Baker, at 10,778 feet, dominates the northern section and is the site of Sherman Crater, where thermal activity began in 1975. The Mount Baker Wilderness surrounds the volcano.

Glacier Peak, at 10,568 feet, towers over the central part of the forest. The Glacier Peak Wilderness lies between Stevens Pass and North Cascades National Park. In the high country between Snoqualmie Pass and Stevens Pass is the Alpine Lakes Wilderness.

Four east-west highways offer scenic drives—I-90, US 2, SR 20 and SR 410. National Scenic Byways include the Mount Baker Highway (SR 542) from Glacier to Artist Point, and the Stevens Pass Highway (US 2) east from Gold Bar to Leavenworth.

The Mountain Loop Highway also is a National Scenic Byway leading into the heart of the western Cascades. From Granite Falls it parallels the South Fork of the Stillaguamish River past Mount Pilchuck, numerous forest service campgrounds and old mine sites. Silverton, 22 miles east of Granite Falls, is an old former mining town. Four miles past Silverton, a 1-mile trail leads to the Big Four Ice Caves (closed until further notice; phone ahead). East of Silverton the road is subject to closure due to weather from November until April or May.

Once past Barlow Pass the partly gravel road, which also is subject to closure due to washouts, leads north to Darrington. The former road to Monte Cristo, an important 1890s gold mining town, is closed indefinitely due to washouts but is accessible to hikers. Check road and trail conditions at the Darrington Ranger Station, 1405 Emens Ave. N.; phone (360) 436-1155.

Wildlife abounds and streams teem with fish. Camping, pack trips and hiking are popular, particularly along the Pacific Crest National Scenic Trail. The Washington portion of the trail runs along the north-south crest of the Cascades for more than 500 miles from the Columbia River to the British Columbia border.

Skiers head to The Summit at Snoqualmie Pass on I-90, Mount Baker on SR 542 and Stevens Pass on US 2. Visitor information is available at ranger stations in Darrington, Enumclaw, North Bend, Sedro-Woolley and Skykomish; public services centers at Glacier and Granite Falls and a visitor center at Snoqualmie Pass are open late May to late September. The Heather Meadows Visitor Center is open from late July to early October, depending on snow conditions.

A Northwest Forest Pass, available at ranger stations, is required for parking at most trailheads in the forest. A day pass costs $5 per vehicle; an annual pass costs $30. For recreation information contact the Outdoor Recreation Information Center, 222 Yale Ave. N., Seattle, WA 98109; phone (206) 470-4060. For further information contact the Forest Supervisor's Office, Mount Baker-Snoqualmie National Forest, 2930 Wetmore Ave., Suite 3A, Everett, WA 98201; phone (425) 783-6000 or (800) 627-0062, ext. 0. (**Note:** This office provides no visitor services or recreation pass sales.) *See Recreation Areas Chart.*

▼GEM MOUNT RAINIER NATIONAL PARK (F-7)
• Hotels p. 88
• Attractions map p. 87

Elevations in the park range from 1,700 ft. at the Carbon River entrance station to 14,411 ft. at the summit of Mount Rainier. Refer to AAA maps for additional elevation information.

Mount Rainier National Park has four entrances: the Nisqually, off SR 706 in the southwest; the Carbon River, on Carbon River Road in the northwest (which is closed indefinitely to vehicles due to flood damage; access is by foot or bicycle only); the White River, on White River Road off SR 410 in the northeast (open seasonally); and the Stevens Canyon Road entrance in the southeast (open seasonally).

Mount Rainier, a towering, ice-clad volcano rising 14,411 feet, is a striking Pacific Northwest landmark. The cap of glacial ice that conceals all but a few crags and ridges makes it doubly impressive. Mount Rainier belongs to the composite class of volcanoes, much like recently awakened Mount St. Helens, and quite conceivably could one day erupt in a similar manner.

Although mere remnants of their former size, Rainier's 35 square miles of glaciers constitute the largest single-peak glacial system in the contiguous United States: 25 glaciers extend down the mountainside. Six of them—Nisqually, Ingraham, Emmons, Winthrop, Kautz and Tahoma—originate in the summit ice cap. Other glaciers are born of snows in valley heads, or cirques, between 10,000 and 12,000 feet; the most notable of these are the Cowlitz, Carbon, Russell, North and South Mowich and Puyallup glaciers.

Forests cover the mountainsides up to 5,000 feet, where subalpine meadows of wildflowers and grass contrast with masses of ice at higher elevations. The timberline is at about 6,500 feet. Deer, bears and mountain goats inhabit the forests, meadows and ridges. Park animals, regardless of size, should not be fed; all food should be kept locked up or out of the reach of wildlife.

Flowers in the high meadows typically bloom from mid-July to mid-August. Huckleberries, vine maple and mountain ash grow throughout the park late summer through early fall; fall colors peak from late September to early October.

More than 100 miles of roads and 270 miles of trails are open to the public. Trail maps are available at all visitor centers. Permits are required for back-country camping. Road opening and closing dates vary from year to year depending on snow conditions.

VISITOR CENTERS are located throughout the park and offer a variety of free information as well as exhibits.

Henry M. Jackson Memorial Visitor Center at Paradise is in Mount Rainier National Park, 18 mi. e. of the Nisqually park entrance via Paradise Rd. The current visitor center replaced the one built in 1966 that many Northwesterners derided for resembling a flying saucer. A soaring 60-foot ceiling and floor-to-roofline windows frame views of Mount Rainier to the north and the jagged Tatoosh Range to the south. Exhibits—many of them hands-on and high-tech—educate visitors about the park's geology, flora and fauna, and a state-of-the-art diorama uses lighting to show various park locations and seasonal closures. You can also watch a 22-minute overview film.

Note: Heavy fog can obscure visibility even in the middle of summer; also be prepared for an often dramatic decrease in temperature with the increase in elevation. **Hours:** Daily 10-7, mid-June to late Sept.; daily 10-5, late Sept. to mid-Oct. and Dec. 23-Jan. 1; Sat.-Sun. and holidays 10-5, rest of year. Phone ahead to confirm schedule. **Cost:** Park admission, valid for 7 days, $25 (per private vehicle); $20 (per motorcycle); $10 (per person on foot or bicycle). **Phone:** (360) 569-6575, or (360) 569-2211 for information about weather and road conditions. 🍴 🏕

Longmire Museum is in Mount Rainier National Park, 6 mi. e. of the Nisqually park entrance via Paradise Rd. The museum has interesting geology, flora and fauna, history and transportation exhibits. **Hours:** Daily 9-5, mid-June through Sept. 30; 9-4:30, rest of year. Phone ahead to confirm schedule. **Cost:** Park admission, valid for 7 days, $25 (per private vehicle); $20 (per motorcycle); $10 (per person on foot or bicycle). **Phone:** (360) 569-6575.

Ohanapecosh Visitor Center is in the s.e. corner of Mount Rainier National Park off SR 123. The visitor

center has exhibits about forest ecology and the history of the park. **Hours:** Daily 9-5, mid-June to mid-Sept. Phone ahead to confirm schedule. **Cost:** Park admission, valid for 7 days, $25 (per private vehicle); $20 (per motorcycle); $10 (per person on foot or bicycle). **Phone:** (360) 569-6581.

Sunrise Visitor Center is in the n.e. section of Mount Rainier National Park, 16 mi. off Mather Memorial Pkwy. (SR 410) via Sunrise Rd. The visitor center presents exhibits on geology, Native American history and subalpine ecology. **Hours:** Daily 9-6, July 1-late Sept. Phone ahead to confirm schedule. **Cost:** Park admission, valid for 7 days, $25 (per private vehicle); $20 (per motorcycle); $10 (per person on foot or bicycle). **Phone:** (360) 663-2425.

General Information and Activities

The park is open daily. Only the Nisqually (southwest) entrance and Nisqually-Longmire-Paradise Road *(see attraction listing)* are open all year, unless storms or avalanches threaten passage. All other roads are closed from late October or the first snowfall, whichever comes first, to somewhere between late April and early July, depending upon the occurrence of snowfalls. Cayuse Pass, between the park's northern boundary on SR 410 to Ohanapecosh, is usually closed from early December to early May. The road between Chinook Pass and Cayuse Pass is closed from mid-November to late May.

Naturalists conduct free guided and illustrated talks from late June through Labor Day at Longmire, Paradise, Sunrise and Ohanapecosh; schedules are posted at visitor centers. Snowshoe walks are conducted at Paradise from late December to late March. Self-guiding nature trails and wayside exhibits are found throughout the park. Wilderness information centers are at Longmire and White River.

Sightseeing flights can be arranged through private operators in Seattle and Puyallup and at nearby airports. Information concerning roads, camps and programs can be obtained by contacting the Park Superintendent's office. For information about the park's inns contact Rainier Guest Services, phone (360) 569-2275 or (360) 569-2400.

Special regulations apply to climbers; details are available from the Park Superintendent. Climbing schools and seminars as well as guided climbs are conducted by Rainier Mountaineering Inc. in Ashford, phone (360) 569-2227 or (888) 892-5462; International Mountain Guides in Ashford, phone (360) 569-2609; and Alpine Ascents International in Seattle, phone (206) 378-1927.

Fishing is permitted without a license in most lakes; check at a ranger station for special regulations. Hunting is prohibited. Winter sports, a snow play area and ranger-led snowshoe walks are available at Paradise (weather permitting). Snowmobiles are permitted only on designated roads. *See Recreation Areas Chart.*

ADMISSION to the park is by weekly pass that costs $30 per private vehicle, $25 per motorcycle or $15 per person on foot or bicycle. Annual passes, valid

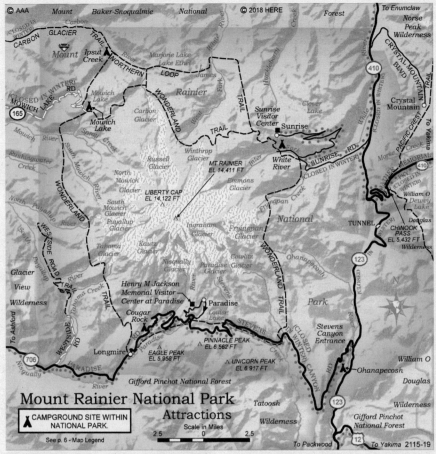

© AAA · Mount Baker-Snoqualmie National Forest · © 2018 HERE

Mount Rainier National Park
Attractions

CAMPGROUND SITE WITHIN NATIONAL PARK.

See p. 6 - Map Legend

Scale in Miles
2.5   0   2.5

for 1 year, cost $55 per vehicle. Campground fees are $20 per private vehicle.

PETS are permitted only if they are on a leash or are otherwise physically restrained at all times. Pets are not permitted on the trails, in the backcountry areas or in buildings.

ADDRESS general inquiries to the Longmire Museum, Mount Rainier National Park, 55210 238th Ave. E., Ashford, WA 98304; phone (360) 569-2211, (360) 569-6575 or TTY (360) 569-2177.

CARBON GLACIER TRAIL is in the n.w. corner of Mount Rainier National Park. A 17-mile trail leads hikers and bicyclists through virgin forests to Ipsut Creek Campground, which has limited hike-in camping facilities and access to back-country trails. A 3.5-mile trail leads hikers from the campground to Carbon Glacier, thought to be the lowest elevation reached by glacier ice in the 48 states. Campers must obtain a wilderness permit, available at ranger stations. **Phone:** (360) 569-2211, (360) 829-9639 or TTY (360) 569-2177.

EAST SIDE ROAD (SR 123) extends across the southeastern section of Mount Rainier National Park

from Ohanapecosh to SR 410 at Cayuse Pass. The Stevens Canyon Road intersection is 2 miles north of Ohanapecosh. Tipsoo Lake and Chinook Pass are 5 miles east of Cayuse Pass on SR 410; there are excellent panoramas of Mount Rainier, Governors Ridge, the Pacific Crest National Scenic Trail and the high country of the Cascade Mountains from this site. **Hours:** Open July 1-early Sept. (weather permitting). **Phone:** (360) 569-2211 or TTY (360) 569-2177.

MOWICH LAKE ROAD is accessible via the SR 165 entrance in Mount Rainier National Park's n.w. corner. Although this dirt and gravel surfaced byway is not a through road, it serves as a trailhead for those taking trips into the park's back country. Primitive, hike-in camping is permitted at a designated campsite along the lake, but campfires are prohibited and potable water is not available. Campers must obtain a wilderness permit, available at ranger stations. **Hours:** Open mid-July to mid-Oct. (weather permitting). **Phone:** (360) 569-2211 or TTY (360) 569-2177.

MOUNT RAINIER GONDOLA is 6 mi. e. of SR 410 at 33914 Crystal Mountain Blvd. at the Crystal Mountain Resort. Eight-passenger gondolas take just under

12 minutes to ascend above meadows and lush forests almost 2,500 vertical feet to the summit of Crystal Mountain. The 6,782-foot mountain top offers a stunning 360-degree panorama that encompasses Mount Rainier and five other Cascade volcanoes. Hike on a mountain trail or enjoy a meal with magnificent views steps away from the gondola at the Summit House, Washington's loftiest restaurant.

Pets on leash permitted only late June to late September. **Time:** Allow 30 minutes minimum. **Hours:** Gondola rides run daily; hours vary, phone ahead. **Cost:** $23; $18 (ages 65+); $12 (ages 4-12). Unlimited Day Pass $33; free (ages 0-3). **Phone:** (360) 663-2265, (360) 663-3085 for the restaurant or (888) 754-6199. 🍴

NISQUALLY-LONGMIRE-PARADISE ROAD extends 18 mi. from the s.w. park entrance of Mount Rainier National Park to Longmire and Paradise. Points of interest along the way to Paradise Valley include a museum at Longmire; Christine Falls; the trail to 320-foot Comet Falls, accessible only in summer; and 168-foot Narada Falls. Tire chains are required in winter months. **Hours:** Nisqually-to-Longmire portion open 24 hours, year-round (weather permitting). Longmire-to-Paradise section open 24 hours, late April-late Oct.; dawn-dusk, rest of year (weather permitting). Phone ahead to confirm schedule. **Phone:** (360) 569-2211 or TTY (360) 569-2177.

NORTHERN LOOP TRAIL runs 25 mi. from Carbon River to Sunrise. It climbs through rugged Windy Gap, intersects with a trail leading to Natural Bridge and passes Lake James, Grand and Berkeley parks and Frozen Lake. Combining the section of the Wonderland Trail from Sunrise past Mystic Lake and the Winthrop Glacier makes for a challenging 42.5-mile loop back to Carbon River. The trail is free of snow only from late July to mid-September. **Phone:** (360) 569-2211 or TTY (360) 569-2177.

STEVENS CANYON ROAD leaves Nisqually-Longmire-Paradise Rd. about 1 mi. beyond Narada Falls. The road provides east-west access within the park seasonally. The effects of glacial and water erosion are apparent at Box Canyon, along the Cowlitz River. Picnicking is permitted a half-mile west of Box Canyon.

There are excellent views of Mount Rainier, Mount Adams and the Tatoosh Range from this route, which intersects East Side Road (SR 123) 2 miles above Ohanapecosh; the best views are westbound. **Hours:** Usually open Memorial Day weekend to mid-Oct. (weather permitting). **Phone:** (360) 569-2211 or TTY (360) 569-2177. 🏕️

WESTSIDE ROAD leaves Nisqually-Longmire-Paradise Rd. 1 mi. from the park entrance. The road, improved but not surfaced, provides access to the west side trailheads. **Hours:** The road is closed indefinitely at Milepost 3; beyond that point the right of way is accessible to hikers and bicyclists. It is not a through road and is often closed due to bad weather

or high water damage. Check for conditions. **Phone:** (360) 569-2211 or TTY (360) 569-2177.

WHITE RIVER/SUNRISE ROAD runs off SR 410 from the n.e. White River entrance to the Sunrise area. It passes Fryingpan Creek; White River Campground and the trail to the Emmons Glacier moraine; and Sunrise Point, offering a panorama stretching from Mount Baker in the north to Mount Hood in the south. Branching out from Sunrise Visitor Center, a variety of trails pass through subalpine scenery with views of Mount Rainier's glaciers. The meadows are known for summer displays of subalpine wildflowers. **Hours:** Open late June or early July-early Oct. (weather permitting). **Phone:** (360) 569-2211 or TTY (360) 569-2177.

WONDERLAND TRAIL encircles Mount Rainier. It is divided into different portions. The 30-mile section from Paradise to Sunrise passes lakes, falls and Box Canyon, which is notable as one of the most unusual slot canyons in America for its glacially polished bedrock. From Sunrise to Carbon River—16.5 miles—hikers enter the park's most primitive area for the opportunity to view Winthrop Glacier, Mystic Lake and Carbon Glacier.

From Carbon River to Longmire, a 39-mile stretch, the trail passes Mowich Lake, Golden Lakes, Sunset Park, Klapatche Park, Indian Henry's Hunting Ground and other points of interest. The 6.5-mile section from Longmire to Paradise passes Carter, Madcap and Narada waterfalls. **Hours:** Travel on the Wonderland Trail is recommended only from mid-July to mid-Sept. **Phone:** (360) 569-2211 or TTY (360) 569-2177.

ALTA CRYSTAL RESORT AT MT RAINIER   360/663-2500
💎💎💎
Hotel
Rates not provided

Address: 68317 SR 410 E 98022 **Location:** 2 mi outside northeast park entrance. **Facility:** 26 kitchen units, some two bedrooms and cabins. 2 stories (no elevator), exterior corridors. **Terms:** check-in 4 pm. **Pool:** heated outdoor. **Activities:** hot tub, cross country skiing, bicycles.

[SAVE] 🛏️ 📶 ✕ 🏋️ 🔌 📺
📷 / SOME UNITS 🐾

💎 MOUNT ST. HELENS NATIONAL VOLCANIC MONUMENT (G-6)

In southwestern Washington, Mount St. Helens National Volcanic Monument contains the volcano and the surrounding area devastated by the 1980 eruption. Access to the 110,000-acre monument is limited; local roads only skirt the region, ending in overlooks providing scenic views. Southeast of the crater FR 25 branches off from FR 90 and continues north, becoming SR 131, then meets US 12 at Randle. Northeast of the volcano FR 99 branches west off FR 25, ending at the Windy Ridge viewpoint, with a view of Mount St. Helens crater and Spirit Lake.

The roads are open from late May or mid-June to late October (weather permitting). Spirit Lake Memorial Highway (SR 504) extends 50 miles from I-5 at Castle Rock to Johnston Ridge. Except for the section between Coldwater Ridge and Johnston Ridge, this road is kept open year-round; however, chains or winter traction devices may be necessary.

Until May 18, 1980, Mount St. Helens was one of Washington's snowcapped crown jewels. Spirit Lake, at its northern base, was a primary recreation center. The surrounding hills of the Gifford Pinchot National Forest *(see place listing p. 67)* beckoned hikers and outdoor recreation enthusiasts, and timber provided a livelihood for loggers.

At 8:32 a.m. an explosion of incredible force blew the top 1,313 feet and much of the bulging north face off Mount St. Helens, shot a dense plume of smoke and ash 80,000 feet into the air and released a mile-wide avalanche that raised Spirit Lake by more than 200 feet and laid over forests as if they had been combed. Mud and logs surged down the Toutle and Cowlitz rivers, temporarily clogging the Columbia River shipping lanes with silt. The pall of ash turned morning into midnight as it fell, halting traffic for a hundred miles and covering parts of three states with a fine gray powder.

The cataclysm was not wholly unexpected. The first puff of steam and ash that appeared nearly two months earlier signaled the end of the mountain's 123-year-long sleep and announced the first volcanic activity in the contiguous 48 states since the initial eruption of California's Mount Lassen in 1914. Mount St. Helens soon became one of the world's most closely monitored volcanoes.

Weeks before the great explosion, increasing seismic phenomena, heat and the swelling north slope had changed *"if* the mountain blows" to *"when* the mountain blows." Despite the renewal of life that has taken hold since the 1980 blast, the watch continues; subsequent, subtle episodes suggest that the volcano might not yet be ready for another extended nap.

General Information and Activities

If you are planning to travel in southwestern Washington, you might wish to check with your local AAA club for the latest highway and recreation area information, then update that information by checking with clubs once you arrive in the Pacific Northwest. Many roads within the Gifford Pinchot National Forest are usually closed from November until April or May; you should check at Forest Service offices before driving on these roads.

More information about the volcanic area can be obtained from the Mount St. Helens National Volcanic Monument Headquarters, 42218 N.E. Yale Bridge Rd., Amboy, WA 98601; phone (360) 449-7800.

Sightseeing helicopter flights are available from several locations along SR 504. Flights also leave daily from Seattle's Boeing Field.

A growing network of hiking trails is becoming accessible around the volcano. It is possible to climb the southern flank of Mount St. Helens, allowing about 7-12 hours for the rigorous trek to the summit and back; a $22 permit is required to climb. For permit and reservation information about the summit climb and information about the hiking trails contact monument headquarters. The Mount St. Helens climbing information line is (360) 449-7861. **Note:** Climbing may be suspended periodically due to volcanic activity.

A much easier way to see part of the blast zone is to stop at the Science and Learning Center at Coldwater; from I-5 exit 49, proceed 43 miles east on SR 504 (Spirit Lake Memorial Highway) to Milepost 43. The center sits atop a ridge offering a spectacular view of the lava dome of Mount St. Helens, 7 miles in the distance. The paved, quarter-mile Winds of Change Trail traverses part of the blast zone, while the Elk Bench and Lakes trails lead to Coldwater Lake. Picnic facilities are available. The center's visitor information station is open Sat.-Sun. 10-6, June-Oct.; Sat.-Sun. 10-4, rest of year; phone (360) 274-2131.

A pass is required at developed sites and visitor centers. A Mount St. Helens National Volcanic Monument Day Pass, available at Johnston Ridge Observatory, costs $8; free (ages 0-15). The America the Beautiful – National Parks and Federal Recreational Lands Passes also are accepted at this visitor center. A National Forest Recreation Pass ($5 per vehicle for a day pass) or a Northwest Forest Pass ($30 for an annual pass) is required at sites on the east and south sides of the monument.

APE CAVE GEOLOGIC SITE is on FR 8303, 1 mi. w. of FR 83. Thought to be the third longest lava tube in North America, the 13,042-foot tunnel was found within a massive lava flow that oozed from the volcano almost 2,000 years ago. Flowing downhill, the stream of lava cooled and formed a hard crust. In time the lava drained and left an intricate, winding lava cave behind. The cave was discovered in 1947 but not explored until the early 1950s by a local Boy Scout troop. The scouts named the cave in honor of their sponsor, the St. Helens Apes.

Visitors should have a minimum of three light sources, extra batteries, sturdy shoes and a jacket; the temperature is a constant 42 degrees Fahrenheit. Rental propane lanterns are available at Ape Headquarters. **Hours:** Cave open daily 6 a.m.-10 p.m. The Ape Cave Headquarters are open daily 10-5, mid-June through Labor Day; Sat.-Sun. 10-5, Memorial Day weekend to mid-June. **Cost:** Admission May-Oct. $5 (per private vehicle). Rental lantern $5. **Phone:** (360) 449-7800.

FOREST LEARNING CENTER AT MOUNT ST. HELENS is off I-5 exit 49, then 33 mi. e. on SR 504 (Spirit Lake Memorial Hwy.) to 17000 Spirit Lake Memorial Hwy. The center offers displays highlighting the eruption of Mount St. Helens and the recovery and reforestation efforts currently under way. Visitors can sit inside the cockpit of a helicopter and take a video tour of Mount St. Helens. Many hands-on displays also are featured, and viewing platforms offer a panorama of the mountain. **Time:** Allow 30 minutes minimum. **Hours:** Indoor exhibits open daily 10-4, mid-May to late Sept. Outdoor exhibits open daily

10-6, mid-May through Sept. 30; 10-5, in Oct. Phone ahead to confirm schedule. **Cost:** Free. **Phone:** (360) 274-7750 or (360) 414-3439.

JOHNSTON RIDGE OBSERVATORY is at the end of Spirit Lake Memorial Hwy. (SR 504) in Mount St. Helens National Volcanic Monument. The observatory is the closest to the crater and lava dome and offers panoramic views. The facility is named for a volcanologist, on duty at the time of the eruption, who was one of the 57 people who lost their lives during this catastrophic event. Interpretive exhibits explain the series of events leading to the eruption of the volcano and the resulting change to the landscape. A 16-minute video presentation re-creates the eruption. A 1.5-mile interpretive trail shows how the eruption shaped the landscape. Ranger-led interpretive walks are offered daily. **Time:** Allow 1 hour minimum. **Hours:** Daily 10-6, May-Oct. (weather permitting). **Cost:** Monument pass $8; free (ages 0-15). **Phone:** (360) 274-2140.

MOUNT ST. HELENS VISITOR CENTER AT SILVER LAKE is on the shore of Silver Lake, 5 mi. e. of I-5 exit 49 to 3029 SR 504 (Spirit Lake Memorial Hwy.). A walk-in model of the volcano illustrates its composition; pictorial and interpretive material and a film highlight the May 18, 1980, eruption. A short trail outside the center leads to a viewpoint overlooking Silver Lake and, 34 miles east, Mount St. Helens. The vegetation along a 1-mile wetlands trail is representative of the local ecosystem's ongoing recovery.

Time: Allow 30 minutes minimum. **Hours:** Daily 9-5, mid-May to mid-Sept.; daily 9-4, Mar. 1 to mid-May and mid-Sept. through Oct. 31; Thurs.-Mon. 9-4, rest of year. Closed Jan. 1, Martin Luther King Jr. Day, Presidents Day, Veterans Day, Thanksgiving and Christmas. **Cost:** $5; $2.50 (ages 7-17); $15 (family). Phone ahead to confirm rates. **Phone:** (360) 274-0962.

SCENIC DRIVES are provided by a network of state and forest roads connecting with I-5 and US 12. Mount St. Helens is visible on clear days from Chehalis to Salem, Ore. A series of Forest Service roads forms a 60-mile link between Cougar and Randle, the principal western and northern gateways into the forest. FR 90, along the southern edge of the volcanic area east of Cougar, is paved as far as the intersection with FR 25, a paved road extending north to Randle.

A number of paved and gravel forest service roads branch off FRs 90 and 25, with viewpoints within the volcanic area. Many forest service roads are closed from October through May or June, depending on snow conditions. A concession stand and portable toilets are available at Cascade Viewpoint on FR 99. Groceries are available at the east end of Swift Reservoir.

Roads, some unpaved, leading into the volcanic area include Cougar Creek Road (FR 8303) from FR 83 to Ape Cave, which crosses a 1,900-year-old lava field with numerous caves and tubes. The first 10 miles of FR 81 from Cougar passes Merrill Lake and Kalama Falls.

A particularly scenic road is Spirit Lake Memorial Highway (SR 504), which follows the north fork of the Toutle River to Johnston Ridge Observatory. Overlooks along the highway provide views of the crater and northwest lava dome, the blast zone, Castle Lake and Coldwater Lake. The road ends 7 miles beyond Coldwater Ridge at Johnston Ridge.

FR 99 branches off FR 25 and travels west past Meta Lake to within 5 miles of the volcano at Windy Ridge. There, at the road's end, visitors have a dramatic view of the devastation stretching from Mount St. Helens' crater to Spirit Lake. **Phone:** (360) 449-7800 for Mount St. Helens National Monument headquarters. ▯

MOUNT VERNON (C-3) pop. 31,743, elev. 23'

Named for President George Washington's Potomac River home, Mount Vernon dates back to a trading post established on the banks of the Skagit River in 1870. In the vicinity is one of the nation's largest commercial bulb growing regions. Bulb farms cluster along county roads branching north and south from SR 20; follow SR 536 west from I-5 exit 226.

Daffodils bloom from mid-March to early April, tulips during the first half of April and irises in early May. Maps pinpointing the location of various flower fields and dates of festival events are available from the chamber of commerce. The chamber also houses a visitor information center.

Tulip season coincides with April's 🌷 Skagit Valley Tulip Festival, celebrated the entire month throughout the Skagit Valley with display gardens, exhibits, food, fairs and shows. Among the largest display gardens are those at Tulip Town and Roozengaarde *(see attraction listings).*

Mount Vernon Chamber of Commerce & Visitor Information Center: 301 W. Kincaid St., P.O. Box 1007, Mount Vernon, WA 98273. **Phone:** (360) 428-8547.

PADILLA BAY NATIONAL ESTUARINE RESEARCH RESERVE AND BREAZEALE INTERPRETIVE CENTER is .2 mi. n. of Bay View State Park at 10441 Bayview-Edison Rd. This 10,600-acre reserve protects habitats ranging from open marine waters, tidal flats, marshes and beaches to wooded uplands and open fields. It is home to a variety of fish, mammals and birds, including nearly 250 visiting bird species. An interpretive center has aquariums and interactive learning modules about estuaries and watersheds. More than 3 miles of trails lead to beach, shoreline and upland areas.

Educational programs are presented periodically. **Time:** Allow 1 hour, 30 minutes minimum. **Hours:** Center open Tues.-Sat. 10-5; closed major holidays. Trails open daily dawn-dusk. **Cost:** Donations. **Phone:** (360) 428-1558. ▭

ROOZENGAARDE is at 15867 Beaver Marsh Rd. The 3-acre display garden is filled with tulips, irises, daffodils and other flowering bulbs. Roozengaarde is a division of the Washington Bulb Co., one of the world's largest growers of tulips, daffodils and irises. The main blooming season is late March-early May. **Hours:** Mon.-Sat. 9-6, Sun. and holidays 11-4. Closed Jan. 1, Thanksgiving and Christmas. **Cost:** In Apr. $7; $6 (military with ID); free (ages 0-5). Rest of year free. **Phone:** (360) 424-8531 or (866) 488-5477. [AAA]

TULIP TOWN is s. of SR 20 at 15002 Bradshaw Rd. Open only during the months of April, September and October, the Skagit Valley Bulb Farm's show garden features indoor and outdoor displays of some 60 varieties of tulips. In recognition of the tulip's status as the "World's Peace Flower," a special exhibit contains varieties from 17 peace gardens around the world. Visitors can walk through the fields or take a tractor trolley ride. Garden paths may be muddy; all-weather shoes are recommended. **Time:** Allow 30 minutes minimum. **Hours:** Daily 9-5, in Apr.; Mon.-Sat. 9-5, Sept.-Oct. Tractor trolley tour daily 10-4, in Apr. (weather permitting). **Cost:** $7; free (ages 0-10). Tractor trolley $2; $1 (ages 0-10). Cash only. **Phone:** (360) 424-8152. [GT]

BEST WESTERN COLLEGE WAY INN   (360)424-4287

▼▼
Hotel
$103-$168

(BW) **Best Western.**

AAA Benefit: Members save up to 15% and earn bonus points!

Address: 300 W College Way 98273 **Location:** I-5 exit 227, just w. **Facility:** 65 units, some kitchens. 2 stories (no elevator), exterior corridors. **Terms:** cancellation fee imposed. **Pool:** heated outdoor. **Activities:** hot tub. **Featured Amenity:** full hot breakfast.

BEST WESTERN PLUS SKAGIT VALLEY INN & CONVENTION CENTER   (360)428-5678

▼▼▼
Hotel
$100-$200

(BW) **Best Western PLUS.**

AAA Benefit: Members save up to 15% and earn bonus points!

Address: 2300 Market St 98273 **Location:** I-5 exit 227, 0.3 mi e on College Way, then 0.5 mi n on Riverside Dr. Located in a commercial area. **Facility:** 120 units. 3 stories, interior corridors. **Terms:** cancellation fee imposed. **Pool:** heated outdoor. **Guest Services:** valet and coin laundry. **Featured Amenity:** continental breakfast.

🅖 **For complete hotel, dining and**
attraction listings:
AAA.com/travelguides

TULIP INN   360/428-5969

▼▼▼
Motel
Rates not provided

Address: 2200 Freeway Dr 98273 **Location:** I-5 exit 227, just w on College Way, then just n. **Facility:** 40 units, some efficiencies. 2 stories (no elevator), exterior corridors. **Featured Amenity:** continental breakfast.

WHERE TO EAT

BURGERMASTER   360/899-4075
▼ Burgers. Quick Serve. **Address:** 2030 Freeway Dr 98273

CALICO CUPBOARD CAFE & BAKERY   360/336-3107
▼▼ American. Casual Dining. **Address:** 121B Freeway Dr 98273

IL GRANAIO   360/419-0674
▼▼ Italian. Casual Dining. **Address:** 100 E Montgomery St 98273

MAX DALE'S STEAK AND CHOP HOUSE   360/424-7171
▼▼ Steak. Casual Dining. **Address:** 2030 Riverside Dr 98273

MEXICO CAFE   360/424-1977
▼▼ Mexican. Casual Dining. **Address:** 1320 Memorial Hwy 98273

RACHAWADEE CAFE   360/336-6699
▼▼ Thai. Casual Dining. **Address:** 410 W Gates St 98273

SKAGIT RIVER BREWERY & RESTAURANT   360/336-2884
▼▼ American. Brewpub. **Address:** 404 S 3rd St 98273

TRUMPETER PUBLIC HOUSE   360/588-4515
▼▼ American. Casual Dining. **Address:** 416 Myrtle St 98273

MUKILTEO (E-3) pop. 20,254, elev. 12'
- Hotels p. 92 • Restaurants p. 92
- Part of Seattle area — see map p. 124

Mukilteo, named for the Suquamish word meaning "good camping ground," was the site of the Point Elliott Treaty of 1855. The document, signed by the leaders of 22 local tribes, relinquished land claims to white settlers. A lighthouse built in 1905 is open to visitors on weekends and holidays from April through September; phone (425) 513-9602. Washington State Ferries connects the mainland with Clinton on Whidbey Island; phone (206) 464-6400, or (888) 808-7977 in Wash.

◤GEM◢ **FUTURE OF FLIGHT AVIATION CENTER & BOEING TOUR** is off I-5 exit 189, then 4.5 mi. w. on SR 526, following signs to 8415 Paine Field Blvd. One of the largest buildings in the world, the Boeing Everett assembly plant employs some 41,000 people. The visitor tour begins with an informational video before you board a bus for a trip to the factory where all the magic takes place.

It's fascinating to watch aircraft—including 747s, 777s and 787s—taking shape before your eyes as the tour guide explains various assembly processes. The facility even has a runway where airplanes are tested. One of the most impressive sights is the four-story-high tail section of a 747 Jumbo Jet.

The center's aviation gallery, which can be visited before or after the plant tour, has learning zones with interactive computer stations that allow you to design and test your own aircraft. There also are changing exhibits that display the latest advances in aerospace technology.

Purses, backpacks and electronic devices such as cellphones and cameras are not permitted on the tour; lockers are available. **Time:** Allow 2 hours, 30 minutes minimum. **Hours:** Open daily 8-7, Memorial Day-Labor Day; 8:30-5:30, rest of year. Tours are given on the hour at 9, 10, 11, 1, 2 and 3 (last tour at 11 a.m., Christmas Eve and Dec. 31). Closed Jan. 1, Thanksgiving and Christmas. **Cost:** Gallery only $12. Tour and aviation gallery $25; $15 (ages 0-15). Children must be at least 48 inches tall to take the tour. Tour reservations are recommended. **Phone:** (425) 438-8100 or (800) 464-1476. ☐ GT ⑪

HISTORIC FLIGHT FOUNDATION is on the w. side of Paine Field, off Mukilteo Speedway (SR 525) to 10719 Bernie Webber Dr., following signs. The foundation collects and restores aircraft from the period between Charles Lindbergh's solo Atlantic crossing (1927) and the first Boeing 707 flight (1957). The hangar displays such meticulously restored aircraft as a DH89 Dragon Rapide, a North American P-51B Mustang and a Waco UPF-7.

Interpretive displays describe each plane's history, and visitors can take advantage of interactive kiosks and video displays that include a 360-degree cockpit view and footage of the aircraft in flight. Guided 30-minute tours are available by request.

Time: Allow 1 hour minimum. **Hours:** Tues.-Sun. 10-5. Closed Jan. 1, Thanksgiving and Christmas. **Cost:** $15; $12 (ages 65+ and military with ID); $10 (ages 11-17). Aircraft ride opportunities are available; reservations are required. **Phone:** (425) 348-3200. GT ✈

HILTON GARDEN INN SEATTLE NORTH EVERETT
425/423-9000
♥♥♥ Hotel. **Address:** 8401 Paine Field Blvd 98275

AAA Benefit:
Members save 5%
or more!

SILVER CLOUD INN MUKILTEO   (425)423-8600
♥♥♥♥ Hotel. **Address:** 718 Front St 98275

STAYBRIDGE SUITES SEATTLE NORTH-EVERETT
(425)493-9500

♥♥♥
Extended Stay Hotel
$149-$219

Address: 9600 Harbour Pl 98275 **Location:** Jct Paine Field Blvd and SR 525 (Mukilteo Speedway). **Facility:** 134 efficiencies, some two bedrooms. 5 stories, interior corridors. **Amenities:** safes. **Pool:** heated indoor. **Activities:** hot tub, exercise room. **Guest Services:** complimentary and valet laundry, area transportation. **Featured Amenity:** full hot breakfast.

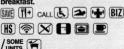

TOWNEPLACE SUITES BY MARRIOTT-MUKILTEO
(425)551-5900
♥♥♥ Extended Stay Hotel. **Address:** 8521 Mukilteo Speedway 98275

AAA Benefit:
Members save 5%
or more!

ARNIES RESTAURANT   425/355-2181
♥♥♥ Seafood. Fine Dining. **Address:** 714 2nd St 98275

IVAR'S MUKILTEO LANDING   425/742-6180
♥♥♥ Seafood. Casual Dining. **Address:** 710 Front St 98275

JOHN'S GRILL   425/347-1068
♥♥ American. Casual Dining. **Address:** 649 5th St 98275

NEWHALEM (C-8) elev. 525'

Derived from a Native American word meaning "goat snare," Newhalem is a company town of frame houses and well-tended yards built to house employees of the Skagit River Hydroelectric Complex. The Skagit Information Center on SR 20 has displays and interpretive material on the Skagit River project and area recreational opportunities.

Nearby is a 1926 Baldwin steam locomotive that operated on the Seattle City Light Railway. Also of interest are the Trail of the Cedars nature walk and Ladder Creek Falls and Rock Garden, where summer evening illumination makes for a pleasant stroll. The North Cascades National Park Complex Visitor Center *(see North Cascades National Park listing)* is just west of town across the Skagit River.

SKAGIT TOURS—SEATTLE CITY LIGHT can be reached by following signs on SR 20 to the Skagit Information Center. The 90-minute Diablo Lake Boat Tour aboard the *Alice Ross IV* focuses on the remote, scenic lake setting and the hydroelectric facilities around SR 20. The entire complex, which centers on the source of Seattle's electricity supply, lies within Ross Lake National Recreation Area.

The Powerhouse Insiders Tour is a two-hour, forty-five minute guided walking tour of the historic company town of Newhalem and the Gorge Powerhouse. An evening tour with dinner also is offered.

Hours: Diablo Lake Afternoon Cruise departs Fri.-Sun. at 1:45, early July-early Sept. Diablo Lake & Lunch Tour departs Thurs.-Mon. at 10:30, late June-late Sept. Powerhouse Insiders Tour departs Sat.-Sun. at 10, early July-early Sept. Phone ahead to confirm schedule. **Cost:** Diablo Lake Afternoon Cruise $30; $28 (ages 62+); $15 (ages 3-12). Diablo Lake & Lunch Tour $42; $40 (ages 62+); $21 (ages 3-12). Powerhouse Insiders Tour (includes lunch) $20; $18 (ages 62+); ages 0-9 not permitted. Reservations are required. **Phone:** (360) 854-2589 for tour information, or (206) 233-2709 for the Skagit Information Center. GT

NEWPORT (D-12) pop. 2,126, elev. 2,142'

Newport faces the Idaho border at the point where the Pend Oreille River enters Washington. A store opened on the Idaho side in 1889, and in 1890 a post office was established with the name Newport, in the hopes that the town would attract river traffic. In 1892 the Great Northern Railroad built a depot on the Washington side of the border and the community shifted west, thriving as an outfitting center for nearby mines.

The original settlement is now Oldtown, Idaho (*see place listing in the Idaho, Montana & Wyoming TourBook*), separated from Newport by State Avenue. Newport also is the Washington entryway to the International Selkirk Loop (*see attraction listing*).

Greater Newport Area Chamber of Commerce: 325 W. 4th St., P.O. Box 2006, Newport, WA 99156. **Phone:** (509) 447-5812.

INTERNATIONAL SELKIRK LOOP is a 280-mile scenic byway in northeastern Washington, northern Idaho and adjoining British Columbia. Starting at Newport, the 74-mile Washington segment follows SR 20 north to Tiger, then SR 31 north to the Canadian border through a sparsely settled part of the state known as "Washington's forgotten corner."

Between Newport and Metaline Falls the route parallels the Pend Oreille (pond-ah-RAY) River, where dense forests of aspen, fir, cedar and pine alternate with patches of farmland. Practically the entire loop follows either a river or a lakeshore, waterways that historically were used for transportation in this remote area. Rising up on both sides of the river, the Selkirk Mountains ascend to heights of 5,000 feet in the south and more than 7,000 feet in the north.

Watch for ospreys and eagles soaring high in the sky before plummeting down to the water to seize fish with their talons. Large bundles of sticks high in the trees denote nesting sites. Big horn sheep also inhabit the Selkirks, and winter foraging brings them down to river level. Moose, deer and elk are other wilderness dwellers that might be spotted during the winter months as they search out tender vegetation hiding beneath a blanket of snow.

An excursion train from Newport takes you through areas that are not accessible by road. For a more exhilarating adventure, embark on a guided kayak trip that negotiates spectacular Z Canyon. Or take your pick of recreational pursuits—golf, fishing, boating, swimming, mountain biking and horseback riding all can be enjoyed. Summer, when wildflowers are in bloom, is a great time to hike the hundreds of miles of trails crisscrossing the rugged, impressively scenic terrain of the Selkirk wilderness region.

Chambers of commerce and visitor centers along the loop provide maps and information. Towns with attraction listings located on the Washington portion of the route are Ione, Metaline Falls and Newport. **Phone:** (208) 267-0822 or (888) 823-2626.

NORTH BEND (E-7) pop. 5,731, elev. 445'
• **Part of Seattle area — see map p. 124**

The chief agricultural center for the upper Snoqualmie Valley, North Bend straddles the South Fork of the Snoqualmie River. The town's proximity to Snoqualmie Pass and the western slopes of the Cascade Range make it a good starting point for trips to both areas.

Mountains have influenced local architecture, much of which sports an alpine motif. Rising nearby is 4,167-foot Mount Si (pronounced "sigh"); a 4-mile trail to the summit ascends 3,500 feet and offers spectacular views. Linking with the 2-mile Rattlesnake Ledge Trail, the 8.8-mile Rattlesnake Mountain Trail provides views of Mount Si, North Bend and the Snoqualmie River Valley. The early 1990s TV series "Twin Peaks" was filmed in North Bend and neighboring Snoqualmie.

Shopping: North Bend Premium Outlets, I-90 exit 31, offers discount shopping in more than 50 stores.

ROARING RIVER BED & BREAKFAST   (425)888-4834
▼▼▼ Bed & Breakfast. **Address:** 46715 SE 129th St 98045

NORTH BONNEVILLE (H-7) pop. 956, elev. 74'

North Bonneville is named for Capt. Benjamin Louis Eulalie Bonneville, a French-born American army officer who explored a large portion of the Northwest in the early 1830s. Bonneville's travels were chronicled in Washington Irving's book "Adventures of Captain Bonneville, U.S.A., in the Rocky Mountains and the Far West," published in 1837.

The town was established in 1933 to house construction workers on the Bonneville Dam. It was relocated to the present site in 1976 to make way for a new powerhouse.

BONNEVILLE LOCK AND DAM— WASHINGTON SHORE VISITOR COMPLEX is 1 mi. e. on SR 14, then 1 mi. s. and e., following signs. At the north end of Bonneville Dam, the complex features the Second Powerhouse Gallery, where windows overlook giant turbines and generators that hum around the clock (from the orientation building, take the enclosed walkway that crosses high above the fish ladder). Gallery exhibits depict the construction of the powerhouse and explain power production, while an adjacent theater screens short films that include an 11-minute video about the dam.

In the Underwater Fish Viewing building next to the dam's fish ladder, exhibits trace the area's fishing history and the use of fish wheels on the Columbia River, a practice outlawed by Oregon in 1926 and Washington in 1934. Six large viewing windows on the lower level permit visitors to observe adult fish migrating through the ladder, which occurs from mid-April to mid-October (peak times are May-June and August-September). Interpretive signs describe species, life cycles, ladders and fish counting.

Note: Public access to the dam can also be reached from the Oregon side off I-84, exit 40. **Time:** Allow 1 hour minimum. **Hours:** Daily 9-5. Free guided tours of the complex and Second Powerhouse are given daily at 10, 1:30 and 3:30, mid-June to early Sept.; 10:30, 1:30 and 3:30, rest of year. Closed Jan. 1, Thanksgiving and Christmas. **Cost:** Free. **Phone:** (509) 427-4281, or (541) 374-8820 for tour information. GT 🅟

NORTH CASCADES NATIONAL PARK
(C-7)

Elevations in the park range from 400 ft. at the western entrance of the park to 9,220 ft. at the summit of Goode Mountain. Refer to AAA maps for additional elevation information.

North Cascades National Park can be reached via trails off the North Cascades Highway (SR 20), from Marblemount on the western side and from Mazama through Okanogan-Wenatchee National Forest on the eastern side. The highway is closed between Diablo Lake and Mazama from the first major snowfall until April or May. From Marblemount, Cascade River Road leads east for 22 miles and is the only accessible road into the park. The park also can be reached by boat via Lake Chelan or from Canada via Ross Lake.

The park embraces 505,000 acres in north-central Washington. Its northern and southern sections, separated by Ross Lake National Recreation Area *(see place listing p. 117)*, are bordered by Okanogan-Wenatchee National Forest *(see place listing p. 96)* to the east and south, Lake Chelan National Recreation Area *(see place listing p. 77)* to the southeast and Mount Baker-Snoqualmie National Forest to the west *(see place listing p. 85)*.

Park terrain is the result of glaciation; more than 300 glaciers remain. Jagged peaks, sheer canyons and many rivers and lakes characterize the landscape.

Mountain goats, deer and black and grizzly bears are among the most common animals in the park. Cougars and wolverines are rarely-seen residents. Smaller mammals and a host of birds, including white-tailed ptarmigans, also inhabit the area. Hunting is prohibited. Several varieties of trout live in park waters.

General Information and Activities

North Cascades National Park is open daily 24 hours, year-round. Highway access is non-existent in winter; however, SR 20 is passable from mid-April to mid-November (weather permitting).

Hiking access and roadside views of the northwest corner of the park are offered from SR 542 east from Bellingham. Lake Chelan Boat Co. *(see attraction listing p. 52)* provides round-trip ferry service between Stehekin, in Lake Chelan National Recreation Area, and Chelan, at the southern end of Lake Chelan. Shuttle bus service transports visitors

from Stehekin to High Bridge and Cottonwood, both in the remote southeast portion of the park, four times a day from late May through early October. One-way shuttle fare is $8 per person, dog or bicycle; $5 (ages 0-12); phone (509) 699-2054.

Trails suitable for hiking and climbing wind through the back country. Primitive campsites are available by free permit issued at most ranger stations; the most developed sites are off SR 20 in the Ross Lake National Recreation Area. Summer activities, including evening programs and guided nature walks, are given at campgrounds in both recreation areas.

The park headquarters, adjoining SR 20 in Sedro-Woolley, is open daily 8-4:30, Memorial Day-Columbus Day; Mon.-Fri. 8-4:30, rest of year. The North Cascades National Park Visitor Center, just west of Newhalem off SR 20, has exhibits and films that focus on the park's natural and cultural history. A short walk from the center's rear deck leads to an excellent view of the rugged Picket Range in the wilderness heart of the park. The center is open daily 9-5, late May-late Sept.; Sat.-Sun. 9-5, early-late May and in Oct. Phone (206) 386-4495, ext. 11.

Weather forecasts, trail conditions and free permits for back-country camping are available at the Chelan, Marblemount, Newhalem, Winthrop and Stehekin ranger stations; for details phone (509) 682-4900 in Chelan, (360) 854-7245 in Marblemount, or (206) 386-4495, ext. 11 in Newhalem. *See Recreation Areas Chart.*

ADMISSION to the park is free.

PETS are permitted in the Lake Chelan and Ross Lake national recreation areas only if they are on a leash or otherwise restricted at all times. Dogs and cats are not permitted on the trails or in buildings.

ADDRESS inquiries to the Park Superintendent's Office, North Cascades National Park, 810 SR 20, Sedro-Woolley, WA 98284; phone (360) 854-7200.

OAK HARBOR (C-2) pop. 22,075, elev. 84'

The largest town on Whidbey Island *(see place listing p. 216)*, Oak Harbor is named for the white oak trees growing in the vicinity. Many of the first settlers were Dutch. Holland Gardens in Neil Park, with its windmill and flower beds, and the Dutch windmill in Oak Harbor Beach Park are examples of the prevailing Dutch influence.

North of Oak Harbor is Whidbey Island Naval Air Station, home to the Navy's electronic warfare squadrons and the Pacific Meteorology and Oceanographic Detachment.

Oak Harbor Chamber of Commerce: 32630 SR 20, Oak Harbor, WA 98277. **Phone:** (360) 675-3755.

DECEPTION PASS STATE PARK is 9 mi. n. to 41020 SR 20. Capt. George Vancouver named the cliff-lined channel that separates Whidbey and Fidalgo islands in 1792. Within the park's 4,134 acres are freshwater lakes, marshland, sand dunes, offshore islands and almost 15 miles of saltwater shoreline. The coastal landscape comprises cliffs, rocky shores, beaches of gravel and sand, tidal flats and hidden coves—and a plethora of spectacular views.

Cedar, Douglas fir, hemlock and spruce form magnificent stands of old-growth forest. Some 38 miles of hiking trails meander through the park. Hike to West Beach, a long, skinny stretch of sand littered with huge bleached logs; it's an exceptionally scenic spot for sunset watching.

Wildlife is abundant, although the animal residents may not always be visible. Mammals include deer, foxes, muskrats, otters and skunks. Among the 174 species of birds are gulls, herons, ducks, owls and bald eagles. Tide pool explorations will uncover clams, crabs and sea cucumbers.

A roadside viewpoint at the southern end of Deception Pass Bridge offers a panorama of Deception Pass, the channel between Whidbey and Fidalgo islands. When the tide changes there often are spectacular displays of churning water and roiling eddies as ocean water pushes and pulls through the narrows. If you're not afraid of heights, take in the view from the bridge's pedestrian walkway (and exercise caution due to the frequent traffic). *See Recreation Areas Chart.* **Hours:** Daily 6:30-dusk, Apr.-Sept.; 8-dusk, rest of year. **Cost:** Park admission $10 (per private vehicle); Discover Pass, valid for 1 year, $30 (per private vehicle). **Phone:** (360) 675-3767. 🅰 🍴 ⊠ 🏕 ⛲

Civilian Conservation Corps Interpretive Center is in Deception Pass State Park, 1 mi. n. of the Deception Pass Bridge at Bowman Bay to 4402 Bowman Bay Rd. The center documents the story of the Civilian Conservation Corps—a federal program that helped support the newly established state park system in the 1930s by building picnic shelters, residences, restrooms and hiking trails in state parks. **Hours:** Daily 10-6, mid-May to Labor Day; by appointment rest of year. **Cost:** Interpretive center free. Park admission $10 (per private vehicle). **Phone:** (360) 675-3767, ext. 31.

BEST WESTERN PLUS HARBOR PLAZA & CONFERENCE CENTER   (360)679-4567

◆◆ **Hotel** $139-$179

🅱🅆 **Best Western PLUS.** **AAA Benefit:** Members save up to 15% and earn bonus points!

Address: 33175 SR 20 98277 **Location:** Just n of town. **Facility:** 80 units. 3 stories, interior corridors. **Terms:** cancellation fee imposed. **Pool:** heated outdoor. **Activities:** hot tub, exercise room. **Featured Amenity:** full hot breakfast.

🆂🅰🆅🅴 🍴➕ CALL 🔉 ➿ 👼 BIZ
🛜 ⊠ 📶 🖥 🖨 / SOME UNITS 🐾

CANDLEWOOD SUITES-OAK HARBOR   360/279-2222
◆◆ Extended Stay Hotel. **Address:** 33221 SR 20 98277

FLYERS RESTAURANT & BREWERY   360/675-5858
◆◆ American. Casual Dining. **Address:** 32295 SR 20 98277

FRASERS GOURMET HIDEAWAY   360/279-1231
◆◆◆ International. Casual Dining. **Address:** 1191 SE Dock St 98277

ZORBA'S RESTAURANT   360/279-8322
◆◆ Greek. Casual Dining. **Address:** 32955 SR 20 98277

OCEAN SHORES (F-4) pop. 5,569, elev. 43'
• Restaurants p. 96

Occupying a sandy peninsula separating Grays Harbor from the Pacific Ocean, Ocean Shores is a popular resort area. More than 6 miles of sandy beach and a network of freshwater lakes and canals lend themselves to swimming, fishing, clamming and kayaking; other leisure activities include horseback riding and golf. Charter fishing trips depart from the Ocean Shores Marina. Damon Point, at the southern tip of the peninsula, is one of the Pacific Northwest's premier sites for bird-watching and is a popular place for beachcombing.

Ocean Shores Visitors Information Center: 120 W. Chance-a-la-Mer St., P.O. Box 1447, Ocean Shores, WA 98569. **Phone:** (360) 289-9586 or (866) 602-6278.

COASTAL INTERPRETIVE CENTER is at 1033 Catala Ave. S.E. The center offers hands-on nature exhibits as well as displays describing indigenous peoples, early pioneers, shipwrecks and such natural phenomena as tsunamis. Video presentations educate visitors about beach safety, erosion, birds, wetlands and area geology. There's also an interpretive walking trail and a children's playground. **Time:** Allow 30 minutes minimum. **Hours:** Daily 11-4, Apr. 1-Labor Day; Sat.-Sun. 11-4, rest of year. **Cost:** Donations. **Phone:** (360) 289-4617.

BEST WESTERN LIGHTHOUSE SUITES INN
    (360)289-2311

◆◆ **Hotel** $120-$229

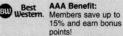

🅱🅆 **Best Western.** **AAA Benefit:** Members save up to 15% and earn bonus points!

Address: 491 Damon Rd NW 98569 **Location:** Oceanfront. Just w of main entrance to town; north end of downtown. **Facility:** 95 units. 4 stories, interior corridors. **Terms:** check-in 4 pm, cancellation fee imposed. **Pool:** heated indoor. **Activities:** sauna, hot tub, exercise room. **Guest Services:** coin laundry. **Featured Amenity:** continental breakfast.

🆂🅰🆅🅴 CALL 🔉 ➿ 👼 BIZ 🛜
⊠ 🏂 📶 🖥 🖨 / SOME UNITS 🐾

THE CANTERBURY INN   (360)289-3317
◆◆ Condominium. **Address:** 643 Ocean Shores Blvd NW 98569

THE POLYNESIAN CONDOMINIUM RESORT   (360)289-3361
◆◆ Condominium. **Address:** 615 Ocean Shores Blvd NW 98569

QUALITY INN OCEAN SHORES   (360)289-2040
♥♥ Hotel. **Address:** 773 Ocean Shores Blvd NW 98569

WHERE TO EAT

ALEC'S BY THE SEA   360/289-4026

♥♥

Seafood
Casual Dining
$11-$30

AAA Inspector Notes: A nice selection of beef, chicken and seafood is offered here. While the menu is well-rounded with choices for all appetites, locals know that the fresh fish options are the way to go. The clam chowder, which has won much acclaim, is a great starter. If oysters, salmon, razor clams or halibut are available, I recommend you stop looking and place your order. Parties with children in tow are welcomed at this casual spot. **Features:** full bar, senior menu, happy hour. **Reservations:** suggested, for dinner. **Address:** 131 E Chance A La Mer Blvd NE 98569 **Location:** Just e of Point Brown Ave. L D

BENNETT'S FISH SHACK   360/289-2847
♥ Seafood. Casual Dining. **Address:** 105 W Chance A La Mer Blvd 98569

GALWAY BAY IRISH RESTAURANT & PUB   360/289-2300
♥♥ Irish. Casual Dining. **Address:** 880 Point Brown Ave NE 98569

HOME PORT RESTAURANT   360/289-2600
♥♥ American. Casual Dining. **Address:** 857 Point Brown Ave NW 98569

MARIAH'S RESTAURANT & LOUNGE   360/289-3315
♥♥ American. Casual Dining. **Address:** 615 Ocean Shores Blvd NW 98569

MIKE'S SEAFOOD   360/289-0532
♥♥ Seafood. Casual Dining. **Address:** 830 Point Brown Ave NE 98569

OKANOGAN-WENATCHEE NATIONAL FOREST (C-8, D-8)

Elevations in the forest range from 778 ft. at Pateros to 9,511 ft. at Bonanza Peak. Refer to AAA maps for additional elevation information.

Extending from the Canadian border to the Goat Rocks Wilderness area south of White Pass, and from North Cascades National Park and Lake Chelan National Recreation Area to the Yakama Nation Reservation, Okanogan-Wenatchee National Forest covers 3,906,000 acres. Smaller sections are east of Oroville and Tonasket. Farther to the north is Pasayten Wilderness, encompassing 529,607 acres. The Lake Chelan-Sawtooth Wilderness covers 145,667 acres.

The main access routes from the north and south are US 2 and US 97, and from the east and west by the North Cascades Highway (SR 20), the forest's outstanding scenic drive. The highway connects Winthrop and Marblemount and is open late April through early November (weather permitting). The Washington Pass Scenic Overlook, 32 miles west of Winthrop, offers a short loop trail to an overlook at an elevation of 5,500 feet, where there are picnic sites as well as a visitor information center.

A narrow gravel road leads to Slate Peak, 19 miles northwest of Mazama. Reaching an elevation of 7,400 feet, the road offers a panorama of the North Cascades. The road, leading to the highest elevation in the state accessible by automobile, is open from July until the first snowfall; it is not suitable for trailers.

Recreational activities include winter sports, hunting, fishing and rockhounding. Trails include 200 miles of the Pacific Crest National Scenic Trail, which runs from the Canadian border to the forest's southern border. The trail is generally free of snow August through September. Also on the North Cascades Highway is the Rainy Lake Trail at Rainy Pass. This paved 1-mile trail is open July through September.

Parts of eight wilderness areas lie within the forest: Pasayten in the north; Alpine Lakes, Glacier Peak, Henry M. Jackson and Lake Chelan-Sawtooth in the central portion; and Goat Rocks, Norse Peak and William O. Douglas in the south. Overnight permits are required in the Enchantments area of the Alpine Lakes Wilderness.

The Summit at Snoqualmie consists of a cluster of four ski areas off I-90 on both sides of Snoqualmie Pass. Mission Ridge Ski Area is 13 miles southwest of Wenatchee; White Pass ski area, off US 12, is 50 miles west of Yakima. This vast region is traversed by some 2,500 miles of trails suitable for hiking, horseback riding and bicycling. Popular recreation areas include Lake Chelan, north of Wenatchee via US 97A; Lake Wenatchee, about 20 miles north of Leavenworth via CR 62; and lakes Cle Elum, Kachess and Keechelus, near I-90 west of Cle Elum. *See Recreation Areas Chart.*

Access to the park is free. A Northwest Forest Pass, available at ranger stations, is required for parking at most trailheads in the forest. Day passes cost $5 per vehicle; an annual pass costs $30 per vehicle. Ranger stations are at Chelan, Cle Elum, Entiat, Leavenworth, Naches, Okanogan, Tonasket, Wenatchee and Winthrop. Information about any of the forest's areas can be obtained by writing the Okanogan Valley Office, Okanogan-Wenatchee National Forest, 1240 Second Ave. S., Okanogan, WA 98840; phone (509) 664-9200.

OLYMPIA (F-6) pop. 46,478, elev. 36'
• Hotels p. 98 • Restaurants p. 98

Settlers first arrived at Budd Inlet at the southern end of Puget Sound in the 1840s. Smithfield, the community they established, became the site of the first U.S. customhouse in the Northwest, and later was renamed Olympia for the magnificent mountains to the northwest.

Washington's capital is the starting point of the Olympic Highway (US 101), which circles the Olympic Peninsula and continues south along the Pacific coast into northern California. Passing many beach and lake resorts, this highway provides access to Olympic National Park and Olympic National Forest.

The well-known Olympia oyster is taken from Puget Sound in this vicinity. The most prolific beds are found west of town in Mud, Oyster and Big and

Little Skookum bays. In September and October salmon can be observed from the Fifth Street Bridge as they swim into Capitol Lake; the fish also can be seen going up the fish ladders on the Deschutes River in Tumwater Falls Park. The Yashiro Japanese Garden, north of Union Avenue at 1010 Plum St., commemorates Olympia's sister city relationship with Yashiro, Japan; phone (360) 753-8380.

Percival Landing Park, on the east side of Budd Bay off Olympia Avenue and Columbia Street N.W., features picnic areas, a playground, public art and a .9-mile boardwalk along the waterfront. The park offers superb views of the Olympic Mountain Range.

Olympia-Lacey-Tumwater Visitor and Convention Bureau Visitor Information Center: 103 Sid Snyder Ave. S.W., Olympia, WA 98501. **Phone:** (360) 704-7544 or (877) 704-7500.

Self-guiding tours: More than 80 installations can be seen on a self-guiding walking tour of downtown public art. Olympia also has a downtown historic district, bordered roughly east and west by Franklin and Water streets and north and south by State and 7th avenues. Pick up brochures and self-guiding tour maps at the visitor and convention bureau.

Shopping: JCPenney, Macy's and REI are the anchor stores at Capital Mall, 2 miles west on Black Lake Boulevard off US 101. The Olympia Farmers Market, 700 N. Capitol Way, is open Thurs.-Sun. 10-3, Apr.-Oct.; Sat.-Sun. 10-3, Nov.-Dec.; Sat. 10-3, rest of year.

HANDS ON CHILDREN'S MUSEUM is at 414 Jefferson St. N.E. The museum features activities and interactive displays geared to kids up to age 10, encouraging learning through hands-on play. Nine themed galleries and more than 150 exhibits focus on art, science and nature. Within the secure Outdoor Discovery Center kids can play while learning about the environment, and in Move It! they can experience the forces of gravity and friction. The museum also has an Early Development Center for toddlers and a child-oriented art studio.

Time: Allow 1 hour minimum. **Hours:** Tues.-Sat. 10-5, Sun.-Mon. 11-5. Closed Easter, July 4, Thanksgiving and Christmas. **Cost:** $12.95; $10.95 (ages

65+ and military with ID); free (ages 0-23 months). **Parking:** $1 per hour. **Phone:** (360) 956-0818. ⓉⓇ

WASHINGTON STATE CAPITOL CAMPUS is w. of I-5 exit 105 to 416 14th Ave. S.E., following signs. Occupying a hill south of downtown, it includes buildings housing state legislative, judicial and administrative offices. For visitors one of the chief attractions is the attractively landscaped grounds, dotted with imposing monuments, memorials and a replica of a Tivoli fountain.

The Legislative Building dominates. Completed in 1928, the capitol's 287-foot-tall masonry dome is one of the largest in the world. Louis Comfort Tiffany designed the chandelier that hangs in the rotunda. The oldest building is the 1908 Georgian-style Governor's Mansion, furnished with fine antiques. The tour desk inside the capitol's main entrance has campus and tour information.

Hours: Capitol building open Mon.-Fri. 7-5:30, Sat.-Sun. and holidays 11-4. Tour desk staffed Mon.-Fri. 10-4, Sat.-Sun. 11-4. Guided public tours of the capitol building depart from the tour desk on the hour Mon.-Fri. 10-3, Sat.-Sun. 11-3. Governor's Mansion tours are available most Wednesdays; reservations are required. Closed Jan. 1, Thanksgiving, day after Thanksgiving and Christmas. **Cost:** Tours free. **Parking:** $2 per hour. **Phone:** (360) 902-8880 for tour information and Governor's Mansion tour reservations, or (360) 725-0018 for botanical tour information. ⒼⓉ

WATER EDUCATION & TECHNOLOGY (WET) SCIENCE CENTER, on the ground floor of the LOTT building at 500 Adams St. N.E., showcases the importance of water with interactive exhibits as well as special activities on Saturdays. Exhibits cover a variety of themes including conservation, wastewater treatment, reclaimed water and the water cycle.

Guided tours of the adjacent Budd Inlet Treatment Plant are offered by appointment; closed-toe shoes are required. **Time:** Allow 30 minutes minimum. **Hours:** Mon.-Sat. 10-4. Closed major holidays. Children under age 10 are not permitted on Budd Inlet Treatment Plant tours. **Cost:** Free. **Parking:** Free in small lot on Thurston Ave. **Phone:** (360) 664-2333. ⒼⓉ Ⓐ

DOUBLETREE BY HILTON-OLYMPIA   (360)570-0555

Hotel
$99-$239

DoubleTree
BY HILTON

AAA Benefit:
Members save 5% or more!

Address: 415 Capitol Way N 98501 **Location:** I-5 exit 105 (City Center) northbound; exit 105A southbound, 0.4 mi w on 14th Ave, then 0.8 mi n. **Facility:** 102 units. 3 stories, interior corridors. **Terms:** check-in 4 pm, 1-7 night minimum stay, 3 day cancellation notice-fee imposed. **Amenities:** safes. **Pool:** heated indoor. **Activities:** hot tub, exercise room. **Guest Services:** valet laundry. *(See ad this page.)*

[SAVE] [CALL] [&] [icons] [BIZ] [wifi] [X] [icons]

HAMPTON INN & SUITES BY HILTON OLYMPIA-LACEY
360/459-5000

Hotel. **Address:** 4301 Martin Way E 98516

AAA Benefit:
Members save 5% or more!

HILTON GARDEN INN OLYMPIA   360/236-9934

Hotel. **Address:** 2101 Henderson Park Ln SE 98501

AAA Benefit:
Members save 5% or more!

HOTEL RL OLYMPIA   360/943-4000

Hotel. **Address:** 2300 Evergreen Park Dr SW 98502

For complete hotel, dining and attraction listings:

AAA.com/travelguides

RAMADA OLYMPIA   (360)459-8866

Hotel
$116-$149

Address: 4520 Martin Way E 98516 **Location:** I-5 exit 109, just sw. **Facility:** 125 units, some efficiencies. 4 stories, interior corridors. **Pool:** heated indoor. **Activities:** hot tub, exercise room. **Guest Services:** valet and coin laundry. **Featured Amenity:** full hot breakfast.

[SAVE] [icons] [BIZ] [HS] [wifi] [X] [icons]

TOWNEPLACE SUITES BY MARRIOTT OLYMPIA
(360)753-8770

Extended Stay Hotel. **Address:** 900 Capitol Way S 98501

AAA Benefit:
Members save 5% or more!

WHERE TO EAT

ANTHONY'S HEARTHFIRE GRILL NORTHPOINT OLYMPIA
360/705-3473

American. Casual Dining. **Address:** 1675 Marine Dr NE 98501

ANTHONY'S HOMEPORT OLYMPIA   360/357-9700

Seafood. Casual Dining. **Address:** 704 Columbia St NW 98501

BASILICO RISTORANTE ITALIANO   360/570-8777

Traditional Italian. Fine Dining. **Address:** 507 Capitol Way S 98501

GARDNER'S RESTAURANT   360/786-8466

Italian Seafood. Casual Dining. **Address:** 111 Thurston Ave NW 98501

GREAT CUISINE OF INDIA   360/943-3442

Indian. Casual Dining. **Address:** 116 4th Ave W 98501

MCMENAMINS SPAR CAFE   360/357-6444

American. Casual Dining. **Address:** 114 4th Ave E 98501

▼ See AAA listing this page ▼

DoubleTree BY HILTON OLYMPIA

415 Capitol Way N., Olympia, WA 98501

- Indoor Pool & Hot Tub
- Press NW Bistro & Bar
- 24 Hour Fitness by Precor
- 24 Hour Business Center
- Wireless High-Speed Internet Access
- Premium HD TV Channels (HBO, CNN & ESPN)
- Downtown Waterfront Location

DoubleTree by Hilton – Olympia
360-570-0555

Olympia.doubletree.com

MERCATO RISTORANTE   360/528-3663
♥♥ Italian. Casual Dining. **Address:** 111 Market St NE 98501

RAMBLIN' JACK'S   360/754-8909
♥♥ American. Casual Dining. **Address:** 520 4th Ave E 98501

OLYMPIC NATIONAL FOREST (D-5, E-1)

Elevations in the forest range from sea level at Hood Canal to 6,988 ft. at Buckhorn Mountain. Refer to AAA maps for additional elevation information.

The 633,600-acre Olympic National Forest, on the Olympic Peninsula, is noted for its rugged mountain terrain, lush rain forests and glacial streams. Roosevelt elk, deer and bears are among the large mammals inhabiting the forest; prominent trees are Douglas fir, western red cedar, western hemlock and big-leaf maple. There also are outstanding seasonal display of rhododendrons and wildflowers.

There are more than 200 miles of trails, with some overlapping into Olympic National Park. Pets are permitted on forest trails. Trout fishing is popular; hunting is permitted in season. Most recreation sites are open May through October. Evidence of early mining activities, railroad logging and exploration remains. *See Recreation Areas Chart.*

Of special interest is the Quinault Rain Forest. Two loop trails into the rain forest begin at the nature trail parking lot off South Shore Road, 2 miles off US 101 at Lake Quinault. Five wilderness areas encompass thousands of acres; Buckhorn is the largest. Permits are not needed to enter the wilderness areas; however, motorized vehicles are not permitted.

The Steel Bridge is 8 miles west of US 101 on Skokomish Valley Road, then 2.4 miles north on gravel FR 2340. It stands 420 feet above the basalt-lined canyon of Vance Creek. Built by the Simpson Timber Co. in 1929 as part of its logging railway, the span was opened to vehicle use in 1964.

Panoramas of the Olympics, Hood Canal and Puget Sound reward a trek to the Mount Walker viewpoint, accessible by a gravel road off US 101 south of Quilcene. Also exceptionally scenic is Seal Rock Beach, along the Hood Canal 2 miles north of Brinnon.

Access is free. A Northwest Forest Pass, available at ranger stations, is required for parking at most trailheads. A day pass costs $5 per vehicle; an annual pass costs $30 per vehicle. Ranger stations are located at Forks, Quilcene and Quinault. For further information contact the Olympic National Forest Supervisor's Office, 1835 Black Lake Blvd. S.W., Suite A, Olympia, WA 98512-5623; phone (360) 956-2402, (360) 956-3203 or TTY (360) 956-2401.

OLYMPIC NATIONAL PARK (E-1)

• Hotels p. 103 • Restaurants p. 103
• Attractions map p. 102

Elevations in the park range from sea level along 73 miles of coastline to 7,980 ft. at Mount Olympus. Refer to AAA maps for additional elevation information.

US 101 forms an inverted U shape encompassing Olympic National Park and the adjacent Olympic National Forest. Paved entrance roads include Hurricane Ridge Road, off Race Street/Mt. Angeles Road in Port Angeles; Olympic Hot Springs Road, 8 miles southwest of Port Angeles; Sol Duc Road, west of Lake Crescent; Hoh Road, 13 miles south of Forks; and North and South Shore roads, along Lake Quinault.

Unpaved roads off US 101 include Deer Park Road, east of Port Angeles, not for use by trailers or recreational vehicles; Queets Road, east of Queets; Staircase Road, west of Hoodsport; and Dosewallips Road (closed due to washout; accessible only on foot or bicycle), west of Brinnon. All of these roads end fewer than 20 miles into the park; due to rugged terrain and to preserve the wilderness, no roads pass through the park's interior.

Olympic National Park is a scenic wilderness of 922,650 acres extending from glacier-clad mountains to ocean shore. Ranging between these borders are coniferous rain forests, glaciers, lakes and streams as well as 73 miles of unspoiled coastline. The wilderness area encompasses the interior of the Olympic Peninsula, between Hood Canal on the east and the Pacific Ocean on the west.

Mount Olympus, at 7,980 feet, is the highest of the park's mountains, which rise within 35 miles of the coast. The range is extremely rugged, with spectacular cliffs and crags and deep, forested valleys. On the upper slopes are glaciers unusual for their formation at such a relatively low elevation and latitude.

Magnificent stands of Sitka spruce, Douglas fir, western hemlock and western red cedar cover the lower mountainsides. On the upper slopes near the timberline, Alaska cedar, mountain hemlock and subalpine fir intermingle with alpine meadows. More than 600 miles of trails run through virgin forests and along stream banks in narrow valleys to ridgetops and mountain passes.

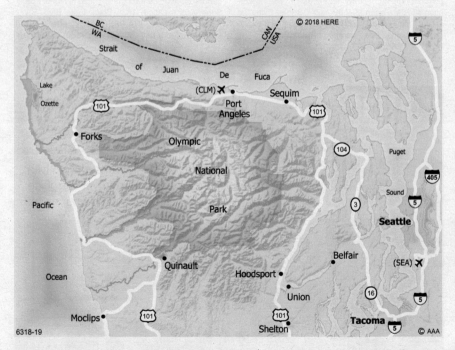

This map shows cities in Olympic National Park where you will find attractions, hotels and restaurants. Cities are listed alphabetically in this book on the following pages.

Snowfall might make passage on some trails difficult; check with the visitor centers and ranger stations in the park. Only experienced mountain climbers should attempt to scale the park's challenging peaks. The Olympic high country can be reached by automobile only from the north side where roads lead to subalpine meadows at Deer Park *(see attraction listing this page)* and Hurricane Ridge *(see attraction listing this page)*.

Rainfall averaging some 140 inches annually nourishes a lush temperate rain forest in the western valleys of the park. The most interesting of these centuries-old forests are found in the valleys of the Hoh, Quinault, Bogachiel and Queets rivers.

The area teems with wildlife. Of the 6,500 elk estimated to inhabit the peninsula, 5,000 are in the park, chiefly on the western slope of the mountains. Blacktail deer and many smaller mammals are common throughout the park. Hunting is prohibited. Among the great variety of birds in the park is the bald eagle.

General Information and Activities

Though the park is open all year, parts of the high country are usually closed by snow from early fall until July. The streams of the Olympic Mountains offer fine fishing; salmon fishing is excellent in the Strait of Juan de Fuca and the ocean. No license is required for fishing within the park boundaries, but steelhead trout and salmon punch cards are required in season; check with the visitor center regarding park fishing regulations. Sol Duc Hot Springs is in the Sol Duc Valley, 12 miles southeast of US 101 *(see attraction listing p. 103)*.

A number of self-guiding nature trails have been developed throughout the park. Rangers/naturalists give interpretive talks late June through Labor Day; check with the visitor centers for schedules. Visitor centers are open all year at Port Angeles and the Hoh Rain Forest. The Kalaloch center is open daily late May-late September. The Storm King (Lake Crescent) ranger station is open mid-June to mid-September; phone for schedule. The Hurricane Ridge Center is open daily, mid-June to mid-September, and also the rest of the year when Hurricane Ridge Road is open. Road conditions prohibit the passage of trailers in some areas of the park. *See Recreation Areas Chart.*

ADMISSION is $30 per vehicle, good for up to 7 consecutive days anywhere in the park. An entrance fee of $25 is charged for those arriving on motorcycle and $15 for those on foot or bicycle. An Olympic Park Annual Pass costs $55. Camping fees range $15-$22. A permit fee of $8 per person per night is charged to camp overnight in the park's back-country wilderness; an annual wilderness pass is $45 per person.

PETS are permitted in developed areas only. Pets must be leashed and may not be left unattended or tied to a stationary object. Leashed pets are permitted only during daylight hours on beaches from Rialto Beach north to Ellen Creek and the beaches between the Hoh and Quinault Indian reservations.

ADDRESS inquiries to the Park Superintendent's Office, Olympic National Park, 600 E. Park Ave., Port Angeles, WA 98362; phone (360) 565-3130, or (360) 565-3131 for recorded road and weather information.

DEER PARK, in Olympic National Park, can be reached via a 17-mi., mountainous, mostly unpaved road 5 mi. e. of Port Angeles; the road is not recommended for trailers. The parkland is mostly subalpine meadow. A short trail leads to the summit of 6,007-foot Blue Mountain, which affords views of the Dungeness Valley, Olympic Mountains, Strait of Juan de Fuca, Vancouver Island and the San Juan Islands.

Hours: Daily 24 hours. The access road is usually closed Oct. to mid-June; check for conditions before starting out. Ranger station hours vary and are posted on the bulletin board at the park entrance. **Cost:** Park admission, valid for 7 days, $25 (per private vehicle); $15 (per motorcycle); $10 (per person arriving on foot or bicycle); free (ages 0-16). **Phone:** (360) 565-3130, or (360) 565-3131 for road conditions, weather information and activities.

ELWHA RIVER VALLEY, in Olympic National Park, is accessible via a paved road off US 101, 8 mi. w. of Port Angeles. The valley extends for 45 miles from the river's headwaters near Mount Olympus to its outlet into the Strait of Juan de Fuca. With the removal of the Glines Canyon Dam, restoration of the Elwha River watershed is currently ongoing. Olympic Hot Springs Road leads to the Glines Canyon Spillway Overlook, the area once flooded by the dam. Interpretive exhibits detail the area's history and ongoing restoration process. Whiskey Bend Road, a 4.5-mile dirt road just past the Elwha Ranger Station, offers access to a trailhead. **Cost:** Park admission, valid for 7 days, $25 (per private vehicle); $15 (per motorcycle); $10 (per person arriving on foot or bicycle); free (ages 0-16). **Phone:** (360) 565-3130, or (360) 565-3131 for road conditions, weather information and activities.

HOH RAIN FOREST, in Olympic National Park, can be reached via a 18-mi. paved road off US 101, 13 mi. s. of Forks. A visitor center features informative displays and serves as a departure point for several self-guiding nature trails, including the frequently photographed Hall of Mosses Trail. **Time:** Allow 1 hour minimum. **Hours:** Visitor center daily 9-5, May-Sept.; hours vary rest of year. **Cost:** Visitor center free. Park admission, valid for 7 days, $25 (per private vehicle); $15 (per motorcycle); $10 (per person arriving on foot or bicycle); free (ages 0-16). **Phone:** (360) 374-6925.

HURRICANE RIDGE, in Olympic National Park, can be reached from Port Angeles via Hurricane Ridge Rd., a roadway with a 7-percent grade. More than 5,200 feet above sea level, Hurricane Ridge features a visitor center from which there are striking views of the Olympic Mountains.

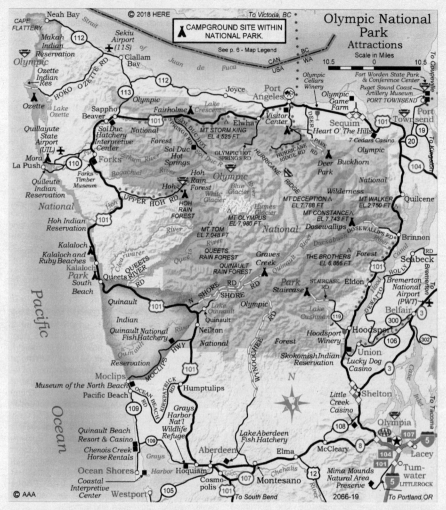

Olympic National Park Attractions

CAMPGROUND SITE WITHIN NATIONAL PARK.

See p. 6 - Map Legend

Scale in Miles

© 2018 HERE

© AAA

2066-19

Nature trails wind through the meadows, where wildflowers bloom from late June through October, and lead to views of the Strait of Juan de Fuca and Vancouver Island. A narrow gravel road leads 8 miles east along the crest to Obstruction Peak.

Naturalist programs are conducted daily from late June through Labor Day. During the ski season rentals and rope tow service are available on weekends (weather permitting). The winter use area also provides cross-country ski and snowshoe trails. **Hours:** Visitor center open daily 9-5, mid-June to mid-Sept. Schedule varies otherwise. **Cost:** Visitor center free. Park admission, valid for 7 days, $25 (per private vehicle); $15 (per motorcycle); $10 (per person arriving on foot or bicycle); free (ages 0-16). **Phone:** (360) 565-3130, or (360) 565-3131 for road conditions, weather information and activities.

KALALOCH AND RUBY BEACHES, in Olympic National Park, can be reached by short trails off US 101 n. of Queets. These are two of the park's most accessible beach areas. Kalaloch, southernmost of the two, has a campground and offers cliff-top views of the coast. Ruby Beach, with its sea arches and offshore islands, is more of a wilderness beach. Smaller beaches in the vicinity are designated by numbers. **Cost:** Park admission, valid for 7 days, $25 (per private vehicle); $15 (per motorcycle); $10 (per person arriving on foot or bicycle); free (ages 0-16). **Phone:** (360) 565-3130, or (360) 565-3131 for road conditions, weather information and activities.

LAKE CRESCENT, in Olympic National Park, is 17 mi. w. of Port Angeles on US 101 to 416 Lake Crescent Rd. This deep freshwater lake was carved by glaciers. Surrounded by high mountains, including 4,534-foot Mt. Storm King, the lake is 12 miles long and 624 feet deep. Near the midpoint just off US 101 is the trailhead for the 1-mile Marymere Falls Trail, an easy hike through dense old-growth forest habitat that leads to 90-foot Marymere Falls. **Cost:** Park admission, valid for 7 days, $25 (per private vehicle); $15 (per motorcycle); $10 (per person arriving on foot or bicycle); free (ages 0-16). **Phone:** (360) 565-3130, or (360) 565-3131 for road conditions, weather information and activities.

LAKE QUINAULT is in the s.w. corner of Olympic National Park and accessible via US 101. The Quinault River rises in the peninsula's interior and flows into 3-mile-long Lake Quinault at an elevation of less than 200 feet above sea level with peaks rising to 4,000 feet surrounding the valley.

Annual rainfall in this region can top 140 inches, which supports a lush temperate rain forest—Douglas fir, Sitka spruce, big-leaf maple and red alder as well as a profusion of mosses, lichens and ferns. The North Shore Road runs east from US 101 along the lake to the Quinault Rain Forest Ranger Station, where the half-mile Maple Glade Rain Forest Trail loops through dense woodlands. **Hours:** Forest Service/Park Service ranger station open Sun.-Thurs. 8-5, Fri.-Sat. 9-6, Memorial Day weekend-Labor Day; hours vary rest of year. **Cost:** Park admission, valid for 7 days, $25 (per private vehicle); $15 (per motorcycle); $10 (per person arriving on foot or bicycle); free (ages 0-16). **Phone:** (360) 288-2444.

OLYMPIC NATIONAL PARK VISITOR CENTER is s. of US 101 via Race St., at 3002 Mount Angeles Rd. The visitor center provides park information, a 25-minute orientation video and a hands-on discovery area for children. Displays relate to wildlife, plants, geology and Northwest Coast Native American culture. Two nature trails are on the premises, one accessible to the physically impaired. **Hours:** Daily 8:30-5, Labor Day-Memorial Day; 9-4, rest of year. Closed Thanksgiving and Christmas. **Cost:** Park admission, valid for 7 days, $25 (per private vehicle); $15 (per motorcycle); $10 (per person arriving on foot or bicycle); free (ages 0-16). **Phone:** (360) 565-3130, or (360) 565-3131 for road conditions, weather information and activities.

RIALTO BEACH, in Olympic National Park, is 14 mi. w. of Forks off SR 110 to Mora Road, following signs. Piles of sun-bleached driftwood lie in twisted heaps on this beach, with huge logs at the extreme high tide line. Climb past the logs and you'll be treated to scenic views of rough surf and sea stacks—giant rock pinnacles with stunted trees growing from their tops—that rise 50 feet or more above the water.

A 1.5-mile hike north along the beach leads to Hole-in-the-Wall, a rocky arch carved by the sea. Check tide tables before visiting, as low tide provides the best opportunity for viewing tide-pool critters and the rocky arch. **Cost:** Park admission, valid for 7 days, $25 (per private vehicle); $15 (per motorcycle); $10 (per person arriving on foot or bicycle); free (ages 0-16). **Phone:** (360) 565-3130, or (360) 565-3131 for road conditions and weather information.

SOL DUC HOT SPRINGS is in Olympic National Park's Sol Duc Valley, 30 mi. w. of Port Angeles and 12 mi. s.e. of US 101. Natural mineral water flows from the springs at a temperature of 128 F and is piped into three outdoor pools ranging in temperature from 99 F to 104 F. Lodging, campsites and RV facilities are available. **Hours:** Pools open daily 9-8, late Mar.-late Oct. **Cost:** Pools $15; $10 (ages 4-12, ages 62+, military with ID and the physically impaired). Pool admission beginning 2 hours before closing $10. Park admission, valid for 7 days, $25 (per private vehicle); $15 (per motorcycle); $10 (per person arriving on foot or bicycle); free (ages 0-16). Locker rental $3.25. Towel rental $3.25. **Phone:** (360) 327-3583 or (800) 204-3116.

KALALOCH LODGE   360/962-2271
Cabin. **Address:** 157151 Hwy 101 98331

WHERE TO EAT

CREEKSIDE DINING ROOM   360/962-2271
American. Casual Dining. **Address:** 157151 Hwy 101 98331

THE SPRINGS RESTAURANT   360/327-3583
American. Casual Dining. **Address:** 12076 Sol Duc Hot Springs Rd 98363

OMAK (D-9) pop. 4,845, elev. 837'

A sister city to Okanogan, Omak derives its name from the Salish word *omache,* meaning "good medicine." Apple orchards are a prime business, as is the growing of baby's breath, a florist industry staple.

Eastside Park *(see Recreation Areas Chart)* is a quarter-mile west of Main Street on Omak Avenue. Nearby attractions reminiscent of the past include several ghost towns that hark back to gold rush days.

Omak Visitor Information Center: 401 Omak Ave., Omak, WA 98841. **Phone:** (509) 826-4218 or (800) 225-6625.

BEST WESTERN PLUS PEPPERTREE INN AT OMAK
(509)422-2088

Hotel
$99-$399

Best Western PLUS

AAA Benefit: Members save up to 15% and earn bonus points!

Address: 820 Koala Ave 98841 **Location:** US 97, just n of Riverside Dr. **Facility:** 117 units, some two bedrooms. 4 stories, interior corridors. **Parking:** winter plug-ins. **Pool:** heated indoor. **Activities:** hot tub, exercise room. **Guest Services:** coin laundry.

WHERE TO EAT

BREADLINE CAFE   509/826-5836
American. Casual Dining. **Address:** 102 S Ash St 98841

RANCHO CHICO   509/826-4757
♥♥ Mexican. Casual Dining. **Address:** 22 N Main St 98841

ORCAS ISLAND (B-1)

One of the islands that make up the San Juan Islands, Orcas Island also is among the largest and most rugged. Washington State Ferries docks at the village of Orcas on the southern shore; phone (206) 464-6400 or (888) 808-7977. Eastsound, at the head of Orcas Island's largest bay, is the major town. Historic buildings now house local commercial enterprises, including the Outlook Inn, which incorporates parts of a fur trappers cottage built in 1838. The Emmanuel Episcopal Church, 242 Main St., dates from 1886; phone (360) 376-2352.

Wildlife Cycles, 350 N. Beach Rd. in Eastsound, offers rental bicycles year-round for self-guiding tours; phone (360) 376-4708.

Turtleback Mountain Preserve lies on the west side of Orcas Island and comprises grasslands, oak woodlands, conifer forests and wetlands. The 1,578-acre preserve's high elevation allows for spectacular views of the Canadian Gulf and San Juan Islands. Visitors can hike on two trails, and bird-watching is a popular activity. Phone (360) 378-4402 for more information.

The Orcas Island Farmers Market sets up Saturdays 10-3 off North Beach Road in Eastsound, May through September, and Saturdays 11-2 at the Odd Fellows Hall at 112 Haven St., October through November. Local farmers offer organic fruits and veggies while artisans showcase handcrafted jewelry, soaps, candles, pottery and art.

Orcas Island Chamber of Commerce and Visitor Center: 65 N. Beach Rd., Eastsound, WA 98245. **Phone:** (360) 376-2273.

THE FUNHOUSE COMMONS is in the village of Eastsound at 30 Pea Patch Ln. (look for the green exterior). This community center is not only a safe haven for kids but a great place to spend a rainy afternoon. There are loads of activities to keep children occupied: hands-on science exhibits; a computer lab; interactive exhibits about sports, geography, music, history and the human body; an art studio; and a climbing wall. Drop-in art classes and various workshops are held throughout the year.

Children under 8 years of age must be accompanied by an adult. **Time:** Allow 2 hours minimum. **Hours:** Mon.-Fri. 1-5, July-Aug.; Mon.-Fri. 3-5:30, rest of year. **Cost:** One-day pass $10; free (ages 0-6); $15 (family, two adults and dependent children). **Phone:** (360) 376-7177. 🎨

🔻 **MORAN STATE PARK** is at 3572 Olga Rd., 13 mi. n.e. of the Orcas village ferry dock via Horseshoe Hwy. One of Washington's scenic gems, this 5,252-acre park occupies land donated in 1920 by former Seattle mayor and shipbuilder Robert Moran. Cloaked in a forest of Douglas fir, western red cedar and western hemlock, it features five freshwater lakes, waterfalls and 2,409-foot Mount

Constitution, the highest peak in the San Juan Islands. Paved roads connect the major sites; hikers, mountain bikers and horseback riders use the 38-mile network of trails, most built by the Civilian Conservation Corps (CCC) in the 1930s.

The day-use area at Cascade Lake has a short interpretive trail. Paddleboat, canoe, kayak and electric-powered fishing boat rentals are available Memorial Day weekend to Labor Day. An easy 2.7-mile trail encircles the lake. Mt. Constitution Road leads to the top of its namesake peak, passing other attractions en route. Cascade Falls is accessible via a short trail. The 100-foot drop, set in an amphitheater of mossy woods, is the highest in the San Juans. Three other waterfalls are within a 0.6-mile hike. Mountain Lake, the park's largest, contains four small islands. An easy 3.9-mile loop trail follows its shoreline.

Beyond Mountain Lake the road ascends the steep flank of Mt. Constitution via a series of six switchbacks. The upper switchbacks offer sweeping views. This narrow roadway is open daylight hours only and is not recommended for trailers or motor homes; it is occasionally closed in winter due to snow.

At the road's end a short trail leads through a forest of lodgepole pine to one of the Northwest's iconic views. Here at the summit the CCC erected a 50-foot observation tower out of native sandstone. Modeled after a 12th-century watchtower in the Caucasus Mountains of southern Russia, its upper levels offer a 360-degree panorama encompassing islands, saltwater channels, the Cascades and the Olympic mountains. The lower two levels contain historical displays about Robert Moran, the establishment of the park, the CCC's labors and the area's natural history. *See Recreation Areas Chart.*

Note: The trail from Cascade Lake to Cascade Falls is closed on and off for reforesting projects; phone ahead to confirm schedule. **Time:** Allow 2 hours minimum. **Hours:** Daily 6:30 a.m.-10 p.m., May-Sept.; 8-dusk, rest of year. **Cost:** Park admission $10 (per private vehicle). **Phone:** (360) 376-2326 or (360) 902-8844. 🅰 🍴 🚫 🐕 🏕

ORCAS ISLAND ECLIPSE CHARTERS AND WHALE WATCH TOURS meets at the Orcas ferry dock, 8368 Orcas Rd. The MV *Orcas Express* tracks orca whales around the San Juan Islands. Other possible sightings include eagles, harbor seals, minke whales, humpback whales, porpoises and seabirds. **Time:** Allow 3 hours, 30 minutes minimum. **Hours:** Cruises depart daily at 12:30, June-Oct.; Fri.-Sun. at 12:30, Apr.-May. Phone ahead to confirm schedule. **Cost:** Fare $99; $64 (ages 3-12); $40 (ages 9 months-3 years). Reservations are required. **Phone:** (360) 376-6566 or (800) 376-6566. 🅶🆃

OUTER ISLAND EXPEDITIONS meets in the main office of Smuggler's Villa Resort, 54 Hunt Rd. Three- to 5-hour whale-watching excursions around the San Juan Islands offer a chance to see bald eagles, otters, seals, porpoises, sea lions and orca, gray, minke and humpback whales. Three-hour and full-day guided kayak tours also are offered.

Hours: Whale-watch tours depart daily at 1 and 5, mid-Apr. through Oct. 31. Three-hour kayak tours depart daily at 10 and 2. Full-day kayak tours depart daily at 9. Phone ahead for schedule rest of year and to confirm departure times. **Cost:** Whale-watch tour $99-$109; $79-$89 (ages 13-17); $59-$69 (ages 7-12); $48-$59 (ages 0-6). Kayak tour $79-$159; $45-$99 (ages 12-16). **Phone:** (360) 376-3711 or (360) 622-6562. [GT]

DEER HARBOR INN   360/376-4110
♥♥ Country Inn. **Address:** 33 Inn Ln 98243

THE INN ON ORCAS ISLAND   360/376-5227
♥♥♥ Bed & Breakfast. **Address:** 114 Channel Rd 98243

LANDMARK ORCAS ISLAND   (360)376-2423
♥♥ Condominium. **Address:** 67 Main St 98245

OTTERS POND BED & BREAKFAST ON ORCAS ISLAND
                                             (360)376-8844
♥♥♥ Bed & Breakfast. **Address:** 100 Tomihi Dr 98245

OUTLOOK INN ON ORCAS ISLAND   (360)376-2200
♥♥ Historic Hotel. **Address:** 171 Main St 98245

TURTLEBACK FARM INN   (360)376-4914
♥♥♥
**Historic Bed
& Breakfast**
$125-$260

Address: 1981 Crow Valley Rd 98245 **Location:** In Eastsound; 4 mi sw of Eastsound on Orcas Rd. Located near Turtleback Mountain Preserve. **Facility:** The lovely restored 1895 farmhouse and annex building sits on 80 acres of forest, ponds and open pasture land. Guests can choose from a wide variety of room styles and sizes. 11 units. 2 stories (no elevator), interior corridors. **Terms:** 2 night minimum stay - seasonal and/or weekends, 15 day cancellation notice-fee imposed. **Featured Amenity: full hot breakfast.**

[SAVE] 🛜 ✕ 🅺 🆆 🅩 / SOME UNITS 🐾 🛗 🖥 📶

WHERE TO EAT

DEER HARBOR INN RESTAURANT   360/376-1040
♥♥ American. Casual Dining. **Address:** 33 Inn Ln 98243

MADRONA BAR & GRILL   360/376-7171
♥♥ American. Casual Dining. **Address:** 310 Main St 98245

NEW LEAF CAFE   360/376-2200
♥♥ American. Casual Dining. **Address:** 171 Main St 98245

ROSE'S BAKERY & CAFE   360/376-4292
♥♥ American. Casual Dining. **Address:** 382 Prune Alley 98245

OROVILLE (C-9) pop. 1,686, elev. 913'

Set in a deep valley flanked by high ridges, Oroville takes its name from the Spanish word for gold for good reason: A strike found near the mouth of the Similkameen River in 1861 resulted in the establishment of the boom town. The arrival of the railroad in 1914 and the construction of irrigation works eventually turned the economic focus to commercial

orchards, the first of which was planted in 1858 by prospector Hiram Smith. Today most of the bounty is in the form of locally grown apples.

The Oroville district also is an emerging wine-producing region, and four wineries in town offer tastings. There are recreational facilities at nearby Osoyoos Lake Veteran's Memorial Park *(see Recreation Areas Chart).*

Oroville Visitor Welcome Center: in the Oroville Depot Museum at 1210 Ironwood St., Oroville, WA 98844. **Phone:** (509) 476-2739 early May to mid-Sept. or (888) 699-5659.

OLD MOLSON GHOST TOWN MUSEUM is 10 mi. e. on Oroville-Chesaw Rd., then 5 mi. n. to 521 Molson Rd. A 5-acre town site founded as a mining venture in 1900, the museum features a collection of early-20th-century buildings including a bank, an assay office and three houses. On display are mining and farming equipment. A church, relocated here in 1922, is 1 block north. **Time:** Allow 1 hour minimum. **Hours:** Daily dawn-dusk, Apr.-Nov. (weather permitting). Molson Schoolhouse Museum daily 10-5, Memorial Day-Labor Day. **Cost:** Donations. **Phone:** (509) 485-3292.

Molson Schoolhouse Museum is 10 mi. e. on Oroville-Chesaw Rd., then 5 mi. n. to 539 Molson Rd. Housed in a 1914 brick school, the museum houses four floors of exhibits and contains several schoolrooms and the original library. Displays feature a horse-drawn equipment, clothing, hand tools, furniture, paintings, player pianos and various pioneer household appliances. **Time:** Allow 1 hour minimum. **Hours:** Daily 10-5, Memorial Day weekend-Labor Day. **Cost:** Donations. **Phone:** (509) 485-3292.

OTHELLO (F-10) pop. 7,364, elev. 1,038'
• Restaurants p. 106

Founded on a Northern Pacific branch rail line in 1902, Othello was named for the Shakespeare play. The town, located in the heart of the Columbia Basin Project, boomed when irrigation waters transformed the surrounding desertlike environment into a productive farming region. Potatoes are a principal crop.

Greater Othello Chamber of Commerce: 33 E. Larch St., P.O. Box 2813, Othello, WA 99344. **Phone:** (509) 488-2683.

QUALITY INN OTHELLO   (509)488-5671
♥♥♥
Hotel
$90-$130

Address: 1020 E Cedar St 99344 **Location:** Jct E Main St and N 10th Ave. **Facility:** 50 units, some efficiencies. 2 stories (no elevator), interior corridors. **Pool:** heated outdoor. **Activities:** sauna, exercise room. **Guest Services:** coin laundry. **Featured Amenity: continental breakfast.**

[SAVE] 🛜 🌊 [BIZ] 🛜 🛗 🖥
📶 / SOME UNITS 🐾

WHERE TO EAT

IRONWORKS CAFE   509/592-9710
▼▼▼ Sandwiches Soup. Casual Dining. **Address:** 335 S Broadway Ave 99344

PACKWOOD pop. 342

COWLITZ RIVER LODGE   (360)494-4444
▼▼ Motel. **Address:** 13069 US 12 98361

CREST TRAIL LODGE   (360)494-4944

| ▼▼▼ Hotel $120-$160 | **Address:** 12729 US 12 98361 **Location:** West end of town. **Facility:** 27 units. 2 stories (no elevator), interior corridors. **Featured Amenity: continental breakfast.** |

SAVE 🛜 ✖ 🛏 🖼 🖳 / SOME UNITS 🐾

PASCO (G-10) pop. 59,781, elev. 380'

Oldest of the Tri-Cities, Pasco traces its beginnings to the 1879 railroad camp of Ainsworth. A construction engineer renamed the settlement for the Peruvian mining town of Cerro de Pasco. Pasco has been a rail center since its early days, and the sprawling BNSF Railway yards still dominate the city's east side. The strategic location at the confluence of the Yakima, Snake and Columbia rivers did not go unnoticed by Lewis and Clark as they passed through the area on their epic expedition decades earlier; the Corps of Discovery camped at the mouth of the Snake River on Oct. 16-17, 1805.

The Tri-Cities form eastern Washington's second largest urban area. Favored with a sunny climate and a brief winter season, this has long been a productive agricultural region. Vineyards in particular proliferate in all directions. A combination of hot summer days, cool nights and rich volcanic soils creates a perfect *terroir* for crafting premium wines. The Columbia Valley American Viticultural Area (AVA) surrounds the Tri-Cities. More than 160 wineries are within an hour's drive, making this a popular base for wine touring.

Downtown Pasco has become the retail hub for the region's sizable Hispanic population. Spanish-language signs and a multitude of ethnic shops and restaurants give it the feel of a small Mexican city. The white-domed Franklin County Courthouse faces shady Volunteer Park, a nice spot for a picnic. On display in the park is a vintage Northern Pacific steam locomotive.

Baseball fans enjoy Tri-City Dust Devils Northwest League Short Season Class A home games at Pasco's Gesa Stadium from late June to early September; phone (509) 544-8789.

The Pasco Farmers Market sets up downtown at Fourth Avenue and Columbia Street. This open-air produce market, the state's largest, is open Wednesday and Saturday mornings from May through October.

BECHTEL NATIONAL PLANETARIUM is off Farm Rd., on the campus of Columbia Basin College (park in the lot next to the soccer fields); the planetarium entrance is on the e. side of Building D, 2600 N. 20th Ave. Housed in a large cylindrical structure, it utilizes a state-of-the-art Spitz SciDome XD projection system and a 36-foot diameter hemispherical projection surface that displays lifelike, extra high-definition images. One-hour shows include a 20- to 30-minute live presentation followed by a 25- to 30-minute full-dome film.

Hours: Presentations are shown Fri. at 7 and 8 p.m., Sat. at 2 and 3. Additional shows are occasionally scheduled. Planetarium opens 30 minutes prior to first show. **Cost:** Double feature $10; $8 (ages 60+); $4.50 (ages 6-12). Single show $6; $5 (ages 60+); $3 (ages 6-12). **Phone:** (509) 542-4515.

FRANKLIN COUNTY HISTORICAL MUSEUM is at 305 N. Fourth Ave. The museum, housed in the former 1910 Carnegie Library, presents exhibits relating to Native American artifacts, the Lewis and Clark expedition, agriculture, railroading and river and air transportation. **Hours:** Tues.-Fri. noon-4, every other Sat. 9:30-3:30. **Cost:** $5; $3 (ages 65+ and active duty military and veterans with ID); $1 (students); free (ages 0-5). **Phone:** (509) 547-3714.

BEST WESTERN PLUS PASCO INN & SUITES
    (509)543-7722

▼▼▼ Hotel $130-$350

 Best Western PLUS **AAA Benefit:** Members save up to 15% and earn bonus points!

Address: 2811 N 20th Ave 99301 **Location:** I-182 exit 12B, just n. **Facility:** 110 units. 3 stories, interior corridors. **Terms:** cancellation fee imposed. **Amenities:** safes. **Pool:** heated indoor. **Activities:** sauna, hot tub, exercise room. **Guest Services:** valet and coin laundry, area transportation. **Featured Amenity: full hot breakfast.**

SAVE ✖ CALL 📞 🔁 👶 BIZ
HS 🛜 ✖ 🛏 🖼 🖳 / SOME UNITS 🐾

HAMPTON INN & SUITES BY HILTON PASCO   509/792-1660
▼▼▼ Contemporary Hotel. **Address:** 6826 Burden Blvd 99301
AAA Benefit: Members save 5% or more!

HOLIDAY INN EXPRESS PASCO/TRI-CITIES AT TRAC
    509/543-7000
▼▼▼ Hotel. **Address:** 4525 Convention Pl 99301

MY PLACE HOTEL PASCO   509/545-2186
▼▼ Extended Stay Hotel. **Address:** 6830 Rodeo Dr 99301

RED LION HOTEL PASCO   509/547-0701
▼▼▼ Hotel. **Address:** 2525 N 20th Ave 99301

SLEEP INN BY CHOICE HOTELS PASCO   (509)545-9554
▼▼ Hotel. **Address:** 9930 Bedford St 99301

WHERE TO EAT

COUSINS' RESTAURANT & SALOON PASCO   509/543-9925
▼▼ American. Casual Dining. **Address:** 4605 Rd 68 99301

FIESTA MEXICAN RESTAURANT   509/543-6884
▼▼ Mexican. Casual Dining. **Address:** 5210 N Road 68 #L 99301

MAGILL'S RESTAURANT   509/547-6448
▼▼ American. Casual Dining. **Address:** 3214 Road 68 99301

PATEROS (D-9) pop. 667, elev. 776'

Located on the Columbia River just above the confluence with the Methow River, Pateros was founded in 1895. First called Ives Landing, the name was changed in 1900 to honor a town in the Philippines where a pioneer settler had served during the Spanish-American War. It prospered as a fruit-growing center after the railroad arrived in 1914.

Pateros was relocated in 1968 when the pool behind Wells Dam flooded the original site. Alta Lake State Park, 3 miles southwest of town, is a popular recreation area *(see Recreation Areas Chart)*; phone (509) 923-2473. River Recreation Inc. offers white-water rafting excursions on Methow River April-September; phone (206) 276-8774 or (800) 464-5899.

PORT ANGELES (D-5) pop. 19,038, elev. 20'
• Part of Olympic National Park area — see map p. 100

In 1791 Spanish captain Francisco Eliza sailed into the natural harbor of what is now Port Angeles and became the first European to see this area. He named the site Puerto de Nuestra Señora de los Angeles, "Port of Our Lady of the Angels," from which the current name is derived. The 4.5-mile sandbar that forms the harbor is called Ediz Hook, which offers a panorama of the city and the Olympic Mountains.

Black Ball Ferry Line operates passenger and automobile ferry service daily between Port Angeles and Victoria, B.C., 18 miles across the Strait of Juan de Fuca; phone (360) 457-4491 or (888) 993-3779.

Shopping: Several antique shops are on W. 1st Street between Oak and Laurel streets, including Port Angeles Antique Mall, 109 W. 1st St.

Port Angeles Regional Chamber of Commerce: 121 E. Railroad Ave., Port Angeles, WA 98362. **Phone:** (360) 452-2363.

PORT ANGELES FINE ARTS CENTER is .2 mi. e. of Race St. at 1203 E. Lauridsen Blvd. The center features changing exhibits of contemporary paintings, sculpture, photographs, drawings and other media. The center also holds lectures, concerts and other performances. The 5-acre grounds are laced with walking trails and also feature Webster's Woods, an outdoor art park containing sculptures and site works by Northwest artists. The grounds offer a panorama of the city, harbor and Strait of Juan de Fuca.

Time: Allow 30 minutes minimum. **Hours:** Grounds open daily dawn-dusk. Center open Thurs.-Sun. 11-5, Mar.-Nov.; Thurs.-Sun. 10-4, rest of year. Closed Jan. 1, July 4, Thanksgiving, day after Thanksgiving, Christmas Eve, Christmas and Dec. 31. **Cost:** Free. **Phone:** (360) 457-3532.

A HIDDEN HAVEN & WATER GARDEN COTTAGES   (360)452-2719
▼▼▼ Cottage. **Address:** 1428 Dan Kelly Rd 98363

COLETTE'S BED & BREAKFAST   360/457-9197

▼▼▼ ▼▼◆
Bed & Breakfast
Rates not provided

Address: 339 Finn Hall Rd 98362 **Location:** Oceanfront. 7 mi e on US 101, 1.5 mi ne on Old Olympic Hwy, just ne on Wild Currant Way, 0.3 mi n on Gehrke Rd, then just e. Located in a secluded rural area. **Facility:** Featuring professionally designed gardens, this 10-acre estate offers finely appointed rooms, all with fireplaces and water views. 5 units. 1 story, interior/exterior corridors. **Terms:** check-in 4 pm, age restrictions may apply. **Featured Amenity:** full hot breakfast.

[SAVE] ⊞ [BIZ] 🛜 ✕ 🖥 🖵

DOMAINE MADELEINE   (360)457-4174
▼▼▼ Bed & Breakfast. **Address:** 146 Wildflower Ln 98362

THE FIVE SEASUNS B & B   (360)452-8248
▼▼▼ Historic Bed & Breakfast. **Address:** 1006 S Lincoln St 98362

OLYMPIC LODGE   360/452-2993
▼▼▼ Hotel. **Address:** 140 Del Guzzi Dr 98362

PORT ANGELES INN   360/452-9285
▼▼ Motel. **Address:** 111 E 2nd St 98362

RED LION HOTEL PORT ANGELES   360/452-9215
▼▼▼ Hotel. **Address:** 221 N Lincoln St 98362

SEA CLIFF GARDENS BED & BREAKFAST   (360)452-2322
▼▼▼ ▼▼ Bed & Breakfast. **Address:** 397 Monterra Dr 98362

SUPER 8 BY WYNDHAM PORT ANGELES AT OLYMPIC PENINSULA   (360)452-8401
▼ Motel. **Address:** 2104 E 1st St 98362

WHERE TO EAT

BELLA ITALIA   360/457-5442

▼▼▼ ▼◆
Italian
Casual Dining
$10-$34

AAA Inspector Notes: Serving cuisine made from fresh ingredients, this eatery presents an exceptional selection of pasta and pizza options. An authentic Italian menu features the freshest Northwest produce and seafood. The large windows and cozy booths make for great people watching or a romantic setting. **Features:** beer & wine. **Reservations:** suggested. **Address:** 118 E 1st St 98362 **Location:** Between N Lincoln and N Laurel sts. **Parking:** street only. [D] [AC]

CAFE GARDEN   360/457-4611
▼▼ American. Casual Dining. **Address:** 1506 E 1st St 98362

C'EST SI BON   360/452-8888
▼▼◆ French. Fine Dining. **Address:** 23 Cedar Park Rd 98362

CHESTNUT COTTAGE RESTAURANT   360/452-8344
▼▼ American. Casual Dining. **Address:** 929 E Front St 98362

DOWNRIGGERS WATERFRONT RESTAURANT   360/452-2700
♥♥ Seafood. Casual Dining. **Address:** 115 E Railroad Ave 98362

DUPUIS RESTAURANT   360/457-8033
♥♥ American. Casual Dining. **Address:** 256861 Hwy 101 98362

FIRST STREET HAVEN   360/457-0352
♥♥ American. Casual Dining. **Address:** 107 E 1st St 98362

KOKOPELLI GRILL   360/457-6040
♥♥♥ Southwestern. Casual Dining. **Address:** 203 E Front St 98362

MICHAEL'S SEAFOOD & STEAKHOUSE   360/417-6929
♥♥♥ American. Casual Dining. **Address:** 117B E 1st St 98362

TRAYLOR'S RESTAURANT   360/452-3833
♥♥ American. Casual Dining. **Address:** 3256 E Hwy 101 98362

PORT ORCHARD (F-2) pop. 11,144, elev. 13'
• Hotels & Restaurants map & index p. 170
• Part of Seattle area — see map p. 124

The first settlers in this area built houses on the wooded shores of Sinclair Inlet in 1854 and named their community Sidney. Sawmills and shipyards powered the town's economy, and in 1903 Sidney was renamed Port Orchard and made the seat of Kitsap County.

The Log Cabin Museum, 416 Sidney Ave., features an early 20th-century log house with period furnishings; phone (360) 876-3693.

Kitsap Live Steamers, 3100 S.E. Marbeth Ln., has more than 4,000 feet of ground-level, 7.5-inch gauge track. Train rides are offered from 10-4 on the second and fourth Saturdays of the month from April through October; phone (206) 718-9401. The train is located in South Kitsap Regional Park, 2841 S.E. Lund Ave. (at Jackson Avenue).

Daily passenger ferry service links Port Orchard and Annapolis to nearby Bremerton; phone (360) 373-2877 for schedule.

Port Orchard Chamber of Commerce: 1014 Bay St., Suite 3, Port Orchard, WA 98366. **Phone:** (360) 876-3505.

Shopping: Antique shopping is popular in Port Orchard. Olde Central Antique Mall, 801 Bay St., has more than 40 dealers. Port Orchard Public Market, 715 Bay St., is a year-round indoor market.

The Port Orchard Farmers Market has a waterfront backdrop in Marina Park and is held Saturdays 9-3 from April to mid-October. The market features locally grown Kitsap Peninsula fruits and vegetables, flowers and plants as well as locally caught fish. An especially scenic way to get there is to take Washington State Ferries to the Bremerton ferry dock, then the Kitsap Transit Foot Ferry to the Port Orchard dock.

COMFORT INN PORT ORCHARD   (360)895-2666 **17**
♥♥♥ Motel $98-$144
Address: 1121 Bay St 98366 **Location:** Waterfront. SR 16 exit Tremont St, 0.9 mi e to Sidney Ave, 1.2 mi n to Bay St, then just e. **Facility:** 62 units. 3 stories (no elevator), exterior corridors. **Activities:** picnic facilities, exercise room. **Guest Services:** valet and coin laundry. **Featured Amenity: continental breakfast.**
[SAVE] [CALL] [♿] [🛏] [BIZ] [📶] [✕]
[▯] [▭] [▱] / SOME UNITS [🐾] [HS]

PORT TOWNSEND (D-2) pop. 9,113, elev. 120'
• Hotels p. 110 • Restaurants p. 110

Founded in the early 1850s, Port Townsend was one of the leading cities on Puget Sound in the late 19th century. The first settlers arrived here in 1851, and by 1853 the customs house was relocated here from Olympia, making it the official point of entry. The port offered safe moorage for the large sailing vessels of the time, and the economy prospered, first from providing supplies to gold seekers bound for British Columbia, then later from speculating on the prospects of attracting a transcontinental railroad line.

The city boasted consulates, banks, large hotels, a streetcar line, shipyards and all manner of commercial establishments—an expansive layout reflecting hope that Port Townsend would become the region's major port and trading center. The population reached 7,000, but when plans for a railroad fizzled in 1895, a long period of decline set in.

Port Townsend owes much of its charm to an impressive collection of Victorian-era architecture. The historic downtown district is filled with homes—a number of them now bed-and-breakfast properties—displaying turrets, pergolas, towers, gingerbread trim and Carpenter Gothic details.

Many of Water Street's brick buildings, now occupied by hotels, restaurants, bars, coffee houses, stores and antique shops, date from the late 1800s. An excellent example of the prevailing architectural eclecticism is the Jefferson County Courthouse on Walker Street. Built in 1892, it combines Romanesque and Gothic styles as well as a nod to the whimsical elements of a fairytale castle.

St. Paul's Church, 1020 Jefferson St., was built in 1865, making it the oldest Episcopal church in the diocese of Olympia. The bell in the tower was donated by a cutter captain on the condition that it be rung on foggy days to help guide sailing vessels into the bay.

The lobby of the 1893 Customs House, Washington and Van Buren streets, displays historic photographs. Haller Fountain, at Washington and Taylor, was originally built for the Mexican exhibit at the 1893 Chicago World's Exhibition. The structure at the top of the bluff above Taylor Street is the old Fire Bell Tower, built in 1885.

The Port Townsend Farmers Market was named Washington's large market of the year in 2011. More than 70 vendors representing some 40 farms offer a variety of seasonal produce, artisan breads and cheeses, cider, cut flowers and specialty foods. Craft vendors sell everything from pottery and ceramics to soy candles. It sets up along Tyler Street (between Lawrence and Clay streets) on Saturday from 9-2, April through October, and 10-1, November through December. To reach the market if you're downtown and on foot, take the steps from the Haller Fountain to the top, then turn left.

The Port Townsend Chamber Music Festival is a major summertime event in a town that has long been home to artists and musicians. World-renowned ensembles play the music of classical masters at the Joseph F. Wheeler Theater at Fort Worden State Park & Conference Center *(see attraction listing this page)*. Public concerts are given in February, April and October; for schedule and ticket information phone (360) 385-3102 or (800) 746-1982

Nearby Fort Townsend Historical State Park *(see Recreation Areas Chart)* includes the site of a U.S. Army post built in 1856 to protect settlers. The fort was abandoned in 1895 after it was destroyed by fire. The site is now a wildlife sanctuary.

Washington State Ferries offers daily service from Port Townsend to Coupeville (Keystone Harbor) on Whidbey Island; phone (206) 464-6400, or (888) 808-7977 in Wash. (**Note:** This run is subject to cancellation during extreme low tides.) Puget Sound Express *(see attraction listing)* provides daily passenger service to the San Juan Islands from May through September.

Port Townsend Visitor Information Center : 2409 Jefferson St., Suite B, Port Townsend, WA 98368. **Phone:** (360) 385-2722.

Shopping: Lining the bay along Water Street, former saloons distinguished by handsome facades are now occupied by antique shops, restaurants, art galleries and specialty shops. Vendors at the Port Townsend Antique Mall, 802 Washington St., sell everything from pricey collectibles to nautical souvenirs.

FORT WORDEN STATE PARK & CONFERENCE CENTER is 1 mi. n. via Cherry St. to 200 Battery Way. The fort within this 434-acre park was part of an important system of coastal fortresses guarding the entrance to Puget Sound established in the 1890s. The large, grassy parade ground remains, and the handsome Victorian houses along Officers' Row have been restored. The rhododendron garden contains more than 1,100 plants. See Recreation Areas Chart.

Centrum, a non-profit center for the arts and creative education, offers a year-round program of events. For information and tickets phone (360) 385-3102. **Hours:** Park open daily 6:30 a.m.-dusk. **Cost:** Park admission $10 (per private vehicle). **Phone:** (360) 344-4400 for the park, or (360) 385-3102 for Centrum. 🅐 🍴 ⊠ 🏠 ⊞

Commanding Officer's Quarters is in Fort Worden State Park at 1 Pershing Ave. Built in 1904 in the Edwardian style, this nearly 5,000-square-foot house features a slate roof and decorated boxed cornices. It has been restored and contains period late Victorian and Edwardian furnishings, providing a glimpse into the lives of a U.S. Army colonel and his family in the first decade of the 20th century. Guided tours are available by appointment.

Time: Allow 30 minutes minimum. **Hours:** Daily noon-5, May-Sept.; occasional Sat.-Sun. noon-5, rest of year. Closed Jan. 1, Thanksgiving and Christmas. Phone ahead to confirm schedule. **Cost:** $6; $5 (ages 65+); $3 (active military); $1 (ages 3-12). **Phone:** (360) 385-1003. GT

Port Townsend Marine Science Center is in Fort Worden State Park at 532 Battery Way. The center has two exhibit buildings. The Marine Science Exhibit on the pier features touch pools displaying local marine life. The Natural History Exhibit on the shore showcases beach rocks, marine animal fossils and sand from around the world; the Learning from Orcas—the Story of Hope exhibit follows the life of a highly contaminated transient orca whale. Daily guided walks and interpretive programs are offered in the summer.

A 3-hour nature and birding boat trip around Protection Island National Wildlife Refuge takes place late April, early May, in July, early August, late September, early October and New Year's Eve; phone ahead for details. **Hours:** Wed.-Mon. 11-5, mid-June through Labor Day; Fri.-Sun. noon-5, early Apr. to mid-June and day after Labor Day-Oct. 31. Natural History Exhibit also open Fri.-Sun. noon-5, Nov.-Mar. Marine Exhibit also open by appointment, Nov.-Mar. **Cost:** $5; $3 (ages 6-17). Park admission $10 (per private vehicle). **Phone:** (360) 385-5582.

Puget Sound Coast Artillery Museum is 1 mi. n. via Cherry St. at the eastern edge of Fort Worden State Park. The museum describes the coastal defense system's history with exhibits of uniforms, guns and historic photographs. Guided tours of the Harbor Entrance Control Post and Artillery Hill are available. **Time:** Allow 30 minutes minimum. **Hours:** Daily 11-4 (also Fri.-Sat. 4-5, Memorial Day weekend-Labor Day weekend). Harbor Entrance Control Post guided tours depart Sat. 11-3. Walking tour of Artillery Hill departs Sat. at 1. **Cost:** $4; $2 (ages 6-12); $10 (family); free (ages 0-5 and active military with ID). **Phone:** (360) 385-0373.

NORTHWEST MARITIME CENTER is at 431 Water St., at the n.e. end of the downtown waterfront. Especially appealing to boating enthusiasts, the center celebrates the region's rich maritime heritage and Port Townsend's wooden boat culture. The Maritime Heritage and Resources Building at the corner of Water and Monroe streets features the Wooden Boat Chandlery, which offers boating equipment and supplies. The H.W. McCurdy Library on the second floor contains nautical books and charts, and an adjoining hall often displays changing exhibits.

A mezzanine in the adjacent Chandler Education Building allows visitors to observe artisans building and repairing wooden boats at the Boatshop. The Commons, a public open space facing the shoreline, has a compass rose, boardwalk, access to a small beach and the center's pier.

Time: Allow 1 hour minimum. **Hours:** Chandlery open daily 10-5. Library open Mon.-Fri. 9-5. Free 1-hour guided tours are available by appointment. Closed Jan. 1, Thanksgiving and Christmas. **Cost:** Free. **Phone:** (360) 385-3628. GT 🅐

PORT TOWNSEND AERO MUSEUM is 5 mi. s. on SR 20, then 1 mi. s. on SR 19 at Jefferson County International Airport, 105 Airport Rd. The main gallery displays 17 rare small planes from a collection numbering 35; most are vintage 1920s to 1940s aircraft. Each has been carefully restored, some from wrecks, and those that are airworthy are flown periodically. Interpretive signs describe each plane's history and performance statistics.

Artwork, historic photographs and model plane displays augment the primary exhibit. A second-floor walkway overlooks the planes, seven of which are suspended from the ceiling. The museum also offers a variety of youth education programs.

Time: Allow 45 minutes minimum. **Hours:** Wed.-Sun. 9-4. Closed Thanksgiving and Christmas. **Cost:** $10; $9 (ages 65+ and active military with ID); $6 (ages 7-12). **Phone:** (360) 379-5244.

PUGET SOUND EXPRESS departs from 227 Jackson St. Offering tours of the Strait of Juan de Fuca, Puget Sound Express makes a 2-hour stop at the picturesque community of Friday Harbor. A naturalist explains the different types of wildlife indigenous to the San Juan archipelago, including bald eagles, seals and orcas.

Hours: Full-day tours to Friday Harbor, including whale watching, depart daily at 9, mid-May to mid-Sept. Four-hour whale-watching tours depart daily at 10, May-Oct. (also at 2:30, mid-June to early Sept.). **Cost:** Round-trip fare $103.50; $65 (ages 2-10). One-way fare $55.50; $35 (ages 2-10). Whale watch tours $95; $65 (ages 2-10). A fuel surcharge may apply; call for details. Reservations are recommended. **Phone:** (360) 385-5288. GT

BISHOP VICTORIAN HOTEL   (360)381-7048
♥♥♥ Historic Hotel. **Address:** 714 Washington St 98368

HARBORSIDE INN   360/385-7909
♥♥ Hotel. **Address:** 330 Benedict St 98368

OLD CONSULATE INN   (360)385-6753
♥♥♥ Historic Bed & Breakfast. **Address:** 313 Walker St 98368

THE SWAN HOTEL   (360)385-1718
♥♥ Motel. **Address:** 222 Monroe St 98368

THE WATER STREET HOTEL   (360)385-5467
♥ Historic Hotel. **Address:** 635 Water St 98368

WHERE TO EAT

THE BELMONT   360/385-3007

♥♥♥ ◆
American
Casual Dining
$10-$34

AAA Inspector Notes: *Historic.* Built in 1885, the waterfront Victorian restaurant and saloon is the only one of its kind left in the area. On the menu is a variety of seafood, beef, poultry and pasta entrées, all served by the friendly staff. During summer, diners can enjoy nice sunsets from seats on the outdoor patio. Meals aren't complete without the signature dessert: a hot and delicious, mixed berry cobbler. **Features:** full bar, patio dining, senior menu. **Reservations:** suggested. **Address:** 925 Water St 98368 **Location:** Between Taylor and Tyler sts. **Parking:** street only. L D 🅙

FOUNTAIN CAFE   360/385-1364
♥♥ Regional American. Casual Dining. **Address:** 920 Washington St 98368

KHU LARB THAI   360/385-5023
♥♥ Thai. Casual Dining. **Address:** 225 Adams St 98368

LANZA'S RISTORANTE/PIZZERIA   360/379-1900
♥♥ Italian. Casual Dining. **Address:** 1020 Lawrence St 98368

THE SILVERWATER CAFE   360/385-6448
♥♥♥ Seafood. Casual Dining. **Address:** 237 Taylor St 98368

POULSBO (E-2) pop. 9,200, elev. 33'
- **Hotels & Restaurants map & index p. 170**
- **Part of Seattle area — see map p. 124**

Set on hillsides overlooking Liberty Bay, Poulsbo is a picturesque port with a strong Scandinavian heritage. The first postmaster called it Paulsbo, meaning "Paul's Place" in Norwegian, but a postal service misspelling ultimately prevailed.

In the 1880s Norwegians comprised 90 percent of the town's population, and Norwegian was commonly heard on city streets well into the 1920s. Today evidence of Poulsbo's heritage can be seen in the Norwegian banners decorating Front Street, cafes that offer Scandinavian delicacies and streets bearing the names of Norwegian royalty. Many buildings feature the decorative architectural motif known as rosemaling, which often incorporates floral designs.

The Poulsbo Farmers Market, 19540 N.E. Front St., is held Saturday 9-2, early April to mid-December.

Poulsbo Visitors Center: 19010 Front St. N.E., Poulsbo, WA 98370. **Phone:** (360) 779-4999.

GUESTHOUSE INTERNATIONAL INN & SUITES
          360/697-4400 **20**
♥♥ Hotel. **Address:** 19801 7th Ave NE 98370

POULSBO INN & SUITES   (360)779-3921 **21**

♥♥
Motel
$93-$140

Address: 18680 SR 305 NE 98370 **Location:** SR 3, 2.3 mi e. Located in a commercial area. **Facility:** 83 units, some kitchens. 1-2 stories (no elevator), exterior corridors. **Terms:** 7 day cancellation notice-fee imposed. **Pool:** heated outdoor. **Activities:** hot tub, playground, exercise room. **Guest Services:** coin laundry. **Featured Amenity:** breakfast buffet.

SAVE 🔌 🍴 BIZ 📶 ✕ 🛏
🖥 💻 / SOME UNITS 🐾

(See map & index p. 170.)

ELMER'S   360/697-2215
♦♦ American. Casual Dining. **Address:** 760 NE Liberty Rd
98370

MOLLY WARD GARDENS   360/779-4471
♦♦ Pacific Northwest. Casual Dining. **Address:** 27462 Big
Valley Rd 98370

PROSSER (G-9) pop. 5,714, elev. 662'

Part of the Yakima Valley's fruit growing district,
Prosser also is a shipping point for cattle and sheep.
The treeless Horse Heaven Hills, where wild horses
once roamed, rise to the south. Horse Heaven Vista,
2.5 miles southeast via SR 221, offers a panorama
of the lower Yakima Valley, the Cascades and the
Yakima River.

Vineyards are plentiful in the area; harvest time is
generally the last 2 weeks in September. More than
30 area wineries offer tastings; for more information
contact the Prosser Visitor Information Center. Vint-
ner's Village, off I-82 exit 80 at 100 Merlot Drive, is
made up of a dozen wineries spread out over a 32-
acre site; phone (509) 786-7401.

Prosser Visitor Information Center: 1230 Bennett
Ave., Prosser, WA 99350. **Phone:** (509) 786-3177
or (866) 343-5101.

BENTON COUNTY HISTORICAL MUSEUM is in
the city park at 1000 Paterson Rd. The museum has
more than 20,000 items, including pioneer and Native
American artifacts, a natural history diorama, Edison
phonographs, a cut glass and porcelain collection, 37
oversized hand-carved model cars, and reconstruc-
tions of a Victorian parlor and an early homestead. A
collection of gowns covers the period 1843-1920.
Time: Allow 1 hour minimum. **Hours:** Tues.-Fri. 11-4,
Sat. noon-3. Guided tours available on request.
Closed Jan. 1, Easter, Thanksgiving and Christmas.
Cost: Donations. **Phone:** (509) 786-3842. GT

WALTER CLORE WINE AND CULINARY CENTER
is off I-82 exit 82 at 2140A Wine Country Rd. The
center includes exhibits that illustrate wine history in
the state and pay tribute to Dr. Walter Clore, considered a pioneer in Washington's wine industry. A large
map behind the tasting bar portrays the major grape
growing regions of the state. Tastings highlight different regions, climates and winemakers each month.
Time: Allow 30 minutes minimum. **Hours:** Daily 11-5.
Closed major holidays. **Cost:** Center free. Wine
tasting $5. **Phone:** (509) 786-1000. GT

WINERIES

• **Hinzerling Winery** is 1.5 mi. from I-82 at jct. Wine
  Country Rd. and Sheridan Ave. **Hours:** Mon.-Sat.
  11-5 (also Sun. 11-4, Mar. 1-late Dec.). Closed
  Jan. 1, Easter and Christmas. **Phone:** (509)
  786-2163 or (800) 727-6702. GT

BEST WESTERN PLUS THE INN AT HORSE HEAVEN
(509)786-7977

◆◆◆
Hotel
$115-$145

BW **Best**
Western
PLUS.

AAA Benefit:
Members save up to
15% and earn bonus
points!

Address: 259 Merlot Dr 99350 **Loca-**
tion: I-82 exit 80 (Gap Rd), just se. **Fa-**
cility: 86 units, some kitchens. 2 stories
(no elevator), interior corridors. **Terms:**
cancellation fee imposed. **Pool:** heated
outdoor, heated indoor. **Activities:**
sauna, hot tub, picnic facilities, exercise
room. **Guest Services:** coin laundry.
Featured Amenity: breakfast buffet.

SAVE [↑] CALL [⟱] [▤] [↺] [BIZ]

HOLIDAY INN EXPRESS & SUITES PROSSER   509/786-1399
♦♦♦ Hotel. **Address:** 680 Wine Country Rd 99350

HORSE HEAVEN SALOON & BREWERY   509/781-6228
♦♦ American. Brewpub. **Address:** 615 6th St 99350

JEREMY'S 1896 PUBLIC HOUSE   509/786-7492
♦♦ American. Casual Dining. **Address:** 1232 Wine Country
Rd 99350

WINE O'CLOCK BISTRO & WINE BAR   509/786-2197
♦♦♦ American. Fine Dining. **Address:** 548 Cabernet Ct
99350

PULLMAN (F-12) pop. 29,799, elev. 2,500'
• Hotels p. 112 • Restaurants p. 112

Fertile, rolling hills perfect for the cultivation of
wheat led to the settlement of Pullman, originally
known as Three Forks because of its location at the
confluence of three streams. The town was renamed in 1884 in honor of railroad sleeping car
manufacturer George Pullman, in what turned out to
be a futile attempt to attract an endowment. In 1890,
when state officials visited Pullman while scouting
out a site for the state's new land grant college, residents dressed in their Sunday best and congregated
on the main street to create an air of prosperity and
civic bustle. The ploy worked, and Washington Agricultural College opened its doors in 1892.

The Bill Chipman Palouse Trail is a 7-mile paved
path following SR 270 between Pullman and
Moscow, Ind. Interpretive panels depict area geology,
settlement and agriculture. Lawson Gardens, 705
Derby St., offers paved and gravel paths that loop
through a sloping site featuring seasonal plantings of
annuals, a reflecting pond, a perennial garden and a
rose garden with more than 600 rose bushes.

Pullman Chamber of Commerce: 415 N. Grand
Ave., Pullman, WA 99163. **Phone:** (509) 334-3565
or (800) 365-6948.

WASHINGTON STATE UNIVERSITY occupies a
hilly, 600-acre site on the e. side of town. Authorized
in 1890 as the Washington Agricultural College, WSU
has grown to become one of the most important universities in the West, renowned for its research and

curriculum in agriculture, veterinary medicine and communications. The attractive campus of red-brick buildings is set against a backdrop of trees and rolling green lawns.

A number of facilities are open to the public. The Holland/Terrell Libraries contain several historical collections. The Museum of Art features changing paintings, photography, sculptures and performances. The Cougars play Pac-12 football in 33,000-seat Martin Stadium; basketball is played at Beasley Coliseum. Both are located on Stadium Way.

At the WSU Bear Center, on Terre View Drive near the intersection with Grimes Way, visitors can observe bears foraging in their exercise yard. In the planning stages is the National Bear Center, a research and educational facility. WSU Creamery dairy products can be sampled at Ferdinand's Ice Cream Shoppe, located in the Food Quality Building, 2 blocks east of Stadium Way on Ferdinand's Lane; phone (509) 335-2141.

A 90-minute campus walking tour, offered Mon.-Fri. at 9 and 1 (also most Sat. at 10, Sept.-Apr. when school is in session), starts at the Lighty Student Services Building, Stadium Way and Wilson Road. Visitor parking permits can be purchased at the Brelsford WSU Visitor Center, 150 E. Spring St. (at E. Main Street); phone (509) 335-4636.

Hours: Visitor Center open Mon.-Fri. 7-5, Sat. 9-2. Museum of Art Mon.-Sat. 10-4 (also Thurs. 4-7), Aug.-May; Tues.-Fri. noon-4, rest of year. **Phone:** (509) 335-1910 for the Museum of Art, (509) 335-1119 for the Bear Center, or (888) 468-6978 for walking tour information. GT

Charles R. Conner Natural History Museum is on the first floor of Abelson Hall on the Washington State University campus. Three galleries display more than 700 mounted birds, mammals, reptiles and amphibians. The museum's research collection numbers more than 65,000 specimens, including displays that were part of Washington state's exhibits at the 1893 Chicago World's Fair. Visitor parking permits can be purchased at the WSU Visitor Center, located at E. Main and N.E. Spring streets. **Time:** Allow 30 minutes minimum. **Hours:** Daily 8-5. Closed major holidays. Phone ahead to confirm schedule. **Cost:** Free. **Phone:** (509) 335-3515.

Geology Museum is in the Webster Physical Sciences Building on the Washington State University campus. The Culver Study Memorial, located in the lobby, displays hundreds of rock and mineral samples from around the world. A booth in Room 124 showcases fluorescent minerals, and the Jacklin Collection includes more than 2,000 cut and polished specimens of petrified wood. Visitor parking permits can be purchased at the WSU Visitor Center, located at E. Main and N.E. Spring streets. **Time:** Allow 30 minutes minimum. **Hours:** Mon.-Fri. 8-5, mid-Aug. to early May; 8-4, rest of year. Closed major holidays. **Cost:** Free. **Phone:** (509) 335-3009.

The Jordan Schnitzer Museum of Art/WSU is at Wilson Rd. across from Stadium Way on the Washington State University Pullman campus. It features changing exhibitions of art from regional, national and international artists. Lectures and guided tours complement the exhibitions. Visitor parking permits can be purchased from WSU Transportation Services, located at Colorado Street and Cougar Way. **Time:** Allow 30 minutes minimum. **Hours:** Tues.-Sat. 10-4 (also first Thurs. 4-7). Hours may vary in summer, phone ahead to confirm schedule. Closed major holidays and university breaks. **Cost:** Free. **Phone:** (509) 335-1910. GT

COAST HILLTOP INN   (509)332-0928
◆◆ Hotel. **Address:** 928 NW Olsen St 99163

COURTYARD BY MARRIOTT PULLMAN   (509)332-1500
◆◆◆ Contemporary Hotel. **Address:** 1295 NE North Fairway Rd 99163   **AAA Benefit:** Members save 5% or more!

HOLIDAY INN EXPRESS & SUITES PULLMAN   (509)334-4437
◆◆◆ Hotel. **Address:** 1190 SE Bishop Blvd 99163

RESIDENCE INN BY MARRIOTT PULLMAN
                                                     (509)332-4400

◆◆◆◆
Extended Stay Contemporary Hotel $64-$339

Residence INN **AAA Benefit:** Members save 5% or more!

Address: 1255 NE North Fairway Rd 99163 **Location:** Jct SR 27 (N Grand Ave) and NE Stadium Way, 0.8 mi se to NE North Fairway Rd, then 0.6 mi ne. Next to Washington State University. **Facility:** 131 efficiencies. 4 stories, interior corridors. *Bath:* shower only. **Terms:** cancellation fee imposed. **Pool:** heated indoor. **Activities:** hot tub, picnic facilities, exercise room. **Guest Services:** valet and coin laundry, boarding pass kiosk, area transportation. **Featured Amenity:** breakfast buffet.

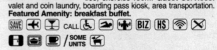

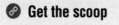

🔗 **Get the scoop**

from AAA inspectors:

AAA.com/travelguides/restaurants

WHERE TO EAT

BIRCH & BARLEY   509/332-0108
◆◆ American. Casual Dining. **Address:** 1360 SE Bishop Blvd 99163

THE BLACK CYPRESS BAR & KITCHEN   509/334-5800
◆◆ Greek. Casual Dining. **Address:** 215 E Main St 99163

COUGAR COUNTRY DRIVE-IN   509/332-7829
💎 Burgers. Quick Serve. **Address:** 760 N Grand Ave 99163

THE OLD EUROPEAN RESTAURANT   509/334-6381
💎💎 European. Casual Dining. **Address:** 455 S Grand Ave 99163

SOUTH FORK PUBLIC HOUSE   509/332-3675
💎💎 American. Gastropub. **Address:** 1680 S Grand Ave 99163

PUYALLUP (G-3) pop. 37,022, elev. 48'
- **Hotels & Restaurants map & index p. 201**
- **Part of Seattle area — see map p. 124**

After crossing the plains in a covered wagon, Ezra Meeker arrived at a site just east of what is now Tacoma and named it for the Puyallup tribe; the name means "generous people." (The proper pronunciation is "Pew-allop.") This homey city lies in the shadow of mighty Mount Rainier, and the Puyallup River flows through downtown. The extremely fertile surrounding region is conducive to the cultivation of spring bulbs, and fields explode with color in spring when daffodils, tulips and irises bloom.

The Daffodil Festival pays tribute to this floral bounty. Daffodils first came to the Puyallup Valley in the 1920s as the area's hop industry was dying out. About 200 varieties are grown, the best known being the King Alfred daffodil. A big parade through downtown is the highlight and takes place in early April. For information about other festival events phone (253) 840-4194.

"Do the Puyallup" at the 🎡 Washington State Fair, held in September. A celebration of life in the Evergreen State, the fair has it all: midway rides, thrill rides (including the looping Rainier Rush roller coaster), big-name concerts, a rodeo, a cattle drive, animal exhibits, interactive games, a beer garden and of course plenty of edibles, from scones to barbecue to a *fleischkuechle* (German meat turnover). It all happens at the Washington State Fair Events Center, 110 9th Ave. S.W.

The holidays are celebrated in traditional style at 🎡 A Victorian Country Christmas Festival, held at the Washington State Fair Events Center in early December. A Victorian-themed village is filled with shops offering ornaments, holiday-themed decorations, toys, jewelry and art. Gourmet food items can be sampled at the Winter Wine Garden, and stage shows and concerts take place at two venues, the Holiday Jubilee Theater and the Victorian Christmas Opry Theater.

Puyallup/Sumner Chamber of Commerce: 323 N. Meridian, Suite A, P.O. Box 1298, Puyallup, WA 98371. **Phone:** (253) 845-6755.

Shopping: The anchor stores at South Hill Mall, a quarter of a mile south of SR 512 at 3500 S. Meridian St., are JCPenney and Macy's. Downtown Puyallup has a dozen or so antique and secondhand shops, mostly along Meridian Street.

MEEKER MANSION, 312 Spring St., is a 17-room Italianate Victorian house that was the home of Ezra Meeker, an entrepreneur and Puyallup's first mayor.

Guided tours of the 1890 mansion reveal ceiling art, handcrafted fireplaces, leaded glass windows and period furnishings. A variety of events are held at the mansion throughout the year.

Time: Allow 30 minutes minimum. **Hours:** Wed.-Sun. noon-4, early Mar. to mid-Dec. Last admission 1 hour before closing. Closed Easter and Thanksgiving. **Cost:** $4; $3 (ages 12-18 and 62+); $2 (ages 0-11). Prices may increase for Christmas tours. **Phone:** (253) 848-1770. GT 🖨 Puyallup, 48

BEST WESTERN PREMIER PLAZA HOTEL & CONFERENCE CENTER   (253)848-1500 ③①

 💎💎💎
Hotel
$119-$289

🅑🅦🅟 PREMIER
BEST WESTERN.
AAA Benefit: Members save up to 15% and earn bonus points!

Address: 620 S Hill Park Dr 98373 **Location:** SR 512 exit S Hill Park Dr southbound; exit 9th St SW northbound, just w. **Facility:** 99 units. 3 stories, interior corridors. **Terms:** cancellation fee imposed. **Amenities:** safes. **Pool:** heated indoor. **Activities:** hot tub, exercise room. **Guest Services:** valet and coin laundry. **Featured Amenity: full hot breakfast.**

SAVE 🍴 ⅄ CALL 🔌 🚗 ♿ BIZ 🛜 ✕ 🔒 📠 🖥 / SOME UNITS 🐾 HS

FAIRFIELD INN & SUITES BY MARRIOTT TACOMA PUYALLUP
     (253)770-3100 ②⑨
💎💎💎 Hotel. **Address:** 202 15th Ave SW 98371
AAA Benefit: Members save 5% or more!

HAMPTON INN & SUITES BY HILTON TACOMA/PUYALLUP
253/770-8880 ③⓪
💎💎💎 Hotel. **Address:** 1515 S Meridian 98371
AAA Benefit: Members save 5% or more!

HOLIDAY INN EXPRESS HOTEL & SUITES
253/848-4900 ③②
💎💎💎 Hotel. **Address:** 812 S Hill Park Dr 98373

WHERE TO EAT

POWERHOUSE RESTAURANT & BREWERY
253/845-1370 ②④
💎💎 American. Brewpub. **Address:** 454 E Main Ave 98372

RAM RESTAURANT AND BREWERY
💎💎 American. Casual Dining.
LOCATIONS:
Address: 103 35th Ave SE 98374 **Phone:** 253/841-3317
Address: 10403 156th St E, Suite 101 98374
Phone: 253/445-1005

QUINAULT (E-5) elev. 305'
- **Part of Olympic National Park area — see map p. 100**

Nestled among towering conifers on the south shore of Lake Quinault, this resort community is a popular stop for visitors to Olympic National Park and the Olympic National Forest. The area's mild, humid climate supports a lush temperate rain forest;

six conifer specimens in the "Valley of the Rain Forest Giants" are recognized as champions by the National Register of Big Trees. A .3-mile walking trail branching off South Shore Road at the east edge of town leads to the world's largest Sitka spruce *(Picea sitchensis);* this 191-foot-tall monarch measures nearly 59 feet in circumference and is estimated to be around 1,000 years old.

The Rain Forest Nature Trail, off South Shore Road at the west end of town, is a half-mile interpretive loop through an old-growth forest of Douglas fir, western hemlock, western red cedar and Sitka spruce. Moss drapes the giant trees and carpets the forest floor, which is crowded with dense growths of sword fern. For information about other area hiking trails and recreational activities contact the Quinault office of the Pacific Ranger District, 353 South Shore Rd., Quinault, WA 98575; phone (360) 288-2525.

REDMOND (E-7) pop. 54,144, elev. 50'
- Hotels & Restaurants map & index p. 160
- Part of Seattle area — see map p. 124

First called Salmonberg for the abundance of salmon in the Sammamish River, Redmond was renamed to honor pioneer settler and first postmaster Luke McRedmond. Redmond is the headquarters of such well-known companies as Microsoft and Nintendo of America.

The city offers miles of bike trails; the paved Sammamish River Trail connects the city with Woodinville, Bothell and Seattle. Other recreation areas include Lake Sammamish State Park *(see Recreation Areas Chart)* in nearby Issaquah and Farrel-McWhirter Farm Park.

A restored, brick-paved section of the Yellowstone Trail is located on 196th Avenue N.E., between SR 202 and N.E. Union Hill Road. This is Washington's longest unaltered stretch of the nation's first northern transcontinental auto road, established in 1913.

OneRedmond Visitor Information Center: 8383 158th Ave. N.E., Suite 225, Redmond, WA 98052. **Phone:** (425) 885-4014.

Shopping: Redmond Town Center, on Redmond Way, has more than 100 stores, including Macy's and REI.

MARYMOOR PARK, .5 mi. s. to 6046 W. Lake Sammamish Pkwy. N.E., is a 642-acre recreation area on the site of Seattle banker James Clise's estate. The park provides facilities for picnicking, tennis, soccer, rugby, lacrosse, rock climbing, horseback riding, softball, baseball and bicycling. The Jerry Baker Velodrome is the scene of international-class bicycling events, and there also is a radio-controlled model airplane field, bird loop and dog park. A summer concert series features national acts. Outdoor movies are offered periodically. **Hours:** Daily 8-dusk. **Cost:** Free. **Parking:** $1. **Phone:** (206) 477-7275. 🗙 🐾 🏛

MICROSOFT VISITOR CENTER is at 15010 N.E. 36th St., Building 92, adjacent to Microsoft's corporate headquarters. The visitor center recounts the software giant's history along with the history of personal computing through a 30-foot-long timeline that includes a large collection of computer memorabilia. Interactive, hands-on product displays showcase current technology and explore possibilities for future Microsoft products. **Time:** Allow 1 hour minimum. **Hours:** Mon.-Fri. 9-7. Phone ahead to confirm schedule. **Cost:** Free. **Phone:** (425) 703-6214.

ALOFT SEATTLE REDMOND HOTEL   (425)636-9922 **50**
🍷🍷🍷 Hotel. **Address:** 15220 NE Shen St, Suite 150 98052

AAA Benefit: Members save 5% or more!

ELEMENT SEATTLE REDMOND HOTEL   (425)636-9942 **51**
🍷🍷🍷 Extended Stay Contemporary Hotel. **Address:** 15220 NE Shen St, Suite 100 98052

AAA Benefit: Members save 5% or more!

HAMPTON INN & SUITES BY HILTON SEATTLE/REDMOND   425/553-1200 **48**
🍷🍷🍷 Hotel. **Address:** 17770 NE 78th Pl 98052

AAA Benefit: Members save 5% or more!

HYATT HOUSE SEATTLE/REDMOND   (425)497-2000 **45**

🍷🍷🍷
Extended Stay Contemporary Hotel
$109-$609

H Y A T T house™

AAA Benefit: Members save 5% or more!

Address: 15785 Bear Creek Pkwy NE 98052 **Location:** I-405 exit 14 (SR 520), 4.5 mi e to W Lake Sammamish Pkwy, just n to Leary Way, just e to Bear Creek Pkwy, then just n. **Facility:** 149 units, some efficiencies. 5 stories, interior corridors. **Pool:** heated indoor. **Activities:** hot tub, bicycles, exercise room. **Guest Services:** valet and coin laundry, area transportation. **Featured Amenity:** breakfast buffet.

[SAVE] 🍴 🍸 CALL 🦽 ➜ 👪 [BIZ] [HS] 📶 🗙 🔲 🖼 🖵 / SOME UNITS 🐾

REDMOND INN   425/883-4900 **49**

🍷🍷🍷
Hotel
Rates not provided

Address: 17601 Redmond Way 98052 **Location:** I-405 exit 14 (SR 520), 5.5 mi e to Redmond Way, then just s. **Facility:** 137 units. 3 stories, interior corridors. **Amenities:** safes. **Pool:** heated outdoor. **Activities:** hot tub, bicycles, exercise room. **Guest Services:** valet and coin laundry, area transportation. **Featured Amenity:** continental breakfast.

[SAVE] 🍴 👪 CALL 🦽 ➜ 👪 [BIZ] [HS] 📶 🗙 🔲 🖼 🖵

RESIDENCE INN BY MARRIOTT SEATTLE EAST / REDMOND   (425)497-9226 **46**
🍷🍷🍷 Extended Stay Hotel. **Address:** 7575 164th Ave NE 98052

AAA Benefit: Members save 5% or more!

(See map & index p. 160.)

SEATTLE MARRIOTT REDMOND   (425)498-4000   **47**

♥♥♥♥ Hotel. **Address:** 7401 164th Ave NE 98052

AAA Benefit: Members save 5% or more!

SILVER CLOUD INN REDMOND   (425)746-8200   **52**

♥♥♥♥ Hotel. **Address:** 2122 152nd Ave NE 98052

WHERE TO EAT

TROPEA RISTORANTE ITALIANO   425/867-1082   **72**

♥♥ Southern Italian. Casual Dining. **Address:** 16156 NE 87th St 98052

WOODBLOCK   425/285-9458   **73**

♥♥ American. Casual Dining. **Address:** 16175 Cleveland St, Suite 109 98052

RENTON (F-3) pop. 90,927, elev. 45'

- Restaurants p. 115
- Hotels & Restaurants map & index p. 160
- Part of Seattle area — see map p. 124

Originally a Duwamish Indian encampment at the southern end of Lake Washington, Renton is a manufacturing city and producer of jet aircraft; Boeing rolled out its first commercial jet, the 707, at its Renton plant.

Gene Coulon Memorial Beach Park, 2 miles north to 1201 N. Lake Washington Blvd., offers freshwater fishing, swimming, boating and a nature trail. Renton River Days, held in July, features arts and crafts, entertainment, rides, games and athletic events. Standing in Greenwood Memorial Park Cemetery, N.E. 4th St. and Monroe Ave. N.E., is a memorial to Seattle-born rock legend Jimi Hendrix.

Renton Chamber of Commerce: 625 S. 4th St., Renton, WA 98057. **Phone:** (425) 226-4560 or (877) 467-3686.

RENTON HISTORY MUSEUM, 235 Mill Ave. S., features exhibits tracing the city's growth from a Duwamish Native American settlement through 19th-century coal mining and lumber producing days to present-day manufacturing. Displays recount Boeing's Renton plant and include a World War I flight simulator. **Time:** Allow 30 minutes minimum. **Hours:** Tues.-Sat. 10-4. Closed major holidays. **Cost:** $5; $2 (ages 9-16); free (ages 0-8 and to all first Wed. and first Sat. of the month). **Phone:** (425) 255-2330. **GT**

HAMPTON INN & SUITES BY HILTON SEATTLE/RENTON
425/524-4440   **86**

♥♥♥♥ Hotel. **Address:** 1300 Lake Washington Blvd N 98056

AAA Benefit: Members save 5% or more!

HILTON GARDEN INN SEATTLE/RENTON   425/430-1414   **91**

♥♥♥ Hotel. **Address:** 1801 E Valley Rd 98057

AAA Benefit: Members save 5% or more!

HYATT REGENCY LAKE WASHINGTON AT SEATTLE'S SOUTHPORT   (425)203-1234   **85**

Contemporary Hotel
$149-$409

HYATT REGENCY
AAA Benefit: Members save 5% or more!

Address: 1053 Lake Washington Blvd N 98056 **Location:** Waterfront. I-405 exit 5, just s on NE Park Dr, then just n. **Facility:** Guests will love the hotel's lakefront location and easy interstate access. The upscale guest rooms reflect modern and minimalist styling; many have incredible lake views. 347 units. 12 stories, interior corridors. **Parking:** on-site (fee) and valet. **Terms:** 3 day cancellation notice-fee imposed. **Amenities:** safes. **Pool:** heated indoor. **Activities:** hot tub, exercise room, spa. **Guest Services:** valet laundry.

[icons] / SOME UNITS

LARKSPUR LANDING RENTON   425/235-1212   **89**

♦♦♦ Extended Stay Hotel
Rates not provided

Address: 1701 E Valley Rd 98057 **Location:** SR 167 exit E Valley Rd, 1 mi nw. **Facility:** 127 efficiencies. 4 stories, interior corridors. **Activities:** exercise room. **Guest Services:** complimentary and valet laundry, area transportation. **Featured Amenity:** continental breakfast.

[icons] / SOME UNITS

QUALITY INN RENTON   (425)226-7600   **87**

♥♥ Hotel. **Address:** 1850 Maple Valley Hwy 98057

SPRINGHILL SUITES BY MARRIOTT SEATTLE SOUTH/ RENTON   (425)226-4100   **90**

♥♥♥♥ Hotel. **Address:** 200 SW 19th St 98057

AAA Benefit: Members save 5% or more!

TOWNEPLACE SUITES BY MARRIOTT SEATTLE SOUTH/RENTON   (425)917-2000   **88**

♦♦ Extended Stay Hotel
$85-$366

TOWNEPLACE SUITES MARRIOTT

AAA Benefit: Members save 5% or more!

Address: 300 SW 19th St 98057 **Location:** SR 167 exit E Valley Rd, 1 mi nw, then just w. Tukwila, 44. **Facility:** 137 kitchen units, some two bedrooms. 4 stories, interior corridors. **Terms:** cancellation fee imposed. **Pool:** heated outdoor. **Activities:** exercise room. **Guest Services:** valet and coin laundry, area transportation. **Featured Amenity:** breakfast buffet.

[icons] / SOME UNITS

WHERE TO EAT

MELROSE GRILL   425/254-0759   **113**

♥♥ Steak. Casual Dining. **Address:** 819 Houser Way S 98057

(See map & index p. 160.)

PLUM DELICIOUS   425/255-8510   (110)
▼▼ American. Casual Dining. **Address:** 3212 NE Sunset Blvd 98056

RIVER ROCK GRILL   425/430-0311
▼▼ Steak Seafood. Casual Dining. **Address:** 4050 Maple Valley Hwy 98058

TORERO'S   425/228-6180   (112)
▼▼ Mexican. Casual Dining. **Address:** 920 N 10th St 98057

WHISTLE STOP ALE HOUSE   425/277-3039   (114)
▼▼ American. Casual Dining. **Address:** 809 S 4th St 98055

WILDFIN AMERICAN GRILL   425/970-3757   (111)
▼▼ American. Casual Dining. **Address:** 727-C N 10th St 98057

RICHLAND (G-10) pop. 48,058, elev. 384'

Prior to World War II, Richland was a tranquil ranching settlement of approximately 200 people. The government selected the vast sage plains north of here as one of the development sites for the Manhattan Project, a top-secret nuclear weapons program which attracted tens of thousands of workers and scientists. After the war, many remained in this planned community. Over the years "Atomic City," as Richland became known, developed into a major center of technological industries.

Free public tours of the B Reactor National Historic Landmark, the nuclear reactor that produced plutonium for the atomic bomb dropped on Nagasaki, Japan, during World War II, are offered by the Department of Energy in partnership with the National Park Service. The four-hour bus tours depart most Mondays through Saturdays, mid-April through mid-November; advance registration is required. For schedule and information, contact the Manhattan Project National Historical Park's Visitor Contact Station at 2000 Logston Blvd., (509) 376-1647.

COURTYARD BY MARRIOTT RICHLAND COLUMBIA POINT
(509)942-9400
▼▼▼ Hotel. **Address:** 480 Columbia Point Dr 99352

AAA Benefit:
Members save 5% or more!

HAMPTON INN BY HILTON RICHLAND   (509)943-4400

▼▼▼
Hotel
$117-$323

Hampton

AAA Benefit:
Members save 5% or more!

Address: 486 Bradley Blvd 99352 **Location:** Waterfront. I-182 exit 5B, 0.5 mi n. Next to Howard Amon Park and the Columbia River. **Facility:** 130 units. 3 stories, interior corridors. **Terms:** 1-7 night minimum stay, 3 day cancellation notice-fee imposed. **Pool:** heated indoor. **Activities:** hot tub, trails, exercise room. **Guest Services:** valet and coin laundry, area transportation. **Featured Amenity:** full hot breakfast.

SAVE ▭ ⊞ TI+ CALL & 🛇 🛉 BIZ 🛜 ✕
▯ ▭ ▭

HOLIDAY INN EXPRESS & SUITES RICHLAND   509/737-8000
▼▼▼ Hotel. **Address:** 1970 Center Pkwy 99352

HOME2 SUITES BY HILTON RICHLAND   509/460-4040
▼▼▼ Extended Stay Contemporary Hotel. **Address:** 2861 Lincoln Landing 99352

AAA Benefit:
Members save 5% or more!

HOMEWOOD SUITES BY HILTON RICHLAND/TRI-CITIES
(509)371-1550

▼▼▼
Extended Stay Hotel
$129-$189

HOMEWOOD SUITES BY HILTON

AAA Benefit:
Members save 5% or more!

Address: 1060 George Washington Way 99352 **Location:** Waterfront. I-182 exit 5B, 2 mi n on SR 240 business route. Located on Columbia River. **Facility:** 115 efficiencies, some two bedrooms. 4 stories, interior corridors. **Terms:** 1-7 night minimum stay, 3 day cancellation notice-fee imposed. **Pool:** heated outdoor. **Activities:** hot tub, game room, picnic facilities, trails, exercise room. **Guest Services:** valet and coin laundry. **Featured Amenity:** full hot breakfast.

SAVE ▭ CALL & 🛇 🛉 BIZ HS 🛜 ✕ ▯
▭ ▭

LODGE AT COLUMBIA POINT   509/713-7423
▼▼▼ Boutique Hotel. **Address:** 530 Columbia Point Dr 99352

TOWNEPLACE SUITES BY MARRIOTT RICHLAND COLUMBIA POINT
(509)943-9800

▼▼▼
Extended Stay Hotel
$85-$197

TOWNEPLACE SUITES MARRIOTT

AAA Benefit:
Members save 5% or more!

Address: 591 Columbia Point Dr 99352 **Location:** I-182 exit 5B, 0.5 mi n to Columbia Point Dr, then 0.8 mi e. **Facility:** 90 efficiencies, some two bedrooms. 4 stories, interior corridors. **Terms:** cancellation fee imposed. **Pool:** heated indoor. **Activities:** hot tub, bicycles, exercise room. **Guest Services:** valet and coin laundry. **Featured Amenity:** continental breakfast.

SAVE TI+ CALL & 🛇 🛉 BIZ HS 🛜 ✕ ▯
▭ ▭ / SOME UNITS 🐾

WHERE TO EAT

3 EYED FISH WINE BAR & TAPAS   509/628-3255
▼▼ Small Plates. Casual Dining. **Address:** 1970 Keene Rd 99352

ANTHONY'S RESTAURANT   509/946-3474
▼▼▼ Seafood. Casual Dining. **Address:** 550 Columbia Point Dr 99352

ATOMIC ALE BREWPUB & EATERY   509/946-5465
▼▼ American. Casual Dining. **Address:** 1015 Lee Blvd 99352

BUDD'S BROILER COLUMBIA POINT   509/946-8178
▼▼▼ Steak Seafood. Fine Dining. **Address:** 450 Columbia Point Dr 99352

CASA MIA ITALIAN RESTAURANT   509/946-0500
▼▼ Italian. Casual Dining. **Address:** 607 George Washington Way 99352

DRUMHELLER?S FOOD & DRINK   509/713-7423
▼▼▼ American. Fine Dining. **Address:** 530 Columbia Point Dr 99352

LU LU CRAFT BAR & KITCHEN   509/713-7880
▼▼▼ American. Casual Dining. **Address:** 606 Columbia Point Dr 99352

MONTEROSSO'S ITALIAN RESTAURANT   509/946-4525
▼▼ American. Casual Dining. **Address:** 1026 Lee Blvd 99352

THREE MARGARITAS FAMILY MEXICAN RESTAURANT
                                            509/946-7755
▼▼ Mexican. Casual Dining. **Address:** 627 Jadwin Ave 99352

RITZVILLE (F-11) pop. 1,673, elev. 1,818'

Located in the heart of Washington's wheat-growing region, Ritzville is named for late 19th-century homesteader Philip Ritz. By 1904 the town was a major wheat shipping point and billed itself—with perhaps a touch of grandiosity—as the "bread-basket of the world."

The Channeled Scablands, north of Ritzville, form a landscape of eroded features created by cataclysmic floods during the last Ice Age.

Ritzville Area Chamber of Commerce: 111 W. Main Ave., P.O. Box 122, Ritzville, WA 99169-0122. **Phone:** (509) 659-1936.

BEST WESTERN BRONCO INN   (509)659-5000

▼▼▼ **Hotel** $100-$125

BW Best Western. **AAA Benefit:** Members save up to 15% and earn bonus points!

Address: 105 W Galbreath Way 99169 **Location:** I-90 exit 221, cross overpass, then second left. **Facility:** 63 units. 3 stories, interior corridors. **Parking:** winter plug-ins. **Terms:** cancellation fee imposed. **Pool:** heated indoor. **Activities:** hot tub, exercise room. **Guest Services:** coin laundry.
[SAVE] [🚭] [📶] [🛎] [⌨] [BIZ] [HS]
[📶] [✕] [🛗] [📷] [🖥]
/ SOME UNITS [🐾]

ROCHESTER (I-1) pop. 2,388, elev. 149'

A historical marker just southeast of Rochester on Sargent Road S.W. designates the site of Fort Henness, a U.S. Army post built on Grand Mound Prairie in 1855 to protect pioneer settlers from a perceived Native American threat. An interpretive panel describes the fort, which once housed more than 200 people. The site has chimney remains; a pioneer cemetery is on the opposite side of the road.

FAIRFIELD INN & SUITES BY MARRIOTT GRAND MOUND
CENTRALIA   (360)858-5757
▼▼▼ Hotel. **Address:** 6223 197th Way SW 98579

AAA Benefit: Members save 5% or more!

ROSS LAKE NATIONAL RECREATION AREA (C-8)

Between the north and south sections of North Cascades National Park, Ross Lake National Recreation Area is shaped like a backward L. For access from the east, west and south, SR 20 parallels the Skagit River through the southern half of the area, continuing southeast into Okanogan-Wenatchee National Forest. This road is normally closed east of Diablo Lake from mid-November to mid-April. Access from the north is possible only through Canada via a secondary road that branches off Hwy. 3 east of Hope, British Columbia.

Ross, Diablo and Gorge lakes are formed by Ross, Diablo and Gorge dams on the Skagit River. The dams are part of a hydroelectric project that supplies Seattle with electricity; an information center is in Newhalem *(see place listing p. 92).* The 3.5-mile Diablo Lake Trail, beginning near Diablo Lake Resort, leads to Ross Dam. From the south, access to Ross Lake is limited to trail and water routes. Seven major trails lead outward from Ross Lake into the back country.

Surrounding the lakes are 118,000 acres of glaciers, mountain peaks and forested valleys providing habitats for a variety of wildlife. Fishing season for Ross Lake, one of the few remaining large lakes in Washington not artificially stocked, is mid-June to late October; state fishing regulations apply and a license is required. Ranger stations are on SR 20 at Marblemount, phone (360) 854-7245, and in Newhalem; phone (206) 386-4495, ext. 11.

For further information contact the Park Superintendent's Office; phone (360) 854-7200. *See Recreation Areas Chart.*

SAN JUAN ISLANDS (B-1)
• Attractions map p. 119

The glaciers that covered northwest Washington approximately 15 million years ago created the San Juan Archipelago, between the mainland and Vancouver Island. As part of this archipelago, the San Juan Islands are made up of 172 islands ranging in size from mere rocky islets to 57-square-mile Orcas Island, with its picturesque bays and steep, forested ridges.

Spanish captain Francisco Eliza charted and named the islands in 1791, 16 years after a previous expedition discovered them. In 1792 Capt. George

Vancouver claimed the islands for Britain, and in 1841 Capt. Charles Wilkes declared them part of America.

The ensuing dispute over ownership of the islands nearly brought the two nations to blows during the infamous Pig War of 1859, in which a stray British pig was shot in an American potato patch. The opposing sides occupied the islands for the next 13 years, but the conflict was solved peacefully through arbitration by German Kaiser Wilhelm I, who ruled in favor of the United States. What remains of the British and American forts are now part of San Juan Island National Historical Park in Friday Harbor.

If you're wondering where to find hotels, restaurants and fun things to do in the San Juan Islands, consider Fidalgo Island, Lopez Island, Orcas Island and San Juan Islands, the largest and most populated of the islands. Recreational opportunities abound. Boating, kayaking, swimming, scuba diving, fishing, hiking, bicycling and camping are among the main activities.

The San Juan Islands are home to more bald eagles than any other region in the 48 contiguous states. Great horned owls, tufted puffins and a variety of other birds and mammals inhabit the islands; salmon, seals, dolphins and orcas thrive in the waters, making whale watching in the San Juan Islands a popular activity. San Juan Islands National Wildlife Refuge comprises 48 other rocks and islands; only Matia and Turn islands are open to the public and offer overnight camping and short hiking trails for those seeking adventurous things to do.

Washington State Ferries provides daily ferry service between the ports of Friday Harbor, Anacortes, Lopez, Shaw and Orcas as well as to Sidney, British Columbia, north of Victoria; phone (206) 464-6400, or (888) 808-7977 in Wash. Passenger ferry service is available early May to late September from Friday Harbor to Port Townsend via the Puget Sound Express *(see attraction listing p. 110)*, (360) 385-5288; to Seattle via Clipper Navigation *(see attraction listing p. 150)*, (206) 448-5000 or (800) 888-2535; and to Bellingham and Victoria via Victoria/San Juan Cruises, (800) 443-4552.

Sightseeing flights are available late May to early October from San Juan Airlines in Friday Harbor; phone (800) 874-4434. If you're headed from Seattle to the San Juan Islands, scheduled air service is available from Bellingham, Seattle-Lake Union or Seattle-Boeing Field via wheeled plane or seaplane. For further information about airlines and travel plans, contact your local AAA travel agency or AAA Washington; phone (800) 562-2582.

San Juan Islands Chamber of Commerce: 165 First St. S., P.O. Box 98, Friday Harbor, WA 98250. **Phone:** (360) 378-5240.

SAN JUAN ISLAND (C-1)
• Hotels p. 120 • Restaurants p. 120

One of the islands that make up the San Juan Islands, this also is the westernmost major island in the archipelago. Rolling hills dotted with small farms and

patches of forest in the east transition to rugged terrain in the west, where Mount Dallas rises to 1,086 feet. Friday Harbor, San Juan Island's largest town, is a bustling port of call for ferries and other boats.

Perched at the island's northwest corner is Roche Harbor, a resort town and popular yachting destination. In a peaceful glen nearby is the Afterglow Vista Mausoleum. It commemorates John S. McMillan, founder of the local limeworks.

San Juan Transit provides regular shuttle service around the island. Narrated tours are available on a limited basis by reservation; phone (360) 378-8887.

LIME KILN POINT STATE PARK is 10 mi. w. of Friday Harbor via Beaverton Valley Rd., West Valley Rd. and Mitchell Bay Rd. to 1567 Westside Rd. Covering 41 acres, Lime Kiln is a living museum of natural and cultural history. Its name derives from the vicinity's former lime kiln operations. A 1.6-mile hiking trail loops through the park, traversing meadows, open woodlands and rocky shores. Look for outcrops of prickly pear, the northernmost species of cactus, and the shaggy-barked Pacific madrone, a beautiful broadleaf evergreen.

The trail overlooks Haro Strait, waters favored by orca and minke whales and Dall's porpoise, and is an excellent vantage point for whale sightings (most likely to occur May through September). Lime Kiln Lighthouse was built in 1919; it is closed to the public except for guided tours on selected days during the summer. The trail continues to a restored lime kiln that operated until 1923. Both the park visitor center and the lighthouse have interpretive displays.

Time: Allow 1 hour minimum. **Hours:** Park open daily 8 a.m.-dusk. Visitor center open daily 11-5, late May-Labor Day. Lighthouse tours given Thurs. and Sat. 7-10 p.m., Memorial Day-Labor Day; phone to confirm staff availability. **Cost:** Park admission $10 (per private vehicle); Discover Pass, valid for 1 year, $30 (per private vehicle). **Phone:** (360) 378-2044 or (360) 902-8844. GT ⒜

MAYA'S LEGACY WHALE WATCHING departs from downtown in Friday Harbor and at San Juan Island's Snug Harbor Resort, 10 mi. w. of Friday Harbor at 1997 Mitchell Bay Rd. The tour provider offers 3-hour narrated small group whale-watch excursions and private charters. Guides describe San Juan Island's history and various types of local wildlife, including the orcas passengers are likely to see. **Time:** Allow 3 hours minimum. **Hours:** Tours depart two to three times daily, Apr.-Sept.; once daily, rest of year. **Cost:** Fare June-Sept. $129. Fare rest of year $119. Reservations are required. **Phone:** (360) 378-7996. GT

SAN JUAN EXCURSIONS WHALE WATCHING departs from Spring Street Landing, a half blk. from the Friday Harbor ferry dock at 40 Spring St. San Juan Excursions offers 3.5- to 4.5-hour whale-watch/wildlife tours in the San Juan and Canadian Gulf islands narrated by two certified naturalists. Passengers see orca

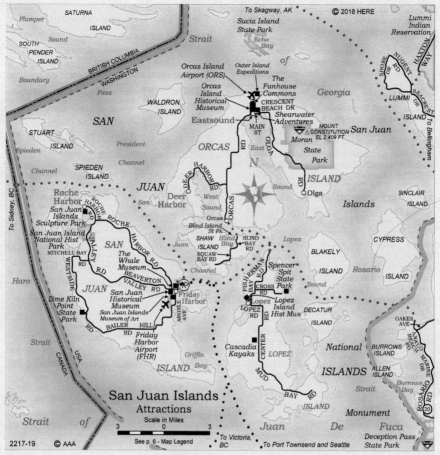

San Juan Islands
Attractions
Scale in Miles
3   0   3

2217-19   © AAA
See p. 6 - Map Legend

whales on most trips (during peak season). Bald eagles, harbor seals and many other marine mammals and birds can be seen on every trip.

Time: Allow 4 hours minimum. **Hours:** Whale watch tours depart daily at noon, early Apr. to mid-June and mid-Sept. to mid-Oct.; at 1:30, mid-June to mid-Sept. **Cost:** Fare $99; $89.10 (ages 65+ and college students, teachers and military with ID); $69 (ages 3-12). Reservations are recommended. **Phone:** (360) 378-6636 or (800) 809-4253. GT

SAN JUAN ISLAND NATIONAL HISTORICAL PARK is on San Juan Island. The park commemorates the British and American struggle for possession of the San Juans—a dispute that culminated in the Pig War of 1859. The lone casualty of the war was a stray pig, and in 1872 arbitration sustained the American claim to the San Juans and set the boundary between the United States and Canada.

The English Camp is 10 miles northwest of Friday Harbor on a cove known as Garrison Bay at 3905 W. Valley Rd. The blockhouse, commissary, hospital, barracks and a formal garden are restored;

only the blockhouse and barracks are open to the public. The American Camp is on the southeastern tip of the island, 6 miles from Friday Harbor at 4668 Cattle Point Rd. Vestiges of the principal American defense work are preserved. The officers' quarters and laundress' quarters have been restored.

Beaches, trails and a small boat dock are within the park; hunting and camping are not permitted. **Hours:** Grounds open daily dawn-11 p.m. Rangers are at the sites daily. Ranger programs are offered daily in summer. American Camp Visitor Center open daily 8:30-5, early June-early Sept.; daily 8:30-4:30, early Sept.-early Oct.; Wed.-Sun. 8:30-4:30, rest of year. American Camp Visitor Center closed Jan. 1, Thanksgiving and Christmas. English Camp Visitor Center open daily 9-5, early June-early Sept. **Cost:** Free. **Phone:** (360) 378-2240, ext. 2226.

WESTERN PRINCE WHALE & WILDLIFE TOURS departs from the Port of Friday Harbor; the office is at 1 Spring St., adjacent to the ferry dock. The company conducts naturalist-guided whale search/wildlife excursions in the San Juan Islands and Canadian Gulf

Islands. Whales are sighted during the great majority of trips, while marine mammals and bald eagles are guaranteed sightings on all trips.

Time: Allow 4 hours minimum. **Hours:** Standard trips lasting 3-4 hours depart daily at 10:30 and 2:15, mid-June to late Sept.; daily at 12:30, mid-Mar. to mid-June and late Sept.-Oct. 31. Adventure trips aboard *Western Explorer* lasting 2.5-3 hours depart daily at 11 and 3, mid-June to late Sept.; at noon, mid-Mar. to mid-June and late Sept.-Oct. 31. Ages 0-5 not permitted on Adventure tour. **Cost:** Standard fare $99; $90 (military and teachers with ID); $69 (ages 2-12). Adventure fare $109; $99 (military and teachers with ID); $85 (ages 6-12). **Phone:** (360) 378-5315 or (800) 757-6722. GT

THE WHALE MUSEUM is 3 blks. n.w. of the ferry landing at 62 First St. N. in Friday Harbor. The museum occupies one of the island's oldest buildings. Exhibits depict the biology, behavior and sounds of whales. Included are a display comparing the skeletons of a human, a river otter and a dolphin; a genealogy exhibit of local resident orcas; and two movies. Complete skeletons of a baby gray whale and an adult orca also are displayed. A children's activity room plus carvings, paintings, lithographs and photographs highlight other whale-related exhibits.

Time: Allow 1 hour minimum. **Hours:** Daily 9-6, Memorial Day-early Oct.; 10-4, rest of year. Closed Jan. 1, Jan. 5-15, Thanksgiving and Christmas. **Cost:** $6; $5 (ages 65+); $3 (ages 5-18 and students with ID). **Phone:** (360) 378-4710 or (800) 946-7227, ext. 30.

ARGYLE HOUSE BED & BREAKFAST   360/378-4084
♦♦ Historic Bed & Breakfast. **Address:** 685 Argyle Ave 98250

EARTHBOX INN & SPA   360/378-4000
♦♦ Hotel. **Address:** 410 Spring St 98250

FRIDAY HARBOR HOUSE   360/378-8455
♦♦♦ Boutique Hotel. **Address:** 130 West St 98250

FRIDAY HARBOR SUITES   360/378-3031

♦♦♦
Hotel
Rates not provided

Address: 680 Spring St 98250 **Location:** In Friday Harbor; 0.7 mi w of ferry dock. **Facility:** 61 units, some two bedrooms and houses. 2 stories, interior corridors. **Terms:** check-in 4 pm. **Activities:** hot tub, exercise room. **Guest Services:** area transportation. **Featured Amenity: breakfast buffet.**

SAVE ⊞ ▥ ⌁ CALL ⌖ ⧖
BIZ 📶 ✕ ⌨ 🖥 ▭ ▯
/SOME UNITS 🐾

HILLSIDE HOUSE BED & BREAKFAST   360/378-4730

♦♦♦
Bed & Breakfast
Rates not provided

Address: 365 Carter Ave 98250 **Location:** In Friday Harbor; just off Guard St. **Facility:** Situated on a small hill overlooking Friday Harbor, this contemporary lodging offers water views from some guest rooms. 7 units. 3 stories (no elevator), interior corridors. **Terms:** check-in 4 pm. **Featured Amenity: full hot breakfast.**

SAVE 📶 ✕ ⌨ ⊡

WHERE TO EAT

THE BEAN CAFÉ   360/370-5858
♦ Coffee/Tea Sandwiches. Quick Serve. **Address:** 150B 1st St 98250

CASK & SCHOONER PUBLIC HOUSE   360/378-2922
♦♦ American. Casual Dining. **Address:** 1 Front St N 98250

COHO RESTAURANT   360/378-6330
♦♦♦ Pacific Northwest. Fine Dining. **Address:** 120 Nichols St 98250

DOWNRIGGER   360/378-2700
♦♦ Seafood. Casual Dining. **Address:** 10 Front St N 98250

DUCK SOUP INN   360/378-4878
♦♦♦ Pacific Northwest. Casual Dining. **Address:** 50 Duck Soup Ln 98250

HALEY'S SPORTS BAR & GRILL   360/378-4434
♦♦ American. Casual Dining. **Address:** 175 Spring St 98250

LIME KILN CAFE   360/378-2155
♦ American. Quick Serve. **Address:** 248 Reuben Memorial Dr 98250

MADRONA BAR & GRILL   360/378-2155
♦♦ American. Casual Dining. **Address:** 248 Reuben Memorial Dr 98250

THE MARKET CHEF   360/378-4546
♦♦ Deli. Quick Serve. **Address:** 225 A St 98250

MCMILLIN'S DINING ROOM   360/378-5757
♦♦♦ American. Casual Dining. **Address:** 248 Reuben Memorial Dr 98250

VIC'S DRIVE-IN   360/378-8427
♦ Burgers. Quick Serve. **Address:** 25 Second St S 98250

VINNY'S RISTORANTE   360/378-1934
♦♦♦ Italian. Casual Dining. **Address:** 165 West St 98250

SEATAC pop. 26,909, elev. 371'
• Restaurants p. 122
• Hotels & Restaurants map & index p. 160
• Part of Seattle area — see map p. 124

ALOFT SEATTLE SEA-TAC AIRPORT (206)241-0260 **118**

Hotel. **Address:** 19030 28th Ave S 98188

AAA Benefit: Members save 5% or more!

BEST WESTERN SEATTLE AIRPORT HOTEL
(206)878-3300 **125**

Hotel
$109-$249

Best Western. **AAA Benefit:** Members save up to 15% and earn bonus points!

Address: 20717 International Blvd (SR 99) 98198 **Location:** Jct SR 518, 3.2 mi s. Angle Lake, 43. **Facility:** 143 units. 3 stories, interior corridors. **Terms:** cancellation fee imposed. **Pool:** heated indoor. **Activities:** hot tub, exercise room. **Guest Services:** coin laundry.

CEDARBROOK LODGE 206/901-9268 **115**

Hotel
Rates not provided

Address: 18525 36th Ave S 98188 **Location:** Jct SR 518, 1.9 mi s on International Blvd (SR 99), just e on 188th St, then just n. SeaTac/Airport, 42. **Facility:** 167 units. 2-5 stories, interior corridors. **Parking:** on-site (fee) and valet. **Terms:** check-in 4 pm. **Amenities:** safes. **Dining:** Copperleaf Restaurant & Bar, see separate listing. **Activities:** hot tub, exercise room, spa. **Guest Services:** valet laundry, area transportation. **Featured Amenity:** full hot breakfast.

CLARION HOTEL (206)242-0200 **110**

Hotel. **Address:** 3000 S 176th St 98188

COAST GATEWAY HOTEL 206/248-8200 **114**

Hotel
Rates not provided

Address: 18415 International Blvd (SR 99) 98188 **Location:** Jct SR 518, 1.7 mi s. SeaTac/Airport, 42. **Facility:** 144 units. 6 stories, interior corridors. **Activities:** exercise room. **Guest Services:** complimentary and valet laundry, boarding pass kiosk, area transportation. **Featured Amenity:** continental breakfast.

COUNTRY INN & SUITES BY RADISSON SEATTLE AIRPORT
206/433-8188 **119**

Hotel. **Address:** 3100 S 192nd St 98188

CROWNE PLAZA SEATTLE AIRPORT (206)248-1000 **109**

Hotel. **Address:** 17338 International Blvd (SR 99) 98188

DOUBLETREE BY HILTON HOTEL SEATTLE AIRPORT
(206)246-8600 **116**

Hotel
$99-$369

DOUBLETREE BY HILTON **AAA Benefit:** Members save 5% or more!

Address: 18740 International Blvd (SR 99) 98188 **Location:** Jct SR 518, 1.7 mi s. Located in a commercial area. SeaTac/Airport, 42. **Facility:** 850 units, some two bedrooms. 3-14 stories, interior corridors. **Parking:** on-site (fee) and valet. **Terms:** 1-7 night minimum stay, 3 day cancellation notice-fee imposed. **Dining:** 2 restaurants. **Pool:** heated outdoor. **Activities:** hot tub, exercise room. **Guest Services:** valet and coin laundry, boarding pass kiosk, area transportation.

FAIRFIELD INN BY MARRIOTT SEATTLE SEA-TAC AIRPORT
(206)824-9909 **123**

Hotel. **Address:** 19631 International Blvd (SR 99) 98188

AAA Benefit: Members save 5% or more!

HAMPTON INN & SUITES BY HILTON SEATTLE AIRPORT - 28TH AVE 206/244-5044 **117**

Hotel. **Address:** 18850 28th Ave S 98188

AAA Benefit: Members save 5% or more!

HAMPTON INN BY HILTON SEATTLE-AIRPORT
(206)878-1700 **120**

Hotel
$112-$277

Hampton **AAA Benefit:** Members save 5% or more!

Address: 19445 International Blvd (SR 99) 98188 **Location:** Jct SR 518, 2.4 mi s. Angle Lake, 43. **Facility:** 128 units. 4 stories, interior corridors. **Terms:** 1-7 night minimum stay, 3 day cancellation notice-fee imposed. **Pool:** heated outdoor. **Activities:** exercise room. **Guest Services:** valet laundry, area transportation. **Featured Amenity:** full hot breakfast.

HILTON SEATTLE AIRPORT & CONFERENCE CENTER
(206)244-4800 **111**

Hotel
$99-$399

Hilton HOTELS & RESORTS **AAA Benefit:** Members save 5% or more!

Address: 17620 International Blvd (SR 99) 98188 **Location:** Jct SR 518, 1.3 mi s. SeaTac/Airport, 42. **Facility:** 396 units. 3-4 stories, interior corridors. **Parking:** on-site (fee) and valet. **Terms:** 1-7 night minimum stay, 3 day cancellation notice-fee imposed. **Amenities:** safes. **Dining:** Spencer's for Steaks and Chops, see separate listing. **Pool:** heated outdoor. **Activities:** hot tub, exercise room. **Guest Services:** valet and coin laundry.

(See map & index p. 160.)

HOLIDAY INN EXPRESS HOTEL & SUITES-SEATTLE SEA-TAC
AIRPORT   206/824-3200   121
◈◈◈ Hotel. Address: 19621 International Blvd (SR 99) 98188

RADISSON HOTEL SEATTLE AIRPORT   (206)244-6666   113
◈◈◈ Hotel. Address: 18118 International Blvd (SR 99) 98188

RED ROOF INN SEATTLE AIRPORT-SEATAC
                                    (206)248-0901   108

◈◈◈
Hotel
$69-$289

Address: 16838 International Blvd (SR 99) 98188 Location: Jct SR 518, 0.8 mi s. ⓜ SeaTac/Airport, 42. Facility: 152 units. 4 stories, interior corridors. Parking: on-site (fee). Terms: cancellation fee imposed, resort fee. Amenities: safes. Activities: limited exercise equipment. Guest Services: coin laundry.

SAVE ⊬ BIZ 🛜 ✕ 🎦 ▣
/ SOME UNITS 🐾 🔋 🖥 🖨

RESIDENCE INN BY MARRIOTT SEATTLE SEA-TAC
AIRPORT   (206)878-6188   122

◈◈◈
Extended Stay Hotel
$95-$318

Residence INN   AAA Benefit:
Members save 5% or more!

Address: 19608 International Blvd (SR 99) 98188 Location: Jct SR 518, 2.5 mi s. ⓜ Angle Lake, 43. Facility: 170 efficiencies. 5 stories, interior corridors. Bath: shower only. Parking: on-site (fee). Terms: cancellation fee imposed. Activities: trails, exercise room. Guest Services: valet and coin laundry, boarding pass kiosk, area transportation. Featured Amenity: full hot breakfast.

SAVE ⊬ CALL ♿ 🌀 BIZ 🛜 ✕ 🔋 🖥 ▣
/ SOME UNITS 🐾 🖨

SEATTLE AIRPORT MARRIOTT   (206)241-2000   112

◈◈◈
Hotel
$89-$352

MARRIOTT
AAA Benefit:
Members save 5% or more!

Address: 3201 S 176th St 98188 Location: Jct SR 518, 1.2 mi s on International Blvd (SR 99), just e. Located in a commercial area. ⓜ SeaTac/Airport, 42. Facility: 459 units. 5-9 stories, interior corridors. Parking: on-site (fee) and valet. Terms: check-in 4 pm, cancellation fee imposed. Pool: heated indoor. Activities: sauna, hot tub, exercise room. Guest Services: valet laundry, boarding pass kiosk, rental car service.

SAVE ⊬ ▯▮ 🛀 ⅄ CALL ♿ 🌀 🗊 BIZ 📶
✕ 🔋 🖥 🚌

SLEEP INN SEATAC AIRPORT   (206)878-3600   124
◈◈ Hotel. Address: 20406 International Blvd (SR 99) 98198

13 COINS RESTAURANT   206/243-9500
◈◈ American. Casual Dining. Address: 18000 International Blvd (SR 99) 98188

COPPERLEAF RESTAURANT & BAR   206/214-4282   126
◈◈◈ Pacific Northwest. Casual Dining. Address: 18525 36th Ave S 98188

DAVE'S DINER & BREW   206/277-7196   125
◈◈ American. Casual Dining. Address: 2825 S 188th St 98188

SPENCER'S FOR STEAKS AND CHOPS   206/248-7153   124
◈◈◈ Steak. Casual Dining. Address: 17620 International Blvd (SR 99) 98188

Seattle

Then & Now

Picture it: Urbane Frasier Crane and his equally urbane brother Niles meet at Café Nervosa to sip caffeinated drinks and discuss opera, ballet and the finer points of a good sherry. Interns and residents juggle medical training, grueling work schedules and messy personal lives at Seattle Grace Hospital. Recently widowed Sam Baldwin moves into a houseboat on the west shore of Lake Union. While the coffee shop and the hospital are fictional, the houseboat from the romantic comedy "Sleepless in Seattle" does exist, and "Frasier's" overall ambience—and all those scenes on "Grey's Anatomy" where rain is a backdrop—leave no doubt as to *exactly* what city you're in.

A vivid sense of place is one of the more charming aspects of this Northwestern metropolis, and geography plays a large part in the natural beauty on display. Puget Sound, a deep-water inlet punctuating the northwest Washington coast, not only provides scenic vistas; its indentations create several harbors that contributed to the area's early growth. The Olympic Peninsula's snowcapped mountains frame the western horizon. And to the southeast lies towering, ice-clad Mount Rainier; on clear days it resembles an ethereal image of a massive mountain. These are just three reasons why Seattle's reputation as a city of spectacular views is fully justified.

Yes, it can be gloomy (locals will tell you that summer finally arrives on July 4). Yes, it can be rainy (the

AAA.com/travelguides—
more ways to look, book and save

kind of light but persistent rain that requires a rain jacket but not an umbrella). But the reward for putting up with this is sweet indeed: the azure blue skies, warm sun and low humidity that characterize the glorious days of midsummer and early fall.

And Seattle's urban green spaces are delightful. Imagine, for instance, happening on Kinnear Park, a wee stretch of green hugging the southwest slope of Queen Anne Hill. A path winds beneath tall, stately trees. Benches invite you to stop and sit for a while. And there are pretty views of the Elliott Bay waterfront. It's a perfect spot to relax and enjoy nature for a few minutes.

"Frasier's" title screen shows a stylized Seattle skyline with an instantly identifiable city landmark. Opened in 1962—just in time for the Century 21 Exposition, more commonly known as the Seattle World's Fair—the Space Needle's futuristic profile remains unmistakable, although five Seattle skyscrapers to date have surpassed its 605-foot height. A trip

(Continued on p. 125.)

Seattle waterfront

Destination Seattle

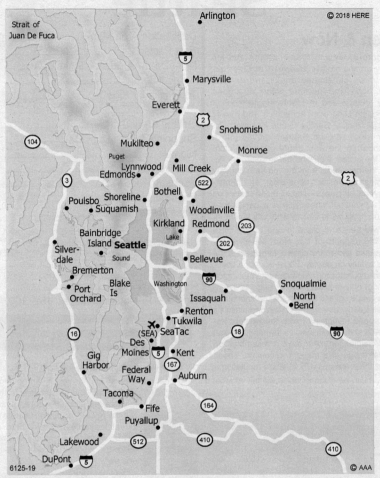

Strait of Juan De Fuca

Arlington

© 2018 HERE

Marysville

Everett

Snohomish

Mukilteo

Monroe

Puget

Lynnwood   Mill Creek

Edmonds

Poulsbo   Shoreline   Bothell

Suquamish   Woodinville

Kirkland   Redmond

Bainbridge   Lake

Island   **Seattle**

Silver-
dale   Sound

Bremerton

Blake
Is   Washington

Port
Orchard

Snoqualmie

Issaquah   North
Bend

Renton

Tukwila

(SEA) SeaTac

Des
Moines   Kent

Gig
Harbor   Federal
Way   Auburn

Tacoma

Fife

Puyallup

Lakewood

DuPont

6125-19   © AAA

This map shows cities in the Seattle vicinity where you will find attractions, hotels and restaurants. Cities are listed alphabetically in this book on the following pages.

Fast Facts

ABOUT THE CITY

POP: 608,660 ▪ **ELEV:** 350 ft.

MONEY

SALES TAX: State and county sales taxes total 10.1 percent in Seattle. A lodging tax of 10.1 to 15.6 percent is levied along with a 17.8 percent rental car tax.

WHOM TO CALL

EMERGENCY: 911

POLICE (non-emergency): (206) 625-5011

HOSPITALS: Harborview Medical Center, (206) 744-3000 ▪ Northwest Hospital & Medical Center, (206) 364-0500 ▪ Swedish Medical Center-First Hill, (206) 386-6000 ▪ University of Washington Medical Center, (206) 598-3300 ▪ Virginia Mason Medical Center, (206) 223-6600.

VISITOR INFORMATION

Visit Seattle: 701 Pike St., Suite 800 (next to the escalators inside the Convention Center), Seattle, WA 98101. **Phone:** (206) 461-5800 or (866) 732-2695.

The convention center location is open daily 9-5, mid-May to mid-Oct.; Mon.-Fri. 9-5, rest of year. An additional visitor information center is located in Pike Place Market at 1st Avenue and Pike Street and is open daily 10-6.

TRANSPORTATION

AIR TRAVEL: Seattle-Tacoma (Sea-Tac) International Airport (SEA) is midway between Seattle and Tacoma on SR 99; most scheduled services and international flights use Sea-Tac; phone (206) 787-5388 or (800) 544-1965. King County International Airport/Boeing Field, south of the city, is a smaller airport used by private and charter planes and some regional carriers. Travel sites including

AAA.com can help you find vacation packages with cheap plane tickets.

Shuttle Express' Downtown Airporter operates express buses daily 24 hours between Seattle-Tacoma International Airport and various downtown hotels. One-way fare is $18; free (ages 0-17 with paying adult). Reservations are required for service from downtown to the airport. Phone (425) 981-7000.

Shuttle Express offers door-to-door van or limousine service to and from Sea-Tac within the Seattle-Everett-Tacoma metropolitan area. One-way fares start at $33. For information and reservations phone (425) 981-7000, or (800) 487-7433 in Wash.

Sound Transit's Central Link light rail line connects the airport with downtown Seattle. *See Getting Around, Public Transportation.*

RENTAL CARS: Hertz offers discounts to AAA members; phone (206) 903-6260 or (800) 654-3080.

 Book and save at AAA.com/hertz

RAIL SERVICE: Amtrak passenger trains, (800) 872-7245, arrive and depart the King Street Station at 303 S. Jackson St. Amtrak also serves Edmonds, Everett, Tacoma and Tukwila.

BUSES: The Greyhound Lines Inc. station is at 503 S. Royal Brougham Way; phone (206) 624-0618 or (800) 231-2222.

TAXIS: Taxis must be contacted by phone or hired while stopped at cab stands. Major companies are Farwest Taxi, (206) 622-1717 ▪ Orange Cab, (206) 522-8800 ▪ and Yellow Cab, (206) 622-6500.

PUBLIC TRANSPORTATION: Transportation by bus, trolley, street car, light rail, monorail and trains is available in Seattle. *See Getting Around, Public Transportation.*

BOATS: Two companies provide water transportation within the greater Seattle area and to British Columbia. *See Arriving, By Boat.*

(Continued from p. 123.)

up to the observation deck for the breathtaking 360-degree panorama is the No. 1 thing on many a tourist's "don't miss" list, so by all means do it.

After you've explored Pike Place Market, that is. There's no better place to be early in the morning, wandering among the produce, seafood, craft and flower vendors as they set up shop. Locally grown raspberries and wood ear mushrooms, sourdough cinnamon rolls, whole Dungeness crab, artisan cheeses, Greek yogurt made from locally sourced ingredients: it's foodie heaven. Noise, crowds and

the salmon-flinging antics of the fishmongers aside, the soul of the city is right here. Not to mention the amazing places to eat.

The market also is the location of the oldest operating Starbucks (1912 Pike Place). It's hard to believe that the global brand of everything from organic beans to specialty brewing equipment had a humble beginning not so long ago—1971 to be exact—as a local coffee roaster. But then again, who can remember life before cellphones and apps? Amazon.com, Costco and Microsoft are just a few of the corporate powerhouses headquartered in the Seattle area.

Must Do: AAA Editor's Picks

- Every Seattle trip should include a stop at ⩔ **Pike Place Market** (spreads out from Pike Street and 1st Avenue). The fishmongers' salmon-flinging antics alone are worth a visit, which makes the gorgeous array of produce, baked goods, prepared foods (a shout-out to the mac 'n cheese at Beecher's) and craft stalls simply icing on the cake when it comes to fun things to do in Seattle.

- On a clear day, your vacation should include a pilgrimage to the observation deck near the top of the 605-foot ⩔ **Space Needle** (400 Broad St.) for the 360-degree panorama of shimmering Puget Sound, the Cascades, the Olympic Mountains and distant Mount Rainier.

- Admire another city view from the vantage point of little **Kerry Park** (211 W. Highland Dr.) on Queen Anne Hill: an unobstructed look at Seattle's impressive downtown skyline, with the Space Needle front-and-center.

- Stroll through ⩔ **Olympic Sculpture Park** (2901 Western Ave.), an expansive green space along the Elliott Bay waterfront, and contemplate Louise Bourgeois' thought-provoking fountain "Father and Son." It's also a peaceful spot to watch a Seattle sunset.

- Wondering what to do today? For a crash course in local history, take the ⩔ **Underground Tour** (608 1st Ave.) in the Pioneer Square Historic District. It's not only fun but educational, and yes—parts of it take place below street level.

- Take a morning walk on the paved path around Green Lake in **Green Lake Park** (7201 E. Green Lake Dr. N.), popular with legions of strolling, jogging and cycling Seattleites.

- Seattle and seafood restaurants go together like yin and yang, so head to **Ivar's Acres of Clams** (1001 Alaskan Way at Pier 54), one of the favorite local restaurants, and feast on their signature dish—Manila clams and red potatoes bathed in a garlic and white wine butter sauce.

- Saunter next door and check out **Ye Olde Curiosity Shop,** a quintessential tourist trap that makes grandma's attic look like a spread in *Architectural Digest.* Every square inch of space—including the walls and ceiling—is crammed with oddities like Siamese twin calves and shrunken heads, and you can purchase everything from fish candy to fart powder.

- While away an afternoon in **Fremont,** the self-proclaimed "center of the universe," and check out the neighborhood's quirky public art installations like the Fremont Troll (which crouches beneath the north end of the Aurora Bridge). It's the place to be on Sundays when the Fremont Sunday Market brings food trucks, antiques and local treasures to the corner of Evanston Avenue and N. 34th Street.

- Watch boats navigate the ⩔ **Hiram M. Chittenden Locks** (3015 N.W. 54th St.) on the Washington Ship Canal, used by all types and sizes of vessels to negotiate a chain of freshwater lakes to saltwater Puget Sound. Then observe migrating salmon in the **Fish Ladder,** a stairway that allows them to bypass the locks en route to their spawning grounds.

- Hop aboard the Washington State Ferry (801 Alaskan Way at Pier 52) to **Bainbridge Island** and feel the wind on your face as the boat crosses Elliott Bay.

- **The Elliott Bay Book Company** (1521 10th Ave.) was a Pioneer Square institution for 36 years before moving to Capitol Hill. The current digs retain the same cedar bookcases, and longtime customers know that this independent store remains one of the city's best places to curl up with a good book.

- Is there really a **Starbucks** on every corner? No, but the popular brand has hundreds of outlets in the Seattle area. Indulge in your favorite concoction at Pike Place Market—the oldest operating location for the coffee chain. If you like views with your latte, visit the location on the 40th floor of the Columbia Center (701 5th Ave.).

Underground Tour

Seattle 1-day Itinerary

AAA editors suggest these activities for a great short vacation experience. Those staying in the area for a longer visit can access a 3-day itinerary at AAA.com/TravelGuides.

Morning

- Spend the morning at ▽ **Pike Place Market** (spreads out from the corner of Pike Street and 1st Avenue). It's the best place in Seattle to meet a friend (the traditional spot is under the neon "Public Market Center" sign) and then wander around looking, smelling, tasting and buying. If you arrive early (before 8 a.m.) you can banter with the vendors while they're setting up and also get first pick at the produce and flower stands.

- Follow your nose to **Daily Dozen Doughnut Co.** (93 Pike St.) and **Three Girls Bakery** (1514 Pike Pl.) and unsuccessfully resist the urge to pick up some mini maple bacon donuts or gooey cinnamon buns to go. Definitely check out the specialty food vendors. **Beecher's Handmade Cheese** (1600 Pike Pl.) makes a tasty grilled cheese panini with tomato and basil; **Uli's Famous Sausage** (1511 Pike Pl.), a classic bratwurst slathered with mustard. Homemade soaps, handcrafted jewelry and souvenir trinkets? You'll find them all here.

- If you still can't tear yourself away from the market (and it's hard), have brunch or an early lunch on the outdoor patio at **Cafe Campagne** (1600 Post Alley). Order the quiche of the day or a *croque-monsieur*, a ham and Gruyère cheese sandwich served on crusty French bread, and you'll think you're in a Parisian cafe.

Afternoon

- From the main market entrance, walk down 1st Avenue to the ▽ **Seattle Art Museum.** The 48-foot-tall "Hammering Man," a black steel sculpture, stands guard outside the entrance, his arm raising and lowering four times a minute every day of the year except Labor Day. SAM's galleries often mix media, concepts, centuries and artists in the same room. Tip: Admission is free the first Thursday of the month.

- On a clear day, you can't beat the sweeping views from the **Sky View Observatory,** on the 73rd floor of the Columbia Center (701 5th Ave.). Take the speedy elevator to the top and admire magnificent views of downtown, Elliott Bay, the Cascade and Olympic mountain ranges and even the Space Needle.

- If the ▽ **Space Needle** is on your bucket list, you're not alone—a visit to the futuristic-looking structure is the No. 1 touristy thing to do in this city and on the top of the list of fun things to do in Seattle. You could easily fill an afternoon exploring the grounds of the ▽ **Seattle Center,** which include Dale Chihuly's glass creations at ▽ **Chihuly Garden and Glass** and the music-focused exhibits at ▽ **MoPOP (Museum of Pop Culture).**

Space Needle

Evening

- Seattle and seafood go together like yin and yang, so fresh dinner options are aplenty. A popular place for seafood is **Ivar's Acres of Clams,** on the waterfront at Pier 54 (1001 Alaskan Way). Consult the daily fresh sheet to see what looks good, but you can't go wrong with the Dungeness crab salad, fish and chips or the deservedly popular clam chowder, brimming with clams, potatoes and bits of bacon. If it's nice outside, order from the Fish Bar walk-up window and sit at one of the picnic tables.

- Another spot for good seafood is across the bay at **Salty's on Alki Beach** (1936 Harbor Ave. S.W. in West Seattle). The restaurant's menu includes local, regional and seasonal specialties, and the view from the dining room—with three walls of windows overlooking Elliott Bay and the city skyline—can't be beat. The most scenic way to get to West Seattle is aboard the King County Water Taxi, a passenger-only ferry which makes the trek across the bay in just 15 minutes.

- Finish off the night in **Capitol Hill,** one of Seattle's hippest, most socially diverse neighborhoods. Nightlife options abound here. Dozens of bars and clubs line E. Pike and Pine streets, the district's main thoroughfares. Grab a cold one at **Capitol Cider** (818 E. Pike St.), where you'll find dozens of hard ciders on tap and even more in a bottle. The basement level has another bar along with board games and live entertainment on some nights. For fancier drinks, head to **Tavern Law** (1406 12th Ave.), a cocktail lounge with an intimate, speakeasy feel.

Top Picks for Kids

Under 13

- At the award-winning ▼ **Woodland Park Zoo** (5500 Phinney Ave. N.), animal lovers can get nose-to-snout with ocelots, grizzly bears, orangutans and other wild residents, where animals roam in impressive naturalistic habitats. On rainy days, the Zoomazium offers nature-themed indoor activities and climbing structures for tots with extra energy to burn.

- Other fun places to go include the lush meadows and shaded nature trails at **Carkeek Park** (950 N.W. Carkeek Park Rd.), where a giant salmon-shaped slide and views of both the Olympic Mountains and Puget Sound beckon. Curious kids can explore tide pools and hunt for seashells at a small beach area, and little ones will get a kick out of waving to train conductors from an elevated pedestrian bridge over the railroad tracks.

- One of the most family-friendly spots to spend a day is ▼ **Seattle Center** (305 Harrison St.). When the sun is out, kids can play in the International Fountain and brave the choreographed water jets that burst in time to music. **Seattle Children's Museum** (305 Harrison St.) offers hands-on, play-based activities and even an art studio. For a thrilling view of the city during your trip, board the Seattle Monorail (picks up next to the Space Needle) and take a quick 2-minute trip to Westlake Center mall.

Teens

Gas Works Park

- Seattle Center's ▼ **MoPOP (Museum of Pop Culture)** (325 5th Ave. N.) is *the* place for teens who speak the language of Jimi Hendrix, the Rolling Stones and other music legends. Interactive exhibits give budding musicians a chance to perform on stage in front of a virtual audience or create a recording in a studio.

- Aviation enthusiasts will find a million things to learn and explore at ▼ **The Museum of Flight** (9404 E. Marginal Way S.), where full-size aircraft and hands-on exhibits explore aviation history. Climb aboard a retired Air Force One 707 jet, or tour the interior of a Concorde supersonic jetliner. The Museum of Flight Tower teaches the basics of air traffic control, and simulators offer flight-ready visitors a chance to pilot a World War I biplane or perform aerial spins in a modern jet.

- Did you know there are tunnels and sidewalks below the streets of the **Pioneer Square Historic District?** Learn this and other Seattle secrets on a guided, 90-minute walking tour with ▼ **Underground Tour** (608 1st Ave.).

All Ages

- Hop aboard the **Washington State Ferry** (801 Alaskan Way at Pier 52) for a scenic trip across Elliott Bay to Bainbridge Island. The 35-minute voyage provides gorgeous views of the skyline and the chance to spot seals, bald eagles and maybe even whales. If stomachs are rumbling, just a short walk from the Bainbridge ferry terminal are many delicious local restaurants, including **The Streamliner Diner** (397 Winslow Way E.). Try the homemade biscuits with strawberry jam if you arrive in time for breakfast.

- Twice as tall as the iconic Space Needle, **Sky View Observatory** (701 5th Ave.) offers a sky-high viewing area with a can't-miss panoramic view of the city. A series of high-speed elevators will whiz you up to the 73rd floor, where you'll look down on CenturyLink Field and the Needle—a unique viewpoint to enjoy during your Seattle vacation.

- On windy days, the grassy hill at **Gas Works Park** (2101 N. Northlake Way) provides the perfect spot for kite flying, a favorite outdoor pastime among Seattleites. Views of the downtown skyline from across Lake Union are stunning, and the park's towering, rusting machinery—the 1950s remains of a manufacturing plant originally built to convert coal to gas—makes for some cool photographs.

- Rain or shine, there is something for everyone at ▼ **Pike Place Market** (Pike Street and 1st Avenue). Dodge fish thrown through the air in the outdoor fish market, or snap a picture with Rachel, the 550-pound bronze piggy bank known as the market's unofficial mascot. Other kid-friendly curiosities include a magic shop; toy stores; and a brick wall covered entirely in chewing gum.

Arriving
By Car

The major north-south route is I-5 from the Canadian border through Seattle to Portland and California. East-west traffic generally follows I-90, which crosses the Cascade Mountains and approaches Seattle over Lake Washington from Spokane and the East. Additional freeway lanes on sections of I-5 and I-90 operate as reversible roadways, inbound during morning hours and outbound afternoons and evenings.

SR 520, which becomes the Governor Albert D. Rosellini–Evergreen Point Bridge, runs east-west from I-5 in Seattle to I-405 in Bellevue. I-405 also runs north-south around Lake Washington and connects to I-5, which runs through the city.

By Boat

Seattle is a popular departure point for cruise ships. The ocean-going vessels dock at Pier 66 at Bell Street Pier, downtown on the waterfront and at Smith Cove Terminal (Pier 91) at the north end of the waterfront.

Washington State Ferries, Colman Dock (Pier 52) at the foot of Marion Street, link Seattle with the Olympic Peninsula via Bremerton and Bainbridge Island. State ferries also leave Fauntleroy Pier in West Seattle for Vashon Island and Southworth. Service also is available from Edmonds to Kingston and from Point Defiance (Tacoma) to Tahlequah (Vashon Island). Phone (206) 464-6400, or (888) 808-7977 in Washington.

Passenger-only ferry service is offered by King County Water Taxi for travel between Pier 50 and either Vashon Island (weekdays only) or West Seattle. Passengers board on a first-come, first-served basis. Phone (206) 4777-3979.

Clipper Navigation (see attraction listing p. 150) provides daily round-trip passenger catamaran service between Seattle's Pier 69 and Victoria, British Columbia, and seasonal service to Friday Harbor in the San Juan Islands. For schedule information phone (206) 448-5000 or (800) 888-2535.

Getting Around
Street System

Seattle's avenues run north and south; they are designated by both numbers and names. Streets, also both numbered and named, run east and west. Most addresses also have area designations—N., S., E., W., N.E., N.W., S.E. or S.W.—that are important in determining correct locations. The portion of downtown south of Denny Way, north of Yesler Way, and west of Melrose Avenue and Broadway has avenues running parallel to Elliott Bay and streets running perpendicular to it.

Many downtown streets are one way. Synchronized traffic lights on northbound 4th Avenue and southbound 2nd Avenue make crossing the city easier. The speed limit is 30 mph or as posted. Right turns are permitted at red lights after a complete stop, unless signs indicate otherwise. Rush hours, 7-9 a.m. and 4-6 p.m., should be avoided if possible.

Washington State Ferry

Portions of I-5 and I-90 have express lanes that change traffic flow during certain times; be aware of highway signs indicating times and directions.

Parking

On-street parking in downtown Seattle costs $2-$4 for 1 hour Mon.-Sat. 8-8; the fare is deposited at one of the curbside pay stations. Parking is prohibited on certain streets during rush hours. There are off-street parking lots throughout the downtown area. Parking garages can be found at Pacific Place (on 6th Avenue between Pine and Olive streets), on Stewart Street between 2nd and 3rd avenues, on 6th Avenue between Union and Pike streets, on Pike Street between 5th and 6th avenues and on 5th Avenue between Seneca and Spring streets. Garage rates range $4-$12 for an hour to $20-$36 for a full day.

Public Transportation

Getting around Seattle and its suburbs without a car is fairly easy thanks to an extensive network of buses, trolleys, streetcars, light rail and even a short monorail line.

King County Metro Transit operates a full schedule of bus and trolley service within the Seattle metropolitan area. Metro service is offered daily, with most schedules beginning in the early morning and ending around midnight; some buses run on a more limited schedule. Passengers pay upon boarding and must have exact fare (cash only) or use a reloadable ORCA Card, available online or at the King Street Center (201 S. Jackson St.). Bus fare is $2.75 per ride; $1.50 (ages 6-18); children under 6 with a fare-paying adult ride free. For information phone (206) 553-3000.

Sound Transit provides Central Link Light Rail service connecting Angle Lake and the Seattle-Tacoma International Airport with downtown Seattle, Capitol Hill and the University of Washington. The trip from Sea-Tac Airport to the University of Washington station is 44 minutes and includes 13 stops in between. Trains arrive every 6 to 15 minutes Mon.-Sat. 5 a.m.-1 a.m. and Sun. and holidays 6 a.m.-midnight. One-way fares depend on distance traveled, but the maximum fares are $3.25, $1.50 (ages 6-18) and $1 (ages 65+ and people with disabilities). Tickets are available at station vending machines which accept cash or credit cards. ORCA cards also are accepted. For information phone (206) 398-5000 or (888) 889-6368.

The Seattle Center Monorail, built for the 1962 Seattle World's Fair, whisks passengers from the Westlake Center station (5th Avenue and Pine Street) to Seattle Center in Lower Queen Anne in just 2 minutes. Service is offered Mon.-Fri. 7:30 a.m.-11 p.m. and Sat.-Sun. 8:30 a.m.-11 p.m. The one-way, cash-only fare is $2.50; $1.25 (ages 5-12, ages 65+, people with disabilities and active military with ID). For information phone (206) 905-2620.

The South Lake Union Streetcar runs between Westlake Center downtown and South Lake Union (Fairview Avenue N. and Campus Drive) with seven stops along the way. It operates on 15-minute intervals Mon.-Thurs. 6 a.m.-9 p.m., Fri.-Sat. 6 a.m.-11 p.m. and Sun. and holidays 10-7. The First Hill Streetcar offers service from Capitol Hill (E. Howell Street and Broadway E.) to Pioneer Square (S. Jackson Street and Occidental Avenue S.) with eight stops along its route through First Hill, Central District, Yesler Terrace and Chinatown. It operates on 10-minute intervals Mon.-Sat. 5 a.m.-1 a.m., Sun. and holidays 10-8. Streetcar fare is $2.25; $1.50 (ages 6-18); $1.00 (ages 65+ and people with disabilities). For information phone King County Metro at (206) 553-3000.

Shopping

Shopping at ✻ Pike Place Market *(see attraction listing p. 143)* is flat-out fun and a must for every vacation in Seattle. Yes, it's touristy. Yes, it can get crowded (especially on Saturday and most other days beginning around 11 a.m. until 2 or 3). Yes, street parking is practically nonexistent (the Pike Place Market Parking Garage at 1531 Western Ave. is your best bet if driving). Yes, it helps to know where the restrooms are (in the Sanitary Market and on the downstairs level at the north and south ends of the Main Arcade).

But these are minor inconveniences in the face of bountiful pleasures and all the fun things to do. Pike Place Market is browsing heaven. The sights, the smells, the sidewalk musicians, the seafood-tossing fishmongers, the places to eat and the ambling crowds all make it a sensory experience of the highest order. Those in the know go early on a weekday morning when the vendors are setting up. A map and directory from the Market Information Booth (on 1st Avenue and Pike Place just east of the neon sign) will help you navigate the mazelike layout of the market.

Fruit, vegetables and flowers are market mainstays, and locally grown so they change with the seasons. **Corner Produce** and **Frank's Quality Produce** (in the Corner Market building near 1st Avenue and Pike Place) are known for offering free samples of mouthwatering peaches, berries or whatever else is in season to passersby. The goods at local restaurants **Three Girls Bakery** (1514 Pike Pl.) are divine, as are the paper sacks full of hot, fresh mini doughnuts from **Daily Dozen Doughnut Co.** (93 Pike St.).

One of only two national retailers in the market, **Sur La Table**'s flagship store (84 Pine St.) offers top-of-the-line cooking supplies and kitchenware. (The other national retailer in Pike Place Market is Starbucks at 1912 Pike Pl., the oldest Starbucks in operation.) Nearby is another popular market mainstay—**Beecher's Handmade Cheese** (1600 Pike Pl.), where a glass-walled kitchen allows visitors to watch as cheesemakers stir giant vats of cheese curds.

Explore the specialty shops "DownUnder" (on the lower floors of the Main Arcade) where you'll find everything from stacks of books (**Lion Heart Book Store**) to comics (**Golden Age Collectables**) to vintage posters and prints (**Old Seattle Paperworks**).

Other interesting shops and fun places to go are located near the market on 1st Avenue, including **Metsker Maps** (1511 1st Ave.), a haven for map lovers and geography enthusiasts. **Hard Rock Cafe** (116 Pike St.) has a variety of rock 'n' roll souvenirs and music memorabilia.

Pike Place Market

If a good old-fashioned tourist trap sounds right up your alley, head to **Ye Olde Curiosity Shop** (1001 Alaskan Way at Pier 54). In business since 1899, this shop bills itself as a museum, but shrunken heads, prehistoric elephant tusks and the Lord's Prayer engraved on a grain of rice all play second fiddle to the merchandise: a hodgepodge of gag gifts, tchotchkes, Native American art and nautically themed collectibles to share with all your friends back home after your travel.

Seattle's downtown retail core is between 3rd and 7th avenues and Pine and University streets. This is where you'll find major department stores like Macy's and Nordstrom (the Seattle location is the brand's largest), familiar names like Old Navy and Gap, and a couple of upscale shopping complexes. The four levels at **Pacific Place** (6th Avenue and Pine Street), offer the usual mix of retailers selling men's and women's apparel, shoes, jewelry and gifts.

There are more stores and nearby restaurants at **Westlake Center** (400 Pine St. between 4th and 5th avenues). For shopping toward the luxury end of the scale—Brooks Brothers, Louis Vuitton and so forth—try **Rainier Square** (5th Avenue and University Street).

Just south of downtown, the **International District** *(see attraction listing p. 140)* is home to some unique shops. The **Yummy House Bakery** (522 6th Ave. S., look for the yellow sign) has all kinds of "Hong Kong-style" cakes and pastries, including squares of feather-light sponge cake—usually sitting on a tray on top of the order counter—egg tarts and a variety of bubble teas. For a one-stop Asian shopping immersion experience, the place to go is **Uwajimaya** (600 5th Ave. S.). It's a combination grocery, gift and housewares emporium with lots of unusual items.

Two Seattle neighborhoods—**Capitol Hill** and **Fremont**—are funky shopping destinations. The shops along Broadway reflect Capitol Hill's friendly but edgy vibe. Avid readers will want to check out **The Elliott Bay Book Company** (1521 10th Ave.) during their trip. The independent bookseller's creaky wood floors, comfy chairs and cedar bookcases make it the perfect place to curl up with a good book.

North of Lake Union, compact Fremont is ideal for strolling and has a wide variety of shops. You'll discover mid-century furniture, collectibles, records and all sorts of memorabilia at **Fremont Vintage Mall** (3419 Fremont Pl. N.). **Portage Bay Goods** (621 N. 35th St.) offers Seattle-inspired gifts, kids' clothing, art and stationery. Nearby is **Ophelia's Books** (3504 Fremont Ave. N.), where bibliophiles hunt for used treasures. The busiest shopping day in Fremont each week is Sunday, when the **Fremont Sunday Market** brings food trucks, antiques and local treasures to N. 34th Street near Evanston Avenue N., rain or shine.

Another popular weekend destination is the **Ballard** neighborhood, where boutiques, shops and restaurants abound. **Bop Street Records** (2220 N.W. Market St.) has more than 500,000 records in stock from the 1920s to the 1990s. The **Ballard**

International District

Farmers Market takes place on Sundays year-round on Ballard Avenue N.W. (between Vernon Place N.W. and 22nd Avenue N.W.).

If you don't consider a shopping trip complete without hitting at least one mall, make it **University Village** (N.E. 45th Street and 25th Avenue E.), especially on a sunny day. This outdoor shopping plaza, sprinkled with fountains and animal sculptures, offers familiar stores like Pottery Barn, Banana Republic, Williams-Sonoma and RH Gallery.

Nightlife

Whether your idea of nightlife at your travel destination is listening to live music at a rowdy venue, sipping cocktails at a cozy bar or watching the sunset from a scenic overlook, Seattle delights with a wide variety of offerings. For deep discounts on food and drink, you can't go wrong with Seattle's weekday happy hours in the downtown area. Many local restaurants and bars offer specials beginning as early as 3 p.m., which means you can fuel up before a night of fun for a lot less money.

Kells Irish Restaurant & Pub, near Pike Place Market at 1916 Post Alley, has a jolly atmosphere, an outdoor patio and live Irish music nightly beginning around 9; phone (206) 728-1916. Just across Post Alley, the lounge at **The Pink Door** (1919 Post Alley) offers live entertainment and fun things to do every night of the week, including a burlesque show on Saturday at 11 p.m. (cover charge is $25 and reservations can be made online); phone (206) 443-3241.

The Triple Door (downtown at 216 Union St., across from Benaroya Hall) features live music (mainly jazz and blues) in The Musicquarium

Lounge and the Mainstage, a sleek, snazzy 300-seat theater. For hungry patrons who wonder where to eat, The Triple Door serves food from the upstairs **Wild Ginger Asian Restaurant & Satay Bar.** Phone (206) 838-4333 for The Triple Door.

Well-known rockers and hip-hoppers play at **The Showbox** (1426 1st Ave.); phone (206) 628-3151. **The Crocodile** (in Belltown at 2200 2nd Ave.) books local and national indie bands as well as a sprinkling of bigger names in a standing-room-only venue; phone (206) 441-4618.

One of the top jazz clubs on the West Coast, **Dimitriou's Jazz Alley Restaurant & Nightclub** (2033 6th Ave.) books big-name acts in a supper club setting. You can have dinner here—the food is pretty good, albeit pricey—or opt to find other places to eat and just see the show (in which case seating is on a first-come, first-served basis). Reservations are recommended; phone (206) 441-9729.

Low lighting and an understated alleyway entrance give **Bathtub Gin & Co.** (2205 2nd Ave.) a speakeasy feel. Mixologists whip up superb Old Fashioneds and other cocktails at this local favorite. To find it, look for the wooden door in an alley off Blanchard Street between 1st and 2nd avenues; phone (206) 728-6069.

The Capitol Hill neighborhood has some cool dive bars and late-night hangouts. The **Cha Cha Lounge** (1013 E. Pike St.) has a great atmosphere: red lighting, sombreros hanging from the ceiling, disco balls and flashy *lucha libre* (Mexican wrestling) paraphernalia everywhere. The crowd tends to be young and painfully hipster. It's in the basement of Bimbo's

Northwest Flower & Garden Show

Cantina; just take the stairs down; phone (206) 322-0703.

If you're looking for some fun things to do with friends, the low-key atmosphere at **Tavern Law** (1406 12th Ave.) is perfect for a quiet drink. Skilled bartenders whip up all sorts of custom cocktails here, from a classic Manhattan to concoctions made with egg whites and lavender. An intimate upstairs bar called Needle and Thread admits guests by reservation only; phone (206) 322-9734 for Tavern Law and (206) 325-0133 for Needle and Thread.

If you lean toward the twangy side of rock, head to the Ballard neighborhood and the **Tractor Tavern** (5213 Ballard Ave. N.W.). The atmosphere is bare bones and the beer comes in plastic cups; this is first and foremost a place to watch alt-country, rockabilly and roots rock bands, with a good view of the stage from every spot in the room; phone (206) 789-3599. The **Sunset Tavern** (5433 Ballard Ave. N.W.) is more unruly: you're cramped and crowded but close to the action, and the bands rock out more (the Sunset supports new and local talent). Don't come here if you're looking for a mellow evening. Phone (206) 784-4880.

In Fremont, the **High Dive** (513 N. 36th St.) is yet another club with shows practically every night—mostly local bands looking to establish themselves—and the cover charge is almost always under $10. Admittance to shows is 21 and over; phone (206) 632-0212.

Get a laid-back start to your evening hanging out at the **Fremont Coffee Company** (459 N. 36th St.). It occupies a rambling old house with a wraparound porch, back deck and several rooms filled with comfy chairs. The barista will create awesome foam art to grace the surface of your latte. It closes at 8 p.m.; phone (206) 632-3633.

And what if you just want peace, quiet and a beautiful setting? Watching the sun drop behind distant mountains at ⛊ **Olympic Sculpture Park** *(see attraction listing p. 143)*, 2901 Western Ave., is a simple yet deeply rewarding pleasure. Or claim a spot at dusk along the wall in little **Kerry Park** *(see attraction listing p. 140)* and marvel as the Seattle skyline starts to light up. The **Sky View Observatory** *(see attraction listing p. 146)* on the 73rd floor of the Columbia Center at 701 5th Ave., offers another option for watching the sunset (with an entrance fee). The observatory's Sky View Café is a great stop for any trip and stays open until 7 p.m., with local beers to sip while you watch the sun dip down.

Big Events

Cold, gray days inevitably lead to thoughts of spring, and the **Northwest Flower & Garden Show** is a great welcome to the coming season. This huge event, one of the many exciting and fun things to do with friends, is held at the Washington State Convention Center in February and has exhibits by practically every plant society and horticultural organization you can think of, plus florist competitions and an orchid show.

Another antidote to the winter blues is provided by **Taste Washington,** a wine and food event in late March. More than 200 wineries from around the Evergreen State show up to pour a taste of their products at this popular event, which also features savory bites prepared by dozens of Pacific Northwest restauranteurs. This can be one of many romantic, memorable things for couples to do.

Seattle celebrates the coming of spring in early May with **Seattle Yacht Club Opening Day Week,** a tradition since 1913 and one of the most interesting things to do in Seattle. The unofficial beginning of boating season, it starts with a cannon blast as the Montlake Bridge is raised. A lively procession of watercraft—from kayaks to sailboats to yachts—then threads through Montlake Cut between Portage and Union bays, bound for Lake Washington.

The **University District StreetFair** in mid-May is the kickoff of Seattle's festival season. Norwegian Constitution Day is celebrated at the **17th of May Festival** with a parade and other activities in the Ballard neighborhood. The well-attended **Seattle International Film Festival** is held over four weeks in late May and early June at venues throughout the city; some 400 films from 80 countries are featured.

Work with your AAA travel agency to ensure you are in Seattle during the **Northwest Folklife Festival.** Held over Memorial Day weekend on the Seattle Center grounds, it is a showcase of traditional and folk arts of more than 100 countries. Music, dancing, craft exhibits and cooking demonstrations are among the activities, some of which are participatory. The ☞ **Fremont Fair** welcomes the summer solstice in mid-June with an old-fashioned street fair, all kinds of live music, a parade and an art car show.

Seattle Center hosts the ☞ **Bite of Seattle** food festival in mid-July, with more than 60 of the city's finest local restaurants as well as outdoor concerts and beer gardens. **Seattle Seafair,** held from mid-June to early August, anchors the summer schedule with street parades, hydroplane races on Lake Washington, tours of naval vessels and an air show. Labor Day weekend boasts **Bumbershoot: Seattle's Music & Arts Festival.** Music, comedy, visual and literary arts, theater and dance are showcased.

The ☞ **Argosy Christmas Ship Festival,** which occurs from late November through late December, has been a Seattle holiday tradition since 1949 and should be included in all AAA travel packages. Illuminated boats sail to Puget Sound waterfront communities, with onboard choirs singing 20-minute performances broadcast via a speaker system while crowds on shore gather around roaring bonfires to listen. It's a fine way to get into the holiday spirit.

Sports & Rec

The NFL's Seattle Seahawks play **football** at CenturyLink Field, 800 Occidental Ave. S. This also is the venue for Seattle Sounders major league **soccer** games; going to a Sounders game is almost a rite of passage for many Seattleites and is one of

Bite of Seattle

the most fun things to do in Seattle for sports fans. Major league **baseball** is represented by the Seattle Mariners, who play at Safeco Field; the 47,898-seat stadium with a retractable roof is at First Avenue S. and S. Atlantic Street.

The Seattle Storm plays WNBA **basketball** in KeyArena at Seattle Center. The Seattle Thunderbirds **hockey** team takes to the ice at the ShoWare Center in Kent. Area college teams participate in all major sports.

Boating can be enjoyed on freshwater Lake Washington, saltwater Puget Sound or both, thanks to the locks and canal connecting the two. A multitude of marinas provides moorage facilities. Any type of craft can be rented, from small sailboats or canoes to large seagoing yachts.

Cast your **fishing** line from piers at Green Lake and Lake Washington, in county parks and at area lakes and streams. Pier 86 on Elliott Bay is a public fishing pier. The Washington State Department of Fish and Wildlife, phone (425) 775-1311, is the best source for freshwater license requirements and information.

Spot Tail Salmon Guides offers private salmon fishing and saltwater fly-fishing trips daily; phone (206) 295-7031. Charters for Puget Sound or deep-sea fishing off the coast can be arranged.

White-water rafting, float trips and bald eagle sightseeing tours are offered on rivers in the Cascades and Olympics. The season for white-water rafting is April through September; bald eagle sightseeing tours take place December through February. Rates vary, but the average fee for a full-day guided trip is normally $60-$100.

Reservations for trips can be made through the following agencies: River Recreation, Inc., (206) 276-8774 or (800) 464-5899; Riverrider.com, (206) 668-7238 or (800) 448-7238; and Rivers Inc., (425) 822-5296.

Lake Union is conveniently located for **kayaking.** Northwest Outdoor Center, on the lake, rents kayaks and organizes tours; phone (206) 281-9694. Moss Bay Row, Kayak, Sail & Paddle Board Center rents kayaks and paddleboards year-round; phone (206) 682-2031. Alki Kayak Tours offers guided sea kayaking trips from Pier 66 at the downtown waterfront and from West Seattle; phone (206) 953-0237.

Looking for things to do in summer? The saltwater beaches at Alki Gardens and Golden Gardens and the freshwater beaches along Lake Washington and Green Lake are suitable for summer **swimming** and **scuba diving.**

Within the city are some 90 miles of signed **bicycling** routes and another 30 miles of bike-pedestrian trails. The free Seattle Bike Map details Seattle's extensive network of bike lanes and trails as well as streets commonly used by bikers. The map is available at area bike shops, branches of the public library, from the City Transportation Department and from the Cascade Bicycle Club; phone (206) 522-3222.

The **Burke-Gilman Trail,** designed for bicycling and hiking, extends 20 miles from 11th Ave. N.W. and Leary Way to Tracy Owen Station Park at 73rd Avenue N.E. and SR 522 and from N.W. 54th St. and 30th Ave. N.W. to Golden Gardens Park. The longer section of the trail skirts the University of Washington campus and offers good views of the area. North of Lake Washington it connects with the **Sammamish**

Seattle Opera

River Trail, which then continues another 12 miles to Marymoor Park *(see Redmond p. 114).*

One of Seattle's most popular bike paths is the nearly 3-mile paved trail encircling **Green Lake.** There are separate lanes for cyclists and pedestrians. Many other bike routes connect with city parks or run along the waterfront. Lake Washington Boulevard is closed to motorized traffic (and open to bikes) on some Sundays from 10-6, mid-May to mid-September. Bikes can be rented at the Montlake Bicycle Shop, 2223 24th Ave. E., phone (206) 329-7333, and at Recycled Cycles, 1007 N.E. Boat St., phone (206) 547-4491.

Miles of **hiking** and **horseback riding** trails are located in nearby mountain and forest areas. The U.S. Forest Service, phone (206) 470-4060, can provide information about trails.

Within a 1- or 2-hour drive are numerous venues for **mountain climbing, skiing** and other adventure travel activities. Guided trips to the summit of Mount Rainier, including instruction in this challenging sport, can be arranged *(see Mount Rainier National Park p. 85).* Major ski areas and resorts are mentioned under the place listings for Snoqualmie Pass, Skykomish and Crystal Mountain.

Golf courses, driving ranges and pitch and putt courses are plentiful. Some private clubs extend reciprocal privileges to visitors who are members of certain out-of-town golf clubs. The Seattle Parks and Recreation Department operates four 18-hole courses; phone (206) 684-2489 or (206) 684-4075 for information.

Fans of **automobile racing** have their choice of two major raceways: Pacific Raceways in Kent, phone (253) 639-5927, and Evergreen Speedway in Monroe, phone (360) 805-6100. Racing schedules vary.

Performing Arts

Seattle Center *(see attraction listing p. 144)* is the cultural focus of metropolitan Seattle. **Marion Oliver McCaw Hall** is the headquarters of the **Seattle Opera,** which presents several opera productions during its August through May season; phone (206) 389-7676 or (800) 426-1619. **Pacific Northwest Ballet** also performs at McCaw Hall, with six productions during its September through June season; phone (206) 441-2424.

The **Seattle Symphony** plays at **Benaroya Hall,** on 2nd Avenue between Union and University streets. Nearly 200 concerts take place between September and July, and these are all fun things to do with friends. Family concerts, recitals and other musical events also are offered. If your travel falls on the right day of the month, you can enjoy a tour of the building; phone (206) 215-4747 or (866) 833-4747 for ticket information, or (206) 215-4856 for tour information.

Bagley Wright Theatre at Seattle Center houses the nationally acclaimed **Seattle Repertory Theatre,** which presents plays from early September through early May; for curtain times phone (206) 443-2222 or (877) 900-9285. **Book-It Repertory**

Theatre presents adaptations of classic and contemporary literature at various Seattle Center stages; phone (206) 216-0833.

Other fun places to go include **The 5th Avenue Theatre**, 1308 5th Ave., for Broadway shows; phone (206) 625-1900. Traveling shows, comedians and popular recording artists (everything from teen pop to hard rock) take the stage at the historic **Paramount Theatre**, downtown at 911 Pine St., the **Moore Theatre**, 1932 2nd Ave., and the **Neptune Theatre**, 1303 N.E. 45th St. Phone (206) 682-1414 for all three theaters.

Popular with summer playgoers are **A Contemporary Theater** (ACT) at 700 Union St., phone (206) 292-7676; and the **Intiman Theatre** at 201 Mercer St., phone (206) 441-7178. Summer brings open-air concerts to the Woodland Park Zoo, the White River Amphitheater in Auburn, Chateau Ste. Michelle Winery in Woodinville and Marymoor Park in Redmond. The free *Seattle Weekly* has information about additional travel spots, places to eat and things to do this weekend in Seattle.

INSIDER INFO:
Seattle CityPASS

Seattle CityPASS *(See ad on inside back cover.)* saves travelers up to 45 percent at 5 of Seattle's top attractions. Prepaid admission includes the Space Needle, Seattle Aquarium, Argosy Cruises Harbor Tour, a choice between the Museum of Pop Culture (MoPOP) or the Woodland Park Zoo, and a choice between Chihuly Garden and Glass or the Pacific Science Center. Seattle CityPASS tickets are 9 consecutive days, including the first day of use. The Seattle CityPASS is available online or from participating attractions.

ATTRACTIONS

For a complete list of attractions, visit AAA.com/travelguides/attractions

 ASIAN ART MUSEUM—see Volunteer Park p. 147.

BALLARD LOCKS—see Hiram M. Chittenden Locks p. 140.

BILL & MELINDA GATES FOUNDATION DISCOVERY CENTER is at 440 Fifth Ave. N., just e. of Seattle Center. Four themed galleries filled with thought-provoking interactive displays offer a look inside the foundation and its partners' work to reduce poverty, promote health, advance education and create opportunity. Visitors are introduced to the foundation's staff, partners and beneficiaries while exploring its history, strategies and innovations. Throughout the galleries visitors are invited to consider what they would do to create positive change.

Video programs offering insight into the foundation's work rotate every half-hour. **Hours:** Tues.-Sat. 10-6, early June-late Aug.; 10-5, rest of year. Phone ahead to confirm schedule. **Cost:** Discovery center free. **Parking:** Pay parking is available in the Seattle Center Fifth Avenue N. parking garage (enter from Harrison or Republican streets). **Phone:** (206) 709-3100, ext. 7100. 🏛 Seattle Center, 4

CENTURYLINK FIELD TOURS is at 800 Occidental Ave. S. Conducted by knowledgeable guides, the 90-minute tours offer a behind-the-scenes look at this state-of-the-art, 72,000-seat football stadium, home of the Seattle Seahawks. Among the areas normally off-limits that are included on the tour are the press box, playing field, visiting team locker room and a luxury suite.

Comfortable walking shoes are recommended. **Hours:** Tours are given daily at 10:30, 12:30 and 2:30, June-Aug.; Fri.-Sun. at 10:30, 12:30 and 2:30, rest of year. Arrive 30 minutes before tour time. Tours may not occur during game days and special events; phone ahead to confirm schedule. **Cost:** $14; $10 (ages 62+ and military with ID); $8 (ages 5-11). **Phone:** (206) 381-7582. GT 🏛 King Street, 31

Public Art at CenturyLink Field is at 800 Occidental Ave. S. Installed primarily outside CenturyLink Field, this collection of fine art includes paintings, photographs, sculpture, bas-reliefs and a video installation. A pamphlet is available for self-guiding tours. **Hours:** Daily 24 hours. **Cost:** Free. **Phone:** (206) 381-7555. 🏛 King Street, 31

DISCOVERY PARK, 3801 Discovery Park Blvd., is entered via Gilman Ave. W./W. Government Way at 36th Ave. W. Named after British explorer George Vancouver's ship the *Discovery,* this 534-acre urban wilderness and wildlife sanctuary is ideal for getting away from it all—if only for an afternoon.

The natural setting is impressive—Magnolia Bluff overlooks Puget Sound, with (in clear weather) views of the Cascade and Olympic mountain ranges. There are cool, shady forest groves, soaring seaside cliffs, 2 miles of protected tidal beaches, sand dunes, open meadows and quiet ponds. Hiking is the best way to enjoy Discovery Park, and many visitors opt for the 2.8-mile Loop Trail that passes through lush stands of Douglas fir, western red cedar and big-leaf maple.

West Point Lighthouse, built in 1881, stands at the park's westernmost tip. The lighthouse grounds are open to the public but parking is limited; check at the visitor center for availability or to take the complimentary shuttle. The Daybreak Star Indian Cultural Center, 5011 Bernie Whitebear Way, has several exhibits of Native American art. Guided bird walks are given during the spring and fall migration seasons; the park's wide variety of habitats shelter more than 230 resident and migrant species.

Time: Allow 2 hours minimum. **Hours:** Park open daily 6 a.m.-11 p.m. Visitor center open Tues.-Sun. 8:30-5. Visitor center closed major holidays. Cultural

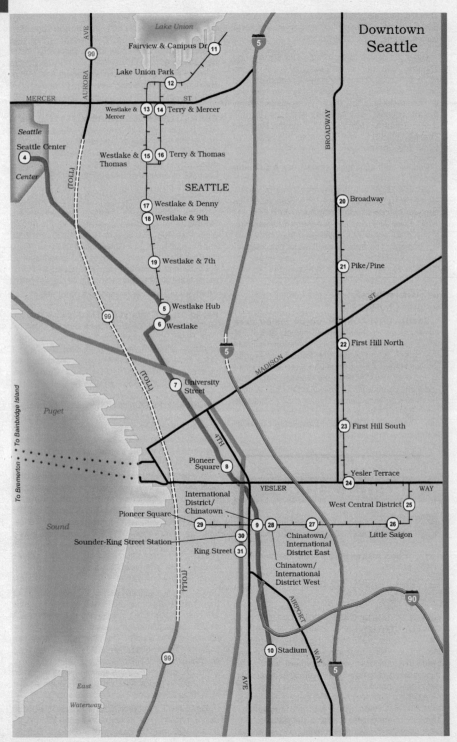

Downtown
Seattle

Lake Union

99

5

Fairview & Campus Dr 11

Lake Union Park 12

MERCER ST

Westlake & Mercer 13 14 Terry & Mercer

BROADWAY

AURORA AVE

Seattle
Seattle Center 4

Center

Westlake & Thomas 15 16 Terry & Thomas

SEATTLE

17 Westlake & Denny

18 Westlake & 9th

20 Broadway

19 Westlake & 7th

21 Pike/Pine

ST

5 Westlake Hub

6 Westlake

99

22 First Hill North

5

Puget

MADISON

7 University Street

To Bremerton • To Bainbridge Island

23 First Hill South

4TH

Pioneer Square 8

24 Yesler Terrace

Sound

YESLER WAY

International District/Chinatown

West Central District 25

Pioneer Square 29

9 28 27

26 Little Saigon

Sounder-King Street Station 30

Chinatown/International District East

King Street 31

Chinatown/International District West

AIRPORT WAY

90

99

10 Stadium

AVE

5

East

Waterway

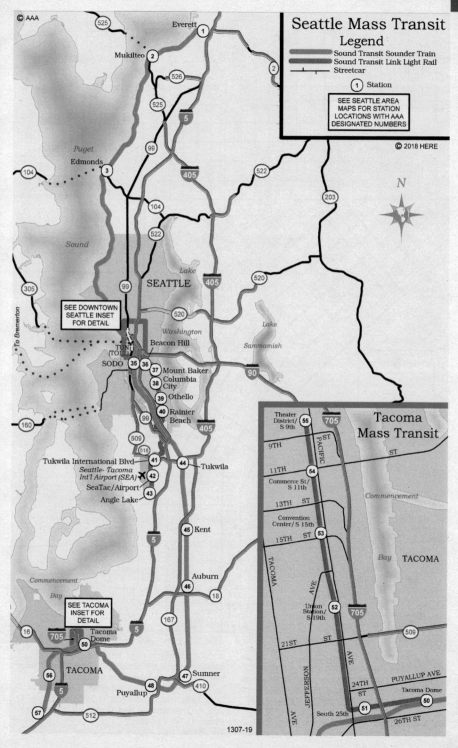

© AAA

Seattle Mass Transit
Legend

— Sound Transit Sounder Train
— Sound Transit Link Light Rail
— Streetcar

(1) Station

SEE SEATTLE AREA
MAPS FOR STATION
LOCATIONS WITH AAA
DESIGNATED NUMBERS

© 2018 HERE

Everett

Mukilteo

Puget

Edmonds

Sound

To Bremerton

SEATTLE

Lake

SEE DOWNTOWN
SEATTLE INSET
FOR DETAIL

Washington

Beacon Hill

Lake
Sammamish

TUN'L
(TOLL)

SODO

Mount Baker
Columbia
City
Othello
Rainier
Beach

Tukwila International Blvd
*Seattle- Tacoma
Int'l Airport (SEA)*
SeaTac/Airport
Angle Lake

Tukwila

Kent

Auburn

Commencement
Bay

SEE TACOMA
INSET FOR
DETAIL

Tacoma
Dome

TACOMA

Sumner

Puyallup

1307-19

N

Tacoma
Mass Transit

Theater
District/
S 9th   55

9TH

11TH

Commerce St/
S 11th   54

13TH

Convention
Center/ S 15th   53

15TH

Commencement

Bay   **TACOMA**

Union
Station/
S 19th   52

21ST

24TH

South 25th   51

26TH ST

PUYALLUP AVE

Tacoma
Dome   50

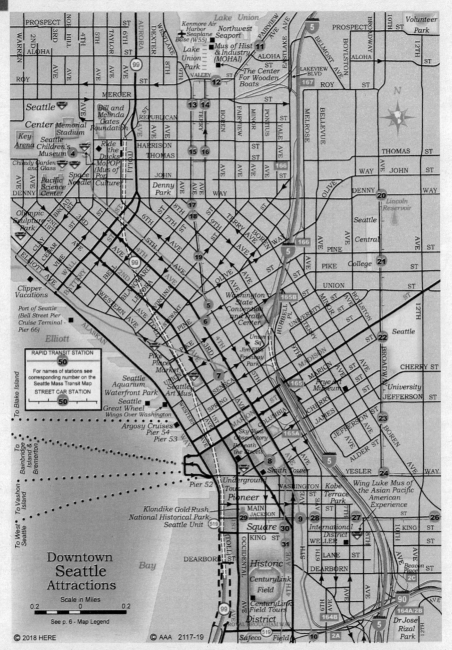

Downtown
Seattle
Attractions

Scale in Miles
0.2   0   0.2

See p. 6 - Map Legend

© 2018 HERE   © AAA 2117-19

center open daily 10-5. Guided, 90-minute nature and bird walks depart from the visitor center on Saturdays during migration season; reservations are required. **Cost:** Free. **Phone:** (206) 386-4236 for the park, or (206) 285-4425 for the cultural center.

FRYE ART MUSEUM is at 704 Terry Ave. The museum displays 19th- and 20th-century European

and American paintings and changing exhibits of contemporary and historical art. **Time:** Allow 1 hour minimum. **Hours:** Tues.-Sun. 11-5 (also Thurs. 5-7). Free guided tours are given Tues.-Sun. at 1 (also Tues. and Sat.-Sun. at 11:30). Closed Jan. 1, July 4, Thanksgiving and Christmas. **Cost:** Free. **Phone:** (206) 622-9250.

GT ⓘ 🚇 Broadway & Terrace, 23

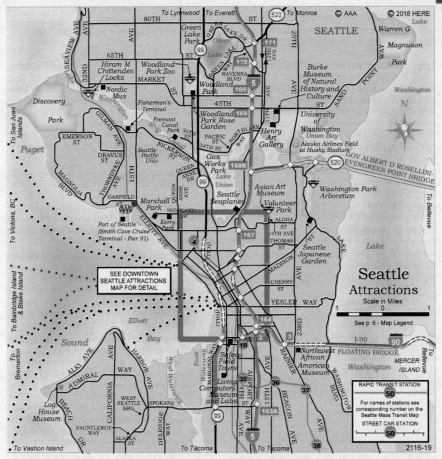

GAS WORKS PARK is at 2101 N. Northlake Way; from I-5, take the 45th St. exit, go w. on N.E. 45th St. to Meridian Ave. N., turn left and proceed s. on Meridian Ave. N. to Northlake Way, then turn right; the parking lot is on the left. A plant to manufacture gas from coal was built in 1906 on this 20-acre expanse along the north shore of Lake Union. By the 1950s natural gas importation had rendered it obsolete, but the machinery still stands and presents a curious sight, looking simultaneously antiquated and futuristic.

While the generator towers remain in ruins, two older wooden structures—the boiler house and the pump house—were restored and converted into a picnic shelter and a children's "play barn." A grassy artificial hill created from construction rubble covered with topsoil is a popular spot for flying kites and watching fireworks; the sundial at its summit was created by two local artists. From this elevated perspective the view south across the lake to the downtown skyline—flanked on the left by Capitol Hill and on the right by Queen Anne Hill—is splendid. **Time:** Allow 30 minutes minimum. **Hours:** Daily 6 a.m.-10 p.m. **Cost:** Free. **Phone:** (206) 684-4075 or TTY (206) 233-1509.

GREEN LAKE PARK is at 7201 E. Green Lake Dr. N.; from I-5 northbound take exit 171 to N.E. 71st St., then w. to E. Green Lake Dr. N. and the main parking lot. This urban 323-acre green space is a favorite destination for walkers and joggers. The lake, carved by a glacial ice sheet, and its banks are a natural preserve for numerous tree and plant species, birds and waterfowl. A path with two lanes—one for ambulatory users and one for cyclists and skaters—encircles the lake. Once around is 2.8 miles, just the right distance for a nice walk. Cedars, weeping willows, lush vegetation and attractive residential homes frame the water views at every turn.

The Green Lake Small Craft Center, at the lake's southwest end at 5900 W. Green Lake Way N., has rowing, canoeing, kayaking and sailing classes, and rowing teams often use the lake for practice. The center doesn't rent boats; you can rent a canoe, kayak, paddleboard, paddleboat or row boat from Green Lake Boat Rental, on the northeast side of the lake. Other facilities include a community center, swimming pool, pitch-and-putt golf course, sports courts, children's play area, beach and amphitheater. The park also is a lovely spot for a lakeside picnic. **Time:** Allow 1 hour minimum. **Hours:** Park open daily 24 hours. **Cost:** Free. **Phone:** (206) 684-4075, (206) 527-0171 for Green Lake Boat Rental or TTY (206) 233-1509. ⊠ 🎋

HIRAM M. CHITTENDEN LOCKS are in the n.w. part of the city, 4 mi. w. of I-5 exit 169 at 3015 N.W. 54th St. Often called the Ballard Locks, construction of these locks and the Lake Washington Ship Canal was completed in 1917. The locks and canal connect the waters of Lake Washington, Lake Union and Salmon Bay with saltwater Puget Sound.

Today the locks are a popular place for sightseeing, as the operation of the locks and the parade of recreational and commercial boat traffic is a fascinating spectacle. Visitors can walk along the lock walls and across the gates when they're closed to access the south side of the canal and the Fish Ladder *(see attraction listing this page)*.

A visitor center just inside the north entrance of the complex has exhibits depicting the history and operation of the ship canal and locks. A downstairs auditorium shows a 12-minute video about the canal every half-hour; the last showing is 30 minutes before closing.

Also on the grounds is the Carl S. English Jr. Botanical Garden, with more than 570 plant species from around the world interspersed with varieties indigenous to the Pacific Northwest, including magnolias, crabapples, flowering cherries, rhododendrons, evergreen oaks, pines, hardy palms and camellias. Grassy slopes offer a view of the locks. A free summer concert series is presented Saturday and Sunday on the grounds at 2 p.m., June through August. **Time:** Allow 45 minutes minimum. **Hours:** Grounds open daily 7 a.m.-9 p.m. Visitor center daily 10-6, May-Sept.; Thurs.-Mon. 10-4, rest of year. Fish ladder viewing room daily 7 a.m.-8:45 p.m. One-hour guided tours of the locks, grounds and fish ladder depart the visitor center daily at 1 and 3 (also Sat.-Sun. at 11), May-Sept.; Thurs.-Mon. at 2, Mar.-Apr. and Oct.-Nov. **Cost:** Free. **Parking:** $2 (per hour in a City of Seattle lot off N.W. 54th St.). **Phone:** (206) 783-7059. GT 🎋

Fish Ladder, at the s. end of the dam at the Hiram M. Chittenden Locks, 3015 N.W. 54th St., is one of few facilities of its kind in the United States located at the confluence of salt and fresh water. This ingenious stairway consists of 21 weirs—each approximately a foot higher than the previous one—that enable migrating salmon to bypass the dam and locks. A viewing gallery features windows looking into the upper weirs, both above and below water level.

Information panels and a wall mural illustrate the natural history of the four salmon species that utilize the ladder. Peak migration varies by species: sockeye (July), chinook (late August) and coho (late September). You may see tribal members fishing near the locks, which is permitted by treaties. **Time:** Allow 30 minutes minimum. **Hours:** Viewing room daily 7 a.m.-8:45 p.m. One-hour guided tours of the fish ladder and Hiram M. Chittenden Locks depart the locks' visitor center daily at 1 and 3 (also Sat.-Sun. at 11), May-Sept.; Thurs.-Mon. at 2, Mar.-Apr. and Oct.-Nov. **Cost:** Free. **Phone:** (206) 783-7059. GT

INTERNATIONAL DISTRICT, or ID, encompasses the blocks from Yesler Way s. to S. Dearborn St. and from 4th Ave. S E. to 12th Ave. S. Seattle's Chinatown actually is a mix of Asian communities adjoining Pioneer Square. The unofficial entry into this bustling neighborhood is through the Chinatown Gate, an archway painted lucky red that straddles S. King Street at 5th Avenue S. The orb that sits atop the gate is a fireball from heaven, a symbol of good luck.

Dragons coiled around light posts give the ID character. Hing Hay Park, at the corner of S. King Street and Maynard Avenue S., is a brick-paved urban space with a lovely pagoda right in the middle and a cool dragon mural that covers the wall of a building. It's a local gathering place where people eat lunch or take a tai chi class.

Kobe Terrace, which you can reach by walking up 7th Avenue S., is a bit of a climb but worth the effort as you gaze down at the neighborhood below from your elevated perch on the terraced hillside. Shady paths wind through the park, passing a community garden, cherry trees and a 200-year-old stone lantern on the hilltop, a gift from Kobe, Japan.

The Great Hall at Union Station, 401 S. Jackson St., was built in 1911 and restored in 1999. It features antique floor tiles, pilasters accented by a series of archways and an impressive barrel-vaulted ceiling. The interior is used for weddings, high school graduation celebrations and public events. Uwajimaya is a combination grocery and department store with a food court that offers everything from burgers to *banh mi,* the yummy Vietnamese sandwich of beef, cilantro, onions and pickled peppers on a baguette. **Hours:** Daily 24 hours. **Cost:** Free. 🍴 🎋 🎐 7th & Jackson, 27

Little Saigon extends from the eastern edge of the International District to Rainier Ave. S. This commercial district, a bit shabby in appearance but with its own distinct character, is filled with grocers, beauty salons, law offices, pho houses and other small, family-owned businesses catering to the city's sizable Vietnamese-American community. Stand at the intersection of S. Jackson Street and 12th Avenue S., the heart of Little Saigon, and look around you; every storefront sports a brightly colored sign in Vietnamese. **Hours:** Daily 24 hours. **Cost:** Free. 🍴 🎐 12th & Jackson, 26

KERRY PARK is 2 blks. w. of Queen Anne Ave. N. at 211 W. Highland Dr. Situated on the south slope of Queen Anne Hill, what this pocket park lacks in size—it's just a 1.25-acre square of grass, a couple of benches and the abstract sculpture "Changing Form"—it makes up for with a sweeping panoramic view of downtown Seattle, Elliott Bay and Mount Rainier. This is a favorite spot for shutterbugs, particularly at sunset when city lights begin twinkling and Mount Rainier shimmers pink and gold.

Stairs lead from the viewpoint down to a children's play area. The park is in a residential neighborhood full of gracious old homes. Residential street parking is available. A coin-operated telescope is provided. **Time:** Allow 30 minutes minimum. **Hours:** Daily 6 a.m.-10 p.m. **Cost:** Free. **Phone:** (206) 684-4075 or TTY (206) 233-1509. 🚹 Seattle Center, 4

KLONDIKE GOLD RUSH NATIONAL HISTORICAL PARK—SEATTLE UNIT is at 319 2nd Ave. S. in the Pioneer Square Historic District. The Cadillac Hotel building houses a two-level visitor center that commemorates Seattle's role in the Klondike Gold Rush of 1897-98 through interactive exhibits, videos, gold panning demonstrations, a replica miner's cabin and general store and displays of gold bars, hardware, clothing and mining artifacts.

Time: Allow 1 hour minimum. **Hours:** Daily 9-5, Memorial Day-Labor Day; 10-5, rest of year. Gold panning demonstrations take place daily at 10 and 3, mid-June through Labor Day. Closed Jan. 1, Thanksgiving and Christmas. **Cost:** Free. **Phone:** (206) 220-4240. 🚹 Occidental Mall, 29

KUBOTA GARDEN is in South Seattle's Rainier Beach neighborhood at 9817 S. 55th Ave. In 1927 Japanese emigrant Fujitaro Kubota bought 5 acres of logged-off swampland and created a family garden that was for many years a center for social and cultural activities in Seattle's Japanese community. This 20-acre site is now a city historical landmark and a serene haven open to the public.

Gravel paths wind among conifers, rhododendrons, Japanese red maples, various shrubs and flowering perennials. The Tom Kubota Stroll Garden has places to sit and admire a striking Weeping Blue Atlas Cedar with powdery silver-blue needles on gracefully drooping branches. The Mountainside, built by the Kubota family to celebrate the 1962 Seattle World's Fair, features waterfalls, carved stones and carefully arranged plantings. **Hours:** Daily 6 a.m.-10 p.m., during DST. **Cost:** Free. **Phone:** (206) 684-4584, (206) 725-5060 for guided tour reservations, (206) 684-4075 or TTY (206) 233-1509. GT 🚹 Rainier Beach, 40

LAKE UNION PARK is at 860 Terry Ave. N. An urban green space that highlights the maritime history of the Pacific Northwest, this 12-acre park lies at the southern end of Lake Union. Features include a restored shoreline and salmon habitat, a beach for canoe or kayak launching and a model boat pond. A pedestrian bridge spans Central Cove. A history trail offers interpretive panels.

The South Lake Union Historic Ships Wharf provides moorage for four time-honored vessels. The former 1941 Naval Reserve Building at the water's edge is the home of the Museum of History & Industry (see attraction listing). The park is a great place to enjoy breezy water views on a sunny summer day. Gas Works Park (see attraction listing) is visible across the lake. **Hours:** Park open daily 4 a.m.-11:30

p.m. **Phone:** (206) 684-7254, (206) 684-4075 or TTY (206) 233-1509. 🚹 🚹 Lake Union Park, 12

The Center For Wooden Boats is at 1010 Valley St., next to Lake Union Park. The center displays more than 50 wooden vessels ranging from replicas to boats over a century old. The collection includes dugout canoes from Native Americans. A Wooden Boat Festival is held the first weekend in July.

Rental sailboats, rowboats, canoes and pedal boats are available. **Time:** Allow 30 minutes minimum. **Hours:** Daily 10-8, late Apr.-early Sept.; daily 10-7, early to late Sept.; Tues.-Sun. 10-6, late Sept.-late Oct.; Tues.-Sun. 10-5, rest of year. Boat rentals daily 12:30-dusk, May-Sept.; Sat.-Sun. 12:30-dusk, rest of year. Closed Thanksgiving and Christmas. **Cost:** Donations. Boat rentals $30-$60 per hour. **Phone:** (206) 382-2628. GT 🚹 Lake Union Park, 12

Museum of History & Industry (MOHAI) is in Lake Union Park, 4 mi. w. of I-5 exit 169 at 860 N. Terry Ave. Housed in the restored Naval Reserve Building, MOHAI explores Seattle's more than 150-year history in its showcase exhibit, True Northwest: The Seattle Journey, which has a compelling assemblage of artifacts, images and oral histories.

Other permanent exhibits include Maritime Seattle, which celebrates the city's long relationship with water through interactive galleries and a working WWII-era periscope, and the Bezos Center for Innovation, where Seattle-made inventions and big ideas are featured. Traveling exhibits, lectures, classes, family events and educational programs augment the main offerings.

Hours: Daily 10-5 (also first Thurs. of the month 5-8). Closed Thanksgiving and Christmas. Phone ahead to confirm schedule. **Cost:** $19.95; $15.95 (ages 62+); $13.95 (students and military with ID); free (ages 0-14 with adult and to all first Thurs. of the month). **Parking:** $5 at Westlake Avenue N. garage or Associated General Contractors building (with validation). **Phone:** (206) 324-1126. 🍽 🚹 Lake Union Park, 12

Northwest Seaport is in Lake Union Park at 860 Terry Ave. N. The seaport features two landmark vessels moored at the end of South Lake Union Historic Ships Wharf. The 1904 Coast Guard lightship Swiftsure once guided commercial and cruise ships entering and leaving the Pacific Ocean. The 1933 salmon troller Twilight is a commercial fishing boat that pulls lines hung from long poles slowly through the water.

Hands-on "Engineer For a Day" experiences, a children's story hour, education programs and sleepovers take place aboard the 1889 tugboat Arthur Foss. In addition to towing barges during the Alaska gold rush and serving in World War II, the tugboat was the Narcissus in the 1933 film "Tugboat Annie." Sea chantey sings and other maritime-themed concerts are offered regularly. Stem-to-stern tours of the 120-foot tug also are given; reservations are required.

Time: Allow 1 hour minimum. **Hours:** Grounds open Wed.-Thurs. noon-3, Fri.-Sun. 11-7, June-Sept.; hours vary rest of year. *Arthur Foss* and *Swiftsure* open Sat.-Sun. noon-4, May-Oct.; phone ahead to confirm schedule. Closed Jan. 1 and Christmas. **Cost:** Donations. **Phone:** (206) 447-9800 for tugboat tour reservations and educational program schedules. GT 🅿 Lake Union Park, 12

LAKE WASHINGTON SHIP CANAL—see Hiram M. Chittenden Locks p. 140.

SAVE **LIVING COMPUTERS: MUSEUM AND LABS** is at 2245 1st Ave. S., .5 mi. s. of Safeco Field. Located on the second floor of a former warehouse, the museum contains computers representing milestones in the evolution of technology. The Exhibit Hall displays computers from the late 1960s through the late 1980s, including a vintage 1964 PDP7, the oldest computer in the collection and the only one of its kind still operating.

The Microsoft Exhibit shows how Microsoft Windows, introduced in 1985, has changed over the years. In the Mainframe Room visitors can observe vintage computers being restored to working order. Take the guided tour, which will enhance the experience. **Time:** Allow 1 hour minimum. **Hours:** Wed.-Sun. 10-5 (also first Thurs. of the month 5-8). Guided tours depart at 11:15, 1:15 and 3:15. Closed Thanksgiving and Christmas. **Cost:** $16; $14 (ages 62+ and students and active military with ID); free (ages 0-5 and to all first Thurs. of the month 5-8). **Phone:** (206) 342-2020. GT 🅿 SODO, 35

The Museum of Flight

LOG HOUSE MUSEUM is at 3003 61st Ave. S.W. The museum is in a renovated turn-of-the-20th-century log building at Alki Point, known as the "birthplace of Seattle." Operated by the Southwest Seattle Historical Society, the museum chronicles the history of the area and features changing exhibits. Of interest is the admiral totem pole. **Time:** Allow 30 minutes minimum. **Hours:** Thurs.-Sun. noon-4. Closed major holidays. **Cost:** $3. **Phone:** (206) 938-5293.

GEM **MOPOP (MUSEUM OF POP CULTURE)**— see Seattle Center p. 145.

GEM **THE MUSEUM OF FLIGHT** is .5 mi. n.w. of I-5 exit 158 at 9404 E. Marginal Way S. The pioneering spirit of aerospace technology begins at the Red Barn (part of the original Boeing airplane factory), where the Boeing story from 1916 to 1958 is told. The Personal Courage Wing explores aircraft from World Wars I and II; 28 fighter planes are on display, some of which can only be seen at the museum.

Cross the skybridge to view a retired Concorde jetliner and an Air Force One jet plane that you can walk through. The T.A. Wilson Great Gallery, a breathtaking 6-story glass and steel structure, displays 43 historic aircraft, including a replica of the 1903 Wright Flyer and a rare Lockheed M-21 Blackbird spy plane. Flight simulators are equipped with state-of-the-art 3-D visuals. Kids can learn the basics of flight through hands-on activities at the Flight Zone. The Tower exhibit, overlooking Boeing Field, contains displays about weather, physics and the natural world. The 3-acre Aviation Pavilion focuses on the airline industry from the 1930s to the present and houses 19 rare military and commercial airplanes. Of interest is the FedEx Air Cargo exhibit.

The Lear Gallery is the permanent home to NASA's Space Shuttle Trainer, used by every shuttle astronaut. A replica of the International Space Station's laboratory gives you a peek at astronaut life on a space mission. Also on display is the Perlan glider used to set the current world altitude record.

Audio guides are available in multiple languages. **Time:** Allow 3 hours minimum. **Hours:** Daily 9-5 (also first Thurs. of the month 5-9). Aviation Pavilion daily 9-8. Closed Thanksgiving and Christmas. **Cost:** $24; $21 (active military and veterans with ID); $20 (ages 65+); $15 (ages 5-17); free (to all first Thurs. of the month 5-9). Audio guides $5. Flight simulator i360 $9 per person, 4D-X simulator $8 per person. Shuttle Trainer tours $30; $25 (ages 10-17); age and height restrictions apply. **Phone:** (206) 764-5700 or TTY (800) 833-6384. GT 🍴 🅿 Rainier Beach, 40

NORDIC MUSEUM is at 2655 N.W. Market St. The museum focuses on Nordic cultural contributions to life in the Pacific Northwest. The Dream of America exhibit traces the journey of early 20th-century Nordic immigrants to America and the Pacific Northwest using photographs, artifacts and sound. Additional galleries focus on the impact of Nordic immigration on the fishing and lumber industries, as well as the heritage of each of the five Nordic countries: Denmark, Finland, Iceland, Norway and Sweden. An art gallery hosts changing exhibits by contemporary Nordic and Nordic-American artists.

Time: Allow 1 hour minimum. **Hours:** Tues.-Sun 10-5 (also Thurs. 5-8). Closed Jan. 1, Easter, Thanksgiving, Christmas Eve and Christmas. **Cost:** $15; $12 (ages 63+); $10 (ages 5-17 and students with ID). **Parking:** $1 per hour. **Phone:** (206) 789-5707.

OLYMPIC SCULPTURE PARK is at 2901 Western Ave. This 9-acre green space boasts an urban waterfront setting and manages to be delightfully scenic despite the industrial presence of a train track and busy Alaskan Way. From an elevated vantage point, the main Z-shaped path zigzags 2,200 feet down a 40-foot slope to the Elliott Bay waterfront. Meadow and forest grove environments are naturally landscaped with native trees, plants and flowers.

The mostly contemporary works of sculpture are a mix of permanent and on-loan installations and include "Eagle," a soaring Alexander Calder steel abstract painted a vivid orange. Perhaps the most provocative work is the "Father and Son" fountain. Nude figures of a man and boy reaching out toward each other are alternately revealed and obscured by gushing water, artist Louise Bourgeois' statement on the vulnerability of familial relationships.

The glass-walled PACCAR Pavilion not only provides refuge on a rainy day but has a second-story landing from which to gaze out on the expansive view of the bay and the distant Olympic Mountains. Paid parking is available beneath the pavilion; enter at Broad St. and Western Ave. Contact Seattle Art Museum (SAM) for a guided tour schedule. Food is available Fri.-Sun. 10-3 from late May through early September.

Time: Allow 1 hour minimum. **Hours:** Park open daily 30 minutes before dawn-30 minutes after dusk. Pavilion open Wed.-Mon. 10-5, Apr.-Oct.; Wed.-Sun. 10-5, rest of year. Pavilion closed most major holidays. **Cost:** Free. **Parking:** Pavilion Mon.-Fri. $6 (up to 2 hours), $8 (2-4 hours), $15 (6-8 hours), $22 (all day); Sat.-Sun. $5 (up to 4 hours), $10 (4-10 hours). **Phone:** (206) 654-3100, (206) 654-3177 or TTY (206) 441-4261. GT 🐾 📷 Seattle Center, 4

PIKE PLACE MARKET spreads out from the corner of Pike St. and 1st Ave. Where else in Seattle can you wander among stall after stall of luscious produce, briny fresh seafood, beautiful cut flowers, gooey mac 'n' cheese, delectable baked goods, crafts galore and restaurants aplenty? Pike Place Market is the city's heart and soul, a market that opened in 1907 as an experiment in bringing together local farmers and consumers.

The Main and North arcades stretch along Pike Place between Pike and Virginia streets. This is where many of the produce vendors, flower sellers and specialty food retailers are located. The fishmongers at Pike Place Fish market, at the south end

Pike Place Market

of the Main Arcade, never fail to draw a crowd with their boisterous banter and penchant for casually tossing a whole salmon or two.

The market's footprint expanded in 2017 with the opening of MarketFront, a $74 million expansion offering additional vendors, food stalls and an outdoor plaza with views of Puget Sound and the Olympic Mountains.

On narrow, pedestrian-only Post Alley is the infamous Gum Wall, a wall covered in colorful chewing gum that's a popular photo op. DownUnder, below the Main Arcade, is a warren of specialty shops selling everything from jewelry to collectibles to vintage comics.

Ethnic groceries, bookstores, meat sellers and small mom 'n' pop businesses also are part of the market fabric. A Starbucks branch (1912 Pike Pl., the chain's oldest in operation), Beecher's Homemade Cheese (1600 Pike Pl., their original store) and Sur La Table (84 Pine St. and also their first store) are the only national retailers. Franchises are not permitted, but several businesses that started in the market have expanded to other locations.

Pedestrian access to the waterfront is via the steps of the Pike Street Hillclimb between Alaskan Way and Western Avenue. **Hours:** Most farm vendor stalls are open daily 8-4; most craft vendors are open 10-4, while others are open 10-6. Individual business hours may vary. Produce and flower sellers, fishmongers, coffee shops and bakeries frequently open by 7 a.m., while some restaurants open as early as 6 a.m. or close as late as 1:30 a.m. Many businesses are closed Thanksgiving and Christmas. **Cost:** Market free. **Parking:** $4 per hour in the Public Market

Parking Garage (1531 Western Ave.) and Market-Front Parking Garage (1901 Western Ave.). **Phone:** (206) 682-7453. GT 🍴 🚇 University Street, 7

SAFECO FIELD TOURS is at jct. 1st Ave. S. and S. Royal Brougham Way at 1250 1st Ave. S. Tours explore the 20-acre, 46,500-seat home of the Seattle Mariners. The 1-hour tour visits the field's Mariners Hall of Fame and the Northwest Baseball Museum, plus areas typically off limits to the public, including the press box, luxury suites, dugouts and the visiting teams' clubhouse.

Comfortable walking shoes are recommended. **Time:** Allow 1 hour, 30 minutes minimum. **Hours:** Tours depart daily at 10:30, 12:30 and 2:30, Apr.-Oct.; Tues.-Sat. at 10:30 and 12:30, Sun. at 12:30 and 2:30, rest of year. Times vary on game day; phone for schedule. **Cost:** $12; $11 (ages 65+); $10 (ages 3-12). **Phone:** (206) 346-4241, (206) 346-4246 or (206) 622-4487. GT 🚇 Stadium, 10

SEATTLE AQUARIUM, 1483 Alaskan Way at Pier 59, features more than 380 species of birds, fish, invertebrates and marine mammals. Highlights include the 400,000-gallon Underwater Dome, a Pacific coral reef exhibit, a tide pool exhibit with touch zones and a section with harbor seals, fur seals and otters.

Window on Washington Waters replicates the rocky, kelp-filled underwater terrain that characterizes Neah Bay, inhabited by salmon, rockfish, sea anemones and other native marine life. Educational activities also are offered.

Time: Allow 1 hour, 30 minutes minimum. **Hours:** Daily 9:30-6. Last admission 1 hour before closing. Window on Washington Waters dive show daily at 10, 11:30 and 12:15. Closed first Friday in June and Christmas. Closed Christmas. **Cost:** $29.95; $27.95 (ages 65+ and persons with disabilities); $27 (active military with ID); $19.95 (ages 4-12). **Phone:** (206) 386-4300. 🍴 🚇 University Street, 7

GEM **SEATTLE ART MUSEUM** (SAM) is at 1300 1st Ave. (enter on 1st Ave. at the corner of Union St.). Jonathan Borofsky's 48-foot-tall, kinetic steel sculpture "Hammering Man" greets visitors outside the entrance. SAM's superbly eclectic collection encompasses American, European, African, Native American and ancient Mediterranean art. The three floors of exhibits are arranged thematically and conceptually rather than chronologically; paintings, sculpture, furniture, wall hangings, found objects and other media are intriguingly juxtaposed in the museum's 35 galleries.

The treasures in the Wyckoff Porcelain Room are arranged by color, shape and artistic theme. Visitors will see painted wood screens created by Tlingit Indians, 18th-century tapestries depicting mythical animals and a coffin in the shape of a Mercedes Benz. Some of the pieces feature videos about their creators. Noteworthy special exhibitions are scheduled throughout the year.

An audio guide to the permanent collection is free with admission. Parking is available at the Russell Investment Center building garage beneath the museum; enter on Union Street between 1st and 2nd avenues. **Time:** Allow 2 hours minimum. **Hours:** Fri.-Sun. and Wed. 10-5, Thurs. 10-9 (also Mon. 10-5, late May-early Sept.). Closed most major holidays. **Cost:** $19.95; $17.95 (ages 62+); $12.95 (ages 13-17 and students with ID); free (ages 0-12, ages 62+ first Fri. of the month, military with ID and to all first Thurs. of the month). **Parking:** Russell Investment Center parking garage fees begin at $7 for the first 20 minutes Mon.-Fri.; $8 (up to additional 4 hours) Sat.-Sun. **Phone:** (206) 654-3100 or TTY (206) 654-3137. GT 🍴 🚇 University Street, 7

GEM **SEATTLE CENTER** is between Denny Way and Mercer St. and 1st and 5th aves. This was the site of the Century 21 Exposition, better known as the 1962 World's Fair. The fair was an exciting window to the future, with exhibit areas like The World of Tomorrow, and also gave Seattle one of its most beloved landmarks, the Space Needle.

After the fair's 6-month run ended the 74-acre grounds remained, along with many of the pavilion buildings and the Seattle Center Monorail, which still runs between stations next to the Space Needle and at Westlake Center Mall, downtown at 5th Avenue and Pine Street. Of course the passage of time has mellowed once-radical ideas introduced by the fair's exhibits, but Seattle Center has persevered as a public meeting place of sorts—on a very large scale.

Several of the city's popular attractions are conveniently gathered here. There are plenty of open spaces for picnics, and landscaped areas centered around plazas, fountains and sculptures offer numerous opportunities for relaxing. Gardens, water features and sculptures enhance the outdoor pathways.

This also is Seattle's No. 1 festival site; Bumbershoot, Bite of Seattle, the Northwest Folklife Festival, Seattle PrideFest and the Seattle International Film Festival are just five of the many popular events held here each year. **Phone:** (206) 684-7200 or TTY (206) 684-7100. 🍴 🚇 Seattle Center, 4

GEM **Chihuly Garden and Glass** is on the Seattle Center grounds next to the Space Needle at 305 Harrison St. Bringing together elements of American artist Dale Chihuly's work, the exhibition features drawings, glass pieces, large architectural installations and personal collections. Exhibits in eight galleries demonstrate how Chihuly pushed the boundaries of glass art in concept, execution and presentation.

The Glasshouse, a 40-foot-tall glass and steel structure filled with natural light, is based on Chihuly's lifelong appreciation of conservatories and showcases one of his largest suspended works, a 100-foot-long assemblage of flowers in hues of red, yellow, orange and amber. In the garden, trees, plants and flowers are a real-life backdrop for glass forms that mimic nature, from reeds and cattails to herons and seal pups that can be seen year-round.

Time: Allow 2 hours minimum. **Hours:** Mon.-Thurs. 8:30-8:30, Fri.-Sun. 8:30 a.m.-9:30 p.m., in summer; Sun.-Thurs. 10-6, Fri.-Sat. 10-7, rest of year. Last admission 1 hour before closing. Opening and closing times vary seasonally and during private events; phone ahead to confirm schedule. **Cost:** $19-$29; $16-$22 (ages 65+); $13-$18 (ages 5-12). Combination ticket with Space Needle Observation Deck $36-$49; $30-$42 (ages 65+); $24-$32 (ages 5-12). Reservations are recommended. **Parking:** In nearby garages (starts at $6 per hour). **Phone:** (206) 753-4940. 🍴 🖼 Seattle Center, 4

MoPOP (Museum of Pop Culture) is on the Seattle Center grounds at 325 5th Ave. N. Exhibits inside this eye-catching building—designed by architect Frank O. Gehry to resemble a smashed guitar—explore the history of music, science fiction and popular culture through state-of-the-art interactive displays and an extensive collection of memorabilia. The Sky Church houses a gigantic LED video screen that constantly pulses with music videos, short films and performances.

The Guitar Gallery follows the evolution of the rock's favorite instrument. Visitors can make their own music in the Sound Lab using a variety of instruments and high-tech musical gear, or become a rock star in On Stage. True rock music fans will pay their respects at exhibits saluting the talents of Jimi Hendrix and other music icons.

The pop culture side of the museum encourages visitors to explore the worlds of fantasy, science fiction, horror, video games, animation, costumes and sports with rotating installations.

Time: Allow 2 hours minimum. **Hours:** Daily 10-7, Memorial Day-Labor Day; 10-5, rest of year. Closed Thanksgiving and Christmas. Phone ahead to confirm schedule. **Cost:** $26-$36; $23-$33 (ages 65+ and students with ID); $20-$30 (military with ID); $17-$27 (ages 5-17). Costs vary seasonally and for special exhibitions; phone ahead to confirm rates. **Phone:** (206) 770-2700. 🍴 🖼 Seattle Center, 4

Pacific Science Center is at 200 2nd Ave. N. adjacent to the Seattle Center grounds. Exhibits run the gamut here, from a Tropical Butterfly House and Insect Village to Professor Wellbody's Academy of Health & Wellness, where interactive inventions, gadgets and experiences promote exercise, diet and hygiene choices to help ensure lifelong health. Scale-model dinosaurs are set in a Mesozoic-era environment. Other highlights include an interactive planetarium, laser light shows and two IMAX theaters with 3-D capability.

Water Works is an outdoor exhibit with pumps, a propeller and a giant water wheel. The High Rail Bicycle teaches riders about the center of mass while taking them on a daring adventure via a rail 1 inch wide and 15 feet above the ground.

Time: Allow 3 hours minimum. **Hours:** Daily 10-6, mid-June through Labor Day; Mon.-Fri. 10-5, Sat.-Sun. 10-6, rest of year. High Rail Bicycle and other outdoor

exhibits open seasonally (weather permitting). Exhibits closed Thanksgiving and Christmas. IMAX closed Christmas. **Cost:** Exhibits $21.95; $19.95 (ages 65+); $15.95 (ages 6-15); $11.95 (ages 3-5). IMAX film $10.75-$16.95; $9.75-$15.95 (ages 65+); $8.75-$14.95 (ages 6-15); $6.75-$11.95 (ages 3-5). Combination exhibits and IMAX documentary film $30.70; $27.70 (ages 65+); $22.70 (ages 6-15); $16.70 (ages 3-5). Planetarium shows free with general admission. Matinee laser shows additional $4. Evening laser shows $12 (Wed. and Fri.-Sun.); $10 (Thurs.). **Phone:** (206) 443-2001 for general information, (206) 443-4629 for IMAX film schedule, or (206) 443-2850 for laser show schedule. 🖼 Seattle Center, 4

Seattle Children's Museum is on the lower level of the Seattle Center Armory, 305 Harrison St., on the Seattle Center grounds. The museum encourages children and adults to participate in hands-on, innovative and educational activities. Interactive exhibits invite children to create an artistic masterpiece, explore a miniature grocery store and discover new cultures. Interpretive workshops complement the exhibits.

Time: Allow 1 hour minimum. **Hours:** Tues.-Sun. 10-5. Last admission 1 hour before closing. Closed Jan. 1, Labor Day weekend, Thanksgiving, Christmas Eve and Christmas. **Cost:** $11.50; $10.50 (grandparents); $9 (active military with ID); free (ages 0-12 months). **Phone:** (206) 441-1768. 🖼 Seattle Center, 4

Space Needle is at 400 Broad St. on the Seattle Center grounds. Standing at a height of 605 feet, the Space Needle has been an iconic part of the Seattle skyline since it was unveiled as the

Space Needle

centerpiece of the 1962 World's Fair. And ironically, the city's instantly identifiable symbol began as a sketch on a napkin.

The Needle was the brainchild of hotel magnate and key World's Fair organizer Edward E. Carlson. While on vacation in Stuttgart, Germany, Carlson—inspired by that city's Stuttgart Tower—sketched his version of a structure that would underscore the 21st-century themes of the upcoming exposition. His prototype, which resembled a flying saucer balanced on top of a very tall tripod, opened on Apr. 21, 1962, and was an immediate hit.

A newly renovated observation area provides panoramas of the city, Puget Sound and—on clear days—the distant Cascade and Olympic mountains from more than 500 feet in the air. Floor-to-ceiling glass walls that angle outward and glass benches dubbed "Skyrisers" make for unique photo ops on the upper level. The lower observation level features The Loupe, said to be the world's first and only rotating glass floor, with adrenaline-inducing views straight down to the Seattle Center grounds below; the floor rotates once every 30 minutes.

Time: Allow 1 hour minimum. **Hours:** Daily 8 a.m.-midnight, Memorial Day-Labor Day; hours vary rest of year. Last admission 30 minutes before closing. Phone ahead to confirm schedule. **Cost:** Observation deck $27.50-$37.50; $25.50-$32.50 (ages 65+); $22.50-$28.50 (ages 5-12). Combination ticket with Chihuly Garden and Glass $49-$54; $41-$49 (ages 65+); $34-$38 (ages 5-12). **Parking:** $26-$32 (with validation). **Phone:** (206) 905-2100 or (800) 937-9582. ⏴️ 🈺 Seattle Center, 4

SEATTLE CHINESE GARDEN is 1.75 mi. w. of I-5 exit 163A (southbound) or exit 163 (northbound) via West Seattle Freeway to the Delridge Way exit, then .5 mi. s. on Delridge Way to S.W. Oregon St./23rd Ave. S.W., then 1 mi. s.e. to South Seattle College, 6000 16th Ave. S.W. Built in the Sichuan style, the garden incorporates a traditional courtyard with a tiled roof gate and beautiful windows, woodwork, stone paving, and river rocks from China, all bearing symbolic meanings. Trees and plants indigenous to China include bamboo, pine, magnolia and a large tree peony garden.

Time: Allow 30 minutes minimum. **Hours:** Garden open daily dawn-dusk. Courtyard open Tues.-Sun. 11:30-5. Closed Jan. 1, Thanksgiving and Christmas. **Cost:** Donations. **Phone:** (206) 934-5219. 🈺

South Seattle College Arboretum is on the South Seattle College campus, 6000 16th Ave. S.W., just w. of the Seattle Chinese Garden. Designed, built and maintained by students in the college's Landscape Horticulture Program, this 6-acre green space is divided into themed areas connected by gravel paths. In addition to collections of dwarf conifers, rhododendrons, ferns, roses and perennials, there is a Sensory Garden showcasing fragrant, textural and edible plants. A gazebo in a landscaped setting overlooks

the Seattle skyline and Elliott Bay. **Time:** Allow 30 minutes minimum. **Hours:** Daily dawn-dusk. **Cost:** Free. **Phone:** (206) 934-5396 or (206) 934-6616.

SEATTLE GREAT WHEEL is at 1301 Alaskan Way, on the downtown waterfront at Pier 57. At 175 feet tall, Seattle's newest landmark is one of the largest observation wheels in the U.S. Located at the end of the pier and extending nearly 40 feet beyond the pier over Elliott Bay, it offers spectacular views of the downtown skyline and waterfront, Puget Sound and the distant Olympic Mountains.

The wheel's 41 eight-passenger enclosed gondolas are climate controlled. The ride lasts approximately 15 minutes and makes three full revolutions. A VIP gondola is tricked out with four leather bucket seats, mood lighting and a glass floor. On selected special occasion evenings (for example, Seattle Seahawks games), the wheel's LED light shows light up the waterfront sky.

Time: Allow 30 minutes minimum. **Hours:** Sun.-Thurs. 10 a.m.-11 p.m., Fri.-Sat. 10 a.m.-midnight, July-Sept. Mon.-Thurs. 11-10, Fri. 11 a.m.-midnight, Sat. 10 a.m.-midnight, Sun. 10-10, rest of year. Closed Christmas. Phone ahead to confirm schedule. **Cost:** $14; $12 (ages 65+); $9 (ages 4-11); free (ages 0-3, although a ticket is still required). VIP gondola $50 per person. Tickets can be purchased at the Pier 57 booth and do not expire until used; reservations are not accepted. **Parking:** Metered lots are on Alaskan Way; pay lots are on Western Avenue. **Phone:** (206) 623-8607. 🈺 University Street, 7

SEWARD PARK is at 5900 Lake Washington Blvd. S. This 300-acre park occupies all of the Bailey Peninsula, a forested finger of land jutting out from the southwestern shore of Lake Washington. The city bought the peninsula in 1911 and named it after William H. Seward, the former U.S. secretary of state responsible for the Alaska Purchase. The peninsula was an island before the Montlake cut of the Lake Washington Ship Canal was completed in 1916, which lowered the lake level by about 9 feet.

There are nearly 6 miles of trails. The flat, 2.4-mile paved loop trail that follows the shoreline is popular with walkers and cyclists. The northern two-thirds of the peninsula is cloaked with old growth forest of Douglas fir, western red cedar, western hemlock, big-leaf maple and madrona; forest trails provide beautifully serene hiking opportunities. Also on the park grounds are a native plant garden, an amphitheater, an art studio, a play area and the Seward Park Environmental & Audubon Center. **Time:** Allow 1 hour minimum. **Hours:** Daily 6 a.m.-10 p.m. **Cost:** Free. **Phone:** (206) 684-4396, (206) 684-4075 or TTY (206) 233-1509. 🈺

SKY VIEW OBSERVATORY is downtown at 700 4th Ave. Located on the 73rd floor of the Columbia Center, this public observation area offers a panoramic view of Seattle and its surrounds. Giant windows provide views of Elliott Bay, Mt. Baker, the

Cascade and Olympic mountains, the Space Needle, Mt. Rainier (on a clear day) and other landmarks.

Wall murals, tablets, video displays and window plaques identify landmarks and provide information about the history and geography of Seattle as well as the construction of the Columbia Center, one of the tallest skyscrapers on the West Coast.

Note: The box office is located inside the 4th Avenue Entrance, with a direct elevator for guests to the Observatory on the 73rd floor. **Time:** Allow 1 hour minimum. **Hours:** Daily 10-10, Memorial Day-Labor Day; 10-8, rest of year. **Cost:** $22; $19 (ages 65+); $16 (ages 5-13). **Phone:** (206) 386-5564. 📶 🍴 🏪 Pioneer Square, 8

SMITH TOWER is at 506 2nd Ave. in Pioneer Square. At 522-feet-tall, this 42-story building was the tallest west of the Mississippi River when it was built in 1914. Guests learn about the tower's history through exhibits in the Legends of Smith Tower experience. The 35th-floor observatory features a speakeasy-themed cocktail bar and cafe as well as an open-air observation deck that offers 360-degree views of Seattle, the Olympics, Mount Rainier and the Cascades.

Timed admission tickets include street-level exhibits as well as a manually operated elevator ride to the observatory level. **Hours:** Admission tickets offered daily 10-6. Entry after 6 p.m. is through the main lobby. Phone ahead to confirm schedule and availability. **Cost:** $19; $15 (ages 5-12, ages 65+ and military and students with ID); $12 (WA residents with ID). **Phone:** (206) 624-0414 or (877) 412-2776. 🍴 🏪 Pioneer Square, 8

SPACE NEEDLE—see Seattle Center p. 145.

UNIVERSITY OF WASHINGTON occupies a 639-acre campus on 15th Ave. N.E. between Portage Bay and N.E. 45th St. With more than 44,000 students, UW is one of the country's largest single-campus schools. In 1909 the university hosted the Alaska-Yukon-Pacific Exposition; its legacy is today's beautifully landscaped campus. The Rainier Vista promenade, centered on Drumheller Fountain, is aligned to provide a perspective of Mt. Rainier.

Red Square, named for its brick pavement, is the heart of the campus. Extending northeast from this square is Pierce Lane, formerly known as The Quad, a shaded promenade flanked by Collegiate Gothic-style brick buildings. The dramatic facade of Suzzallo Library forms the square's east flank. It's the largest of UW's more than two dozen libraries, which collectively contain more than 6.5 million volumes and 7.5 million microforms.

The University of Washington Visitors Center is on the west side of Odegaard Undergraduate Library. Seventy-minute campus tours depart from Schmitz Hall, third floor Admissions Office lobby, at 1410 N.E. Campus Pkwy. **Hours:** Visitor center open Mon.-Fri. 8:30-5. **Cost:** Free. **Phone:** (206)

543-9198 for the visitors center, or (206) 543-9686 for campus tour information. 🅖🅣

Burke Museum of Natural History and Culture is on the University of Washington campus. The museum focuses on the natural and cultural history of the Pacific Rim. Displays draw from a permanent collection numbering more than 16 million objects, while diverse special exhibits portray this part of the world's natural and cultural stories. Family and children's events are scheduled year-round. **Note:** The museum is closed and moving its collection to a new building. It is scheduled to reopen fall 2019.

Henry Art Gallery is on 15th Ave. N.E. at N.E. 41st St on the University of Washington campus. The gallery presents changing exhibits of contemporary art by international artists. **Hours:** Wed. and Fri.-Sun. 11-4, Thurs. 11-9. Closed Jan. 1, July 4, Thanksgiving and Christmas. **Cost:** $10; $6 (ages 62+); free (ages 0-13, students with ID and to all on Sun. and first Thurs. of the month). **Phone:** (206) 543-2280. 🍴

VOLUNTEER PARK is entered at E. Galer St. and 15th Ave. E. or at E. Prospect and 14th Ave. E. The park, designed by the renowned Olmsted Brothers architectural firm and completed in 1912, encompasses 48.3 acres of formal gardens and extensive lawns on Capitol Hill. The Asian Art Museum (see attraction listing) is on the grounds. Volunteer Park Conservatory, 1400 E. Galer St., has a large collection of cactuses, succulents, orchids and tropical and subtropical plants. A spiral stairway leads to the top of the 75-foot Volunteer Park Water Tower for an excellent view of the city, its lakes and nearby mountains. Of interest is Isamu Noguchi's Black Sun sculpture. A wading pool, located near the Conservatory and the Asian Art Museum, is open in summer months.

Hours: Park open daily 6 a.m.-10 p.m. Conservatory open Tues.-Sun. 10-4. Wading pool daily 11-8, late June-early Sept. **Cost:** Free. Conservatory $4; $2 (ages 13-17); free (ages 0-12 and to all the first Thurs. and first Sat. of the month). **Phone:** (206) 684-4075, (206) 684-4743 for the conservatory or TTY (206) 233-1509. 🏪 Fairview & Campus Dr, 11

Asian Art Museum is at 1400 E. Prospect St. in Volunteer Park. The outstanding collection of Asian art emphasizes quality over quantity. The setting is stellar—a magnificent Art Deco-style building built in 1933 and located in luxuriantly leafy Volunteer Park. Approaching the main entrance you pass through the Garden Court, filled with beautiful Hindu and Tibetan sandstone sculptures.

Inside are Chinese calligraphy paintings and Japanese watercolors of cherry blossoms, chickadees and cranes. The collection of Chinese art is particularly extensive—more than 7,000 works covering a range of dynasties (among them Han, Song, Tang and Ming) that includes paintings, sculpture, jade and bronze pieces, textiles, lacquers and ceramics.

Seattle Japanese Garden

Japanese art ranges from prehistory to the present and includes screens, ceramics, textiles and extensive archeological materials. Look for Korean Buddhist paintings, folk art, porcelains and tomb pieces. The Indian paintings are beautifully detailed. Last but not least, posing with the camel in the outdoor courtyard makes for a fun photo op.

Free guided tours are given; inquire in advance for information about tour times and topics. **CLOSURE INFORMATION:** The museum was closed for major renovations at press time; reopening is scheduled for fall 2019. Phone ahead for updates and to confirm hours and admission fees. **Time:** Allow 1 hour minimum. **Hours:** Wed.-Sun. 10-5 (also Thurs. 5-9). **Cost:** $9; $6 (ages 62+ and military with ID); $5 (ages 13-19 and students with ID); free (to all first Thurs. of the month, to all second Thurs. of the month 5-9, ages 62+ first Fri. of the month, and families first Sat. of the month). **Phone:** (206) 654-3100 or TTY (206) 344-5267. GT ⊕ Fairview & Campus Dr, 11

Volunteer Park Conservatory is at 1400 E. Galer St. in Volunteer Park. A Victorian-era glass and iron greenhouse, modeled after London's Crystal Palace, offers a large collection of cactuses, succulents, orchids and tropical and subtropical plants. Popular events include a spring plant sale and a holiday open house featuring festive décor and hot cocoa. **Hours:** Tues.-Sun. 10-4. Guided tours are offered by appointment. **Cost:** $4; $2 (ages 13-17); free (ages 0-12 and to all the first Thurs. and first Sat. of the month). **Phone:** (206) 684-4743. GT ⊕ Fairview & Campus Dr, 11

WASHINGTON PARK ARBORETUM encompasses 230 acres extending from 40th Ave. E. and E. Madison St. n. to SR 520 and Lake Washington. In a city blessed with urban green spaces, Washington Park Arboretum is one of the loveliest. It contains more than 5,500 kinds of plants from around the world—including many species native to the Pacific Northwest—that give the overall impression of a natural but meticulously manicured woodland.

There are notable collections of conifers, maples, rhododendrons, camellias, hollies and magnolias. Spring is a highlight, when the azaleas, dogwoods and cherry blossoms that grace Azalea Way, a promenade three-quarters of a mile long, are in bloom.

Rhododendron Glen, planted on a hillside valley off Arboretum Drive E., has varieties from dwarfs to tree forms and is ablaze with color from April into June. In fall Japanese maples turn a vivid array of reds and purples, and the bright yellow blooms of witch hazel in the Joseph A. Witt Winter Garden prove that not all plants go into cold-season hibernation. **Time:** Allow 1 hour, 30 minutes minimum. **Hours:** Arboretum open daily dawn-dusk; gates at the north and south end of Arboretum Drive E. are closed during non-open hours. Visitor center open daily 9-5; closed most major holidays. Free 60- to 90-minute guided walks depart from the visitor center Sun. at 1, Jan.-Nov. **Cost:** Free. **Phone:** (206) 543-8800. GT 🐾

Seattle Japanese Garden is within Washington Park Arboretum, just off Lake Washington Blvd. E. and just n. of E. Madison St. at 1075 Lake Washington Blvd. E. Designed by a team of landscape architects under the supervision of celebrated Japanese garden designer Juki Iida, this is a world of forests, lakes, mountains and a village compressed into a serene 3.5-acre space. Conifers, maples, flowering cherry trees, rhododendrons, camellias, Japanese irises, ferns and water lilies are among the plants growing in harmony with rocks and water. A copper-shingled tea house, a lake spanned by earthen and plank bridges, an 11-tiered pagoda and an *azumaya*, or sheltered resting place, are integral parts of the garden.

Hours: Mon. noon-5, Tues.-Sun. 10-5, in Mar. and in Oct.; Mon. noon-7, Tues.-Sun. 10-7, May-Aug.; Mon. noon-6, Tues.-Sun. 10-6, in Apr. and in Sept.; Mon. noon-4, Tues.-Sun. 10-4, in Nov. Tours depart daily at 12:30, Apr.-Oct. Forty-minute presentations of Chado, a ritual Japanese tea ceremony, are offered; phone ahead to confirm schedule and make reservations. Garden may close during special events. **Cost:** $8; $6 (city of Seattle residents); $4 (ages 6-17, ages 65+, college students with ID and the physically impaired). Chado tickets $10; $7 (ages 6-17); reservations required. **Phone:** (206) 684-4725. GT

WING LUKE MUSEUM OF THE ASIAN PACIFIC AMERICAN EXPERIENCE, 719 S. King St., documents the achievements as well as the historical struggles of Seattle's prominent Asian-American community. Wing Luke was the city's first Asian-American city councilman, active in the development of the International District.

Local artists have contributed their own visions—such as the front door that features a pair of elegant squiggles as bronze door handles—and an enormous wind-chime chandelier. The main gallery presents changing art exhibits, and a museum marketplace offers artwork, jewelry and other handcrafted items for sale.

Historic artifacts, textiles, photographs, diaries, letters and oral histories can be viewed in the Governor Gary Locke Library and Community Heritage Center on the top floor. Cultural exhibits are contributed by Asian-Pacific communities throughout the Pacific Northwest. The museum also sponsors a Chinatown walking tour (see Walking Tours p. 150).

Time: Allow 1 hour minimum. **Hours:** Tues.-Sun. 10-5 (also first Thurs. of the month 5-8). Guided tour schedule varies; phone ahead. Closed Jan. 1, July 4, Thanksgiving, Christmas Eve and Christmas. **Cost:** $17; $15 (ages 62+); $12.50 (ages 13-18 and students with ID); $10 (ages 5-12); free (ages 0-4 and to all first Thurs. of the month). **Phone:** (206) 623-5124. GT 🍴 ♿ 7th & Jackson, 27

WINGS OVER WASHINGTON is at Pier 57, 1301 Alaskan Way. Visitors gather in a room with native carvings, where they are introduced to the attraction by a "park ranger." Upon entry to the theater, rangers ensure passengers are strapped securely into their moving seats, which provide the sensation of flying or floating through the air during the 20-minute presentation. The virtual experience highlights the state's exquisite scenery, featuring locations such as Mount St. Helens, Snoqualmie Falls and the San Juan Islands. Minimum height is 40 inches; maximum height is 76 inches. Maximum weight is 300 pounds.

Hours: Sun.-Thurs. 10 a.m.-11 p.m., Fri.-Sat. 10 a.m.-midnight, late June to mid-Sept.; Mon.-Thurs. 11-10, Fri. 11 a.m.-midnight, Sat. 10 a.m.-midnight, Sun. 10-10, rest of year. Last ride boards 15 minutes before closing. **Cost:** $17; $15 (ages 65+); $13 (ages 0-11). **Phone:** (206) 602-1808. ♿ University Street, 7

🔻 GEM SAVE **WOODLAND PARK ZOO** has two entrances, at 750 N. 50th St. (south) and 5500 Phinney Ave. N. (west). The zoo is known for its dedication to replicating naturalistic habitats. The Tropical Rain Forest habitat, in addition to offering jaguar and gorilla exhibits, is lush with 700 plant species. The Adaptations Building is home to meerkats and nocturnal animals as well as the world's largest lizard—the endangered Komodo dragon, a native of Indonesia. Northern Trail provides a habitat for grizzly bears, river otters, Roosevelt elk, gray wolves, mountain goats and Steller's sea eagles.

Endangered orangutans, Malayan tapirs and siamangs reside within the Trail of Vines, while hippopotamuses, giraffes, patas monkeys, zebras and lions roam the African Savanna. The Temperate Forest and Wildlife Survival Zone include various waterfowl species, red pandas and maned wolves,

while Bug World thrills kids with the likes of cockroaches, walking sticks and tarantulas.

Humboldt penguins live in a habitat that mimics the desert coast of Peru, complete with cliffs, beaches and crashing waves. Bright pink Chilean flamingos have a salt marsh to call their own. Willawong Station is a walk-through bird enclosure showcasing Australian parrots. Last but not least is Zoomazium, an indoor, all-season nature play space and learning center.

Rental strollers and wheelchairs are available. **Time:** Allow 2 hours minimum. **Hours:** Daily 9:30-6, May-Sept.; 9:30-4, rest of year. Animal contact area open May 1-Sept. 30. Special programs and talks are presented May 1-Sept. 30. Closed Christmas. **Cost:** Admission Apr.-Sept. $20.95; $18.95 (ages 65+ and the physically impaired); $12.95 (ages 3-12). Admission rest of year $14.95; $12.95 (ages 65+ and the physically impaired); $9.95 (ages 3-12). Phone ahead to confirm seasonal rates. Carousel rides $2. **Parking:** $6; $18 (RVs). **Phone:** (206) 548-2500. 🍴 ♿

Woodland Park Rose Garden is in Woodland Park Zoo at 750 N. 50th St. A 2.5-acre cultivated area with more than 5,000 plants representing more than 290 varieties of roses, the garden also features a lily pool, topiary shrubbery, a sensory garden and a gazebo. The peak bloom season is June through September. **Hours:** Daily 7:30 a.m.-dusk. **Cost:** Free. **Parking:** $6 for cars during zoo hours. **Phone:** (206) 548-2500.

Sightseeing

Visitors looking for fun things to do and fun places to go can tour Seattle's eye-catching, glass-and-steel Seattle Central Library, at the corner of Fourth Avenue and Madison Street. The futuristic building, designed by Rem Koolhaas, features stunning glass curtain walls supported by a diamond-shaped grid, cantilevered platforms jutting from a central structure and a soaring nine-level atrium. Self-guiding tour maps and brochures are available at the welcome desk and make it easy to add this stop to your trip. Phone (206) 386-4636.

Learn about architecture, design and other urban issues at the Seattle Architecture Foundation, downtown at 1010 Western Ave. in the Center for Architecture and Design. The foundation offers guided, 2-hour themed walking tours that depart at 10 a.m. some Thursdays, Fridays, Saturdays and Sundays, late April through December. If you know when your vacation is planned, advance reservations are advised. Have your AAA travel agency book you a tour. Phone (206) 667-9184.

The Tillicum Excursion tour offered by Argosy Cruises provides passage across Elliott Bay and Puget Sound to Blake Island Marine State Park, where passengers can visit Tillicum Village (see attraction listing for Argosy Cruises this page).

Boat Tours

ARGOSY CRUISES departs from 1101 Alaskan Way at piers 55 and 56 and from AGC Marina on Lake Union. Departing from the downtown pier, the company offers a 1-hour narrated Harbor Cruise along the waterfront and past the shipyards, a 2.5-hour Locks Cruise through the Hiram Chittenden Locks between Elliott Bay and Lake Union, and the 4- to 5-hour Tillicum Excursion to Blake Island Marine State Park.

Departing from the South Lake Union dock, a 1.5-hour Lake Union Cruise includes a narrated tour of Lake Union, Portage Bay and parts of Lake Washington.

Hours: The 1-hour Harbor Cruise departs daily at 9:25, 10:45, 12:05, 1:25, 2:45, 4:05, 5:25, 6:45 and 8:05 p.m., June 30-Sept. 4; at 10:45, 12:05, 1:25, 2:45, 4:05 and 5:25 (also Fri.-Sat. at 6:45 p.m.), May 19-June 29; at 12:05, 1:25, 2:45 and 4:05 (also Sat.-Sun. at 5:25), Mar. 10-May 18 and Sept. 5-Oct. 8; at 12:05 and 1:25 (also Sat.-Sun. at 2:45), rest of year. Departures times vary for the Locks and Lake Union cruises and the Tillicum Excursion; phone ahead for details. Closed Christmas.

Cost: Harbor Cruise fare $27; $22 (ages 65+); $13 (ages 4-12). Locks Cruise fare $44; $39 (ages 65+); $20 (ages 4-12). Lake Union Cruise fare $32; $27 (ages 65+); $13 (ages 4-12). Tillicum Excursion (includes boat tour, dinner and show) $84; $75 (ages 65+); $32 (ages 4-12). A fuel surcharge may apply. Reservations are recommended. **Phone:** (206) 623-1445 for the Pier 55/56 ticket booth, (206) 285-2886 for the Lake Union ticket booth or (888) 623-1445. GT ⌨ University Street, 7

CLIPPER VACATIONS departs from Pier 69 at 2701 Alaskan Way. On the San Juan Islands Whale Watching & Sealife Search Day Trip, the high-speed passenger vessel travels north through scenic Deception Pass to Friday Harbor in the San Juan Islands, arriving at 11:45. Passengers may disembark or, from mid-May to early October, stay aboard for a 2.5-hour sea life and orca whale-watching excursion complete with onboard naturalist. Whales are sighted more than 90 percent of the time. The trip back to Seattle departs at 5, arriving at 7:45 p.m. Other tour packages also are available.

Note: Passengers should inquire beforehand about payment policy and where to park. **Hours:** Departs daily at 8:15 a.m., mid-June to early Sept.; Thurs.-Mon. at 8:15 a.m., mid-May to mid-June; Sat.-Sun. at 8:15, early Sept.-early Oct. Phone ahead to confirm schedule. **Cost:** Ferry round-trip fare mid-June to early Sept. $100; mid-May to mid-June and early Sept.-early Oct. $94. Ferry and whale watch round-trip fare mid-June to early Sept. $166; mid-May to mid-June and early Sept.-early Oct. $112. Child ages 1-11 $25 with paying adult; otherwise half price. Listed fares require a minimum 1-day advance purchase. Reservations are recommended. **Phone:** (206) 448-5000 or (800) 888-2535. GT ⌨ Seattle Center, 4

Bus and Trolley Tours

Tours Northwest offers 3-hour narrated, interactive mini-coach tours of the city's highlights and spots you must see while you travel, including the waterfront, Pioneer Square, Ballard Locks and various neighborhoods. Door-to-door service is provided from downtown Seattle, Bellevue, SeaTac and

Tukwila hotels; phone (206) 768-1234 or (888) 293-1404 for more information.

Food Tours

SAVOR SEATTLE FOOD TOURS departs from various locations near Pike Place Market and downtown. Two-hour guided culinary tours introduce visitors to the food and culture of Pike Place Market and include 6-8 stops and more than 15 tastings. The Signature Food Tour of Pike Place Market serves as a good introduction to the market's foodie items, while early-access VIP tours offer the chance to sample produce and smoked salmon before the market gets busy. A chocolate tour and other specialty and gourmet tours are offered.

Time: Allow 2 hours, 30 minutes minimum. **Hours:** Signature Food Tour departs daily every half-hour 9:30-11 and 2-3:30. VIP Food Tour departs daily at 8, 8:30 and 9. Availability and tours times may vary; phone ahead or check the website when reserving tickets. **Cost:** Signature Food Tour Fri.-Sun. $43.99; Mon.-Thurs. $41.99. VIP Food Tour Fri.-Sun. $55.99; Mon.-Thurs. $53.99. Reservations are required. **Phone:** (206) 209-5485. GT ⌨ ⌨ Westlake, 6

Show Me Seattle offers guided 2.5-hour culinary and cultural walking tours of the Belltown and Pike Place Market neighborhoods, exploring cuisine, history, architecture and public art as well as shopping and entertainment venues along the way. In addition to enjoying a variety of mouthwatering market goodies during the tour of Pike Place Market, you'll find out how to select fresh fish and when seasonal produce is at its best.

Plane Tours

Kenmore Air Scenic Flight Tours, 950 Westlake Ave. N., offers sightseeing flights via seaplane from downtown Seattle's Lake Union. Flights last approximately 20 minutes. Departures to San Juan Island and Victoria, B.C., also are scheduled daily. Phone (425) 482-2222. Several companies also offer sightseeing flights of the area departing from Renton, at the south end of Lake Washington.

SEATTLE SEAPLANES is off I-5 exit 167 to 1325 Fairview Ave. E. Departing from Lake Union, Seattle Seaplanes offers 20-minute tours highlighting the greater Seattle area. Charter flights also are available to Mount Rainier, Mount St. Helens and San Juan Islands. **Hours:** Daily 8-dusk. **Cost:** Fare $97.50; $8 fuel surcharge. **Phone:** (206) 329-9638 or (800) 637-5553. GT ⌨ Fairview & Campus Dr, 11

Walking Tours

Chinatown Discovery Tours, offered by the Wing Luke Museum of the Asian Pacific American Experience (see attraction listing p. 148), includes a program and a leisurely guided walking tour of Seattle's Chinatown/International District. For information and reservations phone (206) 623-5124.

BENEATH THE STREETS departs from 102 Cherry St. in the Pioneer Square Historic District. Guided tours take visitors below street-level to explore underground passageways created after the Great Seattle Fire of 1889. Historical information and facts are covered along the way, including such topics as early settlers, Chief Seattle and the Duwamish tribe, the Klondike gold rush and the architectural significance of buildings in Pioneer Square.

Note: Tour participants must be able to walk on uneven ground and climb steps. Comfortable walking shoes are recommended. **Hours:** Tours offered daily at 10:30, 11:30, 12:30, 1:30, 2:30 and 3:30 (also Fri.-Sat. at 4:30). Additional tours offered; phone ahead to confirm schedule. Closed Christmas. **Cost:** $19; $17 (ages 13-17, ages 60+ and college students and military with ID); $10 (ages 7-12). **Phone:** (206) 624-1237. ⊞ Pioneer Square, 8

SEATTLE FREE WALKING TOURS departs from Victor Steinbrueck Park, at the north entrance to Pike Place Market. Knowledgeable guides lead guests on 60- to 120-minute walking tours of the city, recounting historical anecdotes and interesting facts along the way. The Seattle 101 tour offers visitors an overview of the downtown area with stops in downtown Seattle, Pioneer Square Historic District and the waterfront. The Market Experience tour focuses on Pike Place Market and its history, with opportunities for sampling and interacting with market vendors.

Comfortable walking shoes and weather-appropriate clothing are recommended. **Hours:** Seattle 101 tour departs daily at 10 and 1, May-Sept.; schedule varies rest of year. The Market Experience tour departs daily 9:30 and 11, May-Sept.; schedule varies rest of year. Phone ahead to confirm schedule. **Cost:** Donations. Reservations are required. **Phone:** (425) 770-6928. ⊞ Westlake, 6

◤GEM **UNDERGROUND TOUR** departs from Doc Maynard's Public House at 614 1st Ave. Tours explore a three-block area—both above and below ground—of the Pioneer Square Historic District. The tour includes subterranean sidewalks and abandoned turn-of-the-20th-century storefronts created when street levels were raised 8 to 35 feet following The Great Seattle Fire in 1889. The guided tour, humorously narrated, highlights Seattle's history in the aftermath of the fire that destroyed 30 blocks of downtown Seattle.

Comfortable walking shoes and weather-appropriate clothing are recommended. Tour participants must be able to walk on uneven ground and climb stairs. **Time:** Allow 1 hour, 30 minutes minimum. **Hours:** Tours depart daily on the hour 9-7 (also on the half-hour, June-Aug.), Apr.-Sept.; 10-6, rest of year. Tickets are available online or on a first-come, first-served basis; arrive early. Closed Thanksgiving and Christmas. **Cost:** $22; $20 (ages 13-17, ages 60+ and college students with ID); $10 (ages 7-12). **Phone:** (206) 682-4646. GT ⏹ ⊞ Pioneer Square, 8

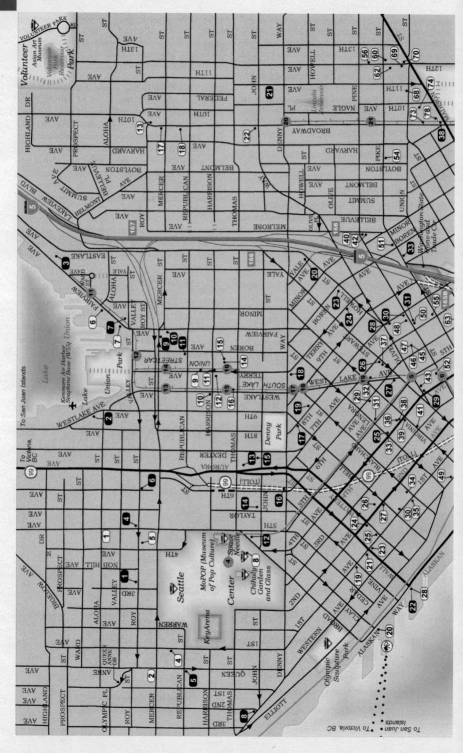

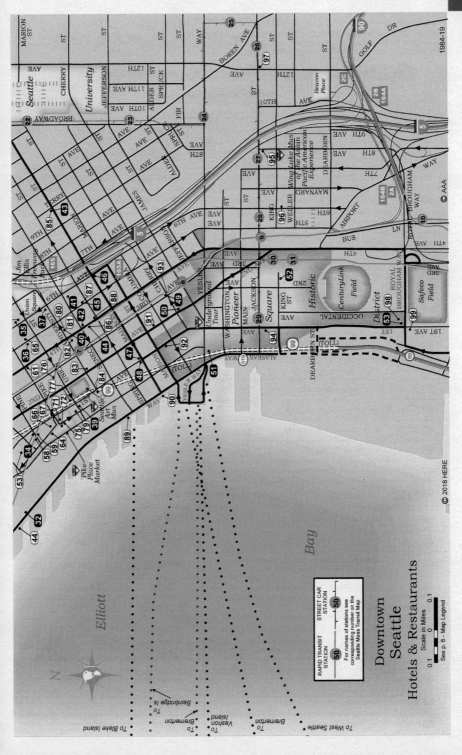

Downtown
Seattle
Hotels & Restaurants

Downtown Seattle

This index helps you "spot" where approved hotels and restaurants are located on the corresponding detailed maps. Hotel daily rate range is for comparison only. Restaurant price range is a combination of lunch and/or dinner. Turn to the listing page for more information and consult display ads for special promotions.

 For more details, rates and reservations: AAA.com/travelguides/hotels

DOWNTOWN SEATTLE

Map Page	Hotels	Diamond Rated	Rate Range	Page
1 p. 152	The Maxwell Hotel	💎💎💎	Rates not provided	174
2 p. 152	Courtyard by Marriott Seattle Downtown/Lake Union	💎💎💎	$89-$483	172
3 p. 152	Silver Cloud Inn Lake Union	💎💎💎	$179-$349	176
4 p. 152	Hampton Inn & Suites by Hilton-Seattle Downtown	💎💎💎	Rates not provided	173
5 p. 152	Mediterranean Inn	💎💎	$129-$399	174
6 p. 152	**Four Points by Sheraton Downtown Seattle Center**	💎💎💎	$150-$659 SAVE	173
7 p. 152	Residence Inn by Marriott Seattle Downtown/Lake Union	💎💎💎	$136-$536	175
8 p. 152	Homewood Suites by Hilton-Seattle Downtown	💎💎💎	Rates not provided	173
9 p. 152	Staybridge Suites Seattle Downtown - South Lake Union	💎💎💎	Rates not provided	176
10 p. 152	EVEN Hotel Seattle Downtown - South Lake Union	💎💎💎	Rates not provided	172
11 p. 152	MOXY Seattle Downtown	💎💎	$104-$379	175
12 p. 152	**Hyatt House Seattle/Downtown**	💎💎💎	$159-$599 SAVE	174
13 p. 152	Holiday Inn Express & Suites	💎💎💎	$109-$299	173
14 p. 152	**Best Western Executive Inn**	💎💎	$89-$499 SAVE	172
15 p. 152	Holiday Inn Seattle Downtown	💎💎💎	$109-$299	173
16 p. 152	**Hyatt Place Seattle/Downtown**	💎💎💎	$159-$599 SAVE	174
17 p. 152	The Loyal Inn	💎💎	Rates not provided	174
18 p. 152	**Pan Pacific Hotel Seattle**	💎💎💎💎	Rates not provided SAVE	175
19 p. 152	La Quinta Inn & Suites Seattle Downtown	💎💎💎	$119-$379	174
20 p. 152	**SpringHill Suites by Marriott Seattle Downtown/South Lake Union**	💎💎💎	$92-$357 SAVE	176
21 p. 152	11th Avenue Inn Bed & Breakfast	💎💎	$99-$249	172
22 p. 152	**The Edgewater**	💎💎💎💎	$179-$529 SAVE	172
23 p. 152	Hilton Garden Inn-Seattle Downtown	💎💎💎	Rates not provided	173
24 p. 152	Residence Inn by Marriott Seattle Downtown/Convention Center	💎💎💎	$114-$370	175
25 p. 152	**Warwick Seattle**	💎💎💎	$149-$449 SAVE	176
26 p. 152	**Hotel Max**	💎💎💎	Rates not provided SAVE	173
27 p. 152	**The Westin Seattle**	💎💎💎💎	$125-$385 SAVE	176

DOWNTOWN SEATTLE (cont'd)

Map Page	Hotels (cont'd)	Diamond Rated	Rate Range	Page
28 p. 152	**Hyatt Olive 8**	◆◆◆◆	$159-$499 SAVE	174
29 p. 152	Mayflower Park Hotel	◆◆◆	Rates not provided	174
30 p. 152	The Paramount Hotel	◆◆◆	Rates not provided	175
31 p. 152	**Grand Hyatt Seattle**	◆◆◆◆	$159-$599 SAVE	173
32 p. 152	**Seattle Marriott Waterfront Hotel**	◆◆◆	$149-$498 SAVE	175
33 p. 152	**Homewood Suites by Hilton Seattle Convention Center/Pike Street**	◆◆◆	$125-$525 SAVE	173
34 p. 152	Inn At The Market	◆◆◆◆	Rates not provided	174
35 p. 152	**Sheraton Grand Seattle**	◆◆◆◆	$198-$435 SAVE	175
36 p. 152	**Motif Seattle**	◆◆◆◆	Rates not provided SAVE	175
37 p. 152	**Hilton Seattle**	◆◆◆	$199-$399 SAVE	173
38 p. 152	Silver Cloud Hotel-Broadway	◆◆◆	$179-$349	176
39 p. 152	Four Seasons Hotel Seattle	◆◆◆◆	$699-$6850	173
40 p. 152	**Fairmont Olympic Hotel**	◆◆◆◆	$199-$499 SAVE	172
41 p. 152	**Crowne Plaza Seattle-Downtown**	◆◆◆	$169-$449 SAVE	172
42 p. 152	**W Seattle**	◆◆◆◆	$128-$417 SAVE	176
43 p. 152	Hotel Sorrento	◆◆◆	Rates not provided	173
44 p. 152	**Kimpton Hotel Monaco Seattle**	◆◆◆◆	Rates not provided SAVE	174
45 p. 152	**Kimpton Hotel Vintage Seattle**	◆◆◆◆	Rates not provided SAVE	174
46 p. 152	**Renaissance Seattle Hotel**	◆◆◆◆	$105-$487 SAVE	175
47 p. 152	Loews Hotel 1000	◆◆◆◆	Rates not provided	174
48 p. 152	**Kimpton Alexis Hotel Seattle**	◆◆◆◆	Rates not provided SAVE	174
49 p. 152	**The Arctic Club Seattle-a DoubleTree by Hilton Hotel**	◆◆◆◆	$259-$499 SAVE	172
50 p. 152	Courtyard by Marriott Seattle Downtown/Pioneer Square	◆◆◆	$116-$612	172
51 p. 152	**Best Western Plus Pioneer Square Hotel**	◆◆	$109-$799 SAVE	172
52 p. 152	Embassy Suites by Hilton Seattle Downtown Pioneer Square	◆◆◆	Rates not provided	172
53 p. 152	Silver Cloud Hotel Seattle-Stadium	◆◆◆	$179-$459	176

Map Page	Restaurants	Diamond Rated	Cuisine	Price Range	Page
1 p. 152	Crow Restaurant & Bar	◆◆	International	$16-$29	177
2 p. 152	Toulouse Petit Kitchen & Lounge	◆◆	Cajun	$12-$55	179
4 p. 152	Chutney's	◆◆	Indian	$11-$23	177
5 p. 152	Bahn Thai Restaurant	◆◆	Thai	$10-$21	176
6 p. 152	Duke's Chowder House	◆◆	Seafood	$12-$35	177

Map Page	Restaurants (cont'd)	Diamond Rated	Cuisine	Price Range	Page
⑦ p. 152	Daniel's Broiler on Lake Union	◈◈◈	Steak	$36-$125	177
⑧ p. 152	The Space Needle - SkyCity Restaurant	fyi	American	$27-$70	178
⑨ p. 152	Veggie Grill	◈	Vegan	$9-$12	179
⑩ p. 152	Serious Pie Westlake & Serious Biscuit	◈◈	Pizza	$7-$20	178
⑪ p. 152	Cactus South Lake Union	◈◈	Tex-Mex	$11-$19	177
⑫ p. 152	Portage Bay Cafe South Lake Union	◈◈	Regional American	$9-$19	178
⑬ p. 152	Poppy	◈◈◈	Pacific Northwest	$24-$32	178
⑭ p. 152	Brave Horse Tavern	◈◈	American	$8-$16	177
⑮ p. 152	Cuoco	◈◈◈	Northern Italian	$15-$42	177
⑯ p. 152	Flying Fish Seattle	◈◈◈	Seafood	$12-$38	177
⑰ p. 152	Aoki Japanese Grill & Sushi Bar	◈◈	Japanese	$7-$20	176
⑱ p. 152	Altura	◈◈◈◈	Italian	$137	176
⑲ p. 152	CJ's Eatery	◈◈	American	$7-$15	177
⑳ p. 152	Aqua by El Gaucho	◈◈◈	Seafood	$32-$98	176
㉑ p. 152	El Gaucho	◈◈◈	Steak	$26-$78	177
㉒ p. 152	Americana	◈◈	Comfort Food	$9-$16	176
㉓ p. 152	Cyclops	◈◈	American	$8-$16	177
㉔ p. 152	Shiro's	◈◈	Sushi	$7-$35	178
㉕ p. 152	Macrina Bakery & Cafe	◈	Breads/Pastries	$5-$14	178
㉖ p. 152	Marrakesh Moroccan Restaurant	◈◈	Moroccan	$22-$33	178
㉗ p. 152	Wasabi	◈◈◈	Japanese	$8-$40	179
㉘ p. 152	Six Seven	◈◈◈	Pacific Northwest	$12-$50	178
㉙ p. 152	Dimitriou's Jazz Alley Restaurant & Nightclub	◈◈	International	$27-$39	177
㉚ p. 152	Umi Sake House	◈◈	Sushi	$6-$18	179
㉛ p. 152	Palace Kitchen	◈◈	American	$20-$32	178
㉜ p. 152	Barolo Ristorante	◈◈◈	Italian	$31-$50	176
㉝ p. 152	**Margaux Restaurant**	◈◈	Pacific Northwest	$10-$35	178
㉞ p. 152	La Fontana Siciliana	◈◈	Italian	$14-$39	177
㉟ p. 152	Queen City Grill	◈◈	American	$15-$34	178
㊱ p. 152	Assaggio Ristorante	◈◈	Italian	$12-$37	176
㊲ p. 152	Miller's Guild	◈◈◈	Steak	$10-$62	178
㊳ p. 152	Lola	◈◈◈	New Greek	$13-$39	178
㊴ p. 152	Dahlia Lounge	◈◈◈	Pacific Northwest	$13-$54	177

Map Page	Restaurants (cont'd)	Diamond Rated	Cuisine	Price Range	Page
40 p. 152	Sitka & Spruce	♦♦♦	New American	$15-$37	178
41 p. 152	Serious Pie Downtown	♦♦	Pizza	$17-$20	178
42 p. 152	Ristorante Machiavelli	♦♦	Italian	$10-$34	178
43 p. 152	Andaluca	♦♦♦	Mediterranean	$25-$45	176
44 p. 152	Anthony's Pier 66	♦♦♦	Seafood	$12-$65	176
45 p. 152	Il Fornaio Panettera/Bakery Cafe	♦	Italian	$8-$15	177
46 p. 152	Il Fornaio	♦♦♦	Italian	$19-$38	177
47 p. 152	Gordon Biersch Brewery Restaurant	♦♦♦	American	$10-$29	177
48 p. 152	Dragonfish Asian Cafe	♦♦	Asian	$10-$17	177
49 p. 152	Etta's	♦♦♦	Seafood	$16-$38	177
50 p. 152	Ruth's Chris Steak House	♦♦♦	Steak	$20-$65	178
51 p. 152	Tango	♦♦♦	Latin American Small Plates	$11-$54	179
52 p. 152	P.F. Chang's China Bistro	♦♦♦	Chinese	$12-$29	178
53 p. 152	The Pink Door	♦♦	Italian	$12-$39	178
54 p. 152	Ayutthaya Thai Restaurant	♦♦	Thai	$9-$22	176
55 p. 152	The Cheesecake Factory	♦♦♦	International	$11-$30	177
56 p. 152	Momiji	♦♦♦	Japanese	$7-$20	178
58 p. 152	Cafe Campagne	♦♦	French	$11-$23	177
59 p. 152	Steelhead Diner	♦♦♦	Pacific Northwest	$14-$37	179
60 p. 152	Elysian Brewing	♦♦	American	$10-$18	177
61 p. 152	RN74	♦♦♦	Regional French	$30-$55	178
62 p. 152	Osteria La Spiga	♦♦♦	Northern Italian	$11-$34	178
63 p. 152	Loulay Kitchen & Bar	♦♦♦	New French	$10-$37	178
64 p. 152	Athenian Seafood Restaurant and Bar	♦♦	Seafood	$10-$35	176
65 p. 152	Palomino Restaurant	♦♦♦	Mediterranean	$13-$39	178
66 p. 152	Matt's in the Market	♦♦♦	American	$15-$48	178
67 p. 152	Hard Rock Cafe	♦♦	American	$13-$34 [SAVE]	177
68 p. 152	Bateau	♦♦♦	Steak	$30-$100	176
69 p. 152	Plum Bistro	♦♦	Vegan	$10-$23	178
70 p. 152	Barrio Mexican Kitchen & Bar	♦♦♦	Mexican	$11-$24	176
71 p. 152	IL Bistro	♦♦♦	Italian	$18-$44	177
72 p. 152	Place Pigalle	♦♦♦	French	$16-$44	178
73 p. 152	Garage	♦♦	American	$11-$15	177
74 p. 152	Lark	♦♦♦	American	$16-$42	178

Map Page	Restaurants (cont'd)	Diamond Rated	Cuisine	Price Range	Page
⑦⑤ p. 152	Sound View Cafe	◆	American	$11-$30	178
⑦⑥ p. 152	Wild Ginger Asian Restaurant & Satay Bar	◆◆◆	Asian	$11-$35	179
⑦⑦ p. 152	Japonessa	◆◆◆	Japanese Sushi	$8-$22	177
⑦⑧ p. 152	Jimmy's on Broadway	◆◆	American	$14-$25	177
⑦⑨ p. 152	The Pike Pub and Brewery	◆◆	American	$10-$45	178
⑧⓪ p. 152	**Shuckers**	◆◆◆	Seafood	$12-$40	178
⑧① p. 152	**The Georgian**	◆◆◆◆	Regional American	$12-$29	177
⑧② p. 152	Purple Cafe and Wine Bar	◆◆	American	$14-$70	178
⑧③ p. 152	The Brooklyn Seafood, Steak & Oyster House	◆◆◆	Seafood Steak	$14-$54	177
⑧④ p. 152	Lecosho	◆◆◆	New American	$12-$30	178
⑧⑤ p. 152	Dunbar Room	◆◆◆	American	$10-$35	177
⑧⑥ p. 152	Outlier	◆◆◆	American	$14-$32	178
⑧⑦ p. 152	Tulio Ristorante	◆◆◆	Regional Italian	$8-$38	179
⑧⑧ p. 152	**Trace**	◆◆◆	American	$14-$34	179
⑧⑨ p. 152	Elliott's Oyster House	◆◆◆	Seafood	$13-$76	177
⑨⓪ p. 152	Ivar's Acres of Clams	◆◆	Seafood	$15-$60	177
⑨① p. 152	Metropolitan Grill	◆◆◆	Steak	$14-$120	178
⑨② p. 152	Fado Irish Pub	◆◆	Irish	$10-$17	177
⑨③ p. 152	Juno	◆◆◆	Pacific Northwest	$14-$40	177
⑨④ p. 152	Il Terrazzo Carmine	◆◆◆	Italian	$13-$57	177
⑨⑤ p. 152	House of Hong	◆◆	Chinese Dim Sum	$8-$18	177
⑨⑥ p. 152	Shanghai Gardens	◆◆	Chinese	$11-$30	178
⑨⑦ p. 152	Huong Binh Restaurant	◆◆	Vietnamese	$9-$15	177
⑨⑧ p. 152	Jimmy's on First	◆◆	American	$11-$34	177
⑨⑨ p. 152	Pyramid Alehouse, Brewery & Restaurant	◆◆	American	$12-$18	178

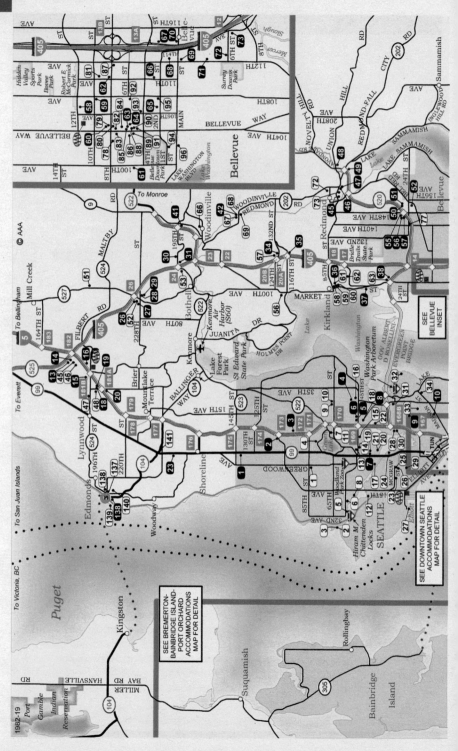

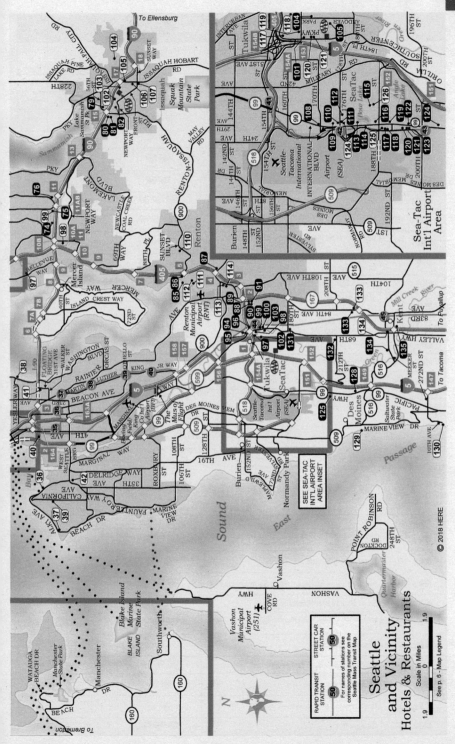

Seattle and Vicinity
Hotels & Restaurants

Scale in Miles

RAPID TRANSIT
STATION

STREET CAR
STATION

For names of stations see
corresponding number on the
Seattle Mass Transit Map

See p. 6 - Map Legend

© 2018 HERE

Sea-Tac
Int'l Airport
Area

SEE SEA-TAC
INT'L AIRPORT
AREA INSET

✈ Airport Hotels

Map Page	SEATTLE-TACOMA INTERNATIONAL (Maximum driving distance from airport: 3.7 mi)	Diamond Rated	Rate Range	Page
118 p. 160	Aloft Seattle Sea-Tac Airport, 2.7 mi	◈◈◈	$95-$263	121
125 p. 160	**Best Western Seattle Airport Hotel, 3.5 mi**	◈◈	$109-$249 SAVE	121
115 p. 160	**Cedarbrook Lodge, 2.7 mi**	◈◈◈	Rates not provided SAVE	121
110 p. 160	Clarion Hotel, 1.5 mi	◈◈	$89-$175	121
114 p. 160	**Coast Gateway Hotel, 1.9 mi**	◈◈	Rates not provided SAVE	121
119 p. 160	Country Inn & Suites By Radisson Seattle Airport, 2.4 mi	◈◈	Rates not provided	121
109 p. 160	Crowne Plaza Seattle Airport, 1.3 mi	◈◈◈	$109-$309	121
116 p. 160	**DoubleTree by Hilton Hotel Seattle Airport, 2.4 mi**	◈◈◈	$99-$369 SAVE	121
123 p. 160	Fairfield Inn by Marriott Seattle Sea-Tac Airport, 2.8 mi	◈◈	$72-$247	121
117 p. 160	Hampton Inn & Suites by Hilton Seattle Airport - 28th Ave, 2.6 mi	◈◈◈	Rates not provided	121
120 p. 160	**Hampton Inn by Hilton Seattle-Airport, 2.6 mi**	◈◈◈	$112-$277 SAVE	121
111 p. 160	**Hilton Seattle Airport & Conference Center, 1.8 mi**	◈◈◈	$99-$399 SAVE	121
121 p. 160	Holiday Inn Express Hotel & Suites-Seattle Sea-Tac Airport, 2.7 mi	◈◈◈	Rates not provided	122
113 p. 160	Radisson Hotel Seattle Airport, 1.8 mi	◈◈◈	$109-$499	122
108 p. 160	**Red Roof Inn Seattle Airport-SeaTac, 1.1 mi**	◈◈	$69-$289 SAVE	122
112 p. 160	**Seattle Airport Marriott, 1.7 mi**	◈◈◈	$89-$352 SAVE	122
124 p. 160	Sleep Inn SeaTac Airport, 3.7 mi	◈◈	$84-$184	122

Seattle and Vicinity

This index helps you "spot" where approved hotels and restaurants are located on the corresponding detailed maps. Hotel daily rate range is for comparison only. Restaurant price range is a combination of lunch and/or dinner. Turn to the listing page for more information and consult display ads for special promotions.

 For more details, rates and reservations: **AAA.com/travelguides/hotels**

SEATTLE

Map Page	Hotels	Diamond Rated	Rate Range	Page
1 p. 160	Holiday Inn Express Hotel & Suites North Seattle/Shoreline	◈◈◈	$129-$375	179
2 p. 160	**Hotel Nexus Seattle**	◈◈	Rates not provided SAVE	179
3 p. 160	Hampton Inn & Suites by Hilton Seattle/Northgate	◈◈◈	Rates not provided	179
4 p. 160	Silver Cloud Hotel-University District	◈◈◈	$179-$329	179
5 p. 160	Residence Inn by Marriott - Seattle/University District	◈◈◈	$123-$461	179
6 p. 160	Graduate Seattle	fyi	Rates not provided	179
7 p. 160	Staybridge Suites - Seattle - Fremont	◈◈◈	$109-$299	179
8 p. 160	University Inn	◈◈	Rates not provided	179
9 p. 160	Mildred's Bed & Breakfast	◈◈	Rates not provided	179
10 p. 160	Gaslight Inn	◈◈◈	$178-$238	179

Map Page	Restaurants	Diamond Rated	Cuisine	Price Range	Page
① p. 160	Gorditos	◈	Mexican	$4-$13	180
② p. 160	Ray's Cafe	◈◈	Seafood	$16-$38	180
③ p. 160	Ray's Boathouse	◈◈◈	Seafood	$20-$59	180
④ p. 160	Duke's Chowder House	◈◈	Seafood	$9-$31	180
⑤ p. 160	Portage Bay Cafe Ballard	◈◈	American	$10-$19	180
⑥ p. 160	La Carta de Oaxaca	◈◈	Mexican	$7-$13	180
⑦ p. 160	Nell's	◈◈◈	Pacific Northwest	$22-$48	180
⑧ p. 160	The Walrus and the Carpenter	◈◈◈	Small Plates Seafood	$10-$16	180
⑨ p. 160	JuneBaby	◈◈◈	Southern	$12-$22	180
⑩ p. 160	Salare	◈◈◈	American	$15-$30	180
⑪ p. 160	Tangletown - Elysian Brewing	◈◈	American	$7-$15	180
⑫ p. 160	Chinook's at Salmon Bay	◈◈	Seafood	$10-$35	180
⑬ p. 160	Bizzaro Italian Cafe	◈◈	Italian	$15-$22	179
⑭ p. 160	Tilth Restaurant	◈◈◈	New American	$17-$95	180
⑮ p. 160	Kabul Afghan Cuisine	◈◈	Afghan	$11-$40	180
⑯ p. 160	Veggie Grill	◈	Vegan	$9-$12	180
⑰ p. 160	Brouwer's Cafe	◈◈	Belgian	$8-$22	179
⑱ p. 160	Portage Bay Cafe Roosevelt	◈◈	Regional American	$9-$16	180
⑲ p. 160	Art of the Table	◈◈◈	New American	$16-$29	179
⑳ p. 160	Joule	◈◈◈	Korean Fusion	$16-$35	180
㉑ p. 160	The Whale Wins	◈◈◈	Continental	$12-$45	180
㉒ p. 160	Le Fournil Ltd	◈◈	French Breads/ Pastries	$5-$12	180
㉓ p. 160	Macrina Bakery & Cafe	◈	Breads/Pastries	$5-$14	180
㉔ p. 160	Canlis	◈◈◈◈	Pacific Northwest	$90-$145	179
㉕ p. 160	Orrapin Thai Cuisine	◈◈	Thai	$8-$14	180
㉖ p. 160	Mezcaleria Oaxaca	◈◈	Regional Mexican	$7-$17	180
㉗ p. 160	Palisade Restaurant	◈◈◈	Seafood	$22-$79	180
㉘ p. 160	Terry's 14 Carrot Café	◈◈	American	$8-$15	180
㉙ p. 160	5 Spot	◈◈	American	$9-$19	179
㉚ p. 160	Serafina	◈◈◈	Italian	$14-$33	180
㉛ p. 160	Cafe Lago	◈◈	Italian	$16-$26	179
㉜ p. 160	Cactus Madison Park	◈◈	Tex-Mex	$10-$19	179
㉝ p. 160	Monsoon	◈◈	Vietnamese	$10-$35	180
㉞ p. 160	Cafe Flora	◈◈	Vegetarian Vegan	$6-$19	179
㊱ p. 160	Salty's on Alki Beach	◈◈◈	Seafood	$22-$75	180
㊲ p. 160	Cactus Alki Beach	◈◈	Tex-Mex	$11-$19	179
㊳ p. 160	Daniel's Broiler - Leschi	◈◈◈	Steak	$30-$115	180

Map Page	Restaurants (cont'd)	Diamond Rated	Cuisine	Price Range	Page
39 p. 160	Circa	◆◆	American	$10-$20	180
40 p. 160	Henry's Tavern Seattle	◆◆	Regional American	$11-$28	180
41 p. 160	That's Amore! Italian Cafe	◆◆	Italian	$16-$25	180
42 p. 160	Luna Park Cafe	◆◆	American	$8-$14	180

LYNNWOOD

Map Page	Hotels	Diamond Rated	Rate Range	Page
13 p. 160	Homewood Suites by Hilton Seattle/Lynnwood	◆◆◆	Rates not provided	82
14 p. 160	Residence Inn by Marriott-Seattle North/Lynnwood	◆◆◆	$98-$344	82
15 p. 160	**Best Western Alderwood**	◆◆	$99-$199 SAVE	81
16 p. 160	Hampton Inn & Suites by Hilton Seattle-North/Lynnwood	◆◆◆	$139-$308	81
17 p. 160	Holiday Inn Express North Seattle Lynwood	◆◆◆	$149-$169	81
18 p. 160	**La Quinta Inn Lynnwood**	◆◆	$69-$159 SAVE	82
19 p. 160	Courtyard by Marriott Seattle North-Lynnwood-Everett	◆◆◆	$80-$323	81
20 p. 160	Embassy Suites by Hilton Hotel Seattle North/Lynnwood	◆◆◆	Rates not provided	81

Map Page	Restaurants	Diamond Rated	Cuisine	Price Range	Page
45 p. 160	P.F. Chang's China Bistro	◆◆◆	Chinese	$10-$28	82
46 p. 160	Anthony's Seafood Grill Alderwood Mall	◆◆	Seafood	$13-$35	82
47 p. 160	Moonshine BBQ	◆◆	Barbecue	$8-$21	82
48 p. 160	Talay Thai Restaurant	◆◆	Thai	$9-$16	82

SHORELINE

Map Page	Hotel	Diamond Rated	Rate Range	Page
23 p. 160	Days Inn by Wyndham - Shoreline	◆◆	$60-$150	181

BOTHELL

Map Page	Hotels	Diamond Rated	Rate Range	Page
26 p. 160	Hilton Garden Inn Seattle/Bothell	◆◆◆	Rates not provided	48
27 p. 160	Extended Stay America-Seattle-Bothell-West	◆◆	Rates not provided	48
28 p. 160	Comfort Inn & Suites	◆◆	$95-$170	48
29 p. 160	Holiday Inn Express Bothell-Canyon Park	◆◆◆	Rates not provided	48
30 p. 160	Residence Inn by Marriott Seattle NE	◆◆◆	$98-$320	48
31 p. 160	Country Inn & Suites by Radisson	◆◆	Rates not provided	48

Map Page	Restaurants	Diamond Rated	Cuisine	Price Range	Page
51 p. 160	Lombardi's	◆◆	Italian	$11-$29	48
52 p. 160	Bonefish Grill	◆◆◆	Seafood	$11-$36	48
53 p. 160	Beardslee Public House	◆◆	American	$10-$22	48

KIRKLAND

Map Page	Hotels	Diamond Rated	Rate Range	Page
34 p. 160	Comfort Inn-Kirkland	◆◆	$89-$178	75
35 p. 160	**Baymont Inn & Suites by Wyndham**	◆◆	$79-$159 SAVE	75
36 p. 160	The Heathman Hotel	◆◆◆◆	Rates not provided	75

KIRKLAND (cont'd)

Map Page	Hotels (cont'd)	Diamond Rated	Rate Range	Page
37 p. 160	**Woodmark Hotel & Still Spa**	♦♦♦♦	$198-$334 SAVE	76
38 p. 160	La Quinta Inn & Suites Seattle Bellevue/Kirkland	♦♦♦	$99-$249	75

Map Page	Restaurants	Diamond Rated	Cuisine	Price Range	Page
56 p. 160	Cafe Juanita	♦♦♦♦	Northern Italian	$15-$45	76
57 p. 160	Cafe Veloce	♦♦	Italian	$10-$20	76
58 p. 160	Ristorante Paradiso	♦♦♦	Regional Italian	$12-$32	76
59 p. 160	Cactus Kirkland	♦♦	Tex-Mex	$10-$19	76
60 p. 160	Hector's	♦♦	American	$15-$28	76
61 p. 160	Trellis	♦♦♦	Pacific Northwest	$13-$36	76
62 p. 160	Shamiana	♦♦	Indian	$8-$19	76
63 p. 160	Big Fish Grill	♦♦	Seafood	$12-$37	76

WOODINVILLE

Map Page	Hotels	Diamond Rated	Rate Range	Page
41 p. 160	Hampton Inn & Suites by Hilton Woodinville	♦♦♦	Rates not provided	218
42 p. 160	Willows Lodge	♦♦♦♦	$269-$499	218

Map Page	Restaurants	Diamond Rated	Cuisine	Price Range	Page
66 p. 160	Big Fish Grill	♦♦	Seafood	$12-$37	218
67 p. 160	**The Herbfarm Restaurant**	♦♦♦♦♦	Continental	$225-$295	218
68 p. 160	Barking Frog at Willows Lodge	♦♦♦	Pacific Northwest	$14-$52	218
69 p. 160	Purple Cafe and Wine Bar	♦♦	American	$14-$70	218

REDMOND

Map Page	Hotels	Diamond Rated	Rate Range	Page
45 p. 160	**Hyatt House Seattle/Redmond**	♦♦♦	$109-$609 SAVE	114
46 p. 160	Residence Inn by Marriott Seattle East / Redmond	♦♦♦	$88-$549	114
47 p. 160	Seattle Marriott Redmond	♦♦♦	$86-$450	115
48 p. 160	Hampton Inn & Suites by Hilton Seattle/Redmond	♦♦♦	Rates not provided	114
49 p. 160	**Redmond Inn**	♦♦♦	Rates not provided SAVE	114
50 p. 160	Aloft Seattle Redmond Hotel	♦♦♦	$140-$384	114
51 p. 160	Element Seattle Redmond Hotel	♦♦♦	$115-$395	114
52 p. 160	Silver Cloud Inn Redmond	♦♦♦	$169-$299	115

Map Page	Restaurants	Diamond Rated	Cuisine	Price Range	Page
72 p. 160	Tropea Ristorante Italiano	♦♦	Southern Italian	$10-$29	115
73 p. 160	Woodblock	♦♦	American	$15-$30	115

BELLEVUE

Map Page	Hotels	Diamond Rated	Rate Range	Page
55 p. 160	Courtyard by Marriott Bellevue/Redmond	♦♦♦	$76-$406	42
56 p. 160	**Fairfield Inn & Suites by Marriott Seattle Bellevue/Redmond**	♦♦♦	$69-$344 SAVE	42
57 p. 160	Residence Inn by Marriott Seattle Bellevue	♦♦♦	$94-$502	43
58 p. 160	Silver Cloud Inn-Bellevue Downtown	♦♦♦	$169-$299	43

BELLEVUE (cont'd)

Map Page	Hotels (cont'd)	Diamond Rated	Rate Range	Page
59 p. 160	Hilton Garden Inn Seattle/Bellevue Downtown	◆◆◆	Rates not provided	42
60 p. 160	**Hyatt Regency Bellevue**	◆◆◆◆	$159-$429 SAVE	43
61 p. 160	**La Residence Suite Hotel**	◆◆	$139-$229 SAVE	43
62 p. 160	**Courtyard by Marriott-Bellevue Downtown**	◆◆◆	$84-$483 SAVE	42
63 p. 160	**The Westin Bellevue**	◆◆◆◆	$175-$435 SAVE	43
64 p. 160	W Bellevue	◆◆◆◆	$188-$457	43
65 p. 160	**AC Hotel by Marriott Seattle Bellevue/Downtown**	◆◆◆	$72-$453 SAVE	42
66 p. 160	Seattle Marriott Bellevue	◆◆◆	$86-$518	43
67 p. 160	Hampton Inn & Suites by Hilton Bellevue Downtown-Seattle	◆◆◆	Rates not provided	42
68 p. 160	**Sheraton Bellevue Hotel**	◆◆◆	$215-$472 SAVE	43
69 p. 160	**Red Lion Hotel Bellevue**	◆◆	$88-$298 SAVE	43
70 p. 160	Extended Stay America-Seattle-Bellevue-Downtown	◆◆	Rates not provided	42
71 p. 160	**Hilton Bellevue**	◆◆◆	$109-$459 SAVE	42
72 p. 160	**Bellevue Club Hotel**	◆◆◆◆	Rates not provided SAVE	42
73 p. 160	Residence Inn by Marriott Seattle Bellevue/ Downtown	◆◆◆	$104-$516	43
74 p. 160	**Hyatt House Seattle/Bellevue**	◆◆◆	$109-$609 SAVE	43
75 p. 160	Silver Cloud Hotel-Bellevue Eastgate	◆◆◆	$169-$329	43
76 p. 160	**Embassy Suites by Hilton Seattle - Bellevue**	◆◆◆	$129-$400 SAVE	42

Map Page	Restaurants	Diamond Rated	Cuisine	Price Range	Page
77 p. 160	Taj Palace of India	◆◆	Indian	$12-$16	44
78 p. 160	Ruth's Chris Steak House	◆◆◆	Steak	$20-$50	44
79 p. 160	Daniel's Broiler, Bellevue Place	◆◆◆	Steak	$14-$115	44
80 p. 160	Maggiano's Little Italy	◆◆◆	Italian	$14-$39	44
81 p. 160	Andiamo Ristorante Italiano	◆◆	Italian	$13-$30	44
82 p. 160	McCormick & Schmick's	◆◆◆	Seafood	$13-$41	44
83 p. 160	P.F. Chang's China Bistro	◆◆◆	Chinese	$10-$28	44
84 p. 160	Pearl Seafood & Oyster Bar	◆◆◆	American	$12-$50	44
85 p. 160	Palomino Restaurant	◆◆◆	Mediterranean	$13-$35	44
86 p. 160	The Cheesecake Factory	◆◆◆	International	$11-$30	44
87 p. 160	John Howie Steak	◆◆◆	Steak	$17-$89	44
88 p. 160	Henry's Tavern Bellevue	◆◆	American	$14-$20	44
89 p. 160	Cactus Bellevue Square	◆◆	Tex-Mex	$9-$19	44
90 p. 160	Wild Ginger Asian Restaurant & Satay Bar	◆◆	Asian	$11-$34	44
91 p. 160	Fogo De Chao	◆◆◆	Brazilian Steak	$26-$54	44
92 p. 160	El Gaucho	◆◆◆	Steak	$26-$78	44
93 p. 160	Purple Cafe and Wine Bar	◆◆	American	$12-$70	44
94 p. 160	Carmine's-Bellevue	◆◆◆	Italian	$15-$50	44
95 p. 160	Seastar Restaurant & Raw Bar	◆◆◆	Seafood	$13-$86	44

Map Page	Restaurants (cont'd)	Diamond Rated	Cuisine	Price Range	Page
96 p. 160	Bis On Main	◈◈◈	International	$14-$61	44
97 p. 160	Chace's-Pancake Corral	◈	American	$6-$10	44
98 p. 160	Goldberg's Famous Delicatessen	◈◈	American	$10-$31	44
99 p. 160	Nine O Bar & Grill	◈◈	American	$10-$30	44

ISSAQUAH

Map Page	Hotels	Diamond Rated	Rate Range	Page
79 p. 160	**Holiday Inn Seattle Issaquah**	◈◈◈	Rates not provided (SAVE)	71
80 p. 160	Homewood Suites by Hilton Seattle/Issaquah	◈◈◈	Rates not provided	71
81 p. 160	Hilton Garden Inn Seattle/Issaquah	◈◈◈	Rates not provided	71
82 p. 160	SpringHill Suites by Marriott Seattle Issaquah	◈◈◈	$88-$345	71

Map Page	Restaurants	Diamond Rated	Cuisine	Price Range	Page
102 p. 160	WildFin American Grill - Issaquah	◈◈	American	$10-$28	71
103 p. 160	Flat Iron Grill	◈◈	American	$12-$39	71
104 p. 160	Big Fish Grill	◈◈	Seafood	$12-$39	71
105 p. 160	Triple XXX Rootbeer Drive-In	◈	Burgers	$7-$15	71
106 p. 160	Fins Bistro	◈◈◈	Seafood	$10-$35	71
107 p. 160	Issaquah Brewhouse	◈◈	American	$8-$18	71

RENTON

Map Page	Hotels	Diamond Rated	Rate Range	Page
85 p. 160	**Hyatt Regency Lake Washington at Seattle's Southport**	◈◈◈◈	$149-$409 (SAVE)	115
86 p. 160	Hampton Inn & Suites by Hilton Seattle/Renton	◈◈◈	Rates not provided	115
87 p. 160	Quality Inn Renton	◈◈	$79-$156	115
88 p. 160	**TownePlace Suites by Marriott Seattle South/Renton**	◈◈	$85-$366 (SAVE)	115
89 p. 160	**Larkspur Landing Renton**	◈◈◈	Rates not provided (SAVE)	115
90 p. 160	SpringHill Suites by Marriott Seattle South/Renton	◈◈◈	$89-$362	115
91 p. 160	Hilton Garden Inn Seattle/Renton	◈◈◈	Rates not provided	115

Map Page	Restaurants	Diamond Rated	Cuisine	Price Range	Page
110 p. 160	Plum Delicious	◈◈	American	$8-$25	116
111 p. 160	WildFin American Grill	◈◈	American	$10-$28	116
112 p. 160	Torero's	◈◈	Mexican	$8-$25	116
113 p. 160	Melrose Grill	◈◈	Steak	$22-$48	115
114 p. 160	Whistle Stop Ale House	◈◈	American	$9-$16	116

TUKWILA

Map Page	Hotels	Diamond Rated	Rate Range	Page
94 p. 160	Homewood Suites by Hilton Seattle Airport - Tukwila	◈◈◈	Rates not provided	206
95 p. 160	**Comfort Suites Airport-Tukwila**	◈◈◈	$76-$239 (SAVE)	205
96 p. 160	**Hampton Inn by Hilton Seattle/Southcenter** (See ad p. 206.)	◈◈◈	$112-$226 (SAVE)	206
97 p. 160	Holiday Inn Express & Suites Seattle South-Tukwila	◈◈◈	Rates not provided	206
98 p. 160	Ramada Tukwila SeaTac Airport	◈◈	$90-$159	206

TUKWILA (cont'd)

Map Page	Hotels (cont'd)	Diamond Rated	Rate Range	Page
99 p. 160	Embassy Suites by Hilton Hotel	◈◈◈	Rates not provided	206
100 p. 160	Courtyard by Marriott/Sea-Tac Area	◈◈◈	$64-$347	205
101 p. 160	DoubleTree Suites by Hilton, Seattle Airport-Southcenter	◈◈◈	Rates not provided	206
102 p. 160	Hotel Interurban	◈◈◈	Rates not provided	206
103 p. 160	Residence Inn by Marriott-Seattle South	◈◈◈	$95-$420	206
104 p. 160	**Courtyard by Marriott-Seattle/Southcenter**	◈◈◈	$83-$406 SAVE	205
105 p. 160	Home2 Suites by Hilton, Seattle Airport	◈◈◈	Rates not provided	206

Map Page	Restaurants	Diamond Rated	Cuisine	Price Range	Page
117 p. 160	Bahama Breeze Island Grille	◈◈◈	Caribbean	$9-$27	206
118 p. 160	Odin Brewing Company	◈	Barbecue	$8-$12	206
119 p. 160	The Cheesecake Factory	◈◈◈	International	$11-$30	206
120 p. 160	Miyabi Sushi	◈◈	Japanese	$10-$38	206
121 p. 160	Bai Tong Thai Restaurant	◈◈	Thai	$10-$22	206

SEATAC

Map Page	Hotels	Diamond Rated	Rate Range	Page
108 p. 160	**Red Roof Inn Seattle Airport-SeaTac**	◈◈	$69-$289 SAVE	122
109 p. 160	Crowne Plaza Seattle Airport	◈◈◈	$109-$309	121
110 p. 160	Clarion Hotel	◈◈	$89-$175	121
111 p. 160	**Hilton Seattle Airport & Conference Center**	◈◈◈	$99-$399	121
112 p. 160	**Seattle Airport Marriott**	◈◈◈	$89-$352 SAVE	122
113 p. 160	Radisson Hotel Seattle Airport	◈◈◈	$109-$499	122
114 p. 160	**Coast Gateway Hotel**	◈◈	Rates not provided SAVE	121
115 p. 160	**Cedarbrook Lodge**	◈◈◈	Rates not provided SAVE	121
116 p. 160	**DoubleTree by Hilton Hotel Seattle Airport**	◈◈◈	$99-$369 SAVE	121
117 p. 160	Hampton Inn & Suites by Hilton Seattle Airport - 28th Ave	◈◈◈	Rates not provided	121
118 p. 160	Aloft Seattle Sea-Tac Airport	◈◈◈	$95-$263	121
119 p. 160	Country Inn & Suites By Radisson Seattle Airport	◈◈	Rates not provided	121
120 p. 160	**Hampton Inn by Hilton Seattle-Airport**	◈◈◈	$112-$277 SAVE	121
121 p. 160	Holiday Inn Express Hotel & Suites-Seattle Sea-Tac Airport	◈◈◈	Rates not provided	122
122 p. 160	**Residence Inn by Marriott Seattle Sea-Tac Airport**	◈◈◈	$95-$318 SAVE	122
123 p. 160	Fairfield Inn by Marriott Seattle Sea-Tac Airport	◈◈	$72-$247	121
124 p. 160	Sleep Inn SeaTac Airport	◈◈	$84-$184	122
125 p. 160	**Best Western Seattle Airport Hotel**	◈◈	$109-$249 SAVE	121

Map Page	Restaurants	Diamond Rated	Cuisine	Price Range	Page
124 p. 160	Spencer's for Steaks and Chops	◈◈◈	Steak	$12-$60	122
125 p. 160	Dave's Diner & Brew	◈◈	American	$7-$21	122
126 p. 160	Copperleaf Restaurant & Bar	◈◈◈	Pacific Northwest	$12-$52	122

DES MOINES

Map Page	Hotel	Diamond Rated	Rate Range	Page
128 p. 160	**Four Points by Sheraton Seattle Airport South**	◈◈◈	$95-$307 SAVE	58

Map Page	Restaurants	Diamond Rated	Cuisine	Price Range	Page
129 p. 160	Anthony's HomePort Des Moines	◈◈◈	Seafood	$8-$24	58
130 p. 160	Salty's at Redondo Beach	◈◈◈	Seafood	$16-$70	58

KENT

Map Page	Hotels	Diamond Rated	Rate Range	Page
131 p. 160	TownePlace Suites by Marriott-Seattle Southcenter	◈◈◈	$76-$279	74
132 p. 160	Hampton Inn & Suites by Hilton Seattle/Kent	◈◈◈	Rates not provided	74
133 p. 160	Comfort Inn Kent	◈◈	$89-$179	74
134 p. 160	**Best Western Plus Plaza by the Green**	◈◈◈	$119-$249 SAVE	74
135 p. 160	Red Lion Inn & Suites Kent	◈◈	Rates not provided	74

Map Page	Restaurants	Diamond Rated	Cuisine	Price Range	Page
133 p. 160	Mitzel's American Kitchen	◈◈	American	$10-$22	74
134 p. 160	Thai Chili Restaurant	◈◈	Thai	$8-$14	74

EDMONDS

Map Page	Hotel	Diamond Rated	Rate Range	Page
136 p. 160	**Best Western Plus Edmonds Harbor Inn** *(See ad p. 61.)*	◈◈◈	$135-$150 SAVE	61

Map Page	Restaurants	Diamond Rated	Cuisine	Price Range	Page
137 p. 160	Chanterelle	◈◈◈	American	$7-$25	61
138 p. 160	Salt & Iron	◈◈◈	American	$13-$62	61
139 p. 160	Arnies at Edmonds	◈◈	Seafood Steak	$9-$51	61
140 p. 160	Girardi's Osteria	◈◈	Italian	$9-$25	61
141 p. 160	Scott's Bar & Grill	◈◈	American	$13-$36	61

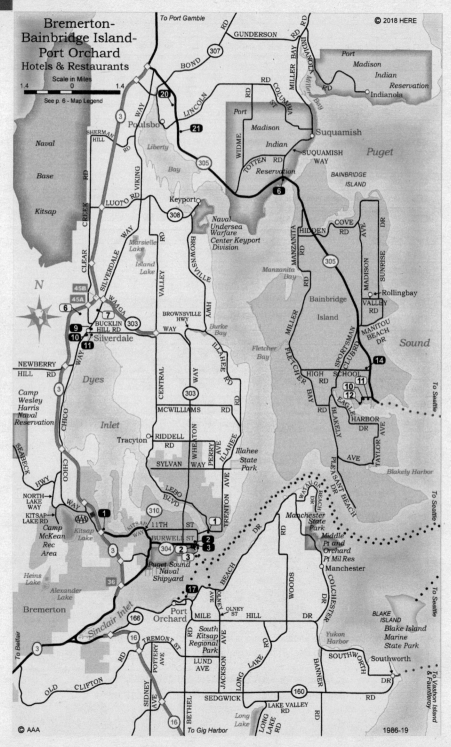

Bremerton-
Bainbridge Island-
Port Orchard
Hotels & Restaurants

Scale in Miles
1.4   0   1.4
See p. 6 - Map Legend

Bremerton-Bainbridge Island-Port Orchard

This index helps you "spot" where approved hotels and restaurants are located on the corresponding detailed maps. Hotel daily rate range is for comparison only. Restaurant price range is a combination of lunch and/or dinner. Turn to the listing page for more information and consult display ads for special promotions.

 For more details, rates and reservations: AAA.com/travelguides/hotels

BREMERTON

Map Page	Hotels	Diamond Rated	Rate Range	Page
❶ p. 170	**Super 8-Bremerton**	◆◆	$70-$80 (SAVE)	49
❷ p. 170	Fairfield Inn & Suites by Marriott Seattle Bremerton	◆◆◆	$98-$202	49
❸ p. 170	Hampton Inn & Suites by Hilton Bremerton	◆◆◆	Rates not provided	49

Map Page	Restaurants	Diamond Rated	Cuisine	Price Range	Page
① p. 170	Boat Shed	◆◆	American	$12-$32	49
② p. 170	Bremerton Bar & Grill	◆◆	American	$12-$25	49
③ p. 170	Anthony's at Sinclair Inlet	◆◆	Seafood	$11-$39	49

SUQUAMISH

Map Page	Hotel	Diamond Rated	Rate Range	Page
❻ p. 170	**Suquamish Clearwater Casino Resort**	◆◆◆	$109-$279 (SAVE)	195

SILVERDALE

Map Page	Hotels	Diamond Rated	Rate Range	Page
❾ p. 170	Quality Inn & Suites	◆◆	$79-$158	182
❿ p. 170	**Oxford Suites Silverdale**	◆◆◆	$89-$700 (SAVE)	182
⓫ p. 170	**Best Western Plus Silverdale Beach Hotel**	◆◆◆	$94-$200 (SAVE)	182

Map Page	Restaurants	Diamond Rated	Cuisine	Price Range	Page
⑥ p. 170	Oak Table Cafe	◆◆	American	$10-$16	182
⑦ p. 170	Silver City Restaurant & Brewery	◆◆	American	$13-$32	182

BAINBRIDGE ISLAND

Map Page	Hotel	Diamond Rated	Rate Range	Page
⓮ p. 170	The Marshall Suites	◆◆◆	$179-$279	39

Map Page	Restaurants	Diamond Rated	Cuisine	Price Range	Page
⑩ p. 170	Hitchcock	◆◆◆	Pacific Northwest	$21-$95	39
⑪ p. 170	The Streamliner Diner	◆◆	American	$6-$28	39
⑫ p. 170	Doc's Marina Grill	◆◆	American	$12-$24	39

PORT ORCHARD

Map Page	Hotel	Diamond Rated	Rate Range	Page
⓱ p. 170	**Comfort Inn Port Orchard**	◆◆	$98-$144 (SAVE)	108

POULSBO

Map Page	Hotels	Diamond Rated	Rate Range	Page
⓴ p. 170	GuestHouse International Inn & Suites	◆◆	Rates not provided	110
㉑ p. 170	**Poulsbo Inn & Suites**	◆◆	$93-$140 (SAVE)	110

DOWNTOWN SEATTLE
- **Restaurants p. 176**
- **Hotels & Restaurants map & index p. 152**

11TH AVENUE INN BED & BREAKFAST   (206)720-7161   **21**
♦♦ Historic Bed & Breakfast. **Address:** 121 11th Ave E 98102

THE ARCTIC CLUB SEATTLE-A DOUBLETREE BY HILTON HOTEL   (206)340-0340   **49**

♦♦♦♦
Historic Hotel
$259-$499

DOUBLETREE
BY HILTON™

AAA Benefit:
Members save 5% or more!

Address: 700 3rd Ave 98104 **Location:** Corner of 3rd Ave and Cherry St. Pioneer Square, 8. **Facility:** Close to sports venues and Pioneer Square, this historic hotel was once a social club for businessmen who found fortune in the Klondike Gold Rush. Look for a dignified lobby and modern guest rooms. 120 units. 10 stories, interior corridors. **Parking:** valet only. **Terms:** check-in 4 pm, 1-7 night minimum stay, 3 day cancellation notice-fee imposed. **Amenities:** safes. **Dining:** Juno, see separate listing. **Activities:** exercise room. **Guest Services:** valet laundry.

BEST WESTERN EXECUTIVE INN   (206)448-9444   **14**

♦♦♦
Hotel
$89-$499

BW Best Western.

AAA Benefit:
Members save up to 15% and earn bonus points!

Address: 200 Taylor Ave N 98109 **Location:** Just n of jct E Denny Ave. Located in a commercial area. Seattle Center, 4. **Facility:** 123 units. 5 stories, interior corridors. **Parking:** on-site (fee). **Terms:** check-in 4 pm, cancellation fee imposed. **Amenities:** safes. **Activities:** exercise room. **Guest Services:** valet and coin laundry.

BEST WESTERN PLUS PIONEER SQUARE HOTEL   (206)340-1234   **51**

♦♦♦
Historic Hotel
$109-$799

BW Best Western PLUS.

AAA Benefit:
Members save up to 15% and earn bonus points!

Address: 77 Yesler Way 98104 **Location:** Just w of 1st Ave. Located in historic Pioneer Square. Occidental Mall, 29. **Facility:** Some rooms at this Romanesque-Victorian hotel are compact or offer limited views, but all are charming and inviting. Parking is available one block away. 75 units. 4 stories, interior corridors. **Parking:** on-site (fee). **Terms:** cancellation fee imposed. **Amenities:** safes. **Guest Services:** valet laundry.

AAA.com/campgrounds—
For overnights under the stars

COURTYARD BY MARRIOTT SEATTLE DOWNTOWN/LAKE UNION   (206)213-0100   **2**
♦♦♦ Hotel. **Address:** 925 Westlake Ave N 98109

AAA Benefit:
Members save 5% or more!

COURTYARD BY MARRIOTT SEATTLE DOWNTOWN/PIONEER SQUARE   (206)625-1111   **50**
♦♦♦ Hotel. **Address:** 612 2nd Ave 98104

AAA Benefit:
Members save 5% or more!

CROWNE PLAZA SEATTLE-DOWNTOWN   (206)464-1980   **41**

♦♦♦
Hotel
$169-$449

Address: 1113 6th Ave 98101 **Location:** Corner of 6th Ave and Seneca St. Located in a business area. University Street, 7. **Facility:** 418 units. 34 stories, interior corridors. **Parking:** valet only. **Terms:** cancellation fee imposed. **Amenities:** safes. **Activities:** exercise room. **Guest Services:** valet laundry.

THE EDGEWATER   (206)728-7000   **22**

♦♦♦♦
Hotel
$179-$529

Address: 2411 Alaskan Way, Pier 67 98121 **Location:** Waterfront. On waterfront at Pier 67; at base of Wall St. Seattle Center, 4. **Facility:** Located on a pier extending over the water, many guest rooms overlook Elliott Bay and the Olympic Mountains; some rooms include a balcony. All rooms have a gas fireplace and a walk-in granite shower. 223 units. 4 stories, interior corridors. **Parking:** valet only. **Terms:** check-in 4 pm, 3 day cancellation notice-fee imposed, resort fee. **Amenities:** safes. **Dining:** Six Seven, see separate listing. **Activities:** bicycles, exercise room. **Guest Services:** valet laundry, area transportation.

EMBASSY SUITES BY HILTON SEATTLE DOWNTOWN PIONEER SQUARE   206/859-4400   **52**
♦♦♦ Hotel. **Address:** 255 S King St 98104

AAA Benefit:
Members save 5% or more!

EVEN HOTEL SEATTLE DOWNTOWN - SOUTH LAKE UNION   206/596-2302   **10**
♦♦♦ Hotel. **Address:** 527 Fairview Ave N 98109

FAIRMONT OLYMPIC HOTEL   (206)621-1700   **40**

♦♦♦♦
Historic Hotel
$199-$499

Address: 411 University St 98101 **Location:** Corner of 4th Ave and University St. Located in the financial and retail districts. University Street, 7. **Facility:** A historic icon, the Italian Renaissance-style hotel is in the heart of the city. It reflects the grandeur of the past but with modern conveniences. Rooms vary significantly in size. 450 units. 12 stories, interior corridors. **Parking:** on-site (fee) and valet. **Terms:** 1-2 night minimum stay. **Amenities:** safes. **Dining:** The Georgian, Shuckers, see separate listings. **Pool:** heated indoor. **Activities:** sauna, hot tub, health club, spa. **Guest Services:** valet laundry, area transportation.

(See map & index p. 152.)

FOUR POINTS BY SHERATON DOWNTOWN SEATTLE CENTER
(206)282-2600 **6**

Hotel
$150-$659

FOUR POINTS BY SHERATON

AAA Benefit: Members save 5% or more!

Address: 601 Roy St 98109 **Location:** Jct SR 99 (Aurora Ave N), just w. Westlake & Mercer, 13. **Facility:** 158 units, some two bedrooms. 4 stories, interior corridors. **Parking:** on-site (fee). **Terms:** check-in 4 pm, cancellation fee imposed. **Amenities:** safes. **Activities:** exercise room. **Guest Services:** valet and coin laundry.

[SAVE] [symbols] CALL [symbols]

[BIZ] [HS] [symbols]

FOUR SEASONS HOTEL SEATTLE
(206)749-7000 **39**
Hotel. **Address:** 99 Union St 98101

GRAND HYATT SEATTLE
(206)774-1234 **31**

Contemporary Hotel
$159-$599

GRAND HYATT

AAA Benefit: Members save 5% or more!

Address: 721 Pine St 98101 **Location:** Corner of 7th Ave and Pine St. Westlake Hub, 5. **Facility:** Guest rooms provide panoramic city views; some offer views of Elliott Bay. Modern amenities, an elegant ambience and contemporary design features provide a luxurious feel for guests. 457 units. 30 stories, interior corridors. **Parking:** on-site (fee) and valet. **Terms:** check-in 4 pm. **Amenities:** safes. **Dining:** 2 restaurants, also, Ruth's Chris Steak House, see separate listing. **Activities:** sauna, hot tub, steamroom, exercise room. **Guest Services:** valet laundry, boarding pass kiosk, rental car service.

[SAVE] [ECO] [symbols] CALL [symbols] [BIZ] [HS] [symbols]
[symbols] / SOME UNITS [symbols]

HAMPTON INN & SUITES BY HILTON-SEATTLE DOWNTOWN
206/282-7700 **4**

Hotel. **Address:** 700 5th Ave N 98109

AAA Benefit: Members save 5% or more!

HILTON GARDEN INN-SEATTLE DOWNTOWN
206/467-7770 **23**

Hotel. **Address:** 1821 Boren Ave 98101

AAA Benefit: Members save 5% or more!

HILTON SEATTLE
(206)624-0500 **37**

Hotel
$199-$399

Hilton
HOTELS & RESORTS

AAA Benefit: Members save 5% or more!

Address: 1301 6th Ave 98101 **Location:** Corner of 6th Ave and University St. Located in a business area. University Street, 7. **Facility:** 239 units. 29 stories, interior corridors. **Parking:** on-site (fee). **Terms:** check-in 4 pm, 1-7 night minimum stay, 3 day cancellation notice-fee imposed. **Amenities:** safes. **Activities:** exercise room. **Guest Services:** valet laundry, rental car service.

[SAVE] [symbols] [BIZ] [symbols]

HOLIDAY INN EXPRESS & SUITES
(206)441-7222 **13**
Hotel. **Address:** 226 Aurora Ave N 98109

HOLIDAY INN SEATTLE DOWNTOWN
(206)728-8123 **15**
Hotel. **Address:** 211 Dexter Ave N 98109

HOMEWOOD SUITES BY HILTON SEATTLE CONVENTION CENTER/PIKE STREET
(206)682-8282 **33**

Extended Stay Hotel
$125-$525

HOMEWOOD SUITES BY HILTON

AAA Benefit: Members save 5% or more!

Address: 1011 Pike St 98101 **Location:** I-5 exit 165 northbound to Pike St via 6th Ave; exit Union St southbound to Pike St. Next to convention center. Westlake Hub, 5. **Facility:** 195 units, some efficiencies and kitchens. 9 stories, interior corridors. **Parking:** on-site (fee). **Terms:** check-in 4 pm, 1-7 night minimum stay, 3 day cancellation notice-fee imposed. **Pool:** heated outdoor. **Activities:** hot tub, game room, exercise room. **Guest Services:** valet and coin laundry, rental car service. **Featured Amenity:** breakfast buffet.

[SAVE] CALL [symbols] [BIZ] [symbols]
/ SOME UNITS [symbols]

HOMEWOOD SUITES BY HILTON-SEATTLE DOWNTOWN
206/281-9393 **8**

Extended Stay Hotel. **Address:** 206 Western Ave W 98119

AAA Benefit: Members save 5% or more!

HOTEL MAX
206/728-6299 **26**

Boutique Contemporary Retro Hotel
Rates not provided

Address: 620 Stewart St 98101 **Location:** Corner of 7th Ave and Stewart St. Located in a business area. Westlake & 7th, 19. **Facility:** Guest rooms are very compact in size but offer retro-cool décor and scaled-down furnishings. While smaller in size, the "sexy" lobby has some comfy seating and a free happy hour pint. 163 units. 10 stories, interior corridors. **Parking:** valet only. **Terms:** check-in 4 pm. **Amenities:** safes. **Dining:** Miller's Guild, see separate listing. **Activities:** bicycles, exercise room. **Guest Services:** valet laundry.

[SAVE] [symbols] CALL [symbols]
[symbols]
/ SOME UNITS [symbols]

HOTEL SORRENTO
206/622-6400 **43**
Historic Boutique Hotel. **Address:** 900 Madison St 98104

(See map & index p. 152.)

HYATT HOUSE SEATTLE/DOWNTOWN

(206)727-1234 **12**

◆◆◆
Extended Stay Contemporary Hotel
$159-$599

AAA Benefit: Members save 5% or more!

Address: 201 5th Ave N 98109 **Location:** Just n of jct E Denny Way. Seattle Center, 4. **Facility:** 172 units, some efficiencies. 8 stories, interior corridors. **Parking:** on-site (fee). **Activities:** exercise room. **Guest Services:** valet and coin laundry, area transportation. **Featured Amenity:** breakfast buffet.

HYATT OLIVE 8

(206)695-1234 **28**

◆◆◆
Contemporary Hotel
$159-$499

HYATT

AAA Benefit: Members save 5% or more!

Address: 1635 8th Ave 98101 **Location:** Between Olive Way and Pine St. Westlake Hub, 5. **Facility:** This modern property is near the convention center and offers stunning Seattle skyline views. 346 units. 17 stories, interior corridors. **Parking:** valet only. **Terms:** check-in 4 pm. **Amenities:** safes. **Dining:** 2 restaurants. **Pool:** heated indoor. **Activities:** sauna, hot tub, steamroom, exercise room, spa. **Guest Services:** valet laundry, boarding pass kiosk.

HYATT PLACE SEATTLE/DOWNTOWN

(206)441-6041 **16**

◆◆◆
Contemporary Hotel
$159-$599

HYATT PLACE

AAA Benefit: Members save 5% or more!

Address: 110 6th Ave N 98109 **Location:** Corner of 6th Ave and Denny Way. Seattle Center, 4. **Facility:** 160 units. 9 stories, interior corridors. **Parking:** on-site (fee). **Pool:** heated indoor. **Activities:** exercise room. **Guest Services:** valet and coin laundry, area transportation. **Featured Amenity:** breakfast buffet.

INN AT THE MARKET
206/443-3600 **34**
◆◆◆◆ Boutique Hotel. **Address:** 86 Pine St 98101

🏨 **For complete hotel, dining and attraction listings:**

AAA.com/travelguides

KIMPTON ALEXIS HOTEL SEATTLE
206/624-4844 **48**

◆◆◆◆◆
Historic Boutique Hotel
Rates not provided

Address: 1007 1st Ave 98104 **Location:** Corner of Madison St and 1st Ave. University Street, 7. **Facility:** This hotel combines two turn-of-the-20th-century buildings. Works by local artists are the focal point of the public spaces. 121 units, some kitchens. 4-6 stories, interior corridors. **Parking:** valet only. **Amenities:** safes. **Activities:** bicycles, exercise room, spa. **Guest Services:** valet laundry.

KIMPTON HOTEL MONACO SEATTLE
206/621-1770 **44**

◆◆◆◆
Contemporary Hotel
Rates not provided

Address: 1101 4th Ave 98101 **Location:** Corner of 4th Ave and Spring St. University Street, 7. **Facility:** This downtown hotel has an expansive lobby decorated with chandeliers and Mediterranean-style frescoes. Upon request, little aquariums stocked with goldfish will keep you company during your stay. 189 units. 11 stories, interior corridors. **Parking:** valet only. **Amenities:** safes. **Dining:** Outlier, see separate listing. **Activities:** bicycles, exercise room, massage. **Guest Services:** valet laundry.

KIMPTON HOTEL VINTAGE SEATTLE
206/624-8000 **45**

◆◆◆◆
Historic Boutique Hotel
Rates not provided

Address: 1100 5th Ave 98101 **Location:** Corner of Spring St and 5th Ave. University Street, 7. **Facility:** A wood-burning fireplace graces the intimate lobby of this European-style downtown hotel. Tastefully decorated and furnished guest rooms are named after Washington wineries. 124 units. 11 stories, interior corridors. **Parking:** valet only. **Amenities:** safes. **Dining:** Tulio Ristorante, see separate listing. **Activities:** bicycles, exercise room, massage. **Guest Services:** valet laundry.

LA QUINTA INN & SUITES SEATTLE DOWNTOWN
(206)624-6820 **19**
◆◆◆ Hotel. **Address:** 2224 8th Ave 98121

LOEWS HOTEL 1000
206/957-1000 **47**
◆◆◆◆ Boutique Contemporary Hotel. **Address:** 1000 1st Ave 98104

THE LOYAL INN
206/682-0200 **17**
◆◆ Hotel. **Address:** 2301 8th Ave 98121

THE MAXWELL HOTEL
206/286-0629 **1**
◆◆◆ Contemporary Hotel. **Address:** 300 Roy St 98109

MAYFLOWER PARK HOTEL
206/623-8700 **29**
◆◆◆ Historic Boutique Hotel. **Address:** 405 Olive Way 98101

MEDITERRANEAN INN
(206)428-4700 **5**
◆◆ Hotel. **Address:** 425 Queen Anne Ave N 98109

(See map & index p. 152.)

MOTIF SEATTLE
206/971-8000   **36**

Contemporary Hotel
Rates not provided

Address: 1415 5th Ave 98101 **Location:** Between Pike and Union sts. Westlake, 6. **Facility:** This hotel is conveniently located in the heart of downtown. Guests will enjoy the upscale accommodations. Most rooms feature fantastic city and water views. 319 units. 20 stories, interior corridors. **Parking:** on-site (fee). **Amenities:** safes. **Activities:** exercise room. **Guest Services:** valet laundry.

SAVE 🍽 📶 ✕ 📷 📁 💻 SOME UNITS 🐾 🖥 🚌

MOXY SEATTLE DOWNTOWN
(206)708-8200   **11**

Hotel. **Address:** 1016 Republican St 98109

AAA Benefit: Members save 5% or more!

PAN PACIFIC HOTEL SEATTLE
206/264-8111   **18**

Contemporary Hotel
Rates not provided

Address: 2125 Terry Ave 98121 **Location:** Just s of jct E Denny Way. Westlake & Denny, 17. **Facility:** Located on the edge of downtown by Seattle's Space Needle, this luxury hotel features seldom-seen African zebra wood walls in its public spaces; ask about the story regarding this wood. 153 units. 14 stories, interior corridors. **Parking:** on-site (fee) and valet. **Terms:** check-in 4 pm. **Amenities:** safes. **Activities:** sauna, hot tub, exercise room. **Guest Services:** valet laundry, area transportation.

SAVE 🍽 📶 ✕ 📷 📁 💻 SOME UNITS 🐾 🖥 🚌

THE PARAMOUNT HOTEL
206/292-9500   **30**

Hotel. **Address:** 724 Pine St 98101

RENAISSANCE SEATTLE HOTEL
(206)583-0300   **46**

Contemporary Hotel
$105-$487

AAA Benefit: Members save 5% or more!

Address: 515 Madison St 98104 **Location:** Corner of Madison St and 6th Ave. University Street, 7. **Facility:** This convention-oriented, high-rise hotel offers many guest rooms with sweeping easterly views. A few guest rooms at the end of the hallways offer a dramatic peek at Elliott Bay. 557 units. 28 stories, interior corridors. **Parking:** on-site (fee) and valet. **Terms:** check-in 4 pm, cancellation fee imposed. **Amenities:** safes. **Dining:** 2 restaurants. **Activities:** exercise room, massage. **Guest Services:** valet laundry.

SAVE 🍽 📶 ✕ CALL 📷 📁 💻 SOME UNITS 🐾 🚌

RESIDENCE INN BY MARRIOTT SEATTLE DOWNTOWN/CONVENTION CENTER
(206)388-1000   **24**

Extended Stay Contemporary Hotel. **Address:** 1815 Terry Ave 98101

AAA Benefit: Members save 5% or more!

RESIDENCE INN BY MARRIOTT SEATTLE DOWNTOWN/LAKE UNION
(206)624-6000   **7**

Extended Stay Hotel. **Address:** 800 Fairview Ave N 98109

AAA Benefit: Members save 5% or more!

SEATTLE MARRIOTT WATERFRONT HOTEL
(206)443-5000   **32**

Hotel
$149-$498

AAA Benefit: Members save 5% or more!

Address: 2100 Alaskan Way 98121 **Location:** Between Wall and Vine sts. Westlake, 6. **Facility:** 361 units. 8 stories, interior corridors. **Parking:** valet only. **Terms:** check-in 4 pm, 3 day cancellation notice-fee imposed. **Amenities:** *Some:* safes. **Pool:** heated outdoor. **Activities:** exercise room. **Guest Services:** complimentary and valet laundry.

SAVE 🍽 📶 ✕ 📷 CALL 🛗 💻 BIZ 📶
✕ 📁 💻 SOME UNITS 🖥 🚌

SHERATON GRAND SEATTLE
(206)621-9000   **35**

Hotel
$198-$435

Sheraton

AAA Benefit: Members save 5% or more!

Address: 1400 6th Ave 98101 **Location:** Between Pike and Union sts. Westlake, 6. **Facility:** Offering great views from its upper floor rooms, this large convention-oriented hotel is within walking distance of the convention center. Most guest rooms feature a comfy chair and ample workspace. 1236 units. 26-35 stories, interior corridors. **Parking:** valet only. **Terms:** 3 day cancellation notice-fee imposed. **Amenities:** safes. **Dining:** Daily Grill, Loulay Kitchen & Bar, see separate listings. **Pool:** heated indoor. **Activities:** exercise room. **Guest Services:** valet laundry, boarding pass kiosk.

SAVE ECO 🍽 📶 ✕ CALL 🛗 💻 BIZ SHS
📶 ✕ 📷 📁 💻 SOME UNITS 🐾 🚌

(See map & index p. 152.)

SILVER CLOUD HOTEL-BROADWAY (206)325-1400 **38**
ⱽⱽⱽ Hotel. **Address:** 1100 Broadway 98122

SILVER CLOUD HOTEL SEATTLE-STADIUM
(206)204-9800 **53**
ⱽⱽⱽ Hotel. **Address:** 1046 1st Ave S 98134

SILVER CLOUD INN LAKE UNION (206)447-9500 **3**
ⱽⱽⱽ Hotel. **Address:** 1150 Fairview Ave N 98109

**SPRINGHILL SUITES BY MARRIOTT SEATTLE
DOWNTOWN/SOUTH LAKE UNION** (206)254-0500 **20**

ⱽⱽⱽ
Hotel
$92-$357

SPRINGHILL SUITES°
MARRIOTT
AAA Benefit:
Members save 5%
or more!

Address: 1800 Yale Ave 98101 **Location:** Jct Stewart St, just se. Westlake & 9th, 18. **Facility:** 234 units. 10 stories, interior corridors. **Parking:** valet only. **Terms:** cancellation fee imposed. **Pool:** heated indoor. **Activities:** hot tub, exercise room. **Guest Services:** valet and coin laundry. **Featured Amenity: full hot breakfast.**

SAVE ECO 🍴 Y 🏊 👟 BIZ
📶 ✕ 🔌 📠 💻 🚌

**STAYBRIDGE SUITES SEATTLE DOWNTOWN - SOUTH LAKE
UNION** 206/596-2301 **9**
ⱽⱽⱽ Extended Stay Hotel. **Address:** 1119 Mercer St 98109

WARWICK SEATTLE (206)443-4300 **25**

ⱽⱽⱽ
Hotel
$149-$449

Address: 401 Lenora St 98121 **Location:** Corner of 4th Ave and Lenora St. Located in a commercial area. Westlake & 7th, 19. **Facility:** 231 units. 18 stories, interior corridors. **Parking:** onsite (fee) and valet. **Terms:** cancellation fee imposed, resort fee. **Amenities:** safes. **Dining:** Margaux Restaurant, see separate listing. **Pool:** heated indoor. **Activities:** hot tub, exercise room. **Guest Services:** valet laundry.

SAVE 🍴 👟 Y 🏊 👟 BIZ
📶 ✕ 🔌 💻 🚌

THE WESTIN SEATTLE (206)728-1000 **27**

ⱽⱽⱽⱽ
Contemporary
Hotel
$125-$385

WESTIN
HOTELS & RESORTS
AAA Benefit:
Members save 5%
or more!

Address: 1900 5th Ave 98101 **Location:** Corner of 5th Ave and Stewart St. Westlake & 7th, 19. **Facility:** The hotel's two distinct cylindrical towers stand out on the downtown skyline. All of the rooms have sweeping views of the city and Elliott Bay. 891 units. 40-47 stories, interior corridors. **Parking:** on-site (fee) and valet. **Terms:** check-in 4 pm, 3 day cancellation notice-fee imposed. **Amenities:** safes. **Pool:** heated indoor. **Activities:** exercise room. **Guest Services:** valet laundry.

SAVE ECO 🍴 👟 Y CALL ♿ 🏊 👟 BIZ sHS

💲 📶 ✕ 🎥 🔌 💻 / SOME UNITS 🐾 🔌 🚌

W SEATTLE (206)264-6000 **42**
ⱽⱽⱽⱽ
Hotel
$128-$417

W
HOTELS
AAA Benefit:
Members save 5% or
more!

Address: 1112 4th Ave 98101 **Location:** Corner of 4th Ave and Seneca St. University Street, 7. **Facility:** A thorough remodeling in 2016 returns a fresh, upscale appeal to the hotel in this notable chrome tower. Guest rooms feature new, high-quality furnishings and stylish décor. 424 units. 26 stories, interior corridors. **Parking:** valet only. **Terms:** check-in 4 pm, 3 day cancellation notice-fee imposed. **Amenities:** safes. **Dining:** Trace, see separate listing. **Activities:** exercise room. **Guest Services:** valet laundry, boarding pass kiosk. **Featured Amenity: full hot breakfast.**

SAVE ECO 🔌 🍴 👟 Y CALL ♿ 👟 BIZ HS
📶 ✕ 🎥 🔌 💻 / SOME UNITS 🐾 🚌

WHERE TO EAT

13 COINS RESTAURANT 206/682-2513
ⱽⱽ American. Casual Dining. **Address:** 255 S King St 98104

ALTURA 206/402-6749 **18**
ⱽⱽⱽⱽ Italian. Fine Dining. **Address:** 617 Broadway E 98102

AMERICANA 206/328-4604 **22**
ⱽⱽ Comfort Food. Casual Dining. **Address:** 219 Broadway Ave E 98102

ANDALUCA 206/382-6999 **43**
ⱽⱽⱽ Mediterranean. Casual Dining. **Address:** 407 Olive Way 98101

ANTHONY'S PIER 66 206/448-6688 **44**
ⱽⱽⱽ Seafood. Casual Dining. **Address:** 2201 Alaskan Way 98121

AOKI JAPANESE GRILL & SUSHI BAR 206/324-3633 **17**
ⱽⱽ Japanese. Casual Dining. **Address:** 621 Broadway E 98102

AQUA BY EL GAUCHO 206/956-9171 **20**
ⱽⱽⱽ Seafood. Fine Dining. **Address:** 2801 Alaskan Way, Pier 70 98121

ASSAGGIO RISTORANTE 206/441-1399 **36**
ⱽⱽⱽ Italian. Casual Dining. **Address:** 2010 4th Ave 98121

ATHENIAN SEAFOOD RESTAURANT AND BAR
206/624-7166 **64**
ⱽⱽ Seafood. Casual Dining. **Address:** 1517 Pike Pl 98101

AYUTTHAYA THAI RESTAURANT 206/324-8833 **54**
ⱽⱽ Thai. Casual Dining. **Address:** 727 E Pike St 98122

BAHN THAI RESTAURANT 206/283-0444 **5**
ⱽⱽ Thai. Casual Dining. **Address:** 409 Roy St 98109

BAROLO RISTORANTE 206/770-9000 **32**
ⱽⱽⱽ Italian. Casual Dining. **Address:** 1940 Westlake Ave 98101

BARRIO MEXICAN KITCHEN & BAR 206/588-8105 **70**
ⱽⱽⱽ Mexican. Casual Dining. **Address:** 1420 12th Ave 98122

BATEAU 206/900-8699 **68**
ⱽⱽⱽ Steak. Casual Dining. **Address:** 1040 E Union St 98122

(See map & index p. 152.)

BRAVE HORSE TAVERN 206/971-0717 (14)
👑👑 American. Casual Dining. **Address:** 310 Terry Ave N 98109

THE BROOKLYN SEAFOOD, STEAK & OYSTER HOUSE
206/224-7000 (83)
👑👑👑 Seafood Steak. Casual Dining. **Address:** 1212 2nd Ave 98101

CACTUS SOUTH LAKE UNION 206/913-2250 (11)
👑👑 Tex-Mex. Casual Dining. **Address:** 350 Terry Ave N 98109

CAFE CAMPAGNE 206/728-2233 (58)
👑👑 French. Casual Dining. **Address:** 1600 Post Alley 98101

THE CHEESECAKE FACTORY 206/652-5400 (55)
👑👑👑 International. Casual Dining. **Address:** 700 Pike St 98101

CHUTNEY'S 206/284-6799 (4)
👑👑 Indian. Casual Dining. **Address:** 519 1st Ave N 98109

CJ'S EATERY 206/728-1648 (19)
👑👑 American. Casual Dining. **Address:** 2619 1st Ave 98121

CROW RESTAURANT & BAR 206/283-8800 (1)
👑👑 International. Casual Dining. **Address:** 823 5th Ave N 98109

CUOCO 206/971-0710 (15)
👑👑👑 Northern Italian. Casual Dining. **Address:** 310 Terry Ave N 98109

CYCLOPS 206/441-1677 (23)
👑👑 American. Casual Dining. **Address:** 2421 1st Ave 98121

DAHLIA LOUNGE 206/682-4142 (39)
👑👑👑 Pacific Northwest. Fine Dining. **Address:** 2001 4th Ave 98121

DAILY GRILL 206/624-8400
👑👑 American. Casual Dining. **Address:** 629 Pike St 98101

DANIEL'S BROILER ON LAKE UNION 206/621-8262 (7)
👑👑👑 Steak. Fine Dining. **Address:** 809 Fairview Pl N 98109

DIMITRIOU'S JAZZ ALLEY RESTAURANT & NIGHTCLUB
206/441-9729 (29)
👑👑 International. Dinner Theatre. **Address:** 2033 6th Ave 98121

DRAGONFISH ASIAN CAFE 206/467-7777 (48)
👑👑 Asian. Casual Dining. **Address:** 722 Pine St 98101

DUKE'S CHOWDER HOUSE 206/382-9963 (6)
👑👑 Seafood. Casual Dining. **Address:** 901 Fairview Ave N 98109

DUNBAR ROOM 206/343-6156 (85)
👑👑👑 American. Casual Dining. **Address:** 900 Madison St 98104

EL GAUCHO 206/728-1337 (21)
👑👑👑 Steak. Fine Dining. **Address:** 2505 1st Ave 98121

ELLIOTT'S OYSTER HOUSE 206/623-4340 (89)
👑👑👑 Seafood. Casual Dining. **Address:** 1201 Pier 56-Alaskan Way, Suite 100 98101

ELYSIAN BREWING 206/860-1920 (60)
👑👑 American. Casual Dining. **Address:** 1221 E Pike St 98122

ETTA'S 206/443-6000 (49)
👑👑👑 Seafood. Casual Dining. **Address:** 2020 Western Ave 98121

FADO IRISH PUB 206/264-2700 (92)
👑👑 Irish. Casual Dining. **Address:** 801 1st Ave 98104

FLYING FISH SEATTLE 206/728-8595 (16)
👑👑👑 Seafood. Casual Dining. **Address:** 300 Westlake Ave N 98109

GARAGE 206/322-2296 (73)
👑👑 American. Casual Dining. **Address:** 1130 Broadway 98122

THE GEORGIAN 206/621-1700 (81)

Regional American Fine Dining $12-$29

AAA Inspector Notes: *Historic.* The grand, elegant dining room is adorned with formal Renaissance appointments and gilded trim. Built in 1924, it's on the National Register of Historic Places. Carefully prepared and creatively presented dishes on the Continental menu are created from fresh, local ingredients. Seafood is always a solid choice in the Northwest, so a good meal might include the steamed halibut with sticky rice and a berry granita for dessert. The traditional afternoon tea is a fun experience. **Features:** full bar. **Reservations:** suggested. **Address:** 411 University St 98101 **Location:** Corner of 4th Ave and University St; in Fairmont Olympic Hotel. 🚇 University Street, 7. **Parking:** on-site (fee) and valet.
B L 🚇

GORDON BIERSCH BREWERY RESTAURANT
206/405-4205 (47)
👑👑👑 American. Casual Dining. **Address:** 600 Pine St 98101

HARD ROCK CAFE 206/204-2233 (67)
👑👑 🆂🅰🆅🅴 American. Casual Dining. **Address:** 116 Pike St 98101

HOUSE OF HONG 206/622-7997 (95)
👑👑 Chinese Dim Sum. Casual Dining. **Address:** 409 8th Ave S 98104

HUONG BINH RESTAURANT 206/720-4907 (97)
👑👑 Vietnamese. Casual Dining. **Address:** 1207 S Jackson St 98144

IL BISTRO 206/682-3049 (71)
👑👑👑 Italian. Casual Dining. **Address:** 93A Pike St 98101

IL FORNAIO 206/264-0994 (46)
👑👑👑 Italian. Fine Dining. **Address:** 600 Pine St 98101

IL FORNAIO PANETTERA/BAKERY CAFE 206/264-0994 (45)
👑 Italian. Quick Serve. **Address:** 600 Pine St 98101

IL TERRAZZO CARMINE 206/467-7797 (94)
👑👑👑 Italian. Fine Dining. **Address:** 411 1st Ave S 98104

IVAR'S ACRES OF CLAMS 206/624-6852 (90)
👑👑 Seafood. Casual Dining. **Address:** 1001 Alaskan Way 98104

JAPONESSA 206/971-7979 (77)
👑👑👑 Japanese Sushi. Casual Dining. **Address:** 1400 1st Ave 98101

JIMMY'S ON BROADWAY 206/204-1188 (78)
👑👑 American. Casual Dining. **Address:** 1100 Broadway 98122

JIMMY'S ON FIRST 206/204-9700 (98)
👑👑 American. Casual Dining. **Address:** 1046 1st Ave S 98134

JUNO 206/631-8080 (93)
👑👑👑 Pacific Northwest. Casual Dining. **Address:** 700 3rd Ave 98104

LA FONTANA SICILIANA 206/441-1045 (34)
👑👑 Italian. Casual Dining. **Address:** 120 Blanchard St 98121

(See map & index p. 152.)

LARK   206/323-5275   (74)
♦♦♦♦ American. Fine Dining. **Address:** 952 E Seneca St 98122

LECOSHO   206/623-2101   (84)
♦♦♦ New American. Casual Dining. **Address:** 89 University St 98101

LOLA   206/441-1430   (38)
♦♦♦♦ New Greek. Casual Dining. **Address:** 2000-B 4th Ave 98121

LOULAY KITCHEN & BAR   206/402-4588   (63)
♦♦♦♦ New French. Fine Dining. **Address:** 600 Union St 98101

MACRINA BAKERY & CAFE   206/448-4032   (25)
♦ Breads/Pastries. Quick Serve. **Address:** 2408 1st Ave 98121

MARGAUX RESTAURANT   206/219-2224   (33)

♦♦ ♦♦

Pacific Northwest Casual Dining $10-$35

AAA Inspector Notes: This restaurant likes to think of itself as Belltown's best-kept secret, featuring Pacific Northwest cuisine with a little bit of a French twist. Stop in for happy hour from 4-7 p.m. while enjoying specially prepared tapas and wonderfully unique cocktails. There's a nightly prix fixe menu for as little as $35. Start your meal with a cup of razor clam chowder and then the maple brined pork chop or maybe the buttermilk marinated turkey cutlets. **Features:** full bar, Sunday brunch, happy hour. **Reservations:** suggested. **Address:** 401 Lenora St 98121 **Location:** Corner of 4th Ave and Lenora St; in Warwick Seattle. 🚇 Westlake & 7th, 19. **Parking:** on-site and valet.

[B] [L] [D] [🚇]

MARRAKESH MOROCCAN RESTAURANT   206/956-0500   (26)
♦♦ Moroccan. Casual Dining. **Address:** 2334 2nd Ave 98121

MATT'S IN THE MARKET   206/467-7909   (66)
♦♦♦ American. Casual Dining. **Address:** 94 Pike St, Suite 32 98101

MCMENAMINS QUEEN ANNE PUB BREWERY   206/285-4722
♦♦♦ American. Brewpub. **Address:** 200 Roy St, Suite 105 98109

METROPOLITAN GRILL   206/624-3287   (91)
♦♦♦ Steak. Casual Dining. **Address:** 820 2nd Ave 98104

MILLER'S GUILD   206/443-3663   (37)
♦♦♦ Steak. Casual Dining. **Address:** 612 Stewart St 98101

MOMIJI   206/457-4068   (56)
♦♦♦ Japanese. Casual Dining. **Address:** 1522 12th Ave 98122

OSTERIA LA SPIGA   206/323-8881   (62)
♦♦♦ Northern Italian. Casual Dining. **Address:** 1429 12th Ave 98122

OUTLIER   206/624-7755   (86)
♦♦♦ American. Casual Dining. **Address:** 1101 4th Ave 98101

PALACE KITCHEN   206/448-2001   (31)
♦♦♦ American. Casual Dining. **Address:** 2030 5th Ave 98121

PALOMINO RESTAURANT   206/623-1300   (65)
♦♦♦ Mediterranean. Fine Dining. **Address:** 1420 5th Ave 98101

P.F. CHANG'S CHINA BISTRO   206/393-0070   (52)
♦♦♦ Chinese. Fine Dining. **Address:** 400 Pine St, Ste 136 98101

THE PIKE PUB AND BREWERY   206/622-6044   (79)
♦♦ American. Brewpub. **Address:** 1415 1st Ave 98101

THE PINK DOOR   206/443-3241   (53)
♦♦ Italian. Casual Dining. **Address:** 1919 Post Alley 98101

PLACE PIGALLE   206/624-1756   (72)
♦♦♦ French. Fine Dining. **Address:** 81 Pike St 98101

PLUM BISTRO   206/838-5333   (69)
♦♦ Vegan. Casual Dining. **Address:** 1429 12th Ave 98122

POPPY   206/324-1108   (13)
♦♦♦ Pacific Northwest. Casual Dining. **Address:** 622 Broadway E 98102

PORTAGE BAY CAFE SOUTH LAKE UNION
    206/462-6400   (12)
♦♦ Regional American. Casual Dining. **Address:** 391 Terry Ave N 98109

PURPLE CAFE AND WINE BAR   206/829-2280   (82)
♦♦ American. Casual Dining. **Address:** 1225 4th Ave 98101

PYRAMID ALEHOUSE, BREWERY & RESTAURANT
    206/682-3377   (99)
♦♦ American. Brewpub. **Address:** 1201 1st Ave S 98134

QUEEN CITY GRILL   206/443-0975   (35)
♦♦ American. Casual Dining. **Address:** 2201 1st Ave 98121

RISTORANTE MACHIAVELLI   206/621-7941   (42)
♦♦ Italian. Casual Dining. **Address:** 1215 Pine St 98101

RN74   206/456-7474   (61)
♦♦♦ Regional French. Casual Dining. **Address:** 1433 4th Ave 98101

RUTH'S CHRIS STEAK HOUSE   206/624-8524   (50)
♦♦♦ Steak. Fine Dining. **Address:** 727 Pine St 98101

SERIOUS PIE DOWNTOWN   206/838-7388   (41)
♦♦ Pizza. Casual Dining. **Address:** 316 Virginia St 98121

SERIOUS PIE WESTLAKE & SERIOUS BISCUIT
    206/436-0050   (10)
♦♦ Pizza. Casual Dining. **Address:** 401 Westlake Ave N 98109

SHANGHAI GARDENS   206/625-1688   (96)
♦♦ Chinese. Casual Dining. **Address:** 524 6th Ave S 98104

SHIRO'S   206/443-9844   (24)
♦♦ Sushi. Casual Dining. **Address:** 2401 2nd Ave 98121

SHUCKERS   206/621-1984   (80)

♦♦ ♦♦

Seafood Casual Dining $12-$40

AAA Inspector Notes: *Historic.* Locally inspired cuisine adorns the menu at this sophisticated pub-style restaurant. The extensive selection of seafood includes their signature fresh oysters, which are prepared in a number of ways. Don't forget to try the locally brewed beer made with honey from the hives on the hotel's roof. **Features:** full bar, patio dining, happy hour. **Reservations:** suggested. **Address:** 411 University St 98101 **Location:** Corner of 4th Ave and University St; in Fairmont Olympic Hotel. 🚇 University Street, 7. **Parking:** on-site (fee) and valet. [L] [D] [🚇]

SITKA & SPRUCE   206/324-0662   (40)
♦♦♦ New American. Casual Dining. **Address:** 1531 Melrose Ave 98122

SIX SEVEN   206/269-4575   (28)
♦♦♦ Pacific Northwest. Casual Dining. **Address:** 2411 Alaskan Way, Pier 67 98121

SOUND VIEW CAFE   206/623-5700   (75)
♦ American. Casual Dining. **Address:** 1501 Pike Place Market, Suite 501 98101

THE SPACE NEEDLE - SKYCITY RESTAURANT
    206/905-2100   (8)
[fyi] American. Fine Dining. Under major renovation, call for details. **Last rated:** ♦♦♦ **Address:** 400 Broad St 98109

(See map & index p. 152.)

STEELHEAD DINER   206/625-0129 (59)
♦♦♦ Pacific Northwest. Casual Dining. **Address:** 95 Pine St 98101

TANGO   206/583-0382 (51)
♦♦♦ Latin American Small Plates. Casual Dining. **Address:** 1100 Pike St 98101

TOULOUSE PETIT KITCHEN & LOUNGE   206/432-9069 (2)
♦♦ Cajun. Casual Dining. **Address:** 601 Queen Anne Ave N 98109

TRACE   206/264-6060 (88)
♦♦♦♦
**American
Casual Dining
$14-$34**

AAA Inspector Notes: This trendy restaurant is adjacent to the living room at W Seattle. The restaurant's focus is to use locally sourced ingredients and Northwest seafood for its "farm-to-table" concept. While there is a nice choice of entrées, the best way to order is by going with a host of small plates, like lemongrass chicken wings, smoked octopus fritters and pork sausage sliders then share with friends. A selection of sushi is offered at dinner. The hotel's W Bar is a popular spot for a trendy cocktail. **Features:** full bar, Sunday brunch, happy hour. **Reservations:** suggested. **Address:** 1112 4th Ave 98101 **Location:** Corner of 4th Ave and Seneca St; in W Seattle. University Street, 7. **Parking:** valet and street only.

[B] [L] [D] CALL [&] [⊞]

CHEF-DRIVEN DISHES, LOCAL/SUSTAINABLE FOCUS, ASIAN HINT

TULIO RISTORANTE   206/624-5500 (87)
♦♦♦ Regional Italian. Casual Dining. **Address:** 1100 5th Ave 98101

UMI SAKE HOUSE   206/374-8717 (30)
♦♦ Sushi. Casual Dining. **Address:** 2230 1st Ave 98121

VEGGIE GRILL   206/623-0336 (9)
♦ Vegan. Quick Serve. **Address:** 446 Terry Ave N 98109

WASABI   206/441-6044 (27)
♦♦♦ Japanese. Casual Dining. **Address:** 2311 2nd Ave 98121

WILD GINGER ASIAN RESTAURANT & SATAY BAR
                                   206/623-4450 (76)
♦♦♦ Asian. Fine Dining. **Address:** 1401 3rd Ave 98101

SEATTLE
• **Hotels & Restaurants map & index p. 160**

GASLIGHT INN   (206)325-3654 (10)
♦♦♦ Historic Bed & Breakfast. **Address:** 1727 15th Ave 98122

GRADUATE SEATTLE   206/634-2000 (6)
[fyi] Boutique Hotel. Under major renovation, call for details. **Last Rated:** ♦♦♦ **Address:** 4507 Brooklyn Ave NE 98105

HAMPTON INN & SUITES BY HILTON SEATTLE/NORTHGATE
                                   206/522-6991 (3)
♦♦♦ Hotel. **Address:** 9550 1st Ave NE 98115

AAA Benefit:
Members save 5% or more!

HOLIDAY INN EXPRESS HOTEL & SUITES NORTH SEATTLE/SHORELINE   (206)365-7777 (1)
♦♦♦ Hotel. **Address:** 14115 Aurora Ave N 98133

HOTEL NEXUS SEATTLE   206/365-0700 (2)
♦♦♦
**Hotel
Rates not provided**

Address: 2140 N Northgate Way 98133 **Location:** I-5 exit 173, just nw. **Facility:** 169 units, some kitchens. 4 stories, exterior corridors. **Terms:** check-in 4 pm. **Pool:** heated outdoor. **Activities:** exercise room. **Guest Services:** complimentary and valet laundry, area transportation. **Featured Amenity:** full hot breakfast.

[SAVE] [📶] CALL [&] [🛄] [♿] [BIZ]
[HS] [📶] [✕] [🎮] [🅿] [🖨] [🖥]
/ SOME UNITS [🐾]

MILDRED'S BED & BREAKFAST   206/325-6072 (9)
♦♦ Bed & Breakfast. **Address:** 1202 15th Ave E 98112

RESIDENCE INN BY MARRIOTT - SEATTLE/UNIVERSITY DISTRICT   (206)322-8887 (5)
♦♦♦ Extended Stay Hotel. **Address:** 4501 12th Ave NE 98105

AAA Benefit:
Members save 5% or more!

SILVER CLOUD HOTEL-UNIVERSITY DISTRICT
                                   (206)526-5200 (4)
♦♦♦ Hotel. **Address:** 5036 25th Ave NE 98105

STAYBRIDGE SUITES - SEATTLE - FREMONT
                                   (206)632-1015 (7)
♦♦♦ Extended Stay Hotel. **Address:** 3926 Aurora Ave N 98103

UNIVERSITY INN   206/632-5055 (8)
♦♦ Hotel. **Address:** 4140 Roosevelt Way NE 98105

WHERE TO EAT

5 SPOT   206/285-7768 (29)
♦♦ American. Casual Dining. **Address:** 1502 Queen Anne Ave N 98109

ART OF THE TABLE   206/282-0942 (19)
♦♦♦ New American. Casual Dining. **Address:** 3801 Stone Way N 98103

BIZZARO ITALIAN CAFE   206/632-7277 (13)
♦♦ Italian. Casual Dining. **Address:** 1307 N 46th St 98103

BROUWER'S CAFE   206/267-2437 (17)
♦♦ Belgian. Casual Dining. **Address:** 400 N 35th St 98103

BURGERMASTER
♦ Burgers. Quick Serve.
LOCATIONS:
Address: 3040 NE 45th St 98105 **Phone:** 206/525-7100
Address: 9820 Aurora Ave N 98103 **Phone:** 206/522-2044

CACTUS ALKI BEACH   206/933-6000 (37)
♦♦ Tex-Mex. Casual Dining. **Address:** 2820 Alki Ave SW 98116

CACTUS MADISON PARK   206/324-4140 (32)
♦♦ Tex-Mex. Casual Dining. **Address:** 4220 E Madison St 98112

CAFE FLORA   206/325-9100 (34)
♦♦ Vegetarian Vegan. Casual Dining. **Address:** 2901 E Madison St 98112

CAFE LAGO   206/329-8005 (31)
♦♦ Italian. Casual Dining. **Address:** 2305 24th Ave E 98112

CANLIS   206/283-3313 (24)
♦♦♦♦ Pacific Northwest. Fine Dining. **Address:** 2576 Aurora Ave N 98109

(See map & index p. 160.)

CHINOOK'S AT SALMON BAY   206/283-4665 (12)
🌑🌑 Seafood. Casual Dining. **Address:** 1900 W Nickerson St 98119

CIRCA   206/923-1102 (39)
🌑🌑 American. Casual Dining. **Address:** 2605 California Ave SW 98116

DANIEL'S BROILER - LESCHI   206/329-4191 (38)
🌑🌑🌑 Steak. Fine Dining. **Address:** 200 Lake Washington Blvd 98122

DUKE'S CHOWDER HOUSE   206/522-4908 (4)
🌑🌑 Seafood. Casual Dining. **Address:** 7850 Green Lake Dr N 98103

GORDITOS   206/706-9352 (1)
🌑 Mexican. Casual Dining. **Address:** 213 N 85th St 98103

HENRY'S TAVERN SEATTLE   206/624-0501 (40)
🌑🌑 Regional American. Casual Dining. **Address:** 1518 1st Ave S 98134

JAK'S GRILL
🌑🌑 Steak. Casual Dining.
LOCATIONS:
Address: 4548 California Ave SW 98116 **Phone:** 206/937-7809
Address: 3701 NE 45th St 98105 **Phone:** 206/985-8545

JOULE   206/632-5685 (20)
🌑🌑🌑 Korean Fusion. Casual Dining. **Address:** 3506 Stone Way N 98103

JUNEBABY   206/257-4470 (9)
🌑🌑 Southern. Casual Dining. **Address:** 2122 NE 65th St 98115

KABUL AFGHAN CUISINE   206/545-9000 (15)
🌑🌑 Afghan. Casual Dining. **Address:** 2301 N 45th St 98103

LA CARTA DE OAXACA   206/782-8722 (6)
🌑🌑 Mexican. Casual Dining. **Address:** 5431 Ballard Ave NW 98107

LE FOURNIL LTD   206/328-6523 (22)
🌑 French Breads/Pastries. Quick Serve. **Address:** 3230 Eastlake Ave E 98102

LUNA PARK CAFE   206/935-7250 (42)
🌑🌑 American. Casual Dining. **Address:** 2918 SW Avalon Way 98126

MACRINA BAKERY & CAFE   206/283-5900 (23)
🌑 Breads/Pastries. Quick Serve. **Address:** 615 W McGraw St 98119

MEZCALERIA OAXACA   206/216-4446 (26)
🌑 Regional Mexican. Casual Dining. **Address:** 2123 Queen Anne Ave N 98109

MONSOON   206/325-2111 (33)
🌑🌑 Vietnamese. Casual Dining. **Address:** 615 19th Ave E 98112

NELL'S   206/524-4044 (7)
🌑🌑🌑 Pacific Northwest. Fine Dining. **Address:** 6804 E Green Lake Way N 98115

ORRAPIN THAI CUISINE   206/283-7118 (25)
🌑🌑 Thai. Casual Dining. **Address:** 10 Boston St 98109

PALISADE RESTAURANT   206/285-1000 (27)
🌑🌑🌑 Seafood. Fine Dining. **Address:** 2601 W Marina Pl 98199

PORTAGE BAY CAFE BALLARD   206/783-1547 (5)
🌑🌑 American. Casual Dining. **Address:** 2825 NW Market St 98107

PORTAGE BAY CAFE ROOSEVELT   206/547-8230 (18)
🌑🌑 Regional American. Casual Dining. **Address:** 4130 Roosevelt Way NE 98105

RAM RESTAURANT & BREWERY
🌑🌑 American. Casual Dining.
LOCATIONS:
Address: 2650 University Village 98105 **Phone:** 206/525-3565
Address: 401 NE Northgate Way, Suite 1102 98125
Phone: 206/364-8000

RAY'S BOATHOUSE   206/789-3770 (3)
🌑🌑🌑 Seafood. Fine Dining. **Address:** 6049 Seaview Ave NW 98107

RAY'S CAFE   206/782-0094 (2)
🌑🌑 Seafood. Casual Dining. **Address:** 6049 Seaview Ave NW 98107

SALARE   206/556-2192 (10)
🌑🌑🌑 American. Casual Dining. **Address:** 2404 NE 65th St 98115

SALTY'S ON ALKI BEACH   206/937-1600 (36)
🌑🌑🌑 Seafood. Fine Dining. **Address:** 1936 Harbor Ave SW 98126

SERAFINA   206/323-0807 (30)
🌑🌑🌑 Italian. Casual Dining. **Address:** 2043 Eastlake Ave E 98102

STANFORD'S RESTAURANT & BAR   206/834-6277
🌑🌑 American. Casual Dining. **Address:** 401 NE Northgate Way 98125

TANGLETOWN - ELYSIAN BREWING   206/547-5929 (11)
🌑🌑 American. Casual Dining. **Address:** 2106 N 55th St 98103

TERRY'S 14 CARROT CAFÉ   206/324-1442 (28)
🌑🌑 American. Casual Dining. **Address:** 2305 Eastlake Ave E 98102

THAT'S AMORE! ITALIAN CAFE   206/322-3677 (41)
🌑🌑 Italian. Casual Dining. **Address:** 1425 31st Ave S 98144

TILTH RESTAURANT   206/633-0801 (14)
🌑🌑🌑 New American. Fine Dining. **Address:** 1411 N 45th St 98103

VEGGIE GRILL   206/523-1961 (16)
🌑 Vegan. Quick Serve. **Address:** 2681 NE University Village St 98105

THE WALRUS AND THE CARPENTER   206/395-9227 (8)
🌑🌑🌑 Small Plates Seafood. Casual Dining. **Address:** 4743 Ballard Ave NW 98107

THE WHALE WINS   206/632-9425 (21)
🌑🌑🌑 Continental. Casual Dining. **Address:** 3506 Stone Way N 98103

SEAVIEW

SHELBURNE HOTEL   360/642-2442
fyi Historic Country Inn. Under major renovation, call for details.
Last Rated: 🌑🌑🌑 **Address:** 4415 Pacific Way 98644

WHERE TO EAT

42ND STREET CAFE & BISTRO   360/642-2323
🌑🌑 American. Casual Dining. **Address:** 4201 Pacific Way 98644

THE DEPOT RESTAURANT   360/642-7880
🌑🌑🌑 Continental. Casual Dining. **Address:** 1208 38th & L Pl 98644

LAURIE'S HOMESTEAD BREAKFAST HOUSE   360/642-7171
♥♥ American. Casual Dining. **Address:** 4214 Pacific Way 98644

SHELBURNE RESTAURANT & PUB   360/642-4150

| fyi | Under major renovation, call for details. |

Pacific Northwest Fine Dining
$10-$28

Under major renovation, call for details. **Last rated:** ♥♥♥ AAA Inspector **Notes:** *Historic.* Diners can unwind in the more upscale dining room or the more casual lounge. Attentive servers will try to accommodate requests in any way they can. A salad with the made-in-house basil-vinaigrette dressing is a fabulous beginning to a meal. Call for winter hours. **Features:** full bar, happy hour. **Address:** 4415 Pacific Way 98644 **Location:** 0.5 mi n of jct US 101 on SR 103; in Shelburne Hotel. B L D 🅰

SEQUIM (D-1) pop. 6,606, elev. 183'
• **Part of Olympic National Park area — see map p. 100**

Sequim (SKWIM), a Klallam Indian word meaning "a place for going to shoot," is a popular retirement area due to the relatively dry, sunny climate and a variety of recreational opportunities. Developed facilities are found at Sequim Bay State Park *(see Recreation Areas Chart).* Dungeness Recreation Area *(see Recreation Areas Chart),* 5 miles northwest, provides camping facilities as well as access to the Dungeness National Wildlife Refuge. John Wayne Marina, 2577 W. Sequim Bay Rd., occupies land donated by the legendary actor so that others could enjoy his favorite fishing spot.

Lavender, which blooms July through August, is an important local crop. Some 40 lavender farms are in the vicinity, and many are open to the public. The summer air is perfumed with its aromatic scent—a perfect time of year for the 🌼 Sequim Lavender Festival. In addition to free, self-guiding tours of eight area lavender farms, there's a street fair that sets up along Fir Street downtown, with more than 150 vendors from across the Pacific Northwest offering lavender-scented products and lavender art, plus live music on an outdoor stage and a food court where you can purchase a glass of lavender wine. This 3-day event is held the third weekend in July.

Sequim-Dungeness Chamber of Commerce: 1192 E. Washington St., P.O. Box 907, Sequim, WA 98382. **Phone:** (360) 683-6197 or (800) 737-8462.

HOLIDAY INN EXPRESS & SUITES CONFERENCE CENTER SEQUIM   360/681-8756
♥♥♥ Hotel. **Address:** 1441 E Washington St 98382

JUAN DE FUCA COTTAGES   (360)683-4433
♥♥♥ Cottage. **Address:** 182 Marine Dr 98382

QUALITY INN & SUITES AT OLYMPIC NATIONAL PARK   (360)683-2800
♥♥ Hotel. **Address:** 134 River Rd 98382

RED LION INN & SUITES SEQUIM AT OLYMPIC NATIONAL PARK   (360)683-1775
♥♥ Hotel. **Address:** 1095 E Washington St 98382

WHERE TO EAT

HI-WAY 101 DINER   360/683-3388
♥♥ Comfort Food. Casual Dining. **Address:** 392 W Washington St 98382

OAK TABLE CAFE   360/683-2179
♥♥ American. Casual Dining. **Address:** 292 W Bell St 98382

SAWADEE THAI CUISINE   360/683-8188
♥♥ Thai. Casual Dining. **Address:** 271 S 7th Ave, Suite 31 98382

SHELTON (G-1) pop. 9,834, elev. 41'
• **Part of Olympic National Park area — see map p. 100**

Shelton, on an inlet of South Puget Sound, is known for Christmas trees and oysters. Between November and mid-December, 3 million Christmas trees are cut, packed and shipped from this area. "Tollie," a 90-ton Shay locomotive that operated in the woods near Shelton from 1924 until 1958, is displayed at Railroad Avenue and Third Street. Its caboose houses a visitor center.

Shelton-Mason County Tourist Information Center: 230 W. Railroad Ave., P.O. Box 2389, Shelton, WA 98584. **Phone:** (360) 426-2021 or (800) 576-2021.

LITTLE CREEK CASINO RESORT   (360)427-7711

Resort Hotel
$59-$299

Address: 91 W SR 108 98584 **Location:** Jct US 101 and SR 108. **Facility:** This resort offers live entertainment year-round, table games, slots, a luxurious spa, a golf course and an inviting pool area. Be sure to stroll the public areas and admire all the great local art. 190 units. 5 stories, interior corridors. **Parking:** on-site and valet. **Terms:** check-in 4 pm, cancellation fee imposed. **Amenities:** safes. **Dining:** 4 restaurants, also, Island Grille, see separate listing, entertainment. **Pool:** heated indoor. **Activities:** hot tub, regulation golf, game room, exercise room, spa. **Guest Services:** valet and coin laundry. **Featured Amenity:** breakfast buffet.

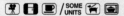

SUPER 8 OF SHELTON   (360)426-1654
♥♥ Motel. **Address:** 2943 Northview Cir 98584

WHERE TO EAT

ISLAND GRILLE   360/427-7711
♥♥ American. Casual Dining. **Address:** 91 W SR 108 98584

SHORELINE (E-3) pop. 53,007, elev. 475'
• **Hotels & Restaurants map & index p. 160**
• **Part of Seattle area — see map p. 124**

Just north of Seattle, Shoreline is primarily a residential community. Richmond Beach, 3 miles west of SR 99 via N. 185th Street and Richmond Beach Road, offers one of the largest sand beaches on Puget Sound.

Shoreline Chamber of Commerce: 18560 First Ave. N.E., Shoreline, WA 98155. **Phone:** (206) 361-2260.

DAYS INN BY WYNDHAM - SHORELINE   (206)542-6300   **23**
♥♥ Hotel. **Address:** 19527 Aurora Ave N 98133

SILVERDALE pop. 19,204

- Hotels & Restaurants map & index p. 170
- Part of Seattle area — see map p. 124

BEST WESTERN PLUS SILVERDALE BEACH HOTEL
(360)698-1000 **11**

▼▼▼
Hotel
$94-$200

Best Western PLUS **AAA Benefit:** Members save up to 15% and earn bonus points!

Address: 3073 NW Bucklin Hill Rd 98383 **Location:** Oceanfront. SR 3 exit Newberry Hill Rd, just e, 1 mi n on Silverdale Way, then just e. **Facility:** 151 units. 3 stories, interior corridors. **Terms:** check-in 4 pm, cancellation fee imposed. **Amenities:** *Some:* safes. **Pool:** heated indoor. **Activities:** sauna, hot tub, bicycles, exercise room. **Guest Services:** valet and coin laundry.

[icons] SAVE 🍴 🍸 ⊃ ⊞ BIZ 📶 ✕ 🔲 🖼 🖵
/ SOME UNITS 🐾

OXFORD SUITES SILVERDALE
(360)698-9550 **10**

▼▼▼
Contemporary Hotel
$89-$700

Address: 9550 NW Silverdale Way 98383 **Location:** Waterfront. SR 3 exit Newberry Hill Rd, just e, then 0.9 mi n. **Facility:** 104 units, some efficiencies. 5 stories, interior corridors. **Terms:** check-in 4 pm, 2-14 night minimum stay - seasonal and/or weekends, 30 day cancellation notice-fee imposed. **Pool:** heated indoor. **Activities:** sauna, hot tub, steamroom, exercise room. **Guest Services:** valet and coin laundry, area transportation. **Featured Amenity:** breakfast buffet.

[icons] SAVE 🍴 🍸 CALL ♿ ⊃ ⊞
BIZ HS 📶 ✕ 🔲 🖼 🖵
/ SOME UNITS 🐾

QUALITY INN & SUITES
(360)692-7777 **9**
▼▼ Hotel. **Address:** 9734 NW Silverdale Way 98383

WHERE TO EAT

OAK TABLE CAFE
360/204-5198 **6**
▼▼ American. Casual Dining. **Address:** 3290 NW Mount Vintage Way 98383

SILVER CITY RESTAURANT & BREWERY
360/698-5879 **7**
▼▼ American. Brewpub. **Address:** 2799 NW Myhre Rd 98383

SNOHOMISH (D-7) pop. 9,098, elev. 64'
- Part of Seattle area — see map p. 124

Founded in 1859 at the confluence of the Pilchuck and Snohomish rivers, Snohomish's rich history is reflected in its homes and commercial buildings. The residential area north of 2nd Street has some substantial Victorians, and a number of 19th-century buildings along 1st Street and the riverbank have been restored. The Snohomish County Tourism Bureau Visitor Center, a replica of a turn-of-the-20th-century railroad station, provides an interpretive exhibit and a 10-minute video about the town's history.

The Blackman House Museum, 118 Ave. B, was built in 1878 by Snohomish's first mayor, Hyrcanus Blackman. Subsequently enlarged and remodeled in 1895, the house and its furnishings are restored to reflect the Victorian period. Phone (360) 568-5235 or (425) 315-2258.

The 30-mile Centennial Trail, a paved path for pedestrians and bicyclists, was built on the abandoned Burlington Northern Railroad right-of-way.

Snohomish County Tourism Bureau Visitor Center: 1301 First St., Snohomish, WA 98290. **Phone:** (360) 862-9609 or (888) 338-0976.

Self-guiding tours: Driving or walking tour maps of Snohomish are available from the visitor center.

Shopping: In keeping with the prevailing Victorian-era atmosphere, the town bills itself as the "Antique Capital of the Northwest." Antique malls provide space for dealers in the historic business district, centered on First Street between Cedar Avenue and Avenue D. Restored buildings also house restaurants and specialty shops.

INN AT SNOHOMISH
360/568-2208

▼▼
Motel
Rates not provided

Address: 323 2nd St 98290 **Location:** Just e; corner of Pine St. **Facility:** 26 units. 2 stories (no elevator), exterior corridors.

[icons] SAVE 📶 ✕ 🔲 🖼 🖵
/ SOME UNITS 🐾

WHERE TO EAT

COLLECTOR'S CHOICE RESTAURANT
360/568-1277

▼▼
American Casual Dining
$9-$33

AAA Inspector Notes: Located behind the Rite Aid, this restaurant offers a wide array of dining options, including a daily lunch special. Guests will enjoy that breakfast is served through lunch. The Monte Cristo is a great option. Desserts like Key lime pie and peanut butter pie are made in house and are a great a finish to any meal. During the warmer months try dining on the spacious outdoor deck; it overlooks the Pilchuck River. **Features:** full bar, patio dining, happy hour. **Reservations:** suggested, for dinner. **Address:** 215 Cypress Ave 98290 **Location:** Jct 2nd St and Pine Ave, just ne.

[icons] B L D CALL ♿

SNOQUALMIE (E-7) pop. 10,670, elev. 423'
- Part of Seattle area — see map p. 124

Like most of the towns in this part of the state, Snoqualmie got its start as a lumbering center and prospered further when the railroad arrived in 1889. The completion of I-90 in the 1970s brought easy access, and in the first decade of the 21st century Snoqualmie was one of Washington's fastest-growing cities. If you're a rail buff, a treasure trove of historic railway rolling stock stands on the tracks that parallel SR 202 on the west side of town. An 1890 depot is among several historic buildings in the central business district along Railroad Avenue.

Snoqualmie Valley Chamber of Commerce: 38767 S.E. River St., Snoqualmie, WA 98065. **Phone:** (425) 888-6362.

SNOQUALMIE FALLS is 1.5 mi. n.w. on SR 202. Plunging 268 feet over a basalt cliff, this is one of Washington's most popular natural attractions. Volume varies depending on the flow of the same-named river, and is at its most impressive after heavy rains that occur periodically from November through March. When the river is at flood stage it flows across the entire precipice and is an awesome sight.

Much of the river's flow is diverted into two power plants. A 1,215-foot tunnel channels water into a power plant located 270 feet beneath the surface; built in 1898, it was the world's first completely underground facility of its kind. A second plant a quarter of a mile downstream was built in 1910 and enlarged in 1957.

There's a landscaped park on the north side of the falls, and a covered gazebo—perched at the edge of the cliff 300 feet above the river—overlooks the plunge. The half-mile River Trail follows a steep descending course down to the river and the base of the falls. **Note:** Dogs are not permitted in the park. **Time:** Allow 1 hour minimum. **Hours:** Daily dawn-dusk. **Cost:** Free. **Phone:** (425) 888-4440 or (425) 326-2563. ⊺⊺ ⋒

SALISH LODGE & SPA   425/888-2556
♥♥♥♥ Hotel. **Address:** 6501 Railroad Ave SE 98065

WHERE TO EAT

THE DINING ROOM - SALISH LODGE & SPA   425/888-2556
♥♥♥♥ Pacific Northwest. Fine Dining. **Address:** 6501 Railroad Ave SE 98065

SOAP LAKE (E-9) pop. 1,514, elev. 1,074'

Native Americans called Soap Lake Smokiam, meaning "healing waters." The 2-mile-long lake stands at the southern entrance to cliff-lined Grand Coulee. Its waters are highly mineralized; early maps labeled it Alkali Lake. The present name refers to the fringe of suds that occasionally forms along the shoreline in windy weather.

Settlers moved into this region with the coming of the Great Northern Railroad in the mid-1880s. A sanitarium hotel capitalizing on the alleged therapeutic benefits of bathing in the lake's waters opened in 1905, and was quickly followed by several others. Soap Lake became a busy resort and health spa that attracted people from around the country, especially those with skin ailments, arthritis and rheumatism. Medical advances made these resorts less popular by the mid-20th century, and irrigation water seeping into the lake over time has altered its mineral content.

East Beach Park on SR 17 provides public access to Soap Lake. A notable feature in the park is a giant sundial called "Calling the Healing Waters." The 15-foot-tall bronze sculpture of a Native American couple underscores the lake's importance to the region's first inhabitants. The male figure's outstretched wings serve as the sundial's pointer.

SOAP LAKE NATURAL SPA & RESORT   509/246-1132
♥♥ Motel. **Address:** 236 E Main Ave 98851

SOUTH BEND (F-5) pop. 1,637, elev. 11'

The development of rich timberland established South Bend as the key point in the water and stagecoach transportation system of Washington Territory in the late 1800s. After the arrival of the railroad in 1893, the town became an important shipping point for oysters to Eastern markets, and oyster processing has been an important local industry since the 1930s.

A descriptive marker 7.7 miles west on US 101 defines the site of Bruceville, settled in 1851 by the crew of the oyster schooner Robert Bruce, which burned near the site. Bruceville, later called Bruceport, was one of the pioneering oyster communities on Willapa Bay.

PACIFIC COUNTY COURTHOUSE is 2 blks. s. of US 101 at 300 Memorial Dr. Once described as a gilded palace of extravagance, the 1911 courthouse is an excellent example of Second Renaissance Revival architecture. The rotunda is lit by a stained-glass dome 35 feet in diameter. Waterfalls and a duck pond are on the grounds. **Hours:** Mon.-Fri. 8-5. **Cost:** Free. **Phone:** (360) 875-9337.

SPOKANE (E-12) pop. 208,916, elev. 1,898'
• Hotels p. 190 • Restaurants p. 192
• Hotels & Restaurants map & index p. 187

Early settlers quickly spread the word that a trip to Spokane (spo-CAN) House meant warm hospitality as well as profitable business dealings. The active little trading post was the first non-Native American habitation of the Pacific Northwest. Spokane has since grown into the state's second largest city without losing its pioneering spirit.

The Northwest Fur Co. operation, established in 1810 soon after the Lewis and Clark expedition, was actually alongside the Little Spokane River about 10 miles from the present city. It was not until 1872 that the nucleus of today's Spokane was established at Spokane Falls. Grain and lumber mills replaced fur trading as the major business; the appearance of railroads coincided with a gold rush to the Coeur d'Alene district.

One of downtown Spokane's most convenient features is its system of enclosed skywalks that allows pedestrians to visit many downtown establishments without having to brave the winter cold. Historic residential neighborhoods, such as Browne's Addition, just west of downtown, and South Hill, south of I-90, feature grand mansions from the late 19th and early 20th centuries, including half a dozen designed by renowned Spokane architect Kirtland Kelsey Cutter.

Spokane Falls thunder through downtown during the spring and early summer runoff periods. The 130-foot-high series of cascades can be seen from various observation points in Riverfront Park (see attraction listing p. 185), Huntington Park, points along Spokane Falls Boulevard, from the walkway on the east side of the Monroe Street Bridge and

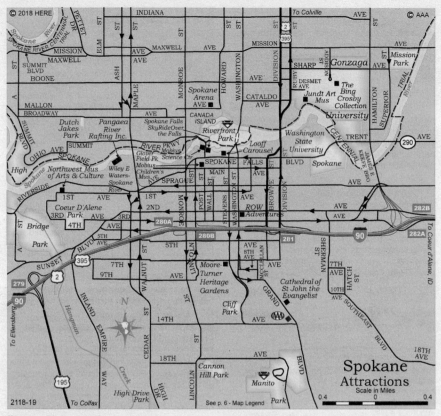

© 2018 HERE

© AAA

Spokane Attractions
Scale in Miles
0.4   0   0.4

2118-19   To Colfax   See p. 6 - Map Legend

(See map & index p. 187.)

from the Post Street Bridge. The closest views are in Huntington Park, where a path just west of City Hall on Spokane Falls Boulevard leads down to the park. For a unique view consider Spokane Falls SkyRide Over the Falls *(see attraction listing p. 186)*.

Downtown Spokane celebrates the Lilac Festival in mid-May when lilacs are in full bloom. The highlight of the festivities is the Armed Forces Torchlight Parade; phone (509) 535-4554.

"The best basketball weekend on Earth" is one way to describe Hoopfest: more than 6,000 teams from around the country play on 450 courts that span 45 city blocks. For non-hoops players the festival offers shopping, food and interactive games. Hoopfest takes place in late June; for more information phone (509) 624-2414.

Native American petroglyphs are northwest of town near Rutter Bridge. From US 395 (Division Street) take SR 291 (Francis Avenue) west 2 miles to Indian Trail Road, then proceed north on Indian Trail Road about 4 miles.

Skiing and snowboarding are popular at Mount Spokane in Mount Spokane State Park *(see Recreation Areas Chart)*, which is 29 miles northeast of the city. Six local wineries offer tours and tastings;

contact the convention and visitors bureau for more information.

Visit Spokane Visitor Center: 808 W. Main Ave., Spokane, WA 99201. **Phone:** (509) 747-3230 or (888) 776-5263.

Self-guiding tours: Information about the City Tour is available from the visitor center. Distinctive brown-and-white arrowhead signs are posted along the 32-mile route, which loops through the southern and western parts of Spokane.

Shopping: Anchor stores at Northtown Mall, 4 miles north of I-90 on US 2/395 at 4750 N. Division St., are JCPenney, Kohl's, Macy's and Sears. The Flour Mill, downtown at 621 W. Mallon Ave., has a collection of specialty shops.

Fifteen blocks of downtown Spokane are connected by enclosed skywalks, providing climate-controlled access to hotels, the convention center and Nordstrom at River Park Square. The former railroad-centric Hillyard District now features a collection of antique and secondhand shops; mostly along Market Street between Wellesley and Francis avenues. Antiques also can be found in the Monroe Street Antique District, which extends from Bridge Avenue north to Cleveland Avenue.

(See map & index p. 187.)

GONZAGA UNIVERSITY, 502 E. Boone Ave., 4 blks. e. of US 2/395, occupies a 131-acre landscaped campus along the Spokane River on the northeast edge of downtown. The university traces its origins to 1883, when Father Joseph M. Cataldo established a Native American boarding school for boys at the site. Named for the 16th-century Italian Jesuit saint Aloysius Gonzaga, patron of youth, it is the largest institute of private learning in the inland Northwest. Gonzaga's law school in one of only three in Washington.

St. Aloysius Church, with its twin steeples, is a campus landmark. The interior features oak woodwork, Italian marble, stained-glass windows and an authentic pipe organ with 37 ranks of keys. Just east of the church is College Hall, a four-story brick building erected in 1898. The Foley Center Library's Cowles Rare Book Room contains a collection of tomes up to 600 years old.

Hours: St. Aloysius Church is open for self-guiding tours daily during daylight hours. The Foley Center Library is open to non-students Mon.-Fri. 8 p.m.-9 p.m. **Phone:** (509) 328-4220 for campus information, (509) 313-6532 for the Foley Center Library, or (509) 313-5896 for St. Aloysius Church.

The Bing Crosby Collection is in the Crosby House on the Gonzaga University campus at 508 E. Sharp Ave. The boyhood home of Bing Crosby contains more than 150 items relating to the crooner's life, including his Oscar, gold and platinum records, photographs and trophies. Crosby attended Gonzaga University and was awarded an honorary doctorate in 1937. **Time:** Allow 1 hour minimum. **Hours:** Mon.-Fri. 10-4, Sat. 1-4, Mar.-Oct.; Mon.-Fri. 10-4, Sat. 1-3, rest of year. Closed major holidays. **Cost:** Free. **Phone:** (509) 313-3847 or (509) 313-5931.

Jundt Art Museum is at 202 E. Cataldo Ave. on the Gonzaga University campus. The museum features a 2,800-square-foot main gallery that houses traveling exhibits as well as rotating displays from the museum's permanent collection. The permanent collection includes glass art by Dale Chihuly and bronze sculpture by Auguste Rodin along with paintings, prints, ceramics, photographs and tapestries. Suspended within the museum's spire is Chihuly's work "The Gonzaga Red Chandelier." **Time:** Allow 1 hour minimum. **Hours:** Mon.-Sat. 10-4. Closed federal and university holidays. **Cost:** Free. **Phone:** (509) 313-6843. **GT**

MANITO PARK is between 17th and 25th aves at 1702 S. Grand Blvd. Spokane's beloved greensward is the perfect place to while away a sunny afternoon: The park's 98 acres feature spacious lawns, groves of trees, walking and bicycle paths, historic buildings and five theme gardens.

The Renaissance-style Duncan Garden, centered around a fountain and gazebo, has a formal layout designed for the display of bedding plants. Rose Hill is an All American Rose Selections test garden that contains more than 1,500 bushes and 150 varieties of roses. The Nishinomiya Tsutakawa Japanese Garden, named for Spokane's sister city, contains a waterfall, koi pond and graceful statuary. The Joel E. Ferris Perennial Garden offers a changing display of flowering plants throughout the growing season.

The Gaiser Conservatory houses plants native to tropical, subtropical and temperate regions around the world; the displays of flowering plants are changed seasonally. Other gardens showcase lilacs—the city's official flower—dahlias, irises, shade plants and hardy fuschias. Flowering season for the Duncan Garden is June through September; the Joel E. Ferris Perennial Garden is in bloom mid-April through October; Rose Hill blooms June through September. Complementing all the greenery are several Craftsman-style buildings, topiary shrubs, playgrounds, a splash pad, two-acre Mirror Pond and a historic stone bridge built in the early 1930s. A free concert series is offered Fridays June through August.

Food is available seasonally. **Time:** Allow 2 hours minimum. **Hours:** Park open daily 5 a.m.-11 p.m., Apr. 1-late Oct.; 5 a.m.-10 p.m., rest of year. Conservatory open daily 8-7, mid-May to mid-Sept.; 8-6, first day of DST to mid-May; 8-5, mid-Sept. through Oct. 31; 8-3:30, rest of year. Conservatory closed Jan. 1, Martin Luther King Jr. Day, Thanksgiving and Christmas. Japanese Garden open 8 a.m. to half hour before dusk, Apr. 1-Nov. 1. **Cost:** Free. **Phone:** (509) 625-6200, (509) 363-5422, or (509) 625-6601 for concert information. **[†]**

MOBIUS SCIENCE CENTER is at 331 N. Post St. across the street from Riverfront Park. The center encourages visitors ages 8 and up to explore basic scientific and technological concepts through more than 100 changing interactive exhibits and activities. Visitors also can take advantage of special events and a lecture series. **Time:** Allow 1 hour minimum. **Hours:** Tues.-Sat. 10-5. Closed major holidays. **Cost:** $8; $7 (ages 65+ and military and students with ID); free (ages 0-1). **Phone:** (509) 321-7133.

SAVE NORTHWEST MUSEUM OF ARTS & CULTURE is at 2316 W. 1st Ave. in the historic Browne's Addition neighborhood. The museum displays visual art in five underground galleries, as well as exhibits pertaining to regional history and Native American and other cultures. The restored Campbell House, next to the museum, is representative of Spokane's turn-of-the-20th-century "Age of Elegance."

Time: Allow 2 hours minimum. **Hours:** Tues.-Sun. 10-5 (also Wed. 5-8 p.m.). Guided house tours depart at noon, 1, 2 and 3; advance registration is required. Closed major holidays. **Cost:** $10; $7.50 (ages 60+); $5 (students with ID). **Phone:** (509) 456-3931, or (509) 363-5315 for recorded information. **GT** **[†]**

RIVERFRONT PARK is off I-90 at 507 N. Howard St. The centerpiece of this 100-acre park is the Spokane River, which forms a series of

(See map & index p. 187.)

cataracts before plunging over the main drop of Spokane Falls. Prior to 1974, industrial activities and rail yards dominated the site, which was cleared and redeveloped for Expo '74. The park offers a mix of green spaces and attractions built for and after the world's fair.

Spokane Falls SkyRide Over the Falls *(see attraction listing)* affords scenic views of the falls and park. A network of walkways links all sections of the park. Pedestrian bridges lead to Havermale Island, featuring the former U.S. Pavilion and a Clock Tower, part of the former 1902 Great Northern Depot. Other attractions are an interactive fountain, the Spokane Sculpture Walk, a giant Red Wagon play structure and an outdoor skating ribbon open to roller skates, non-motorized scooters and skateboards. Ice-skating is offered in winter. Special events take place throughout the year.

Note: The park is undergoing construction through 2019. Some attractions may be unavailable; phone ahead for details. **Time:** Allow 2 hours minimum. **Hours:** Park grounds open daily 5 a.m.-midnight. Sky-Ride open Sun., Mon. and Thurs. 11-6, Fri.-Sat. 11-7. Skating ribbon and carousel open Sun.-Thurs. 11-6, Fri.-Sat. 11-7. Phone for schedule of seasonal attractions. **Cost:** Park grounds free. SkyRide $7.75; $5.75 (ages 2-12). Skate rental $6.50 (per hour); scooter rental $8.50 (per hour). Carousel $2.50; free (ages 0-2 with adult). **Phone:** (509) 625-6601, or (509) 625-6608 Oct.-Feb. for the Ice Palace. 🍴 ☒ 🍽

Looff Carousel is on the s. side of Riverfront Park at 507 N. Howard St. People of all ages love this hand-carved treasure built in 1909 by Charles Looff, who also created the first carousel for New York's Coney Island. **Hours:** Daily 10-7. **Cost:** Individual ride $2; free (ages 0-2 with adult). **Phone:** (509) 625-6600.

Spokane Falls SkyRide Over the Falls leaves from the w. edge of Riverfront Park, 507 N. Howard St., and carries visitors over the Spokane River and falls within enclosed six-person, wheelchair-accessible gondolas. The best views can be seen Mar.-June when Spokane Falls is strongest. **Hours:** Sun., Mon. and Thurs. 11-6, Fri.-Sat. 11-7 (weather permitting). **Cost:** Fare $7.75; $5.75 (ages 2-12). Ages 0-15 must be accompanied by an adult. **Phone:** (509) 625-6601.

WINERIES

- **Arbor Crest Wine Cellars** is on Fruithill Rd.; from I-90 exit 287, go n. 1.75 mi. on Argonne Rd., then 1.1 mi. e. on Upriver Rd., then 1 mi. n.e. on Fruithill Rd., following signs. The 75-acre estate features landscaped grounds and the historic Cliff House, perched atop a bluff overlooking Spokane. Self-guiding tours of the grounds and tasting room are offered. **Hours:** Daily noon-5. Closed Jan. 1, Thanksgiving and Christmas. **Cost:** Tastings start at $7. **Phone:** (509) 927-9463. GT

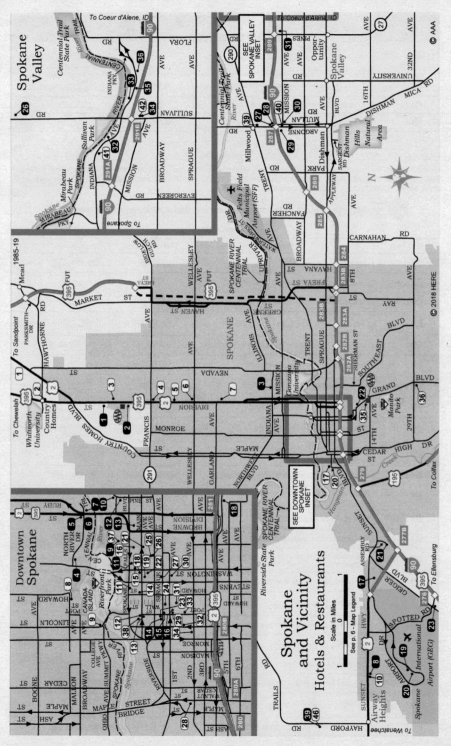

Map Page	✈ **Airport Hotels**			
	SPOKANE INTERNATIONAL (Maximum driving distance from airport: 2.8 mi)	Diamond Rated	Rate Range	Page
⑰ p. 187	Holiday Inn Spokane Airport, 2.8 mi	◈◈◈	Rates not provided	192
⑳ p. 187	Ramada at Spokane Airport, 0.3 mi	◈◈	$105-$125	192
⑲ p. 187	Wingate by Wyndham Spokane Airport, 0.4 mi	◈◈◈	$103-$189	192

Spokane

This index helps you "spot" where approved hotels and restaurants are located on the corresponding detailed maps. Hotel daily rate range is for comparison only. Restaurant price range is a combination of lunch and/or dinner. Turn to the listing page for more information and consult display ads for special promotions.

 For more details, rates and reservations: AAA.com/travelguides/hotels

SPOKANE

Map Page	Hotels	Diamond Rated	Rate Range	Page
❶ p. 187	**Quality Inn Oakwood**	◈◈	$95-$205 [SAVE]	192
❷ p. 187	Ramada North Spokane	◈◈	$95-$230	192
❸ p. 187	1908 Marianna Stoltz House Bed & Breakfast	◈◈	$95-$125	190
❹ p. 187	Centennial Hotel Spokane	◈◈◈	Rates not provided	190
❺ p. 187	Holiday Inn Express-Downtown	◈◈◈	$119-$299	192
❻ p. 187	**Oxford Suites-Downtown Spokane**	◈◈◈	$89-$755 [SAVE]	192
❼ p. 187	Red Lion River Inn-Spokane	◈◈	Rates not provided	192
❽ p. 187	**Hilton Garden Inn Spokane Airport**	◈◈◈	$112-$308 [SAVE]	191
❾ p. 187	DoubleTree by Hilton Spokane City Center	◈◈◈	Rates not provided	191
❿ p. 187	Courtyard by Marriott Spokane Downtown at the Convention Center	◈◈◈	$73-$280	191
⓫ p. 187	**The Davenport Grand, Autograph Collection**	◈◈◈◈	$92-$333 [SAVE]	191
⓬ p. 187	Fairfield Inn & Suites by Marriott Spokane Downtown	◈◈◈	$82-$304	191
⓭ p. 187	**Best Western Plus City Center**	◈◈	$95-$295 [SAVE]	190
⓮ p. 187	**The Davenport Lusso, Autograph Collection**	◈◈◈	$95-$306 [SAVE]	191
⓯ p. 187	**The Historic Davenport Hotel, Autograph Collection**	◈◈◈◈	$116-$380 [SAVE]	192
⓰ p. 187	**The Davenport Tower, Autograph Collection**	◈◈◈◈	$90-$315 [SAVE]	191
⓱ p. 187	Holiday Inn Spokane Airport	◈◈◈	Rates not provided	192
⓲ p. 187	**Quality Inn Downtown 4th Avenue**	◈◈	$88-$168 [SAVE]	192
⓳ p. 187	Wingate by Wyndham Spokane Airport	◈◈◈	$103-$189	192
⓴ p. 187	Ramada at Spokane Airport	◈◈	$105-$125	192
㉑ p. 187	**Hampton Inn by Hilton Spokane Airport**	◈◈◈	$123-$385 [SAVE]	191
㉒ p. 187	The Madison Inn by Riversage	◈◈	Rates not provided	192
㉓ p. 187	**Best Western Plus Peppertree Airport Inn**	◈◈◈	$99-$399 [SAVE]	190

Map Page	Restaurants	Diamond Rated	Cuisine	Price Range	Page
① p. 187	Frank's Diner	◈◈	American	$6-$19	192
② p. 187	Wasabi Bistro	◈◈	Asian Sushi	$7-$38	193
③ p. 187	The Old European Restaurant	◈◈	European Breakfast	$7-$12	193
④ p. 187	Tomato Street	◈◈	Italian	$10-$20	193
⑤ p. 187	Thai Bamboo	◈◈	Thai	$10-$20	193
⑥ p. 187	The Mustard Seed Asian Cafe	◈◈	Asian	$8-$20	193
⑦ p. 187	The Cathay Inn	◈◈	Chinese	$9-$20	192
⑧ p. 187	Clinkerdagger	◈◈◈	American	$8-$48	192
⑨ p. 187	Anthony's Restaurant	◈◈◈	Seafood	$12-$43	192
⑩ p. 187	The Rusty Moose Bar & Grill	◈◈	American	$13-$30	193
⑪ p. 187	O'Doherty's Irish Grill	◈◈	Irish	$7-$18	193
⑫ p. 187	Twigs Bistro & Martini Bar	◈◈◈	International	$11-$34	193
⑬ p. 187	P.F. Chang's China Bistro	◈◈◈	Chinese	$9-$28	193
⑭ p. 187	Mizuna Restaurant & Wine Bar	◈◈	International	$12-$36	193
⑮ p. 187	Table 13	◈◈◈	American	$22-$38	193
⑯ p. 187	La Costa Azteca Mexican Restaurant	◈◈	Mexican	$8-$23	193
⑰ p. 187	Elk Public House	◈◈	American	$7-$13	192
⑱ p. 187	Santé Restaurant & Charcuterie	◈◈◈	Continental	$6-$29	193
⑲ p. 187	Madeleine's Cafe & Patisserie	◈	French	$8-$20	193
⑳ p. 187	Italia Trattoria	◈◈◈	Italian	$10-$27	193
㉑ p. 187	Luigi's	◈◈	Italian	$14-$33	193
㉒ p. 187	Herbal Essence Cafe	◈◈◈	American	$8-$30	192
㉓ p. 187	Post Street Ale House	◈◈	American	$9-$15	193
㉔ p. 187	Domini Sandwiches	◈	Sandwiches	$8-$14	192
㉕ p. 187	Italian Kitchen	◈◈	Italian	$10-$31	193
㉖ p. 187	The Onion	◈◈	American	$7-$26	193
㉗ p. 187	Chicken-N-Mo	◈	American	$5-$19	192
㉘ p. 187	Frank's Diner	◈◈	American	$7-$14	192
㉙ p. 187	Palm Court Grill	◈◈◈	American	$10-$46	193
㉚ p. 187	Thai on 1st	◈◈	Thai	$11-$30	193
㉛ p. 187	Europa Pizzaria & Bakery	◈◈◈	Italian	$9-$25	192
㉜ p. 187	Steam Plant Grill	◈◈	New American	$14-$40	193
㉝ p. 187	Churchill's Steakhouse	◈◈◈	Steak	$29-$65	192
㉞ p. 187	Wild Sage American Bistro	◈◈◈	Regional Pacific Northwest	$16-$42	193
㉟ p. 187	Ginger	◈◈	Asian Sushi	$7-$22	192

Map Page	Restaurants (cont'd)	Diamond Rated	Cuisine	Price Range	Page
36 p. 187	Gordy's Sichuan Cafe	♦♦	Chinese	$7-$22	192
37 p. 187	Spencer's for Steaks & Chops	♦♦♦	Steak	$25-$65	193
38 p. 187	Tortilla Union Southwest Grill	♦♦	Southwestern	$10-$15	193

SPOKANE VALLEY

Map Page	Hotels	Diamond Rated	Rate Range	Page
26 p. 187	La Quinta Inn & Suites Spokane Valley	♦♦♦	$79-$159	194
27 p. 187	Super 8	♦♦	$58-$122	194
28 p. 187	Baymont Inn & Suites	♦♦	$99-$139	194
29 p. 187	Fairfield Inn & Suites Spokane Valley	♦♦♦	$75-$186	194
30 p. 187	Holiday Inn Express-Valley	♦♦♦	Rates not provided	194
31 p. 187	Comfort Inn & Suites at Spokane Valley	♦♦♦	$84-$188	194
32 p. 187	**Oxford Suites Spokane Valley**	♦♦♦	$85-$755 [SAVE]	194
33 p. 187	**Residence Inn by Marriott**	♦♦♦	$90-$261 [SAVE]	194
34 p. 187	**Mirabeau Park Hotel & Convention Center**	♦♦♦	Rates not provided [SAVE]	194
35 p. 187	My Place Hotel-Spokane Valley	♦♦	Rates not provided	194
36 p. 187	Hampton Inn & Suites by Hilton Spokane Valley	♦♦♦	Rates not provided	194

Map Page	Restaurants	Diamond Rated	Cuisine	Price Range	Page
39 p. 187	Ambrosia Bistro & Wine Bar	♦♦♦	International	$12-$29	194
40 p. 187	Casa De Oro	♦♦	Mexican	$11-$19	194
41 p. 187	Twigs Bistro & Martini Bar	♦♦♦	American	$11-$37	194
42 p. 187	MAX at Mirabeau Restaurant & Lounge	♦♦♦	American	$8-$40	194

AIRWAY HEIGHTS

Map Page	Hotel	Diamond Rated	Rate Range	Page
39 p. 187	**Northern Quest Resort & Casino**	♦♦♦♦	$179-$369 [SAVE]	36

Map Page	Restaurant	Diamond Rated	Cuisine	Price Range	Page
46 p. 187	**Masselow's Steakhouse**	♦♦♦♦	Pacific Northwest	$23-$53	36

1908 MARIANNA STOLTZ HOUSE BED & BREAKFAST
(509)483-4316 **3**
♦♦ Historic Bed & Breakfast. **Address:** 427 E Indiana Ave 99207

BEST WESTERN PLUS CITY CENTER
(509)623-9727 **13**

♦♦
Hotel
$95-$295

Address: 33 W Spokane Falls Blvd 99201 **Location:** I-90 exit 281 (Division St), 0.5 mi n, then just w. **Facility:** 81 units. 4 stories, interior corridors. **Terms:** cancellation fee imposed. **Activities:** exercise room. **Guest Services:** coin laundry. **Featured Amenity:** breakfast buffet.

BEST WESTERN PLUS PEPPERTREE AIRPORT INN
(509)624-4655 **23**

♦♦♦
Hotel
$99-$399

Address: 3711 S Geiger Blvd 99224 **Location:** I-90 exit 276 (Geiger Field), 1.3 mi n, 0.8 mi s, 0.4 mi e, then just s. **Facility:** 100 units, some efficiencies. 3 stories, interior corridors. **Terms:** check-in 4 pm. **Pool:** heated indoor. **Activities:** hot tub, exercise room. **Guest Services:** valet and coin laundry, area transportation.

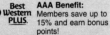

CENTENNIAL HOTEL SPOKANE   509/326-8000 **4**
♦♦♦ Hotel. **Address:** 303 W North River Dr 99201

(See map & index p. 187.)

COURTYARD BY MARRIOTT SPOKANE DOWNTOWN AT THE CONVENTION CENTER
(509)456-7600 **10**

WWW Hotel. **Address:** 401 N River-
point Blvd 99202

AAA Benefit:
Members save 5%
or more!

THE DAVENPORT GRAND, AUTOGRAPH COLLECTION
(509)458-3330 **11**

Hotel
$92-$333

AUTOGRAPH
COLLECTION®
HOTELS

AAA Benefit:
Members save 5%
or more!

Address: 333 W Spokane Falls Blvd
99201 **Location:** At N Washington St;
downtown. Across from convention
center. **Facility:** The Davenport Group's
newest hotel, located downtown right
next to the convention center, offers contemporary and luxurious rooms. Relax
by the fire pits outside on the deck area
during a cool night. 716 units. 2-16 stories, interior corridors. **Parking:** on-site
(fee) and valet. **Terms:** check-in 4 pm, cancellation fee imposed,
resort fee. **Amenities:** safes. **Dining:** 2 restaurants, also, Table
13, see separate listing. **Activities:** bicycles, exercise room.
Guest Services: valet laundry, area transportation.

SAVE 🔌 ➡️ 🍴 ▼ CALL 🧑‍🦽 👨‍👩‍👧 BIZ HS
🛜 ✖️ 🎦 💻 /SOME UNITS 🛗 🖨️

THE DAVENPORT LUSSO, AUTOGRAPH COLLECTION
(509)747-9750 **14**

**Historic Boutique
Hotel**
$95-$306

AUTOGRAPH
COLLECTION®
HOTELS

AAA Benefit:
Members save 5%
or more!

Address: 808 W Sprague Ave 99201
Location: At Post St; downtown. **Facility:** This luxurious boutique hotel is in
the heart of downtown. You'll find quaint
hallways leading to rooms with decorative furnishings. The bathrooms are tiled
from floor to ceiling. 48 units. 5 stories,
interior corridors. **Parking:** on-site (fee)
and street. **Terms:** check-in 4 pm, cancellation fee imposed, resort fee. **Ame-
nities:** safes. **Dining:** Post Street Ale House, see separate
listing. **Activities:** exercise room. **Guest Services:** valet laundry,
area transportation.

SAVE ➡️ 🍴 ▼ CALL 🧑‍🦽 👨‍👩‍👧 BIZ 🛜 ✖️ 🎦
🛗 💻 /SOME UNITS 🖨️

THE DAVENPORT TOWER, AUTOGRAPH COLLECTION
(509)789-6965 **16**

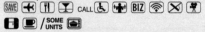
Hotel
$90-$315

AUTOGRAPH
COLLECTION®
HOTELS

AAA Benefit:
Members save 5%
or more!

Address: 111 S Post St 99201 **Location:** Center. **Facility:** This impressive
hotel sports a fun and elegant safari
motif with rich marble floors, stained
glass and custom-built furniture. 328
units. 21 stories, interior corridors.
Parking: on-site (fee) and valet. **Terms:**
check-in 4 pm, cancellation fee imposed,
resort fee. **Amenities:** safes. **Pool:**
heated indoor. **Activities:** hot tub, bicycles, exercise room. **Guest Services:** valet laundry, area
transportation.

SAVE ➡️ 🍴 👨‍👩‍👧 ▼ CALL 🧑‍🦽 � 👨‍👩‍👧 BIZ HS
🛜 ✖️ 🎦 💻 /SOME UNITS 🛗 🖨️

DOUBLETREE BY HILTON SPOKANE CITY CENTER
(509)455-9600 **9**

WWW Hotel. **Address:** 322 N Spokane Falls Ct 99201

AAA Benefit:
Members save 5%
or more!

FAIRFIELD INN & SUITES BY MARRIOTT SPOKANE DOWNTOWN
(509)747-9131 **12**

WWW Hotel. **Address:** 311 N River-
point Blvd 99202

AAA Benefit:
Members save 5%
or more!

HAMPTON INN BY HILTON SPOKANE AIRPORT
(509)747-1100 **21**

Hotel
$123-$385

AAA Benefit:
Members save 5%
or more!

Address: 2010 S Assembly Rd 99224
Location: I-90 exit 277A eastbound, 1 mi
ne to Sunset Hwy, just w to Assembly Rd,
then just s; exit 277 westbound, just e to
Rustle St, just n to Sunset Hwy, just w to
Assembly Rd, then just s. **Facility:** 129
units. 3 stories, interior corridors. **Terms:**
check-in 4 pm, 1-7 night minimum stay, 3
day cancellation notice-fee imposed.
Pool: heated indoor. **Activities:** hot tub,
exercise room. **Guest Services:** valet and coin laundry, area
transportation. **Featured Amenity: full hot breakfast.**

SAVE 🔌 ➡️ 🍴 CALL 🧑‍🦽 🚏 👨‍👩‍👧 BIZ 🛜 ✖️
🎦 🛗 🖨️ 💻

HILTON GARDEN INN SPOKANE AIRPORT
(509)244-5866 **8**

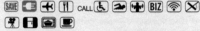
Hotel
$112-$308

Hilton
Garden Inn

AAA Benefit:
Members save 5%
or more!

Address: 9015 W Hwy 2 99224 **Location:** I-90 exit 277B eastbound; exit 277
westbound, 3 mi w. **Facility:** 120 units. 3
stories, interior corridors. **Terms:**
check-in 4 pm, 1-7 night minimum stay,
3 day cancellation notice-fee imposed.
Pool: heated indoor. **Activities:** hot tub,
exercise room. **Guest Services:** coin
laundry, area transportation.

SAVE 🔌 ➡️ 🍴 ▼ CALL 🧑‍🦽
🚏 👨‍👩‍👧 BIZ HS 🛜 ✖️ 🛗 🖨️ 💻

(See map & index p. 187.)

THE HISTORIC DAVENPORT HOTEL, AUTOGRAPH COLLECTION
(509)455-8888 **15**

Classic Historic Hotel
$116-$380

AUTOGRAPH COLLECTION® HOTELS **AAA Benefit:** Members save 5% or more!

Address: 10 S Post St 99201 **Location:** Downtown. **Facility:** Built in 1914, this Grand Old Lady has been restored to all its original and impressive glory. The rooms are adorned in elegant furnishings and boast upscale artwork. 284 units, some two and three bedrooms. 3-12 stories, interior corridors. **Parking:** on-site (fee) and valet. **Terms:** check-in 4 pm, cancellation fee imposed, resort fee. **Amenities:** safes. **Dining:** Palm Court Grill, see separate listing. **Pool:** heated indoor. **Activities:** hot tub, bicycles, exercise room, spa. **Guest Services:** valet laundry, area transportation.

`SAVE` `ECO` `[symbols]` `CALL` `/SOME UNITS` `[symbols]`

HOLIDAY INN EXPRESS-DOWNTOWN   (509)328-8505 **5**
Hotel. **Address:** 801 N Division St 99202

HOLIDAY INN SPOKANE AIRPORT   509/838-1170 **17**
Hotel. **Address:** 1616 S Windsor Dr 99224

THE MADISON INN BY RIVERSAGE   509/474-4200 **22**
Hotel. **Address:** 15 W Rockwood Blvd 99204

OXFORD SUITES-DOWNTOWN SPOKANE
(509)353-9000 **6**

Hotel
$89-$755

Address: 115 W North River Dr 99201 **Location:** I-90 exit 281 (Division St), 1 mi n, then just n. Adjacent to Centennial Trail. **Facility:** 125 units, some two bedrooms and efficiencies. 5 stories, interior corridors. **Terms:** 2-14 night minimum stay - seasonal and/or weekends, 31 day cancellation notice-fee imposed. **Pool:** heated indoor. **Activities:** sauna, hot tub, steamroom, exercise room. **Guest Services:** valet and coin laundry, area transportation. **Featured Amenity:** breakfast buffet.

`SAVE` `[symbols]` `BIZ` `HS` `[symbols]`

`/SOME UNITS` `[symbol]`

QUALITY INN DOWNTOWN 4TH AVENUE
(509)838-6101 **18**

Hotel
$88-$168

Address: 110 E 4th Ave 99202 **Location:** I-90 exit 281 (Division St), just n to 2nd Ave, just w to Browne St, just s to 4th Ave W, then just e. **Facility:** 132 units, some two bedrooms. 6 stories, interior corridors. **Pool:** heated outdoor. **Activities:** exercise room. **Guest Services:** valet and coin laundry, area transportation. **Featured Amenity:** breakfast buffet.

`SAVE` `[symbols]` `CALL` `[symbols]` `BIZ` `[symbols]`

🔗 **Get member rates and reservations at AAA.com/hertz**

QUALITY INN OAKWOOD
(509)467-4900 **1**

Hotel
$95-$205

Address: 7919 N Division St 99208 **Location:** I-90 exit 281 (Division St), 6.5 mi n. **Facility:** 128 units, some two bedrooms. 3 stories, interior corridors. **Terms:** check-in 4 pm. **Pool:** heated indoor. **Activities:** hot tub, exercise room. **Guest Services:** valet and coin laundry. **Featured Amenity:** full hot breakfast.

`SAVE` `[symbols]` `BIZ` `[symbols]` `/SOME UNITS`

RAMADA AT SPOKANE AIRPORT   (509)838-5211 **20**
Hotel. **Address:** 8909 Airport Dr 99224

RAMADA NORTH SPOKANE   (509)467-7111 **2**
Hotel. **Address:** 7111 N Division St 99208

RED LION RIVER INN-SPOKANE   509/326-5577 **7**
Hotel. **Address:** 700 N Division St 99202

WINGATE BY WYNDHAM SPOKANE AIRPORT
(509)838-3226 **19**
Hotel. **Address:** 2726 S Flint Rd 99201

WHERE TO EAT

ANTHONY'S RESTAURANT   509/328-9009 **9**
Seafood. Casual Dining. **Address:** 510 N Lincoln St 99201

THE CATHAY INN   509/326-2226 **7**
Chinese. Casual Dining. **Address:** 3714 N Division St 99207

CHICKEN-N-MO   509/838-5071 **27**
American. Quick Serve. **Address:** 414 1/2 W Sprague 99201

CHURCHILL'S STEAKHOUSE   509/474-9888 **33**
Steak. Fine Dining. **Address:** 165 S Post St 99201

CLINKERDAGGER   509/328-5965 **8**
American. Fine Dining. **Address:** 621 W Mallon St 99201

DOMINI SANDWICHES   509/747-2324 **24**
Sandwiches. Quick Serve. **Address:** 703 W Sprague Ave 99201

ELK PUBLIC HOUSE   509/363-1973 **17**
American. Casual Dining. **Address:** 1931 W Pacific Ave 99204

EUROPA PIZZARIA & BAKERY   509/455-4051 **31**
Italian. Casual Dining. **Address:** 125 S Wall St 99201

FRANK'S DINER   509/747-8798 **28**
American. Casual Dining. **Address:** 1516 W 2nd Ave 99201

FRANK'S DINER   509/465-2464 **1**
American. Casual Dining. **Address:** 10929 N Newport Hwy 99218

GINGER   509/315-5201 **35**
Asian Sushi. Casual Dining. **Address:** 1228 S Grand Blvd 99202

GORDY'S SICHUAN CAFE   509/747-1170 **36**
Chinese. Casual Dining. **Address:** 501 E 30th Ave 99203

HERBAL ESSENCE CAFE   509/838-4600 **22**
American. Casual Dining. **Address:** 115 N Washington St 99201

(See map & index p. 187.)

ITALIAN KITCHEN 509/363-1210 ㉕
♦♦ Italian. Casual Dining. **Address:** 113 N Bernard St 99201

ITALIA TRATTORIA 509/459-6000 ⑳
♦♦♦ Italian. Casual Dining. **Address:** 144 S Cannon St 99201

LA COSTA AZTECA MEXICAN RESTAURANT
509/456-0350 ⑯
♦♦ Mexican. Casual Dining. **Address:** 245 W Spokane Falls Blvd 99201

LATAH BISTRO 509/838-8338
♦♦ Regional American. Casual Dining. **Address:** 4241 S Cheney-Spokane Rd, Suite C 99224

LUIGI'S 509/624-5226 ㉑
♦♦ Italian. Casual Dining. **Address:** 245 W Main Ave 99202

LUNA 509/448-2383
♦♦♦ Regional American. Casual Dining. **Address:** 5620 S Perry St 99223

MACKENZIE RIVER PIZZA 509/315-9466
♦♦ Pizza. Casual Dining. **Address:** 2910 E 57th Ave, Suite E 99223

MADELEINE'S CAFE & PATISSERIE 509/624-2253 ⑲
♦ French. Quick Serve. **Address:** 415 W Main Ave 99201

MIZUNA RESTAURANT & WINE BAR 509/747-2004 ⑭
♦♦ International. Casual Dining. **Address:** 214 N Howard St 99201

THE MUSTARD SEED ASIAN CAFE 509/483-1500 ⑥
♦ Asian. Casual Dining. **Address:** 4750 N Division St 99207

O'DOHERTY'S IRISH GRILL 509/747-0322 ⑪
♦ Irish. Casual Dining. **Address:** 525 W Spokane Falls Blvd 99201

THE OLD EUROPEAN RESTAURANT 509/467-5987 ③
♦♦ European Breakfast. Casual Dining. **Address:** 7640 N Division St 99208

THE ONION 509/747-3852 ㉖
♦♦ American. Casual Dining. **Address:** 302 W Riverside Ave 99201

PALM COURT GRILL 509/789-6848 ㉙
♦♦♦ American. Fine Dining. **Address:** 10 S Post St 99201

P.F. CHANG'S CHINA BISTRO 509/456-2166 ⑬
♦♦ Chinese. Fine Dining. **Address:** 801 W Main Ave 99201

POST STREET ALE HOUSE 509/789-6900 ㉓
♦♦ American. Casual Dining. **Address:** 1 N Post St 99201

ROCK CITY GRILL 509/455-4400
♦♦ International. Casual Dining. **Address:** 2911 E 57th Ave 99223

THE RUSTY MOOSE BAR & GRILL 509/747-5579 ⑩
♦♦ American. Casual Dining. **Address:** 9105 W SR 2 99224

SANTÉ RESTAURANT & CHARCUTERIE 509/315-4613 ⑱
♦♦ Continental. Casual Dining. **Address:** 404 W Main Ave 99201

SPENCER'S FOR STEAKS & CHOPS 509/744-2372 ㊲
♦♦♦ Steak. Fine Dining. **Address:** 322 N Spokane Falls Ct 99201

STEAM PLANT GRILL 509/777-3900 ㉜
♦♦ New American. Casual Dining. **Address:** 159 S Lincoln St 99201

TABLE 13 509/598-4300 ⑮
♦♦♦ American. Fine Dining. **Address:** 333 W Spokane Falls Blvd 99201

THAI BAMBOO 509/777-8424 ⑤
♦♦ Thai. Casual Dining. **Address:** 5406 N Division St 99207

THAI ON 1ST 509/455-4288 ㉚
♦♦ Thai. Casual Dining. **Address:** 411 W 1st Ave 99201

TOMATO STREET 509/484-4500 ④
♦♦ Italian. Casual Dining. **Address:** 6220 N Division St 99207

TORTILLA UNION SOUTHWEST GRILL 509/381-5162 ㊳
♦♦ Southwestern. Casual Dining. **Address:** 808 W Main Ave 99201

TWIGS BISTRO & MARTINI BAR 509/232-3376 ⑫
♦♦♦ International. Casual Dining. **Address:** 808 W Main Ave 99201

TWIGS BISTRO & MARTINI BAR 509/465-8794
♦♦ International. Casual Dining. **Address:** 401 E Farwell Rd 99218

TWIGS BISTRO & MARTINI BAR 509/443-8000
♦♦ American. Casual Dining. **Address:** 4320 S Regal St 99223

WASABI BISTRO 509/290-5699 ②
♦♦ Asian Sushi. Casual Dining. **Address:** 10208 N Division St, Suite 105 99208

WILD SAGE AMERICAN BISTRO 509/456-7575 ㉞
♦♦♦ Regional Pacific Northwest. Casual Dining. **Address:** 916 W 2nd Ave 99201

SPOKANE VALLEY (E-12) pop. 89,755, elev. 2,020'

- **Hotels p. 194 • Restaurants p. 194**
- **Hotels & Restaurants map & index p. 187**

The eastern suburbs of Spokane, including the communities of Opportunity, Dishman, Greenacres and Veradale, formed the city of Spokane Valley in 2003. The paved Centennial Trail passes through the city, and float trips on the Spokane River are popular in summer.

Greater Spokane Valley Chamber of Commerce: 1421 N. Meadowwood Ln., Suite 10, Liberty Lake, WA 99019. **Phone:** (509) 924-4994 or (866) 475-1436.

Shopping: The anchor stores at Spokane Valley Mall, I-90 exit 291 at 14700 E. Indiana Ave., are JC-Penney, Macy's and Sears.

SPLASHDOWN FAMILY WATERPARK is off I-90 exit 289, then s. to 11127 E. Mission Ave. in Valley Mission Park. Nine water slides and a children's play area help visitors of all ages beat the heat; two hot tubs also are available. **Hours:** Mon.-Sat. 11-6 (also Tues. and Thurs. 6-8 p.m.), Sun. noon-6, mid-June through Labor Day; Sat. 11-6, Sun. noon-6, Memorial Day weekend to mid-June. The park does not operate on cloudy days when the air temperature is below 70 degrees; phone ahead to confirm. **Cost:** $20 (spectators receive $5 refundable deposit); $15 (under 48 inches tall); free (ages 0-3 and 65+ with

(See map & index p. 187.)

ID). Tues. and Thurs. 4-8 p.m. $9; free (ages 0-3 and 65+ with ID). **Phone:** (509) 924-3079. [T|]

BAYMONT INN & SUITES (509)922-9002 **28**
[▼▼] Hotel. **Address:** 2016 N Argonne Rd 99212

COMFORT INN & SUITES AT SPOKANE VALLEY
(509)926-7432 **31**
[▼▼▼] Hotel. **Address:** 12415 E Mission Ave 99216

FAIRFIELD INN & SUITES SPOKANE VALLEY
(509)928-5218 **29**
[▼▼▼] Hotel. **Address:** 8923 E Mission Ave 99212

AAA Benefit:
Members save 5% or more!

HAMPTON INN & SUITES BY HILTON SPOKANE VALLEY
509/928-6900 **36**
[▼▼▼] Hotel. **Address:** 16418 E Indiana Ave 99216

AAA Benefit:
Members save 5% or more!

HOLIDAY INN EXPRESS-VALLEY 509/927-7100 **30**
[▼▼▼] Hotel. **Address:** 9220 E Mission Ave 99206

LA QUINTA INN & SUITES SPOKANE VALLEY
(509)893-0955 **26**
[▼▼▼] Hotel. **Address:** 3808 N Sullivan Rd 99216

MIRABEAU PARK HOTEL & CONVENTION CENTER
509/924-9000 **34**
[▼▼▼] Hotel. Rates not provided

Address: 1100 N Sullivan Rd 99037 **Location:** I-90 exit 291B, just s. **Facility:** 235 units, some kitchens. 2-3 stories, interior corridors. **Amenities:** safes. **Pool:** heated outdoor. **Activities:** hot tub, exercise room. **Guest Services:** valet and coin laundry, area transportation.

[SAVE] [◄►] [T|] [🛏] [Y] [▶] [♿]
[BIZ] [🛜] [✕] [🗄] [📷] [📶]
[/SOME UNITS] [🐾] [HS]

MY PLACE HOTEL-SPOKANE VALLEY 509/228-6105 **35**
[▼▼] Extended Stay Hotel. **Address:** 16106 E Indiana Ave 99216

OXFORD SUITES SPOKANE VALLEY
(509)847-1000 **32**
[▼▼▼] Hotel. $85-$755

Address: 15015 E Indiana Ave 99216 **Location:** I-90 exit 291A eastbound; exit 291B westbound, just nw. Across from Spokane Valley Mall. **Facility:** 129 units. 5 stories, interior corridors. **Terms:** check-in 4 pm, 2-14 night minimum stay - seasonal and/or weekends, 31 day cancellation notice-fee imposed. **Pool:** heated indoor. **Activities:** sauna, hot tub, steamroom, exercise room. **Guest Services:** valet and coin laundry, area transportation. **Featured Amenity:** breakfast buffet.

[SAVE] [🍽] [◄►] [T|] [Y] CALL [♿]
[▶] [♿] [BIZ] [HS] [🛜] [✕] [🗄]
[📷] [📶] [/SOME UNITS] [🐾]

RESIDENCE INN BY MARRIOTT (509)892-9300 **33**

Extended Stay Hotel $90-$261

Residence INN. **AAA Benefit:**
Members save 5% or more!

Address: 15915 E Indiana Ave 99216 **Location:** I-90 exit 291 westbound, just e; exit 291B eastbound, just n, then just e. **Facility:** 84 units, some two bedrooms, efficiencies and kitchens. 3 stories, interior corridors. **Parking:** winter plug-ins. **Terms:** cancellation fee imposed. **Pool:** heated indoor. **Activities:** hot tub, bicycles, exercise room. **Guest Services:** valet and coin laundry.

[SAVE] [T|] CALL [♿] [▶] [♿] [BIZ] [🛜] [✕] [🗄] [📷]
[📶] [/SOME UNITS] [🐾]

SUPER 8 (509)928-4888 **27**
[▼▼] Motel. **Address:** 2020 N Argonne Rd 99212

WHERE TO EAT

AMBROSIA BISTRO & WINE BAR 509/928-3222 **39**
[▼▼▼] International. Casual Dining. **Address:** 9211 E Montgomery Ave 99206

CASA DE ORO 509/921-2122 **40**
[▼▼] Mexican. Casual Dining. **Address:** 1611 N Mullan Rd 99206

MAX AT MIRABEAU RESTAURANT & LOUNGE
509/922-6252 **42**
[▼▼▼] American. Casual Dining. **Address:** 1100 N Sullivan Rd 99037

TWIGS BISTRO & MARTINI BAR 509/290-5636 **41**
[▼▼▼] American. Casual Dining. **Address:** 14728 E Indiana Ave 99216

STEVENSON pop. 1,465, elev. 103'

The Upper Cascades of the Columbia River, 2 miles west of Stevenson, were the site of a portage where pioneers reassembled their wagons after rafting down the river from The Dalles, Ore. After steamboats began to ply the upper river, the town of Upper Cascades served as the transfer point from steamboat to portage for all traffic between Portland and the Inland Empire.

Skamania County Chamber of Commerce: 167 N.W. 2nd Ave., P.O. Box 1037, Stevenson, WA 98648. **Phone:** (509) 427-8911 or (800) 989-9178.

[▼GEM] **COLUMBIA GORGE INTERPRETIVE CENTER MUSEUM**—see Columbia River Gorge National Scenic Area p. 55.

SKAMANIA LODGE

509/427-7700

Resort Hotel
Rates not provided

Address: 1131 SW Skamania Lodge Way 98648 **Location:** 1 mi w on SR 14, just n on Rock Creek Dr, then just w. **Facility:** Settle in for a lazy weekend and enjoy the food, recreation and tranquility of this peaceful retreat. The panoramic views are delightful. Some guest rooms have balconies. 258 units, some cabins. 4 stories, interior corridors. **Parking:** on-site and valet. **Terms:** check-in 4 pm. **Dining:** 2 restaurants. **Pool:** heated indoor. **Activities:** sauna, hot tub, fishing, regulation golf, tennis, recreation programs, bicycles, playground, exercise room, spa.

WHERE TO EAT

BIG RIVER GRILL   509/427-4888
American. Casual Dining. **Address:** 192 SW 2nd St 98648

THE CASCADE DINING ROOM   509/427-2508
Pacific Northwest. Casual Dining. **Address:** 1131 SW Skamania Lodge Way 98648

WALKING MAN BREWING   509/427-5520
American. Brewpub. **Address:** 240 SW 1st St 98648

SUNNYSIDE (G-9) pop. 15,858, elev. 743'

Sunnyside is known as the asparagus capital of the Northwest, although local farms and orchards produce more than 50 other crops, including grapes processed in area wineries. The 1859 Ben Snipes Cabin, across the street from the Sunnyside Historical Museum, was built by a pioneer cattleman and is reputedly the oldest homestead in the Yakima Valley. A statue of Snipes stands near the cabin. The Sunnyside State Wildlife Recreation Area, south of the city off SR 241 and McGee Road, occupies land along the Yakima River and is a haven for shorebirds.

BEST WESTERN PLUS GRAPEVINE INN (509)839-6070

Hotel
$120-$140

AAA Benefit: Members save up to 15% and earn bonus points!

Address: 1849 Quail Ln 98944 **Location:** I-82 exit 69, just nw. **Facility:** 54 units, some kitchens. 2 stories, interior corridors. **Terms:** cancellation fee imposed. **Pool:** heated indoor. **Activities:** hot tub, picnic facilities, exercise room. **Guest Services:** coin laundry.

WHERE TO EAT

GREEN OLIVE CAFE   509/837-9009
American. Casual Dining. **Address:** 2926 Covey Ln 98944

SNIPES MOUNTAIN BREWERY & RESTAURANT
                                               509/837-2739
American. Brewpub. **Address:** 905 Yakima Valley Hwy 98944

SUQUAMISH (E-2) pop. 4,140, elev. 202'

- Hotels & Restaurants map & index p. 170
- Part of Seattle area — see map p. 124

Suquamish Memorial Cemetery is the burial site of one of the most important Native American leaders of the Northwest—Chief Sealth, better known today as Chief Seattle. Sealth's father, Schweabe, was a Suquamish chief; his mother was the daughter of a Duwamish chief.

As a young man Sealth gained renown as a warrior and leader, controlling regional tribes but maintaining friendly relations with early American and European settlers, protecting them from Native American attack. He also formed a personal friendship with local entrepreneur David Swinson "Doc" Maynard. Chief Sealth died in 1866 at the age of 80. In honor of their friendship, Maynard urged other settlers to name in his honor the fledgling community that later became the city and seaport of Seattle.

An interpretive marker at the west end of Agate Pass off SR 305 marks the former site of The Old Man House, which once housed eight Native American chiefs and their families.

SUQUAMISH MUSEUM, 6861 N.E. South St., depicts the history and culture of the Suquamish tribe through photographs, manuscripts and interactive exhibits in a modern building. Particularly fascinating are the audio and visual elements, which integrate Lushootseed, the language of the Suquamish and other Coast Salish tribes.

Time: Allow 30 minutes minimum. **Hours:** Daily 10-5. Closed Jan. 1, July 4, Thanksgiving and Christmas. **Cost:** $5; $3 (ages 5-17 and 55+); $15 (family). **Phone:** (360) 394-8499.

SUQUAMISH CLEARWATER CASINO RESORT

(360)598-8700 6

Hotel
$109-$279

Address: 15347 Suquamish Way 98392 **Location:** Waterfront. SR 3 exit SR 305, 6.2 mi se. **Facility:** The hotel is divided into two sections. Choose one of the modern rooms in the beautiful tower area or classic room with views in the quieter resort building. 184 units, some two bedrooms and houses. 4-6 stories, interior corridors. **Terms:** check-in 4 pm, cancellation fee imposed. **Amenities:** safes. **Dining:** 5 restaurants, entertainment. **Pool:** heated indoor. **Activities:** hot tub, exercise room, spa. **Guest Services:** area transportation.

TACOMA (E-6) pop. 198,397, elev. 87'

- Hotels p. 203 • Restaurants p. 204
- Hotels & Restaurants map & index p. 201
- Part of Seattle area — see map p. 124

Tacoma is defined in part by a nickname: "The City of Destiny." Early settlers coined the name in hopes

(See map & index p. 201.)

that their community—established in 1852 when a Swedish immigrant built a water-powered sawmill on a creek near the head of Commencement Bay—would rise to greatness by being designated the end of the line for the Northern Pacific Railroad. The bay was indeed chosen as the western terminus in 1873, but the company built its depot on a spot 2 miles south, dubbing it "New Tacoma." By the time the transcontinental link finally came through in 1887 the two towns had merged to become one Tacoma.

"The aroma of Tacoma" is another sobriquet. The Tacoma copper smelter operated by the American Smelting and Refining Company (ASARCO) was finally shut down in 1985 due to its controversial arsenic emissions (the site is being cleaned up for redevelopment, including the waterfront area at Point Defiance Park), but the paper mills that are still a defining part of the downtown waterfront continue to provide olfactory proof.

"Diamond in the rough," however, best describes Tacoma today, since it's often overlooked by travelers who are more familiar with the Space Needle, Pike Place Market and Pioneer Square than the Bridge of Glass, the Spanish Steps and Bob's Java Jive. For one thing, glass sculptor extraordinaire Dale Chihuly is a Tacoma native. His abstract blown-glass creations—explosions of color and shape inspired in part by the plants and flowers in his mother's garden—are exhibited in museums, galleries and public spaces around the world.

The artist lives and works in a studio on Seattle's Lake Union but maintains close ties with his home-town, and the city thus boasts a bevy of Chihuly installations that can be explored on a guided or self-guiding walking excursion. If you want to learn a little more about the man and his art, take the "Ear for Art" cellphone tour, which features audio commentary by the artist at 13 tour stops (enter the three-digit number listed on the Ear for Art label at each stop). To begin the tour, dial (888) 411-4220. Guided tours of the installations are offered on select days each month by the Museum of Glass (see attraction listing p. 199).

Union Station was built in 1911 and functioned as a train station until the early 1980s. This copper-domed brick building currently serves as a federal courthouse, but inside there are five Chihuly installations. In particular, check out the orange glass flowers adorning the half moon-shaped Monarch Window on the second floor and the chandelier hanging from the skylight in the dome, which resembles a mass of writhing, multicolored snakes.

The Bridge of Glass passes over I-705, connecting the waterfront and Pacific Avenue. This pedestrian walkway is a must for Chihuly lovers. The display pieces individually showcased along the Venetian Wall conjure up everything from vases to decanters to Martian life forms, all rendered exquisitely in colored glass.

Tacoma is a great theater town, and the Theater District, centered along—aptly enough—Broadway, spotlights two grandly restored dames and a state-of-the-art facility, all under the banner of the

Broadway Center For the Performing Arts. The Pantages Theater (S. 9th Street and Broadway), built in 1918, was modeled after the lavishly opulent theater in the Palace of Versailles in France. Restored in 1983, it is home to the Tacoma Opera, the Tacoma City Ballet and the Tacoma Symphony Orchestra.

The Rialto Theater (a block up from the Pantages at S. 9th and Market streets), also restored, is a Beaux Arts jewel box of a building and former movie palace that presents performances by the Northwest Sinfonietta chamber orchestra and the Tacoma Youth Symphony, among others. The intimate Theatre on the Square, next to the Pantages, mounts an annual schedule of dramas, comedies and musicals. Close-to-the-stage seating, a come-as-you-are atmosphere and such events as "brewpub previews" all aim to make theatergoing an accessible experience here. Contact the Broadway Center for the Performing Arts for schedule, ticket information and details about free theater tours; phone (253) 591-5894 or (800) 291-7593.

Another artsy touch in the Theater District is the masks that are installed on the outside walls of surrounding buildings. The Woolworth Windows (on Broadway near the corner of S. 11th Street) houses cool art installations in a former Woolworth's five-and-dime store. The Tollbooth Gallery (corner of Broadway and S. 11th Street) is a street kiosk that provides a tiny space for offbeat, mixed-media installations.

Downtown Tacoma has reminders of the past, too. The Spanish Steps, the stairway that connects Broadway with Commerce Street below, were intended to be used as a fire escape. Designed after the Spanish Steps in Rome that climb from the Piazza di Spagna up to the Trinità dei Monti church, Tacoma's stairway was adorned with flowers and landscaping during its heyday, but over the course of decades time and city soot have both been unkind. The good news is that the steps are still around, the beneficiary of an ongoing renovation project. The tall, ancient-looking evergreen growing at the top of the steps is a Monkey Puzzle tree (Araucaria araucana), an ornamental native to Chile and Argentina.

Stadium High School, 111 N. E St. (between 1st Street and Division Avenue), was built in 1906 and was originally going to be a luxury hotel. The turreted brick walls and narrow windows give "the castle on the hill" a decidedly Gothic look. The sunken football stadium is where Heath Ledger serenaded Julia Stiles in the 1999 movie "10 Things I Hate About You," a remake of Shakespeare's "The Taming of the Shrew" set in a contemporary high school. And the vista looking out over Commencement Bay from the top of the bleachers is spectacular.

Local universities contribute significantly to Tacoma's vibrant performing arts scene, thanks to venues like the newly renovated Karen Hille Phillips Center for the Performing Arts at Pacific Lutheran University, 12180 Park Ave. S. The Pacific Lutheran University Jazz Ensemble performs at this state-of-the-art facility, on Red Square in the center of the campus. For information phone (253) 531-6900. The Jacobsen

(See map & index p. 201.)

Series, named in honor of the former chair of the Piano Department, brings classical and chamber music concerts to the University of Puget Sound, 1500 N. Warner St. Performances are given in the 500-seat Schneebeck Concert Hall, on campus at N. 14th Street and Union Avenue. For schedule information phone the Office of Public Events at (253) 879-3555; to purchase tickets phone (253) 879-6013.

Take advantage of Sound Transit's Tacoma Link light-rail system to explore the city. Link trains connect the Tacoma Dome station on E. 25th Street—a regional hub for bus and commuter train service—with stops at Union Station, the Convention Center and the Theater District—a convenient way to navigate downtown without driving. They run every 12 to 24 minutes Mon.-Fri. 5 a.m.-10 p.m., every 12 minutes Sat. 7:48 a.m.-10:10 p.m., and every 24 minutes Sun. and holidays 9:48-5:58. For more information phone (888) 889-6368.

Two local institutions stand out. Rather than a tempest in a teapot, Bob's Java Jive (2102 S. Tacoma Way) is a teapot plunked down in a rather grimy industrial neighborhood on the south side of town—which makes its offbeat charm stand out all the more. It's hard to find, but you can't miss this round white edifice complete with red spout and handle.

Above the door are the words "world famous," and Bob's certainly does have an intriguing past. It began life in 1927 as the Coffee Pot, a restaurant that during the Prohibition years had a little back room, accessed through a secret door, where patrons partook of liquor and gambling. A local businessman bought the restaurant in 1955 and renamed it the Java Jive after a popular jukebox selection by vocal group the Ink Spots. The teapot opens at 8 p.m., and for a mere $5 cover you get pool, pinball, darts, nightly karaoke, a "jungle room" (a jungle mural painted around an addition added to the back of the teapot), beer and rowdy rock 'n roll.

You can't miss the classic '50s-era neon sign sitting atop a candy-cane pole at Frisko Freeze, a walk-up hamburger stand at 1201 N. Division Ave. (3 blocks west of Wright Park). It opened in 1950—and little has changed since, from the time-honored menu of burgers, fries, onion rings and "fish wiches" to milk shakes so thick a spoon stands up with absolutely no problem. There are Seattleites who will drive 45 minutes out of their way for one of these shakes.

Since there's nary an outdoor seat at Frisko Freeze, you'll have to eat in your car. Better yet, get a milk shake to go and head down Division Avenue to Wright Park, a lovely green rectangle shaded by beautiful old trees. Amble along the paths and listen to the kids playing; this is the sort of genteel urban scene developers were aiming for when land donated to the city in 1886 was developed into a public park modeled after the classic English design.

Other parks take advantage of the city's scenic setting. Fireman's Park, 801 A St. at S. 8th Street, overlooks Commencement Bay and the Port of Tacoma. The park's 105-foot totem (82 feet stand above ground) was carved out of red cedar by Alaskan Indians in 1903. For more panoramic views of the bay, head to Ruston Way Park, where a 2-mile-long paved walkway runs along the waterfront between Point Defiance and the North Tacoma neighborhood. On clear days you can see Vashon Island and the Olympic Mountains. Anglers can drop their lines at Les Davis Pier and the Old Town Dock. For additional information phone Metro Parks Tacoma at (253) 305-1000.

Spectator sports? You can choose between professional baseball and ice hockey. The Tacoma Rainiers play class AAA Pacific Coast League baseball at Cheney Stadium; phone (253) 752-7707. For information about other events phone the Tacoma Dome ticket office at (253) 272-3663 or the event hotline at (253) 572-3663

Although Tacoma has long dwelled in Seattle's formidable shadow, it does trump its bigger sibling in at least one respect: the view of 14,411-foot Mount Rainier. While it's a prominent feature of the southern horizon in most of metro Seattle, the loftiest peak in the Cascade Range has—even on clear days—a surreal, somewhat ethereal presence, looking rather like a ghostly painting. But here there's no mistaking the mountain; it soars majestically above the City of Destiny, a definitive visual backdrop.

Travel Tacoma + Pierce County: 1516 Commerce St., Tacoma, WA 98402. **Phone:** (253) 284-3254 or (800) 272-2662.

Shopping: Antique Row is a concentration of more than a dozen shops along Broadway and St. Helens Avenue between S. 7th and S. 9th streets. Old Town, the original business district at McCarver Street and Ruston Way, has shops and restaurants. JCPenney, Macy's and Nordstrom are the anchor stores at Tacoma Mall, west of I-5 exits 130 and 131 on Tacoma Mall Boulevard.

The Proctor District, on N. Proctor and N. 26th streets, features more than 60 shops and restaurants. Freighthouse Square, 1 block north of the Tacoma Dome at 25th and East D streets, is a public market that features restaurants, specialty stores and a full calendar of events.

CHILDREN'S MUSEUM OF TACOMA, 1501 Pacific Ave., features hands-on displays and programs about literature, the arts and creative play. Changing interactive exhibits also are featured. **Time:** Allow 1 hour minimum. **Hours:** Wed.-Sun. 10-4 (also third Thurs. of the month 4-7). Closed Jan. 1, July 4, Labor Day, Thanksgiving, Christmas Eve and Christmas. **Cost:** Donations. **Phone:** (253) 627-6031. GT ⓘ 🅿 Convention Center/S 15th, 53

THE KARPELES MANUSCRIPT LIBRARY MUSEUM, 407 S. G St., preserves original handwritten documents and manuscripts created by noted historical figures. Exhibits change every 3 months. **Hours:** Tues.-Fri. 10-4. Closed major holidays. **Cost:** Free. **Phone:** (253) 383-2575. 🅿 Theater District/S 9th, 55

© 2018 HERE

Tacoma
Attractions

Scale in Miles

0.8   0   0.8

See p. 6 - Map Legend

RAPID TRANSIT STATION   STREET CAR STATION

50   50

For names of stations see
corresponding number on the
Seattle Mass Transit Map

2014-19

(See map & index p. 201.)

LEMAY—AMERICA'S CAR MUSEUM is n. of I-5 exit 133 (I-705 to the E. 26th St. exit) at 2702 E. D St., just w. of the Tacoma Dome. The 9-acre campus is a technologically advanced, inter-active automotive and education center. An international destination for families and auto enthusiasts, the museum explores and celebrates America's love affair with the automobile and how it shaped society.

The museum's centerpiece is the four-level, 165,000-square-foot main building. This cavernous, wood-ribbed space showcases hundreds of contem-porary and futuristic cars with brand names that span the more than 100-year history of the automobile. The four floors are accessed by ramps on each side of the showroom; walk down all four ramps on one side and back up the ramps on the opposite side so as not to miss any of the gleaming machines on dis-play. Exhibits and vehicles are rotated regularly.

The NAPA Auto Care Center is a garage area with multiple bays where visitors can view museum vehicles being preserved and prepared for displays, exhibits and events. The Speed Zone features

racing simulators and a slot car track. The 3.5-acre Haub Family Field is a multipurpose outdoor venue for car shows, auctions, swap meets, car club events, concerts and new model launches.

Time: Allow 2 hours minimum. **Hours:** Daily 10-5. Guided tours depart Mon.-Fri. at 11. Closes at 3 p.m. day before Thanksgiving and Dec. 24 and 31. Closed Thanksgiving and Christmas. Phone ahead to con-firm schedule. **Cost:** $18; $16 (ages 65+ and active military with ID); $14 (students with ID); $10 (ages 6-12). Racing simulator $8. Slot car track $3. All-Access Pit Pass (includes museum admission, two Speed Zone vouchers, store discount, 50 percent off Race Night admission and food voucher) $39; $34 (ages 6-12). **Parking:** $5 (up to 3 hours and after 5 p.m.); $10 (3-6 hours). **Phone:** (253) 779-8490 or (877) 902-8490. GT 🍴 ♿ Tacoma Dome, 50

THE LEMAY FAMILY COLLECTION FOUN-DATION is at 325 152nd St. E. Harold LeMay certainly loved cars, as he managed to amass more than 3,000 automobiles, trucks and motorcycles as well as countless items of vehicle-related memorabilia over a 40-year period. This

(See map & index p. 201.)

treasure trove is housed in several buildings on the 80-acre grounds of historic Marymount Academy. A number of the vehicles in this collection have been donated to LeMay—America's Car Museum *(see attraction listing).*

There's still plenty to see here, however. The guided tour takes you on a joy ride through a century of American-made cars, from vintage models like the 1931 Stutz Boattail Speedster to the muscle cars of the 1970s to such whimsical one-off designs as the SeaWorld Manta Ray, which suggests a future conveyance that might be used to explore the sea floor frontier.

Layered clothing and comfortable walking shoes are recommended for the guided tour. **Time:** Allow 2 hours minimum. **Hours:** Tues.-Sat. 9-5, Sun. noon-5. Last tour begins 2 hours before closing. Closed Thanksgiving, Christmas Eve and Christmas. **Cost:** $15; $12 (ages 65+ and active military with ID); $5 (ages 6-17); free (ages 0-5 and to all third Thurs. of the month 3-5). Reservations are recommended. **Phone:** (253) 272-2336. GT

MUSEUM OF GLASS is at 1801 Dock St. Housed in a striking building distinguished by a 90-foot-high cone sheathed in diamond-shaped stainless steel tiles, this art museum is exclusively devoted to changing exhibitions of contemporary and frequently edgy works executed in glass. One of the most enchanting exhibitions features kids' drawings brought to life as glass sculptures.

Within the cone is the Jane Russell Hot Shop, where visitors can watch glassblowers create beautiful works of art from molten glass. Outside, three outdoor plazas feature art installations, tranquil reflecting pools and views of the Thea Foss Waterway.

A highlight is Martin Blank's "Fluent Steps." Spanning the length of the 210-foot-long Main Plaza reflecting pool, 754 individually hand-sculpted pieces of glass form several islands of clear-glass sculpture. One glass grouping resembles mist rising from a meadow; another appears as a cascading waterfall. Appearances change frequently thanks to the interplay of light and shadow caused by the Pacific Northwest's frequently capricious weather.

Just past Howard Ben Tre's "Water Forest," a broad staircase winds around the cone, leading up to the rooftop plaza and the 500-foot-long Chihuly Bridge of Glass *(see attraction listing).* Visitors can walk across the bridge to other museums, shops and restaurants. One-hour walking tours of downtown Tacoma's Chihuly art installations are offered and depart from the museum.

Time: Allow 1 hour minimum. **Hours:** Mon.-Sat. 10-5 (also third Thurs. of the month 5-8), Sun. noon-5, Memorial Day weekend-Labor Day; Wed.-Sat. 10-5 (also third Thurs. of the month 5-8), Sun. noon-5, rest of year. Downtown walking tours offered on select days each month; phone for tour schedule. Closed Jan. 1, Thanksgiving and Christmas. **Cost:** $17; $14 (ages 65+ and students and military with ID); $5 (ages

6-12); free (ages 0-5, to all third Thurs. of the month 5-8 and to college students with ID Sun.). Downtown walking tour (includes museum admission) $27; $19 (ages 65+ and students and military with ID); $15 (ages 6-12). **Parking:** $5 (0-3 hours); $10 (all day). **Phone:** (253) 284-4750 or (866) 468-7386. GT 🍴 ♿ Union Station/S 19th, 52

Chihuly Bridge of Glass spans I-705 between the Museum of Glass, 1801 E. Dock St., and Union Station. This footbridge features three installations of Dale Chihuly's glass art. The ceiling of the Seaform Pavilion suspends more than 2,300 colorful glass objects above the heads of pedestrians. The two translucent, ice-blue Crystal Towers rise 40 feet above the bridge's midpoint. Farther along, the Venetian Wall showcases 109 delicate Chihuly sculptures. **Hours:** Daily 24 hours. **Cost:** Free. **Phone:** (253) 284-4750 or (866) 468-7386. ♿ Union Station/S 19th, 52

POINT DEFIANCE PARK, 5400 N. Pearl St., is a 760-acre park with miles of woodland trails through old growth forest, eight scenic gardens, public beaches with stunning Puget Sound and island views, a museum, a visitor center and a zoo/aquarium. Resident wildlife includes deer, bald eagles and red foxes.

A Japanese Garden with a Shinto shrine commemorates Kitakyushu, Tacoma's sister city. The Northwest Native Garden showcases indigenous plants. Other gardens are dedicated to herbs, irises, rhododendrons, roses and dahlias.

The Point Defiance Marina Complex has a shoreline promenade, a public fishing pier, rental boats and fishing gear, and an eight-lane public boat launch. A Washington State Ferry terminal also is located at the marina. *See Recreation Areas Chart.* **Hours:** Park daily 30 minutes before dawn-30 minutes after dusk. Visitor center open Thurs.-Sun. 10-5, Memorial Day weekend-Labor Day weekend. **Cost:** Free. Individual fees for attractions and rentals vary. **Phone:** (253) 305-1032, or (253) 305-1088 for the visitor center. 🍴 ⊗ 🐾 ⛲

Fort Nisqually Living History Museum is in Point Defiance Park at 5400 N. Pearl St. #11. The museum, the site of an outpost of the Hudson's Bay Co. and the first non-Native settlement on Puget Sound, features one of the oldest standing structures in the state. Changing exhibits describe Washington's fur trading era and Northwest life in the 1800s. **Hours:** Daily 11-5, May-Sept.; Wed.-Sun. 11-4, rest of year. Closed Jan. 1, Thanksgiving and Christmas. **Cost:** $8; $7 (ages 65+ and military with ID); $5 (ages 4-17); $22 (family, two adults and up to six children). **Phone:** (253) 591-5339.

Point Defiance Zoo & Aquarium, in Point Defiance Park at 5400 N. Pearl St., is the only combined zoo and aquarium in the Northwest. Most of the zoo's animal residents are native to the Pacific Rim.

The 5-acre Asian Forest Sanctuary provides a lush habitat for its denizens, which include Sumatran tigers, clouded leopards, siamangs and Asian

(See map & index p. 201.)

elephants. The Rocky Shores habitat is home to seals, walruses, otters and puffins. The Arctic Tundra exhibit features such cold weather-loving mammals as polar bears, Arctic foxes and musk oxen, a shaggy-haired, formidably horned relative of sheep and goats that is native to the Arctic areas of Canada and Greenland. Kids' Zone is an interactive play area for children that has animals from around the world.

The Pacific Seas Aquarium showcases the myriad marine creatures that inhabit Puget Sound, including sea horses and pink anemones. The South Pacific Aquarium displays tropical fish, eels, sharks and stingrays.

The Wild Wonders Outdoor Theater features performing animal shows. During the summer visitors can ride a camel or feed budgies (courtesy of a feed stick) in a walk-through aviary. From late November through January 1, evenings bring the Zoolights display with more than 500,000 lights providing the illuminated outlines for life-size replicas of zoo animals. **Time:** Allow 2 hours minimum. **Hours:** Opens daily at 9:30 a.m., Mar. 1-Oct. 31 and mid-Dec. through Jan. 1; Thurs.-Mon. at 9:30, rest of year. Zoolights daily 5-9 p.m., Nov. 24-Jan. 1. Closing time varies by season; phone ahead to confirm schedule. Closed Thanksgiving and Christmas. **Cost:** $20; $19 (ages 65+); $18 (military with ID) $16 (ages 5-12); $12 (ages 3-4). **Phone:** (253) 591-5337.

TACOMA ART MUSEUM is downtown at 1701 Pacific Ave. The museum presents rotating art exhibitions. A large collection of Chihuly glass is on view, along with other national and regional movements. Of interest is the collection of Western American art. The TAM Studio allows visitors of all ages to create their own art. An audio tour is available. **Time:** Allow 1 hour minimum. **Hours:** Tues.-Sun. 10-5 (also third Thurs. of the month 5-8). Closed most major holidays; phone ahead to confirm schedule. **Cost:** $15; $13 (ages 65+ and students with ID); free (ages 0-5 and to ages 0-18 on Sat.); $40 (family, two adults and up to four children under 18). **Phone:** (253) 272-4258. Convention Center/S 15th, 53

UNION STATION, 1717 Pacific Ave., is a restored 1911 railway station built by the Great Northern, Northern Pacific and Union Pacific railways. The Beaux Arts-style building features some noteworthy Chihuly glass installations. **Time:** Allow 30 minutes minimum. **Hours:** Station open Mon.-Fri. 8-5. **Cost:** Free. **Phone:** (253) 572-9310. Union Station/S 19th, 52

WASHINGTON STATE HISTORY MUSEUM, 1911 Pacific Ave., offers a comprehensive overview of the Evergreen State's past and present. The museum building, modeled after Tacoma's historic Union Station, was the winning design in an architectural competition. Inside visitors will find hands-on exhibits, walk-through settings and interactive computer displays that replicate the Evergreen State's natural setting, the lifestyles and cultures of its first inhabitants, early exploration and settlement of the land, and the significant individuals and events that were instrumental in shaping the state.

The Great Hall of Washington History takes you on a journey from past to present. Other highlights are walking through a traditional Coast Salish plank house, safely touching a 52-foot electrical tower, riding down the Columbia River courtesy of a large-screen video and one of the state's largest and coolest model train layouts. The view from the outdoor plaza overlooks Thea Foss Waterway, the historic red brick Warehouse District and adjacent Union Station, with indomitable Mount Rainier presiding over all.

Time: Allow 1 hour minimum. **Hours:** Tues.-Sun. 10-5 (also third Thurs. of the month 5-8). Closed July 4, Labor Day, Thanksgiving, Christmas Eve and Christmas. **Cost:** $14; $11 (ages 6-17, ages 65+ and students and military with ID); free (ages 0-5 and to all third Thurs. of the month 3-8); $40 (family, two adults and up to four children ages 0-17). **Parking:** Mon.-Fri. $4-$13, Sat.-Sun. $4-$10. **Phone:** (253) 272-3500 or (253) 272-9747. Union Station/S 19th, 52

WRIGHT PARK is bounded by Division and 6th aves. and I and G sts. The land for the park was donated to the city in 1886. Designed in the classic tradition of a pastoral English public park, this is a delightful urban green space with rolling green lawns shaded by horse chestnut, maple, pine and Pacific madrona trees, blue spruces and deodar cedars.

Wright Park has some interesting statues. Reproductions of Antonio Canova's "Dancing Girl" statues flank the Division Avenue entrance. They, along with the two lions guarding the 6th Avenue entrance, were gifts to the city in 1892. A bronze bust of Henrik Ibsen was dedicated May 17, 1913, the 99th anniversary of Norway's independence. The sculpture "Trilogy" stands on an island in the middle of a small duck pond; it depicts three youngsters romping hand in hand, just like their real-life running, swinging and playing counterparts. **Hours:** Park open daily 30 minutes before dawn-30 minutes after dusk. **Cost:** Free. **Phone:** (253) 591-5330. Theater District/S 9th, 55

W.W. Seymour Botanical Conservatory is in Wright Park at 316 S. G St. This small glass conservatory has a distinctive 12-sided central dome and contains unusual tropical plants, orchids and seasonal flower displays. Cyclamen, azaleas and primroses brighten the winter months; salvia, begonias and fragrant lilies celebrate summer; chrysanthemums and ornamental peppers put on a fall show; and the holidays bring vivid poinsettias. Wander among the flowers for half an hour and you're bound to walk out smiling.

Hours: Tues.-Sun. and Mon. holidays 10-4:30 (also third Thurs. of the month 4:30-7). Closed Jan. 1, Thanksgiving and Christmas. **Cost:** Donations. **Phone:** (253) 591-5330. Theater District/S 9th, 55

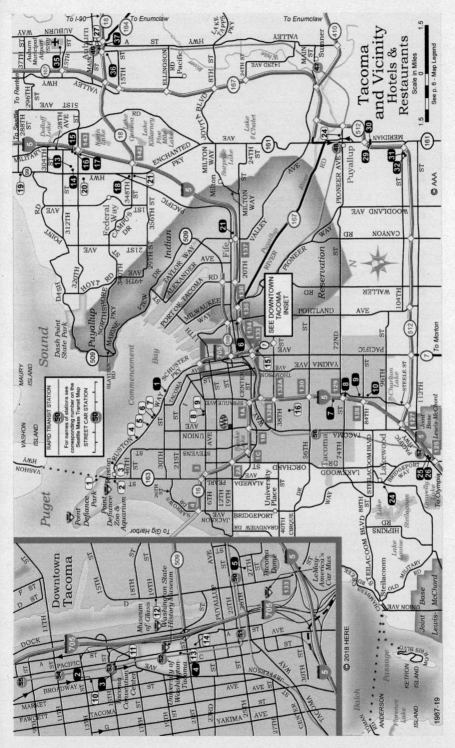

Tacoma and Vicinity Hotels & Restaurants

See p. 6 - Map Legend

Scale in Miles

RAPID TRANSIT STATION
50
For names of stations see corresponding number on the Seattle Mass Transit Map
STREET CAR STATION
50

Downtown Tacoma

© 2018 HERE

1987-19

Tacoma and Vicinity

This index helps you "spot" where approved hotels and restaurants are located on the corresponding detailed maps. Hotel daily rate range is for comparison only. Restaurant price range is a combination of lunch and/or dinner. Turn to the listing page for more information and consult display ads for special promotions.

 For more details, rates and reservations: AAA.com/travelguides/hotels

TACOMA

Map Page	Hotels	Diamond Rated	Rate Range	Page
1 p. 201	Silver Cloud Inn Tacoma	◈◈◈	$179-$329	204
2 p. 201	**Hotel Murano**	◈◈◈	$109-$429 SAVE	204
3 p. 201	Courtyard by Marriott-Tacoma Downtown	◈◈◈	$116-$484	203
4 p. 201	Holiday Inn Express & Suites-Tacoma Downtown	◈◈◈	Rates not provided	204
5 p. 201	**Best Western Plus Tacoma Dome Hotel**	◈◈◈	$129-$189 SAVE	203
6 p. 201	La Quinta Inn & Suites Tacoma Seattle	◈◈	$89-$199	204
7 p. 201	**Clarion Inn Near JBLM**	◈◈	$75-$135 SAVE	203
8 p. 201	Shilo Inn & Suites-Tacoma	◈◈	Rates not provided	204
9 p. 201	**Hampton Inn & Suites by Hilton, Tacoma**	◈◈◈	$112-$195 SAVE	204
10 p. 201	**Holiday Inn Express Hotel & Suites**	◈◈	Rates not provided SAVE	204

Map Page	Restaurants	Diamond Rated	Cuisine	Price Range	Page
① p. 201	Anthony's Restaurant	◈◈◈	Seafood	$13-$27	204
② p. 201	Antique Sandwich Company	◈	Deli	$4-$11	204
③ p. 201	WildFin American Grill - Tacoma	◈◈	American	$10-$28	204
④ p. 201	**Lobster Shop on Commencement Bay**	◈◈◈	Seafood	$12-$65	204
⑤ p. 201	Duke's Chowder House	◈◈	Seafood	$13-$34	204
⑥ p. 201	CI Shenanigans	◈◈◈	Steak Seafood	$14-$48	204
⑦ p. 201	Harbor Lights	◈◈	Seafood	$10-$40	204
⑧ p. 201	Engine House #9	◈◈	American	$10-$17	204
⑨ p. 201	Primo Grill	◈◈	American	$18-$35	204
⑩ p. 201	Bite	◈◈	American	$10-$32	204
⑪ p. 201	Pacific Grill	◈◈◈	Seafood Steak	$13-$46	204
⑫ p. 201	Johnny's Dock Restaurant	◈◈	Seafood	$12-$37	204
⑬ p. 201	Harmon Restaurant & Brewery	◈◈	American	$12-$29	204
⑭ p. 201	El Gaucho	◈◈◈	Steak	$26-$98	204
⑮ p. 201	Stanley & Seaforts	◈◈◈	American	$12-$56	204
⑯ p. 201	The Cheesecake Factory	◈◈◈	International	$11-$30	204

FEDERAL WAY

Map Page	Hotels	Diamond Rated	Rate Range	Page
13 p. 201	Clarion Hotel Federal Way-Seattle	◈◈	$99-$169	65
14 p. 201	Comfort Inn Federal Way-Seattle	◈◈	$99-$169	65
15 p. 201	Hampton Inn & Suites by Hilton Federal Way	◈◈◈	Rates not provided	66
16 p. 201	Courtyard by Marriott Seattle-Federal Way	◈◈◈	$104-$373	66
17 p. 201	**Best Western Plus Seattle/Federal Way**	◈◈◈	$129-$189 SAVE	65

FEDERAL WAY (cont'd)

Map Page	Hotels (cont'd)	Diamond Rated	Rate Range	Page
18 p. 201	Quality Inn & Suites	◇◇	$90-$160 SAVE	66

Map Page	Restaurants	Diamond Rated	Cuisine	Price Range	Page
19 p. 201	Verrazanos Italian Restaurant	◇◇	Italian	$10-$39	66
20 p. 201	Billy McHale's	◇◇	American	$10-$25	66
21 p. 201	The Rock, Wood Fired Pizza & Spirits	◇◇	Pizza	$9-$25	66

FIFE

Map Page	Hotel	Diamond Rated	Rate Range	Page
21 p. 201	Emerald Queen Hotel & Casino	◇◇◇	$121-$259 SAVE	67

LAKEWOOD

Map Page	Hotels	Diamond Rated	Rate Range	Page
24 p. 201	Best Western Lakewood	◇◇	$99-$250 SAVE	78
25 p. 201	TownePlace Suites by Marriott Tacoma Lakewood	◇◇◇	$89-$184	78
26 p. 201	Holiday Inn Express Hotel & Suites Tacoma South-Lakewood	◇◇◇	Rates not provided	78

PUYALLUP

Map Page	Hotels	Diamond Rated	Rate Range	Page
29 p. 201	Fairfield Inn & Suites by Marriott Tacoma Puyallup	◇◇◇	$99-$258	113
30 p. 201	Hampton Inn & Suites by Hilton Tacoma/Puyallup	◇◇◇	Rates not provided	113
31 p. 201	Best Western Premier Plaza Hotel & Conference Center	◇◇◇	$119-$289 SAVE	113
32 p. 201	Holiday Inn Express Hotel & Suites	◇◇◇	Rates not provided	113

Map Page	Restaurant	Diamond Rated	Cuisine	Price Range	Page
24 p. 201	Powerhouse Restaurant & Brewery	◇◇	American	$8-$15	113

AUBURN

Map Page	Hotels	Diamond Rated	Rate Range	Page
35 p. 201	Comfort Inn-Auburn	◇◇	$94-$199	39
36 p. 201	Best Western Plus Mountain View Auburn Inn	◇◇◇	$99-$309 SAVE	39
37 p. 201	La Quinta Inn & Suites Auburn	◇◇◇	$99-$179	39

Map Page	Restaurant	Diamond Rated	Cuisine	Price Range	Page
27 p. 201	Sun Break Cafe	◇	American	$11-$30	39

BEST WESTERN PLUS TACOMA DOME HOTEL
(253)272-7737 **5**

◇◇◇ Hotel $129-$189

 Best Western PLUS **AAA Benefit:** Members save up to 15% and earn bonus points!

Address: 2611 E E St 98421 **Location:** I-5 exit 133 (City Center), follow E 26th St/Tacoma Dome lanes, just n on E 26th St, then just e. Adjacent to the Tacoma Dome. Tacoma Dome, 50. **Facility:** 160 units. 6 stories, interior corridors. **Terms:** cancellation fee imposed. **Activities:** sauna, exercise room. **Guest Services:** valet and coin laundry, area transportation.

CLARION INN NEAR JBLM
(253)475-5900 **7**

◇◇ Hotel $75-$135

Address: 6802 Tacoma Mall Blvd 98409 **Location:** I-5 exit 129, 0.3 mi nw. **Facility:** 128 units. 2 stories (no elevator), interior corridors. **Pool:** outdoor. **Activities:** exercise room. **Guest Services:** valet laundry. **Featured Amenity:** breakfast buffet.

COURTYARD BY MARRIOTT-TACOMA DOWNTOWN
(253)591-9100 **3**

◇◇◇ Hotel. **Address:** 1515 Commerce St 98402

AAA Benefit: Members save 5% or more!

(See map & index p. 201.)

HAMPTON INN & SUITES BY HILTON, TACOMA
(253)539-2288   **9**

Hotel
$112-$195

AAA Benefit:
Members save 5%
or more!

Address: 8203 S Hosmer St 98408 **Location:** I-5 exit 128 northbound, just ne; exit 129 southbound, just e on 72nd St, then 1 mi s. **Facility:** 146 units. 4 stories, interior corridors. **Terms:** 1-7 night minimum stay, 3 day cancellation notice-fee imposed. **Pool:** heated indoor. **Activities:** hot tub, exercise room. **Guest Services:** valet and coin laundry. **Featured Amenity: full hot breakfast.**

SAVE 🛏 🛗 BIZ HS 🛜 ✕ 🍴 🖥 💻

HOLIDAY INN EXPRESS & SUITES-TACOMA DOWNTOWN
253/272-2434   **4**

Hotel. **Address:** 2102 S C St 98402

HOLIDAY INN EXPRESS HOTEL & SUITES
253/539-2020   **10**

Hotel
Rates not provided

Address: 8601 S Hosmer St 98444 **Location:** I-5 exit 128 northbound, just e; exit 129 southbound, just e on 72nd St, then 0.9 mi s. **Facility:** 79 units. 4 stories, interior corridors. **Pool:** heated indoor. **Activities:** sauna, hot tub, limited exercise equipment. **Guest Services:** valet and coin laundry. **Featured Amenity: full hot breakfast.**

SAVE 🍴 CALL ♿ 🛏 BIZ 🛜
✕ 🍴 🖥 💻

HOTEL MURANO
(253)238-8000   **2**

Contemporary Hotel
$109-$429

Address: 1320 Broadway Plaza 98402 **Location:** I-5 exit 133 (City Center) to I-705 N exit A St, just w on 11th St, then just s; downtown. Adjacent to Tacoma Convention & Trade Center. 🏢 Convention Center/S 15th, 53. **Facility:** 319 units. 26 stories, interior corridors. **Parking:** on-site (fee) and valet. **Terms:** cancellation fee imposed. **Amenities:** safes. **Dining:** Bite, see separate listing. **Activities:** exercise room, spa. **Guest Services:** valet laundry.

SAVE 🍴 🛗 🍸 🛗 HS 🛜
✕ 🍴 💻
/ SOME UNITS 🐾 🖥 🛗

LA QUINTA INN & SUITES TACOMA SEATTLE
(253)383-0146   **6**

Hotel. **Address:** 1425 E 27th St 98421

SHILO INN & SUITES-TACOMA
253/475-4020   **8**

Hotel. **Address:** 7414 S Hosmer St 98408

SILVER CLOUD INN TACOMA
(253)272-1300   **1**

Hotel. **Address:** 2317 N Ruston Way 98402

WHERE TO EAT

ANTHONY'S RESTAURANT
253/752-9700   **1**

Seafood. Casual Dining. **Address:** 5910 N Waterfront Dr 98407

ANTIQUE SANDWICH COMPANY
253/752-4069   **2**

Deli. Quick Serve. **Address:** 5102 N Pearl St 98407

BITE
253/572-3200   **10**

American. Casual Dining. **Address:** 1320 Broadway Plaza 98402

THE CHEESECAKE FACTORY
253/474-1112   **16**

International. Casual Dining. **Address:** 4502 S Steele St 98409

CI SHENANIGANS
253/752-8811   **6**

Steak Seafood. Casual Dining. **Address:** 3017 Ruston Way 98402

DUKE'S CHOWDER HOUSE
253/752-5444   **5**

Seafood. Casual Dining. **Address:** 3327 Ruston Way 98402

EL GAUCHO
253/272-1510   **14**

Steak. Fine Dining. **Address:** 2119 Pacific Ave 98402

ELMER'S
253/473-0855

American. Casual Dining. **Address:** 7427 S Hosmer St 98408

ENGINE HOUSE #9
253/272-3435   **8**

American. Brewpub. **Address:** 611 N Pine St 98406

HARBOR LIGHTS
253/752-8600   **7**

Seafood. Casual Dining. **Address:** 2761 N Ruston Way 98402

HARMON RESTAURANT & BREWERY
253/383-2739   **13**

American. Brewpub. **Address:** 1938 Pacific Ave S 98402

JOHNNY'S DOCK RESTAURANT
253/627-3186   **12**

Seafood. Casual Dining. **Address:** 1900 E D St 98421

LOBSTER SHOP ON COMMENCEMENT BAY
253/759-2165   **4**

Seafood
Casual Dining
$12-$65

AAA Inspector Notes: Classic Northwest seafood dishes are the emphasis, with selections such as fresh wild salmon and blackened tuna. In season, the outdoor deck offers a spectacular view of the Olympic Mountains rising high above Commencement Bay. **Features:** full bar, patio dining, early bird specials, Sunday brunch, happy hour. **Reservations:** suggested. **Address:** 4015 Ruston Way 98402 **Location:** I-5 exit 133 (City Center), 5 mi nw via Schuster Pkwy and Ruston Way. L D CALL ♿

PACIFIC GRILL
253/627-3535   **11**

Seafood Steak. Casual Dining. **Address:** 1502 Pacific Ave 98402

PRIMO GRILL
253/383-7000   **9**

American. Casual Dining. **Address:** 2701 S 6th Ave 98406

RAM RESTAURANT AND BREWERY
253/756-7886

American. Casual Dining. **Address:** 3001 Ruston Way 98402

STANLEY & SEAFORTS
253/473-7300   **15**

American. Fine Dining. **Address:** 115 E 34th St 98404

WILDFIN AMERICAN GRILL - TACOMA
253/267-1772   **3**

American. Casual Dining. **Address:** 5115 Grand Loop 98407

TOPPENISH (G-9) pop. 8,949, elev. 757'

Toppenish is the headquarters of the Yakama Nation tribes, whose land covers more than a million acres. Artists have transformed the outside walls of many buildings in town with more than 75 colorful murals depicting pioneer life in the area. A new mural is dedicated annually on the first Saturday in June. Horse-drawn wagon tours are available May through September; phone (509) 697-8995.

Toppenish Chamber of Commerce: 504 S. Elm St., P.O. Box 28, Toppenish, WA 98948. **Phone:** (509) 865-3262.

Self-guiding tours: For information about the town murals and a self-guiding walking tour brochure, contact the chamber of commerce.

AMERICAN HOP MUSEUM is at 22 S. B St. Housed in a building with a trompe l'oeil exterior, the museum contains exhibits tracing the history of the hop industry from its commercial beginnings in New York in the 17th century to present-day Yakima Valley operations. Displays include historic photographs, memorabilia, publications, and antique and modern hop equipment. **Hours:** Wed.-Sat. 10-4, Sun. 11-4, May-Sept.; by appointment rest of year (minimum 10 people required). **Cost:** $3; $2 (ages 6-12); $7 (family). **Phone:** (509) 865-4677.

YAKAMA NATION CULTURAL HERITAGE CENTER is .5 mi. n.w. on US 97, s.w. on Buster Rd., then w. to 100 Spiel-yi Loop. It contains a winter lodge/meeting hall, theater, library and research center. The 76-foot-high Winter Lodge, a stylized version of an ancient Yakama design, dominates the campus. Dioramas and exhibits in the 12,000-square-foot Yakama Nation Museum chronicle the history of the Yakama Nation's tribes. There are additional displays on Native American leaders and dwellings inhabited by the Plateau People, along with historical photographs, audio narrations and music.

Time: Allow 1 hour minimum. **Hours:** Museum open Mon.-Fri. 8-5, Sat.-Sun. 9-5. Guided tours Mon.-Fri. by appointment. Closed Jan. 1, Thanksgiving, day after Thanksgiving and Christmas. **Cost:** $6; $4 (ages 11-64, ages 55+ and active military with ID); $2 (ages 0-10); $15 (family, two adults and two children ages 0-17). Guided tour additional $25. **Phone:** (509) 865-2800. GT ⬛

TOUCHET pop. 421

CAMEO HEIGHTS MANSION BED & BREAKFAST
509/394-0211

◆◆◆◆
Country Inn
Rates not provided

Address: 1072 Oasis Rd 99360 **Location:** 25 mi w of Walla Walla; off SR 12. **Facility:** A winding driveway leads to this romantic retreat which sits on a bluff overlooking a river. The beautiful mansion includes a 400-acre orchard and vineyard. Each room is luxuriously appointed. 7 units, some efficiencies. 4 stories (no elevator), interior corridors. **Terms:** age restrictions may apply. **Dining:** The Vine at Cameo Heights Mansion, see separate listing. **Pool:** outdoor. **Activities:** hot tub, game room, trails. **Featured Amenity: full hot breakfast.**

WHERE TO EAT

THE VINE AT CAMEO HEIGHTS MANSION   509/394-0211
◆◆◆◆ American. Fine Dining. **Address:** 1072 Oasis Rd 99360

TUKWILA (F-3) pop. 19,107, elev. 144'
• Restaurants p. 206
• Hotels & Restaurants map & index p. 160
• Part of Seattle area — see map p. 124

Just 12 miles south of Seattle, 17 miles north of Tacoma and 4 miles east of Seattle-Tacoma International Airport, Tukwila is conveniently close to some of the Pacific Northwest's most popular cities. Residents are employed by such corporations as Boeing, Microsoft, Savvis and the University of Washington.

Take in cool outdoor air and stunning scenery on one of several trails, including the 14.7-mile Interurban Trail and the 10.5-mile Duwamish-Green River Trail. Play at Fort Dent Park (6800 Fort Dent Way), whose 54 acres hold two playgrounds, picnic tables, hiking trails, a soccer field and a duck pond; phone (206) 768-2822. The Rainier Symphony brings music to your ears throughout the year at the Foster Performing Arts Center (4242 S. 144th St.); phone (206) 781-5618.

COMFORT SUITES AIRPORT-TUKWILA
(425)227-7200 95

◆◆◆◆
Hotel
$76-$239

Address: 7200 Fun Center Way 98188 **Location:** I-405 exit 1 (SR 181), just n on Interurban Ave, then just e. Adjacent to Bullwinkle's Amusement Park. Tukwila, 44. **Facility:** 138 units, some two bedrooms. 4 stories, interior corridors. **Pool:** heated indoor. **Activities:** hot tub, exercise room. **Guest Services:** valet and coin laundry, area transportation. **Featured Amenity: continental breakfast.**

SAVE 🚭 ➰ ⬛ BIZ HS 📶
✕ 🛄 ⬛ 💻 🚐

COURTYARD BY MARRIOTT/SEA-TAC AREA
(425)255-0300 100
◆◆◆◆ Hotel. **Address:** 16038 W Valley Hwy 98188

AAA Benefit: Members save 5% or more!

COURTYARD BY MARRIOTT-SEATTLE/SOUTHCENTER
(206)575-2500 104

◆◆◆◆
Hotel
$83-$406

COURTYARD' AAA Benefit: Members save 5% or more!

Address: 400 Andover Park W 98188 **Location:** I-5 exit 153 northbound, s on Southcenter Pkwy, e on Strander Blvd, then s; exit 154B southbound, 0.5 mi s on Southcenter Blvd, just s on 61st Ave, just e on Tukwila Pkwy, then just s. Located in a commercial area. Tukwila, 44. **Facility:** 149 units. 3 stories, interior corridors. **Terms:** cancellation fee imposed. **Pool:** heated indoor. **Activities:** hot tub, exercise room. **Guest Services:** valet and coin laundry, boarding pass kiosk, area transportation.

SAVE ECO 🚭 ⬛ 🍸 CALL 🐾 ➰ ⬛ BIZ 📶
✕ 🛄 💻 SOME UNITS ⬛ 🚐

(See map & index p. 160.)

DOUBLETREE SUITES BY HILTON, SEATTLE AIRPORT-SOUTHCENTER   206/575-8220 **101**
♦♦♦ Hotel. **Address:** 16500 Southcenter Pkwy 98188

AAA Benefit: Members save 5% or more!

EMBASSY SUITES BY HILTON HOTEL   425/227-8844 **99**
♦♦♦ Hotel. **Address:** 15920 W Valley Hwy 98188

AAA Benefit: Members save 5% or more!

HAMPTON INN BY HILTON SEATTLE/SOUTHCENTER   (425)228-5800 **96**

◆◆◆
Hotel
$112-$226

Hampton by Hilton

AAA Benefit: Members save 5% or more!

Address: 7200 S 156th St 98188 **Location:** I-405 exit 1 (SR 181), just s. Tukwila, 44. **Facility:** 153 units. 4 stories, interior corridors. **Terms:** 1-7 night minimum stay, 3 day cancellation notice-fee imposed. **Amenities:** safes. **Pool:** heated outdoor. **Activities:** hot tub, exercise room. **Guest Services:** valet and coin laundry, area transportation. **Featured Amenity:** breakfast buffet. *(See ad this page.)*

[SAVE] ✈ 🚐 🚐 [BIZ] 📶 ✕ 🛏 🖼 ☕ 🚌

HOLIDAY INN EXPRESS & SUITES SEATTLE SOUTH-TUKWILA   206/294-3700 **97**
♦♦♦ Hotel. **Address:** 90 Andover Park E 98188

HOME2 SUITES BY HILTON, SEATTLE AIRPORT   206/623-7300 **105**
♦♦♦ Extended Stay Hotel. **Address:** 380 Upland Dr 98188

AAA Benefit: Members save 5% or more!

HOMEWOOD SUITES BY HILTON SEATTLE AIRPORT - TUKWILA   206/433-8000 **94**
♦♦♦ Extended Stay Hotel. **Address:** 6955 Fort Dent Way 98188

AAA Benefit: Members save 5% or more!

HOTEL INTERURBAN   206/278-7800 **102**
♦♦♦ Hotel. **Address:** 223 Andover Park E 98188

RAMADA TUKWILA SEATAC AIRPORT   (425)226-1812 **98**
♦♦ Hotel. **Address:** 15901 W Valley Hwy 98188

RESIDENCE INN BY MARRIOTT-SEATTLE SOUTH   (425)226-5500 **103**
♦♦♦ Extended Stay Hotel. **Address:** 16201 W Valley Hwy 98188

AAA Benefit: Members save 5% or more!

WHERE TO EAT

BAHAMA BREEZE ISLAND GRILLE   206/241-4448 **117**
♦♦♦ Caribbean. Casual Dining. **Address:** 15700 Southcenter Pkwy 98188

BAI TONG THAI RESTAURANT   206/575-3366 **121**
♦♦♦ Thai. Casual Dining. **Address:** 16876 Southcenter Pkwy 98188

THE CHEESECAKE FACTORY   206/246-7300 **119**
♦♦♦ International. Casual Dining. **Address:** 230 Strander Blvd 98188

CLAIM JUMPER   206/575-3918
♦♦ American. Casual Dining. **Address:** 5901 S 180th St 98188

MIYABI SUSHI   206/575-6815 **120**
♦♦ Japanese. Casual Dining. **Address:** 16820 Southcenter Pkwy 98188

ODIN BREWING COMPANY   206/241-1013 **118**
♦ Barbecue. Brewpub. **Address:** 402 Baker Blvd 98188

STANFORD'S RESTAURANT & BAR   206/575-7454
♦♦ American. Casual Dining. **Address:** 17380 Southcenter Pkwy 98188

▼ *See AAA listing this page* ▼

TUMWATER (H-2) pop. 17,371, elev. 115'

Founded in 1845, Tumwater was the first American settlement north of Fort Vancouver. Waterpower harnessed from the Deschutes River for a brewery, mills and other industries was the key to Tumwater's prosperity in the early 1900s. The original town site, off Deschutes Way at the foot of Grant Street, is now 17-acre Tumwater Historical Park, which includes the 1858 Crosby House, built by Bing Crosby's grandparents, and the 1905 Henderson House (closed to the public); phone (360) 943-9884 or (360) 754-4160. Within adjacent 15-acre Tumwater Falls Park are waterfalls, hiking trails and a fish hatchery.

Tumwater Area Chamber of Commerce: 1520A Irving St. S.W., Tumwater, WA 98512. **Phone:** (360) 357-5153.

BEST WESTERN TUMWATER-OLYMPIA INN
(360)956-1235

Hotel
$104-$149

Best Western. **AAA Benefit:** Members save up to 15% and earn bonus points!

Address: 5188 Capitol Blvd 98501 **Location:** I-5 exit 102, just e. **Facility:** 89 units. 2 stories (no elevator), interior corridors. **Terms:** cancellation fee imposed. **Activities:** hot tub, exercise room. **Guest Services:** coin laundry.

EXTENDED STAY AMERICA - OLYMPIA/TUMWATER
360/754-6063

Extended Stay Hotel. **Address:** 1675 Mottman Rd SW 98512

LA QUINTA INN & SUITES TUMWATER/OLYMPIA
(360)352-5433

Hotel. **Address:** 4600 Capitol Blvd SE 98501

WHERE TO EAT

FALLS TERRACE RESTAURANT
360/943-7830

American. Casual Dining. **Address:** 106 Deschutes Way SW 98501

UNION pop. 631
• Part of Olympic National Park area — see map p. 100

ALDERBROOK RESORT & SPA
360/898-2200

Resort Hotel. **Address:** 7101 E SR 106 98592

WHERE TO EAT

THE RESTAURANT AT ALDERBROOK
360/898-5500

Regional American. Fine Dining. **Address:** 10 E Alderbrook Dr 98592

UNION GAP (G-8) pop. 6,047, elev. 980'

Union Gap takes its name from the natural pass, or gap, carved over time by the Yakima River through high, barren hills. This gap divides the Yakima Valley into upper and lower portions. The settlement of Yakima City was established in 1861 and renamed Union Gap in 1918.

CENTRAL WASHINGTON AGRICULTURAL MUSEUM, 4508 Main St. in Fulbright Park, features 21 display buildings containing farm machinery and equipment. The Magness Hand Tool collection contains more than 6,000 items. Also on the grounds are a restored 1917 log cabin and a railroad boxcar. **Time:** Allow 2 hours minimum. **Hours:** Grounds open daily dawn-dusk. Buildings open Tues.-Sat. 10-4, Sun. 1-4, Apr.-Oct. **Cost:** Donations. **Phone:** (509) 457-8735.

BEST WESTERN PLUS AHTANUM INN   (509)248-9700

Hotel
$100-$210

Best Western PLUS. **AAA Benefit:** Members save up to 15% and earn bonus points!

Address: 2408 Rudkin Rd 98903 **Location:** I-82 exit 36, just nw. **Facility:** 117 units, some efficiencies. 2 stories, interior/exterior corridors. **Terms:** cancellation fee imposed. **Pool:** heated outdoor. **Activities:** picnic facilities, exercise room. **Guest Services:** valet and coin laundry.

HOLIDAY INN EXPRESS & SUITES UNION GAP - YAKIMA AREA
(509)902-8000

Hotel. **Address:** 1215 Ahtanum Ridge Dr 98903

WHERE TO EAT

EL PORTON
509/248-4015

Mexican. Casual Dining. **Address:** 2512 Main St 98903

JEAN'S COTTAGE INN
509/575-9709

American. Casual Dining. **Address:** 3211 Main St 98903

VANCOUVER (H-6) pop. 161,791, elev. 42'
• Hotels p. 210 • Restaurants p. 212
• Hotels & Restaurants map & index p. 209

At the head of deepwater navigation on the Columbia River, Vancouver is the oldest city in Washington. It was founded in 1824 as Fort Vancouver by the Hudson's Bay Co. During the 1860s the young town prospered from the gold rushes to eastern Washington and Idaho. The Kaiser Co. shipyard, constructed in 1942 after the United States entered World War II, employed approximately 36,000 people in three separate shifts and built about 140 vessels that were used in Pacific warfare.

Within Esther Short Park, at the corner of W. Columbia and 8th streets, is the state's oldest town square. It includes the 1867 Slocum House, a Rhode Island-style home now used as a community theater; an impressively large woodcarving of a Native American; and a bronze monument to pioneer women. A free concert and movie series takes place July through August; for schedule information phone (360) 487-8600 or (360) 487-8311.

(See map & index p. 209.)

The Vancouver Farmers Market is one of Washington's largest, with vendors offering locally grown fruits and vegetables, flowers, plants, baked goods and prepared foods. There's live music, and it's dog-friendly as well. The market sets up at 605 Esther St. between W. 6th and W. 8th streets. It operates Sat. 9-3, Sun. 10-3, mid-March through October.

Old Apple Tree Park, 112 Columbia Way, preserves what is believed to be the Pacific Northwest's oldest apple tree, planted in 1826 by residents of the Hudson's Bay Co. trading post. The paved 5-mile Waterfront Renaissance Trail runs from the southern end of Columbia Street in downtown Vancouver east along the Columbia River and Columbia Way to 12.5-acre Wintler Community Park, 6400 Beach Dr., which offers a beach area and observation decks; phone (360) 487-8311.

Covington Historical House, 4201 Main St., is an 1848 log cabin said to be the first schoolhouse in the Oregon Territory north of the Columbia River; phone (360) 695-5602.

Fort Vancouver Visitor Center: 1501 E. Evergreen Blvd., Vancouver, WA 98661. **Phone:** (360) 816-6230, (877) 600-0800 in the off-season or (877) 224-4214.

Shopping: In addition to JCPenney and Macy's, Westfield Vancouver Mall, just west of I-205 exit 30 on SR 500, offers 120 other retailers and Cinetopia, a state-of-the-art, 23-screen multiplex.

VANCOUVER NATIONAL HISTORIC RESERVE

encompasses nearly a dozen sites; a visitor center is at 1501 E. Evergreen Blvd. Collectively these sites represent the settlement of the Vancouver area from the mid-19th century to the present.

The upper portion of the reserve includes the reconstructed Fort Vancouver, Vancouver Barracks, the Pearson Air Museum and Officers Row. The lower portion is made up of the Water Resources Education Center, Waterfront Park, Kaiser Shipyard Overlook, Old Apple Tree Park and a section of Discovery Trail. The Vancouver Land Bridge, a pedestrian bridge designed by Johnpaul Jones with assistance from Maya Lin, spans SR 14 and connects the reserve's two sections. Seven installations along the way commemorate the 1804-06 Lewis and Clark Expedition. A series of guided Lantern Tours is offered October through February; reservations are required.

Hours: Grounds daily dawn-dusk. Visitor center Tues.-Sat. 9-5. Phone for individual site schedules. Lantern Tour departs at 7 p.m. Closed Jan. 1, Thanksgiving, Christmas Eve, Christmas and Dec. 31. **Cost:** Fort Vancouver (valid for 7 days) $7; free (ages 0-15). Visitor center, Officers Row, Pearson Air Museum and Water Resources Education Center free. Lantern Tour $15; $10 (ages 10-15);

tour not recommended for children under 10. **Phone:** (360) 816-6230. GT

Fort Vancouver National Historic Site is e. on Mill Plain Blvd. off I-5 exit 1C, then s. on Ft. Vancouver Way and e. to 1001 E. 5th St., within Vancouver National Historic Reserve. Between 1825 and 1860 the 200-acre site was the center of the Hudson's Bay Co.'s fur-trading empire. In 1849 the first U.S. military post in the Pacific Northwest was founded nearby. The Hudson's Bay Co. stockade and several other buildings are reconstructed and furnished in period. The visitor center at 1501 E. Evergreen Blvd. contains historical exhibits.

Time: Allow 1 hour minimum. **Hours:** Grounds daily dawn-dusk. Fort and visitor center open Tues.-Sat. 9-5. Closed Jan. 1, Thanksgiving, Christmas Eve, Christmas and Dec. 31. **Cost:** Fort (valid for 7 days) $7; free (ages 0-15). Visitor center free. **Phone:** (360) 816-6200.

Officers Row National Historic District is at 1301 Officers Row within Vancouver National Historic Reserve. The 21 Victorian homes, formerly the residences of officers at the U.S. Army post, were built 1849-1906.

The 1886 Marshall House, 1301 Officers Row, is named for Gen. George C. Marshall, author of the post-World War II European recovery plan. A tour includes a 25-minute video about Officers Row and the history of Vancouver since 1850. **Time:** Allow 30 minutes minimum. **Hours:** Mon.-Sat. 9-5. Phone ahead to confirm Sat. schedule. Closed Jan. 1, Thanksgiving, Christmas Eve and Christmas. **Cost:** Free. **Phone:** (360) 693-3103. GT

Pearson Air Museum is 1 mi. s.e. of I-5 exit 1C at 1115 E. 5th St., within Fort Vancouver National Historic Site. An exhibit about the birth of Pearson Field, the oldest airport in the Pacific Northwest, traces its military roots. Also on display are replicas of two encampments that offer a glimpse into the life of spruce mill workers during World War I.

A monument next to the museum marks the site where three Soviet aviators completed the first transpolar flight and the first non-stop flight from Russia to the United States in 1937. The flight took 63 hours and 16 minutes. **Time:** Allow 1 hour minimum. **Hours:** Tues.-Sat. 9-5. Closed Jan. 1, Thanksgiving, Christmas and Dec. 31. **Cost:** Free. **Phone:** (360) 816-6232.

Water Resources Education Center is at 4600 S.E. Columbia Way at the e. end of Marine Park, within Vancouver National Historic Site. It has hands-on exhibits about water usage and conservation and a 350-gallon aquarium. Computer programs explain what happens after water goes down the drain. A demonstration garden and waterfront trail are on the grounds. **Time:** Allow 1 hour minimum. **Hours:** Mon.-Fri. 9-4, Sat. noon-4. Closed Jan. 1, Memorial Day, July 4, Labor Day, Thanksgiving and Christmas. **Cost:** Free. **Phone:** (360) 487-7111.

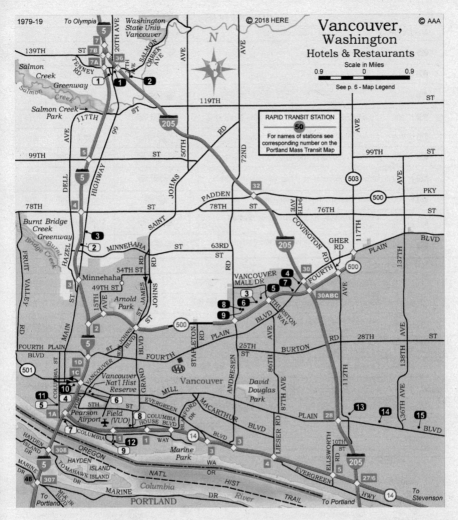

© 2018 HERE

© AAA

Vancouver, Washington
Hotels & Restaurants

Scale in Miles

See p. 6 - Map Legend

RAPID TRANSIT STATION
50
For names of stations see corresponding number on the Portland Mass Transit Map

Vancouver, WA

This index helps you "spot" where approved hotels and restaurants are located on the corresponding detailed maps. Hotel daily rate range is for comparison only. Restaurant price range is a combination of lunch and/or dinner. Turn to the listing page for more information and consult display ads for special promotions.

For more details, rates and reservations: AAA.com/travelguides/hotels

VANCOUVER

Map Page	Hotels	Diamond Rated	Rate Range	Page
1 this page	Quality Inn & Suites	◈◈	$79-$179	211
2 this page	Holiday Inn Express Vancouver North-Salmon Creek	◈◈◈	Rates not provided	211
3 this page	Quality Inn & Suites	◈◈	$72-$163	211
4 this page	**Best Western Plus Vancouver Mall Drive Hotel & Suites**	◈◈◈	$100-$180 SAVE	210
5 this page	**Sonesta ES Suites Portland-Vancouver**	◈◈◈	Rates not provided SAVE	212

VANCOUVER (cont'd)

Map Page	Hotels (cont'd)	Diamond Rated	Rate Range	Page
6 p. 209	The Heathman Lodge	◆◆◆	Rates not provided	211
7 p. 209	Comfort Suites	◆◆	$94-$179	211
8 p. 209	Holiday Inn Express & Suites Vancouver Mall/Portland Area	◆◆◆	Rates not provided	211
9 p. 209	Staybridge Suites Vancouver-Portland Metro Area	◆◆◆	$119-$399	212
10 p. 209	Comfort Inn & Suites Downtown Vancouver	◆◆	$92-$153	210
11 p. 209	Hilton Vancouver Washington	◆◆◆	$149-$283 [SAVE]	211
12 p. 209	Homewood Suites by Hilton Vancouver/Portland	◆◆◆	Rates not provided	211
13 p. 209	Best Western Inn of Vancouver	◆◆	$90-$200 [SAVE]	210
14 p. 209	DoubleTree by Hilton Vancouver (See ad p. 211.)	◆◆◆	$129-$349 [SAVE]	211
15 p. 209	Hampton Inn & Suites by Hilton Portland/Vancouver	◆◆◆	$184-$329 [SAVE]	211

Map Page	Restaurants	Diamond Rated	Cuisine	Price Range	Page
1 p. 209	Billygan's Roadhouse	◆◆	American	$10-$29	212
2 p. 209	Peachtree Restaurant & Pie House	◆◆	American	$7-$20	212
3 p. 209	Hudson's Bar & Grill at The Heathman Lodge	◆◆	Pacific Northwest	$8-$26	212
4 p. 209	Tommy O's	◆◆	Pacific Rim	$8-$28	212
5 p. 209	Grays	◆◆◆	American	$8-$35	212
6 p. 209	Eatery at the Grant House	◆◆◆	American	$8-$35	212
7 p. 209	Who-Song & Larry's	◆◆	Mexican	$12-$22	212
8 p. 209	Lapellah	◆◆	American	$14-$30	212
9 p. 209	Beaches Restaurant & Bar	◆◆	American	$10-$33	212

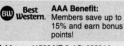

(See map & index p. 209.)

COMFORT SUITES   (360)253-3100   **7**
◆◆ Hotel. **Address:** 4714 NE 94th Ave 98662

DOUBLETREE BY HILTON VANCOUVER
                                        (360)891-9777   **14**

◆◆◆
Hotel
$129-$349

AAA Benefit:
Members save 5% or
more!

Address: 12712 SE 2nd Cir 98684 **Location:** I-205 exit 28 (E Mill Plain Blvd),
0.8 mi e, then just n on SE 126th Ave.
Facility: 98 units. 3 stories, interior corridors. **Terms:** 1-7 night minimum stay, 3
day cancellation notice-fee imposed.
Amenities: safes. **Pool:** heated indoor.
Activities: hot tub, exercise room.
Guest Services: valet laundry, area
transportation. *(See ad this page.)*

HAMPTON INN & SUITES BY HILTON PORTLAND/
VANCOUVER   (360)891-3000   **15**

◆◆◆
Hotel
$184-$329

AAA Benefit:
Members save 5%
or more!

Address: 315 SE Olympia Dr 98684
Location: I-205 exit 28 (E Mill Plain
Blvd), 1.5 mi e, then just n. **Facility:** 99
units. 4 stories, interior corridors. **Terms:**
1-7 night minimum stay, 3 day cancellation notice-fee imposed. **Pool:** heated
indoor. **Activities:** hot tub, exercise
room. **Guest Services:** valet and coin
laundry, area transportation. **Featured
Amenity:** breakfast buffet.

THE HEATHMAN LODGE   360/254-3100   **6**
◆◆◆ Hotel. **Address:** 7801 NE Greenwood Dr 98662

HILTON VANCOUVER WASHINGTON
                                        (360)993-4500   **11**

◆◆◆
Hotel
$149-$283

Hilton
HOTELS & RESORTS

AAA Benefit:
Members save 5% or
more!

Address: 301 W 6th St 98660 **Location:** I-5 exit 1C (E Mill Plain Blvd) southbound, 0.3 mi w, then 0.3 mi s on W
Columbia St; exit 1B northbound, 0.5 mi
sw, follow signs to City Center/6th St.
Facility: 226 units. 7 stories, interior corridors. **Parking:** on-site (fee) and valet.
Terms: 1-7 night minimum stay, 3 day
cancellation notice-fee imposed. **Dining:**
Grays, see separate listing. **Pool:**
heated indoor. **Activities:** hot tub, exercise room. **Guest Services:** valet laundry.

HOLIDAY INN EXPRESS & SUITES VANCOUVER MALL/
PORTLAND AREA   360/253-0500   **8**
◆◆◆ Hotel. **Address:** 7205 NE 41st St 98662

HOLIDAY INN EXPRESS VANCOUVER NORTH-SALMON
CREEK   360/576-1040   **2**
◆◆◆ Hotel. **Address:** 13101 NE 27th Ave 98686

HOMEWOOD SUITES BY HILTON VANCOUVER/PORTLAND
                                        360/750-1100   **12**
◆◆◆ Extended Stay Hotel. **Address:** 701 SE Columbia Shores Blvd
98661

AAA Benefit:
Members save 5%
or more!

QUALITY INN & SUITES   (360)696-0516   **3**
◆◆ Hotel. **Address:** 7001 NE Hwy 99 98665

QUALITY INN & SUITES   (360)574-6000   **1**
◆◆ Hotel. **Address:** 13207 NE 20th Ave 98686

▼ *See AAA listing this page* ▼

(See map & index p. 209.)

SONESTA ES SUITES PORTLAND-VANCOUVER

360/253-4800 5

Extended Stay Hotel
Rates not provided

Address: 8005 NE Parkway Dr 98662 **Location:** I-205 exit 30 (SR 500 W), 0.5 mi w to Thurston Way, just n to NE Parkway Dr, then just w. **Facility:** 120 kitchen units, some two bedrooms. 2 stories (no elevator), exterior corridors. **Amenities:** video games. **Pool:** heated outdoor. **Activities:** hot tub, exercise room. **Guest Services:** valet and coin laundry. **Featured Amenity:** breakfast buffet.

SAVE ✈ ❗️ CALL 🚻 🌊 🏊
BIZ 🛜 ✖️ 🎤 🔌 📺 💻
/ SOME UNITS 🐾

SPRINGHILL SUITES BY MARRIOTT VANCOUVER COLUMBIA TECH CENTER   (360)260-1000
Hotel. **Address:** 1421 SE Tech Center Dr 98683

AAA Benefit:
Members save 5% or more!

STAYBRIDGE SUITES VANCOUVER-PORTLAND METRO AREA   (360)891-8282 9
Extended Stay Hotel. **Address:** 7301 NE 41st St 98662

TOWNEPLACE SUITES BY MARRIOTT PORTLAND VANCOUVER   (360)260-9000
Extended Stay Hotel. **Address:** 17717 SE Mill Plain Blvd 98683

AAA Benefit:
Members save 5% or more!

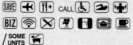

WHERE TO EAT

ARAWAN THAI CUISINE   360/882-8118
Thai. Casual Dining. **Address:** 700 SE 160th Ave 98684

BEACHES RESTAURANT & BAR   360/699-1592 9
American. Casual Dining. **Address:** 1919 SE Columbia River Dr 98661

BILLYGAN'S ROADHOUSE   360/573-2711 1
American. Casual Dining. **Address:** 13200 NE Hwy 99 98686

BURGERVILLE
American. Quick Serve.
LOCATIONS:
Address: 11704 SE Mill Plain Blvd 98684 **Phone:** 360/254-9301
Address: 13309 NE Hwy 99 98686 **Phone:** 360/573-8223
Address: 16416 SE McGillivray Blvd 98683 **Phone:** 360/253-9433
Address: 8320 NE Vancouver Plaza Dr 98662 **Phone:** 360/944-6230

CATHEDRAL TAPATIA MEXICAN RESTAURANT 360/891-0055
Mexican. Casual Dining. **Address:** 707 SE 164th Ave 98684

EATERY AT THE GRANT HOUSE   360/906-1101 6
American. Casual Dining. **Address:** 1101 Officers Row 98661

ELMER'S
American. Casual Dining.
LOCATIONS:
Address: 11310 SE Mill Plain Blvd 98684 **Phone:** 360/256-0808
Address: 7105 NE 40th St 98661 **Phone:** 360/260-1008

GRAYS   360/828-4343 5
American. Casual Dining. **Address:** 301 W 6th St 98660

GUSTAV'S PUB & GRILL   360/883-0222
German. Casual Dining. **Address:** 1705 SE 164th Ave 98683

HOPWORKS URBAN BREWERY   360/828-5139
American. Brewpub. **Address:** 17707 SE Mill Plain Blvd 98683

HUDSON'S BAR & GRILL AT THE HEATHMAN LODGE
360/816-6100 3
Pacific Northwest. Casual Dining. **Address:** 7801 NE Greenwood Dr 98662

JOE'S CRAB SHACK   360/693-9211
Seafood. Casual Dining. **Address:** 101 E Columbia Way 98661

LAPELLAH   360/828-7911 8
American. Casual Dining. **Address:** 2520 Columbia House Blvd 98661

MCGRATH'S FISH HOUSE   360/514-9555
Seafood. Casual Dining. **Address:** 12501 SE 2nd Cir 98684

MCMENAMINS EAST VANCOUVER   360/254-3950
American. Casual Dining. **Address:** 1900 NE 162nd Ave 98684

MCMENAMINS ON THE COLUMBIA   360/699-1521
American. Casual Dining. **Address:** 1801 SE Columbia River Dr 98661

PEACHTREE RESTAURANT & PIE HOUSE
360/693-6736 2
American. Casual Dining. **Address:** 6600 NE Hwy 99 98665

THAI ORCHID RESTAURANT   360/695-7786
Thai. Casual Dining. **Address:** 213 W 11th St 98660

TOMMY O'S   360/694-5107 4
Pacific Rim. Casual Dining. **Address:** 801 Washington St 98660

WHO-SONG & LARRY'S   360/695-1198 7
Mexican. Casual Dining. **Address:** 111 SE Columbia Way 98661

WALLA WALLA pop. 31,731, elev. 949'

In 1836 Dr. Marcus Whitman and his wife, Narcissa, established the first permanent settlers' home in the Pacific Northwest in the Walla Walla Valley. First known as Steptoeville, the city traces its founding to Fort Walla Walla in 1856. The name is a Native American word meaning "many waters" or "small rapid stream."

During the 1860s Walla Walla prospered as a departure point for central Idaho gold rush fortune seekers and also was the western terminus of the pioneer Mullan Road to Fort Benton, on the upper Missouri River in Montana. Wheat farming began in the 1870s, but after 1883 Walla Walla played second fiddle to Spokane, the site of Northern Pacific's transcontinental rail line.

Early settlers planted an abundance of ornamental trees on city streets as reminders of their Eastern and Midwestern hometowns. Along Main

Street downtown stand dozens of preserved late 19th- and early 20th-century buildings.

The valley is noted for rich agricultural productivity; specialty crops include grapes and onions. The famous Walla Walla sweet—a large, round hybrid developed from an Italian sweet onion—is celebrated for its flavor. Commercial wine production began in 1977, and today there are more than 100 wineries in the area. Most specialize in such red wines as Cabernet Sauvignon, Merlot, Sangiovese, Syrah and various blends. The Walla Walla Valley Wine Alliance has information about area wineries; phone (509) 526-3117.

Pioneer Park, 940 E. Alder St., is a 58-acre recreation area with a duck pond, bandstand, rose garden, playground, swimming pool, tennis courts and an aviary featuring exotic bird species; phone (509) 527-4527.

Walla Walla Valley Chamber of Commerce: 29 E. Sumach St., P.O. Box 644, Walla Walla, WA 99362. **Phone:** (509) 525-0850.

WHITMAN MISSION NATIONAL HISTORIC SITE—see place listing p. 216.

BEST WESTERN PLUS WALLA WALLA SUITES INN
(509)525-4700

Hotel
$93-$275

/ SOME
UNITS 🐄

Best Western PLUS
AAA Benefit: Members save up to 15% and earn bonus points!

Address: 7 E Oak St 99362 **Location:** US 12 exit 2nd Ave, just s. **Facility:** 77 units. 3 stories, interior corridors. **Terms:** cancellation fee imposed. **Pool:** heated indoor. **Activities:** hot tub, exercise room. **Guest Services:** valet and coin laundry. **Featured Amenity:** breakfast buffet.

SAVE 🍽️ CALL 👨‍🦽 🛥️ 👷 BIZ
📶 ✕ 🛢️ 🖥️ 💻

COMFORT INN & SUITES BY CHOICE HOTELS   509/522-3500
🔸🔸 Hotel. **Address:** 1419 W Pine St 99362

COURTYARD BY MARRIOTT WALLA WALLA   (509)876-8100
🔸🔸🔸 Contemporary Hotel. **Address:** 550 W Rose St 99362
AAA Benefit: Members save 5% or more!

HAMPTON INN & SUITES BY HILTON WALLA WALLA
509/525-1398
🔸🔸🔸 Contemporary Hotel. **Address:** 1531 Kelly Pl 99362
AAA Benefit: Members save 5% or more!

🔗 **Dreaming of s'mores and starry nights?**
AAA.com/campgrounds

HOLIDAY INN EXPRESS WALLA WALLA   (509)525-6200

Hotel
$94-$250

Address: 1433 W Pine St 99362 **Location:** From US 12 exit SR 125/Prescott/Pendleton, just e on Myra Rd/W Pine St. **Facility:** 81 units. 3 stories, interior corridors. **Terms:** resort fee. **Pool:** heated indoor. **Activities:** hot tub, picnic facilities, exercise room. **Guest Services:** valet and coin laundry. **Featured Amenity:** full hot breakfast.

SAVE 🍽️ CALL 👨‍🦽 🛥️ 👷 BIZ
HS 📶 ✕ 🛢️ 🖥️ 💻
/ SOME UNITS 🐄

LA QUINTA INN & SUITES WALLA WALLA   (509)394-8815
🔸🔸🔸 Contemporary Hotel. **Address:** 776 Silverstone Dr 99362

MARCUS WHITMAN HOTEL & CONFERENCE CENTER
(509)525-2200
🔸🔸🔸 Classic Hotel. **Address:** 6 W Rose St 99362

QUALITY INN & SUITES   509)525-2522
🔸🔸 Hotel. **Address:** 520 N 2nd Ave 99362

WHERE TO EAT

BACON AND EGGS   509/876-4553
🔸🔸 Breakfast Sandwiches. Casual Dining. **Address:** 57 E Main St 99362

BRASSERIE FOUR   509/529-2011
🔸🔸🔸 French. Casual Dining. **Address:** 4 E Main St 99362

CLARETTE'S RESTAURANT   509/529-3430
🔸🔸 Comfort Food. Casual Dining. **Address:** 15 S Touchet St 99362

EL SOMBRERO MEXICAN RESTAURANT   509/522-4984
🔸🔸 Mexican. Casual Dining. **Address:** 4 W Oak St 99362

GRAZE WALLA WALLA   509/522-9991
🔸 Sandwiches Deli. Quick Serve. **Address:** 5 S Colville St 99362

MAPLE COUNTER CAFE   509/876-2527
🔸 Breakfast Sandwiches. Casual Dining. **Address:** 209 E Alder St 99362

THE MARC   509/525-2200
🔸🔸🔸🔸
American Fine Dining
$10-$40
AAA Inspector Notes: Expect beautifully prepared food with flavors that will heighten your senses. Using seasonal ingredients, including micro-greens from the on-site garden, the restaurant continues to place an emphasis on creative and artistic appetizers, salads, steaks and seafood. **Features:** full bar, happy hour. **Address:** 6 W Rose St 99362 **Location:** At N 2nd Ave and W Rose St; downtown; in Marcus Whitman Hotel & Conference Center.
B D

OLIVE MARKETPLACE & CAFE   509/526-0200
🔸 American. Quick Serve. **Address:** 21 E Main St 99362

PUBLIC HOUSE 124   509/876-4511
🔸🔸 Small Plates Sandwiches. Gastropub. **Address:** 124 E Main St 99362

SAFFRON MEDITERRANEAN KITCHEN   509/525-2112
🔸🔸🔸 Mediterranean. Fine Dining. **Address:** 125 W Alder St 99362

SWEET BASIL PIZZERIA   509/529-1950
🔸 Pizza. Quick Serve. **Address:** 5 S 1st Ave 99362

T. MACCARONE'S   509/522-4776
🔸🔸🔸 Italian. Fine Dining. **Address:** 4 N Colville St 99362

WHITEHOUSE-CRAWFORD RESTAURANT   509/525-2222
▼▼▼ American. Fine Dining. **Address:** 55 W Cherry St 99362

WASHOUGAL (H-6) pop. 14,095, elev. 65'

Washougal straddles a peninsula between the Columbia and its namesake river. Bearing a Native American name meaning "rushing water," the town is the Washington gateway to the Columbia Gorge. At Reed Island, 3 miles southeast, the crew of the HMS *Chatham* claimed the Columbia River for England in October 1792. The expedition's leader, William Broughton, also named Mt. Hood.

Lewis and Clark camped at Cottonwood Beach on the Washougal River (then called the Seal River) in March 1806. Settlement began in the late 1840s, after American possession of the Oregon Country north of the Columbia River was established in 1846. Mount Pleasant Grange Hall, 6.5 miles east on SR 14, is the oldest continuously used grange hall in the state; the grange movement began in the late 19th century as a fraternal organization and political forum for farmers.

Camas-Washougal Chamber of Commerce: 422 N.E. 4th Ave., P.O. Box 919, Camas, WA 98607. **Phone:** (360) 834-2472.

BEST WESTERN PLUS PARKERSVILLE INN & SUITES
(360)835-9292

▼▼▼
Hotel
$99-$299

Ⓑⓦ **Best Western PLUS.**

AAA Benefit: Members save up to 15% and earn bonus points!

Address: 121 S 2nd St 98671 **Location:** Jct SR 14 and 2nd St, just s. **Facility:** 79 units. 4 stories, interior corridors. **Terms:** cancellation fee imposed. **Amenities:** safes. **Pool:** heated indoor. **Activities:** sauna, hot tub, exercise room. **Guest Services:** coin laundry.

SAVE CALL 🅖 ⊅ 🎗 BIZ HS
📶 ⊠ 🅙 📷 📺

WENATCHEE (E-9) pop. 31,925, elev. 651'

Wenatchee spreads along the Columbia River just below the confluence with its namesake stream. Despite its rich volcanic soil, the Wenatchee Valley was too arid for farming until the Highline Canal was built in 1903. Once irrigated, the land was planted with apple trees, and Wenatchee emerged as one of the world's largest producers of the fruit.

Wenatchee's proximity to the Okanogan-Wenatchee National Forest *(see place listing p. 96)* makes it a prime area for all-year recreation, from hiking in summer to skiing in winter. Pick up tourist-related literature at the Wenatchee Valley Chamber of Commerce.

A string of parks extends along the city's Columbia River shore. Wenatchee Riverfront Park, off Wenatchee Avenue at 501 Fifth St., features a xeriscape demonstration garden and railroad displays that include a World War II switcher, a diesel locomotive and a caboose. A miniature railway, 155 N. Worthen St., offers passenger rides approximately twice a month on weekends, April through August (weather permitting); phone (509) 661-4551 for park information or (509) 888-6240 for train schedule information.

North of the city, Walla Walla Point Park and Wenatchee Confluence State Park *(see Recreation Areas Chart)* offer swimming beaches, playing fields and hiking trails. The Apple Capital Loop Trail, an 11-mile paved circuit linked by bridges to the east bank of the Columbia River, connects this string of parks. The trail, lighted until midnight on the Wenatchee side, is popular with pedestrians, bicyclists and roller skaters.

Wenatchee Valley Chamber of Commerce: 1 S. Wenatchee Ave., Wenatchee, WA 98801. **Phone:** (509) 662-2116 or (800) 572-7753.

Shopping: JCPenney is the anchor store at Valley North Center, 1300 N. Miller St. Macy's anchors Wenatchee Valley Mall, 511 Valley Mall Pkwy. in East Wenatchee. A cluster of antique shops and boutiques line Wenatchee Avenue between Kittitas and 2nd streets.

The Pybus Public Market, 3 N. Worthen St. opposite Riverfront Park, houses restaurants, specialty shops, vendors and the Wenatchee Valley Farmers Market. The farmers market sets up Sat. 8-1, May through October.

OHME GARDENS, 3327 Ohme Rd., consists of 9 acres of alpine-type gardens built on a rocky bluff overlooking the Wenatchee Valley and Columbia River. Evergreen trees and low-growing plants blend with rugged rock formations to create effects ranging from the lush growth of a rain forest to the variegated patterns of an alpine meadow. Stone pathways connect the garden levels, leading to such features as fern-bordered pools, rustic shelters, a wishing well and a lookout at the park's highest point.

Time: Allow 1 hour minimum. **Hours:** Daily 9-7, Memorial Day-Labor Day; 9-6, Apr. 15-day before Memorial Day and day after Labor Day-Oct. 15. Last admission 45 minutes before closing. **Cost:** $8; $4 (ages 6-17). **Phone:** (509) 662-5785.

ROCKY REACH DAM, 7 mi. n. to 6001 US 97A, is a Z-shaped structure 2,860 feet long. A viewpoint enables visitors to watch migrating fish ascend the mile-long juvenile fish bypass. In the powerhouse is the Museum of the Columbia, which traces life along the river beginning 10,000 years ago and also covers the history of local railroads. Other displays include portraits of Nez Perce Indians, Thomas Edison memorabilia, an overlook onto the generation floor and changing art exhibits.

The Rocky Reach Visitor Center has exhibits about dam building and a fish viewing area. Movies are shown throughout the day in the 90-seat theater. Gardens, picnic shelters and a playground are on the grounds. Guided tours are given March through

October. **Time:** Allow 30 minutes minimum. **Hours:** Grounds open daily 9-9, May-Aug.; 9-6, Mar.-Apr. and Sept.-Oct. Visitor center open daily 9-4, Mar.-Oct. Museum open daily 9-3:30, Mar.-Oct. **Cost:** Free. **Phone:** (509) 663-7522. (GT) (⏸) (🅿)

BEST WESTERN CHIEFTAIN INN (509)665-8585

◈◈◈
Hotel
$105-$170

(BW) **Best Western.** **AAA Benefit:** Members save up to 15% and earn bonus points!

Address: 1017 N Wenatchee Ave 98801 **Location:** Downtown. **Facility:** 77 units. 2 stories (no elevator), interior corridors. **Terms:** check-in 4 pm, cancellation fee imposed. **Pool:** heated outdoor. **Activities:** hot tub, exercise room. **Guest Services:** valet and coin laundry.

(SAVE) (⏸) CALL(♿) (🛆) (➕) (BIZ) (📶) (✕) (🛋) (📷) (📺) / SOME UNITS (HS)

COAST WENATCHEE CENTER HOTEL (509)662-1234
◈◈◈ Hotel. **Address:** 201 N Wenatchee Ave 98801

COMFORT SUITES AT THE PARK (509)662-1818

◈◈◈
Hotel
$118-$198

Address: 195 E Penny Rd 98801 **Location:** US 2 E/97, just s on Easy St, then just e. **Facility:** 84 units. 3 stories, interior corridors. **Parking:** winter plug-ins. **Pool:** heated indoor. **Activities:** hot tub, exercise room. **Guest Services:** valet and coin laundry. **Featured Amenity:** breakfast buffet.

(SAVE) (✈) (⏸) (🛆) (➕) (BIZ) (HS) (📶) (✕) (🛋) (📷) (📺)

HOLIDAY INN EXPRESS 509/663-6355
◈◈◈ Hotel. **Address:** 1921 N Wenatchee Ave 98801

LA QUINTA INN & SUITES WENATCHEE (509)664-6565
◈◈ Hotel. **Address:** 1905 N Wenatchee Ave 98801

SPRINGHILL SUITES BY MARRIOTT WENATCHEE
(509)667-2775
◈◈◈ Hotel. **Address:** 1730 N Wenatchee Ave 98801

AAA Benefit: Members save 5% or more!

SUPER 8 BY WYNDHAM WENATCHEE (509)293-7336

◈◈
Hotel
$55-$160

Address: 1401 N Miller St 98801 **Location:** 1.5 mi n on US 2. **Facility:** 102 units. 3 stories, interior corridors. **Terms:** cancellation fee imposed. **Pool:** heated outdoor. **Activities:** hot tub. **Guest Services:** coin laundry. **Featured Amenity:** continental breakfast.

(SAVE) (⏸) (🛆) (BIZ) (📶) (✕) (🛋) (📷) (📺) / SOME UNITS (🐾)

WHERE TO EAT

CASA HERRADURA 509/470-9414
◈◈ Mexican. Casual Dining. **Address:** 601 S Mission St 98801

CHATEAU GRILL 509/667-9463
◈◈◈ American. Casual Dining. **Address:** 1 Vineyard Way 98801

THE COTTAGE INN 509/663-4435
◈◈ Steak Seafood. Casual Dining. **Address:** 134 Easy St 98801

GARLINI'S NAPOLETANA 509/884-1707
◈◈ Italian Pizza. Casual Dining. **Address:** 212 Fifth St 98801

INNA'S CUISINE 509/888-4662
◈◈ International. Casual Dining. **Address:** 26 N Wenatchee Ave 98801

LA FUENTE 509/664-1910
◈◈ Mexican. Casual Dining. **Address:** 816 S Mission St 98801

MCGLINN'S PUBLIC HOUSE 509/663-9073
◈◈ American. Casual Dining. **Address:** 111 Orondo Ave 98801

SHAKTI'S 509/662-3321
◈◈ Northern Italian. Fine Dining. **Address:** 218 N Mission St 98801

THE THAI RESTAURANT 509/662-8077
◈◈ Thai. Casual Dining. **Address:** 1211 N Mission St 98801

VISCONTI'S - WENATCHEE 509/662-5013
◈◈ Italian. Casual Dining. **Address:** 1737 N Wenatchee Ave 98801

VN PHO 509/667-8650
◈◈ Vietnamese. Casual Dining. **Address:** 1010 Springwater Ave 98801

THE WILD HUCKLEBERRY 509/663-1013
◈◈ American. Casual Dining. **Address:** 302 S Mission St 98801

THE WINDMILL 509/665-9529
◈◈ Steak. Casual Dining. **Address:** 1501 N Wenatchee Ave 98801

WESTPORT (F-4) pop. 2,099, elev. 12'
• Hotels p. 216 • Restaurants p. 216

Westport is at the north end of an 18-mile-long beach popular for surf fishing, clam digging, crabbing or just wading. Surfers ride the waves on both sides of the Westport jetty. Saltwater fishing—particularly for salmon, halibut and tuna—is excellent, and the Westport Marina, at the foot of Wilson Street, is the base for a large sport fishing fleet. Nearly a dozen charter operators provide guided fishing trips; for information contact the chamber of commerce; phone (360) 268-9422.

An 1,800-foot walk and bridge enables anglers to fish from the breakwater area as well as from the jetties. The Lighthouse Trail extends 1.5 miles south from the jetty and follows the beach; interpretive panels along the way describe the natural history of the beach and dunes.

Westport-Grayland Chamber of Commerce: 2985 S. Montesano St., P.O. Box 306, Westport, WA 98595-0306. **Phone:** (360) 268-9422 or (800) 345-6223.

WESTPORT MARITIME MUSEUM is at 2201 Westhaven Dr. Housed in a former 1930s Coast Guard lifeboat station, the museum features displays of marine mammal skeletons as well as exhibits about life in a fishing port. Coast Guard and shipwreck history and a children's discovery room also are featured. A separate building houses a lens from the Destruction Island lighthouse. Eight rooms of displays cover such topics as ecology, shellfish, logging and cranberries.

Time: Allow 30 minutes minimum. **Hours:** Thurs.-Mon. 10-4, Apr.-Sept.; noon-4, rest of year. Phone ahead to confirm schedule. **Cost:** $5; $4 (military with ID); $3 (ages 13-18); $2 (ages 6-12); free (ages 0-5 and Coast Guard with ID). **Phone:** (360) 268-0078.

CHATEAU WESTPORT RESORT   360/268-9101
♦♦ Hotel. **Address:** 710 W Hancock St 98595

WHERE TO EAT

BENNETT'S FISH SHACK   360/268-7380
♦ Seafood. Casual Dining. **Address:** 2581 Westhaven Dr 98595

WHIDBEY ISLAND (C-2)

The largest island in Puget Sound, Whidbey Island has extensive tracts of farmland and forest, scenic shoreline vistas and abundant parkland. Numerous bays and coves are popular with boaters and fishermen. Capt. George Vancouver discovered the island in 1792, naming it after Joseph Whidbey, his sailing master. Whidbey proved the island was not a peninsula by navigating Deception Pass.

Deception Pass Bridge and ferries from Mukilteo and Port Townsend provide access to the island; for ferry information phone (206) 464-6400, or (888) 808-7977 in Wash. Whidbey Island communities include Coupeville—one of the oldest towns in the state—Greenbank and picturesque Langley, which retains a historic atmosphere *(see place listings p. 57)*. The island's largest town is Oak Harbor *(see place listing p. 94)*.

Ebey's Landing National Historical Reserve—the nation's first historical reserve—protects a rural working landscape in the central part of the island. The reserve's 17,500 acres include woodlands, shorelines and fertile agricultural prairies, a landscape that looks much as it did more than 100 years ago. Forests are still harvested, and farms that have been in existence for a century still thrive. Spectacular beach, water and mountain views make Ebey's Landing especially popular with hikers and cyclists.

SR 20, SR 525 and county roads link the reserve's eight major areas: Coupeville, Smith Prairie, Crockett Lake and Uplands, Ebey's Landing, Grassers Hill and Lagoon, Monroe Landing, and Fort Casey Historical and Fort Ebey state parks *(see Recreation Areas Chart)*. A self-guiding driving tour map is available at the Island County Historical Museum in Coupeville. For further information about the reserve phone (360) 678-6084.

Within Fort Casey Historical State Park, 3 miles south of Coupeville off SR 20 at 1280 Engle Rd., are late 19th-century fortifications. The two 10-inch disappearing guns on display are thought to be the only ones of their size still in existence; phone (360) 678-4519.

The park's red-roofed Admiralty Head Lighthouse was built in 1903, replacing a wooden Civil War-era structure. It remained a working lighthouse until 1922, when most ships were steam powered and the Admiralty Inlet route favored by sailing ships was no longer heavily used. The park is open daily 8-dusk. The lighthouse is open daily 11-5, June through August; hours vary rest of year. Phone (360) 678-4519 for the park, or (360) 678-1186 for the lighthouse.

WHITE SALMON (H-7) pop. 2,224, elev. 640'

White Salmon's location, atop a bench 500 feet above the Columbia River, affords panoramic views across the water to the Hood River Valley, with majestic Mount Hood as a backdrop. A glockenspiel—one of the few in the western United States—is a nod to the German heritage of many of the area's early settlers. The clock tower is part of City Hall, at the corner of Main Avenue and Jewett Boulevard. The White Salmon River empties into the Columbia several miles to the west; multitudes of pale-hued, spawned-out salmon, formerly quite abundant but less so now, once gave the waterway a whitish color in the fall.

Mt. Adams Chamber of Commerce: 1 Heritage Plaza, P.O. Box 449, White Salmon, WA 98672. **Phone:** (509) 493-3630.

EVERYBODY'S BREWING   509/637-2774
♦♦ American. Casual Dining. **Address:** 177 E Jewett Blvd (SR 141) 98672

WHITE SWAN (G-8) pop. 793, elev. 973'

FORT SIMCOE STATE PARK is 7 mi. w. of White Swan, following signs to 5150 Fort Simcoe Rd. It was one of two interior Washington Territory army posts established as a result of hostilities between settlers and the Yakama Nation in the fall of 1856. Two blockhouses, a guardhouse and barracks are replicated. Officers Row includes four original houses and a blockhouse.

Hours: Park open daily 6:30 a.m.-dusk, Apr.-Oct. Museum and interpretive center open Wed.-Sun. 9:30-4:30, Apr.-Sept.; by appointment rest of year. **Cost:** Park admission $10 (per private vehicle); Discover Pass, valid for 1 year, $30 (per private vehicle). **Phone:** (509) 874-2372. 🎁

WHITMAN MISSION NATIONAL HISTORIC SITE (G-11)

Seven miles west of Walla Walla off US 12 at 328 Whitman Mission Rd., the 98-acre Whitman Mission

National Historic Site, a unit of the Nez Perce National Historical Park, memorializes a Protestant mission established in 1836 by Dr. Marcus Whitman and his wife.

The mission, one of the first mission stations of its kind in the old Oregon country, operated among the Cayuse tribe until 1847, when a measles epidemic killed half of the village population. Village leaders decided to eliminate the source of the measles infection by killing the Whitmans and other settlers. The attack horrified Americans in the east and focused attention on the status of the Oregon Territory.

Today visitors can explore the grounds of the mission, which include excavations showing the outlined sites of early buildings, a grave where the Whitmans are buried and a visitor center with a small museum. On display in the museum are Cayuse tools and clothing as well as historic items found on the site. A 25-minute movie is shown on request at the visitor center. Junior ranger programs are offered daily during the summer months.

A paved, 1-mile self-guiding trail leads to former building sites, a restored millpond, an apple orchard, an irrigation ditch, a portion of the Oregon Trail, the Whitman Memorial Shaft and the Great Grave. Audio stations provide historical perspective. Picnic facilities are on the grounds. Pets on leash are permitted on trails.

Allow 1 hour minimum. Grounds open daily 8-4:30; closed federal holidays Sept.-Apr. Visitor center open daily 9-4, Memorial Day weekend-Labor Day; Wed.-Sun. 9-4, Feb. 1-day before Memorial Day weekend and day after Labor Day weekend-Nov. 30. Visitor center closed Thanksgiving and federal holidays Sept.-Apr. Admission is free. Phone (509) 522-6360.

WINTHROP (D-9) pop. 394, elev. 1,765'

Winthrop manages to recapture the spirit of the Old West with a colorful main street that has rows of false-fronted buildings, wooden sidewalks and old-fashioned streetlights. It's all reminiscent of the 1890s, when a mining boom brought many new settlers to the area. Poet and author Owen Wister lived in Winthrop in the early 1900s and described some of the town's sites and citizens in his novel "The Virginian."

Winthrop Chamber of Commerce: 202 SR 20, P.O. Box 39, Winthrop, WA 98862. **Phone:** (509) 996-2125.

THE CHEWUCH INN & CABINS   509/996-3107
🏵🏵🏵 Bed & Breakfast. **Address:** 223 White Ave 98862

HOTEL RIO VISTA   (509)996-3535
🏵🏵 Motel. **Address:** 285 Riverside Ave 98862

RIVER RUN INN   509/996-2173
🏵🏵 Motel. **Address:** 27 Rader Rd 98862

SUN MOUNTAIN LODGE   (509)996-2211

🏵🏵🏵
Resort Hotel
$175-$725

Address: 604 Patterson Lake Rd 98862 **Location:** SR 20, 1.8 mi w on Twin Lakes Rd, then 6.2 mi sw, follow signs. Located in a quiet rural area. **Facility:** Mountaintop serenity, sweeping panoramic views and a myriad of activities makes any visit a pleasant experience. This casually elegant resort is perfect for a romantic getaway in the summer or winter. 112 units, some cabins. 2-3 stories, interior/exterior corridors. **Terms:** check-in 4 pm, 2-3 night minimum stay - seasonal and/or weekends, 10 day cancellation notice. **Amenities:** safes. **Dining:** Sun Mountain Lodge Dining Room, see separate listing. **Pool:** heated outdoor. **Activities:** hot tub, tennis, cross country skiing, recreation programs, bicycles, playground, game room, lawn sports, trails, exercise room, spa. **Guest Services:** complimentary laundry.

WINTHROP INN   509-996-2217
🏵🏵 Motel. **Address:** 960 Hwy 20 98862

WHERE TO EAT

ARROWLEAF BISTRO   509/996-3919
🏵🏵🏵 American. Fine Dining. **Address:** 207 White Ave 98862

DUCK BRAND RESTAURANT HOTEL & CANTINA
                509/996-2408
🏵🏵 American. Casual Dining. **Address:** 248 Riverside Ave 98862

SUN MOUNTAIN LODGE DINING ROOM 509/996-4707
🏵🏵🏵
Regional Pacific Northwest Fine Dining
$29-$51
AAA Inspector Notes: Perched high in a mountain retreat overlooking the Methow Valley, the restaurant features plenty of locally grown produce and locally farmed beef, free-range chicken and lamb. The extensive wine list highlights many of the superb wines of Pacific Northwest. The highlight of this restaurant has to be the view. **Features:** full bar. **Reservations:** suggested. **Address:** 604 Patterson Lake Rd 98862 **Location:** SR 20, 1.8 mi w on Twin Lakes Rd, then 6.2 mi sw, follow signs; in Sun Mountain Lodge. B D CALL 🦽

WOODINVILLE (E-3) pop. 10,938, elev. 39'
• Hotels p. 218 • Restaurants p. 218
• Hotels & Restaurants map & index p. 160
• Part of Seattle area — see map p. 124

Located on the Sammamish River, Woodinville takes its name from pioneer Ira Woodin, who settled here in 1871. In the surrounding area is the largest collection of wineries in western Washington, at last count numbering more than 100. Most have tasting rooms. For additional information contact Woodinville Wine Country; phone (425) 205-4394.

Molbak's, 13625 N.E. 175th St., is one of the largest nurseries in the state. Annuals, perennials, vegetables and herbs are all grown on the nursery's own farm. Stimulate your green thumb with a leisurely stroll through their conservatory of tropical plants. Special events from plant seminars to harvest festivals take place regularly; for details phone (425) 483-5000 or (866) 466-5225. For more strenuous exercise, the 12-mile Sammamish River Trail, a popular bicycling route, links Woodinville with Lake Washington and Redmond.

(See map & index p. 160.)

Woodinville Chamber of Commerce: 17401 133rd Ave. N.E., Woodinville, WA 98072. **Phone:** (425) 481-8300.

Woodinville Visitor Center: 14700 148th Ave. N.E., Woodinville, WA 98072. **Phone:** (425) 287-6820.

RED HOOK ALE BREWERY, I-405 exit 23 to 14300 N.E. 145th St., offers one-hour tours explaining the brewing and bottling processes, including tastings and a souvenir glass. **Hours:** Tours Fri.-Sun. at 1 and 3. Closed Thanksgiving and Christmas. Phone ahead to confirm schedule. **Cost:** $6. **Phone:** (425) 483-3232. [GT] [†]

WINERIES

• **Chateau Ste. Michelle,** 2 mi. s. on SR 202 at 14111 N.E. 145th St. **Hours:** Daily 10-5. Tours are given 10:30-4:30. Closed Jan. 1, Easter, Thanksgiving and Christmas. **Phone:** (425) 488-1133 or (800) 267-6793. [GT]

HAMPTON INN & SUITES BY HILTON WOODINVILLE
                                    425/788-9247 **41**
▼▼▼ Hotel. **Address:** 19211 Woodinville Snohomish Rd NE 98072   **AAA Benefit:** Members save 5% or more!

WILLOWS LODGE   (425)424-3900 **42**
▼▼▼▼ Boutique Hotel. **Address:** 14580 NE 145th St 98072

WHERE TO EAT

BARKING FROG AT WILLOWS LODGE   425/424-2999 **68**
◆◆◆ Pacific Northwest. Fine Dining. **Address:** 14580 NE 145th St 98072

BIG FISH GRILL   425/487-3474 **66**
▼▼ Seafood. Casual Dining. **Address:** 13706 NE 175th St 98072

THE HERBFARM RESTAURANT   425/485-5300 **67**
◆◆◆◆◆ **AAA Inspector Notes:** Accomplished
Continental Fine Dining chefs rely on the fresh, prime ingredients available in the Northwest to create
$225-$295 decadent nine-course meals accompanied with five to six paired wines. Meals are given a seasonal theme in advance, but specific menu items are not finalized until a few hours before preparation. Plan to arrive early to peruse the extensive wine cellar and join in on a walking tour of the herb gardens. Reservations are required for the complete experience, which takes 4 to 5 hours. **Features:** beer & wine. **Reservations:** required. **Address:** 14590 NE 145th St 98072 **Location:** I-405 exit 20B (NE 124th St), 0.9 mi e, 1.3 mi n on 132nd Ave, 0.6 mi e on NE 143rd Pl, then just e. **Parking:** on-site and valet. [D]

PURPLE CAFE AND WINE BAR   425/483-7129 **69**
▼▼ American. Casual Dining. **Address:** 14459 Woodinville-Redmond Rd NE 98072

WOODLAND (H-6) pop. 5,509, elev. 25'

Settled in the mid-1800s, Woodland soon developed into a bustling center for the surrounding farming, dairying and poultry-raising area. Logging was a major industry in the early 20th century. An interpretive marker on Finn Hall Road, 4 miles east of I-5 on SR 503, describes the Old Finn Hall, a community center built in 1916 by Finnish immigrants.

The Cedar Creek Grist Mill, 9 miles east of I-5 exit 21 via N.W. Hayes Road and Cedar Creek Road, is the oldest structure of its kind in the Evergreen State. Built in 1874, the mill still operates and is open on weekends; phone (360) 225-5832. The adjacent covered bridge was built in 1995 on the site of an earlier span.

Woodland Chamber of Commerce & Tourism: 900 Goerig St., P.O. Box 1012, Woodland, WA 98674. **Phone:** (360) 225-9552.

BEST WESTERN WOODLAND INN   (360)225-1000

◆◆ Hotel $80-$219

Best Western. **AAA Benefit:** Members save up to 15% and earn bonus points!

Address: 1380 Atlantic Ave 98674 **Location:** I-5 exit 21, just ne. **Facility:** 51 units. 2 stories, interior corridors. **Terms:** cancellation fee imposed. **Pool:** heated indoor. **Activities:** hot tub, exercise room. **Guest Services:** coin laundry. **Featured Amenity:** full hot breakfast.

SAVE ⊷ (♥) [BIZ] 🛜 [X] 🔲
🔲 🔲 / SOME UNITS 🐾

LEWIS RIVER INN   (360)225-6257
▼▼ Motel. **Address:** 1100 Lewis River Rd 98674

WHERE TO EAT

BURGERVILLE   360/225-7965
▼ American. Quick Serve. **Address:** 1120 Lewis River Rd 98674

YAKIMA (F-8) pop. 91,067, elev. 1,065'
• Restaurants p. 220

Yakima (YACK-i-mah) occupies the west bank of its namesake river. The town grew up around a Northern Pacific Railroad depot established in 1884. Originally called North Yakima, the state legislature dropped North from the town's name in 1918. The valley's irrigated fields provide a verdant contrast to the surrounding arid foothills. Fruit warehouses and packing sheds lining the railroad tracks west of First Street, historically known as Produce Row, attest to Yakima's importance as a food processing and shipping center.

The city is the northern gateway to Yakima Valley wine country, where there are more than 70 wineries. Downtown offers several tasting rooms. Wine Yakima Valley has information about area wineries; phone (509) 965-5201 or (800) 258-7270.

Yakima River Canyon, north to I-82 exit 26, then north on SR 821, is popular with rockhounds and offers fine trout fishing along the Yakima River. About 6 miles north of the city the Fred G. Redmon Memorial Bridge, one of the longest concrete arch spans in the nation, carries I-82 over Selah Creek Canyon.

Adjacent viewpoints offer a panorama of the 330-foot-deep gorge and distant views of Mount Rainier and Mount Adams.

The Yakima Greenway, which extends 18 miles along the Yakima and Naches rivers, features a 9-mile paved walking and bicycling path stretching from Selah on the north to Union Gap on the south. For recreation information phone (509) 453-8280.

The Capitol Theatre, a restored vaudeville house at 19 S. 3rd St., presents a variety of performances. A guided tour of the theater also can be taken. Phone (509) 853-8000 for event information, (877) 330-2787 for tickets.

Yakima Valley Visitor Information Center: 101 N. Fair Ave., Yakima, WA 98901. **Phone:** (509) 573-3388 or (800) 221-0751.

Shopping: The anchor stores at Valley Mall, 3 miles south of downtown via S. 1st Street, are Kohl's, Macy's and Sears. Yesterday's Village Antique Mall, 15 W. Yakima Ave., has a number of specialty and craft shops under one roof; phone (509) 457-4981. There are more specialty shops in the historic district along N. Front Street. Glenwood Square, 5110 Tieton Dr., is a former apple warehouse that contains restaurants and a few shops.

HILLSIDE DESERT BOTANICAL GARDENS is at 3405 Hillside Pl.; from I-82 exit 36, take E. Valley Mall Blvd. w. to Main St.; .5 mi. s. on Main St. to W. Ahtanum Rd.; 1.25 mi. w. on W. Ahtanum Rd. to Goodman Rd., which curves w. and becomes Meadowbrook Rd.; 2 blks. s. on S. 5th Ave., then 2 blks. w. on Hillside Dr. to Hillside Pl.

This half-acre backyard garden is the result of the owner's 40 years of experimentation with a wide variety of desert plants to test their tolerance of the region's climatic extremes (hot summers, cold winters and average annual precipitation of only around 6 inches). Twenty raised beds contain about 300 varieties of cacti and other succulents. A greenhouse displays exotic succulents from around the world. Peak bloom is from May into July.

Time: Allow 30 minutes minimum. **Hours:** Mon.-Sat. 9-5, Sun. 1-dusk, May 1 to mid-July; phone for schedule rest of year. Phone at least 1 day in advance for guided tour appointments. Closed major holidays. Phone ahead to confirm schedule. **Cost:** Donations. **Phone:** (509) 248-1742. [GT]

YAKIMA AREA ARBORETUM, I-82 exit 34, .3 mi. e. on Nob Hill Blvd., then n. on S. 22nd St. and w. on Birchfield Dr. to 1401 Arboretum Dr., is a 46-acre reserve containing more than 2,000 species of native and non-native plants and vegetation. The flowering tree collection is at its peak in April and May. **Hours:** Grounds open daily dawn-dusk. Jewett Interpretive Center open Mon.-Sat. 9-5; otherwise by appointment. Closed major holidays. **Cost:** Donations. **Phone:** (509) 248-7337. [🐾]

YAKIMA VALLEY MUSEUM is 1.25 mi. w. on Yakima Ave., then .25 mi. s. on S. 16th Ave., then .3 mi. w. to 2105 Tieton Dr. (next to Franklin Park). It features a large collection of carriages, coaches and wagons. Other exhibits include Yakama Indian artifacts, agricultural equipment, a working soda fountain and a hands-on children's center.

The William O. Douglas Memorial Exhibit includes the U.S. Supreme Court justice's office. Children's Underground offers hands-on activities for kids. **Time:** Allow 1 hour minimum. **Hours:** Tues.-Sat. 10-5. Closed major holidays. **Cost:** $5; $3 (ages 6-18, ages 60+ and students with ID); $12 (family). **Phone:** (509) 248-0747. [🍴]

HOTEL MAISON   509/571-1900

♥♥♥ Historic Boutique Hotel. **Address:** 321 E Yakima Ave 98901

LEDGESTONE SUITES HOTEL YAKIMA   509/453-3151

♥♥♥ Extended Stay Contemporary Hotel. **Address:** 107 N Fair Ave 98901

OXFORD SUITES YAKIMA   (509)457-9000

♥♥♥
Hotel
$89-$755

Address: 1701 E Yakima Ave 98901 **Location:** Waterfront. I-82 exit 33 westbound; exit 33B eastbound. Adjacent to Greenway Trail. **Facility:** 108 units, some kitchens. 4 stories, interior corridors. **Terms:** check-in 4 pm, 2-14 night minimum stay - seasonal and/or weekends, 31 day cancellation notice-fee imposed. **Pool:** heated indoor. **Activities:** hot tub, picnic facilities, trails, exercise room. **Guest Services:** valet and coin laundry, area transportation. **Featured Amenity: breakfast buffet.**

SAVE ✈ ❘❙ ⬜ CALL ♿ ⬗
⬙ BIZ HS 🛜 ✉ 🔋 📷
⬛ / SOME UNITS 🐾

WHERE TO EAT

BOB'S BURGERS & BREW   509/895-7199

♥♥ American. Casual Dining. **Address:** 121 N Fair Ave 98901

CAROUSEL RESTAURANT & BISTRO   509/248-6720

♥♥♥ French. Fine Dining. **Address:** 25 N Front St 98901

COWICHE CANYON KITCHEN & ICE HOUSE   509/457-2007

♥♥♥ American. Casual Dining. **Address:** 202 E Yakima Ave 98901

CREEKSIDE WEST BAR & GRILLE   509/853-1057

♥♥ American. Casual Dining. **Address:** 4000 W Creekside Loop 98908

EL PORTON YAKIMA   509/965-5422

♥♥ Mexican. Casual Dining. **Address:** 420 S 48th Ave 98908

GASPERETTI'S RESTAURANT   509/248-0628

♥♥♥ Northern Italian. Fine Dining. **Address:** 1013 N 1st St 98901

NORM'S OF YAKIMA   509/902-1505

♥♥ American. Casual Dining. **Address:** 5 N Front St 98901

RUSSILLO'S PIZZA & GELATO   509/453-0325

♥♥ Pizza Sandwiches. Casual Dining. **Address:** 32 N Front St 98901

SANTIAGO'S ON THE AVE   509/453-1644

♥♥ Mexican. Casual Dining. **Address:** 111 E Yakima Ave 98901

SECOND STREET GRILL   509/469-1486

♥♥ American. Casual Dining. **Address:** 28 N 2nd St 98901

ZESTA CUCINA   509/972-2000

♥♥♥ Italian. Casual Dining. **Address:** 5110 Tieton Dr 98908

ZILLAH (G-9) pop. 2,964, elev. 821'

Zillah, incorporated in 1911 and named for the daughter of the president of the Northern Pacific Railroad, is in the heart of the Yakima Valley's orchard and vineyard district. The Fruit Loop is a winery and farm itinerary; contact the chamber of commerce for information, phone (509) 829-5055.

A local architectural oddity is the Teapot Dome, which stands in a small park half a mile east of I-82 exit 52 at 117 First Ave., a block east of Cheyne Road. Built in the 1920s as a parody of the then-current Teapot Dome petroleum lease scandal, the squat, circular, red-and-white structure served as a gas station until 2004 and was relocated to the present site in 2012. Instead of fuel, this National Historic Landmark now dispenses tourist information.

Zillah Chamber of Commerce: 605 1st Ave., P.O. Box 1294, Zillah, WA 98953. **Phone:** (509) 829-5055.

WINERIES

• **Bonair Winery** is at 500 S. Bonair Rd. **Hours:** Daily 10-5, Easter Sun.-Oct. 31; noon-4, rest of year. Closed Thanksgiving and Christmas. **Cost:** One-hour guided winery tour $10. Ninety-minute guided vineyard tour $20; maximum of 4 people. Reservations are required for tours. **Phone:** (509) 829-6027. GT

BEST WESTERN PLUS VINTAGE VALLEY INN
(509)829-3399

♥♥♥
Hotel
$150-$160

BW Best Western PLUS. **AAA Benefit:** Members save up to 15% and earn bonus points!

Address: 911 Vintage Valley Pkwy 98953 **Location:** I-82 exit 52, just nw. **Facility:** 69 units, some kitchens. 2 stories, interior corridors. **Parking:** winter plug-ins. **Terms:** cancellation fee imposed. **Pool:** heated indoor. **Activities:** hot tub, exercise room. **Guest Services:** coin laundry. **Featured Amenity: breakfast buffet.**

SAVE ❘❙ CALL ♿ ⬗ ⬙ BIZ
🛜 ✉ 🔋 📷 ⬛ / SOME UNITS 🐾 HS

WHERE TO EAT

EL PORTON   509/829-9100

♥♥ Mexican. Casual Dining. **Address:** 905 Vintage Valley Pkwy 98953

SQUEEZE INN RESTAURANT & LOUNGE   509/790-7041

♥♥ American. Casual Dining. **Address:** 611 1st Ave 98953

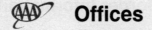

Offices

Main office listings are shown in **BOLD TYPE** and toll-free member service numbers appear in *ITALIC TYPE*.
All are closed Saturdays, Sundays and holidays unless otherwise indicated.
The addresses, phone numbers and hours for any AAA/CAA office are subject to change.
The type of service provided is designated below the name of the city where the office is located:

✦ Auto travel services, including books and maps, and on-demand TripTik ® routings.
● Auto travel services, including selected books and maps, and on-demand TripTik ® routings.
■ Books/maps only, no marked maps or on-demand TripTik ® routings.
▲ Travel Agency Services, cruise, tour, air, car and rail reservations; domestic and international hotel reservations; passport photo services; international and domestic travel guides and maps; travel money products; and International Driving Permits. In addition, assistance with travel related insurance products including trip cancellation, travel accident, lost luggage, trip delay and assistance products.
✪ Insurance services provided. If only this icon appears, only insurance services are provided at that office.
C Car Care Plus Facility provides car care services.
▭ Electric vehicle charging station on premises.

AAA NATIONAL OFFICE: 1000 AAA DRIVE, HEATHROW, FLORIDA 32746-5063, (407) 444-7000

WASHINGTON

BATTLE GROUND—AAA WASHINGTON, 2401 W MAIN STR ST 105, 98604. WEEKDAYS (M-F) 9:00-6:00. (360) 369-7005 ✪

BELLEVUE—AAA WASHINGTON, 1100 BELLEVUE WAY NE #7, 98004. WEEKDAYS (M-F) 9:00-6:00, SAT 10:00-5:00. (425) 455-3933, *(877) 477-4221.* ✦▲✪

BELLEVUE—AAA WASHINGTON, 3605 132ND AVE SE, 98006. WEEKDAYS (M-F) 8:30-5:00. (425) 462-2222, *(800) 562-2582.*

BELLINGHAM—AAA WASHINGTON, 4280 MERIDIAN ST STE 106, 98226. WEEKDAYS (M-F) 9:00-6:00. (360) 733-2740, *(877) 477-4222.* ✦▲✪

BOTHELL—AAA WASHINGTON, 19125 N CREEK PKWY ST 146, 98011. WEEKDAYS (M-F) 9:00-5:00. (425) 329-2594 ✪

BREMERTON—AAA WASHINGTON, 5700 KITSAP WAY, 98312. WEEKDAYS (M-F) 9:00-6:00. (360) 377-0081, *(877) 802-6894.* ✦▲✪

ISSAQUAH—AAA WASHINGTON, 405 NW GILMAN BLVD #102, 98027. WEEKDAYS (M-F) 9:00-6:00. (425) 557-0222, *(866) 756-1049.* ✦▲✪

KENNEWICK—AAA WASHINGTON, 6501 W GRANDRIDGE BLVD #G, 99336. WEEKDAYS (M-F) 8:30-5:30. (509) 735-6351, *(877) 802-6907.* ✦▲✪

LONGVIEW—AAA WASHINGTON, 1339 COMMERCE AVE # 310 C, 98632. WEEKDAYS (M-F) 9:00-6:00. (360) 636-5000 ✪

LYNNWOOD—AAA WASHINGTON, 3000 196TH ST SW, 98036. WEEKDAYS (M-F) 9:00-6:00, SAT 10:00-5:00. (425) 775-3571, *(877) 802-6896.* ✦▲✪✪

MOUNT VERNON—AAA WASHINGTON, 1600 E COLLEGE WAY STE A, 98273. WEEKDAYS (M-F) 9:00-6:00. (360) 428-5800, *(800) 743-1703.* ✦▲✪

OLYMPIA—AAA WASHINGTON, 2627 CAPITAL MALL DR SW 1, 98502. WEEKDAYS (M-F) 9:00-6:00. (360) 357-5561, *(877) 802-6897.* ✦▲✪

SEATTLE—AAA WASHINGTON, 1523 15TH AVE W, 98119. WEEKDAYS (M-F) 9:00-6:00, SAT 10:00-5:00. (206) 218-1222, *(800) 420-0513.* ✦▲✪

SEATTLE—AAA WASHINGTON, 1700 WESTLAKE AVE N # 724, 98109. WEEKDAYS (M-F) 8:00-4:30. (206) 269-5200 ✪

SEATTLE—AAA WASHINGTON, 320 NE 97TH ST STE C, 98115. WEEKDAYS (M-F) 9:00-6:00. (206) 529-2700, *(877) 222-4678.* ✪

SPOKANE—AAA WASHINGTON, 1314 S GRAND BLVD UNIT 1, 99202. WEEKDAYS (M-F) 8:30-5:30. (509) 358-6900, *(800) 456-3222.* ✦▲✪

SPOKANE—AAA WASHINGTON, 7307 N DIVISION ST STE103, 99208. WEEKDAYS (M-F) 8:30-5:30. (509) 358-7050, *(800) 439-9290.* ✦▲✪

TACOMA—AAA WASHINGTON, 1801 S UNION AVE, 98405. WEEKDAYS (M-F) 9:00-6:00, SAT 10:00-5:00. (253) 756-3033, *(877) 802-6906.* ✦▲✪

TUKWILA—AAA WASHINGTON, 17250 SOUTHCENTER PY S112, 98188. WEEKDAYS (M-F) 9:00-6:00, SAT 10:00-5:00. (425) 251-6040, *(877) 802-6898.* ✦▲✪

VANCOUVER—AAA WASHINGTON, 4301 E 4TH PLAIN BLVD, 98661. WEEKDAYS (M-F) 9:00-6:00. (360) 696-4081, *(877) 802-6908.* ✦▲✪

WENATCHEE—AAA WASHINGTON, 221 N MISSION ST, 98801. WEEKDAYS (M-F) 8:30-5:30. (509) 662-8550, *(800) 487-3273.* ✦▲✪

YAKIMA—AAA WASHINGTON, 2301 W NOB HILL BLVD STE1, 98902. WEEKDAYS (M-F) 8:30-5:30. (509) 248-6520, *(800) 898-6524.* ✦▲✪

YAKIMA—AAA WASHINGTON, 3502 SUMMITVIEW AVE, 98902. WEEKDAYS (M-F) 9:00-6:00. (509) 837-9335 ✪

Border Information

U.S. Residents Traveling to Canada

Border crossing requirements: Travelers are required to present proper travel documents in order to enter Canada and return to the U.S.

Air travel: A U.S. passport is required.

Land or sea travel: Proof of citizenship and proof of identity are required. Approved documents include a passport or passport card, Enhanced Driver's License or NEXUS trusted traveler program card. Visit the U.S. Department of State website travel.state.gov for the most current information on these requirements. Canadian citizens should refer to the Canada Border Services Agency website www.cbsa-asfc.gc.ca.

U.S. resident aliens: An Alien Registration Receipt Card (Green Card) as well as a passport from the country of citizenship is required.

Children: All children must provide their own travel documents. In lieu of a U.S. passport or passport card, children under 16 traveling to Canada by land or sea may present an original or copy of their birth certificate, a Report of Birth Abroad obtained from a U.S. Consulate or a Naturalization Certificate. Minors must be accompanied by both parents; if one parent is absent, a notarized letter of consent from the absent parent giving permission to go on the trip is required.

Legal Issues: Persons with felony convictions, DUI convictions or other offenses may be denied entry into Canada.

Firearms: Canada has strict laws regarding the importing, exporting, possession, use, storage, display and transportation of firearms. These are federal laws that apply across the country. Firearms are divided into classes: non-restricted (most ordinary rifles and shotguns); restricted (mainly handguns) and prohibited (full and converted automatics and certain handguns, among others).

To bring a non-restricted or restricted firearm into Canada you must:
- Be 18 years of age or older
- Declare firearm(s) in writing at the first point of entry
- Obtain an Authorization to Transport (ATT) from a provincial or territorial Chief Firearms Officer prior to arrival at the point of entry; contact the Canadian Firearms Centre at (800) 731-4000 for additional details.

Hunters may bring in, duty-free, 200 rounds of ammunition; a valid license or declaration to purchase ammunition is required. Those planning to hunt in multiple provinces or territories must obtain a hunting license from each one.

Firearms are forbidden in many of Canada's national and provincial parks, game reserves and adjacent areas. For additional information regarding the temporary importation and use of firearms consult the Canada Border Services Agency website.

Personal items: Clothing, personal items, sports and recreational equipment, automobiles, snowmobiles, cameras, personal computers and food products appropriate for the purpose and duration of the visit may be brought into Canada duty and tax-free. Customs may require a refundable security deposit at the time of entry.

Tobacco products: Those meeting age requirements (18 years in Alberta, Manitoba, Northwest Territories, Nunavut, Saskatchewan, Quebec and Yukon; 19 years

in other provinces) may bring in up to 50 cigars, 200 cigarettes, 200 grams of tobacco and 200 tobacco sticks.

Alcohol: Those meeting age requirements (18 years in Alberta, Manitoba and Quebec; 19 years in other provinces and territories) may bring in limited alcoholic beverages: 40 fluid ounces (1.14 litres) of liquor, 53 fluid ounces (1.5 litres) of wine (about two 750-ml bottles) or 287 fluid ounces (8.5 litres) of beer or ale (the equivalent of 24 12-ounce bottles or cans).

- Amounts exceeding the allowable quantities are subject to federal duty and taxes, and provincial/territorial liquor fees.
- Provincial fees are paid at customs at the time of entry in all provinces and Yukon.
- It is illegal to bring more than the allowable alcohol quantity into the Northwest Territories or Nunavut.

Purchases: Articles purchased at Canadian duty-free shops are subject to U.S. Customs exemptions and restrictions; those purchased at U.S. duty-free shops before entering Canada are subject to duty if brought back into the United States.

Prescription drugs: Persons requiring medication while visiting Canada are permitted to bring it for their own use. Medication should be in the original packaging with a label listing the drug and its intended use. Bring a copy of the prescription and the prescribing doctor's phone number.

Gifts: Items not exceeding $60 (CAN) in value (excluding tobacco, alcoholic beverages and advertising matter) taken into or mailed to Canada are allowed free entry. Gifts valued at more than $60 are subject to regular duty and taxes on the excess amount.

Pets: You must have a certificate for a dog or cat 3 months and older. It must clearly describe the animal, declare that the animal is currently vaccinated against rabies and include a licensed veterinarian signature.

- Collar tags are not sufficient proof of immunization.
- Be sure the vaccination does not expire while traveling in Canada.
- The certificate is also required to bring the animal back into the U.S.

Exemptions: Service animals; healthy puppies and kittens under 3 months old with a health certificate signed by a licensed veterinarian indicating that the animal is too young to vaccinate.

Vehicles
- Vehicles entering Canada for leisure travel, including trailers not exceeding 8 feet 6 inches (2.6 m) in width, are generally subject to quick and routine entry procedures.
- To temporarily leave or store a car, trailer or other goods in Canada if you must leave the country, you must pay an import duty and taxes or present a valid permit. Canadian Customs officials issue vehicle permits at the point of entry.
- You are required to carry your vehicle registration document when traveling in Canada.
- If driving a car other than your own, you must have written permission from the owner.
- If driving a rented car, you must provide a copy of the rental contract.
- A valid U.S. driver's license is valid in Canada.
- In all Canadian provinces and territories except Alberta, British Columbia and Saskatchewan, it is illegal to use radar detectors, even if unplugged.
- Seat belt use is required for the driver and all passengers.

Financial Responsibility Laws in Canada: When an accident involves death, injury or property damage, Canadian provinces and territories require evidence of financial responsibility.

U.S. motorists should check with their insurance company regarding whether they are required to obtain and carry a yellow Non-Resident Inter-Province Motor Vehicle Liability Insurance Card (accepted as evidence of financial responsibility throughout Canada). Those not carrying proper proof may be subject to a substantial fine. If renting a vehicle, check with the rental car company.

U.S. Residents Returning to the U.S.

U.S. citizens returning to the U.S. from Canada by air must have a valid passport. Those returning by land or sea are required to present the appropriate travel documents outlined above.

Every individual seeking entry into the United States—foreign visitors, U.S. citizens or lawful permanent residents—must be inspected at the point of entry and each family (persons living in the same household related by blood, marriage, domestic partnership or adoption) must complete a declarations form. Random searches may be conducted by U.S. Customs and Border Protection agents.

U.S. Exemptions for a Stay in Canada of 48 Hours or More

- Each individual may bring back tax- and duty-free articles not exceeding $800 in retail value.
- Any amount over the $800 exemption is subject to duty.
- The exemption is allowed once every 31 days.
- A family may combine purchases to avoid exceeding individual exemption limits.
- Exemptions are based on fair retail value (keep receipts of all purchases as proof).
- Exemptions apply to articles acquired only for personal or household use or as gifts and not intended for sale.
- The exemption may include 100 cigars, 200 cigarettes and 1 litre (33.8 fluid ounces) of liquor per person over age 21. Customs enforces state liquor laws.
- All articles must accompany you on your return.

U.S. Exemptions for a Stay in Canada Less Than 48 Hours

- Each individual may bring back tax- and duty-free articles not exceeding $200 in retail value.
- The exemption may include no more than 10 cigars, 50 cigarettes, 150 millilitres (5 fluid ounces) of alcohol or 150 millilitres of perfume containing alcohol.
- A family may not combine purchases.
- If purchases exceed the $200 exemption, you forfeit the exemption and all purchases become subject to duty.
- All articles must be declared and accompany you upon return.

Gifts

- Gifts up to $100 fair retail value may be sent to friends or relatives in the United States provided no recipient receives more than one gift per day (gifts do not have to be included in the $800 exemption).
- Gifts of tobacco products, alcoholic beverages or perfume containing alcohol valued at more than $5 retail are excluded from this provision.
- Mark the contents, retail value and "Unsolicited Gift" on the outside of the package.

Prohibited: Narcotics and dangerous drugs, drug paraphernalia, obscene articles and publications, seditious or treasonable matter, lottery tickets, hazardous items (fireworks, dangerous toys, toxic or poisonous substances) citrus products and switchblade knives. Also prohibited are any goods originating in embargoed countries.

Canadian Residents Traveling to the U.S.

Canadian citizens entering the U.S. by air must have a valid passport. Canadian citizens entering the U.S. by land or sea are required to present the appropriate travel documents; refer to the Canada Border Services Agency website www.cbsa-asfc.gc.ca or travel.state.gov for the most current information on these requirements.

If traveling to the United States with a minor 15 years or younger, carry documentation proving your custodial rights. A person under age 18 traveling to the United States alone or with only one parent or another adult must carry certified documentation proving that the trip is permitted by both parents.

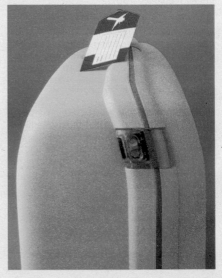

U.S. Customs permits Canadian residents to bring—duty-free for personal use and not intended for sale—the following: clothing, personal items and equipment appropriate to the trip, up to 200 cigarettes, 50 cigars or 2 kilograms of tobacco, and 1 litre of liquor.

Canadian Residents Returning to Canada

There are no exemptions for same-day cross-border shoppers.

Canadian residents may claim a $200 (CAN) exemption on goods, excluding alcoholic beverages and tobacco products, if returning after less than 48 hours and not using any other exemption. This exemption may apply any number of times in a year. No tobacco or alcohol may be brought back if returning from a visit of less than 48 hours.

For each absence of 48 hours or more (but fewer than seven days), residents may bring back, free of duty and taxes, goods valued up to $800 (CAN) any number of times a year, provided the visit to the United States is 48 hours or more and all goods accompany the purchaser (a written declaration may be required).

If returning after 7 days or more (not counting the departure day from Canada) you may claim up to a $800 (CAN) exemption, but goods other than alcohol and tobacco products need not accompany you (a written declaration may be required).

Permitted within the $200 and $800 exemptions: up to 50 cigars, 200 cigarettes, 200 tobacco sticks and 200 grams of tobacco; and up to 1.14 litres (40 fluid ounces) of liquor, 1.5 litres (53 fluid ounces) of wine (about two 750-ml bottles) or 8.5 litres (287 fluid ounces) of beer or ale (the equivalent of 24 12-ounce bottles or cans). You must meet the minimum age requirement of the province or territory entered to claim alcohol or tobacco products.

While AAA makes every effort to provide accurate and complete information, AAA makes no warranty, express or implied, and assumes no legal liability or responsibility for the accuracy or completeness of any information contained herein.

Photo Credits

Page numbers are in bold type. Picture credit abbreviations are as follows:
- (i) numeric sequence from top to bottom, left to right ▪ (AAA) AAA Travel library.

Show You Care

You know how valuable your AAA/CAA card is. Now give this gift of security, value, and peace of mind. **Give a AAA/CAA membership.**

With roadside assistance, vacation planning, maps, travel guides, exclusive savings, and much more, a AAA/CAA Gift Membership makes the perfect gift.

To purchase a AAA/CAA Gift Membership, contact your local club office, visit **AAA.com** or **CAA.ca**, or call **800-Join-AAA** (564-6222).

Hit the Road with Identity Theft Protection

Identity thieves don't take vacations. Ensure you're protected before you leave.

Visit your local AAA/CAA office or online at
AAA.com/IDTheft • CAA.ca

All products not available at all locations.

Hands-Free
IS NOT Risk-Free

Not all voice-activated technologies are equal.
Complicated interactions can take your
attention away from the road.

Use hands-free systems cautiously
and keep your focus on the
road when driving.

AAA.com/**Distraction**

Bring It Home

You always want the best for those you care about. Extend the same benefits you enjoy with a **AAA/CAA Associate Membership.** With roadside assistance, vacation planning, travel guides, exclusive savings, and much more, they can rely on AAA/CAA.

To purchase an Associate Membership, contact your local club office, visit **AAA.com** or **CAA.ca**, or call **800-Join-AAA** (564-6222).

Get INVOLVED and Keep Teens Safe

Exploring the countryside or visiting nearby cities can be perfect opportunities to teach your teens good habits and rules of the road — before and after they learn to drive.

TeenDriving.AAA.com
DriveRight.CAA.ca

Let Your Voice Be Heard

We Want To Hear From You

- If a AAA listed establishment doesn't meet your expectations, send us the details so we can look into it.
- Or, if you've got a favorite hotel, restaurant or attraction you'd like us to consider for AAA inspection, send us your recommendation.

Visit us at **AAA.com/MemberFeedback**

GET YOUR DRIVE TRIP BACK ON TRACK

When a drive trip takes an unexpected turn, use the **MOBILE APP** or go **ONLINE** to quickly request roadside service.

- New, more intuitive user interface
- Easier service request submissions
- Frequent status updates
- Service Tracker feature to follow service vehicle en route to your location

AAA.com/mobile
CAA.ca/mobile

We're here to get you there.

AAA members get more with Hertz.*

- Up to 20% savings on the base rate of all rentals
- Additional driver fee waived for AAA members
- Complimentary use of one child safety seat
- Young Renter fee waived for AAA members ages 20-24
- Free Hertz Gold Plus Rewards® membership with exclusive bonus points
- Discounted NeverLost® navigation system and satellite radio
- 10% off prepay fuel option

Click: AAA.com/hertz
Call: 1-800-654-3080
Visit: Your local AAA branch or Hertz neighborhood location.